The Logical Structure
of Linguistic Theory

Noam Chomsky

The Logical Structure
of Linguistic Theory

PLENUM PRESS • NEW YORK AND LONDON

Library of Congress Cataloging in Publication Data

Chomsky, Noam.
  The logical structure of linguistic theory.

  Bibliography: p.
  Includes index.
  1. Generative grammar.   2. Grammar, Comparative and general.   3. English
language—Grammar, Generative. I. Title.
P158.C5   415   75-26985
ISBN 0-306-30760-X

Plenum Press, New York
A Division of Plenum Publishing Corporation
227 West 17th Street, New York, N.Y. 10011

United Kingdom edition published by Plenum Press, London
A Division of Plenum Publishing Company, Ltd.
Davis House (4th Floor), 8 Scrubs Lane, Harlesden, London, NW10 6SE, England

Printed in the United States of America

CONTENTS

Introduction 1973   1

The Logical Structure of Linguistic Theory

Preface   57

Chapter I. Summary   61

Chapter II. The nature of linguistic theory   77

Chapter III. Linguistic levels   105

Chapter IV. Simplicity and the form of grammars   113

Chapter V. Grammaticalness   129

Chapter VI. Lower levels of grammatical structure   157

Chapter VII. Phrase structure   171

Chapter VIII. Description in terms of phrase structure   223

Chapter IX. Transformational analysis   293

Chapter X. Tranformational analysis of English   401

Bibliography   571

Index   575

INTRODUCTION

This manuscript has a rather unusual status, which should be clearly understood by the reader. In the first place, it dates from 20 years ago. Secondly, the manuscript was never actually prepared for publication. It is hardly necessary to point out that a great deal has been learned about the topics discussed here in the intervening years. If I were to rewrite it today, I would naturally introduce quite a few modifications, though I still regard the general approach and much of the specific substance as valid. In editing the manuscript for publication now, I have made no attempt to bring it up to date or to introduce revisions in the light of subsequent work. The editing has been limited to correction of some obvious minor errors, standardization of notations and terminology, a few clarifying comments, and deletion of a fair amount of material (major deletions are indicated in the text, in some cases, with a brief paraphrase of the omitted material).

Given the unfinished character of the manuscript and its date, I have, for several years, refused offers to publish it, and have now agreed only with some reluctance. A number of colleagues have informed me that they find it useful and have suggested publication. The manuscript has, in fact, been fairly widely distributed in several duplicated and microfilm versions, varying somewhat in text, and there are quite a few references to it in the literature. I have attempted nothing so comprehensive since, and the general approach developed here lies in the immediate background of much of my own work, and perhaps that of some others as well. I hope that publication now will be of some use to students of transformational generative grammar, but I want to emphasize again the special features of this manuscript.

In this introduction, I will review the several versions, noting the differences among them, and will explain the exact status of the manuscript published here, in an effort to avoid confusions that might arise (§I). I will also outline the central concepts of the manuscript (henceforth,

1

LSLT) and will discuss briefly some of the theoretical modifications introduced in work since (§II). The remainder of the introduction will be devoted to an effort to reconstruct what I had in mind in writing *LSLT* (§III). There has been a fair amount written recently about the origins of transformational generative grammar, along with a number of complaints that more complete information has not been made available, and I have repeatedly been asked to discuss the matter. I will not comment directly on the various accounts that have appeared, but will simply describe the stages in the early development of this work, to the best of my recollection, in the hope that this will be useful to those who seem interested in the topic.

There is a certain amount of redundancy in this exposition, as several topics are taken up in §II and then again in the different context of §III. In the interest of clarity, I have let the redundancy stand, avoiding repeated cross-reference.

I   The first and most widely circulated version of *LSLT* was completed and duplicated in the spring of 1955. Chapter IX of the manuscript published here, with some background commentary, was my Ph.D. dissertation in linguistics at the University of Pennsylvania, entitled *Transformational Analysis*. At that time. I was just completing my fourth year as a Junior Fellow of the Society of Fellows at Harvard University. These years were an extraordinary opportunity for me. I was able to pursue a line of inquiry that seemed to many professional linguists unpromising if not exotic, free from external pressures and with the resources of Harvard University available to me. It would be difficult to imagine more ideal circumstances for graduate study and research. I would like to express my gratitude to the Senior Fellows of the Society, to Nelson Goodman, who nominated me for this appointment, and to many teachers, colleagues, and friends whose help I will discuss shortly.

In the fall of 1955, I began teaching at MIT in the Modern Languages Department, with a joint appointment in the Research Laboratory of Electronics. Again, I was most fortunate to have conditions for teaching and research that were virtually ideal. I was able to teach some undergraduate courses in linguistics, logic, and philosophy of language. The Research Laboratory of Electronics, then under the direction of Jerome Wiesner, provided a most stimulating interdisciplinary environment for research of the sort that I wanted to pursue. I was also able to continue working with Morris Halle, who had been at MIT for several years and had initiated my appointment there.

During the fall semester of 1955, I revised several chapters of *LSLT*. At that time, two microfilms were made by Harvard Libraries, one of the 1955 version and one of the partially edited and revised January 1956 version. It is these two microfilms and the duplicated 1955 version that have been distributed over the years. I have not kept count, but there must be several hundred copies.

In the spring of 1956, I began to revise the manuscript for publication. In the original, the tenth and final chapter was a summary. In the version that I was preparing for publication, I placed the summary chapter first, otherwise leaving the chapter order unaltered. During that year I did manage to rewrite the new summary chapter (Chapter I) and the first five chapters of the original (Chapters II–VI). The manuscript as published here consists of a preface written in 1956 and the chapters (here numbered I–VI) of this edited version. Chapters VII and VIII, dealing with the theory of phrase structure, are from the January 1956 version. Chapters IX and X are the originals from the 1955 version (numbered there as Chapters VIII and IX). For the remainder of this discussion, I will refer only to the present chapter arrangement.

After the revisions described were completed, I submitted parts of the manuscript to the Technology Press of MIT for consideration for potential publication. It was rejected, with the not unreasonable observation that an unknown author taking a rather unconventional approach should submit articles based on this material to professional journals before planning to publish such a comprehensive and detailed manuscript as a book. This was no easy matter, however. The one article I had submitted on this material to a linguistics journal had been rejected, virtually by return mail. I had lectured on some of this material at several universities, but as far as I could determine, there was little interest in these topics among professional linguists. Possibilities for publication seemed remote, although I did publish articles in the proceedings of several conferences in 1955 and 1956.[1]

In 1956, at the suggestion of Morris Halle, I showed some of my lecture notes for an undergraduate course at MIT to Cornelis Van Schoonefeld, the editor of the *Janua Linguarum* series of Mouton, and he offered to publish them. A slightly revised version appeared in 1957, under the title *Syntactic Structures (SS)*. This was a sketchy and informal outline of some of the material in *LSLT*, along with some material on finite-state grammars and formal properties of grammars from 1956. I suspect that there would have been little notice in the profession had it not been for a provocative and extensive review article by Robert Lees that appeared almost simultaneously with the publication of *SS*.[2] In 1958 and again in 1959 I was invited to participate in conferences at the

---

[1] The notes to the Introduction will be found starting on page 46.

University of Texas, and had an opportunity to discuss problems of transformational generative grammar there.[3] In 1960, Lees published his 1960 MIT Ph.D. dissertation, the first published book on transformational generative grammar.[4] E. S. Klima and G. H. Matthews were also engaged in important work in this area that appeared in the next few years.[5] Meanwhile, Zellig Harris had published his 1955 Presidential Address to the Linguistic Society on a somewhat different approach to transformational analysis,[6] expanding on earlier proposals.[7] Within a few years, quite a number of linguists were working on transformational grammar, and important theoretical contributions as well as descriptive studies of various languages began to appear.

In 1958–9, I spent a year in research at the Institute for Advanced Study in Princeton and undertook a full-scale revision of *LSLT*, this time in a form for publication. Six chapters were completed, containing some new material and a good deal of technical improvement over the original. However, by the spring of 1959 I found myself deeply involved in work on generative phonology, applying to English an approach that had been presented in my *Morphophonemics of Modern Hebrew* (*MMH*) in 1951, which I had planned to include as an appendix to Chapter VII of *LSLT*.[8] After I returned to MIT in the fall, this and other work took precedence, and I never did return to the revision of the remaining chapters. In preparing the manuscript for publication now, I thought for a time that I would use these revised chapters instead of the 1956 version, but the point of view was sufficiently different so that I found it difficult to integrate this material with the still unedited earlier versions. Furthermore, some of what appears in the revision has been published in one or another form, and other parts are no longer of much current interest, to judge by the literature since.[9] For these reasons, I decided not to include the 1958–9 revision here but to publish rather the 1955–6 version, which is unified and integrated, and not very different in its essential substance in any event.

While working on *LSLT* I discussed all aspects of this material frequently and in great detail with Zellig Harris, whose influence is obvious throughout. I also received some encouragement from Bernard Bloch, who was sufficiently interested in this work to request that I submit a copy of *MMH* and *LSLT* to the Yale Linguistics Library. I discussed parts of this material with Nelson Goodman, with whom I had studied philosophy at the University of Pennsylvania, and whose influence I will outline shortly. I also discussed the whole project with Paul Halmos of the University of Chicago Mathematics Department, after I had presented material on grammaticalness and degrees of grammaticalness (Chapter V) at a summer Linguistics Institute in

Chicago in 1954. From 1951 to 1956 I also had many opportunities to discuss this and related work with teachers and friends in Cambridge: Yehoshua Bar-Hillel, Peter Elias, Morris Halle, Henry Hiż, Anatol Holt, Roman Jakobson, Eric Lenneberg, Israel Scheffler, and W. V. O. Quine, to all of whom I owe a considerable debt, not only for their encouragement but also for many ideas and criticisms.

LSLT is concerned with three fundamental and closely related concepts: language, grammar, and structure (cf. §56.1). A language L is understood to be a set (in general infinite) of finite strings of symbols drawn from a finite "alphabet." Each such string is a sentence of L. The alphabet of primitive symbols is determined by general linguistic theory, in particular, by universal phonetics, which specifies the minimal elements available for any human language and provides some conditions on their choice and combination. A grammar of L is a system of rules that specifies the set of sentences of L and assigns to each sentence a structural description. The structural description of a sentence S constitutes, in principle, a full account of the elements of S and their organization. By the "structure of L," then, we mean the set of structural descriptions of sentences in L. The notion "grammar" is to be defined in general linguistic theory in such a way that, given a grammar G, the language generated by G and its structure are explicitly determined by general principles of linguistic theory. It is appropriate, in my opinion, to regard the grammar of L as a representation of fundamental aspects of the knowledge of L possessed by the speaker-hearer who has mastered L.

II

To use some terminology introduced several years later, we may say that a grammar *weakly generates* a language and *strongly generates* a structure. The notions "strong generation" and "weak generation" are to be defined in general linguistic theory for the set of grammars postulated as "possible grammars for human languages." The notion of central interest, of course, is "strong generation." In the first version of *LSLT*, in 1955, there was no discussion at all of weak generation. In *SS*, the concept is discussed briefly, and in subsequent years there has been a good deal of investigation of the weak generative capacity of phrase-structure grammars and other properties of these systems. See references of Note 24.

It is assumed in *LSLT* (as in *SS*) that the theory developed is to be embedded in a broader semiotic theory which will make use of the structure of L, as here defined, to determine the meaning and reference of expressions and the conditions on their appropriate use, and will also encompass other investigations (statistical linguistics, etc.).

The fundamental notion of "structure" is approached in *LSLT* in the following way. We define, in general linguistic theory, a system of levels of representation. A level of representation consists of elementary units (primes), an operation of concatenation by which strings of primes can be constructed, and various relations defined on primes, strings of primes, and sets and sequences of these strings. Among the abstract objects constructed on the level **L** are **L**-markers that are associated with sentences. The **L**-marker of a sentence S is the representation of S on the level **L**. A grammar of a language, then, will characterize the set of **L**-markers for each level **L** and will determine the assignment of **L**-markers to sentences. The levels considered in *LSLT* are the following: phonetics, phonemics, word, syntactic category, morphemics, morphophonemics, phrase structure, transformations. The major task of linguistic theory, as here understood, is to present an abstract and precise account of these levels and of the set of possible grammars for human languages, and to provide the general principles that determine fully, for each such grammar, the sets that are weakly and strongly generated by this grammar—respectively, the language it generates and the structural descriptions of the sentences of this language.

The purpose of *LSLT*, as described at various points in the manuscript "is to construct an integrated and systematic theory, which, when applied rigorously to linguistic material, gives the correct analysis for the cases where intuition (or experiment, under more desirable circumstances) makes a clear decision" (§93.2, p. 415). "Our problem is to carry out this development, to bring to light the formal patterns underlying the sentences of a language, and to show how these observed regularities might account for particular decisions about which sequences are grammatical and how these are to be understood" (Introduction, p. 63). The term "grammar" is understood here in a narrow sense, as pure theory of form, thus incorporating syntax and phonology (*ibid.*).[10] The primary question for linguistic theory is: how can speakers produce and understand new sentences? (§75, p. 293)? The fundamental long-term task is to provide "an explanation for the general process of projection by which speakers extend their limited linguistic experience to new and immediately acceptable forms" (§110, p. 519).

It has been common in various fields concerned with language to describe linguistic behavior as "the use of words." In Saussurean structuralism, syntactic theory barely extended beyond this characterization,[11] and similar notions appear in the philosophy of language and in developments motivated by the mathematical theory of communication, which had achieved some currency by the early 1950s. The theory of finite-state Markov sources, as developed by Shannon and others, might reasonably be taken as a precise characterization (at the syntactic level) of the vague proposal that linguistic behavior is a matter of "the use of words." In *LSLT* this topic is not considered at all. However, in *SS* and other work of the time, it was shown that the models studied in the mathematical theory of communication, whatever their value, could not serve the purpose of linguistic theory, as had been proposed by a number of linguists and many psychologists and engineers.[12] We may, of course, continue to hold the virtually empty view that finite-state sources serve as a model for the speaker or hearer, i.e., for linguistic performance. This is merely to say that the user of language is a finitely specifiable organism and that language use can be described as a discrete temporal process. But from these truisms it does not follow that the grammar represented in the mind of the speaker-hearer is a "device" of this character, and observation of the facts of language shows clearly that it is not.

The terms "performance" and "competence" do not appear in *LSLT* or *SS*, but the distinction is clear throughout. In *SS*, it appears explicitly at this point in the discussion. Linguistic competence, in the sense of this phrase introduced in later work,[13] is understood as the speaker-hearer's knowledge of his language as represented by a generative grammar. It is merely a conceptual confusion to fail to distinguish competence, in this sense, from performance, in the sense of linguistic behavior, the actual use of language. The use of language undoubtedly involves many factors beyond the grammar that represents fundamental properties of the speaker's knowledge of his language. It is natural to suppose that models of the speaker and hearer will incorporate the "competence grammar" as a basic element; that is, such models will incorporate the system of rules and principles that determines the language that the language user employs and its structure. In fact, virtually all serious work on language use makes some such assumption, either implicitly or explicitly. It should be clear, then, that a generative grammar does not take the point of view of the speaker or hearer. Rather, it is a description, in the most neutral possible terms, of knowledge possessed by the speaker-hearer and put to use in normal discourse. A generative grammar is a theory of competence.

The related distinction between "acceptable" and "grammatical" utterances is also drawn in *LSLT* (cf., e.g., §100.2). We may take "acceptability" to be a concept of the theory of performance, and "grammaticalness" a related notion of the theory of competence. The sentences generated by the grammar directly are the "grammatical" (or "highest-degree grammatical") sentences of the language. Among them are sentences that are true, false, amusing, unintelligible, meaningless, trivial, etc. It may be quite appropriate on particular occasions to construct and use utterances that deviate from grammatical rule in one or another respect, and there may well be general principles for interpreting such sentences—consider, e.g., the case of personification metaphor, perhaps the most obvious case of appropriate but formally deviant structures. In *LSLT* there is considerable discussion of levels of grammaticalness and deviation, particularly at the level of syntactic categories.[14] We may say that the grammar "derivatively generates" sentences that deviate in specified respects from the rules, and that these sentences are at lower levels of grammaticalness. Sentences are acceptable (or perhaps acceptable under particular circumstances) if they are suitable, appropriate, adequate to the purpose at hand, etc. The competence grammar contributes to determining acceptability, but the latter concept involves many other factors.

In *LSLT*, the theory of phrase structure is developed in an effort to capture essential ideas of traditional and structuralist theories of categories and constituents, within the new framework of generative grammar. It is argued that phrase-structure grammars are inadequate in strong generative capacity (I emphasize again that strong generative capacity is the sole concern here; problems of weak generation were considered only later). The theory of phrase structure, as developed here, does not suffice for the characterization of linguistic competence, of what the language user knows. It is suggested that linguistic theory requires a new and more abstract level of description, the level of grammatical transformations, and a richer concept of grammar. The level of transformations is constructed and applied to English. It is then argued that with this elaboration of linguistic theory, some of the essential and crucial defects of the theory of phrase structure are overcome. The grammars developed in these terms and the structural descriptions that they generate express rather subtle aspects of the form and interpretation of sentences. Furthermore, it seems possible to formulate general principles that lead to the selection of the correct grammar on the basis of the kind of data that might be available to the linguist and the language learner, a matter to which I return directly.

A particular theory of grammar, such as the *LSLT* version of transformational generative grammar, provides general principles that determine the generative capacity of the grammars postulated by this theory as "possible human grammars." In contrast, conventional structuralist grammars or traditional grammars do not attempt to determine explicitly the sentences of a language or the structural descriptions of these sentences. Rather, such grammars describe elements and categories of various types, and provide examples and hints to enable the intelligent reader to determine the form and structure of sentences not actually presented in the grammar. Such grammars are written for the intelligent reader. To determine what they say about sentences one must have an intuitive grasp of certain principles of linguistic structure. These principles, which remain implicit and unexpressed, are presupposed in the construction and interpretation of such grammars. While perhaps perfectly adequate for their particular purposes, such grammars do not attempt to account for the ability of the intelligent reader to understand the grammar. The theory of generative grammar, in contrast, is concerned precisely to make explicit the "contribution of the intelligent reader," though the problem is not posed in just these terms. The theory of generative grammar is concerned with the human language faculty as such. A grammar constructed in accordance with the principles postulated in such a theory gives an explicit characterization of a language and its structure—and within the broader semiotic theory envisioned but not developed here, an explicit characterization as well of the meaning and reference of expressions and conditions of appropriate use. So construed, the theory can be accurately described as a study of one aspect of human intelligence, and thus constitutes a particular subbranch of cognitive psychology.

Note that there are two levels of theory under discussion here. The grammar of L is a theory of L, incorporating the linguist's hypotheses concerning the elements and rules of L. This grammar is an account of knowledge of L that has been attained by the speaker-hearer who has mastered L. The theory of transformational generative grammar (or some other general linguistic theory) expresses a hypothesis concerning the "essence of language," the defining properties of human language. We may regard a general linguistic theory, so construed, as a theory of the innate, intrinsic language faculty that provides the basis for the acquisition of knowledge of language. The child, in his "initial state," is uninformed as to the language of the speech community[15] in which he lives. Plainly, he is endowed with some set of mechanisms (what we may call his "language faculty") for determining this language, that is, for achieving a "final state" in which he knows the language. General linguistic theory describes his initial state; the grammar of his language describes his final state. General linguistic theory can appropriately be regarded as an explanatory theory, in that it seeks to explain how a child in a speech community comes to know the language of this community, and to know innumerable particular facts with regard to the form and meaning of particular expressions, and much else.

In an entirely analogous way, one might investigate other aspects of human intelligence. Consider some system of knowledge or belief that a person has developed on the basis of some data. We may attempt to characterize this system, constructing a "grammar" for it. We may inquire into the mechanisms by which the system was acquired. If, in fact, acquisition of this system is, like acquisition of language, a normal biological function of humans, we may seek to characterize the initial state that is a common human attribute. The empirical condition that must be met by this characterization is that a "device" in this initial state, given data of the sort available to a person who acquires a given system of knowledge or belief, will attain a final state in which this system is represented. The general theory that characterizes this initial state, if it meets the empirical condition, is an explanatory theory of a particular human cognitive faculty. Were such theories available for various cognitive systems, we might proceed to investigate the general structure of human intelligence. That is, we might inquire into the interaction and relations of various cognitive systems, the general principles (if there are such) by which they operate, the relative independence of one system from another, and so on.

It is often speculated that there exist "generalized learning mechanisms" of which the linguistic faculty is merely a special case. But in the absence of any serious research along the lines just sketched, there are no substantive and plausible proposals in this regard to be examined for adequacy. It may well be the case, as has often been speculated in the past, that the human language faculty is relatively independent of other faculties of the mind and is also a unique human attribute. Certainly such a conclusion should not surprise the biologist. The matter need not, of course, be left with so vague and inconclusive a formulation. In fact, any explicit linguistic theory that offers a definition of "language," "grammar," and "structure," along the general lines sketched earlier, constitutes a specific proposal as to the nature of the language faculty, to be examined for its empirical adequacy in accounting for the facts of language. I am not aware of any evidence that there are significant analogues in other areas of cognitive function or in other organisms— note that the unexplained notion "significant" bears a considerable burden in this assertion.

It is a historical curiosity that the experimental investigation of human behavior has often departed from the general methods and approaches of the natural sciences, and has insisted on certain *a priori* conditions on "legitimate theory construction." The several varieties of behaviorism (excluding here certain empty versions that do not merit discussion) are, in effect, defined by the arbitrary conditions that they impose on permissible theory construction. We need not go into the historical reasons for this tendency. Because of its considerable impact, it seems strange to many psychologists to describe the theory of generative grammar as a part of psychology, since its concepts and the principles postulated in an effort to explain the facts of language form, interpretation, use, and acquisition, generally depart from the *a priori* constraints imposed by one or another variety of behavioral theory. Some have argued that the approach outlined here is "circular," failing to see that if this were true, the various empirical principles postulated within theories of generative grammar would be irrefutable, whereas they are, in fact, all too refutable and have been repeatedly modified in the light of new discoveries and observations. Exactly the same is true of a theory of language acquisition that takes the principles of general linguistic theory to be an innate schematism, brought to bear by the child in language learning. Plainly, an explicit proposal of this sort can easily be disconfirmed, say, by the discovery that the data of some language are inconsistent with the postulated principles. Or, such a theory might be abandoned if it were shown that some simpler or deeper theory can account for the acquisition of language.

The construction of a grammar of a language by a linguist is in some respects analogous to the acquisition of language by the child. The linguist has a corpus of data; the child is presented with unanalyzed data of language use. The linguist tries to formulate the rules of the language; the child constructs a mental representation of the grammar of the language. The linguist applies certain principles and assumptions to select a grammar among the many possible candidates compatible with his data; the child must also select among the grammars compatible with the data. General linguistic theory, which is concerned with discovering and exhibiting the principles, conditions, and procedures that the child brings to bear in attaining his knowledge of language, can also be construed as an account of the methodology of linguistic investigation, the methods by which a linguist arrives at a grammar.

Within structural linguistics there were serious and important efforts to deal with some of the problems just mentioned. Harris, Bloch, Trubetzkoy, Pike, and others attempted, with varying degrees of explicitness, to analyze the procedures by which the linguist might arrive at a grammar (or parts of a grammar), given a corpus of data. But the notion "generative grammar," in the sense of the foregoing discussion, was never clearly developed.[16] Were it possible to formulate procedures that can be applied to a corpus of data to yield a generative grammar, these procedures could be formulated as an empirical hypothesis with regard to the language faculty. It would be appropriate to postulate that the child acquires language by applying procedures of this sort to the data available to him.[17] We would then have something explicit to investigate in place of vague and near vacuous discussions of the child's unspecified "dispositions," which are not uncommon in the literature.

LSLT adopts this general approach, suggesting, however, that structural linguistics was investigating the problem in a way that is not quite correct and is unlikely to be successful.[18] The theories of structural linguistics, insofar as they deal with the matter at hand, take the view that the linguist's methods (and, if one adopts the analogy just discussed, the child's language faculty) provide a system of taxonomic procedures that can be applied to a corpus of data to determine a grammar, a system that incorporates principles of segmentation, substitution, classification, generalization, and analogy. In contrast, it is suggested in *LSLT* that linguistic theory characterizes a system of levels, a class of potential grammars, and an evaluation procedure with the following property: given data from language L and several grammars with the properties required by linguistic theory, the procedure of evaluation selects the highest-valued of these. It is thus suggested that the language learner (analogously, the linguist) approaches the problem of language acquisition (grammar construction) with a schematism that determines in advance the general properties of human language and the general properties of the grammars that may be constructed to account for linguistic phenomena. His task is to select the highest-valued grammar of the appropriate form compatible with available data. Having done so, he knows the language it generates. His knowledge may thus extend far beyond what might be provided by principles of induction, generalization, analogy, substitution, segmentation, and classification of the sort examined in any of the explicit theories of acquisition of language that had been proposed.

Furthermore, the process of language acquisition (grammar construction) may, and in general will, involve a revision of the data base itself. The actual data presented to the language learner or the linguist are degenerate in various respects, quite apart from limitations of scope. The grammar that is constructed is an idealization. General linguistic theory, then, must provide the characterization of grammars, linguistic levels, the principles that determine the generation of structural descriptions, the principles of idealization that are in fact applied by the language learner (analogously, the linguist) in arriving at an explicit generative grammar, and the method for selecting a set of potential grammars to be evaluated.

We have here two rather different approaches to what I take to be the fundamental problem of linguistic theory, the problem of determining how it is possible for a child to acquire knowledge of a language. In later work, I and others have suggested that these two distinct approaches, each of which can be made precise in various ways, express certain leading ideas in empiricist and rationalist theories of knowledge, respectively. Traditional empiricism may be understood as an elementary "data-processing approach." The mind contains a system of properties that provide an initial analysis of the data of sense.[19] Systems of knowledge and belief are developed by the procedures of generalization, analogy, induction, association, and habit formation that are developed in the several varieties of empiricist psychology and philosophy. It is, I believe, appropriate to regard the procedural approaches of structural linguistics as an unusually refined, detailed, and sophisticated development of a theory of this general character.

Rationalist approaches, in contrast, assume that the form of the systems of acquired knowledge is determined by *a priori* principles of mind. It is important to bear in mind that traditional rationalism did not distinguish clearly between necessary and contingent properties in the modern sense. Thus the theories of perception sketched by Descartes and the English Platonists—paradigm examples of a rationalist approach —postulated principles of mind and concepts of innate structure that would surely be regarded as empirical hypotheses regarding contingent properties of mind, in the modern understanding of these notions. Analogously, the linguistic theory developed in *LSLT* presents certain empirical hypotheses concerning the structure of language that can likewise be regarded as hypotheses concerning the properties of mind, specifically, concerning the initial state of the organism in the sense described earlier. These hypotheses aim to characterize the schematism that the mind imposes in examining the data of sense and acquiring knowledge of language on the basis of the evidence produced by such an examination and analysis.

These matters are not discussed in *LSLT*, but the issues lie in the immediate background of this work and have been the subject of considerable discussion and controversy since. In my personal view, the general intellectual interest of the work in generative grammar lies primarily in its contribution to the understanding of these issues.[20]

Pursuing the program of investigation outlined here, the linguistic theorist will attempt to construct generative grammars for particular languages and a general linguistic theory that meets the following empirical conditions: it must be sufficiently narrow and restrictive so that, as a characterization of the initial state of the organism, it suffices to explain how the final state in which knowledge of language is represented is attained on the basis of available data; and it must be sufficiently abstract so that all "humanly possible languages"—in particular, the attested natural languages—are provided with descriptively adequate grammars, in conformity with this theory. Thus there is an upper bound and a lower bound, empirically constrained, on the richness and specificity of this general linguistic theory. A general principle of language structure is a candidate for incorporation into such a theory if it is consistent with what is known of the variety of human languages.

In practice, the real problem faced by the linguistic theorist is to devise a system of principles sufficiently restrictive so that it succeeds in accounting for the transition from the initial to the final state, in the case of particular languages. We will naturally seek to construct the general theory that is most susceptible to disconfirmation by empirical evidence, the theory that makes the strongest claims with regard to the nature of language, while also meeting other methodological conditions common to all intellectual endeavor—conditions of simplicity, elegance, naturalness, and so on that are, unfortunately, quite vague and poorly understood. Methodological considerations and the empirical requirements of linguistic investigation thus converge on the enterprise of devising a linguistic theory that narrowly circumscribes the class of humanly possible grammars, while precisely determining how such grammars generate languages and their structures. Given a theory that narrowly circumscribes the class of attainable grammars, we may hope to be able to provide an evaluation procedure that selects among those compatible with rich enough data. Much of the work on linguistic theory since the mid-1950s has been devoted to circumscribing and delimiting the class of potential generative grammars and determining how they function, in an effort to meet this goal and thus to solve the fundamental problem of linguistic theory as outlined earlier: the problem of characterizing the language faculty and thus accounting for the acquisition of knowledge of language (and, analogously, the problem of justifying the grammars proposed by the linguist for particular languages).

The terms "deep structures" and "surface structure," familiar in later discussion (cf. *ATS*), do not appear in *LSLT*. In the *LSLT* version of syntactic theory, a phrase-structure grammar generates terminal strings and assigns them **P**-markers, representations on the level **P** of phrase structure.[21] A **P**-marker is a set of strings, representable as a labeled bracketing or a tree diagram, which assigns a phrase-structure interpretation to the terminal string, determining its phrases and the categories to which they belong. More generally, the notion of "phrase-structure interpretation" is defined in such a way that a set of strings of a particular type on the level **P**, containing a single terminal string, assigns a phrase-structure interpretation to this terminal string whether or not it is generated by the phrase-structure grammar. **P**-markers are a special case, generated by the phrase-structure grammar,[22] and assigned by a mapping Φ to a restricted class of sentences, called the "kernel sentences." The mapping Φ can be decomposed into a sequence of elementary components, each of which is an obligatory grammatical transformation. The kernel sentences are simple declarative sentences with no complex phrases. Optional grammatical transformations can be interspersed among the components of the mapping Φ; thus other sentences (passives, interrogatives, etc.) are derived. Furthermore, a "generalized transformation" may apply to a sequence of **P**-interpretations, generating a sentence with complex phrases that are themselves ultimately based on terminal strings generated by the phrase-structure grammar. In this manner, it is argued in detail, the problems that arise in phrase-structure grammar can be overcome and a broad class of complex sentences can be generated with structural descriptions that provide a basis for explaining the use and understanding of language.

Furthermore, it is argued that given the class of transformational grammars, it may be possible to undertake, now with some hope of success, an investigation of the problem of justifying the selection of a grammar and, analogously, accounting for language acquisition. In an interesting class of cases, the transformational grammar that captures linguistic intuition and presents a revealing account of what the speaker-hearer knows appears to be the highest-valued transformational grammar in terms of procedures of evaluation of the sort that are investigated in Chapter IV, though many open questions, both conceptual and empirical, are noted.

Note that in the *LSLT* theory, transformations are required to complete the development of the level **P** of phrase structure, since the components of Φ are transformations, in the sense developed in Chapter IX (cf. §88).

Each grammatical transformation, including the components of Φ, applies to a string with a phrase-structure interpretation, forming a new string with a new phrase-structure interpretation (a "derived constituent structure," in the terminology that is often used). Thus transformations are iterable, as required. By application of transformations in the manner permitted by the transformational component of the grammar, we derive ultimately a string with its derived phrase-structure interpretation, also representable as a labeled bracketing or tree diagram. The latter is the "surface structure" of the generated sentence, in the sense of *ATS*.

In *LSLT*, the level **T** of transformations is developed as a level of representation in the sense of the earlier discussion. The **T**-marker of a sentence S provides a record of the **P**-markers of the elementary strings from which S is derived (its "**P**-basis") and also a record of the "history of derivation" of S. Kernel sentences are those with the minimal **T**-marker, namely, just the components of Φ. It is also proposed that these components provide a kind of fixed "skeleton" for more complex **T**-markers, in a manner which is discussed in some detail in Chapter IX.

The nearest analogue to the notion "deep structure" in the *LSLT* theory is the **T**-marker of the generated sentence. An important theoretical innovation in later work is the principle of cyclic application of rules. In accordance with this principle, transformations are first applied to the minimal sentences (phrases of the category Sentence) in a **P**-marker, then to sentences including these, etc., until the maximal sentence (viz., the full **P**-marker) is reached. (In later modifications, Noun Phrases and Adjective Phrases are also considered "cyclic categories," serving as the domain of transformations in accordance with the principle of the cycle.) This cyclic principle makes possible a reconstruction of syntactic theory without generalized transformations or a level of transformations in which **T**-markers are assigned to sentences (cf. *ATS*, Chapter 3). Given this modification, it was natural to introduce the notion "deep structure," referring to the underlying phrase marker generated by the rules of the phrase-structure grammar, to which transformations are applied, forming ultimately a surface structure. The deep structure is a **P**-marker which now incorporates all of the elementary terminal strings generated by the phrase-structure grammar in the earlier sense, each in the place in which it would have been inserted, in earlier theory, by a generalized transformation. The recursive property of the grammar, the property of generating an infinite class of structures, now is assigned to the phrase-structure grammar, instead of (as before) the transformational component of the grammar. The importance of this modification cannot be readily understood in terms of the informal account in *SS*, but in the far more detailed development of the theory in *LSLT* numerous problems arose that are overcome by postulation of the principle of the transformational cycle, as a general principle of linguistic theory.[23]

Perhaps it should be stressed that the concept "deep structure" is a technical notion that is developed within a specific theory of transformational-generative grammar, namely, the *ATS* theory (and others like it in the relevant respects). In other versions of the theory of transformational-generative grammar, there is no precise analogue to this notion. Thus in the *LSLT* version, for example, the notion "deep structure" in the sense of *ATS* is not definable. There are, nevertheless, loosely related notions, such as the notions "**T**-marker" and "**P**-basis." In informal discussions of generative grammar, I have at times noticed a much looser use of the term "deep structure," referring to abstract underlying structures of various sorts that are distinguished from surface structures, or, occasionally, to structures that meet conditions imposed by the postulated universal principles of linguistic theories, or even to these principles themselves. With this vague (and, I believe, quite confused usage), it may seem that the existence of "deep structure" is a profound question on which the legitimacy and justification of the whole approach somehow turns. But if the notion "deep structure" is properly understood, the question of existence of "deep structure" is a technical question—an important one—to which various answers might be suggested within the framework of transformational-generative grammar. The matter is further confused by the fact that there is no unanimity as to which of the various properties of "deep structure," as the notion is developed in *ATS*, are to be taken as defining properties, and which are to be understood as empirical assumptions concerning the notion defined. As a result, debate over the existence of deep structure and over the properties of deep structures (should they exist) is often inconclusive. I will not attempt here to clarify the matter further, but merely make these remarks as a *caveat* to the reader who wishes to explore further.

The *LSLT* version of the theory of generative grammar postulated that lexical items are introduced by "context-sensitive" rules of the phrase-structure grammar that permit a category to be replaced in a derivation by a lexical item. Thus the rules would convert a string such as ...*Verb*... to the string ...*convince*..., where the context ...———... meets the conditions defined by the context-sensitive rule introducing the verb *convince*. In this case, the context might be NP —— $NP\ S$, where the two *NP*s are human, so that we might derive "John convinced Bill that the world is flat." Another modification in the *ATS* theory was the development of a system of syntactic features of various sorts, permitting a sharp separation of the lexicon from the remainder of the phrase-structure grammar. In this framework, the "base" of the grammar consists of a lexicon and a "categorial component," the latter being a set of phrase-structure rules that operate independently of context (thus a "context-free grammar," of a sort that has been widely studied).[24] The lexicon is a collection of lexical items, each of which fully specifies the phonological, semantic, and syntactic properties of a particular lexical item. "Lexical transformations" insert lexical items in structures generated by the categorial component, governed by the features of the lexical item. Thus the base generates deep structures.

The theory of linguistic structure that incorporates these and related modifications is now often referred to as the "standard theory."

The grammar of a language determines an association between sound and meaning in the sense that it strongly generates structural descriptions which determine the phonetic representations of utterances and provide the elements that enter into a description of their meaning and appropriate use. On the matter of phonetic representation, Halle, Lukoff, and I showed that cyclic application of very simple rules, proceeding from smaller to larger phrases of the surface structure, determines the stress contours of a complex class of English sentences (cf. Note 8). In later work, Halle and I extended this approach much more generally, and in *SPE*, a comprehensive theory of generative phonology incorporating the principle of cyclic application of rules is outlined. Joan Bresnan has argued persuasively that the phonological rules should apply, not to surface structure as we had postulated, but rather within the transformational cycle.[25] Thus we may assume that the base generates a deep structure, and that transformational and phonological rules are applied in accordance with the principle of the cycle, ultimately yielding the phonetic representation of a sentence, with its surface structure.

Consider now the vexing question of semantic interpretation. In the *SS–LSLT* version of the theory of grammar, it was observed that there are, obviously, striking correspondences between syntactic and semantic properties of utterances, and that "these correspondences should be studied in some more general theory of language that will include a theory of linguistic form and a theory of the use of language as subparts" (*SS*, p. 102). The theory of linguistic form, understood here as incorporating syntax and phonology, studies language "as an instrument or a tool, attempting to describe its structure with no explicit reference to the way in which this instrument is put to use," the reason for this "self-imposed formality requirement" being that "there seems to be no other basis that will yield a rigorous, effective, and 'revealing' theory of linguistic structure." The study of "the structure of language as an instrument may be expected to provide insight into the actual use of language" (*SS*, p. 103). In particular, to understand a sentence we must know its analysis on each linguistic level, the representations in terms of phrase structure and transformational structure serving as "the major syntactic devices available in language for organization and expression of content." Semantics is concerned with problems of meaning and reference, and with the systematic use of the syntactic devices available in the language (*ibid.*).

The same point of view is assumed throughout in *LSLT*, as already noted (see p. 5). Linguistic theory aims to provide an explanation for particular linguistic facts, a justification for particular decisions concerning the grammatical status of sequences, their structure, and how they are to be understood. Thus the grammar is to provide the means for semantic description, and should fall in place in a broader semiotic theory in which this promissory note is made good. Semantic criteria are essential for determining the soundness of the general approach, since the grammar is to provide the means to account for the use and understanding of language (§68.4). For example, it is argued in Chapter X that on grounds internal to grammatical theory we can justify the strong generation of sentences such as "his suggestion was to become famous" or "the policemen must stop drinking after midnight" with structural descriptions that provide a clear basis for explaining the various senses of these expressions. These results thus serve to justify the assumptions with regard to linguistic form that led to the choice of grammar (*ibid.*). But it is further argued that semantic criteria and intuitive judgments with regard to form are not required for the analysis directly, in the sense that the criteria for selecting the analysis need not be framed in terms of these notions, and that there in fact appears to be no way to make systematic use of them as primitive concepts of linguistic theory (in the narrow sense of this discussion; see Note 10).

The published literature (and similarly, *LSLT*) is clear and explicit on this score.[26] Nevertheless, the concept of "independence of syntax" discussed here has frequently been misunderstood as implying that there are no interesting connections between the study of linguistic form and the study of meaning and use, or even that the latter is somehow not part of the study of language. Precisely the opposite position was expressed throughout this work, however. The question of "independence of syntax" arose in a specific context of discussion and had to do with an important technical question: can such notions as "phonemic distinctness," "grammaticalness," "syntactic category," "word," and other notions of grammatical theory, be defined in a general and systematic way in terms of a basis of primitive notions including "synonymy" and "significance" (meaningfulness), or other notions of semantic theory? It was argued that addition of these notions to the primitive basis for the definition of the linguistic notions in question solves none of the problems that arise when the problem of defining these notions is seriously faced.[27] This is the thesis of "independence of syntax" as developed in the work of this period. To refute the thesis, it is only necessary to show how problems that arise are overcome if semantic notions are added to the basis of primitives. I am aware of no serious proposal in the intervening years.

It may well be, as assumed in *LSLT*, that such notions as "noun" and "verb" cannot be defined within this system of grammar, though it may still be possible to define "category" in such a way that nouns and verbs will prove to be categories, as also argued in *LSLT*. But even if this is so, one cannot draw the conclusion, without further argument, that there is a semantic basis for these notions. There is no difference between a system of definitions in which "noun" is taken as a primitive notion, and another system in which "noun" is defined in terms of the "semantic property" *is-a-Noun*, no matter how solemnly the latter is intoned.

To take another case, the approach to phonology (morphophonemics) in *MMH* and *SPE* introduces the notion "related word" in the following sense. The pair *declare-declarative* are taken to be related words, and phonological processes are designed to account for the regularities in the system exemplified by such pairs. But *hear-ear* or *train-truck-trip-travel-trail...* are not taken to be related words, and no phonological processes are constructed to deal with the formal-semantic systems in which these sets appear (plainly, there are such "systems"; cf. my review, cited in Note 18, for some discussion and examples). It has been argued that phonology in the sense of *MMH* and *SPE* is "semantically-based" in that it relies on the semantic notion of "related word." The contention that "related word" is a semantic notion is, in one sense, unexceptionable, at least if the *SS–LSLT* theory is accepted. Thus it is maintained in this theory that every linguistic notion is "semantic" in that it has semantic import; the overarching semiotic theory in which the theory of linguistic form is embedded must develop and explain how the notions constructed and applied in the investigation of linguistic form contribute to determining meaning and conditions of appropriate use. But apparently more than this is intended when the contention is advanced that the *SPE* approach to phonology is semantically-based, though precisely what the further claim is has never been made clear.

Perhaps the claim is that "related word" is a primitive semantic notion of general linguistic theory that can be applied to data (say, by a cross-linguistic operational test) quite apart from consideration of the system of grammatical rules, and that applies to the set *declare-declarative* but not *hear-ear* or *train-truck...* . Thus the semantic relation between *declare* and *declarative* (as in "declarative sentence") is determined by some general language-independent and grammar-independent principle of semantic theory, but the semantic relations in the other sets are not. If so, this primitive semantic notion, "related word," might be applied to provide a preliminary analysis of the data, prior to the construction of grammar. But this claim is surely highly dubious, if not completely outlandish. Surely no argument has ever been presented to support it.

A weaker and more plausible contention might be advanced. One might take "semantic relatedness" to be a primitive notion (language-and grammar-independent) holding for all the sets mentioned. We might then take "related words" to be those that are semantically related and are furthermore derived from the same base form by rules of the grammar. The notion "related word," so construed, is a theoretical concept; its extension in a language is determined in part by application of the primitive notion "semantic relatedness" and in part by systematic properties of grammars. The advocate of "semantically-based phonology" must now demonstrate that the notion "semantic relatedness" enters into the choice among grammars. He must demonstrate that unless this notion is brought to bear, the optimal grammar will, in specific cases, generate improperly related words from the same base form by phonological rules. If this can be shown, we will have an argument in support of the contention that phonology is semantically-based. But such a demonstration, though perhaps possible, has never even been attempted. Thus there is no reason to suppose that grammatical theory can make use of the notion "semantic relatedness," let alone that it *must* make use of these notions.

The *SS–LSLT* approach to these questions is agnostic. It is argued that there is no point issuing manifestos for or against any choice of primitives. Rather, it is necessary to show how some proposed primitive notion enters into the choice among grammars. It is further emphasized that the tendency to characterize each poorly understood property as "semantic" simply indicates a refusal to take problems of semantics at all seriously. I know of no reason to question these conclusions.

There has been considerable discussion in recent years of some thesis of "autonomy of syntax" that is allegedly in dispute, but the thesis itself is rarely formulated.[28] If it is the thesis of *SS–LSLT* and related work, then one can only conclude that the thesis is not even under consideration, surely not refuted or supported by recent discussion. I will merely emphasize again that the "legitimacy of semantics" (whatever that might mean) has never, to my knowledge, been challenged, nor has there ever been any question of the importance of incorporating a study of reference, meaning, language use, and related topics within a full theory of language that will deal, in particular, with the highly significant relations between formal structure and semantic interpretation. The appeal to meaning must be clearly distinguished from the study of meaning. The latter enterprise is unquestionably central to the general theory of language, and a major goal of the *SS–LSLT* approach is to advance it by showing how a sufficiently rich theory of linguistic form can provide structural descriptions that provide the basis for the fruitful investigation of semantic questions. But the appeal to meaning within the theory of linguistic form has all too often served simply as a way of side-stepping serious inquiry. I will return to this matter in another context in §III.

A few years after the publication of *SS*, Fodor and Katz undertook the first systematic effort to develop a theory that would relate questions of meaning to transformational generative grammar.[29] The *SS–LSLT* approach was vague about the notion "semantic representation." A "use theory of meaning" was implicit in the very inadequate discussion of these topics. Fodor and Katz suggested that a theory of semantic representation might be constructed, more or less analogous to the theory of phonetic representation, and that each sentence might be assigned a representation in "semantic space" by compositional projection rules. The general theory of language, then, will characterize the "possible meanings" much as it characterizes the "possible forms" in the theory of universal phonetics. This line of investigation was carried further by Katz and Postal,[30] who proposed that transformations make no contribution to the determination of meaning. In the "standard theory" (see p. 17, above) it was proposed that the deep structure of a sentence fully determines its meaning in some important sense of this notion, though it was noted that some aspects of the interpretation of sentences seem to relate directly to surface structure.[31] Work by Jackendoff and others suggested that the semantic contribution of deep structure is limited to the role of deep structure grammatical relations (subject–verb, verb–object, etc.) in determining such semantic relations as agency, instrument, etc.[32] The designation "extended standard theory" has been suggested for the modification of the standard theory that postulates that semantic representation is determined by deep and surface structure, where the grammatical relations of deep structure and the particular properties of lexical items determine semantic relations, and all other properties (e.g., anaphoric relations, the scope of negation and quantifiers, and other aspects of what might be called "logical form") are determined by rules operating on surface structure.[33]

There are, I believe, good reasons for postulating that transformations that move expressions leave a "trace" in the position from which the item was moved: this abstract trace can be regarded as a bound variable, in effect.[34] In accordance with such a theory of transformations, a surface structure is in interesting respects analogous to an expression in conventional systems of logic, and in many cases can be converted into such an expression by fairly simple rules. It seems to me reasonable to think of the system of grammatical transformations as, in essence, a mapping of a system of grammatical relations (expressed by deep structure) onto a logical form (determined by surface structure).

Katz has perhaps been the clearest advocate of the view that linguistic theory provides a system for representation of meaning, and that the rules of grammar literally map formal structure into representations of meaning.[35] My own view is more skeptical. In *ATS* it is argued that the line of demarcation (if there is one) between syntax and semantics is most unclear, and that it is also questionable whether the theory of meaning can be divorced from the study of other cognitive structures (*ATS*, p. 159; also references of Note 26). I suspect that Katz's approach is legitimate over an interesting range, but that much of what is often regarded as central to the study of meaning cannot be dissociated from systems of belief in any natural way. However, I will not pursue the matter here, my purpose being merely to indicate some of the lines of inquiry that have been pursued in recent years.[36]

A further theoretical innovation of the 1960s is the investigation of abstract conditions on the operation of transformational rules. The theory of transformations as developed in *LSLT* was far too unrestricted. It seems that there are much narrower conditions that determine the applicability of transformations and the kinds of mapping that they can perform. The first proposals on this matter appear in *CILT*. A very important study by Ross carries the investigation much further.[37] I have attempted a further extension and revision of the theory in "Conditions on transformations" (cf. Note 34), and a number of linguists have important further work in progress.

Related studies have suggested that the set of possible transformations can be restricted considerably beyond what is suggested in *SS* and *LSLT*. Emonds has proposed[38] that transformations fall into three major categories: cyclic transformations, root transformations, and minor movement rules. All movement rules among the cyclic transformations are "structure-preserving," in that items of category X can only be moved to a position dominated by the category X. Thus Noun Phrases can be moved to a Noun Phrase position, etc. Root transformations apply only at the final or near-final stage of cyclic application, in a manner that Emonds defines more carefully. Minor movement rules are permutations of adjacent phrases, one of which at least is a word or morpheme category. Others have made more radical though still inexplicit and quite tentative proposals.[39]

For reasons that I have already mentioned, it is crucial to restrict the class of transformational grammars if we are to deal with the fundamental question of justifying grammars and accounting for the human ability to acquire knowledge of language. This is true if we approach the matter from a methodological standpoint, seeking to construct the most restrictive theory with the strongest claims, hence the theory that is most subject to empirical disconfirmation and that makes the most significant contribution to the justification of the linguist's grammars. It is also true if we adopt the alternative psychological perspective, attempting to characterize the "initial state" of the organism capable of acquiring human language, the innate schematism and mechanisms that are applied in the analysis of the data of sense. Investigations of the sort that I have briefly mentioned here are contributions to this problem.

Some linguists have argued, in contrast, that the conditions on grammar must be considerably weakened. It has been proposed that linguistic theory (apart from phonology) can do no more than characterize the notions "surface structure" and "semantic representation," and that beyond this, arbitrary rules (called "derivational constraints," in this theory) must be permitted.[40] The various approaches within so-called "generative semantics" seem to lead in a similar direction. I have argued elsewhere (*SSGG*, Chapter 3) that generative semantics, insofar as it has been clearly formulated, differs from the extended standard theory only in that it weakens certain empirical assumptions of the latter: in particular, it drops the requirement that lexical and nonlexical transformations be segregated,[41] and it permits rules relating steps of derivations quite freely ("derivational constraints"), whereas the extended standard theory permits only rules relating adjacent steps and rules determining semantic interpretation from deep and surface structure.[42] The empirical arguments that have been offered for abandoning a more restrictive (hence preferable) theory seem to me unconvincing. On the contrary, the more restrictive assumptions of the extended standard theory are supported by empirical evidence. For discussion, see *SSGG*, particularly Chapter 3 (which also appears in P. S. Peters, ed., *op. cit.*).

I have made no attempt here to summarize or even to mention the many important contributions in recent years to linguistic theory and the theory of particular languages, but only to indicate some of the essential respects in which further work suggests modification of the *LSLT* theory of generative grammar. Again, it must be stressed that all of these topics are the subject of controversy and that any conclusions that can now be offered are highly tentative. Many new ideas are being explored and a wide range of linguistic phenomena, in a variety of domains of language structure and use, is being actively investigated. The extended standard theory seems to me to be the most promising current version of the theory of generative grammar. I think that it does indeed offer the possibility of approaching the deeper problems sketched earlier.

After this brief sketch of some of the major concepts in *LSLT* and
developments since, I will now turn to the final topic of this introduction,
the origins of the work presented in *LSLT*. I am afraid that this account
will have to be more or less autobiographical, since I was working at the
time in isolation to a considerable extent.

My formal introduction to the field of linguistics was in 1947, when
Zellig Harris gave me the proofs of his *Methods in Structural Linguistics*[43]
to read. I found it very intriguing and, after some stimulating discussions
with Harris, decided to major in linguistics as an undergraduate at the
University of Pennsylvania. I had some informal acquaintance with
historical linguistics and medieval Hebrew grammar, based on my
father's work in these fields,[44] and at the time was studying Arabic
with Giorgio Levi Della Vida. Apart from some introductory work in
logic and philosophy, I had studied nothing else related to the material
under consideration here.

Harris suggested that I undertake a systematic structural grammar
of some language. I chose Hebrew, which I knew fairly well. For a time,
I worked with an informant and applied methods of structural linguistics
as I was then coming to understand them. The results, however, seemed
to me rather dull and unsatisfying. Having no very clear idea as to how
to proceed further, I abandoned these efforts and did what seemed
natural; namely, I tried to construct a system of rules for generating the
phonetic forms of sentences, that is, what is now called a generative
grammar. I thought it might be possible to devise a system of recursive
rules to describe the form and structure of sentences, recasting the
devices in Harris's *Methods* for this purpose,[45] and thus perhaps to
achieve the kind of explanatory force that I recalled from historical
grammar.[46] I had in mind such specific examples as the following.
The Hebrew root *mlk* ("king") enters into such forms as *malki* ("my
king"), *malka* ("queen"), *mlaxim* ("kings"). The change of *k* to *x* in
mlaxim results from a general process of spirantization in post-vocalic
position. But consider the construct state form *malxey* ("kings of").
Here we have *x* in a phonological context in which we would expect *k*
(cf. *malki*, *malka*). The anomaly can be explained if we assume that
spirantization preceded a process of vowel reduction that converted
malaxim to *mlaxim* and *malaxey-X* ("kings of *X*," where *X* contains the
main stress) to *malxey-X*. The processes of spirantization and reduction
(generally, antepretonic) are motivated independently, and by assuming
the historical order to be spirantization–reduction, one can explain the
arrangement of forms *malki*, *malka*, *malxey*, *mlaxim*. It seemed only
natural to construct a synchronic grammar with ordering of rules such
as spirantization and reduction to explain the distribution of existing

forms. Pursuing this idea, I constructed a detailed grammar, concentrating on the rules for deriving phonetic forms from abstract morphophonemic representations. A version of this was submitted as an undergraduate thesis in 1949, and a more extensive version as a master's thesis in 1951. A further revision of fall 1951 was to be the Appendix to Chapter VII, below.[47]

The syntactic component of the grammar was rudimentary. It consisted of phrase structure rules modeled on Harris's morpheme-to-utterance formulas (cf. *Methods*, Chapter 16), reconstructed and modified to serve as rules for generating the syntactic structures of the strings submitted to the morphophonemic component of the grammar, with extensive utilization of long components to express interconnections and selectional relations among phrases. The morphophonemic component was quite detailed, consisting of 45 general rules, most of which have many subrules. The rules were presented in a linear order and applied in that order to derive "phonemic" forms from morphophonemic forms—to use more recent terminology (cf. *SPE*), to derive systematic phonetic representations from phonological representations. The ordering was partial—that is, some reordering was possible without modifying the mapping defined by the system of rules—but extensive.

Since the purpose of this grammar was to provide explanations for the distribution of phonetic forms, it was obvious that there must be some general method for selecting one grammar over others that would serve as well to enumerate these forms. This is particularly clear in a finite system such as morphophonemics, with no recursive devices. Thus a standard phonemic analysis would serve to enumerate the forms, though in a rather unenlightening way, as is perhaps evident even from the single example cited earlier.

The obvious means for selecting among grammars is in terms of the degree of significant generalization that they achieve. In the conventional sense of the term, a generalization is a single rule about many elements. Generalizing this notion, we might measure the degree of generalization attained by a grammar in terms of the formal similarity among its generative rules, the extent to which they say similar things about elements of various sorts. It was no difficult matter to devise a sytem for amalgamating similar rules, so that grammars with a greater degree of similarity among rules become, literally, shorter than others which express the same mapping from morphophonemic to phonetic representation. This system of representation defines a "notational transformation" that assigns to each grammar a number, its length when rules are amalgamated. The system for amalgamating rules expresses a hypothesis as to the relations among rules that constitute linguistically significant generalizations. To illustrate, in *MMH*, notations were defined in such a way that the sequence of morphophonemic rules **I** could be reformulated as **II**:

I   *ABCDF*
        ABCEF
        ACDF
        ACEF

II $A(B) \, C \begin{Bmatrix} D \\ E \end{Bmatrix} F$

The "simplicity measure" of **I** is thus 6, since there are six symbols in **II**. Under the same system of notations, the sequence of rules **III** could be reformulated as **IV** with simplicity measure 7, and the sequence **V** cannot be reformulated at all, so that its simplicity measure is 18:

III   *ABCDF*
        ABCFE
        ACDF
        ACFE

IV $A(B) \, C \begin{Bmatrix} DF \\ FE \end{Bmatrix}$

V   *ABCDE*
        EABCD
        ACDE
        EACD

These notations thus express the empirical hypothesis that the cyclic property of the morphophonemic rules **V** is a mere accident, reflecting no principle of organization of language, whereas the properties exhibited by **I** and **III** are significant, and that the degree of significant generalization of the rules **I** is greater than that of the rules **III**. For further discussion, see *MMH*, *ATS*, *SPE*, and references cited there.

   A system for measuring simplicity in this sense is sometimes called an "evaluation procedure" for grammars. Note that if linguistic theory is so restrictive that it does not permit alternative grammars compatible with a body of data of reasonable size and diversity (where by "reasonable" we mean of an order comparable to what suffices for language learning), then an evaluation procedure need not be constructed as part of linguistic theory (*ATS*, pp. 36–37). Occasionally, it has been argued that evaluation procedures are not necessary. This is to say that linguistic theory can be constrained in the manner indicated. Since there have been no serious attempts to give substance to such proposals, it is impossible to pursue the matter. It is a logical possibility (*ibid.*), though an unlikely one, it appears to me.

Note again that the evaluation procedure proposed in *MMH* (similarly, *ATS*, *SPE*, and other work) constitutes an empirical hypothesis with regard to the "essence of human language," specifically, with regard to the principles of organization that are taken to be fundamental in that the generalizations that express them are defined as "linguistically significant" and contribute to the selection of grammars. Thus, suppose someone were to propose that curly brackets as in **II, IV** should not be permitted in the evaluation procedure. This proposal (which one can find in the literature, without further clarification) amounts to the empirical hypothesis that, e.g., there is no linguistic significance to the principle of organization expressed by **II** as compared with **IV**. In contrast, the notation described, as part of an evaluation measure, expresses the hypothesis that the similarity of rules in **I** as compared with **III** is linguistically significant and reflects a true generalization. Similar remarks apply with regard to other features of an evaluation measure. See the sources mentioned earlier for discussion.

For an approach of the sort just outlined to be meaningful, we must characterize precisely not only the "notational transformation" which implicitly defines "linguistically significant generalization," but also the set of admissible grammars to which the evaluation procedure is to be applied. Linguistic theory, so conceived, thus becomes a theory of the system of permissible grammars, the structures generated by those grammars, and the principles of linguistically significant generalization, to be captured in the evaluation procedure (see Note 10).

Note finally that the "simplicity measure" is global; it is a measure that can be applied only to a completed grammar. There can be no step-by-step procedure to determine the highest-valued grammar. Thus the approach of *MMH* represented a sharp break with the procedural theories of structural linguistics in any of the clearly formulated versions of this approach (Harris, Bloch, Trubetzkoy, *et al.*).

In the 1949 and 1951 versions of *MMH*, these notions are investigated and an evaluation procedure is proposed. I investigated one aspect of "simplicity" in considerable detail, namely, the effect of rule ordering, showing that the grammar as presented is at a "local maximum" in simplicity in that if any two rules adjacent in the ordering[48] were interchanged, the grammar would have to be revised in such a way as to increase complexity as measured by the formal evaluation measure. This analysis was applied, however, only to the morphophonemic component of the grammar, the only component that had any real explanatory force. If we define "depth of ordering" to mean the length of the maximal subsequence of rules no two of which can be interchanged without a modification that will decrease simplicity, then the demonstrated depth of ordering in the morphophonemic component of 45 general rules was 25; subrules were also ordered in the same sense, but the problem of demonstrating ordering was not pursued to this level of detail.

It became obvious that in strictly applying a procedure of evaluation that appeared to express a natural concept of "linguistically significant generalization" I was being driven to more abstract underlying forms which were, in many cases, historically more primitive as well. Furthermore, many of the rules suggested familiar historical processes. Thus there was a certain loose resemblance between the synchronic grammar, selected by application of a formal evaluation measure, and a historical grammar such as Harris's *Development of the Canaanite Dialects.*[49] In 1951, Bar-Hillel suggested to me that I put aside my hesitations on the matter and postulate something very much like the reconstructed historical forms on the abstract morphophonemic level. It was with this in mind that I carried out the revision to the final 1951 version. I was struck by the fact that it led to considerable improvement.

While I found this work intriguing and exciting, I thought of it as more or less of a private hobby, having no relationship to "real linguistics." Part of my skepticism about this work derived from the fact that as the grammar was improved in terms of its explanatory force and degree of generalization, it became more and more difficult to isolate anything approximating a phonemic representation, and I took for granted that phonemic analysis was the unchallengeable core of linguistic theory. More generally, I was firmly committed to the belief that the procedural analysis of Harris's *Methods* and similar work should really provide complete and accurate grammars if properly refined and elaborated. But the elements that I was led to postulate in studying the generative grammar of Hebrew were plainly not within the range of such procedures. However refined, these were essentially procedures of segmentation and classification. They were designed to isolate classes of phones, sequences of these classes, classes of these sequences, etc., until, ultimately, sentences are characterized in terms of their constituents.[50] But the elements that were needed in the optimal generative grammar simply did not have this character. They were not classes, sequences of classes, or anything of the sort, but were simply abstract elements forming strings that could be mapped into phonetic representation by deeply ordered rules of considerable generality. I therefore assumed that whatever I was doing, it was not real scientific linguistics, but something else, obscure in status. This feeling was reinforced by the almost total lack of interest in *MMH* on the part of linguists whose work I respected.[51]

The work that I took more seriously was devoted to the problem of revising and extending procedures of analysis so as to overcome difficulties that arose when they were strictly applied. The critical difficulties arose at the level of syntactic description. Obviously, syntax is an infinite system, but the inductive step that would lead to a description of syntactic structure was plainly lacking, though there were hints, which I felt could be made precise, in Harris's *Methods*. I will not recount the various efforts I made from 1947 until 1953 to try to overcome this and related problems.[52]

While working on "discovery procedures" for linguistics, I was troubled by a number of nagging doubts. In the first place, if (as I assumed) refinements with no far-reaching conceptual change would suffice to provide a complete and formalized system of procedures, then linguistics as a theoretical field would have a kind of "terminal character." That is, by applying these methods, we would be able to derive mechanically the grammar of any language, given an adequate corpus. Obviously, it must be possible to achieve such a result; every child serves as an "existence proof," in that he acquires knowledge of his language, and the knowledge acquired is, to a very good approximation, identical to that acquired by others on the basis of their equally limited and somewhat different experience. Nevertheless, it seemed impossible that grammars derived by methods of the sort under investigation could really express and characterize knowledge of language, which posed innumerable mysteries. My own work on Hebrew, though only rudimentary beyond the morphophonemic level, sufficed to suggest to me that something central was missing. The failure of inductive, data-processing procedures at the syntactic level became more obvious the more I worked on the problem. Shortly after arriving in Cambridge in the fall of 1951, I met Morris Halle, then a student of Roman Jakobson's at Harvard and on the teaching staff at MIT. We disagreed sharply about the merits of procedural approaches in phonology, morphology, and morphophonemics, and though I was not convinced by his arguments, his skepticism about the point of such work led to further doubts.

By 1952, I was working on generative grammar of English, and shortly obtained results that I found quite exciting, though they were entirely divorced from the systems of procedures of analysis on which

I was working at the same time; in particular, results on the system of auxiliary verbs in simple declaratives, interrogatives, negatives, passives, and on complex verb constructions such as "want (*NP*) to *VP*," "consider *NP* (to be) *Predicate*,"[53] etc. As in the case of my earlier work on morphophonemics of Hebrew, it was possible, so it became clear, to discover systems of rules that made sense of the distribution of forms, principles that served to explain a collection of superficially chaotic and anomalous facts. In this case, too, investigation led to more abstract underlying structures that were far removed from anything that might be obtained by systematic application of procedures of analysis of the sort that I was investigating. Again, interest and encouragement on the part of a few friends (in particular, Halle and Bar-Hillel) stimulated me to further work in this area.

My efforts to characterize the missing "inductive step" in procedural analysis led in a similar direction. A natural first step is to construct a system of categories such as Noun, Verb, etc. We may take a "grammatical sentence form" to be a sequence of categories formed from a sentence of the corpus by replacing each word by the category to which it belongs. This system of categories projects the corpus to the set of sentences which are, item by item, members of the categories of a grammatical sentence form. However, although there is frequent reference in the literature of linguistics, psychology, and philosophy of language to inductive procedures, methods of abstraction, analogy and analogical synthesis, generalization, and the like, the fundamental inadequacy of these suggestions is obscured only by their unclarity.[54] The same is true of the substitution procedures developed by linguists in an effort to come to grips with these problems (cf. §§34–35).

It became increasingly clear to me that the methodological limitation to procedures based on substitution, matching, and similar "taxonomic" operations was arbitrary and unwarranted. One might approach the problem of projecting a corpus to a language of grammatical sentences in an entirely different way, with a procedure for evaluating a completed system of categories rather than a procedure for constructing these categories step by step by taxonomic methods. I began to explore several methods of the former sort (cf. Chapter V). Discussions with Peter Elias, a specialist in information theory then also a Junior Fellow at Harvard, led to an approach suggested by an information measure, and several exploratory empirical investigations of various category systems in these terms seemed promising,[55] considerably more so than the taxonomic studies to which I had previously devoted much effort. Two approaches to the specific problem of defining syntactic categories were thus counterposed: a constructive, taxonomic approach and an alternative, no less rigorous or formalizable, that was concerned essentially with the properties of a completed solution.

It was clear at once that the problem of defining syntactic categories was only a special case. The taxonomic approach, which encompassed all theoretical studies of language known to me that were concerned with the fundamental problem of projection and with the precise characterization of the general concepts of linguistics, sought to define such concepts as "phoneme," "morpheme," "category," etc., by procedures of segmentation and classification applied at successive levels of generality, providing what might reasonably be called "a grammar of lists."[56] Alternatively, one might try to define the notion "grammar" directly in terms of a set of primitive notions applicable to a corpus of data; the phonemes, morphemes, categories, etc., would then be the elements that appear in the highest-valued grammar of the appropriate form meeting the empirical conditions determined by application of the primitive notions to a corpus of data. There would now be no reason to regard phonemes, morphemes, categories, and other elements to be segments, classes of segments, sequences of classes, sets of phenomenal properties (e.g., phonetic distinctive features), and so on. Rather, they would be elements in various abstract systems of representation.

Given a system of syntactic categories of various levels of abstractness, selected by an evaluation measure, it seemed possible to make inroads into defining "grammaticalness" and "degree of grammaticalness" ("deviation from grammaticalness"). One might further consider the system of syntactic categories to be one of several "levels of representation," each providing certain descriptive mechanisms that are in principle available for grammar construction. The language and its structure, then, might be determined, given an adequate corpus, by a system of general principles of language structure that characterize linguistic levels, the form of possible grammars, the structures (systems of levels) generated by a grammar, and the evaluation procedure for selecting among such grammars. In this way, I gradually came to believe, one might not only solve the "inductive problem" (now abandoning all inductive methods, in a strict sense), but also, more important, develop and justify grammars with a range of explanatory power that clearly escaped the limits of taxonomic theory.

I was particularly struck by the fact that by adopting this nontaxonomic approach I could bring together the two apparently distinct lines of inquiry that I had been pursuing since beginning the study of linguistics: the attempt to define precisely the notions of linguistic theory in such a way as to overcome the empirical inadequacies of existing approaches; and the study of generative grammars such as my

Hebrew grammar and the grammar of English that I was then working on seriously. The notion "generative grammar" would, in this non-taxonomic approach, be the central notion of linguistic theory, along with the notions "linguistic level" and "evaluation procedure."

By 1953, I had abandoned any hope of formulating taxonomic "discovery procedures" and turned my attention entirely to the problems of generative grammar, in theory and in application. It was at that point that I began writing *LSLT*, bringing together and extending the work I had begun on various aspects of generative grammar, but now with conviction as well as enthusiasm.

At Harris's suggestion, I had begun to study logic, philosophy, and foundations of mathematics more seriously as a graduate student at the University of Pennsylvania, and later at Harvard. I was particularly impressed by Nelson Goodman's work on constructional systems (see his *Structure of Appearance*, Harvard University Press, 1951). In its general character, this work was in some ways similar to Harris's, and seemed to me to provide the appropriate intellectual background for the investigations of taxonomic procedures that I then regarded as central to linguistic theory. But Goodman's ongoing critique of induction seemed to point in a rather different direction, suggesting the inadequacy in principle of inductive approaches.[57] Goodman's investigations of the simplicity of systems[58] also suggested (to me at least) possibilities for a nontaxonomic approach to linguistic theory. Quine's critique of logical empiricism also gave some reason to believe that this line of inquiry might be a plausible one. Quine argued that the principles of scientific theory are confronted with experience as a systematic complex, with adjustments possible at various points, governed by such factors as general simplicity.[59] Perhaps, then, analogous considerations hold for "the fundamental problem of linguistic theory" (see above, p. 12).

LSLT was an attempt to show how linguistic theory might be developed in terms of an initial schematism that determines the set of possible grammars and the structures that they generate. In terms of these notions, one might define the concepts of linguistic theory: phoneme, morpheme, category, phrase, etc. The phonemes (etc.) would be the elements that appear at the appropriate place in the levels of description generated by the highest-valued grammar of the type permitted by the initial schematism The empirical constraints on grammar selection are to be provided by a set of primitive notions, in terms of which all definitions are framed These primitives are to be applicable to a corpus of linguistic data. If the project were successful, we would thus have a constructional system in which all notions are defined ultimately in terms of an acceptable set of primitives, but the definitions will be "indirect," mediated in terms of the more central concepts of "grammar," "structure," and "procedure of evaluation." Applying the primitives to a corpus of data, all linguistic notions for the language of which the corpus is a sample would be defined, though no taxonomic, data-processing procedures would be available for determining the application of these concepts directly.

One consequence of approaching linguistic theory in this way is that the problem of "separation of levels" disappears. Our goal is to define the concepts of linguistic theory in terms of a set of primitive notions. Clearly, circularity must be avoided, if the application of the concepts is to be fixed when the primitives are applied. If concepts are defined by taxonomic procedures, it is necessary that elements (sequences, classes, sequences of classes, etc.) be constructed on "lower levels" before "higher-level" elements are constructed as classes, sequences, etc., of these lower-level elements. The problem had been approached in various ways,[60] and evidently could not be ignored. However, in the framework of *LSLT* the problem does not arise. The grammar of a language L is the most highly-valued system of the permitted form compatible with the data available from L, where "compatibility" is determined by the primitive notions of linguistic theory. The linguistic levels of L are determined by the grammar, and may be interrelated in a variety of ways. The notions "higher level" and "lower level" are now a kind of metaphor, though, as noted in the text, they retain some suggestive value.

Since our goal is to provide as full and systematic an account of the interconnections among concepts as possible, we naturally want to find the "simplest system" of primitive notions.[61] Operational tests should be sought to apply the primitive notions to the data.[62] Suppose we take "phonemically distinct" ("contrasts") to be a fundamental notion of linguistic theory. We may then seek to define it in terms of primitives,[63] or we may take it as a primitive notion itself and seek an operational test for it. The paired-utterance test, discussed by Harris, is a good first approximation to an operational test for phonemic distinctness of utterance tokens, which might be refined in a number of ways. In practice, some variant of this test must be used when a nontrivial problem of determining contrast arises, and it does appear to capture presystematic intuitions fairly well. As noted earlier, it was widely assumed in the early 1950s that grammar depends on meaning in the sense that such notions as "contrast" must be defined in terms of "synonymy" ("difference of meaning" or "differential meaning" was the term often preferred). As far as I could make out, there was not then (nor is there now) any coherent formulation of this proposal, or of other proposals that the concepts of syntax and phonology must (or even can) be defined in terms of semantic primitives.[64] The matter is discussed briefly in *LSLT* (cf. §13).[65]

Similarly, consider the notion of "substitutable," which might be expected to play a role in the definition of "syntactic category" (and elsewhere). We might take "substitutable" as a primitive concept, thus in effect taking as unanalyzed a particular notion of projection of a corpus to a tentative set of grammatical sentences. Alternatively, we might try to explain this first step of projection by defining the relevant notion of "substitutable" in other terms. Since "the purpose of a theory is to investigate to the fullest extent the relations between the notions that enter into the theory," the latter course is preferable, if feasible (§34.2). "Complete success in unearthing and expressing these interrelations is marked by the elimination of terms from the primitive basis" (*ibid.*); partial success, by conditions relating terms taken as primitive, i.e., postulates of the constructional system. See also Note 6, Chapter II.

Given a constructional system of the sort just outlined, we can suggest a way to approach the fundamental problem of linguistic theory (cf. above, p. 12): how does a child come to know the language of his speech community?[66] We might reasonably propose that the human mind is innately endowed with the structures of the postulated con-structional system and with a procedure for applying the primitive notions to the data of sense. If the constructional system is sufficiently restrictive, the number of potential grammars available as sufficiently highly-valued to be submitted to the evaluation procedure might be fairly small. Thus a grammar would be selected, determining the child's knowledge of language. In such a way, we might hope to come to understand how it is that knowledge of language has two striking qualita-tive properties: first, as the normal use of language indicates, it is vast and rich as compared with the limited experience on the basis of which it is acquired; and second, it is narrowly determined and comparable to the knowledge acquired by others on the basis of somewhat different experience. Furthermore, just as selection of the highest-valued grammar may lead us to project the corpus of data in such a way as to exclude parts of it as deviant (see Chapter V), so the language-learner must deal with experience that is degenerate in the sense that it may contain errors and slips, deviant (though appropriate) forms, and so on. Again, this is a striking and obvious property of language-learning.

In *LSLT* the "psychological analogue" to the methodological problem of constructing linguistic theory is not discussed, but it lay in the immediate background of my own thinking. To raise this issue seemed to me, at the time, too audacious. It was, however, raised explicitly in the review article by Lees published in 1957 (see Note 2). In rewriting *LSLT* for publication in 1958–9 (see above, p. 4), I presented this alternative psychological interpretation as the framework for the entire study, and in later work have continued to do so.

We thus have two variants of the fundamental problem of linguistics, as it was conceived in this work: under the methodological interpretation, the problem is taken to be the justification of grammars; under the psychological interpretation, the problem is to account for language acquisition. A linguistic theory, under either conception, is explanatory in a proper and appropriate sense. Given such a theory and certain "boundary conditions" fixed by a corpus of data with a preliminary analysis determined by the application of the primitives of the theory, a grammar is selected. Under the methodological interpretation, the selected grammar is the linguist's grammar, justified by the theory. Under the psychological interpretation, it is the speaker-hearer's grammar, chosen by the evaluation procedure from among the potential grammars permitted by the theory and compatible with the data as represented in terms of the preliminary analysis. In either case, the grammar determines a range of linguistic facts relating to the structure of sentences. The speaker-hearer's judgments that the facts are as determined by the grammar are thus explained by the linguistic theory; correspondingly, the theory is refuted if the judgments are not in accord with the predictions of the grammar.[67]

As already noted, the procedural approaches developed and applied to varied language material are among the most sophisticated and interesting efforts undertaken within a significant (i.e., nonvacuous) empiricist framework. There was some unclarity, in this work, as to exactly what was at stake. Procedures are sometimes presented simply as a device for giving a more organized and less redundant characterization of the linguist's corpus of data. Thus one set of procedures, and the results they provide, are in principle no better or worse than others, apart from their utility for particular purposes. No empirical claim is associated with a particular system of procedures, under this interpretation. However, a careful review of the work in question seems to me to show that a different and more interesting conception was implicit, despite disclaimers: namely, that the procedures determined the true structure of language, a system with "psychological reality."[68] On other grounds, it is difficult to explain why investigators continually found it necessary to revise and modify their procedures in the light of results that were, in some unexplained sense, "unacceptable," though in no way inconsistent with the corpus of data (rather, the results were obtained by applying the procedures in question to the data). The problems become acute in syntactic investigation, where the subject matter is unbounded in scope and the problem of accuracy of prediction is thus unavoidable.

In *LSLT*, the "realist" position is taken for granted. That is, I assumed that the procedural theories I was attempting to refine, extend, and correct did make an empirical claim. A grammar determined by a linguistic theory (given data) constitutes a hypothesis concerning the speaker-hearer's knowledge of his language and is to be confirmed or disconfirmed in terms of empirical evidence drawn, ultimately, from investigation of the linguistic intuitions of the language-user (which might, in principle, be analyzed in terms of operational tests; cf. §§12–15, below). The general theory, now regarded as an explanatory theory, is likewise to be understood as a psychological theory that attempts to characterize the innate human "language faculty," and that can be tested in terms of its consequences in particular languages. Thus I wanted to resolve the tension that I sensed in structuralist theory in a specific way, which seemed to me inconsistent with the announced intentions and understanding (if not, perhaps, the implicit assumptions) of some of the linguists whose work I was attempting to develop further.

The search for an explanatory linguistic theory, now understood in the "realist" sense, is, naturally, closely related to the investigation of linguistic universals. General properties of language, if not merely historical accident and thus of no real interest, must be attributable to an interaction of (1) genetically determined mechanisms of mind and (2) uniformities in the empirical conditions of language use and acquisition. An explicit linguistic theory of either the taxonomic or nontaxonomic variety can be understood as an empirical hypothesis concerning factors of the former sort. It postulates intrinsic properties of mind, genetically determined, though no doubt requiring external stimulation to come into operation in their distinctive way, and perhaps developing through maturational stages, again interacting with external conditions. Thus if one takes a realist interpretation of the work of post-Bloomfieldian theorists, they are proposing certain quite deep linguistic universals: the principles implied by their procedural methods. Under this interpretation, it is postulated that human languages must have the properties determined by application of these procedures to a corpus of data. My own decision to abandon taxonomic approaches resulted from an increasingly firm belief that languages simply do not have these properties. As my work on transformational generative grammar of English proceeded from 1952, I was increasingly convinced by this conclusion, and was thus able to take more seriously the earlier work that I had done on a (nontransformational) generative grammar of Hebrew, and the related theoretical notions. It could not be, I felt, that the explanations of varied and complex phenomena that could be developed in terms of transformational generative grammar were mere accidents. Furthermore, as apparent anomalies and arbitrary features of language structure became comprehensible in these terms, it became increasingly difficult to accept the assumption (which is, after all, arbitrary and not independently motivated) that linguistic universals are as postulated in the realist interpretation of taxonomic theories.

Under the realist interpretation of linguistic theory, it is a natural—in fact, obligatory—task to compare alternative linguistic theories in terms of their empirical consequences. Insofar as these theories are precisely formulated, this task becomes a feasible one. In *LSLT* the central topic of investigation is the comparison of two nontaxonomic generative theories: the theory of phrase structure and transformational theory.[69] I attempted to press to the limits an explicit theory of phrase structure (with a characterization of phrase-structure grammar, the level of phrase structure, the relation between the two, the relation of phrase structure to other levels, and an evaluation procedure), and to show that it was unable to account for the facts of language. I also attempted to show that the inadequacies revealed could be overcome by theory of transformational generative grammar and a level of transformational structure. Chapters VII through X of *LSLT*, which constitute the bulk of this manuscript, are devoted to this problem.

This effort may well be inexplicable to someone who adopts a nonrealist interpretation of linguistic theory. Harris, for example, seems to regard it as a curious aberration, perhaps to be explained in sociological terms.[70] In his view, there are no "competing theories," and "pitting of one linguistic tool against another" is senseless. Alternative theories are equally valid, as alternative procedures of analysis are equally valid. Each can be applied as a "basis for a description of the whole language" and "sentences exhibit simultaneously all of [the] properties" determined by application of these theories (*ibid.*). This is, I believe, a faithful interpretation of post-Bloomfieldian structuralism in its more explicit varieties, though, as noted, it leaves much unexplained in the practice of theorists of this persuasion.

If one adopts the realist interpretation, linguistic theory provides a justification for particular generative grammars that made explicit empirical claims, true or false. Formalization of alternative linguistic theories is undertaken in an effort to determine precisely what such theories imply, so that they can be accepted, rejected, or modified in terms of their empirical consequences. It is important to avoid obscure and intuition-bound notions and to apply linguistic theory strictly, avoiding *ad hoc* adjustments or loose formulation. Absurd consequences, if they result, are important, in that they indicate the necessity for a revision of the theory. The same is true of failure to provide explanations for the phenomena of language. There are "competing theories," and "pitting of one . . . against another," in an effort to discover which of several alternatives is valid, is of the very essence of the inquiry. *LSLT* is devoted to an exploration of this realist interpretation of linguistic theory, primarily in the area of syntax, and to the choice between theories that are plainly in conflict.

At this level of discussion, there is no question of "right or wrong." It is merely a question of where one's interests lie. If someone prefers not to adopt a "realist interpretation" of linguistic theory, and thus to make no claim for the empirical validity of the theoretical principles he adopts, I see no argument that could demonstrate to him that this conception must be abandoned. Or conversely.

Perhaps a word might usefully be added on the general intellectual climate in Cambridge at the time when *LSLT* was written.[71] Inter-disciplinary approaches to language, communication, and human behavior were much the vogue—thus it was hardly surprising that a student in Cambridge in the early 1950s should have come to think of linguistics as, in effect, a branch of cognitive psychology concerned with the language faculty and its exercise. Roman Jakobson's work was well known and influential. Oxford ordinary language analysis and Wittgen-stein's later work were attracting great interest. The problem of recon-ciling these approaches (if possible) with Quine's provocative ideas on language and knowledge troubled many students. Mathematical logic, in particular recursive function theory and metamathematics, were becoming more generally accessible, and developments in these areas seemed to provide tools for a more precise study of natural language as well. All of this I personally found most stimulating.

At the same time electronic computers were just beginning to make their impact. The mathematical theory of communication, cybernetics, sound spectrography, psychophysics, and experimental psychology were in a period of rapid development and much exuberance. Their contribu-tions lent an aura of science and mathematics to the study of language and aroused much enthusiasm, in particular, among those who were attracted by the ideas then current concerning the unity of science. A technology of machine translation, automatic abstracting, and informa-tion retrieval was put forward as a practical prospect. It was confidently expected by many that automatic speech recognition would soon be feasible as well. It was widely believed that B. F. Skinner's William James lectures of 1947[72] offered an account of some of the most complex products of human intelligence in terms of the science of behavior, grounding this study in a system of intelligible concepts and principles verified in animal psychology.[73]

My personal reaction to this particular complex of beliefs, interests, and expectations was almost wholly negative. The behaviorist framework seemed to me a dead end, if not an intellectual scandal. The models of language that were being discussed and investigated had little plausibility, so far as I could see, and I had no personal interest in the experimental studies and technological advances. The latter seemed to me in some respects harmful in their impact, in that they tended to direct research toward problems suggested by the available technology, though of little interest and importance in themselves. As for machine translation and related enterprises, they seemed to me pointless as well as probably quite hopeless. As a graduate student interested in linguistics, logic, and philosophy, I could not fail to be aware of the ferment and excitement. But I felt myself no part of it and gave these matters little serious thought during the years when I was working on *LSLT*. I have been surprised since to read repeated and confident accounts of how work in generative grammar developed out of an interest in computers, machine translation, and related matters. At least as far as my own work is concerned, this is quite false.

Shortly after *LSLT* was completed I did become interested in some of these questions and made several attempts to clarify the issues. For example, virtually every engineer or psychologist with whom I had any contact, and many professional linguists as well,[74] took for granted that the formal models of language proposed in the mathematical theory of communication provided the appropriate framework for general linguistic theory. But this assumption was not correct.[75] Later, I wrote an extensive review of Skinner's *Verbal Behavior*,[76] convincing myself, at least, that there was no hope along these lines.

I have so far been discussing the concepts of generative grammar and of a nontaxonomic theory of language structure, but have as yet said nothing about the specific form of generative grammar developed in *LSLT*. As noted earlier, my *MMH* was an explicit generative grammar, but not a transformational grammar. Rather, its rudimentary syntactic component was a modified phrase-structure grammar with extensive use of long components, essentially, indices carried on grammatically related categories and transmitted to the categories that they dominate. When I began to investigate generative syntax more seriously a few years later, I was able to adapt for this purpose a new concept that had been developed by Zellig Harris and some of his students, namely, the concept of "grammatical transformation." It was quickly apparent that with this new concept, many of the inadequacies of the model that I had used earlier could be overcome.

The concept of "grammatical transformation" developed out of Harris's work on discourse analysis.[77] In about 1948—that is, after the completion of his *Methods in Structural Linguistics*—Harris turned to the investigation of the structure of extended discourse, raising the question whether application of procedures analogous to those developed in his *Methods* might yield some fruitful results. Evidently, the substitution procedures that had been developed for sentence-length units in a corpus (expandable by experiment, if an informant is available) could not be applied to a discourse with its fixed and highly varied sentence forms. However, Harris suggested that it might be possible to apply substitution procedures to a "normalized discourse" formed by applying certain transformations to the sentences of the discourse. Thus, ". . . the complexity of many sentences makes discourse analysis hardly applicable unless the text has first been normalized by transformations,"[78] but once transformations have converted the original sentences into more uniform structures, taxonomic procedures might become applicable. Suppose, for example, that a discourse contained sentences of the general form **1**:

1   (i) $N_1 V N_2$
       (ii) N_3 *is Ved by* N_1
       (iii)   *It is* N_3 *that* $N_4 V$

Suppose that we furthermore have certain relations, as in **2**:

2   (i) $N_x V N_y \leftrightarrow N_y$ *is Ved by* N_x (the passive transformation)
       (ii) $N_x V N_y \leftrightarrow$ *it is* N_y *that* $N_x V$ (the cleft transformation)

Then applying these operations to the text **1** we derive the "normalized" text **3**:

3   (i) $N_1 V N_2$ $(= \text{1i})$
       (ii) $N_1 V N_3$ $(= \text{1ii, under the passive transformation})$
       (iii) $N_4 V N_3$ $(= \text{1iii, under the cleft transformation})$

We might then apply conventional substitution operations to **3**, determining on the basis of (i) and (ii) that N_2 and N_3 belong to the same substitution class, and on the basis of (ii) and (iii) that N_1 and N_4 belong to the same substitution class. Thus we would be able to say that the sentences of **1** are of the form $N_\alpha V N_\beta$ (where N_α contains N_1 and N_4, and N_β contains N_2 and N_3). The substitution classes N_α and N_β are not categories of the language, but rather of this discourse. Examining texts in this way, one might hope to discover properties of structural organization that extend to connected discourse.[79]

Transformational relations such as those of **2** were to be established on the basis of co-occurrence relations. Thus **2i** is a transformation of English if for any choice of nouns N_x and N_y , the sequence $N_x V N_y$ is as acceptable to an informant as is N_y-*is-Ved-by*-N_x .[80]

Note that so understood, each transformation is simply an unordered pair of sentence forms, and the relation "is transformationally related to" is an equivalence relation on sentence forms. If we understand N_x and N_y in **2** to be noun phrases (not necessarily nouns), then each transformation is a relation defined on surface structures. Or, if we take N_x and N_y to be nouns, we may think of the strings related in **2** as a framework converted into actual sentences by adjunction of determiners, particles, adverbs, and so on.[81]

Understood in these terms, transformational analysis is a procedure supplementary to the procedures of structural linguistics, which are complete in themselves. Thus in undertaking transformational analysis, we may assume that the methods of structural linguistics (say, those of Harris's *Methods*) have been applied, along with elicitation techniques if an informant is available. In Harris's original formulation, "we will assume the whole of the usual structural grammar of the language . . ." and then turn to "one of the few types of outside questions that are still relevant to it" ("Co-occurrence," pp. 293, 286), namely, determination of co-occurrence sets (these questions are relevant to structural linguistics in that they "are couched in terms of the raw data of structural morphology"). Having applied the procedures of structural linguistics, the linguist can apply the further procedures of transformational analysis and then turn to discourse analysis and other applications, selecting those transformational relations that are useful for the purpose at hand.

Relations such as **2** are essentially incorrigible once established. Thus "a transformation once established is not normally falsifiable by further research" ("Transformational theory," p. 383). The reason is that each transformation is simply a pairing of two sentence forms that are related by the principle of co-occurrence, as determined by observation and experiment with informants. Each such transformation stands or falls independently of what may be true elsewhere in the language. "It is thus possible to find a precise set of transformations in a language without having to state a precise set of sentences for the language" (*ibid.*, p. 371). This fact is important, since Harris is skeptical about the latter enterprise. It is, he asserts, a "fact that there is no well-defined set of sentences in a language" (*ibid.*, p. 370).

Elsewhere Harris develops a point of view that seems to me somewhat different and perhaps incompatible with these ideas. He suggests that "the grammar which is made to generate all the sentences of [a finite] sample will be found to generate also many other sentences, and unboundedly many sentences of unbounded length" ("Co-occurrence," pp. 338–339). Thus a grammar provides a "well-formedness requirement" ("Transformational theory," p. 384*f*). "There is a family of elementary (axiomatic) sentence forms" (the "kernel"), which satisfy a well-formedness requirement given by a list of sentence forms. For nonkernel sentences, there is "a secondary well-formedness requirement derived from kernel well-formedness." But there is a problem in this formulation. The definition of transformation in terms of observed co-occurrence relations provides no means for the generation of new structures. Nor do the procedures of *Methods*, so far as I can determine, make any explicit provision for the projection of a corpus to a set of grammatical sentences with their structures, as already discussed. In my opinion, these problems relate to the unclarity concerning the "realist interpretation" of linguistic theory discussed earlier.[82]

The "secondary well-formedness requirement" for nonkernel sentences "could as well be expressed in string or other terms as in transformational terms" ("Transformational theory," p. 384); "string analysis" is in effect a variant of phrase-structure description "in which each sentence is segmented into one center string and a number of adjunct strings which are adjoined to the center or adjunct strings" (*ibid.*, p. 363). Thus traditional constituent analysis, string analysis, and transformational analysis are "not competing theories, but rather complement each other in the description of sentences." They focus on different properties, and "each of these properties can be used as a basis for a description of the whole language . . ." (*ibid.*, p. 365). To summarize, transformations are independent of one another, each being a pairing of sentence forms defined in terms of observed co-occurrence, though systems of kernel and "derived" sentences can be set up (presumably, in various ways, for particular purposes and with various criteria). Furthermore, the method of transformational analysis is one of several methods, each complete in itself, each focusing on a particular property of language.

In *LSLT*, transformations are understood in a very different sense; it probably would have been preferable to select a different terminology instead of adapting Harris's in this rather different context. A transformation in *LSLT* is not a relation between sentence forms, or between surface structures, or between centers and the surface structures associated with them by addition of modifiers and other adjuncts. Rather, transformations are rules of a certain type that appear in generative grammars. Each transformation maps abstract representations of phrase structure into other such representations. An initial set of abstract phrase-structure representations (**P**-markers) is provided by rules of a different kind. Application of transformations (including the obligatory operations that are the components of the mapping Φ) yields ultimately the phrase-structure representation (surface structure) of a string of morphemes and words. The term "kernel sentence" was also borrowed from Harris but necessarily given a somewhat different sense; kernel sentences are those with the minimal **T**-marker, namely, the **T**-marker consisting solely of the transformations that are components of Φ. Each kernel sentence results from application of just these transformations to a **P**-marker; no transformations apply to kernel sentences. In Harris's formulation, kernel sentences are characterized by a list of sentence forms; no transformations apply in the generation of kernel sentences and all sentences are related to arrangements of kernel sentences by means of the transformational equivalences (though they could as well be described by the alternative methods of constituent or string analysis).

In the *LSLT* framework, a transformation is definitely falsifiable by further research, since a transformation is not the statement of a particular observed co-occurrence relation, but rather forms part of a system, a generative grammar, which as a whole has certain empirical consequences. Such a system may be refuted by new evidence or may be replaced by a more highly-valued grammar with a different choice of transformations and other rules. No matter how well established a transformation appears today, tomorrow's discoveries may reveal that it was entirely misconceived. Transformations do participate in "stat[ing] a precise set of sentences for the language"; it is assumed that such a specification is possible, as an idealization, to be sure. Thus it is assumed that there is a correct generative grammar which determines the structural characteristics of any string, including those that deviate from well-formedness in various respects, and that the problem of the linguist is to discover this grammar and to discover the linguistic theory that determines possible grammars and incorporates universals of language.

In the *LSLT* framework, a co-occurrence relation between sentence forms may suggest that they derive from the same or related underlying structures by transformation. In Harris's framework, on the contrary, such a relation defines a transformation. For example, in the discussion of verbs with complements below it is noted that "transformational analysis is suggested wherever the complement and the object have the same selectional relation as appears in some simple kernel sentence" (Chapter X, p. 505). In Harris's framework, a transformational relation would be defined in such a case, and the decision would be modified only if further investigation of co-occurrence showed that the co-occurrence relation did not in fact hold. In the *LSLT* theory, the "suggestion" may prove incorrect, so that the transformational analysis will be abandoned.

We have here two quite different conceptions, though they are plainly not unrelated. The differences turn on the notion "generative grammar," and, it appears, on some perhaps deep-seated assumptions concerning the legitimacy of various abstractions and idealizations, and concerning also the goals of linguistic research. The distinctions have been noted repeatedly within both schools of transformational theory. Thus Harris points out that in the alternative *LSLT* theory, transformations "are set up formally not as a relation between sentences but as instructions in the course of generating sentences (from already generated simpler sentences)".[83] Nevertheless, confusions are not rare. I hope that these comments help to clarify the matter.

To summarize these remarks: *LSLT* is an attempt to develop a theory of transformational generative grammar. The "realist interpretation" of linguistic theory is assumed throughout, and it is argued that the competence attained by the normal speaker-hearer is represented by a transformational generative grammar, which determines the representation of each sentence on the levels of phrase structure and transformational structure (*inter alia*). These representations are then employed in the use and understanding of language, and provide the basis for the more general theory of language that will be concerned with meaning and reference, the conditions of appropriate use of language, how sentences are understood, performance in concrete social situations, and in general, the exercise of linguistic competence in thought and communication. The principles of this theory specify the schematism brought to bear by the child in language acquisition. They define the linguistic universals that constitute "the essence of language" (as distinct from accidental properties or properties determined by the exigencies of language use), and thus can be taken as one fundamental element in the characterization of the innate "language faculty." Work by many investigators since has enriched and modified many of the notions developed here and developed the framework that is only implicit in *LSLT*, and has placed it in a rich tradition that was entirely unknown to me at the time.

I hope that this discussion will answer at least some of the many questions that have been raised about the background of this work and will suffice to overcome misunderstandings that might arise by the publication, in 1975, of work that was essentially completed 20 years earlier.

Cambridge, Massachusetts
September 1973

NOTES

1. "Semantic considerations in grammar," Monograph No. 8, The Institute of Languages and Linguistics, Georgetown University (1955); "Three models for the description of language," *I.R.E. Transactions on Information Theory*, Vol. IT-2, Proceedings of the symposium on information theory, September, 1956; "Logical structures in language," *American Documentation* **8**, No. 4, October, 1957.

2. Robert Lees, "Review of Noam Chomsky's *Syntactic Structures*," *Language* **33**, No. 3, 1957.

3. See "A transformational approach to syntax," in Proceedings of the Third Texas Conference on Problems of Linguistic Analysis in English, 1958, A. A. Hill, ed., Texas, 1962; "The transformational basis of syntax," submitted to the Fourth Texas Conference, 1959, unpublished.

4. *The Grammar of English Nominalizations*, Bloomington, 1960. See also his "A multiply ambiguous adjectival construction in English," *Language* **36**, 1960; and Lees and Klima, Note 5.

5. E. S. Klima, "Negation in English," in Jerry F. Fodor and Jerrold J. Katz, eds., *The Structure of Language*, Prentice-Hall, 1964; G. H. Matthews, *Hidatsa Syntax*, Mouton, 1964; R. B. Lees and E. S. Klima, "Rules for English pronominalization," *Language* **39**, 1963.

6. "Co-occurrence and transformation in linguistic structure," *Language* **33**, 1957. I return to this in §III of the Introduction.

7. "Discourse analysis," *Language* **28**, 1952; "Discourse analysis: a sample text," *ibid.*

8. Some of the work on generative phonology of English was presented at the 1959 Texas conference; see Note 3. This work on segmental phonology was intended to complement the study of stress contours presented in N. Chomsky, M. Halle, and F. Lukoff, "On accent and juncture in English," in M. Halle, H. Lunt, and H. MacLean, eds., *For Roman Jakobson*, Mouton, 1956. Halle and I had been working on these problems for several years; there is a reference to an unpublished 1956 paper of ours in Chapter VI, below, Note 11. This work was finally published as *Sound Pattern of English* (*SPE*), Harper and Row, 1968.

9. In particular, a detailed critique of European structuralist theories of meaning and phonology, and a defense of Bloch's work against criticism from these and other sources.

10. Similarly, the term "linguistic theory" is used here throughout for the theory of linguistic form, a subpart of the more general semiotic theory that includes other topics as well. As noted explicitly (cf. Chapter IV, Note 15), the terminology is in no way intended to imply that linguistic theory in the broader sense is somehow beyond the scope of linguistics, though there is no attempt here to develop it in a systematic way.

11. See my *Current Issues in Linguistic Theory* (*CILT*), Mouton, 1964, §1.1.
12. See C. F. Hockett, *A Manual of Phonology*, Indiana University Publications in Anthropology and Linguistics, 1955.
13. See my *Aspects of the Theory of Syntax* (*ATS*), MIT Press, 1965.
14. See also *ATS*, Chapter 4; J. J. Katz, "Semi-sentences," in J. Fodor and J. J. Katz, eds., *op. cit.*; and many other studies.
15. We consider here the simplest case; namely, a homogeneous speech community. See Note 66.
16. See, however, the remarks in Z. S. Harris's, *Methods in Structural Linguistics*, pp. 365–366, on a grammar as a device for "synthesizing" utterances. Bloomfield's "Menomini morphophonemics," *Travaux du cercle linguistique de Prague*, 1939, might be regarded as a segment of a generative grammar in approximately this sense. My *MMH* was written, I regret to say, in ignorance of Bloomfield's study. Some of Sapir's ideas on phonology tended in a similar direction. See Zellig S. Harris, "Review of Mandelbaum (ed.), *Selected Writings of Edward Sapir*," *Language* **27**, 1951.
17. I do not mean to imply that the structural linguists who investigated procedures of analysis would have accepted this interpretation of their work. Some of them at least surely would not have done so.
18. For critical discussion of various procedural approaches, see Lees, *op.* cit.; my review of Joseph Greenberg's *Essays in Linguistics*, *Word* **15**, 202–218, 1959; my *CILT*; Paul M. Postal, *Constituent Structure*, Mouton, 1964, and his *Aspects of Phonological Theory*, Harper and Row, 1968.
19. Distinctive feature theory, in the sense of the Prague circle, might be regarded as such a system. Jakobson, in particular, has developed in numerous works the view that such features are perceived as phenomenal properties, and that acquisition of a phonological system develops in a systematic and fairly uniform way by refinement and elaboration of a feature system. However, insofar as distinctive feature theory postulates certain universal conditions that a grammar must satisfy, it must be considered as a "rationalist" rather than an "empiricist" model in the rational reconstruction of these notions discussed here, and it is interpreted in this manner in *ATS* (p. 55) and elsewhere.

    Perhaps I should mention that in reconstructing an "empiricist" approach, I omit any mention of vacuous versions. For example, one could have no quarrel with (or interest in) a variety of "empiricism" that holds only that knowledge and belief are acquired by "eliminative induction," i.e., selection among theories devised in some unspecified manner on the basis of confirming or disconfirming evidence. Nor am I considering here varieties of "behaviorism" that interpret this doctrine merely as the insistence that scientific laws must somehow be subjected to empirical test. There are real and important questions concerning the relation between systems of knowledge and belief, on the one hand, and the preliminary organization of the data of sense, on the other. It is these questions that I am concerned with here.
20. For further discussion, see my "Review of Skinner, *Verbal Behavior*," *Language* **35**, 1959; "Explanatory models in linguistics," in E. Nagel, P. Suppes, and A. Tarski, eds., *Logic, Methodology, and Philosophy of Science*, Stanford University Press, 1962; *ATS*; *Cartesian Linguistics*, Harper and Row, 1966; *Language and Mind*, Harcourt, Brace, Jovanovich, 1968; *Problems of Knowledge and Freedom*, Pantheon, 1971; "Language and freedom," in *For Reasons of State*, Pantheon, 1973; J. J. Katz, *Philosophy of Language*, Harper and Row, 1966; *Semantic Theory*, Harper and Row, 1972; C. Graves, J. J. Katz, *et al.*, "Tacit knowledge," *Journal of Philosophy* **70**, No. 11, 7 June 1973; L. Jonathan Cohen, *The Diversity of Meaning*, second edition,

Methuen, 1966; R. Edgley, "Innate ideas," in G.N.A. Vesey, ed., *Knowledge and Necessity*, Royal Institute of Philosophy, St. Martin's Press, 1970; H. Bracken, "Chomsky's Cartesianism," *Language Sciences*, October 1972; various contributions to S. Hook, ed., *Philosophy and Language*, NYU Press, 1969; S. Stich, "What every speaker knows," *Philosophical Review* 80, No. 4, October 1971; "Grammar, psychology, and indeterminacy," *Journal of Philosophy* 69, No. 22, 7 Dec. 1972; D. Cooper, "Innateness: old and new," *Philosophical Review*, October 1972; N. Chomsky and J. J. Katz, "What the linguist is talking about," *Journal of Philosophy* 71, No. 12, 27 June 1974; "On innateness: a reply to Cooper," *Philosophical Review* 84, No. 1, January 1975; and many other publications.

21. In the *LSLT* theory, the phrase-structure grammar generates derivations, which determine **P**-markers. Alternatively, one might interpret the rules of the phrase-structure grammar as "tree conditions" that determine the set of **P**-markers in a way that one could proceed to define. Plainly, nothing is at stake in this choice of interpretations. Occasionally, it has been argued that under the *LSLT* procedure, all endocentric constructions are excluded. This is incorrect, however. A narrow (and, to my knowledge, totally uninteresting) class of endocentric constructions must be ruled out if we want a **P**-marker to be uniquely determined by a derivation, as in the *LSLT* theory, where the definition of "generation" is extended to a broad class of systems. There are other ways of defining "generation of **P**-markers" in terms of the rules of the phrase-structure grammar to avoid this nonuniqueness, if this should be desired, and obviously it makes no difference whether in one or the other of such formulations we consider the rules to be rewriting rules or "tree conditions." Serious problems of principle (problems of decidability) arise if the phrase-structure grammar is infinite in generative power, but this is not the case in *LSLT*. In later work, other conditions serve to avoid these problems, which are, again, common to the alternative interpretations.

22. There is some variation in terminology in this connection. In *LSLT* the term "**P**-marker" is used as indicated here. In other publications, the term is used in the more general sense of "phrase-structure interpretation," i.e., it is used to apply to **P**-markers of terminal strings generated by the phrase-structure grammar or the "derived constituent interpretation" (see below) of strings generated by transformation.

23. See in particular the complex of problems involving Condition 5 of §91.5, Chapter IX. A number of these are discussed in §111.2 and §111.5–111.8 in Chapter X. All of these problems relate to the question of how the components of the mapping Φ form a "skeleton" for a **T**-marker. The problems arise when we consider generalized transformations, in which obligatory mappings of Φ must apply separately in the several branches of the **T**-marker.

24. See my "Formal properties of grammars," in R. D. Luce, R. R. Bush, and E. Galanter, eds., *Handbook of Mathematical Psychology*, Vol. II, Wiley, 1963; N. Chomsky and M. P. Schützenberger, "The algebraic theory of context-free languages," in P. Braffort and D. Hirschberg, eds., *Computer Programming and Formal Systems, Studies in Logic*, North-Holland, 1963; S. Ginsburg, *The Mathematical Theory of Context-Free Languages*, McGraw-Hill, 1966; J. Hopcroft and J. D. Ullman, *Formal Languages and Their Relation to Automata*, Addison-Wesley, 1969; J. Kimball, *The Formal Theory of Grammar*, Prentice-Hall, 1973; M. Gross and A. Lentin, *Introduction to Formal Grammars*, Springer-Verlag, 1970; P. S. Peters and R. W. Ritchie, "On the generative power of transformational grammars," *Information Sciences* 6, 49–83, 1973.

25. J. Bresnan, "Sentence stress and syntactic transformations," *Language* 47, No. 2, 1971; "Stress and syntax: a reply," *Language* 48, No. 2, 1972.

26. See, e.g., *SS*, Chapters 8, 9; *CILT*, §2.3; my "Some methodological remarks on generative grammar," *Word* **17**, 1961; and many other sources.

27. In the standard theory (see above, p. 17), as developed, e.g., in *ATS*, it is postulated that deep structure determines meaning. Thus nonsynonymous sentences cannot be assigned the same deep structure. In this respect, semantic considerations provide a partial criterion for the selection of grammars, contrary to what might be suggested by remarks in *ATS*, p. 226, Note 15 (though whether this observation constitutes a "serious proposal" in any relevant respect remains another question).

28. Occasionally, a specific thesis is formulated, but without supporting argument. Virtually the only clear argument against a thesis of autonomy of syntax, to my knowledge, is one offered by George Lakoff, "Linguistics and natural logic," in D. Davidson and. G. Harman, eds. *Semantics of Natural Language*, Reidel, 1972 pp. 547–549. The issue, as he formulates it, is whether "the rules of grammar, which generate the grammatical sentences of English, filtering out the ungrammatical sentences, are . . . distinct from the rules relating the surface forms of English sentences to their corresponding logical forms." Lakoff concludes from an investigation of the rule of Adverb-preposing (A-P) that they are not distinct. He considers such sequences as the following: (1) "I mentioned that Sam smoked pot last night," (2) "Last night, I mentioned that Sam smoked pot," (3) "I mentioned that Sam will smoke pot tomorrow," (4) "Tomorrow, I mentioned that Sam will smoke pot." His argument is that A-P is a rule of grammar, distinguishing grammatical from ungrammatical sentences [cf. (3), (4)]. But A-P is also a rule relating surface structures to logical form [cf. (1), (2); thus A-P serves the function of assigning (2) the same meaning as (5) "I mentioned last night that Sam smoked pot," from which (2) derives by A-P]. Lakoff then argues that under the autonomy thesis, we must set up two distinct rules, one grammatical and the other semantic, which do the work of A-P. On these grounds he concludes that the autonomy thesis must be rejected in favor of the approach of generative semantics. But the argument is hopelessly in error. In the standard theory, there will be one rule A-P for these cases, mapping (5) into (2) and inapplicable to (3), exactly as in Lakoff's account. The deep structures postulated to distinguish the grammatical from the ungrammatical cases under A-P will be just those required to give the senses of the surface forms, and Lakoff's conclusion is at once refuted. To my knowledge, other arguments that appear in the literature fare no better, even when some actual thesis of "autonomy" is formulated.

29. J. J. Katz and J. Fodor, "The structure of a semantic theory," *Language* **39**, No. 2 (Pt. 1), 1963. There was other related work at the time; cf. Paul Ziff, *Semantic Analysis*, Cornell University Press, 1960.

30. J. J. Katz and P. M. Postal, *An Integrated Theory of Linguistic Description*, MIT Press, 1964.

31. See *ATS*, pp. 221, 224–225, and my "The formal nature of language," appendix to E. H. Lenneberg, *Biological Foundations of Language*, Wiley, 1967, which was actually submitted for publication in 1965.

32. See R. S. Jackendoff, *Semantic Interpretation in Generative Grammar*, MIT Press, 1972, for a full exposition of Jackendoff's theory.

33. See my *Studies on Semantics in Generative Grammar* (*SSGG*), Mouton, 1972, and references cited there.

34. See my "Conditions on transformations," in S. Anderson and P. Kiparsky, eds., *Festschrift for Morris Halle*, Holt, Rinehart, and Winston, 1973. For further arguments in support of a trace theory of movement rules, see T. Wasow, *Anaphoric Relations in English*, unpublished Ph.D. thesis, MIT, 1972; E. Selkirk, *The Phrase Phonology of English and French*, unpublished Ph.D. thesis, MIT, 1972.

35. See his *Semantic Theory*, and "Generative semantics *is* interpretive semantics," *Linguistic Inquiry* 2, No. 3, 1971; "Interpretive semantics meets the zombies," *Foundations of Language*, March 1973; "Logic and language: an examination of recent criticisms of intensionalism," in K. Gunderson and G. Maxwell, eds., *Minnesota Studies in the Philosophy of Science* **VI**, in press.

36. There is now an extensive literature on questions of language structure and meaning, and much controversy. For some indication of the range of proposals and debate, see several recent anthologies: Jay F. Rosenberg and Charles Travis, eds., *Readings in the Philosophy of Language*, Prentice-Hall, 1971; Danny Steinberg and Leon Jakobovits, eds., *Semantics, an Interdisciplinary Reader*, Cambridge University Press, 1971; Charles Fillmore and Terence Langendoen, eds., *Studies in Linguistic Semantics*, Holt, Rinehart, and Winston, 1971; Donald Davidson and Gilbert Harman, eds., *Semantics of Natural Language*, Reidel, 1972.

37. J. R. Ross, *Constraints on Variables in Syntax*, unpublished Ph.D. thesis, MIT, 1967.

38. See J. Emonds, *Root and Structure-Preserving Transformations*, unpublished Ph.D. thesis, MIT, 1970.

39. See S. Peters, "The projection problem: how is a grammar to be selected?" in in S. Peters, ed., *Goals of Linguistic Theory*, Prentice-Hall, 1972.

40. I take it that this is what is implied in the "homogeneous theory," as outlined in P. M. Postal, "The best theory," in Peters, ed., *op. cit.* The derivational constraints are to be subject to conditions of various sorts. Postal gives empirical arguments in support of his general contention, and argues that this homogeneous theory is the best on methodological grounds, since it is conceptually the simplest. I do not believe that the empirical arguments are at all convincing, and the methodological arguments are surely incorrect. On the contrary, the theory he proposes is the least refutable, since it permits the broadest class of possible grammars and imposes the fewest conditions on such grammars (and correspondingly reduces to a minimum the possibility of undertaking the investigation of the fundamental problem of linguistics, as here defined). While it is conceivable that empirical considerations might force us to accept a "homogeneous theory" of the sort that Postal proposes, surely this would be a most unfortunate result, and one which is, in my opinion, in no way required or suggested by the empirical facts now available. Postal, in this article, expresses a very pessimistic view about the possibilities for constructing linguistic theory, one which in my opinion is quite unwarranted.

41. This implies that the notion "deep structure" in the sense of the (extended) standard theory no longer exists.

42. See the references of Note 35 for discussion of these matters with a somewhat different interpretation of what is at stake. See also C. L. Baker and M. Brame, " 'Global rules': a rejoinder," in *Language* **48**, No. 1, 1972; Selkirk, *op. cit.*; Carlos Quicoli, *Aspects of Portuguese Complementation*, unpublished SUNY (Buffalo) Ph.D. thesis, 1972; J. Emonds, "Alternatives to global constraints," *Glossa* **7**, No. 1, 1973. This work demonstrates that at least the existing arguments in favor of global rules can be met in far more restrictive theories that make a limited and quite natural use of well-motivated features.

43. University of Chicago Press, 1951.

44. See particularly William Chomsky, *David Kimhi's Hebrew Grammar* (Mikhlol), Bloch, 1952; I had in fact read proofs many years earlier.

45. See Note 16. Harris did not elaborate on the suggestion that a grammar can be regarded as a device for "synthesizing utterances," an idea that does not, strictly speaking, seem compatible with the general approach of *Methods*. This tension, or

perhaps incompatibility, troubled me for quite a few years, as will be explained directly. A similar tension can be found in Bloomfield's work. Thus his "Menomini morphophonemics" (cf. Note16) is virtually a generative grammar with ordered rules, but Bloomfield seemed quite skeptical of the notions that he made use of in this study. For example, in his *Language* (Holt, 1933, p. 213) he described ordering as an artifact invented by the linguist, as compared with order of constituents, which is "part of language." See *CILT*, p. 70n.

46. Thus the historical analogy discussed briefly in §56.2 was actually the source of my own work in generative grammar.

47. This is the study entitled *Morphophonemics of Modern Hebrew (MMH)*, referred to earlier.

48. Recall that the rules were only partially ordered, so that certain interchanges of rules are irrelevant to this analysis.

49. Zellig S. Harris, *Development of the Canaanite Dialects*, American Oriental Society, New Haven, 1939.

50. In the theory developed in Harris's *Methods* there is provision for a kind of "cyclic application" of procedures, i.e., for revising "lower levels" in terms of results obtained at "higher levels," and similar ideas were discussed by Pike and others. But none of this changed the essential character of the procedures, methods, and concepts that were under investigation. The conception of linguistic theory as "taxonomic," that is, based on procedures of segmentation and classification, can be traced to de Saussure. See the references of Note 18. The general point of view appears in several forms. To mention one important example, it is implicit in Jakobson's general theory of language as based on two modes of arrangement, combination, and selection. See Roman Jakobson and Morris Halle, *Fundamentals of Language*, Mouton, 1956.

51. With the exception of Henry Hoenigswald, who read the work carefully and made helpful comments.

52. See my "Systems of syntactic analysis," *Journal of Symbolic Logic*, 18, 242–256 (1953) for the results of one line of investigation.

53. The careful reader will note some inconsistencies in the discussion of sentences with complements (COMP), such as "John considered him to be a nice fellow." These are not very serious, and are pretty well cleared up in "A transformational approach to syntax" (cf. Note 3). I have not revised the text here to clarify the matter. There are also inconsistencies in the discussion of some other examples (e.g., "the man in the corner," where in some instances "the man" is described as a *NP*, and in some cases, the whole structure is described as of the form *Article-N-PP*, with no category assigned to *Article-N*. Again, in these and a few other cases I have left the original text as is, and not proceeded to resolve ambiguities and inconsistencies.

54. Similar observations apply to the notions "habit," "habit structure," "disposition," etc.

55. Some of this material is presented in the 1955 version of *LSLT* [as an appendix to Chapter IV (here Chapter V)], but is omitted here.

56. See Harris, *Methods*, p. 374.

57. See his *Fact, Fiction and Forecast*, Harvard University Press, Cambridge, 1955. Goodman presents a tentative "constructive" solution in this book, but it seemed to me then, and still does, quite hopeless. Goodman accepts the strong empiricist view that the mind, initially uninformed, strikes randomly in arbitrary directions, fixing on certain properties as a framework for later inductive steps on the basis of earlier successes. But his own arguments surely suffice to undermine any such conception.

58. See *Structure of Appearance*, Harvard University Press, Cambridge, 1951.

59. See, e.g., his "Two dogmas of empiricism," *Philosophical Review*, Jan. 1951, and other essays reprinted along with a revised version of this in W.V.O. Quine, *From a Logical Point of View*, Harvard University Press, Cambridge, 1953.

60. See Note 50. Many approaches insisted on strict separation of levels, with no revision of lower-level concepts in terms of characteristics of higher levels. This was a primary reason why investigation of syntax was deferred in much structuralist work.

61. See Note 58.

62. Obviously, there is no guarantee that an operational test will characterize the notion that we have in mind. See below, §15, and also *CILT*, §3. One might also want to construct operational tests for defined notions. We then have the choice between regarding the definitions as theses (true or false, depending on the outcome of the tests) or regarding the tests as characterizations (correct or incorrect) of the notions related by the definitions.

63. As in Bernard Bloch's careful efforts. See, in particular, his "Studies in colloquial Japanese. IV. Phonemics," *Language* 26, 86–512, 1950.

64. It is a curiosity that criticism of Bloch's work (cf. Note 63) was often taken as demonstrating that "contrast" must be defined in terms of "synonymy," an obvious *non sequitur* (whatever the validity of the criticism). For some comment, see *CILT*, p. 83, Note 17.

65. As remarked in Note 9, a much more detailed analysis, from the later 1958–9 version, is omitted here.

66. We consider here the simplest case, highly idealized, in which the speech community is homogeneous. In the real world, the situation is more complex, but not in any way that affects this discussion. Thus I assume that there is an innate psychological property, call it P, such that a child with P in a homogeneous speech community can acquire its language. In the real world of overlapping styles and dialects, P is supplemented by other mechanisms that are surely a legitimate topic of investigation. That there is such a property P will be denied only by someone who takes the position that language learning is impossible in principle in a homogeneous speech community. Apart from this rather outlandish consideration, there can be no objection, so far as I can see, to the idealization. On the contrary, it would be only natural to expect that investigation of the more complex real situation will be successful only insofar as it is based on a tentative theory with regard to the property P. In practice, linguistic and sociolinguistic studies adopt this assumption, I believe, though there has been a certain amount of controversy. The matter is not discussed in *LSLT* (but is, briefly, in *ATS*), since the legitimacy of the idealization seemed to me entirely obvious.

67. Note that there is a further idealization here, in that we abstract away from other factors that may interact with knowledge of language to determine judgments. See the discussion of competence and performance, above, p. 7.

68. This conception was, of course, explicit in the work of Sapir, Jakobson, Whorf, and others. It seems to me that one can detect a negative correlation, by and large, between commitment to the psychological reality of the linguistic structures postulated and the concern for explicit formulation of procedures of analysis, though there is no logical reason why this should be so. Troubetzkoy is perhaps an exception to this remark, in that he was committed to the psychological reality of his constructs and was also an early advocate of a procedural approach.

69. Note that the theory of phrase structure as developed in *LSLT* is nontaxonomic, as distinct from other approaches to constituent analysis current at the time and later, e.g., those discussed in Postal, *Constituent Structure* (cf. Note 18). The *LSLT* theory of phrase structure encompasses a mapping Φ, transformational in character, that

assigns an abstract structure generated by the phrase-structure grammar to a string of words. In fact, the system of syntactic categories proposed (constituting, in effect, an elementary subcomponent of the phrase-structure system) was itself nontaxonomic, as already explained (cf. Chapter V). The same was true of the "lower levels" of linguistic structure, as described here (cf. Chapter VI). The theory of transformations involved still more abstract structures, and a still more extreme departure from taxonomic assumptions.

70. See his "Transformational theory," *Language* 41, No. 3, Part 1, July–September, 1965, pp. 363–401, Note 6.
71. I have briefly discussed this in *Language and Mind*, Chapter 1.
72. Later published as *Verbal Behavior*, Appleton-Century-Crofts, 1957. See also his *Science and Human Behavior*, Macmillan, 1953.
73. For a clear and accurate picture of the prevailing intellectual atmosphere, see G. A. Miller, *Language and Communication*, McGraw-Hill, 1951, and the reports of the 1950 and 1952 speech conferences reprinted in the *Journal of the Acoustical Society of America* 22, No. 6, Nov. 1950 and 24, No. 6, Nov. 1952. For more on this period see Y. Bar-Hillel, introduction to *Language and Information*, Addison-Wesley, 1964.
74. See Note 12 and my review of Hockett's *Manual* in the *International Journal of American Linguistics* XXIII, No. 3, p. 223, July 1957. It should be stressed, however, that Hockett was stating clearly and explicitly what many investigators assumed to be the case.
75. *Ibid.*; also *SS*, and my "Three models for the description of language." As noted above (cf. p. 7), the organization of *SS* may have misled a number of observers in this respect. The first topic discussed there is the inadequacy of finite-state grammars in weak generative capacity. But this was an afterthought in my own work, and in *LSLT* there is no mention of finite-state grammars or the question of weak generative capacity. In the 1956 version of *LSLT*, the appendix to Chapter VI, omitted here, was devoted to formal properties of grammars and problems of weak generative capacity.
76. See Note 20.
77. As a student of Harris's, I participated in seminars on discourse analysis from the outset until leaving for Harvard in 1951, along with Fred Lukoff, A. F. Brown, and a few others.
78. Harris, "Co-occurrence and transformations in linguistic structure" p. 340. See Note 6.
79. See Note 7. Also Z. S. Harris, *Discourse Analysis Reprints*, Mouton, 1963.
80. For further development of this approach to grammatical transformations, see Harris, "Co-occurrence and transformations in linguistic structure" (see Note 6), and "Transformational theory," *Language* 41, No. 3, 1965.
81. See Z. S. Harris, *String Analysis of Sentence Structure*, Mouton, 1962.
82. See also Note 81. Note that even if the methods of structural linguistics were so developed that they led to a generative grammar of unbounded scope, still this would not be true of transformational analysis, at least as the notion of "transformation" is defined. But these two approaches are each assumed to be exhaustive and independent of one another.
83. "Transformational theory," p. 370n. The parenthesized expression is not literally accurate, however.

THE LOGICAL
STRUCTURE OF
LINGUISTIC THEORY

PREFACE

Linguistic theory has two major subdivisions, syntax and semantics. Syntax is the study of linguistic form. Its fundamental notion is "grammatical," and its primary concern is to determine the grammatical sentences of any given language and to bring to light their underlying formal structure. The goal of syntactic study is to show that the complexity of natural languages, which appears superficially to be so formidable, can be analyzed into simple components; that is, that this complexity is the result of repeated application of principles of sentence construction that are in themselves quite simple. Semantics, on the other hand, is concerned with the meaning and reference of linguistic expressions. It is thus the study of how this instrument, whose formal structure and potentialities of expression are the subject of syntactic investigation, is actually put to use in a speech community. Syntax and semantics are distinct fields of investigation. How much each draws from the other is not known, or at least has never been clearly stated. The subject of investigation in the following pages will be syntactic structure, and we shall study it as an independent aspect of linguistic theory.

In part, our decision to place no reliance on meaning in systematic developments is motivated by a feeling that the theory of meaning fails to meet certain minimum requirements of objectivity and operational verifiability. We need not enter into this question, however, since a much more important motivation is that semantic notions, if taken seriously, appear to assist in no way in the solution of the problems that we will be investigating. We will see, however, that syntactic study has considerable import for semantics. This is not surprising. Any reasonable study of the way language is actually put to work will have to be based on a clear understanding of the nature of the syntactic devices which are available for the organization and expression of content. As we will see below, the purely formal investigation of language does provide significant insights into the way language is employed and understood.

57

There can be no definitive formulation of syntactic theory at this point, and in the course of these investigations many more questions are asked than answered. Lack of data is the fundamental reason for this. There simply is not enough detailed syntactic work available, in the proper form, to allow for empirical confirmation of certain theoretical developments. On the other hand, the scarcity of appropriate syntactic material is no doubt a result of the overwhelming complexity of the syntactic structure of natural languages. I will attempt to show that a good deal of this complexity is the result of the inadequacy of our analytic tools, and that it can be substantially reduced if we approach language with a more elaborate syntactic theory. Theoretical investigation and collection and organization of data are interdependent activities. One cannot describe a linguistic system in any meaningful way without some conception of the nature of such a system and the properties and purposes of a grammatical description. The development of a conceptually complete theory of linguistic structure may be an essential step toward obtaining the evidence which will ultimately give this theory its empirical support. It would thus be pointless and self-defeating to insist that theoretical studies in syntax are premature because of the paucity of descriptive material.

In developing a linguistic theory, it is important to formulate clear and precise criteria and to apply these with complete rigor and consistency, even when it appears likely that they are only partially adequate. In this way we may hope to expose the source and exact location of this inadequacy. Pushing a precise but inadequate formulation to an absurd conclusion may be an important method of discovery. Below we will see that careful pursuit of this course exposes a gap in linguistic theory, and leads to the construction of a theory of transformations. Obscure and intuition-bound conceptions can of course never be pushed to absurd conclusions, but this can scarcely be regarded as a point in their favor.

It is quite incorrect, then, to regard formalization as an activity that occupies the researcher after he has developed an effective theory. On the contrary, formalization can play a very productive role in the process of discovery itself, as we will have occasion to see below. We will find that certain familiar conceptions of linguistic structure, when formalized, literally cannot provide an English grammar, and that others can do so, if at all, only at an intolerably great cost. In this way, we develop a succession of increasingly complex theories of linguistic structure corresponding to more and more powerful grammars until we finally reach a theory which seems to provide an adequate grammar for English.

The sketch of a linguistic theory presented below should be understood as suggesting a specific model for syntactic description to be tested and elaborated. Since certain of the formal developments are necessarily rather tentative, the motivation for a construction is often more important than the actual construction itself. For this reason, general requirements that a construction must meet will often be discussed in some detail before the presentation of what seems to be the most natural way of meeting these requirements.

Some of the major points that will be elaborated below are presented schematically and informally in my *Syntactic Structures* (The Hague, 1957). The reader may find this a helpful introduction to the present work.

SUMMARY I

In the following chapters we will sketch some of the fundamental 1
features of a theory of linguistic form and investigate its empirical
consequences. We will try to show how an abstract theory of linguistic
structure can be developed within a framework that admits of operational
interpretation, and how such a theory can lead to a practical mechanical
procedure by which, given a corpus of linguistic material, various
proposed grammars can be compared and the best of them selected.
This is not a clear statement of a proposed investigation, because the
notion of "a grammar" is not antecedently clear. But a field of investigation cannot be clearly delimited in advance of the theory dealing with
this subject matter; in fact, it is one of the functions of a theory to give
such a precise delimitation. Before we have constructed a linguistic
theory we can only have certain vaguely formulated questions to guide
the development of the theory. A simple and natural theory, once
established, determines the precise formulation of the questions that
originally motivated it, and leads to the formulation and resolution of
new problems that could not previously have been raised. We are
antecedently interested in developing a theory that will shed some light
on such facts as the following:

1   A speaker of a language has observed a certain limited set of
    utterances in his language. On the basis of this finite linguistic
    experience he can produce an indefinite number of new utter-
    ances which are immediately acceptable to other members of
    his speech community. He can also distinguish a certain set of
    "grammatical" utterances, among utterances that he has never
    heard and might never produce. He thus projects his past
    linguistic experience to include certain new strings while
    excluding others.

2   Furthermore, the speaker has developed a large store of knowledge about his language and a mass of feelings and understandings that we might call "intuitions about linguistic form." For example, any speaker of English knows that

(a)   "keep" and "coop" begin with the same "sound," while "keep" and "top" (despite experimentally demonstrated acoustic similarity) do not;

(b)   "see" has a special relation to "sight" that it does not have to "seat." This is a relation similar to that between "refuse" and "refusal." Both "flee" and "fly" are related in this way to "flight";

(c)   "are they coming?" is the question corresponding to "they are coming." Similarly, "did they come?" is the question corresponding to "they came" and not (despite the similarity in morphemic constitution) to "they *did* come";

(d)   "John read the book" and "my friend plays tennis" are sentences of the same type (declaratives) as opposed to "did John read the book?" and "who plays tennis?" (interrogatives). "Who read the book?" and "what did John read?" are instances of the same sentence subtype (a particular subclass of interrogatives) as opposed to "did you see the see the book?";

(e)   many sentences can be understood in several different ways, e.g., "they are flying planes" ("my friends are . . .," "those specks on the horizon are . . .") or "they don't know how good meat tastes" ("since they are vegetarians and never eat it," "since they can afford only the cheaper cuts"). Many other sentences are ambiguous (e.g., "take off the shoe" can refer to footwear or tires), but in quite a different manner;

(f)   despite superficial similarities, the sentences "the children laughed at the clown" and "John worked at the office" are structurally quite distinct. "He scoffs at the theater" is ambiguous, being understandable in either of these distinct ways.

Although it may not be too difficult to find an *ad hoc* explanation for each decision about grammaticalness and each particular intuitive judgment, it will require quite an elaborate development of linguistic theory to give a *general* account of projection, ambiguity, sentence type, etc., that will provide automatically for each of these and thousands of other intuitions about linguistic form. Our problem is to carry out this development, to bring to light the formal patterns underlying the sentences of a language, and to show how these observed regularities might account for particular decisions about which sequences are grammatical and how these are to be understood.

By "the grammar of a language *L*" we mean that theory of *L* that attempts to deal with such problems as these wholly in terms of the formal properties of utterances. And by "the general theory of linguistic form" we mean the abstract theory in which the basic concepts of grammar are developed, and by means of which each proposed grammar can be evaluated. It might be supposed that there is no such field of investigation as grammar, in this sense, and no such theory as general linguistic theory. That is, it might be supposed that in order to deal with such topics it is necessary to take into account the meaning and reference of expressions, the particular history of reinforcement of the participating individuals, the sociocultural context of speech, etc. We will see, on the contrary, that a great many aspects of linguistic behavior do fall under grammar in this sense of the word. We conclude that a theory of linguistic form constructed upon a "distributional" basis[1] does delimit an interesting and significant area of linguistic behavior, and that it can be an adequate instrument for the exploration and investigation of this area.

2 A language is an enormously complex system. Linguistic theory attempts to reduce this immense complexity to manageable proportions by the construction of a system of *linguistic levels*, each of which makes a certain descriptive apparatus available for the characterization of linguistic structure. A grammar reconstructs the total complexity of a language stepwise, separating out the contribution of each linguistic level. The adequacy of a linguistic theory containing a given set of abstractly formulated levels can be tested by determining whether the grammars resulting from rigorous application of this theory

3 meet certain formal conditions of simplicity;

4 lead to intuitively satisfactory analyses—i.e., offer explanations on formal grounds for the linguistic intuition of the native speaker.

But such an investigation of the adequacy of a proposed general theory is of course possible only under the condition that "intuition" and

[1] See the next-to-last paragraph of §29 for a brief characterization of the sense in which we use this term, borrowed from Harris (cf. his *Methods of Structural Linguistics*, 1951, for an account of distributional procedures in linguistic analysis).

similarly obscure terms do not appear in the theory itself. If they do, we cannot determine which grammars result from application of the theory.

Our main conclusion will be that familiar linguistic theory has only a limited adequacy—i.e., that it is attempting to do too much with too little theoretical equipment. The specific deficiencies of familiar linguistic theory will be explored by making this theory (or one form of it) explicit and investigating the empirical consequences of rigorous application of the devices available in this theory. It appears that if the set of sentences covered by the grammatical description is artificially restricted in a manner which is intuitively significant, but which cannot be characterized in any independent and systematically significant way within this theory, then the grammars provided by this theory have desirable formal properties and can provide formal grounds for linguistic intuition. But any attempt to carry the description beyond these limits leads to grammars which are intolerably complex (in statable respects) and to counterintuitive analyses. We will argue that the remedy for these deficiencies is not to be found in the extension of the distributional basis for linguistic theory to include meaning, situational context, etc., nor, apparently in the introduction of probabilistic and statistical conceptions. Instead, a new level of transformational analysis is proposed as a higher level of linguistic structure. It will be shown that the theory of transformational analysis can be formulated in the same completely distributional terms that are required anyway for lower levels, and that a large and important class of problems that arise in the rigorous application of familiar linguistic theory disappears when it is extended to include transformational analysis.

An argument of this sort is impossible without a careful construction of the theories being investigated. Hence the first task is to construct the theory of linguistic structure that is implicit in current syntactic work. Chapters II–V are devoted to some general questions concerning the nature and scope of linguistic theory. In Chapter VI, we sketch the formal development of the lower levels of phonemes, morphemes, and words, emphasizing the logical status of these constructions. Chapters V and VI also treat the level of syntactic categories in greater detail. Chapter VII contains a considerably more detailed account of the level of phrase structure, and Chapter VIII is concerned with the application of the theory of phrase structure (constituent analysis) to English. In Chapter IX, the theory of transformations is developed, and in Chapter X it is applied to English.

In terms of the notion of "linguistic level," we will attempt to formulate an approach to the problems raised in §1. We will construct certain linguistic levels with recursive devices so that a description in terms of them generates an infinite set of sentences. We will see that many of the decisions of a speaker of English about grammaticalness are just those that would result if he were to give the best account (in a definable sense) of his past experience in terms of these levels, and then accept as grammatical all those sentences consistent with this description. We will also find evidence that ambiguous sentences are those represented in alternative ways in this description, that the structural type of a sentence can be determined by its behavior under transformations and by the history of its transformational development, and that grounds for many other cases of linguistic intuition can be found in the details of level structure.

In Chapter II, we discuss three major areas of linguistic interest: the construction of grammars of particular languages, the development of an abstract theory of linguistic structure, and the problem of justification of grammars. These three tasks are interdependent. Each grammar can be regarded as essentially the science of a particular subject matter (a given language). For the grammar of each language we can set up certain fairly vague "external criteria of adequacy" that the grammar must meet. Within these broad limits, a grammar is justified by showing that it follows from a given abstract theory of linguistic structure. This abstract theory must provide a practical and mechanical evaluation procedure for grammars. The abstract theory must have the property that for each language, the highest-valued grammar for that language meets the external criteria of adequacy set up for the given language. The fact that certain clear cases must be adequately and simply described in the case of many languages is a fairly heavy condition on the general theory (though it is a weak condition on the grammar of each particular language). In fact, we are far from having an abstract theory that is not hopelessly *ad hoc*, and that leads to an adequate grammar of even one language. Our goal is to construct an abstract theory that is not *ad hoc* (i.e., that does develop in a simple and internally motivated way) and that leads to a revealing and intuitively adequate English grammar, with a relatively simple structure, as its highest-valued interpretation for English, under an evaluation procedure to be developed as part of the theory.

Since we wish to apply the general theory to the evaluation of particular grammars, it must have a basis of primitive notions for which we can supply cross-culturally valid operational tests. In the present state of our knowledge, this requirement already excludes meaning. But a closer study shows that if we grant the availability of *all* semantic knowledge, then it becomes even more apparent that a semantic basis for this theory must be excluded. In particular, it seems that knowledge of sameness of meaning does not aid in determining phonemic distinctness; nor are the sentences to be generated by the grammar characterized, apparently, by a semantic property of significance. There is an effective and widely used operational test for phonemic distinctness, and much of this study is devoted to the development of a systematic account of grammaticalness in terms of the formal notion of "linguistic level." But nowhere in the systematic development does it appear useful to introduce semantic considerations.

4   Chapter III is devoted to a general description of the notion of "linguistic level." Each level is essentially a system of spelling. It contains an "alphabet" of symbols (called "primes") which can be combined by an operation called "concatenation" to form strings. Among the strings on each level are those representing utterances of the language. The grammar is concerned to distinguish these.

We will find it necessary to distinguish at least the following levels for linguistic description: phonemes (**Pm**), morphemes (**M**), words (**W**), syntactic categories (**C**), phrase structure (**P**), and transformations (**T**). The grammar must indicate the structure of each utterance on each of these levels. To accomplish this end, we construct on each level **L** certain elements that we call "**L**-markers" and we construct a mapping called "Φ^L" that assigns these **L**-markers to utterances. The **L**-marker assigned to an utterance gives us complete information as to the structure of this utterance on the level **L**. On certain levels, markers are just strings (e.g., the level of phonemes for English has among its primes the symbols p, i, n, which can be concatenated to form the string $p^\frown i^\frown n$,[2] which is the **Pm**-marker of "pin"). On the levels **C** and **P** the markers will be sets of strings of these levels. The mapping that assigns **L**-markers to utterances will vary in character and complexity from level to level. The levels themselves differ in their internal algebraic properties, and are related to each other in various ways by "conditions of compatibility." Ambiguity arises when an utterance is assigned more than one **L**-marker by the mapping Φ^L.

5   Every factor relevant to the choice among grammars must be built into linguistic theory. The simplicity of a grammar is one such factor, and in Chapter IV we discuss the possibility of defining simplicity of grammar within linguistic theory. We can approach such a conception

---

[2] On the nature of these primes, see Chapter VI.

by providing notations for grammatical description which convert considerations of simplicity into considerations of length by permitting coalescence of similar grammatical statements. This favors grammars that contain generalizations. We have a generalization when we can replace a set of statements, each about one element, by a single statement about the whole set of elements. More generally, we have a partial generalization when we have a set of similar (not identical) statements about distinct elements. By devising notations that permit coalescence of similar statements, we can measure the amount of generalization in a grammar by length. Other features of simplicity can also be measured in a natural way in terms of length. For this approach to be significant, we must develop a fixed set of notations in linguistic theory, and a fixed form for grammatical statement. The definition of these notations (essentially, the construction of a "language of grammar") constitutes the basic part of the definition of simplicity.

It remains to characterize the form of grammars explicitly. A grammar is a device for generating sentences. As an initial step, we take a grammar to be a sequence (not a set—order of statements can be used to effect major simplifications in the grammar) of statements of the form

5 $X_i \rightarrow Y_i$ $(i = 1,..., N)$

interpreted as the instruction "rewrite X_i as Y_i," where X_i and Y_i are strings. Suppose that we have such a sequence, and suppose that X_1 is the element *Sentence* (one of the primes of the level **P**). Call each statement of the form **5** a *conversion*. Then certain conversions are obligatory and certain conversions are merely permitted, and we can construct a *derivation* of any sentence by running through the list of conversions, applying each obligatory conversion and certain permitted ones, until the result is a string of phones. In the first tentative formulation of the theory we provide for the possibility of running through the grammar indefinitely many times on the level **P** to allow for infinite generation. This possibility is eliminated when transformational analysis provides alternative means for sentence generation.

A derivation is roughly analogous to a proof, with *Sentence* playing the role of the single axiom, and the conversions corresponding roughly to rules of inference. We can measure the simplicity of a grammar by measuring the length in symbols of the sequence of conversions, under the "notational transformations" that have been designed to convert considerations of complexity (generalization, etc.) into considerations of length. For each linguistic level, we show how the information about utterances provided on this level can be presented as a sequence of conversions, and how the underlying algebra (i.e., the structure of the level) can be reconstructed from the sequence of conversions. Suppose now that we have given

6　　(i)　the abstract structure of each level, and a statement of the relations of compatibility between levels;

　　　(ii)　an abstract characterization of a bi-unique relation between a set of levels and a sequence of conversions;

　　　(iii)　a measure of simplicity for a sequence of conversions.

Then, given a corpus, we can construct a set of compatible levels, each with the proper internal structure, and such that the correlated sequence of conversions produces the corpus (along with much else). The "structure of the language" is given by that set of levels which is associated (by **6**ii) with the simplest sequence of conversions. We guard against triviality (e.g., simple grammars that generate all sequences) by imposing formal conditions that a level must meet, given a corpus, as part of the abstract definition of this level. For example, the level of syntactic categories must give a minimal projection of the corpus (in a sense defined in Chapter V), and other levels can project further only in a specified way. The grammatical sentences of the language are those that are generated by the associated sequence of conversions. Thus each level makes a certain contribution to defining this set. We can develop a notion of "degree of grammaticalness," and state methods for excluding parts of the corpus (e.g., mistakes, idioms, certain figurative and metaphoric statements, etc.) from the set of fully grammatical sentences. In other words we utilize the descriptive apparatus available on each higher level to draw more precisely the boundaries of this set, introducing the sentences that fit the patterns established when this level is designed to account for the already given grammatical sentences, and assigning lower degrees of grammaticalness to sentences of the corpus that are instances of inadequately represented patterns (i.e., "exceptions").

　　In our study of phrase structure we will see that grammars of the form **5** are not sufficiently powerful for the description of English. Recognition of this inadequacy leads to the construction of the level **T**, which does not reduce to a sequence of conversions in the sense of **6**ii, but the approach to simplicity that we develop in Chapter IV seems to carry over to transformational grammars as well.

　　It is important to note that despite the very great amount of important grammatical work done in the last few decades, there are unfortunately no published grammars which we can use as they stand as data for determining the adequacy of these theoretical constructions concerning simplicity and the form of grammars. The reason is that none of the existing grammars provides a literally mechanical method for generating sentences. Even though it may be intuitively evident to every reader how to use these grammars to generate utterances we cannot know how much the formulation of the missing steps will add to the complexity of the grammar. The difficulty of presenting a really mechanical grammar can be easily underestimated. But it is absolutely crucial to develop such grammars if we wish to investigate seriously the role of such notions as simplicity of grammar in linguistic theory.

In Chapter VII we develop the level **P** of phrase structure. Like all other levels, **P** provides us with ways of representing utterances. Among the primes of **P**, for English, we will have such symbols as *Sentence, Noun Phrase (NP), Verb Phrase (VP), Noun (N), John, ing,* etc. There is a relation ρ, read "represents," defined on the strings of the system **P**. This holds, e.g., between *Sentence* and $NP^\frown VP$, between *Sentence* and $John^\frown came^\frown home$, between *NP* and $my^\frown friend$, etc. It is irreflexive, asymmetrical, transitive, and nonconnected. Furthermore, if X represents Y [i.e., if $\rho(X, Y)$], then $Z^\frown X^\frown W$ represents $Z^\frown Y^\frown W$. There is a unique prime *Sentence* which is "first" in the partial ordering given by ρ, in a sense that will be defined. There is a set of *terminal* strings that are "last" in the ordering, in the sense that they bear ρ to no string. The terminal strings correspond (in a loose way) to strings of words and morphemes.

The first problem on the level **P** is to define the notion of "constituent"; i.e., the notion of "significant occurrence" of a string X in a containing string Z. Thus "called up" is a constituent of "I called up my friends" but not of "I called up the stairs."[3] We must also be able to tell what sort of a constituent a given phrase is. For example, "called up" is a *Verb* above. We will find that these notions can be defined in terms of ρ. We must then construct **P**-markers in such a way that the **P**-marker assigned to a sentence Z will carry all the information about the constituent structure of Z. We find that a **P**-marker can be defined as a certain set of strings that represents a terminal string associated with Z. The **P**-marker of a sentence Z gives a "consistent interpretation" of Z in the sense that two substrings of Z that overlap can be constituents, in terms of this **P**-marker, just in case one is included in the other. Thus the analysis given by a **P**-marker is that of a properly

6

---

[3] There may be a difference in stress and pitch in this case.

parenthesized expression, where each parenthesized part is represented by a prime that states what sort of constituent it is.

The remainder of Chapter VII is largely devoted to showing how a system **P** can be reduced to a sequence of conversions from which the structure of **P** can be uniquely recovered, as required in **6**ii, above. A grammar corresponding to the level **P** contains an initial string *Sentence* and a finite set of instructions of the form $X \rightarrow Y$ interpreted "rewrite X as Y," as in **5**. From this grammar we can construct derivations which end in terminal strings. In Chapter VI we discuss lower levels of linguistic structure, and point out that these can apparently be reduced to a grammar of conversions of the form **5**. Thus we have a sequence of conversions by which we can derive terminal strings from *Sentence*, and a sequence of conversions by which we can derive strings of phones (each of which gives the physical description of an utterance) from strings of morphemes. Our theory would be complete if we could

7   (a)   characterize the mapping $\Phi^{\mathbf{P}}$ that leads from terminal strings to strings of morphemes by a sequence of conversions;

       (b)   account for all the terminal strings (i.e., one at least for each grammatical sentence) by the conversions corresponding to the level **P**.

Our investigation of English phrase structure in Chapter VIII leads to the conclusion that neither of these goals can be achieved, and this will provide the motivation for developing a transformational level that, in fact, is not reducible to a sequence of conversions of the form **5**.

Representation of utterances in terms of **P** is essentially different from representation on any lower level, though both **P** and lower levels can be reduced to a sequence of conversions. On the level of phonemes or morphemes, the marker of an utterance is a certain string of primes, and there is a good sense in which one of these levels is "higher" than the other. On the level **P**, however, each utterance is assigned a **P**-marker which is a set of representing strings. The elements of the level **P** cannot be subdivided into a set of sublevels, ordered into a hierarchy. For example, there is no way of establishing a relation similar to the phoneme–morpheme relation between such elements as *Noun Phrase* (*NP*) and *Verb Phrase* (*VP*); *NP*s are contained within *VP*s and *VP*s within *NP*s in English. Hence phrase structure must be considered a single level of a more abstract character than lower levels.

In Chapters VI and VII we construct various levels of representation and show how we can construct grammars corresponding to these algebras. The appendix to Chapter VII represents a change of emphasis. Here we study the relative power of grammars of various types. In particular, we ask whether, simplicity aside, it is *possible* to construct a grammar for English that is of a more elementary type than a grammar of conversions, and that does not lead to a level of the type **P**. We define a *language* to be a set (in general, infinite) of strings in a finite alphabet, each string being of finite length. We define a *grammar* of the language L as a finite device which generates all and only the strings of L in a determinate way. A class C of grammars is more *powerful* than a class C' of grammars if every language generated by a grammar of C' can be generated by a grammar of C, but not conversely. We now consider grammars that generate strings a symbol at a time from "left to right"; i.e., grammars that correspond to levels of the elementary type of phonemes, morphemes, and words. We find that it is impossible to construct a grammar of English with this restriction, and that phrase-structure grammars are essentially more powerful, and do not fail in the same way. We thus have a very strong motivation for the development of a level of phrase structure. We go on to state several other theorems about the relative power of various types of grammars and to describe certain severe limitations on phrase-structure grammars that will prove to have serious consequences for the description of English, and that will lead us to develop the essentially more powerful class of transformational grammars.

In Chapter VIII we apply the theory of phrase structure to English syntax. We find that if the phrase-structure grammar is arbitrarily limited to a certain subset of simple declarative sentences, then the highest-valued grammar is both intuitively and systematically adequate. But any attempt to go beyond these bounds leads to excessive complexity and many formal and intuitive deficiencies. These are summarized in the introductory section of Chapter IX. Briefly, we find that when the theory of phrase structure is applied to English, there are cases of structural ambiguity with no formal correlate, cases of formal constructional homonymity with no intuitive support, and analyses that are obviously intuitively incorrect. Furthermore, there is a whole class of notions that cannot be developed within this theory, including the notions of sentence type (declarative, interrogative, etc.), relations between sentences (active–passive, question–answer, etc.), and centrality of structure (actives more central than passives, declaratives more central than questions, etc.). Finally, it is impossible to account for all grammatical sentences without an overwhelmingly complex grammar. Thus the theory fails both criteria **3** and **4** of §2. We note that these are the kinds of difficulties that would have been faced by a theory that broke off at the level of words. The fact that they still arise, though in a diminished form, when the level of phrase structure is added, suggests that our theoretical apparatus is still too meager to account properly for the facts of English structure, and that a still higher level of syntactic analysis should be developed as a part of linguistic theory. Transformational analysis is proposed as a higher level.

In the abstract development of the level of transformational analysis, we construct a set of "grammatical transformations" each of which converts a string with phrase structure into a string with derived phrase structure. We consider a set of formal conditions that grammatical transformations must meet and develop a system of grammatical transformations meeting these conditions. If transformations are to appear in a grammar which is evaluated in terms of simplicity, there must be a fixed way to state transformations (just as the form of grammar must be fixed on every other level). We find that each grammatical transformation T is determined by a finitely statable *elementary transformation* and a finite *restricting class*, where the latter is a class of sequences of strings that determines the domain of applicability of T, and the former determines the structural revisions that T effects. We go on to investigate the algebra of transformations and the problem of assigning constituent structure to transforms, and we develop a procedure for compounding transformations. Grammatical transformations are then generalized so that a transformation may apply to a sequence of strings with phrase structure. This extension provides the means for generating such sentences as "proving that theorem was difficult," "I saw him coming," etc., which cause considerable difficulty when incorporated directly into the grammar of lower levels, and which are intuitively clearly derivative from several simple sentences.

In the transformational analysis of a language, we select a *kernel* of basic sentences for which a simple system of phrase structure can be provided, and in which all grammatical and selectional relations are found. Every grammatical sentence not in the kernel must be derived by means of the transformations set up for the language in question. A *syntactic description* then consists of a system of phrase structure for the kernel and a system of transformations. These systems jointly exhaust grammatical sentences.

Transformational analysis can be formulated as a linguistic level. In this formulation, a compound transformation is represented as a string of the grammatical transformations of which it is a compound, in the proper order. A generalized transformation can be represented in a natural manner as a string with substrings, each providing for the transformational development of one of the component kernel strings. Just as on lower levels we can represent a sentence as a sequence of phonemes, morphemes, words, syntactic categories, and (in various ways) phrases, so we can, on the transformational level, represent each sentence as a sequence of operations by which it is derived from the kernel. Each such sequence of operations, interpreted as a string in a concatenation algebra and originating ultimately from a fixed sequence of kernel elements, is a **T**-marker. We have a case of constructional homonymity when, in the simplest syntactic description, a given sentence can be derived from the kernel by several different routes, i.e., when it is assigned two different **T**-markers. Hence structural ambiguity on the level **T** has the same character as on other levels. We say that a *syntactic relation* holds between two sets of sentences if some transformation set up for the language carries one set into the other. Such relations as that of active–passive can receive a formal grounding in this way. The notion of "centrality of structure" can be explained wherever we can show that transformations are irreversible. Sentence types and subtypes can be identified with particular transformations and subsidiary transformations of transforms. The complexity of the grammatical statement is substantially reduced, since sentences with complex phrases and involved structure can be constructed transformationally out of already formed simpler sentences.

The development of transformational analysis incidentally provides the means for characterizing the mapping Φ^P of **P**-markers into strings of words. We find in Chapter VIII that this cannot be represented by a sequence of conversions applying to a terminal string, but it turns out that it can be represented as a compound transformation. It can thus appear in a **T**-marker. In fact, we require that the components of Φ^P provide a kind of skeletal structure for each **T**-marker. The minimal **T**-marker contains only Φ^P. This is the **T**-marker of a kernel sentence.

We now revise the picture of a grammar given in §5. A grammar consists of a sequence of conversions and a list of **T**-markers. The conversions are divided into two parts, the first leading from *Sentence* to terminal strings, the second from strings of words to strings of phonemes. We generate a sentence in the following manner:

8   (i)   Derive a terminal string from *Sentence* by the first part of the sequence of conversions. From this derivation, we can reconstruct uniquely the **P**-marker of this string.

        (ii) Select a **T**-marker and apply it to the terminal string with the given phrase structure. If the **T**-marker is just Φ^P, we have a kernel string; otherwise, a transform. In either case, we have a string of words.

(iii)   Derive a string of phones from this string of words by the remaining conversions. From this derivation we can reconstruct the lower-level representations of the derived string.

    Actually, **8** must be generalized. In step (i) we may derive a sequence of strings, and in step (ii) we may apply a generalized transformation to these, giving a string with complex transformational origin. **T**-markers are formulated in such a way that they can apply to transforms as well as kernel sentences. Thus the process of transformational generation is recursive—infinitely many sentences can be generated. Allowing them to run on freely, we complete the characterization of grammatical sentences.

    The earliest investigations of transformational structure were motivated by certain problems that arose in the attempt to extend linguistic techniques to the analysis of connected discourse.[4] We cannot claim that the problems of discourse analysis are solved by this theoretical study of linguistic structure, but it does appear to be the case that one of the basic operations required is the inverse of transformation. Transformational analysis, as a part of linguistic theory, enables us to construct derivative and complex sentences out of central simple ones. Reversing the process, it may be possible to use the same transformational development to recover from an ordinary discourse the sequence of simple sentences of which the given text is a "transform," in an extended sense of the term. That is, we reconstruct from the text a sequence of kernel sentences (with their phrase structure marked) from which the text can be derived. This reconstruction will be unique except in cases of constructional homonymity on the transformational level. The given text can be recovered from the sequence of reconstructed kernel sentences and the sequence of associated transformations. It will be fairly clear from the examples given in Chapter X that by this process we manage, by and large, to "factor out" the elementary content elements of the text as underlying and very simple kernel sentences. This question deserves more serious investigation, as it may prove to be of considerable independent significance.

8   In the last chapter, we turn to the transformational analysis of English. Investigating English structure in terms of the apparatus provided on

---

[4] See Z. S. Harris, "Discourse analysis"; "Discourse analysis: a sample text."

this new level, we find that the scope and efficiency of grammatical description are considerably increased, and that the specific deficiencies that arise when we attempt to extend lower levels beyond their natural boundaries are eliminated in a natural way. We find a finite kernel of basic sentences in which all the fundamental selectional and grammatical relations are found. The choice of the kernel is dictated, apparently to uniqueness, by rather obvious considerations of simplicity. That is, given two sets of sentences related by a transformation, we invariably seem to find very strong reasons for carrying out the transformation in one direction rather than the other. We can build up the rest of the language outside the kernel step by step, introducing new classes of sentences transformationally, and thus carrying the selectional and grammatical relations of the kernel into new forms and arrangements. We will see that this process enables us to develop very complex sentence forms by a sequence of elementary operations, thus reducing the apparent complexity of linguistic structure to simple components. It also supplies formal grounds in a great many cases for strong intuitions about linguistic structure, e.g., about ambiguity. It thus provides a basis for a description of how, in fact, language is used and understood. Furthermore, we will see that many phenomena that appear to be irregular and exceptional when viewed in terms of lower levels, become automatic consequences of the simplest transformational description of the "regular" cases, and are thus shown to be higher-level regularities. We also find that the behavior of sentences under transformation can throw a good deal of light on their phrase structure, and that, in fact, many of the major criteria for constituent analysis are transformational in origin. Finally, we find that no new notions are needed to develop the level **T** or to validate its application. The major transformations discussed in Chapter X can be established on the most rudimentary assumptions about grammaticalness, and as the analysis of grammaticalness becomes more refined, transformational analysis seems to become continually more revealing.

THE NATURE OF
LINGUISTIC THEORY *II*

Descriptive linguistics is concerned with three fundamental problems. On the one hand, the descriptive linguist is interested in constructing grammars for particular languages. At the same time, he is interested in giving a general theory of linguistic structure of which each of these grammars is an exemplification. Finally, he must be concerned with the problem of justifying and validating the results of his inquiries, and demonstrating that the grammars that he constructs are in some sense the correct ones. All three of these problems will occupy us in this investigation of linguistic structure. Before proceeding with proposals for the construction of linguistic theory, we must determine quite clearly just what is the nature of each of these three projects, and how they are interrelated. **9**

A grammar of a particular language can be considered, in what seems to me a perfectly good sense, to be a complete scientific theory of a particular subject matter, and if given in precise enough form, a formalized theory. Any interesting scientific theory will seek to relate observable events by formulating general laws in terms of hypothetical constructs, and providing a demonstration that certain observable events follow as consequences of these laws. In a particular grammar, the observable events are that such and such is an utterance of the language, and the demonstration that this event is a consequence of the theory consists in stating the structure of this predicted utterance on each linguistic level, and showing that this structure conforms to the grammatical rules, or the laws, of the theory. The grammar thus gives a theory of these utterances in terms of such hypothetical constructs as the particular phonemes, words, phrases, etc. of the language in question. As in the case of any **10.1** scientific theory, only a certain subset of the observable events will have been observed at any given time. In the case of a grammar, we have, at any time, only a finite corpus of utterances[1] out of an infinite set of grammatical utterances.

With its law-like rules for the combination of elements, a grammar can thus be said to "generate" a certain set of utterances on the basis of a given observed sample. Below, we will consider just how this process of generation operates. As an analogue, consider a possible formulation of a part of chemical theory in which, on the basis of such theoretical notions as "electron," "valence," and so on, all possible chemical compounds might be described.[2]

If we had such grammars for every language, we could attempt to abstract from them and to construct a general theory of the elements of which languages are composed. Thus in a certain sense, the complete realization of the first goal, the construction of particular grammars, would lead directly to a general theory of linguistic structure.

10.2   On the other hand, we can scarcely describe a language at all except in terms of some previously assumed theory of linguistic structure. For this reason, a large part of the work in modern structural linguistics has been directed toward providing a methodology for the analysis and description of linguistic behavior, that is, a methodology for the construction of these particular scientific theories. The purpose of these methodological investigations has been, in part, to provide an essentially mechanical method for constructing an appropriate grammar for each language, that is, a method in which the linguist's intuition and other intangibles play no role. If the second goal, that of developing a general theory, were achieved in a strong enough form, the constructing of particular grammars would be a mechanical matter, requiring no ingenuity. Thus these two goals are in a sense interdependent. Given

---

[1] But note that not all utterances of the corpus need be considered grammatical, just as not every recorded observation need be accepted as a datum. We return to this question in Chapter V.

[2] A grammar presented in a different form, such that given an utterance, the grammar will mechanically provided an analysis of it in terms of each level, could be considered roughly analogous to a formalized system of qualitative analysis. This is essentially the "operational" form of grammar discussed by Bar-Hillel, "A quasi-arithmetical notation for syntactic description." Several methods of presenting grammars of the first type are discussed by Harris, *Methods in Structural Linguistics*, §20.3; cf. Bloomfield, "Menomini morphophonemics," Jakobson, "Russian conjugation," as examples of grammars of this general form.

particular grammars, we could generalize to an abstract theory. Given a sufficiently powerful abstract theory, we could automatically derive grammars for particular languages.

Actually, of course, neither goal can be achieved independently. In **10.3** constructing particular grammars, the linguist leans heavily on a pre-conception of linguistic structure, and any general characterization of linguistic structure must show itself adequate to the description of each natural language. The circularity is not vicious, however. The fact is simply that linguistic theory has two interdependent aspects. At any given point in its development, we can present a noncircular account, giving the general theory as an abstract formal system, and showing how each grammars is a particular example of it. Change can come in two ways—either by refining the formalism and finding new and deeper underpinnings for the general theory, or by finding out new facts about languages and simpler ways of describing them.

There are several possible ways of construing the relationships between particular grammars and the general theory. Certainly every grammar must be compatible with the theory in the sense that the elements set up in the grammar must exhibit the general properties required by the theory. This is the weakest possible requirement. At the other extreme, the strongest requirement would be that the theory provide a practical means for literally constructing the grammar out of the raw data. Thus, given a sufficient corpus, such a theory will lead us directly to a grammatical description of the language, in some practical way, requiring no ingenuity or intuition on the part of the linguist. It provides what might be called a "practical discovery procedure" for grammars. A weaker requirement than this would be that given a grammar, the theory must provide a practical mechanical way of vali-dating it, i.e., of showing that it is in fact the best grammar of the language, in a sense specified by the theory. Such a theory provides a practical decision procedure for the notion "grammar of a language." A still weaker requirement would be that the theory provide a method of evaluating any proposed grammar, so that, given two proposed grammars, there would be a practical and mechanical way for deter-mining which is the better of the two. Note that this last is still a strong requirement, much stronger than those imposed in natural sciences, where no one would seriously consider the possibility of a general, practical, mechanical method for deciding between two theories, each compatible with the available evidence. But in linguistics, given the nature of the data, it seems natural that our sights should be set at least that high. Each of these three kinds of relation has been qualified by the word "practical." The significance for linguistics of this vague qualification will become clearer below.[3]

10.4 To recapitulate so far, we see that linguistic research has two aspects. It aims to provide for each language a theory of the structure of that language (i.e., a grammar), and at the same time to develop a general theory of linguistic structure of which each of these grammars will present a model. The particular grammars and the general theory must be closely enough related so that some practical technique is available for deciding which of two proposed grammars better exemplifies the general theory.

11.1 Consider now the problem of justifying a grammar. It is clear in the first place that the form of the justification will vary with the purposes of the grammar. Thus a pedagogic grammar may be justified in terms of teaching success. But such considerations are obviously irrelevant for a linguistic grammar with no such special purposes, a grammar which purports to show the "structure" of the language.

A theory is justified by relating it to data. In the case of a linguistic grammar, we surely require that it meet certain external conditions of adequacy, that the generated sentences be acceptable to the native speaker, that the elements of the language as constructed in the grammar have certain observable correlates, etc. Let us assume[4] that such criteria, however vague and incomplete, have been established for grammars. We then face the problem of choosing among a vast number of different grammars, each giving a different structure, and all meeting these vague and incomplete external criteria. This is the facet of the problem of justification which is most interesting at the present stage of linguistic research, and to which we will devote our primary attention in this study. But to this question, an answer has already been suggested in §10. The grammar can be justified by relating it to the general theory and showing that exactly the structure described arises from the data, given the general theory (or that the given grammar has the highest value in terms of the general theory). The general theory must meet the condition that all grammars to which it leads must satisfy whatever external

---

[3] We return to the matter in Chapters IV and V. It may be worth mentioning that the importance of the vague distinction between a discovery procedure and a practical discovery procedure is not unique to linguistics. One obvious example is in the theory of design of switching circuits, where it is important to find the shortest equivalent of a given truth functional expression. There is a mechanical method, but a good deal of effort has been expended in discovering a practical method.

[4] We return to this assumption below in §15.

criteria of adequacy we can establish. Such a conception of the process of validation means that one indispensable aspect of the validation of a grammar of a given language is the construction of grammars for other languages. This conclusion follows from the conception of a valid grammar as one conforming to a linguistic theory which in turn must produce grammars meeting the external conditions of adequacy. It is important to recognize that even weak conditions of adequacy may impose severe restrictions on the choice of grammars for a given language L_1. While many grammars of L_1 may meet these conditions when L_1 is considered in isolation, it may be the case that very few of these grammars follow from some general theory that leads to grammars of the languages L_2, L_3,..., all of which meet these conditions of adequacy. The fact that grammars of L_2, L_3,... play a part in the evaluation of the grammar of L_1 is as it should be, since we are interested not only in grammars of particular languages, but also in developing a general theory of linguistic structure. Whether or not we can determine grammars to uniqueness in this manner depends on how limiting are the conditions of adequacy and how stringent is the formulation of the general theory (which can in a sense be regarded as the definition of "language").[5]

It appears then that there are two factors involved in determining the validity of a grammar: the necessity to meet the external conditions of adequacy and to conform to the general theory. The first factor cannot be eliminated, or there are no constraints whatsoever on grammar construction; the simplest grammar for L will simply identify a grammatical sentence in L as any phone sequence. Elimination of the second factor leaves us free to choose at will among a vast number of mutually conflicting grammars.

There has been some discussion recently as to whether the linguist "plays mathematical games" or "descibes reality" in linguistic analysis of particular languages, where the phrase "playing mathematical games" often appears to refer to the conscious development of a theory of linguistic structure for use in constructing and validating grammars. If by "describing reality" is meant meeting the external conditions of adequacy, then in order to give content and significance to the requirement that the linguist must describe reality, it is necessary to give independent (i.e., outside the particular grammar) characterizations of these conditions, e.g., for sentencehood, by constructing informant response tests to determine the degree of acceptability or evocability of

---

[5] This definition must be restrictive at least to some extent—no one confuses language with basket making—but exactly how much behavior should be called linguistic is a question to be determined in part by the possibilities for constructing an integrated linguistic theory.

sequences. But within whatever bounds can be clearly set independently, the linguist's goal can only be to construct for each language a simple grammar related to other grammars in such a way as to lead to a revealing general theory of which all are exemplifications. There seems to be no reason to consider the constructs established in pursuit of these goals as being in some sense invalid. If the methods developed with these goals in mind lead to unacceptable results, it is important to show this. But the alternative to ineffective methods is not abandonment of theoretical inquiry.[6]

11.2   What are the practical implications of this conception of validation for the program of building an objective science of linguistics? Suppose that a linguist constructs a grammar of a language in terms of such and such elements and rules of combination. To validate this grammar, it is not sufficient merely to give a formal characterization of the elements that have been constructed. Given any set of phonemes, words, etc., we can easily find purely formal and operational ways to derive just this set from the data, e.g., by listing, which is as precise and formal a procedure as can be found. To justify the contention that such and such are, e.g., the syntactic categories of the language, it is necessary to give a completely general characterization of the notion of syntactic category, and to show that the chosen categories satisfy this definition, whereas others do not. If the linguist wishes to justify a given assignment of words to syntactic categories in one language by appeal to a certain definition of the notion of syntactic category, formal or otherwise, he must be prepared to set up syntactic categories in every other language by exactly the same definition.[7] This condition rules out listing, but it

---

[6] If, for some particular linguistic element or relation, it is possible to set up an unambiguous, cross-culturally valid, and effective behavioral test, then this element or relation can be characterized in the general theory by this test (i.e., by an appropriate primitive). But even where elements and relations can be characterized in this way, it is still necessary to carry out theoretical studies in terms of patterning, simplicity, etc., so as to discover how apparently independent notions are interrelated, and to give a rational account and explanation of linguistic intuitions. It is immaterial whether these tests, where available, are given as criteria of adequacy for defined terms or as operational accounts of primitive terms of the theory, in which case the relations between these terms will be expressed by theorems rather than definitions. What is important is that the relationships be expressed in the theory. See also §34.2.

[7] Of course, such a definition may have many cases. It may apply to one language in one way and to another in a different way. But it must be formulated abstractly if it is to be significant. We must be able to determine somehow from other characteristics of the language which case of the definition applies. The difficulty of giving an abstract formulation for some criterion suggested for linguistic analysis can easily be underestimated.

also leads us to reevaluate many other customary types of descriptive statement that may have been intended to provide justification for grammars. Thus a proposal that Adjective in English be defined as the class of words to which "er" and "est" can be added, though it provides a perfectly adequate specification of a class of linguistic elements, sheds no light on the syntactic categories or morpheme classes of English, since no general notion of syntactic category (or morpheme class) tells us that just these suffixes should be taken as defining a category. Similarly, the proposal that Word or Phrase in English be defined by certain (not all) suprasegmental features, that a certain syntactic category be defined by the fact of its exclusive occurrence in a certain "diagnostic environment," and many other suggestions become suspect. Such suggestions do not provide a significant demonstration that these and not some other elements should have been set up in the grammar. They may be legitimate if understood as a shorthand way of saying that these formal features are chosen because they lead to the simplest grammar. But now the real source of validation is simplicity, and it becomes necessary to analyze this notion, if the validation is to have any significance.

There is a certain vagueness in the word "formal" and the notion **11.3** "formal justification," which should perhaps be commented upon here. In the strict sense of the word, an argument, a characterization, a theory, etc. is "formal" if it deals with form as opposed to meaning, that is, if it deals solely with the shape and arrangement of symbols. In this sense, any distributional theory or argument is formal. But the word "formal" has misleading connotations, implying "rigorous," "clear," etc. Suppose that we use instead the word "formalized" when we have this latter sense in mind. A formalized theory, then, is one that is formulated in accordance with certain clear canons of rigor and precision; definitions are given explicitly in such a way that defined terms are always eliminable, and the axioms and methods of proof are precisely stated. We can thus have a formalized theory purporting to be about form or about meaning. A formalized theory is, of course, not necessarily an acceptable or enlightening theory. And the fact that a certain subject matter is stated to constitute the intended interpretation of a presented formalized theory does not confer any desirable properties upon this subject matter, or upon the theory. It is possible to construct a formalized theory with no interesting interpretation, or with intuition, ghosts, etc., in its intended interpretation. What concerns us here is the possibility of a formalized theory of linguistic form, and the problems involved in constructing such a theory.

A possible instance of equivocation between these two senses of "formal" is the case of formal justification discussed above. We cannot justify the choice of a linguistic element (or category) as grammatically significant for a given language by offering some distributional criterion for this element. Any element or category will have *some* formal property, and a purported justification of this kind merely bypasses the only interesting question, namely, why the particular distributional property was selected as significant or "criterial" in the case in question. The fact that such constructions are formal (in the sense of nonsemantic) does not justify them. To reiterate our earlier conclusion, the discovery of formal markers is not to the point insofar as we are interested in avoiding recourse to intuition in constructing or validating grammars. To do this significantly, it is necessary to demonstrate that the grammar follows from a general and abstract theory of linguistic structure.[8]

This ambiguity may also lead to some confusion in considering the relevance of symbolic logic to linguistic theory. It is sometimes argued that syntactic treatments of systems of logic, or other so-called "artificial languages," with their formation and transformation rules, their syntactic categories, etc., may serve as useful models for the study of linguistic form. Although this could conceivably be so, it does not seem to me that it has been shown in any interesting sense, or that whatever similarities can be found offer any promising line of study. It may be that some of the conviction carried by the argument that linguistics should model itself on logical syntax is due to an equivocation in the word "formal." It is certainly correct that logic is indispensable for formalizing theories, of linguistics or anything else, but this fact gives us no insight into what sort of systems form the subject matter for linguistics, or how it should treat them. Neither from this fact, nor from the indisputable fact that work in logic has incidentally led to important insights into the use of language,[9] can it be argued that the study of the formal (or semantic) properties of natural languages should model itself on the study of the formal (or semantic) properties of logic and artificial languages. Though logic can be applied with profit to the construction of a formalized linguistic theory, it does not follow that this theory is in any sense about logic or any other formalized system.[10]

[8] It should be noted that there can be no basic quarrel between the linguist who attempts to justify his grammar in this way and the linguist who is satisfied to present the grammar without any such justification, and to utilize it or explore its implications for other purposes. They are simply interested in different problems.

[9] For example, the distinction between meaning and reference, use and mention, ordinary and counterfactual conditionals, etc.

[10] For differing views on the relation of linguistics to logic, see Bar-Hillel, "Logical syntax and semantics" and Chomsky, "Logical syntax and semantics: their linguistic relevance."

We have seen that one requirement that justifications must meet if they   12.1
are to be convincing is that of generality. Since the problem of justification
and that of constructing a general theory of linguistic structure are,
in part at least, essentially the same, another look at the structure of the
general theory may clarify further requirements for justification of
particular grammars.

The general theory will ultimately assume the form of a system
of definitions, in which "phoneme," "word," "sentence," etc., are
defined, and their general properties and interrelations specified. A
system of definitions introducing a certain set of concepts must be based
on some set of primitive, undefined terms. The interest and explanatory
power of this theory will depend directly on the clarity and applicability
of these primitive notions.

Among the primitive notions of this general theory of linguistic
structure we might expect to find such terms as "precedes" (so-and-so
precedes such-and-such), "is a fricative," etc. Suppose now that we
know how to apply the primitive notions of this general theory to
actual language material, i.e., we know which form precedes which
other form, which form is a fricative, etc. Then assuming that the definitions in the theory meet appropriate formal requirements, we will have
a mechanical procedure for discovering a grammar of the language. If
"phoneme," "word," "sentence," etc. are each defined in terms of a set
of notions $P, Q, R, \ldots$, and if we know in fact what are the Ps, the Qs,
the Rs, etc., of a given sample of the language, we can determine automatically the phonemes, words, and sentences. Thus, if given in a strong
enough form, linguistic theory may actually provide a literal discovery
procedure for grammars, though perhaps not a practical discovery
procedure.

The form of theory that we have just described, where every notion
appearing in the theory is completely analyzed in terms of a set of
operational primitives, is a very strong one. A broader conception of
the role of theoretical terms in scientific theory can be given.[11] But it
seems to me that this is a correct way to state the goal of that aspect of
linguistic theory that we are here considering.

Wells has pointed out recently[12] that philosophers have, by and
large, rejected, as a general criterion of significance, the strong kind of
reductionism that we are suggesting as appropriate for our particular
purposes. He offers this in apparent criticism of Bloomfield's program

---

[11] See, for instance, Quine, "Two dogmas of empiricism" (reprinted with minor revisions
as Chapter 2 of *From a Logical Point of View*), or Hempel, "A logical appraisal of
operationism."

[12] R. S. Wells, "Meaning and use," p. 241.

of avoiding mentalistic foundations for linguistic theory. It is true that many philosophers have given up, as a *general* requirement for significance, the kind of reductionism that our restatement of Bloomfield's program has as its goal, and have held that dispositional terms and other theoretical constructs must be introduced into scientific theory even if not amenable to the kind of analysis once sought. However, I do not believe that this is relevant to Bloomfield's antimentalism, or to the approach to linguistic theory that we have outlined. The fact that a certain general criterion of significance has been abandoned does not mean that the bars are down and that "ideas" and "meanings" become proper terms for linguistics. If this rejection of an old criterion is not followed by construction of a new one, then it simply has no bearing on the selection of legitimate terms for a scientific theory. If it is followed by a new analysis of "significance," then if this is at all adequate, it seems to me that it will rule out mentalism for what were essentially Bloomfield's reasons, i.e., its obscurity and inherent untestability. Thus Quine rejects reductionism, suggests an alternative, and rejects mentalism.[13]

12.2 We have suggested that a grammar is justified by showing that it follows from application to the corpus of a properly formulated general theory. Clearly, for such a justification of a grammar to carry any conviction, it must be framed in terms of notions whose applicability can be determined in particular cases. Or, to put the same thing differently, if we are to use an explicit and formalized theory of linguistic structure in validating grammars, it will be necessary that the data be presented to it in a certain form. What form this must be is determined by the primitive notions of this theory. The theory is significant just to the extent that we can demonstrate that the data do have the prescribed form, that is, just to the extent that we have unambiguous, cross-culturally valid tests for applying the undefined notions to data. Thus if one of the basic undefined terms of linguistic theory is "intuition," and if we define phonemes in this theory as elements which our intuition perceives in a language, then the notion of phoneme is as clear and precise as is "intuition." We will be able to discover the phonemes of a language by applying this theory just in case our intuition applies without equivocation. And

---

[13] Quine, *From a Logical Point of View*, p. 48. See also, Goodman, *Fact, Fiction and Forecast* for a discussion of the problems touched on in these remarks. As Goodman puts it (p. 58), "Lack of a general theory of goodness does not turn vice into virtue; and lack of a general theory of significance does not turn empty verbiage into illuminating discourse."

the justification of the grammatical description at which we arrive will be as convincing to others as are our intuitions.

It should be clear, then, why the linguist interested in constructing a general theory of linguistic structure, in justifying given grammars, or (to put the matter in its more usual form) in constructing procedures of analysis should try to avoid such notions as "intuition," and others which fail in precisely the same way. With this in mind, we can turn to the question of what is an acceptable basis for linguistic theory.

13.1 The first question that arises in this connection is that of the role of meaning in linguistic analysis. This has been the subject of much debate in recent years. If this debate has not been conclusive, the reason may be in part that the wrong question has been argued. I think that this is in fact the case, and that a fresh approach can shed some new light on this problem.

The central objection to meaning as a criterion of analysis has always been the obscurity of semantic notions. I think it is indeed fair to say that we are currently in pretty much the same state of unclarity with regard to meaning as we are with regard to intuition. And this is a sufficient reason for refusing to admit meaning into linguistic theory. Suppose that we do manage to develop effective and unambiguous cross-culturally valid tests for synonymy, meaningfulness, and related concepts. Would this mean that the description of grammatical structure may be based on semantic notions? I think that it would not—that in fact there is a deeper motivation for refusing to base the theory of linguistic form on semantic notions than merely the obscurity of such a foundation. What I would like to argue here is that semantic notions are of no assistance in the determination of formal structure, that only their unclarity disguises their irrelevance, and that when the claim is put forth that linguistic analysis cannot be carried out without the use of meaning, what is really expressed is that it cannot be carried out without intuition.

13.2 The linguist who claims that linguistic analysis can be done without meaning must demonstrate that the notions which he wishes to apply in describing languages can be given a completely general and abstract characterization in terms of a set of operational[14] primitive notions, not including "synonymity," etc. This is a formidable task. Suppose that he fails, conclusively. Does this mean that it has been shown that

---

[14] This is by no means a clear term—cf. Hempel, *op. cit.*; but we may take it for granted for our limited purposes.

linguistic analysis must be based on meaning? Not at all. To show this it is necessary to carry out a parallel procedure, constructing a system in which the terms of grammatical description are defined and terms involving meaning *do* appear as primitives. The immediate availability of such a theory is often, quite mistakenly, taken for granted. The customary challenge "how can you construct a grammar with no appeal to meaning" begs an important question, by implication, in the unspoken assumption that naturally one can construct a grammar *with* appeal to meaning. But I think an investigation of this latter thesis will show that it is in fact not correct. It is impossible to give a literal demonstration that linguistic analysis cannot be based on semantic notions. But it is both possible and important to investigate in more detail some of the particular cases where, it is urged, linguistics must (or can) rely on meaning.

It is almost a linguistic cliché, even among those linguists who consciously attempt to avoid meaning in their descriptive work, that in order to construct a phonemic system we must know whether or not expressions are different in meaning, and this view has often been reiterated by representatives of neighboring fields. Let us put aside for the moment the question of whether we can determine synonymy relations in some clear and unambiguous way, and assume that we have as much knowledge about synonymy as we please. Can we use this knowledge in constructing a phonemic system?

We are concerned with one aspect of the fundamental problem of determining the subject matter of grammatical description. There are several reasons why this cannot be identified directly as the linguist's corpus of observed utterances. For one thing, we cannot know, from merely observing the physical properties of observed utterances, which of these are repetitions of one another, which utterance tokens are instances of the same utterance type. Suppose, for instance, that an English corpus contains the three utterance tokens "I found the boy," "I found the boy," and "I found the toy," three distinct physical events. Our problem is to develop an operational test or analytic technique that will enable us to determine that the second of these utterances is a repetition of the first, but not the third. If we carry out careful measurements, we find, of course, that the three are distinct from one another in their physical properties. The problem, then, is one of determining which phonetic differences are significant in the language in question in that they determine nonrepetition, or as we will call it, phonemic distinctness. To determine this, it is argued, we must determine which pairs of utterance tokens differ in meaning. The claim seems to be that given two utterance tokens U_1 and U_2,

1   U_1 is phonemically distinct from U_2 if and only if U_1 differs in meaning from U_2.[15]

But it seems that because of homonyms on the one hand and synonyms on the other, this proposed equivalence is simply false in both directions. Let U_1 be the utterance "I saw him by the bank" (meaning the bank of the river) and let U_2 be "I saw him by the bank" (the savings bank). Then U_1 and U_2 differ in meaning and are phonemically identical. And such pairs of words as "advértisement"–"advertísement," /ræšən/–/reyšən/ ("ration"), etc., which often coexist in one style of speech and are clearly synonyms, show that difference in meaning is not a necessary condition for phonemic distinctness. We cannot circumvent this argument by maintaining that 1 holds for all cases except the rather special case of homonyms and synonyms. For one thing, these are by no means peripheral phenomena. For another, homonymity and synonymity are simply the names we give to exceptions to this rule, and any rule works except for its exceptions. We are forced to conclude that knowledge of the meaning of utterance tokens does not enable us to classify these correctly into utterance types in the simple way proposed in 1.

We might try to establish a relation between synonymy and phonemic distinctness by reinterpreting the term "meaning" in 1. Let us define the "ambiguous meaning" of an utterance token not as its actual meaning as it was produced, but as the set of meanings that it *might have had*, produced under any possible circumstances. Hoping to avoid the homonymity problem at least, we can now rephrase 1 with distinctness of ambiguous meaning proposed as a sufficient condition for phonemic distinctness.

In this form, this revision cannot be taken seriously. It requires that to determine phonemic distinctness, we must not only be able to discover the meanings of tokens, but also to analyze the dispositional notion "could have such and such a meaning" (and this without reliance on the notion of "repetition" or "utterance type," if we are to avoid circularity). The prospects for this seem so hopeless that we can safely disregard this proposal as it stands.

We can, however, reformulate this approach making a weaker claim for relevance of meaning than 1. Suppose that we have an *a priori* system of phonetic transcription equipped with a guarantee that, with this system, any utterance token in any language can be transcribed in

---

[15] Almost every descriptive linguist concerned with phonemics has on some occasion maintained this position, and this view has been reiterated by representatives of neighboring fields.

one and only one way, and any two phonemically distinct utterances will be differently transcribed (though not the converse, of course). Naturally, transcription of any one language will reveal an enormous amount of irrelevant detail.

Suppose that we transcribe each utterance token of a corpus in terms of this system, assigning to it its meaning, which we assume once more to be known unambiguously. But now certain distinct utterances will be transcribed in the same way, since only certain distinctions can be recognized by this fixed system of transcription. But it is presumably the case that if two sounds are assigned to different phonemes in a given language, then substitution of one for the other will lead to a difference in meaning in some context. Now that we are assuming part of the problem of phonemic distinctness to be solved on an *a priori*, purely physical basis, we can attempt to use this semantic property to complete the characterization of phonemic distinctness. We might now replace 1 by the condition that two differently transcribed tokens are assigned to different phonemes if there are two utterance tokens that differ in meaning but are identically transcribed except for the transcriptions of the tokens in question. But the problem of homonymity again stands in the way of this formulation, since many phonemically identical tokens will be differently transcribed. Hence homonyms will often be differently transcribed, and the new criterion breaks down just as the old one did. We might revise the proposed condition, then, requiring for phonemic distinctness that *every* two utterance tokens differing just in the transcription of the tokens in question be distinct in meaning. But this will not do, because of the existence of synonyms, for exactly the reasons we discussed above. We must require, then, that there be a *sufficient* number of such pairs of utterances, in some sense that does not seem easy to clarify.

This discussion has been based on the assumption that we can unambiguously determine when two utterance tokens have the same meaning. But clearly in making this assumption, we have granted far too much. Surely this is a far more difficult problem than the problem of determining sameness or difference of linguistic form that we hope to solve in terms of it. Furthermore, there is a conceptual difficulty that seems to undermine the whole approach in a more fundamental manner. We have not dealt with the question of whether the meanings assigned to distinct (but phonemically identical) tokens are identical, or merely very similar. If the latter, then all the difficulties of phonemic distinctness reappear, in a more obscure form, in the determination of sameness of meaning. We must provide a method for determining when two slightly different meanings are *sufficiently* similar. If, on the other hand, we try

to maintain the position that the meanings are identical in each occurrence, then a charge of circularity seems warranted. It seems that the
only way to uphold such a position would be to conceive of the meaning
of a token as the way in which tokens of this type are (or can be) properly
used, the type of response they normally evoke, the type of change in the
organism they normally induce, or something of this sort. But it is
difficult to make any sense at all out of such a conception without the
prior establishment of utterance types (nor is it easy even with this
prior notion). The degree of unclarity in this discussion makes the
attempt to define phonemic distinctness in these terms appear rather
pointless.

We have seen that its vagueness and unclarity make the notion of   **13.3**
meaning an ineffective tool for grammatical analysis, and that it is
difficult to imagine how it might be employed without vicious circularity.
Furthermore, if we take meaning seriously enough to assign meanings
correctly to utterances, we seem to learn very little about phonemic
distinctness. It is important to add that when we actually run into a
problem of determining phonemic distinctness, we in fact do not rely
on meaning in any way.

    Suppose, for example, that in the study of English we record the
utterances "I saw him by the bank" (meaning "river bank"), "I saw him
by the bank (meaning "savings bank"), and "I saw him buy the bank."
It happens that the third of these is phonemically distinct from the
first two, which are phonemically identical. There seems to be only
one basic method that a linguist can actually employ to determine how
these three tokens are phonemically related, namely, the paired utterance
test[16] in one form or another. To perform this test we take two utterances,

---

[16] See Harris, *Methods*, p. 33. It might be argued that a semantic alternative to the paired
utterance test is to ask the informant whether the utterances in question are the same
or different in meaning. It is difficult to comment on this proposal, because it clearly
fails the minimal standards for any procedure designed to determine the application
of a notion of linguistic theory; that is, this procedure is based not on observation of
the speaker's behavior but on his reports about the basis for a distinction he is making.
This leaves us completely in the dark as to the status of the linguistic notion in question.
Suppose that this procedure is proposed as the method of applying the notion "phonemically distinct." Has the speaker actually utilized any semantic information in
giving his answer? This is a question which we obviously cannot answer. Hence this
procedure sheds no light on the question of the relation between meaning and phonemic
distinctness. If we try to introspect, it seems most reasonable to assume that the
informant who is asked whether "bank" and "bank" differ in meaning reinterprets
the question as: are "bank" and "bank" the same word? (i.e., are they phonemically
distinct?). This then is no procedure at all. It amounts to asking the informant to do

let us say recorded on tape and labeled U_1 and U_2, play them repeatedly in random order to an informant, and see whether he can consistently and correctly identify them as U_1 and U_2. Of course we know that the three utterances given above differ in meaning, but this information seems quite irrelevant to solving the problem at hand. Knowing it, we still must determine whether these tokens are phonemically distinct. And the linguist in the field must employ some such nonsemantic device as the paired utterance test to determine this.

The paired utterance test is one of the operational cornerstones for linguistic theory, and as such it deserves much more study and elaboration. Its effectiveness can easily be determined by experiment, and many variations can be developed. Suppose for example that U_1 and U_2 are in free variation, but that the speaker in fact perceives the distinction. It is possible in this case to have the speaker make a series of repetitions of U_1 and U_2 and to run through the test again with these repetitions. If the speaker can consistently distinguish U_1 and U_2 with repetitions and other elaborations, then there is some linguistically relevant distinction between them. What this distinction is and where it lies, of course, the paired utterance test cannot tell us. It is the task of the developed linguistic theory to determine this.

There are certain more complicated ways of attempting to determine phonemic distinctness in terms of meaning, but I think it can be shown that these simply amount to special variations on the paired utterance test, with a spurious explanation of the results of the test thrown in. The compulsion to give some such explanation seems to arise from a feeling that even if this test operationally makes the distinction we require between utterances, it still does not answer the question: in what respect are these utterances distinct? But to this question the answer can only be the tautology: in phonemic constitution. It is not clear what further answer could be required. There is no more need for a semantic explanation for the fact that "bill" is phonemically identical with "bill" than for the equally indisputable fact that "bill" rhymes with "pill." If in fact difference in meaning did correspond exactly to distinctness as defined by the paired utterance test, this would be an interesting correlation between independent notions. But since only the latter gives an operational account of the intuitive sense of distinctness of utterances that we are attempting to reconstruct in linguistic theory, only the latter is taken as the test of phonemic distinctness.

---

the linguist's work, and to do it in a way that is not open to observation. Consider furthermore how the speaker would react if asked whether such phonemically distinct forms as "ádult" and "adúlt," etc., differ in meaning.

Careful investigation seems to show that differential meaning has 13.4 nothing to do with the concrete problem of determining phonemic distinctness. One way to explain the wide acceptance of the claim that it does is to assume that there is a confusion here between "meaning" and "intuition about linguistic form." The real content of the claim that a certain linguistic element is established on the basis of meaning often seems to be that this element must be established on the basis of intuition. But intuition about linguistic form is not meaning. Before we develop an objective and effective technique for constructing a phonemic system, we have only our intuition that "pit" and "pull" begin with the same phoneme, while "pit" and "bit" do not. But there is nothing semantic about this intuition. This confusion of meaning with intuition indicates a failure to take meaning itself very seriously. The only thing that meaning and intuition have in common is their obscurity. Fortunately, in the case of phonemic distinctness the paired utterance test enables us to avoid this reliance on intuition. And the major goal of methodological work in linguistics is to enable us to avoid intuition about linguistic form wherever we find it, replacing it by some explicit and systematic account. If the appeal to meaning proves to be similarly irrelevant at other points in the theory of linguistic form, then we will be entitled to say that this appeal functions as a dangerous bypass, in the sense that it simply indicates lack of interest in the problem of characterizing explicitly the linguistic notion in question—a dangerous bypass, because (as distinct from open recourse to intuition) it gives the illusion of being a real explanation, not merely avoidance of the problem.

Of course, we have not shown that meaning can play no role anywhere in phonemic theory. It is impossible to give a proof for such a negative proposition. But once we have recognized that a semantically oriented theory is by no means an immediately available alternative to a nonsemantic theory, the semantic orientation loses much of its attractiveness. In place of the customary challenge "how can you carry out linguistic analysis with no recourse to meaning" it is perfectly proper to ask where semantic notions can play some part in determining grammatical notions. It is not at all evident that there is any way to meet this challenge.

Until we are presented with some interesting and promising way to meet this challenge, we should certainly avoid such statements as "so-and-so is attempting to construct a grammatical theory or a grammar with no appeal to meaning." Even if this is literally true, it is quite misleading, since the implication that there is an alternative has not been demonstrated. Similarly, we can afford to be quite skeptical about the often-voiced claim that even if we can proceed without meaning, it is much easier to proceed *with* reliance on meaning, using this as a heuristic device to be eliminated in careful reconstruction and validation of the results of linguistic analysis. It is certainly true that our intuitions about linguistic form may be useful in the actual process of gathering and organizing grammatical data, but this is not to say that our intuitions about meaning serve the same purpose. Whatever meaning is, it certainly is not intuition about form. This point is easily obscured in vague statements to the effect that to actually construct a grammar it is useful to know the language under analysis. If "knowledge (or understanding) of a language" includes knowledge of the grammar, this statement is trivially true. If not, I see no reason to assume that it is true at all.

13.5   It is difficult to evaluate many other suggestions about the role of meaning in grammar, largely because it is difficult to pin down the notion of meaning. However, I think that within the limits posed by the obscurity of these notions, it is reasonable to suggest "intuition about linguistic form" as a more proper locution than "meaning," wherever such suggestions are made.

Quine[17] distinguishes two major notions in the theory of meaning, "synonymy" and "significance," and suggests that grammar relies on both for the determination of the subject matter of a linguistic description. The linguist must determine how many distinct forms constitute his corpus, and which forms not in his corpus must be described by the grammar. In the first case, he relies on synonymy (i.e., on difference in meaning), and in the second, on significance (i.e., the grammar must describe exactly the significant or meaningful sentences). The first point we have already discussed.

The grammar must generate a set of grammatical sentences on the basis of a limited corpus: Is it correct to identify "grammaticalness" with "significance"? I think that it is not. If we take "meaningfulness" or "significance" seriously, I think we must admit that

2   *colorless green ideas sleep furiously*

is thoroughly meaningless and nonsignificant, but it seems to me that as a speaker of English, I would regard this as a "grammatical" sentence, and it can certainly be argued that the establishment of its nonsignificance falls outside the domain of grammar. Furthermore, it hardly seems to the point to suggest that the reason why

---

[17] *Op. cit.*, "Meaning in linguistics."

3   *colorless green ideas sleeps furiously*

on the other hand, is not to be generated by the grammar is because it is nonsignificant in some semantic sense. It seems that **3** is more correctly described as an utterance that fails to meet certain formal requirements.

The situation we face is roughly this. We know that a speaker of the language can select, among sequence that he has never heard, certain grammatical sentences, and that he will do this in much the same way as other speakers. We might test this by a direct determination of some sort of "bizarreness reaction," or in various indirect ways. Note for instance that a speaker of English, given **2**, will normally read it with the standard intonation pattern of an English sentence. But given some permutation of the words of **2**, e.g., the sequence formed by reading **2** from back to front,

4   *furiously sleep ideas green colorless*

he will read it with the intonation pattern characteristic of a list of unrelated words, each word with a falling intonation. Yet he has presumably never heard either **2** or **4**, nor even any of the parts of these sequences, in connected discourse.

How can we describe this ability? The only thing we can say directly is that the speaker has an "intuitive sense of grammaticalness." But to say this is simply to state a problem. Suppose that we can (i) construct a linguistic theory in which "grammaticalness" is defined, (ii) apply this linguistic theory in a rigorous way to a finite sample of linguistic behavior thus generating a set of "grammatical" sentences, and (iii) demonstrate that the set of grammatical sentences thus generated, in the case of language after language, corresponds to the "intuitive sense of grammaticalness" of the native speaker. In this case, we will have succeeded in giving a rational account of this behavior, i.e., a theory of the speaker's linguistic intuition. This is the goal of linguistic theory. It is by no means obvious that it can be done, limiting ourselves to formal analysis. It is even more difficult to see how any semantic notion can be of any assistance in this program. In any event, there seems no reason to introduce the notion of "significance" into this account.[18] We

---

[18] Further evidence that no element of significance is involved here comes from noting a similar phenomenon on the phonemic level. Here too, we can distinguish "grammatical nonsense" (e.g., "glip") from ungrammatical nonsense (e.g., "ligp"). It seems reasonable to suppose that the processes involved have the same character, schematically at least. But surely no notion of significance is involved in the phonological process. A

begin by recognizing the existence of an intuition about linguistic form, which, if I am correct, does not correspond to the intuition about significance. We end, if successful, by giving an objective theory which, in a certain sense, explains this intuition. Before a linguistic theory is constructed, the subject matter for linguistic description is determined not by significance and synonymy, but simply by reference to the speaker's intuitions about which forms are grammatical and which pairs phonemically distinct. After a successful theory has been constructed, the subject matter for linguistic description is determined by the theory itself. The success of the theory is determined in part by its efficacy in reconstructing intuition. Naturally, if it generates **4** but not **2** as grammatical, when we apply it to English, it will be judged unsuccessful. Insofar as any argument turning on words like "meaning" and "intuition" can be convincing, I think it is fair to say that in this case, too, any semantic reference is irrelevant to formulating or resolving the problem.

If we keep clearly in mind the distinction between the task of constructing a general theory of linguistic structure and that of constructing particular grammars, we can clarify Quine's contention that in order to set the grammarian's task, we must solve the "problem of defining the general notion of significant sequence."[19] If we replace "significant" by "grammatical," this statement is correct, where the grammarian's task is understood as the construction of a grammar for a particular language. For this to be a significant project, we need a prior notion of "grammatical." But if we understand the grammarian's task as the construction of a general theory, this definition is not something needed to set his task, rather it is this task, or an integral part of it. The point is simply that the twofold program of linguistic research has as distinct but interrelated goals the construction of a general theory, in which terms like "grammatical" are defined, and the construction of grammars validated in part by the demonstration that they follow from the theory. This dual program is significantly achieved only when it provides a systematic and integrated account of a good deal of linguistic behavior, an explanation of linguistic intuition, etc.

13.6   I have argued that the appeal to meaning in the determination of grammatical structure is actually a misnomer for the appeal to intuition, and hence is to be avoided. But it is important to distinguish sharply between

---

nonsemantic characterization of both processes makes it possible to seek a generalization.

[19] *Op. cit.*, p. 53.

the *appeal* to meaning and the *study* of meaning. The latter is an essential task for linguistics. It is certainly important to find some way of describing language in use. But this is not the study of grammatical structure. When these parallel studies are sufficiently advanced, it will be possible to explore the many indisputable connections between them.[20] Exactly where the boundaries are between these studies, it is not easy to determine. We will see below that as the theory of linguistic form becomes more advanced, it can incorporate some of what might have been thought to belong to the theory of meaning.[21] The important thing to remember in constructing a theory of linguistic form is that no matter what difficulties beset this endeavor, these difficulties in themselves in no way indicate that the theory should be based on meaning, or on any other given notion. It may be the case that a certain basis is too narrow for the development of linguistic theory. But to show that some particular notion should be added to this basis, it is necessary to demonstrate that when this notion is added, the difficulties fall away. In the case of meaning, this essential step is generally overlooked.

At this stage of our understanding of linguistic structure there seems to be little point in issuing manifestoes for or against the dependence of the theory of linguistic structure on meaning. We can only try to construct such a theory and investigate its adequacy, a part of this investigation centering around its clarity and operational interpretability. If we find that a certain notion cannot be given distributional grounds, but can be given clear semantic grounds, we can either decide that this notion does not belong to grammar, or that grammar has, in part, a semantic basis. If we make the former decision in too many cases, grammar will simply not be an interesting subject. At present, it seems to me proper to say that whereas we know of many grammatical notions that have no semantic basis, we know of none for which a significant and general semantic analysis is forthcoming. This justifies the tentative assertion that the theory of linguistic form does not have semantic foundations.

To return now to the question posed in §2, we must select a basis of **14.1** operationally analyzable notions that can serve as the foundation for

---

[20] See Harris, "Distributional structure," for discussion of the parallel and lack of parallel between grammatical and semantic study, and for other comments bearing on the topic of this section.

[21] In this connection, it is interesting to note a proposal to incorporate parts of the theory of meaning into the theory of reference. See Goodman, "On likeness of meaning" and "On some differences about meaning." Part of the difficulty with the theory of meaning is that "meaning" tends to be used as a catch-all term to include every aspect of language that we know very little about. Insofar as this is correct, we can expect various aspects of this theory to be claimed by other approaches to language.

linguistic theory. We have already seen that one of our primitive notions must be a relation of *conformity* among utterances, operationally interpreted by the paired utterance test (which can and should be elaborated). This gives us a classification of utterance tokens into utterance types. To apply this test we must have an initial segmentation of the corpus into sentence tokens. These sentence tokens are further segmented into discrete units which may be called "phone tokens." We might extend the primitive notion of conformity to cover all sequences of one or more phone tokens, deriving the notion of phone type and phone sequence type. Conformity of utterance tokens will then be a special case of conformity of phone sequence tokens, though we have suggested an operational interpretation only for this special case.

The next step in the development of linguistic theory is the definition of the notion "phoneme." The major research in structural linguistics has been devoted to this problem, which lies outside the scope of our investigations.[22] Exactly what foundation should be chosen for linguistic theory naturally depends on what sort of phonemic theory is adopted. With the rise of acoustic phonetics, it seems likely that acoustically defined properties, the paired utterance test, and an operational account of segmentation might provide an objective and empirical foundation for linguistic theory.

14.2   However phonemic theory is constructed, the result of a phonemic analysis can be regarded as a certain system for representing the utterances of the language under analysis. Within linguistic theory, we can either attempt to define phonemes directly as certain classes of phone tokens, or we can proceed indirectly, stating the conditions (both formal and phonetic) that a system of phonemic representation must meet, and defining phonemes as the elements which appear in a system of phonemic representation. The customary approach is the direct one, but it leads to rather serious difficulties, some of which we will discuss below. The indirect approach is no less rigorous, and seems to lead to a much simpler and more unified linguistic theory. If we proceed in this way, we do not consider phonemes to be literally constructed out of segments of utterances, i.e., to have direct phonetic content, but rather as the symbols of an "alphabet" of a certain type by which all utterances can be described. In some cases we may not be able to say which physical segments of a represented utterance are associated with a particular letter (phoneme) of this alphabet.

The development of a system of phonemic representation does not

---

[22] See references of Chapter VI, §§42–44.

conclude the process of linguistic analysis. We also want to discover the morphemes, words, and phrases of the language, and to determine principles of sentence construction that could hardly be stated directly in terms of phonemes. Instead of giving a direct definition of these further notions within linguistic theory, we can continue to construct systems of representation for sentence tokens, calling these systems "linguistic levels." A sentence token can be represented as a sequence of phonemes; but it can also be represented as a sequence of morphemes, words, and phrases. Thus each sentence token will have associated with it a whole set of representations, each representation being its "spelling" in terms of elements of one linguistic level. We will see below that some of these levels of representation must be quite abstract in character if we are to be able to meet the aims of grammatical description.

A grammar of a language must tell us exactly what are the grammatical sentence tokens, and exactly how these are represented on each level. Just how a grammar provides this information is an important problem, which will occupy us below. Linguistic theory, in this view, becomes the theory in which these systems of representation are constructed and studied in an abstract manner, and the relations between them explicitly characterized. By studying systems of representation and their interconnections, and formulating linguistic theory in these terms, we avoid the necessity for giving a very complex account of linguistic elements as classes, sequences of classes, classes of these sequences, etc. The definition of linguistic elements and the discussion of the relations between them would become very unwieldy and elaborate if this direct course were followed, particularly in the light of the considerations of Chapter III.[23]

The motivation behind level construction can be briefly restated in terms of the twofold program of constructing grammars and developing a theory of linguistic structure. In the case of a particular grammar, our first problem is to determine the subject matter of the description; that is, to determine which sequences are grammatical (whether or not they occur in the corpus) and which pairs are phonemically distinct. This completed, we want to present a description of this subject matter. Similarly in linguistic theory, we must define "grammatical sentence" (cf. Chapter V) and characterize distinctness (by the paired utterance test), and then construct a precise and general definition for each term entering into this further description.

A language is an extremely complex system. If we were to attempt

14.3

---

[23] See Hockett, *A Manual of Phonology*, for a similar approach to linguistic levels.

to give a direct description of the set of grammatical sequences of phonemes, we would be faced with an immense and unmanageable task. Instead of attempting this, we analyze phoneme sequences into morphemes, morpheme sequences into words and phrases, etc., and we state the restrictions on occurrence of these elements which enter more directly into the process of sentence construction. We thus rebuild the complexity of the system piecemeal, extracting and separating out the contribution to this complexity of each linguistic level. In linguistic theory, we face the problem of constructing this system of levels in an abstract manner, in such a way that a simple grammar will result when this complex of abstract structures is given an interpretation in actual linguistic material. We need not require that an element on one level have actual "content" on lower levels; e.g., a morpheme need not have any specific sequence of phonemes (or set of such sequences) as its phonemic content, though given a sequence of morphemes that represent an utterance, the grammar must enable us to construct the corresponding sequence of phonemes. Since higher levels are not literally constructed out of lower ones, in this view, we are quite free to construct levels of a high degree of interdependence, i.e., with heavy conditions of compatibility between them, without the fear of circularity that has been so widely stressed in recent theoretical work in linguistics.[24]

14.4   Although reduction of the complexity of grammar is the major motivation behind level construction, we find that there are important secondary effects. On lower levels sentence tokens are identically represented just in case they conform. But on higher levels, conforming sentences may have different representations, and nonconforming tokens may have identical representations. For instance, on the morphemic level the phoneme sequence /əneym/ may be represented either as "an aim" or "a name," and both the phoneme sequences /wayf/ and /wayv/ (as in "wives") are represented as "wife." On the level of phrase structure, identical representation of nonconforming tokens is the rule. "John ate his lunch" and "Bill reads books" are both instances of the syntactic construction *Noun Phrase–Verb Phrase*, and will be so represented on this

---

[24] See Bar-Hillel, "On recursive definitions in empirical sciences" and "Logical syntax and semantics," for a discussion of the possibility of using noncircular recursive definitions in linguistics. My own feeling is that Bar-Hillel is much too optimistic about the possibility of using recursive definitions to reconstruct the kind of interplay between levels that we find in actual procedures of linguistic analysis. And if we limit our goals to the establishment of a practical evaluation procedure, rather than a practical discovery procedure, then the method described here will avoid circularity with only direct definitions.

level. The converse case is also common on this level. Thus "they are flying planes" can be represented as *Noun Phrase–are–Noun Phrase* (with noun phrase "flying planes") or as *Noun Phrase–Verb–Noun Phrase* (with verb "are flying" and object "planes"), and is correspondingly ambiguous. Thus we can find higher-level similarity of construction between phonetically dissimilar tokens, and higher-level dissimilarities (i.e., alternative analyses) between conforming tokens. The latter case will be termed "constructional homonymity." We will find that constructional homonymity appears on every level with interesting consequences. In general, in these and other ways, establishment of higher levels permits us to account for many intuitions of the native speaker, and this is an important additional motivation for constructing linguistic theory in these terms.

In §11.1 we pointed out that if linguistic research is to have content, **15.1** there must be certain criteria of adequacy for each grammar, outside of those internal to linguistic theory. But we have said very little about what these criteria may be. Actually, there seems to be very little to say about this that is not uncomfortably vague. Clearly the sequences generated by the grammar as grammatical sentences must be acceptable, in some sense, to the native speaker, and the processes described must conform somehow to his "habits." Above, in §13.5, we construed the linguist's task as one of reconstructing in some systematic and inspectable way the speaker's "linguistic intuition." Thus if a theory of grammatical structure applied to English gave "furiously sleep ideas green colorless" (= **4**) as grammatical, we would no doubt reject it as inadequate. Our reaction would be similar if the definition of "word" put only one word boundary in "John finished eating," perhaps between "finish" and "ed," or in some even less natural place, or if "morpheme" were so defined that "er" in "mother," "father," "brother," "sister" were isolated as a morpheme. The speaker's intuition about form (sometimes misleadingly spoken of as "semantic") poses, for each language, conditions that must be met by linguistic theory. And, broadly speaking, we will regard a linguistic theory as successful if it manages to explicate and give formal justification and support for our strong intuitions about linguistic form within the framework of an integrated, systematic, and internally motivated theory.

But intuition, of course, is an extremely weak support. The program of linguistic research would be a much clearer one if we could show experimentally that these intuitions have distinct behavioral correlates. Thus in §13.5, we noted a behavioral correlate for certain instances of the presystematic intuitive notion of "grammatical sentence." Whenever we have strong intuitions about language, it is reasonable to search from some testable and observable correlate to these intuitions. If we can develop a mass of data about the use and reaction to language, then we can evaluate a linguistic theory not only in terms of its ability to reconstruct intuition about grammatical form, but in terms of its success in providing explanatory support and formal correlates for this independently derived material.

But we must be careful not to exaggerate the extent to which a behavioral reinterpretation of intuition about form will actually clarify the situation. Thus suppose we found some behavioral test corresponding to the analysis of "John finished eating" suggested above. Or, to choose a more interesting case, suppose that we manage to develop some operational account of synonymy and significance. As we have seen in §13, if this is successful and to the point, then the notions characterized will not correspond to the notions of identity of phonemic constitution and grammaticalness, respectively. Thus it would be an error to suggest correspondence to the now presumably operational concept of synonymy as a criterion of adequacy for "identity of phonemic constitution," or to suggest generation of the class of significant sentences as a condition for the theoretical construction of "grammaticalness." As a final example, consider the notion of order of statistical approximation to language, recently shown by Miller and Selfridge[25] to have interesting behavioral correlates. We might thus be tempted to identify grammaticalness in English with high order of approximation to English, and nongrammaticalness with low order of approximation. But if we do this, though we will be characterizing something, it will not be grammaticalness, in the presystematic sense of this term. Perfectly grammatical English sentences can have a reasonable probability of occurrence only in zero-order approximations to English, and as we move to higher orders of approximation, we simply exclude more and more grammatical sequences. Hence these particular behavioral correlates are apparently not relevant to the characterization of grammaticalness.

It appears then that in a certain sense the ultimate criterion remains the speaker's intuition about linguistic form, since only this can tell us which behavioral tests are to the point. We might hope that some more general account of the whole process of linguistic communication than we possess now may permit us to reconstruct the criteria of adequacy for linguistic theory in more convincing and acceptable terms. But for the present, it seems that we must rely, at least to some extent,[26] on the speaker's intuitive conception of linguistic form.

[25] "Verbal context and the recall of meaningful material."
[26] We have mentioned above that even a slight reliance on the clear cases may impose

The point of departure below will thus often be intuition. As motivation for the elaboration of linguistic theory, we will cite cases where previously constructed theory leads to counterintuitive results, and will try to develop a natural reformulation which, among other gains, will lead to a significant correspondence with intuition, i.e., will supply formal grounds for intuition. But it is important to keep clearly in mind that this does not mean that linguistic theory itself is based on intuition, that "intuition" and such notions appear in its basis of primitive terms. On the contrary, this basis is composed of the clearest and most objective notions we can find. Only in this way can linguistic theory serve the purpose of explicating our grammatical intuitions.

If a linguistic theory dictates counterintuitive solutions for a language, we have two possible courses of action. We may disregard the intuition as fallacious (or as an intuition about something other than grammatical form), or we may reconstruct the theory. Between these two poles of reliance on the results of a given theory and reliance on intuition, there are many possible positions and attitudes. In this connection, we can return to the question of whether the linguist "plays mathematical games" or "describes reality" (cf. above, §11.1). To the extent that this discussion has any meaning at all, it seems to reduce to the question of where between these poles the proper approach lies. In the absence of clear criteria of adequacy and relevance, behavioral or otherwise, for theories, it is difficult to determine a correct position. The danger in the "God's truth" approach[27] is that it sometimes verges on mysticism,[28] and tends to blur the fact that the rational way out of this difficulty lies in the program of, on the one hand, formulating behavioral criteria to replace intuitive judgments, and on the other, of constructing a rigorous account of linguistic structure and determining its implications for particular grammars.

15.2

---

stringent limitations on linguistic theory, since this must be adequate to provide grammars meeting these relatively clear conditions for many languages. For further discussion of this problem, often referred to as the problem of the psychological reality of linguistic elements, see Sapir, "La réalité psychologique des phonèmes," translated in Mandelbaum, ed., *Selected Writings of Edward Sapir*. Also Harris and Voegelin "Eliciting"; Harris, "Distributional structure." Aside from correspondence to intuition, we have other (equally vague) criteria that grammars and linguistic theory, like any scientific theory, must meet, e.g., simplicity, naturalness, etc.

[27] As the alternative to "playing mathematical games" has been styled by Householder, "Review of Harris, *Methods*."

[28] Thus the linguist is enjoined not to be misled by theories, but just to describe "the facts," the "real structure" of language.

LINGUISTIC
LEVELS   *III*

In considering the nature of linguistic theory, we have been led to regard   16
the theory of linguistic structure as being, essentially, the abstract study
of "levels of representation." Before going on to develop certain of the
specific structures of linguistic theory, we will investigate the general
nature of such systems and develop some simple ideas that will be useful
later on.[1]

A linguistic level is a system **L** in which we construct unidimensional
representations of utterances. Thus a level has a certain fixed and finite
"alphabet" of elements, which we will call its "primes." Given two
primes of **L** we can form a new element of **L** by an operation called
"concatenation," symbolized by the arch $\frown$. Thus if a and b are (not
necessarily distinct) primes of **L**, we can form $a \frown b$ and $b \frown a$ as new
elements of **L**. Concatenation is essentially the process of spelling, where
primes are taken as letters. Given the element $a \frown b$ and the prime c,
we can form a new element $(a \frown b) \frown c$. This is exactly the element formed
by concatenating a and the element $b \frown c$, i.e., $a \frown (b \frown c) = (a \frown b) \frown c$.
Because of this property of *associativity* of concatenation, we can drop
the parentheses and write this element as $a \frown b \frown c$.

In general, given two elements X and Y of **L**, whether primes or not,
we can form by concatenation new elements $X \frown Y$ and $Y \frown X$, and
concatenation is associative for such compound elements. The elements

---

[1] The particular form of these constructions was suggested by an unpublished paper of
Henry Hiż, entitled "Positional algebras and structural linguistics." In the details of
notation and axiomatization, we generally follow P. Rosenbloom, *The Elements of Mathematical Logic*, Appendix 2, "The algebraic approach to language."

of the system **L** will be called *strings* in **L**.[2] Every nonprime string has a unique spelling in terms of primes.

It is convenient to assume that the system **L** contains an *identity* element which when concatenated with any string X yields again the string X. We will call this element, which is unique on each level, the unit U of **L**. Thus for any string X,

$$1 \qquad X^\frown U = U^\frown X = X$$

We will see that the postulation of a unit element on each level greatly simplifies the construction of levels.

The unit element U of **L** must not be confused with any so-called "zero elements" that may be set up as primes of **L**. (U will not be considered a prime, but of course it is also not a compound string.) We can characterize a zero element of the level **L** as a prime of **L** that happens to correspond to the unit element of some lower level. For example, consider the two levels **Pm** and **M**, the phonemic and morphemic levels. We can "spell" a certain utterance in terms of phonemes or in terms of morphemes;[3] i.e., we can associate with this utterance a certain string in **Pm** and a certain string in **M**. But these strings are related. The "morphophonemic rules" tell us which string of phonemes corresponds to a given string of morphemes. If a certain morpheme corresponds, under these rules, to the unit U of the phonemic level, i.e., if it disappears on this lower level, then we call this morpheme a "zero morpheme" and we write it with the symbol Ø (perhaps with subscripts). We might say, then, that the element Ø has real morphemic content, but no phonemic content. Thus a string of zero morphemes has a perfectly clear meaning. Zero morphemes cannot be added or dropped at will in representations on the level **M**, and they are established on the same grounds as other morphemes.

17   A linguistic level is not determined completely by the statement that it is a concatenation algebra. We must also specify its relations to other levels (i.e., the conditions of compatibility between levels), and there may be further algebraic structure within the given level.

---

[2] A string is regarded as a single "object," distinct from a sequence. Thus the string $X_1{}^\frown X_2{}^\frown ...^\frown X_n$ must be sharply distinguished from the sequence $X_1 ,..., X_n$, or the sequence $X_1{}^\frown X_2 , X_3{}^\frown X_4 ,..., X_{n-1}{}^\frown X_n$, etc. We might develop concatenation theory differently without making this distinction. This would give a more economical theory, but would require certain artificial devices (cf. Quine, *Mathematical Logic*, §56).

[3] The distinction between these representations is sometimes confused by the fact that morphemes are generally given in phonemic spelling.

We have already noted that a grammar of a language must state the structure of each grammatical utterance of the language on each linguistic level. In carrying out linguistic analysis, then, we must construct on each level **L** a set of elements (which we will call "**L**-markers"), one of which is assigned to each grammatical utterance. The **L**-marker of a given utterance T must contain within it all information as to the structure of T on the level **L**. The construction of **L**-markers, for each level **L**, is thus the fundamental task in linguistic analysis, and in the abstract construction of linguistic theory we must determine what sort of elements appear as markers on each level. In the case of most levels, markers will simply be strings. Thus on the level **Pm** of phonemes, each grammatical utterance will be presented as a string of phonemes; the **Pm**-marker of "pin" in English will be just the string $p^\frown i^\frown n$. However, markers are not always simply strings. We will see in Chapter VII that it is necessary on the level **P** of phrase structure to take as **P**-markers certain *sets* of strings in **P**, if we are to provide complete information about the structure of each utterance on this level.[4]

In addition to **L**-markers, we may want to define other elements in **L**, as well as to state various relations among the elements of this level. The relations between **L** and other levels can conveniently be described as mappings which associate elements of **L** with elements of other levels. One mapping of particular importance carries the **L**-markers into grammatical utterances. This mapping we will denote by "Φ." Φ thus assigns **L**-markers to utterances of the language (though **L**-markers may be only a proper part of its domain).

It is not necessary in general to describe the mapping Φ as a mapping of **L**-markers directly into grammatical utterances. If on some level **L'** the mapping $\Phi^{L'}$ has been defined from **L'**-markers to grammatical utterances, then Φ^L can be defined from **L**-markers to **L'**-markers—e.g., **P**-markers can be mapped into strings of words (**W**-markers). Thus levels can be arranged in a hierarchy.[5]

---

[4] So far we have provided only one way of constructing elements in **L**, namely, concatenation. But we will assume with no further question (or mention) that each level includes a full set theory, so that we can also form sets of strings, sequences of strings, etc. This assumption may be dispensable, but it simplifies our constructional task (or at least the exposition of it). See Quine, *Mathematical Logic*, Chapter 7, for general background on various kinds of concatenation theory, and Chomsky, "Systems of syntactic analysis," for discussion of the possibility of constructing linguistic theory with very meager formal apparatus, using many devices developed by Goodman (cf. *The Structure of Appearance*) and Goodman and Quine (cf. "Steps towards a constructive nominalism").

[5] We need not require that the values of Φ exhaust the set of grammatical utterances on

In terms of the mapping Φ and the notion of **L**-marker, we can give a clear and general sense to the important notion of *constructional homonymity* (see §14.5, above). We have a case of constructional homonymity on the level **L** when the mapping Φ assigns two or more **L**-markers to a single utterance. This utterance then falls in the overlap of two distinct patterns, and, if our theory is adequate, such utterances should be, intuitively, cases of structural ambiguity.

18 In very general terms, then, a level **L** is a system

2 $\mathbf{L} = [L, \frown, R_1, ..., R_m, \mu, \Phi, \varphi_1, ..., \varphi_n]$

> where (i) **L** is a concatenation algebra with L its set of primes
>
> (ii) $R_1, ..., R_m$ are classes and relations defined within **L**. R_1 is the identity relation $=$
>
> (iii) μ is a set of **L**-markers—elements of some sort constructed in **L**
>
> (iv) Φ is a mapping which, in particular, maps μ into the set of grammatical utterances
>
> (v) $\varphi_1, ..., \varphi_n$ express the relations between **L** and other levels

In linguistic theory, then, we construct abstractly a set of levels of the general form **2**. The notions developed in each level must be fully characterized in terms of the primitive basis of linguistic theory. The resulting system of levels can be understood as offering a definition of "language,"[6] and the operational tests for the primitives delimit the area of behavior that, in terms of the theory, can properly be called linguistic.

19 It is interesting to inquire into the question of how closely we can specify the primes of the various levels within general linguistic theory. The program of developing a general linguistic theory is reminiscent, in certain respects, of much earlier attempts to develop a universal grammar. These attempts have generally concerned themselves with such questions as, e.g., whether such categories as Noun, Verb, etc., are universally applicable. We can restate this as the question of whether it is possible,

---

each level. Below, we will see the usefulness of constructing the level of phrase structure in such a way that certain utterances have no markers on this level, though these utterances acquire phrase-structure descriptions in other ways.

[6] Certain levels may be missing in the analysis of particular languages. The exact conditions under which this may be the case are unclear.

within general linguistic theory, to construct a fixed set of elements which must (or may) appear as primes on some level in the interpretation of the theory for every language.

For example, in the abstract development of the level of syntactic categories, we might attempt actually to define "Noun," "Verb," etc., as primes of this level, fixed elements that may occur in the description of many languages. Or we may simply define "syntactic category" in such a way that the nouns of English, for instance, turn out to constitute a single syntactic category, though there is no way of associating this category with some category in another language that we might also like to consider to be nouns. The former result would of course be a much more powerful one. In our discussion of syntactic categories and phrase structure we will not be able to approach such a construction. We will merely suggest certain formal conditions that the primes of these levels must meet, and we will make no attempt to construct primes with, in some sense, a fixed "content" for all languages. It is not clear what sort of basis of primitives would be required for this much more ambitious undertaking. In the discussion of transformational structure, however, we will be able to give a much more concrete interpretation of certain of the primes of this level, and it will make sense to ask, in some cases, whether distinct languages have the same transformations.

Suppose that we have, as primes of the word level **W** for English, the elements "New," "York," "City," "is," "in," "State." Then we can form various strings by concatenation of these elements, e.g.,[7]

20

3   *New⌢York⌢City⌢is⌢in⌢New⌢York⌢State*

3 is a string in **W**, in fact, a **W**-marker of the utterance "New York City is in New York State."

For many purposes we need a notion of "occurrence," which will enable us to refer unambiguously to the second occurrence of "new" in **3**, etc. Using a device of Quine's,[8] we can identify an occurrence of a prime X in a string Y as that initial substring of Y that ends in X. Thus the second occurrence of "York" in **3** would be, literally, the string

4   *New⌢York⌢City⌢is⌢in⌢New⌢York*

---

[7] Henceforth we will denote a linguistic expression either by that expression within quotes, or by the expression italicized, whichever is more convenient.

[8] *Mathematical Logic*, third edition, p. 297.

We will also have to speak of the occurrences of nonprimes and it is convenient to construe **4** as being, simultaneously, an occurrence of *York*, *New⌢York*, *in⌢New⌢York*, ..., and of itself.

Definition 1. Z is an *occurrence* of X in Y if there is a W_1, W_2 such that $Y = W_1 {}^\frown X {}^\frown W_2 = Z {}^\frown W_2$

Any of these elements may be the unit element. If $W_1 = U$, then $Z = X$; that is, X is an initial substring of Y and is thus an occurrence of itself. If $X = U$, then $W_1 = Z$. Thus any initial substring of Y (including, in particular, Y itself) is an occurrence of U in Y.

Through this method of introducing the notion of occurrence is somewhat artificial, it appears to be adequate for our purposes. A different approach would be to develop an inscriptional concatenation theory, in which **3** would be considered as a string of eight distinct primes, each a unique occurrence of itself. One of the relations on each level would then be an equivalence relation holding, for instance, between the first and the sixth primes of **3**.[9] While this approach is more natural, it requires somewhat more elaborate constructions, and for this reason we have not followed it in this study.

21   Substitutability is the major distributional relation that will concern us below. Given a string X, and an occurrence Z of W in X, we will often require a notation for denoting the string that differs from X only in that Y is substituted for W. We will denote this new string by the symbol

$$"X\left[\frac{Y}{(W, Z)}\right]."$$

Definition 2. $X\left[\dfrac{Y}{(W, Z)}\right]$ is the string $\bar{X}$ such that either for some Z_1, Z_2

(i) $X = Z_1 {}^\frown W {}^\frown Z_2 = Z {}^\frown Z_2$
(ii) $\bar{X} = Z_1 {}^\frown Y {}^\frown Z_2$

or there is no Z_1, Z_2 such that (i), and

$$\bar{X} = X$$

Thus if W actually is part of X (occurs in X), then Z is an occurrence of W in X ($Z = Z_1 {}^\frown W$), and $Z_1 {}^\frown Y$ is an occurrence of Y in

---

[9] See Chomsky, *op. cit.*, for some elaboration of this inscriptional approach to developing linguistic theory.

$\bar{X} = X\left[\frac{Y}{(W, Z)}\right]$. If W does not occur in X, then $X\left[\frac{Y}{(W, Z)}\right] = X$.
If, for example, $X = 3$, $W = New \frown York$, $Z = 4$, and $Y = an \frown Eastern$,
then $X\left[\frac{Y}{(W, Z)}\right]$ will be

5   *New York City is in an Eastern State*

In the discussion above, then, we have given no actual content to the   22
elements or relations of any linguistic level, but have left the matter
open for specific constructions. The requirements that a level must
meet are quite broad, and we are free to develop the formal structure
of the various levels in many different ways.

In particular, though the representations that we construct on any
linguistic level are unidimensional, we have not required that left-to-right
order of representation correspond directly to temporal order in the
represented utterance. Discontinuous elements provide a common
instance (though not the only one) of noncorrespondence between order
of representation and temporal order. Thus Semitic stems are composed
of discontinuous roots and vowel patterns (e.g., Hebrew "yeled" is
broken down into two morphemes, the root "y...l...d" and the vowel
pattern "...e...e..."), but they can be represented quite adequately as
having the order root–vowel pattern (or *vice versa*). Many other cases of
temporal discontinuity of elements can be handled easily. On the other
hand, the general case of discontinuity presents problems.[10] By accepting
a linear system of representation, we rule out the possibility of certain
kinds of discontinuity. If more general kinds of discontinuity than we
can handle occur in language, a more complicated theory of representations will be necessary.[11]

As long as we have made no requirement that Φ be an order-
preserving mapping, we are free to regard as a linguistic level any
structure of the form **2**. We will make use of this freedom to suggest
transformational analysis as an additional linguistic level. Here the order

[10] For discussion of these problems, see Hockett, "A formal statement of morphemic
analysis," *Studies in Linguistics*; "Two models for grammatical description,"
Linguistics Today, §3.2; and Chomsky, *op. cit.*, §4.

[11] In this study, suprasegmental features (pitch, stress, juncture) have not been seriously
considered. Ultimately, of course, these phenomena must be incorporated into any
full syntactic theory, and it may be that this extension still require a more elaborate
system of representation (cf. Hockett, "Two models," for some discussion of this
possibility). See Chomsky, Halle, and Lukoff, "On accent and juncture in English,"
for discussion of a phonemic transcription for English that includes stress and juncture,
but preserves linearity of representation in a natural way.

of representation bears no relation whatever to temporal order, though it will appear below that there is motivation for interpreting this system in the manner of **2**. It would be possible to require as a condition on levels that Φ be order-preserving, or partially so, but I see no motivation for this, and, as we will see below, there are phenomena on every level, even the phonemic, that would make such a requirement difficult to formulate and to satisfy.

SIMPLICITY AND
THE FORM OF
GRAMMARS   IV

The grammar of a language must specify precisely the set of grammatical   23
utterances constituting this language, and it must do this in such a way
that for each level **L** the **L**-markers of these utterances are mechanically
recoverable. Let us assume that the **L**-marker of an utterance S can be
mechanically reconstructed from the strings in **L** that represent S.[1]
In determining the form of grammars, then, we must make clear exactly
how a grammar provides the set of representations on each level for
each grammatical utterance.

Linguistic theory must enable us to choose among proposed
grammars, and every consideration relevant to this choice must be built
into the theory. So far, the only condition that we have placed on a
grammar is that the system of levels it determines (in a manner yet to
be given) must be of the form required by linguistic theory. But this
formulation leaves out one of the most important and characteristic
features of grammar construction. In careful descriptive work, we almost
always find that one of the considerations involved in choosing among
alternative analyses is the simplicity of the resulting grammar. If we can
set up elements in such a way that very few rules need be given about
their distribution, or that these rules are very similar to the rules for
other elements, this fact certainly seems to be a valid support for the
analysis in question. It seems reasonable, then, to inquire into the

---

[1] This will always be the case in our constructions. See §17, above, for the notion of
L-marker.

possibility of defining linguistic notions in the general theory partly in terms of such properties of grammar as simplicity. If this course is to be followed, then we must give a precise specification for the form that a grammar may assume.[2]

24   We must be able to recover from a grammar a sequence of representations $(R_1, ..., R_n)$ for each sentence, where R_1 is the representation *Sentence*, R_n is a phonetic spelling, and $R_2, ..., R_{n-1}$ are intermediate representations in terms of phrases, words, phonemes, etc. We can generate these representation sequences by rules of the form

1 $X \to Y$

interpreted as the instruction "rewrite X as Y." We call each such rule a *conversion*. The string $Z^\frown Y^\frown W$ is said to *follow from* the string $Z^\frown X^\frown W$ (where Z, W, or both may be the identity element U) by the conversion 1. We say that the sequence $(R_1, ..., R_n)$ is a *derivation* of R_n, *generated* by a set C of conversions, if R_1 is *Sentence* and for each i $(1 \leqslant i < n)$, R_{i+1} follows from R_i by one of the conversions of C. If many ith-level representations are carried into lower-level representations in the same way, we can achieve a good deal of economy by giving a single conversion applying in all cases, and we can hope to generate infinitely many derivations by a finite grammar of conversions.

We may introduce a level of representation solely because it enables us to replace a great many rules by a single rule about a single element of this new level. Morphophonemic representation provides a good example of this. Suppose that English sentences are represented in terms of morphemes and phonemes. Instead of associating with each morpheme a set of phoneme strings,[3] along with the conditions dictating the occurrence of each, it is often possible to rewrite each morpheme as a string of invented elements called morphophonemes in such a way that a relatively small number of statements about the phonemic forms that

---

[2] It is important, incidentally, to recognize that considerations of simplicity are not trivial or "merely esthetic." It has been remarked in the case of philosophical systems that the motives for the demand for economy are in many ways the same as those behind the demand that there be a system at all. See Goodman, "On the simplicity of ideas," where the reference is to economy in the basis of primitives. It seems to me that the same is true of grammatical systems, and of the special sense of simplicity that will concern us directly. See Quine, *From a Logical Point of View*, for recent discussion of the role of simplicity in the choice of scientific theories.

[3] Where each of these phoneme strings is called an "allomorph" of the given morpheme. As we have pointed out above, there is no necessity to associate allomorphs (i.e., phonemic content) directly with morphemes, but only with morpheme strings.

these assume in various contexts will suffice to determine many conversions of morphemes into phonemic representation. In English, for instance, we have the rules

2   (a) $wife\frown pl \rightarrow /wayv/\frown pl$ (ultimately, "wives")
    (b) $wife\frown X \rightarrow /wayf/\frown X$ (where $X \neq pl$)

3   (a) $knife\frown pl \rightarrow /nayv/\frown pl$ (ultimately, "knives")
    (b) $knife\frown X \rightarrow /nayf/\frown X$ (where $X \neq pl$)

4   (a) $leaf\frown pl \rightarrow /liyv/\frown pl$ (ultimately, "leaves")
    (b) $leaf\frown X \rightarrow /liyf/\frown X$ (where $X \neq pl$)
    etc.

where pl is the plural morpheme, and "/.../" encloses phonemic representations.[4] A much simpler description would be to "spell" these morphemes in terms of morphophonemes by the conversions

5   $wife \rightarrow w\frown a\frown y\frown F$

6   $knife \rightarrow n\frown a\frown y\frown F$

7   $leaf \rightarrow l\frown i\frown y\frown F$
    etc.

We can then convert morphophonemes into phonemes by such rules as

8   (a) $F\frown pl \rightarrow /v/\frown pl$
    (b) $F\frown X \rightarrow /f/\frown X$ (where $X \neq pl$)

Words that are not subject to this change (e.g., "fife," "fifes") are spelled with the element f on the morphophonemic level.[5]

The same kind of argument can be used to motivate and justify the introduction of the level of phrase structure. If there were no inter-

---

[4] We will generally use this customary convention for phonemic representation, suppressing the arch within slant lines.

[5] Note that phonemes can often be "embedded" in the morphophonemic level as primes of this level. English, in fact, is a poor source for interesting morphological examples, and the simplification effected by morphophonemic analysis in this case is rather small. But in many languages where such morphophonemes have wide distribution and are complexly interconnected, such analysis can lead to very great economy. See Bloomfield, "Menomini morphophonemics," my *Morphophonemics of Modern Hebrew,* and many other linguistic studies.

vening representations between *Sentence* and words, the grammar would have to contain a vast (in fact, infinite) number of conversions of the form *Sentence* → *X*, where *X* is a permissible string of words. However, we find that it is possible to classify strings of words into phrases in such a way that sentence structure can be stated in terms of phrase strings, and phrase structure in terms of word strings, in a rather simple way. Furthermore, a phrase of a given type can be included within a phrase of the same type,[6] so that a finite number of conversions will generate an infinite number of strings of words.

25 We see then how considerations of simplicity can function in determining linguistic structure. Given a measure of simplicity defined in the general theory, we can define linguistic elements of a given level **L** as being those that satisfy the axioms of **L** (and are properly related to other levels), and that furthermore appear in the simplest grammar of the language under analysis. Linguistic theory is thus constructed in a meta-meta-language to any natural language, and a metalanguage to the language in which grammars are constructed. In applying this theory to actual linguistic material, we must construct a grammar of the proper form, and demonstrate that the elements reconstructed from this grammar satisfy the conditions of level structure laid down in the general theory. Among all grammars meeting this condition, we select the simplest. The measure of simplicity must be defined in such a way that we will be able to evaluate directly the simplicity of any proposed grammar.

Suppose that we have constructed linguistic theory in such a way that given a corpus of utterances for which we know in advance that there is some grammar, it is the case that

9   (i)   all systems having the prescribed form of grammars, given this corpus, can be enumerated in order of increasing complexity;

       (ii) given any such system, it is possible to determine in a mechanical way whether the generated set of derivations provides a proper level structure.

In this case, the general theory will provide a discovery procedure for grammars, though of course not a practical one. The theory we discuss below is too sketchy and incomplete for us to be able to discuss it seriously in these terms, but it seems possible that such a goal can be reached by linguistic theory. If a simplicity measure of the sort we discuss

---

[6] For example, the noun phrase "difficult theorems" is contained within the noun phrase subject of "proving difficult theorems is his chief joy in life."

below proves adequate, condition (i) will be met. And in Chapter X (§110) we will see that though there are infinitely many grammatical sentences, the adequacy of a grammar can perhaps be conclusively determined by investigation of a fixed, finite set of derivations, so that (ii) can be met as well.

These remarks have no practical importance. We are far from being able to construct a satisfactory linguistic theory of even a much weaker kind. But it is important to keep in mind that such a program is by no means unthinkable.

Having developed a rough conception of the form of grammars, we can now turn to the problem of measuring the simplicity of such grammars. That is, we ask what features of grammars are to be taken into account in choosing among them.   **26**

In constructing a grammar, we try to set up elements having regular, similarly patterned, and easily statable distributions, and which are subject to similar variations under similar conditions; in other words, elements about which a good deal of generalization is possible and few special restrictions need be stated. It is interesting to note that any simplification along these lines is immediately reflected in the length of the grammar. We have a generalization when we replace a set of statements, each about a single element, by a single statement about the whole set of elements. We can generalize the notion of generalization to cover the situation where we have a set of statements (each about a single element) which are identical in part. Then the common substatement can be extracted out and stated only once, applying to all elements, with a consequent shortening of the grammar. The demand for "patterning" would appear, in many instances, to be interpretable as a demand for generalization in this broader sense.

It is tempting, then, to consider the possibility of devising a notational system which converts considerations of simplicity into considerations of length. This would amount to constructing a set of "notational transformations," to be applied to grammars which are sets of conversions of the form 1, in such a way that the simplicity of such grammars is a function of the number of symbols in the grammar. (More generally, simplicity might be determined as a weighted function of the number of symbols, the weighting devised so as to favor reductions in certain parts of the grammar.) Full generalization and elimination of special restrictions automatically reduce the length of grammars, and the notational system can be so constructed as to facilitate "extracting out" of common components of distinct statements by the use of brackets and parentheses in fairly familiar ways.

It is important to recognize that we are not interested in reduction of the length of grammars for its own sake. Our aim is rather to permit just those reductions in length which reflect real simplicity, that is, which will turn simpler grammars (in some partially understood, presystematic sense of this notion) into shorter grammars. Within linguistic theory, we must define once and for all the "notational transformations" that are to be available for evaluating the complexity of grammars. It can easily be seen that to permit notations to be devised anew for each particular grammar would quickly lead to absurdity. Suppose, for instance, that a language has n phones $a_1 ,..., a_n$. We might express the grammar in as complicated a way as we like, say, as $Q(a_1 ,..., a_n)$, where Q is some immensely complicated schema. Then defining "$f(x_1 ,..., x_n)$" as "$Q(x_1 ,..., x_n)$", we could construct the extremely short grammar, literally, "$f(a_1 ,..., a_n)$." It is clear that restrictions must be placed on the notations available for grammar construction so as to exclude such grammars as "$f(a_1 ,..., a_n)$," allowing only notations which in general serve to consolidate similar statements, etc. Thus the choice among grammars for a given language is not only influenced by the grammars of other languages (as we have seen above, §11.1), but also by the choice of notations available in the metalanguage. When length, under notational transformations, is used as a measure of simplicity, we can adjust our notations so as to reflect different senses of the notion of simplicity, thus affecting the choice among grammars, and consequently, altering our conception of the grammatical structure of given languages.

The problem of choosing the correct notations is much like that of evaluating a physical constant. Given criteria of adequacy for grammars of certain languages,[7] we can arrive empirically at notations with the property that the grammars meeting the criteria of adequacy are in fact the shortest, given these notations. In other words, we define simplicity so that, in certain clear cases, the simplest grammars are in fact the correct ones. As long as we do not take simplicity to be an absolute ideal, thoroughly understood and specified in advance of theory construction, this procedure is no stranger than attempting to define "morpheme" in such a way that what we know to be morphemes in some language turn out to be morphemes when we apply the theory to a corpus of utterances in this language. This program can be realized in a nontrivial fashion if we can give a general and abstract definition of "simplicity" (just as of "morpheme) which in the case of particular languages leads

---

[7] That is, we begin by investigating languages where we are so insistent on certain results that giving these can be taken as a criterion of adequacy for the general theory (cf. Chapter II).

to adequate grammars, and if the general theory of grammatical structure in which this definition appears meets certain considerations of significance that apply to any scientific theory. For instance, the theory must have internal systematic motivation for its constructions (it cannot be simply a list of all known results, as would be the case if it permitted such notations as "*f*," or permitted the validation of elements by the discovery of formal markers; cf. §11), it must have predictive power (i.e., in the case of new languages, it must lead to correct grammars), etc. These considerations of significance and simplicity are of course not specific to linguistic theory. Note that when we speak of the simplicity of linguistic theory, we are using "simplicity" in the still vague sense in which simplicity is an ideal for any science, whereas when we speak of the simplicity of grammars, we are using it in a sense which we hope to make as precise as the definition of "phoneme" or "morpheme." The simplicity of linguistic theory is a notion to be analyzed in the general study of philosophy of science; the simplicity of grammars is a notion defined within linguistic theory.

An analogy can be drawn between philosophy of science and linguistic theory. Philosophy of science deals with all sciences—physics, chemistry, linguistic theory, etc.—and seeks to determine, among other things, the considerations that lead to the construction of theories and the choice among conflicting theories in the case of each of these sciences. Linguistic theory deals with a set of rather special scientific theories called "grammars" and seeks to establish rigorous principles that apply in the construction and choice of grammars for particular languages. In linguistic theory, where the material under investigation is relatively clear and limited, we may hope to carry out the task of defining simplicity for the theories in question, namely, grammars, and of setting up an effective evaluation procedure for these theories in terms of criteria of simplicity.

To evaluate a grammar of conversions of the form 1 in terms of its simplicity, we construct notations which permit the consolidation of similar statements and we then measure "degree of generalization" (which we have tentatively taken as the measure of simplicity) as length of the consolidated grammar. The determination of correct notations will involve detailed study of the effects of various choices on really mechanical grammars. Almost no work has been done in this important direction. Hence we can make only the most tentative constructions. In this section we will introduce certain notations for subsequent use in pursuing this type of inquiry with actual language material. These notations must be introduced in such a way that a consolidated grammar

27.1

using them can be mechanically expanded into a set of conversions. Since we will later find that order of statements is an important feature of grammars, we will require further that a consolidated grammar must be uniquely expansible into a sequence of conversions.

Suppose that we have a conversion $X \rightarrow Y$, where $X = a \frown b \frown c$ and $Y = a \frown b' \frown c$. Then we say that $b \rightarrow b'$ in the environment a–c.

Definition 1. The statement

$$\text{(i)} \qquad b \rightarrow b' \text{ in env. } a \text{———} c$$

stands for

$$\text{(ii)} \qquad a \frown b \frown c \rightarrow a \frown b' \frown c$$

(ii) is of the form **1**; thus Definition 1 tells us how to restate anything of the form (i) as a conversion. When we have a statement of the form (i), we call a–c the *conditioning context* for the conversion $b \rightarrow b'$, where a is the *initial conditioning context* and c the *final conditioning context*.

We will use brackets to group elements which figure in the same way in a rule. For example, the statement

10 $\qquad \ldots \begin{Bmatrix} a \\ b \\ c \end{Bmatrix} \ldots$

will be an abbreviation for the sequence of statements

11 $\qquad$ (i) $\ldots a \ldots$
$\qquad$ (ii) $\ldots b \ldots$
$\qquad$ (iii) $\ldots c \ldots$

in this order. If more than one set of brackets with the same number of rows occurs, then in the expansion, the ith row of the first corresponds to the ith row of the second. Thus

12 $\qquad \ldots \begin{Bmatrix} a \\ b \\ c \end{Bmatrix} \ldots \begin{Bmatrix} d \\ e \\ f \end{Bmatrix} \ldots \begin{Bmatrix} g \\ h \\ i \end{Bmatrix} \ldots$

will be an abbreviation for the sequence of statements

13 $\qquad$ (i) $\ldots a \ldots d \ldots g \ldots$
$\qquad$ (ii) $\ldots b \ldots e \ldots h$
$\qquad$ (iii) $\ldots c \ldots f \ldots i \ldots$

and expansion is carried out in the same way in all cases of two or more sets of brackets.

Very commonly we find it necessary to indicate that each of a certain set of elements occurs with any element of a second set. To facilitate such statements, we introduce several types of brackets, and limit expansion on the principle of **12–13** to the case in which the brackets are of the same type. In other cases, we expand the brackets separately, each according to the principle **10–11**. Thus

14 $\ldots \begin{Bmatrix} a \\ b \\ c \end{Bmatrix} \ldots \begin{bmatrix} d \\ e \end{bmatrix} \ldots$

is an abbreviation for the sequence of statements

15   (i)   ...*a*...*d*...
        (ii)   ...*a*...*e*...
        (iii) ...*b*...*d*...
        (iv) ...*b*...*e*...
        (v)   ...*c*...*d*...
        (vi) ...*c*...*e*...

Note that in this case we expanded the brackets { } of **14** before expanding [ ]. We will always follow this convention.[8] Note also that if brackets of the same type occur, they have the same number of rows, as in **12** (i.e., this is the only case we consider), and the process of eliminating them is similar to matrix multiplication. If brackets of different types occur, they may have different numbers of rows, and elimination is analogous to formation of the Cartesian product.

We will use angles $\langle \ \rangle$ to indicate that an element may or may not be present. Thus **16** stands for the sequence **17**:

16 $a\langle b\rangle c$

17   (i) $a^\frown b^\frown c$
        (ii) $a^\frown c$

---

[8] More generally, instead of brackets of different form, we can consider the language of grammar to contain brackets of infinitely many orders, with higher-order brackets expanded before lower-order ones. The convention of the text, with { } taken as higher-order brackets than [ ], will generally suffice, since more than two types of brackets are rarely necessary, at least in the cases I have investigated.

where, again, the order (i), (ii) must be preserved. In case several angled elements occur within a statement, any order of expansion will be permitted as long as each statement in which a given angled element appears precedes all statements in which that element does not appear, generalizing **16–17**. Further specification should be given, but happens never to be relevant below. Brackets of any type will always be expanded before angles.

27.2   These conventions can be summarized in the following rules, which give an explicit step-by-step procedure for expanding any consolidated statement in which these notations appear into a sequence of conversions.

Given a consolidated statement Σ, we define *main* brackets (angles) as paired brackets (angles) not contained within the scope of other paired brackets or angles.

Rule 1.   Only main brackets or angles are expanded at any step.

Rule 2.   if Σ contains main angles, and no main brackets, then these angles are eliminated as in **16–17**.

Rule 3.   If Σ contains main brackets of the type { }, then these are expanded as in **12–13** if there is more than one main pair, or as in **10–11** if there is only one.

Rule 4.   If Σ contains main brackets of the type [ ], and none of the type { }, then these brackets [ ] are expanded exactly as { } are expanded by Rule 3.

Rule 5.   A pair of brackets or angles and the enclosed expression are treated as a single element when inside containing brackets or angles.[9]

Rule 6.   If Σ is of the form $b \to b'$ in env. a–c, where b, b', a, c are strings, rewrite it as $a^\frown b^\frown c \to a^\frown b'^\frown c$, as in Definition 1.

To indicate how many rows a pair of brackets contains, we will sometimes use "---" if no element is present.[10] For example, both paired brackets in **18** have three rows and expansion gives **19**.

---

[9] For example, the main brackets { } in **20**, below, contain two rows. Similarly in **10–15**, the letters a, b, stand for expressions of any internal complexity.

[10] Equivalently, we might use the unit element U.

18 $\begin{Bmatrix} a \\ b \\ c \end{Bmatrix} d \begin{Bmatrix} e \\ --- \\ f \end{Bmatrix} g$

19   (i) $a^\frown d^\frown e^\frown g$
    (ii) $b^\frown d^\frown g$
    (iii) $c^\frown d^\frown f^\frown g$

As an example of the functioning of these rules of expansion consider the following case:

20 $\begin{Bmatrix} \begin{bmatrix} \langle a \rangle & b \\ & c \end{bmatrix} \\ d & \langle e \rangle \end{Bmatrix} \rightarrow \begin{bmatrix} f \\ g \end{bmatrix}$

The expansion is given step by step, with the rule governing each step, as follows:

21   (i)   1: $\begin{bmatrix} \langle a \rangle & b \\ & c \end{bmatrix} \rightarrow \begin{bmatrix} f \\ g \end{bmatrix}$
                                                                      by Rules 1, 3, applied to **20**
           2:   $d \quad \langle e \rangle \rightarrow \begin{bmatrix} f \\ g \end{bmatrix}$

    (ii)   11: $\langle a \rangle \quad b \rightarrow f$
           12: $\qquad c \rightarrow g$ by Rules 1, 4, applied to 1

           21: $d \quad \langle e \rangle \rightarrow f$
           22: $d \quad \langle e \rangle \rightarrow g$ by Rule 4, applied to 2

    (iii) 111: $a^\frown b \rightarrow f$
           112: $\quad b \rightarrow f$ by Rule 2, applied to 11

           12:   $\quad c \rightarrow g$

           211: $d^\frown e \rightarrow f$
           212: $\quad d \rightarrow f$ by Rule 2, applied to 21

           221: $d^\frown e \rightarrow g$
           222: $\quad d \rightarrow g$ by Rule 2, applied to 22

Thus **20** is expanded to **21**iii, in the given order. The use of five pairs of brackets and angles in **20** permits the elimination of ten occurrences of $a, b,...$, which may themselves be long and complex expressions.

27.3   We can now convert a consolidated grammar into a unique sequence of conversions. The notational devices we have introduced permit certain selected features of similarity among statements of the grammar (i.e., certains types of partial generalization) to effect a decrease in length, so that grammars whose rules have these features are more highly valued. Thus these constructions can be understood as offering an analysis for certain aspects of simplicity. Whether they provide a correct or sufficient account can only be determined by investigating the effects of using them in actual grammatical work.[11]

28 We have seen (in §24) how a grammar of conversions can provide derivations for utterances, and how a measure of simplicity for such a grammar might be devised. Our task in later chapters will be, in part, to show how (and whether) the structural information corresponding to each linguistic level can be reconstructed from a grammar of conversions.

Note that each conversion must be marked in some way to indicate to which level it refers, if level structure is to be recoverable from the grammar. There is, furthermore, a natural grouping of conversions by order of application; e.g., rules that convert phrases into morphemes must apply before those converting morphemes into phonemes. We can thus indicate the level to which each conversion refers by arranging them in a sequence in order of application, and marking the place in the sequence where a new level begins.

Any attempt to construct a mechanical grammar of conversions corresponding to a part of some natural language quickly brings out the necessity for restrictions on order of application of conversions even within a level, if large-scale redundancy is to be avoided in the grammatical statement. Suppose, in particular, that an element a is converted into b in the context c——d, and into b' in every other context. That is, we have rules

22   R1: $a \rightarrow b$ in env. c——d
    R2: $a \rightarrow b'$ in env. c'——d'

where c'——d' is a specification of all other contexts. We can drop the specification "in env. c'——d'," which will in general be quite complex, from R2, if we indicate in the grammar that R1 must precede R2. Suppose further that R3, R4,... are various rules that convert c——d into a variety of complex forms. Then R1 must be extended to cover every form that the conditioning context c——d may assume, or else R2 will

---

[11] Such notations are quite familiar in grammars, but are rarely used systematically. We will use only these notational devices in the syntactic studies of Chapters VIII and X. In the morphophonemic study of the appendix to Chapter VI, several elaborations are made.

(incorrectly) apply in the case where R3, R4,... are applied before R1. Again, we can avoid a complex extension of R1 if we require that it apply before R3, R4,..., so that only c——d, and not all of the forms that these elements may assume in further development, need be stated as the conditioning context for the conversion $a \rightarrow b$. Since such situations are quite standard, it is clear that we can effect a considerable simplification by ordering the rules in a proper way.

There is a great advantage in giving the principle of ordering once and for all in the general theory. Otherwise, the gain in economy resulting from ordering of rules in a particular grammar will be much reduced because of the need to specify, within that grammar, the order of application of rules. The most favorable situation is one in which we can linearly order the conversions in such a way that all derivations can be formed by running through this sequence from beginning to end.[12] At the same time, given such a rule as R1 of **22**, we would like to have this appear in the sequence before the rules that convert its conditioning context c——d beyond the form relevant to determining the conversion of a to b.[13] These considerations suggest certain *optimality conditions* for grammars. Putting it roughly, a grammar will meet these conditions if, when the rules are given in the maximally condensed form, it is possible to arrange the resulting statements in a sequence in such a way that

23   (i)   we can form all derivations by running through the sequence of rules from beginning to end;

(ii)   no conversion $X \rightarrow Y$ will appear twice in the sequence (i.e., no rule need be repeated in several forms at various places in the grammar);

(iii)   each conditioning context is developed to exactly the extent relevant for the application of the rule in which it appears.

This statement is too vague to be literally applicable to the evaluation of grammars, but such an optimality condition can be given in a more refined and explicit manner. This seems to me to be a worthwhile endeavor, but one which is perhaps premature before much more

---

[12] Repeating this procedure indefinitely often, if infinitely many derivations must be generated by the sequence of conversions. We will disregard, for the moment, various problems connected with recursive generation, returning to them below when we discuss linguistic levels. Note that the decision to introduce ordering into grammar necessitates certain extensions of our description of the form of grammars. Thus we must make a distinction between obligatory and optional conversions if the ordering is to have any effect. This matter will also occupy us below.

[13] Of course, R1 must follow the rules that produce c, d from earlier elements.

experimentation with various notations for grammars (i.e., various definitions of "simplicity").

Nevertheless, we can use this crudely stated optimality condition as a guide to the correctness of analyses. It is not at all evident that it is possible to set up grammars meeting such a stringent condition, with such a rigid hierarchy of statements even within a level. When we find it possible to construct a linguistic level, for a given language, in such a way as to meet or approach this condition, we have good reason to suspect that we are on the right track.

These considerations of ordering of grammatical statements add a new feature to the analysis of simplicity. Now a given description of a language is more highly valued not only if it permits generalizations, but also if it leads to a simple, but quite rigid, hierarchy of grammatical processes; in particular, if it meets such optimality conditions as **23**. This development of grammatical theory was motivated by the recognition that in many familiar situations the grammar can be simplified in a natural and effective way if certain restrictions on order of application of conversions are imposed. And, like other aspects of the characterization of simplicity, its acceptability will ultimately turn on the question of its effect on the choice of grammars for particular languages.[14]

29   We have seen that as a consequence of the decision to consider the simplicity of grammar as a factor in the choice among grammars, and hence a factor in the determination of linguistic structure, we find it necessary to make a detailed study of the form of grammars and the method by which structural information is derived from a grammar. We have outlined a conception of a grammar as a sequence of conversions of the form $X \rightarrow Y$, and we have discussed the question of how such a grammar might be evaluated with respect to its simplicity. Derivations of sentences are constructed by running through this sequence of conversions from beginning to end, perhaps repeatedly, applying appropriate rules to the last-produced string to produce a new string (cf. §24). This conception is incomplete in many respects. For one thing, we have not really stated an evaluation procedure, but only indicated how one might be stated. To complete the statement, we would have to indicate exactly how the symbols of the grammar should be weighted; e.g., should brackets and angles count in calculating length, should a simplification on the phonemic level be counted as more important than

---

[14] See my *Morphophonemics of Modern Hebrew* for a detailed study of the effect of ordering statements in a complex morphological description and the prospects for meeting such optimality requirements as **23**.

a simplification on the syntactic level, etc. Relevant here is the question of how much complexity should be tolerated on each level. The addition of a statement of fixed length to the description of a very simple structure will no doubt be judged far more serious than the addition of a statement of the same length to the description of an already complicated structure. Some of the most interesting questions in grammar construction, as we will see below, concern just this problem of weighting complication of one level against complication of another.

It would be quite easy to fill in these gaps one way or another, but it would also be pointless, at this stage of our knowledge. There is no reason to prefer any one number of different ways of completing the construction. Our approach from this point on will be experimental. We will test the workability of these notions by attempting to apply them to linguistic material, and determining whether the results of this application are acceptable, illuminating, and suggestive. When a great deal of such material has been collected, it will be possible to make some more rational decision as to how to proceed further with the constructional task. In particular, this problem of weighting the contribution to the total complexity of the description of each level is an important problem for investigation.

While the problems briefly cited above are unresolved, it seems that they can be accommodated within the present framework. But other defects of our analysis of simplicity are more serious. There are unquestionably many facets of simplicity not covered by the simple conception sketched above, and it is quite important to investigate these. But it will appear that even on the basis of this limited conception, we can go quite far in studying language structure.

With this, we complete our preliminary investigation of the program and tools of linguistic research. The notions that enter into linguistic theory[15] are those concerned with the physical properties of utterances, the formal arrangement of parts of utterances, conformity of utterance tokens (as determined by the pair test), and finally, formal properties of systems of representation and of grammars. Considerations of other kinds can be admitted if shown to be clear and relevant. We will refer to linguistic analysis carried out in these terms as "distributional analysis." This usage seems to me to correspond to the practice of what has been called distributional analysis.

---

[15] More precisely, that central area of linguistic theory concerned with grammar. There are other legitimate areas of linguistic research with other purposes and other tools. It would perhaps be preferable to replace "linguistic" by "grammatical" throughout this discussion.

Before entering into the direct analysis of the level structure of language, we must study the crucial question of determining "possible" or "grammatical" sentences. This will occupy us in the next chapter.

30   *Appendix to Chapter IV: Formal Construction of the Language of Grammar* [omitted here].

GRAMMATICALNESS *V*

The first problem that the linguist must face in constructing the **31**
grammar of a language is that of determining the subject matter of
his description. Given a corpus of sentences, this problem breaks down
into two parts, as we have already seen in §13. First, he must determine
which of these utterances are phonemically distinct. Second, he must
determine which utterances, whether in the corpus or not, are
grammatical, hence to be described in the grammar to be generated in
the manner discussed in Chapter IV. We have suggested that the first
problem can be met by such devices as the paired utterance test (cf.
§13.3); the second will concern us now.

It is clear that the set of grammatical sentences cannot be identified
with the linguist's corpus of observed sentences. Not only are there
many (in fact, infinitely many) nonobserved grammatical sentences, but,
in addition, certain sentences of the corpus may be ruled out as ungrammatical, e.g., as slips of the tongue. Thus we must project[1] the class of
observed sentences to a larger, in fact, infinite class of grammatical
sentences. And within linguistic theory we must define "grammatical
sentence" in terms of "actual, observed sentence."

Investigating the conditions that we want this definition to meet, we **32.1**
find that a partition of utterances into just two classes, grammatical and
nongrammatical, will not be sufficient to permit the construction of
adequate grammars in terms of what we have broadly described as
distributional analysis. If we wish to distinguish between two elements X

---

[1] We will use the word "project" in a broad sense, it being understood that the projection
of a class to a new class may drop some of the members of the original class. In the
particular kind of projection that we are discussing in this chapter, the deletions will
necessarily be of a minor and peripheral character. But the projection being discussed
here is only a special case, a first stage in a series of projections. And in later stages
(e.g., on the morphological level), the projection may be primarily deletion (cf. §47).

and Y in distributional terms, we must be able to exhibit a significant class[2] K of contexts such that either X or Y (but not both) occurs in the contexts of K to form grammatical sentences. A difficulty arises when X occurs regularly in K, and occurrence of Y in K is somehow "near-grammatical." If Y is excluded from K, we lose the grounds for distinguishing these near-grammatical sequences from completely ungrammatical nonsense, while if occurrence of Y in K is ruled grammatical, we lose the distributional grounds for distinguishing X from Y.

This problem arises, for example, in the case of various subclasses of nouns in English. Clearly, any adequate grammar of English would have to distinguish proper nouns like "Jones," "Bill," etc., on the one hand, from "sincerity," "golf," etc. This requires a discriminatory class K of contexts, including, presumably such contexts as

1   (a)   ——*admires Tom*
     (b)   ——*had lunch with Tom yesterday*

in which "Jones" occurs to form grammatical sentences. But now consider the sentences formed by placing "sincerity" or "golf" in the blanks of 1. If these are considered grammatical, we lose the distributional grounds for distinguishing the class of proper nouns. But if they are ruled ungrammatical (as in some sense they surely are), we will have failed to indicated that these sentences are by no means as remote from English as, e.g., "the admires Tom," or "of had lunch with Tom."

To choose a somewhat different sort of example, an adequate grammar would certainly have to register the fact that the relation between "bring" and "brought" is the same as that between "like" and "liked." We might try to show this on the basis of such contexts as

2   *they——it today*

3   *they——it yesterday*

Clearly, "like" and "bring" occur in 2, and "liked" and "brought" in 3. But even if we agree that it is proper to exclude "like" and "bring" from 3, we face the further difficulty that "break" can occur in 2 and "brought" in 3. How, then, do we establish that the proper pairing is "bring"–"brought," "break"–"broke" rather than "bring"–"broke,"

---

[2] The particular theory that we develop will determine what qualifies as a significant class.

"break"–"brought."[3] The most reasonable distributional grounds for the correct pairing would seem to be that "bring," "brought" can occur in such contexts as **4**, and "break," "broke" in such contexts as **5**:

4   *wars——disease and famine*

5   *they——into the store*

But now consider the class of sentences formed by placing "break," "broke" in the contexts **4**, etc., and "bring," "brought" in the contexts **5**, etc. Clearly these are somehow "more grammatical" than the sequences formed by placing, e.g., "Jones" in these contexts. On the other hand, if they are considered fully grammatical, we lose the basis for making a correct distributional analysis of the verbs in question (and, at the same time, we admit some rather odd sentences into the language).

This leads us to observe that an adequate linguistic theory will have to recognize degrees of grammaticalness, so that substitution of "Jones" in **1**, "bring" in **4**, and "break" in **5** gives fully grammatical sentences; substitution of "sincerity" in **1**, "break" in **4**, and "bring" in **5** gives partially grammatical sentences; and substitution of "brought" in **1** and "Jones" in **4**, **5** gives completely ungrammatical sequences.

We can approach this matter in somewhat different terms. A primary **32.2** motivation for this study is the remarkable ability of any speaker of a language to produce utterances which are new both to him and to other speakers, but which are immediately recognizable as sentences of the language. We would like to reconstruct this ability within linguistic theory by developing a method of analysis that will enable us to abstract from a corpus of sentences a certain structural pattern, and to construct, from the old materials, new sentences conforming to this pattern, just as the speaker does.[4]

But we must be quite careful in determining just what we are to reconstruct. In the only presystematic terms we have (cf. §§13.5, 15), we can say that we are trying to explicate that intuitive concept of linguistic form that enables a speaker to distinguish such grammatical sentences as "colorless green ideas sleep furiously" from such non-grammatical sequences as "furiously sleep ideas green colorless."

---

[3] We might try to argue this on the grounds that the correct pairing minimizes the number of consonant changes. But, on the other hand, we might argue that the incorrect pairing gives the parallelism *break–brought, take–taught.*

[4] See Chapter I. We will try to attach more content to such rather figurative modes of expression below.

But more generally, there is little doubt that speakers can fairly consistently order new utterances, never previously heard, with respect to their degree of "belongingness" to the language, as in the cases discussed above. Similarly, the following sequences may all be new in English:

6   (a)   *look at the cross-eyed elephant*
     (b)   *look at the cross-eyed kindness*
     (c)   *look at the cross-eyed from*

but I think it is clear that any one would arrange them in this order with respect to "belongingness" to English. In other words, we might say that the speaker projects his past linguistic experience to a set of more and more comprehensive extensions. Correspondingly, within linguistic theory we must develop a notion of "degree of conformity to the structural pattern," so that, given a reasonable sample of English not containing **6**, we would be able to predict that **6a** is perfectly grammatical, **6b** partially so, and **6c** not grammatical at all.

Thus from several points of view, we are led to consider as the goal of our reconstruction the notion of "degree of grammaticalness."

33.1   The notion of "syntactic category" provides a first approach to the reconstruction of this process of projection. Let us assume that we have a finite corpus of sentences with word division marked. It might contain, for example,

7   (a)   *John came*
     (b)   *Bill ate*
     (c)   *John saw Bill*

We assign these words to categories. Let us call this assignment a *syntactic analysis* of the words of the language. We can now associate with each sequence of words a sequence of categories, replacing each word by the category to which it belongs. Thus if we assign "John," "Bill" to the category N, and "came," "ate," "saw" to the category V, we will have NV, NV, and NVN corresponding, respectively, to **7a**, **7b**, and **7c**. There will in general be many fewer sequences of categories than sequences of words. Each sequence of categories may be called a *sentence form*, and we can construe the generated language of grammatical (but perhaps nonoccurring) sentences as those which conform to one of these sentence forms. In this example, for instance, "John ate," "Bill saw John," etc., would be sentences, perhaps not in the corpus, but conforming to the sentence forms *NV*, *NVN* constructed from the syntactic analysis.

The notion of degree of conformity to the structural pattern is easily derived. Instead of considering only one syntactic analysis of words into categories, we consider several analyses of various *orders*. That is, we have broad syntactic categories like Noun and Verb, subcategories of these, subsubcategories, etc. Thus we might have a first order syntactic analysis into several hundred categories, a second-order analysis into perhaps fifty categories, etc., down to an analysis into a single category. For each order of syntactic analysis we have a set of sentence forms in terms of the categories of that order. For an order with many categories, hence small categories, we have sentence forms that are more selective and generate few sequences. For an order with few categories, hence large categories, we have sentence forms that generate a great many sequences. A nonoccurring sequence then has a higher degree of grammaticalness if it conforms to the more selective sentence forms stated in terms of a many-category analysis.

Referring to the previous example, suppose that

6   (d)   *look at the cross-eyed man*

does occur in the corpus. We see that **6a** has a high degree of grammaticalness, since "man" and "elephant" are presumably comembers of the small category of Animate Common Noun. **6b** is less grammatical, since "man" and "kindness" are comembers of no syntactic category smaller than Noun, and **6c** is still less grammatical, since the only syntactic category containing both "man" and "from" is presumably the class of all words.

More precisely, we have a system $\mathscr{C}$ of classes of words,   33.2

8 $\mathscr{C} = \{C_{n_i}^n\}$,

where   (i) $1 \leqslant n \leqslant N;\ 1 \leqslant n_i \leqslant a_n$
           (ii) $a_1 > a_2 > \cdots > a_N$
           (iii) $w \in C_{n_i}^n \Rightarrow w$ is a word[5]
           (iv) $C_{n_i}^n$ is non-null; $C_{n_i}^n \subset C_{n_j}^n \Rightarrow i = j$

There are many other conditions that we can put on $\mathscr{C}$, but this will suffice for our immediate discussion.

---

[5] When we fit this discussion directly into our system of levels, this stipulation will mean that w corresponds to a prime of a certain level **W**.

For each n, the set $\mathscr{C}^n = \{C_1^n, ..., C_{a_n}^n\}$ will be called the *syntactic analysis* of order n, and the C_i^n are called *categories of order n*.

We are given a corpus K which we take to be a set of strings of words. A sequence $C_{\alpha_i}^n, ..., C_{\alpha_m}^n$ of categories of order n is said to *generate* the word string $w_1 {}^\frown ... {}^\frown w_m$ if $w_1 \in C_{\alpha_i}^n, ..., w_m \in C_{\alpha_m}^n$. Thus the set of word sequences generated by a category sequence is, essentially, the Cartesian product of the categories.

A sequence of categories of order n is said to be a *grammatical sentence form* of order n if one of the word sequences generated by it is in K.

The sentences of order n are those generated by the grammatical sentence forms of order n. Thus the highest-degree grammatical sentences are those of order 1, the order with the largest number of categories. If $a_N = 1$, then all sequences (of the length of members of K) are grammatical of order N.

34.1 Our immediate problem, then, is to construct a formal and abstract notion of syntactic category that will lead to an appropriate system of categories when we are presented with an adequate sample of linguistic material. Or, to put it differently, we must develop a procedure such that given a corpus of sentences with word division marked (i.e., a set K, as in §33.2), we can, by means of this procedure, construct a system of classes $\mathscr{C}$ which will give the correct account of grammaticalness.

The most obvious approach to this problem seems to be some sort of substitution technique. The very nature of our goal dictates that these categories C_i^n be classes of elements that are, in some sense, mutually substitutable. But attempts to clarify this sense run up against serious difficulties. We will now briefly consider some of these difficulties and the possibilities of elaborating a direct substitution technique in such a way as to avoid them. Then, in §35, we will discuss in greater detail a somewhat different approach to the problem.

34.2 Consider first the problem of constructing the smallest categories, the categories $C_1^1, ..., C_{a_1}^1$, of order 1. This is the problem of defining highest-degree grammaticalness. The use of a substitution technique for this construction faces two immediate difficulties. In any sample of linguistic material, no two words can be expected to have exactly the same set of contexts. On the other hand, many words which should be in different categories will have some context in common. There are contexts like

9   *it is* ———

where elements of many different categories can appear (e.g., "John," "red," "mine," "likely," "up," "here," "not"). Thus substitution is either too narrow, if we require complete mutual substitutability for comembership in a syntactic category C_i^1, or too broad, if we require only that some context be shared. Thus neither of the simplest approaches to substitution is adequate without elaboration.

Though we can scarcely hope to find two words mutually substitutable everywhere in a linguistic corpus, we might find some behavioral test for mutual substitutability, so that we could run through our (finite) corpus testing every pair of words for this property in each context. Then the C_i^1 could be defined as classes of words among whose members complete mutual substitutability holds.

The unacceptability of this approach lies in the fact that it simply avoids the very question with which we are concerned. An operational test for grammaticalness would simply record the speaker's ability to project, but a definition of "grammatical sentence" in terms of rules of combination set up for observed utterances would give some insight into the nature and source of this ability, and as such, it would represent a fundamental contribution to our understanding of linguistic behavior. Replacing a systematic account of grammaticalness by a behavioral test would mean abandoning this goal, which is both important and, it seems, quite possible to attain.

To put if differently, this approach amounts to taking first-order grammaticalness as a primitive notion in linguistic theory. The purpose of a theory is to investigate to the fullest extent the relations between the notions that enter into the theory. Complete success in unearthing and expressing these interrelations is marked by the elimination of terms from the primitive basis. The discovery of an effective behavioral test for first-order grammaticalness, then, should be taken as posing (rather than solving) the problem of accounting for this fact (now presumably behaviorally marked) of first-order projection (cf. Note 6, Chapter II).

Even if such contexts as **9** can be excluded as illegitimate on some grounds, the difficulties faced by a substitution technique are not at an end. It is evident that substitutability is directly relevant only to the establishment of the smallest categories. For words which belongs to the same higher-order (i.e., larger and less selective) category, e.g., the nouns "horse" and "justice," it would be difficult to find any natural sentence in which they can replace one another.

For this reason, it is necessary to develop the methods of substitution somewhat further. One way to do this is as follows. If we find two words in the same legitimate context, we assign them to the same category.

34.3

We now rewrite the corpus, replacing words assigned to the same category by a single symbol everywhere they occur. In other words, we disregard the distinction between words assigned to the same category. This reduces the number of distinct contexts, so that new pairs of words become mutually substitutable, and we can build larger categories. We can thus proceed to analyze the corpus in a constructive manner, using the information obtained at each step in determining substitutability relations for the succeeding step. Such a procedure will lead to a system of categories from which the system $\mathscr{C}$ may be selected. Although the problem of defining grammaticalness is thus not completely solved, given such a technique, it is tremendously reduced in scope.

It seems that a substitution technique must be at least as powerful as this if it is to be effective. Extension to include substitutability of phrases (i.e., sequences of words) is possible, leading to a generalization of the notion of syntactic category to cover at least a partial analysis of phrase structure. One important result of this extension is that now the projection of the corpus can include sentences longer than those of the original corpus. We may be able to develop the infinite generative power required for a full account of grammaticalness by continually repeating the analysis for the successive projections of the corpus.[6]

The extension to include substitution of word sequences raises a further problem of segmentation. We cannot freely allow substitution of word sequences for one another. Thus we cannot set up a category containing "from New York was here" and "left," even though both occur in the context "my friend ——." Thus it may be necessary not only to exclude certain contexts as illegitimate, but also to rule out certain sequences as improper substituends.

34.4 A final difficulty for a substitution technique is the problem of homonyms. Such words as "will," /tuw/ ("to," "too," "two"), /riyd/ ("read," "reed"), etc., are best understood as belonging simultaneously to several categories of the same order. Hence the technique of substitution must be designed in such a way as to lead to a system $\mathscr{C}$ with the categories of a given order overlapping in the syntactic homonyms.[7]

The problem of homonymity is an important one. In preparation for later discussions of homonymity, we note now that only certain cases of homonymity are relevant to grammar, namely those that can

---

[6] For a detailed introductory study of the topics touched on in this section, and certain related problems (e.g., investigation of the equivalence of alternative formulations of such substitution techniques for various kinds of language), see Chomsky, "Systems of syntactic analysis."

[7] See Harris, *Methods*, for discussion of this problem.

be interpreted syntactically by assignment of the words in question to the overlap of syntactic categories of some order. Thus "will," /tuw/, and /riyd/ are instances of syntactic homonyms in this sense, while /sən/ ("son," "sun") or "will" in its various nominal uses are perhaps not. To a certain extent, this distinction is relative to the subtlety of our grammatical analysis. Thus a more refined account of highest-order grammaticalness may convert certain cases of apparent purely semantic homonymity into cases with syntactic correlates.

Among the syntactic homonyms, there is one further distinction of importance. In the overlap of Noun and Verb, we find both "walk" and /riyd/, but clearly these are very different kinds of homonyms. In the first case, we are inclined to say that we have to do with a single word which is in two categories, while in the second, we are more inclined to describe this as a case of two words, one a noun, one a verb, with the same phonemic shape. This distinction might be felt to be a wholly semantic one. We cannot deal with it at this stage in our investigations, but below, we will suggest syntactic grounds for it (§107, Chapter X).

34.5 It is apparent that substitution procedures require for their success that we make an intelligent choice of contexts and substituends, passing over such contexts as **9** and beginning our investigation of distribution with nonhomonyms. There are many quite obvious suggestions for a precise and orderly specification of this element of "intelligent choice," and with the increasing availability of high-speed computers, it may be possible to put some of them to the test.

A somewhat less "constructive" (and perhaps more promising) way to approach this complex of problems is through the analysis of clustering. We define the *distribution* of a word as the set of contexts of the corpus in which it occurs, and the distributional *distance* between two words as the number of contexts they share divided by the total number in which either can occur. More generally, we can define the *cohesion* of the class of words $w_1, ..., w_n$, with distributions $D_1, ..., D_n$, as the cardinal number of the logical product of $D_1, ..., D_n$ divided by that of the logical sum.

We are interested in choosing categories in such a way as to maximize the amount of mutual substitutability among the words belonging to the given category. Let us call the quantity that we would like to maximize the *cluster value* of the category. We can determine the cluster value of a category as a function of the cohesions of its subsets. There are various ways in which this can be done, each making precise a certain sense of the vague notion of mutual substitutability. Suppose we fix on one such function. We might then define the *joint cluster value* of a set of categories as a function of the cluster values of the categories in this set, e.g., their average. Given such a definition we would choose the set of categories as the set with the highest *joint cluster value*.

This only gives us the best analysis into n categories for each n. Thus we still have the problem of selecting a system $\mathscr{C}$ from this system of classes by choosing the n's for which the n-class analysis is to be selected as a syntactic order. This might be done, for instance, by considering, for each n, what the best joint cluster value of an n-class analysis would be if words were distributed randomly in sentences, and choosing those n's for which the deviation of the joint cluster value from this value is above a certain amount. or is at a relative maximum, etc.

If we can develop an effective notion of clustering of sets, this can be used either to establish a system $\mathscr{C}$ directly, or to provide a basis for application of a system of the kind outlined in §34.3. We might use cluster analysis to exclude contexts like **9** (these being characterized by the fact that elements belonging to several clusters appear in them) and to determine homonyms (as elements belonging to several clusters).

This outline can be filled in with formal detail in several different ways. We would be led to favor one of thse formulations if it were shown to have particularly interesting formal properties or (and this is the ultimate test) the correct empirical consequences. A certain amount of formal investigation has not led to any conclusive reason for choosing one of several formulations, and it would clearly require a tremendous amount of data to present even the most fragmentary empirical validation. For these reasons, I will not go on to present in detail any one of the various ways of realizing the program just outlined. Nevertheless, the study of this complex of notions seems to be of considerable importance and promise for distributional analysis, and despite its difficulties and unclarities, it should certainly be pursued further.[8]

34.6   The line of reasoning that underlies the discussion of §34.5 can be generalized beyond substitution techniques. Given any distributional property φ of words (or words and phrases), we can attempt so set up syntactic categories on the basis of φ by defining (i) the distance between words (or the cohesion of a set of words), (ii) the cluster value of a category of words, and (iii) the joint cluster value of a set of categories, all in terms of φ. We have been considering the total distribution of a word in the corpus (unweighted by frequencies) to be the relevant distributional characteristic φ. But there are many other distributional

---

[8] A special case of this problem, the case of clustering of points on a line, has been investigated by A. W. Holt in an unpublished MIT master's thesis (mathematics).

characteristics which are reasonable candidates for this type of category analysis. For example,[9] we can define the *gap* between two word tokens, x and y, as the number of words occurring between them, and we can study the frequency distribution of gaps throughout the corpus for each ordered pair of words (here, word types). Fitting such a study into our framework, we note that for each word w_i there is a set of such frequency distributions, two for each word $w_1, ..., w_n$ in a corpus of n distinct word types. We can take this set of distributions (or certain of them) as the characteristic φ, and can then attempt to define distance between two words in terms of the pairwise similarity between the associated gap distributions.

There are many other distributionally defined properties that deserve consideration here. Thus we might consider morphological criteria as being particularly crucial, or we might assign a special status to words of higher frequency like "the," "of," etc. There is no logical necessity to limit ourselves to one criterion. Some combination of these or other distributional properties may be selected as ϕ.

The correct choice of a distributional characteristic φ as the basic datum for category analysis will be determined, ultimately, by the empirical consequences of that choice. But whatever choice is made, it seems that the line of reasoning sketched in (i)–(iii) above, or something quite similar, will have to be followed, in order to determine the empirical consequences. The investigation of φ alone is of limited interest, in this connection, until we state how a set of categories is to be derived from it.

34.7   The purpose of the rather unorganized remarks about substitution techniques and the like has been to indicate briefly the kind of problem that must be faced by such procedures, and to suggest that there is a large variety of ways of attacking these problems that have not been sufficiently studied. However, it is not surprising that such a technique should be so elusive and difficult to obtain.

If we could formulate a substitution procedure properly, we would have succeeded in meeting the strongest requirement for correspondence between the general theory and particular grammars (cf. §10.3). The approaches we have considered so far aim to provide a practical and mechanical discovery procedure for syntactic categories. In other words, in each case the intention was to enable the syntactic categories to be constructed directly from the raw data by observation of some simple distributional property.

[9] Following a suggestion of V. Yngve, "Gap analysis and syntax."

In view of the difficulties involved in carrying through such an ambitious program, I think it can prove interesting to lower our aims to the weaker correspondence between theory and particular grammars, and to try to construct a definition of syntactic category that begins not with an easily observable distributional characteristic of words, but with some measurable characteristic of completed syntactic solutions; that is, a definition that merely enables us to assign a value, say a number, to each proposed analysis, and thus to decide mechanically between two proposed analyses, with no concern as to how these analyses were arrived at. In accordance with this weaker aim, I would like to sketch a conception of syntactic category that seems to undercut many of the difficulties cited.

35.1   Suppose that we consider once again the method given in §33 for generating sentences once we have a set of categories of a certain order.[10] We rewrite each sentence of the corpus as a sequence of categories, replacing each word by the category to which it belongs. This gives a set of sentence forms, and we may now generate all sentences of these forms. This gives a great many new sentences, since along with each original sentence we now have all sentences of the same form as this original sentence, whether or not they appeared in the corpus.

Let us suppose now, for the sake of simplicity of exposition, that all the sentences of the corpus are of the same length. We also assume, for the moment, that we are discussing only a given fixed order of syntactic categories, with a preassigned number of categories. We return to the latter assumption in §35.2 and to the former in §35.3.

Suppose that the categories of a proposed syntactic analysis are set up on the basis of complete mutual substitutability. That is, two words are members of the same category only if in the original sample, each word occurs in every position in which the other occurs. It is clear that for such a syntactic analysis, no sentence can be generated if it did not already appear in the original sample. Thus no new sentences are generated.

In general, it is clear that more new sentences will be generated to the extent that the distributions of the elements within a category differ. The number of sentences generated by an analysis thus gives some measure of the extent to which elements in the same category have similar distributions, and it seems reasonable to measure the value of

---

[10] For many of the ideas of this section, I am indebted to Peter Elias. In the case of non-overlapping categories, the measure described for evaluating an analysis is the same as what Harwood calls "measure of negative fit" of an analysis to a corpus; "Axiomatic syntax; the construction and evaluation of a syntactic calculus."

a syntactic analysis by the number of sentences that it generates, fewer sentences being generated by a better analysis. Thus we evaluate an analysis by seeing how good an approximation it gives to the original corpus—how few sentences it generates beyond those of the original corpus.

The foremost problem faced by a substitution technique was seen to be the difficulty of deciding how many contexts must be shared for two elements to be in the same category. Such questions are avoided here, since this technique does not built categories step by step, but rather provides a procedure for evaluating a completed solution. Elements may be in the same category in the highest-valued analysis even if they share no context. This property is important, since in actual linguistic material, the selectional restrictions on distribution are extremely heavy, and literal substitutivity is distinctly the exception rather than the rule. Nevertheless different nouns do substitute for each other in the sense that they all occur with *some* verb, though rarely with the same verb. Similarly, individual verbs are substitutable in contexts defined by the categories Noun, Adjective, etc., though rarely in the context of particular nouns and adjectives. This approach, as distinct from a substitution procedure, permits us to use this fact by, as it were, setting up these classes simultaneously.

Consider now the problem of homonyms. This is essentially the problem of when to put a word into two or more of the categories of the syntactic analysis. If a word is put into more than one category, there is always a loss in the value of the analysis in one respect. To see this, not that each time a certain category appears in a grammatical sentence form, a set of sentences is generated for each word in that category. Hence the more words in a category, the more sentences are generated, and the lower the value of the syntactic analysis. When a word is put into a second category, this second category now has an extra member, and it follows that more sentences are generated wherever this second category occurs, with a corresponding drop in the value of the analysis.

On the other hand, if the element is a real homonym, there may be a compensating saving in the following way. Consider an English homonym like /tuw/ ("to," "two," "too"). If this word is put only into the category of prepositions, then, since /tuw/ can appear in such sentences as: "there are two books on the table," it follows that all prepositions will occur in the numeral position in the generated language. But if /tuw/ is put in both the preposition and numeral categories, then a given occurrence of the word can be classed either as a numeral or as a preposition. Since the category of numerals will occur anyway in "there are —— books on the table," no new sentence forms are generated if this occurrence of /tuw/ is classed as a numeral, and there is consequently a considerable saving in the number of generated sentences. We see that assignment of a word to several categories may increase the value of the analysis. This suggests a way of deciding when to consider a word to be in fact a set of homonyms. We do this if the loss incurred in assigning it to several categories is more than offset by the gain; and there is always a numerical answer to this.

It must be shown, of course, that in terms of presystematic criteria, the solution of the homonym problem given by this approach is the correct one. Certain preliminary empirical investigations of this have been hopeful, but the task of properly validating this (or any other) conception of "syntactic category" is of course an immense one.

35.2   We can now determine, for each n, the best analysis in terms of n categories. As n increases, the categories become smaller, and projection is more limited and selective. Thus the degree of grammaticalness of the projected sentences will be higher. Where n is the number of words in the corpus, the set of sentence forms is exactly the corpus itself, and no new sentences are generated. Where $n = 1$, there is only one sentence form, but every possible sequence is generated in terms of it. The number of sentences generated is thus a nonincreasing function of the number of categories.

However, we still have the problem of selecting a system $\mathscr{C}$ from this set of analyses. This is the problem of determining for which n we actually set up the n-category analysis as an order of the system $\mathscr{C}$, i.e., a set $\mathscr{C}^n$ (cf. §33.2). Our aim here is to select a certain n such that the n-category analysis compares very favorably with the $(n-1)$-category analysis, but is not much worse than the $(n+1)$-category analysis. In other words, we are interested in minimizing a certain function of n and the number of sentences generated by the n-category analysis. At this point we can only speculate about which function should be chosen for minimization. There are several possible candidates, and at this point there seems to be no compelling reason for making a choice one way or another. This decision turns upon the empirical consequences of the various choices, and we simply do not have the requisite data at this stage of our knowledge.[11] But it seems reasonable to hope that this is no defect in principle, and that the proper

[11] Perhaps it is worth emphasizing once again that the unavailability of such data is not a reason for judging such theorizing as we have been engaged in to be pointless. We cannot know what kind of data to collect until we have a theory that offers some hope of solving the difficulties that we know in advance to exist. The purpose of these remarks, of course, is to suggest such a theory (cf. Chapter I).

kind of empirical investigation may lead directly to a decision, thus filling in the remaining gap.

Whatever function we do minimize, it must be remembered that we are interested in relative minima, since we would like to construct several orders of analysis. We will see below (§39), however, that the absolute minimum, and the dichotomous partition that it imposes on sequences, may have a special significance.

We have seen how, given a set of sentences of fixed length λ, we can **35.3** determine, for each n, the best analysis into n categories of the words of which these sentences are composed. It would seem reasonable to assume that for any n, λ_i, λ_j,[12] the optimal n-category analysis for sentences of length λ_i and of length λ_j will be identical, since we would hardly expect the basic principles of sentence construction to vary markedly from one sentence length to another. If this assumption is granted, then investigation of a single sentence length will be sufficient for determination of the system $\mathscr{C}$.

Alternatively, we may consider the break between sentences to be a "word" assigned to a special category $\#$, and we define a "discourse form" as any sequence of sufficiently long[12] sentence forms, with sentence break marked.[13] We can then measure the value of an analysis in terms of the number of discourses it generates (generation of discourses from discourse forms being exactly like generation of sentences from sentence forms).

More precisely, we define an "initial discourse form" as the beginning of any discourse form (with a discourse form as a special case), and we let S_λ be the number of strings generated by a given syntactic analysis from the set of all initial discourse forms of length λ.[14] The natural way to define the value of a given syntactic analysis A is as

10 $$\mathrm{Val}(A) = \lim_{\lambda \to \infty} \frac{\log S_\lambda}{\lambda}$$

We choose as the best analysis into n categories that analysis A for which $\mathrm{Val}(A)$ is minimal.

---

[12] λ_i and λ_j being greater than some fixed λ_0. That is, we will not investigate the very shortest sentences, where little grammatical structure appears, in determining $\mathscr{C}$.

[13] Our theory has not yet been extended to account for prosodic features. A more complete account would no doubt identify sentence breaks with intonation morphemes belonging to a special category.

[14] Since there is a finite upper bound to sentence length in our present discussion, it turns

35.4   This conception of syntactic analysis has an information-theoretic interpretation; in fact, it was initially suggested and motivated by this interpretation. We have in fact defined the best analysis as the one that minimizes the information per word in the generated language of grammatical discourses. We have to do here with a very special and elementary case of information, since the frequency of words and word sequences is nowhere considered.

An elaboration of this interpretation may prove illuminating. By the *redundancy* of language is meant, essentially, the restriction on the freedom of the choice of elements in discourse, and in our present context, it can be undertstood as a measure of restriction on the freedom of choice of words. We might picture this redundancy as being broken down into two factors, the first involving the restrictions provided by the grammatical structure of the language, and the second, those provided by all other factors, including the content of discourse and all its extra-grammatical concomitants. In other words, at every point in the stream of discourse the speaker must choose a particular single word, and it makes sense to ask to what extent his choice of a particular word was governed by the grammatical structure of the language, and to what extent it was governed by other factors. The more rigid the grammatical structure, the fewer discourses are permissible altogether (for each length), and the larger the share of the constraints contributed by the grammatical structure. Essentially, the conception of syntactic analysis given above has been designed in such a way as to minimize the number of possible discourses of each length, consistent in a special sense with the corpus, and thus to maximize the contribution of the formal grammatical structure to the total redundancy. As we move to lower, less selective degrees of grammaticalness, this contribution decreases. Even for highest-degree grammaticalness, we should expect it to be relatively slight.

36.1   This interpretation for the proposed constructions focuses attention on a characteristic feature of the linguist's ordinary conception of grammar. I have in mind the sharp distinction maintained between grammatical and statistical structure. In view of recent interest in statistical methods in linguistics, it seems important to give a somewhat more systematic statement of this distinction and its consequences, even at the cost of some repetition.

---

out that as λ increases, the contribution of sentence fragments to S_λ diminishes, so that in the limiting case we are still measuring only the contribution of complete sentences, as is required.

Customarily, the linguist carrying out grammatical analysis disregards all questions of frequency and simply notes the occurrence or nonoccurrence of each element in each context in his observed materials. A consequence of this approach is that the resulting grammar sets up a sharp division between a class G of grammatical sentences and a class $\bar{G}$ of ungrammatical sequences.[15] The formal properties of language might be studied in other ways. Instead of noting merely occurrence and nonoccurrence, we might present a statistical analysis of the corpus, tabulating the probability of occurrence of each element in each context or the conditional probability of occurrence of each element as the nth element of a sequence, given the first $n-1$ elements, etc.

The grammatical approach thus contrasts with a statistical approach that leads to an ordering of sequences from more to less probable, rather than a sharp division into two classes within which no such gradations are marked. This literally correct statement of two different approaches can be misleading. It would be easy to picture the grammatical approach as an attempt, motivated by the complexity of the statistical data, to impose a rough approximation to the full statistical variation, with all sequences of higher than a certain probability being assigned to G and all others to $\bar{G}$. But this would be a gross misconception. We have already noted that if our theory is to begin to satisfy the demands that led to its construction, then G will have to include such sentences as 11, while such sentences as 12 are assigned to $\bar{G}$

11   *colorless green ideas sleep furiously*

12   *furiously sleep ideas green colorless*

But clearly these strings are not distinguished by their assigned probabilities. If probability is to be based on an estimate of frequency in some English corpus, then this probability will be zero in both cases. Nor can they be distinguished, in some more sophisticated way, in terms of the probability of their parts. The full statistical picture is not a direct generalization of the grammatical analysis with its simple yes–no system of constraints. There is no obvious tie-up between the two approaches. If we somehow rank sequences of English words in terms of their probability,[16] we will find grammatical sentences scattered freely throughout the list. The grammatical approach cannot be interpreted

[15] For simplicity of exposition, we will temporarily disregard the notion of degree of grammaticalness.

[16] For example, in terms of order of approximation (cf. Note 36, Chapter II).

as giving a schematized and simplified description of the full variety of the "actual" language. Nor can the generalization to degrees of grammaticalness be understood as simply a closer approximation to this variety.

This is a simple but important point, and failure to appreciate it has occasionally led to serious misunderstanding of the nature of grammar.[17] The linguist uses such words as "pattern" and "structure" quite freely in describing his own activities. He says that he is interested in describing the structure of the language, the pattern to which its utterances conform. The distinction between two kinds of nonsense, grammatical nonsense like **11** and ungrammatical nonsense like **12**, can serve as a simple illustration of the significance of this reference to pattern and structure. Here we have two sequences of words, no part of which may ever have occurred in connected discourse. Yet any speaker of English will recognize at once that **11** is an absurd English sentence,[18] while **12** is no English sentence at all, and he will consequently give the normal intonation pattern of an English sentence to **11** but not to **12** (cf. above, §13.5). Such examples as this give empirical content to the linguist's search for pattern and structure. The distinction between grammatical and ungrammatical nonsense cannot be explained by simply giving a more and more detailed description of observed linguistic behavior, ultimately, let us say, a tabulation of the probability of occurrence of each item in each context. In terms of such a description alone, both **11** and **12** will be excluded as equally remote from observed English. This distinction can be made (in this case, but not in many others that will concern us) by demonstrating that **11** is an instance of the sentence form *Adjective-Adjective-Noun-Verb-Adverb*, which is grammatical by virtue of such sentences as

13   *revolutionary new ideas appear infrequently*

that might well occur in normal English.

36.2   The custom of calling *G* the class of "possible" sentences, or those that "can occur," is no doubt responsible for much confusion here. It is natural to understand "possible" as "highly probable," and "impossible" as "highly improbable." When this interpretation is rejected, as it obviously must be, it becomes equally natural to take the next step of rejecting the notion "possible sentence" as mere mysticism.

---

[17] See, for example, Hockett, *A Manual of Phonology*, pp. 3–17.

[18] More properly, an absurd semi-English sentence, when we have set up degrees of grammaticalness.

Actually, although the notion of grammaticalness is undoubtedly complex and difficulty to reconstruct, it is by no means mystical, and we have a good idea as to how to go about reconstructing it. Given a corpus of sentences, we define the set G to be the set of sentences conforming to the rules established for describing this corpus, whether or not these sentences happen to occur in the corpus. The problem of constructing G, then, is the problem of determining how to provide a proper description for a fixed linguistic corpus—it is the problem of constructing a linguistic theory as we have several times described this project above. Linguistic theory must provide us with the system of formal structures that can be realized in language and with a procedure for evaluating any proposed realization of this system based on a given corpus. To construct such a theory is no mean task, but it is important to recognize that there is no difficulty in principle.

The system $\mathscr{C}$ is one such structure that can be given an explicit interpretation, given an adequate corpus, and in §35 we have suggested one way in which any interpretation might be evaluated. Describing a corpus in terms of $\mathscr{C}$ automatically produces a certain projection of the corpus. Further projection will be discussed below in terms of other structures. Whether or not any of our explicit proposals prove ultimately to be adequate, they do indicate that there is nothing mysterious about the project.

We have frequently noted that the problems of projection and phonemic distinctness are twin aspects of the problem of determining the subject matter of grammatical description. Such goals as that of distinguishing between grammatical and ungrammatical nonsense serve as a principle of relevance for linguistic description in that they determine the degree of detail to which it is necessary to analyze the corpus in the study of grammatical structure. Similarly, the paired utterance test (cf. §13.3, above) offers a principle of relevance on the phonemic level. There is no limit to the detail in which it is possible to characterize the phonetic shape of sounds, and such study may be perfectly proper. But it is also perfectly in order to draw the line just at the point where differences fail to be significant in the sense provided by the paired utterance test. Phonemic theory is developed by drawing the line at just that point.

36.3

Though we have strong reasons for a nonstatistical conception of the form of grammar, it might turn out to be the case that statistical considerations are relevant to establishing, e.g., the absolute, nonstatistical distinction between G and $\bar{G}$ (cf. §36.1). As mentioned in §34.6, the relevant distributional criterion φ may turn out to be statistical in nature. There is no *a priori* way to determine whether the extradistributional information utilized by a statistical approach to grammaticalness will prove essential, or whether it simply blurs important distinctions with irrelevant detail. At the present stage of our knowledge we must surely keep an open mind on this matter.[19]

37   The notion of level of grammaticalness has some further implications that might be explored with profit. If we drop a certain sentence from the corpus, and apply the analysis to the corpus minus this sentence, we would ordinarily expect that this sentence will be generated at the highest degree of grammaticalness (i.e., by generation in terms of first-order categories). But for certain sequences, this will not be the case. Suppose, for instance, that a certain sequence of the corpus is a slip of the tongue, or is an interrupted sentence, or the like. Then if it is struck out of the corpus, it will not be reintroduced by the process of generation at any level of grammaticalness at all, above the lowest. Or consider a sentence like

14   *misery loves company*

This may be the only sentence of the form *Abstract Noun-Verb$_k$-Abstract Noun*, where *Verb$_k$* is a certain class of verbs that occur otherwise only in such contexts as *Proper Noun——Abstract Noun*, etc. If **14** is dropped out of the corpus, then it will not be reintroduced at the highest level of grammaticalness, but only at some lower level, i.e., at the level at which "misery" and "John" are in the same category, since "John loves company" will surely be generated at the highest level. This suggests that we need not consider all occurring sentences as of the highest degree of grammaticalness just because they occur. Above, we

---

[19] Note the similarity between this discussion of statistical approaches to grammaticalness and the discussion of semantic approaches in §13. In both case we have to deal with positions that are often ardently maintained, though never carefully formulated. In both cases, our attempt to formulate them seems to show that they are quite beside the point. We must, of course, remain open to the possibility that there is some more significant formulation.

Note that there is no question being raised here as to the legitimacy of a probabilistic study of language, just as the legitimacy of the study of meaning was in no way brought into question when we pointed out (§13.7) that projection cannot be defined in semantic terms. Whether or not the statistical study of language can contribute to grammar, it surely can be justified on quite independent grounds. These three approaches to language (grammatical, semantic, statistical) are independently important. In particular, none of them requires for its justification that it lead to solutions for problems which arise from pursuing one of the other approaches. Nevertheless, these three approaches are in some way related. The object of investigation is ultimately the same, and ultimately, we might expect them to fall into place in some larger semiotic theory.

were concerned with assigning highest-degree grammaticalness to certain nonoccurring sequences; now we have a way to assign some lower degree of grammaticalness to certain occurring sequences. The method is to strike them out of the corpus, redo the analysis on the reduced corpus, and see at what point the eliminated sentences are reintroduced. More generally, if a certain sentence form is inadequately represented, in some sense that must be defined precisely, we can drop it and investigate the level at which its instances are regenerated. Though this account is oversimplified, it points out the possibility that certain idioms or metaphors[20] might be characterizable as sentences which occur, but are not of the highest degree of grammaticalness, and that mistakes might be characterizable as occurring sentences of the lowest degree of grammaticalness. In this way we may be able to develop a method of projection of the kind originally discussed in §31.

We see that in terms of the system $\mathscr{C}$, such sentences as **14** have a special and exceptional status. They belong to sentence forms that are quite inadequately represented. $\mathscr{C}$ is just one of the systems in terms of which we describe linguistic structure. We will see below (§117) that **14** has an exceptional status in the light of higher-level structures as well. We will also find other sources, on higher levels, for cases of semi-grammaticalness of a different sort.[21]

---

[20] And, for that matter, many other sentences. Partially grammatical sentences play a role in discourse and often have an important literary effect. For example, consider Veblen's phrase "perform leisure" or "conformable individuals." Such locutions are not infrequent in the writings of certain authors. A recent tendency within philosophy has been to seek the source of philosophical perplexity and error in bad grammatical analogies. Here too, the statements criticized often appear to be semigrammatical.

[21] Note that "conformable individuals," in the preceding footnote, is of a different type. Note that when we call a sentence "partially grammatical" we are not excluding it from consideration or declaring it meaningless. We will consider the grammar of a language L to be a device that generates the highest-degree grammatical sentences of L, but if we have a system $\mathscr{C}$ as a linguistic level, it will be possible to recover semigrammatical sentences from the grammar.

A familiar problem in linguistics, similar in many ways to that posed by semigrammatical but occurring sentences, is the problem of determining "analytic norms" (cf. Hockett, *Manual*, and my review of this book). An attempt to construct discovery procedures for grammar is faced by the difficulty that it must deal in a neutral manner with the total linguistic behavior of the informant, including slips, slurred speech, interrupted utterances, etc. A more limited approach will be satisfied with a grammatical description of a partially hypothetical language underlying actual speech in the sense that actual linguistic behavior can easily be characterized as a special deviation from underlying norms. In general, phonemic analysis is the study of fairly slow speech. It is possible to characterize rapid speech as a "blurred" variant of this, though the opposite procedure is out of the question. Similarly, interrupted fragments, semigrammatical statements,

38 The proposed analysis of the notion of syntactic category was introduced in §34.7 as having a more modest aim than what we have called a "procedural" formulation, since it provides a method for evaluating a proposed analysis, but not for arriving at the correct analysis directly. But this is not literally correct. Given a finite corpus, there is a finite (but astronomical) number of ways in which the words can be arranged into n classes, and the procedure of systematically running through these, evaluating each one, and choosing the best is of course a terminating procedure. But it is clear that this is not the sense in which we speak of a procedural definition or technique (cf. §§10.3, 25). However, the difference is not easy to characterize. It is not the difference between finite and infinite, but the more elusive difference between too large and not too large.

Clearly the definition we have constructed can never in fact provide a procedure for discovering the correct grammar, though it can provide a practical procdure for evaluating a given proposal. In this respect, it is much like the measure of simplicity discussed in Chapter IV. These constructions meet the requirements for linguistic theory laid down in §10. Nevertheless, it is interesting to investigate the possibility of actually constructing a stronger theory, i.e., of converting this evaluation procedure into a practical discovery procedure. A combination of the ideas of §§34, 35 might be useful to this end. The procedures discussed in §§34.3, 34.4 can be applied directly to data to provide a complex system of classes from which a system $\mathscr{C}$ can be selected in various ways. Applying the evaluation procedure to these various proposals, we can select the best of them. Even though the substitution procedure will not lead directly to the system $\mathscr{C}$, it may reduce significantly the number of alternative analyses that have to be evaluated. Hence if we do have an effective evaluation procedure, it becomes quite important to develop substitution procedures (or other procedures of the general type outlined in §34.6) even if these prove to be only partially effective in themselves.

Of course the method of §35 cannot guarantee uniqueness of the best analysis in terms of n categories, unless we lay down certain formal restrictions on the sets of symbol sequences that are eligible for consideration as a linguistic corpus. The problem of stating the formal requirements that symbolic systems must meet to qualify as "language" is an important one. In a sense, it is the goal of linguistic theory to solve exactly this problem.

---

etc., can be explained in terms of the underlying constructed norms. This more hopeful approach is open to us once we have lowered our aims from the construction of discovery procedures to the development of procedures of evaluation in terms of simplicity, etc.

Once we have constructed a system $\mathscr{C}$ for a given language, we can give 39
a relative sense to the expression "X and Y have the same grammatical
form," where X and Y are sequences of words of the same length. In
this case, we can say that X and Y have the same n-order grammatical
form if the lowest order of categories in terms of which they are instances
of the same sentence form is the order n. Thus any two sentences of the
same length have the same grammatical form on some order, since at
least they are instances of the same sentence form in terms of the one-
category analysis C_1^N (cf. §33.2). It will also be necessary to give an absolute
sense to the expression "same grammatical form." The reasons for this
are already evident from our discussion of grammatical and ungrammatical nonsense in §35, and further reasons will appear below, in
succeeding chapters.

In §35.2 we suggested that the n's for which an n-category analysis is
to be constructed as an order $\mathscr{C}^i$ of $\mathscr{C}$ be selected by determining the
relative minima of a certain function f (which we left unspecified,
pending further empirical investigation) of the number of categories and
the number of sentences generated. We might then take the absolute
minimum[22] of the function f as defining the *absolute order of grammaticalness* and the *absolute categories*, as we will refer to them below.

Speculating, it would seem reasonable to suppose that a proper
choice of f will give as the absolute order a set of fairly large classes, so
that the absolute order will not correspond to one of the higher degrees
of grammaticalness. The absolute analysis embodies the major grammatical restrictions. Presumably these will be stated in terms of such
classes as Noun, Verb, Preposition, etc. There will be many further
grammatical restrictions that have to do with limited and special
contexts, and that will presumably, be reflected in superior degrees of
grammaticalness (i.e., smaller, lower-order categories). These further
restrictions correspond in part to what Harris has called *selection*.[23]
Thus *selectional restrictions* can be defined as those which refer to an
account of grammaticalness which is more detailed and specific than that
provided by the absolute analysis. Although Preposition may well turn
out to be a class of the abolute analysis for English, there will be subclasses of prepositions that occur with different nouns and verbs, etc.,
and at the first order, we may even find that although many of the
categories are still quite large, the categories of prepositions may be
extremely small, even unit classes.

Below we will find it necessary to make assumptions about absolute

---

[22] Further specification is necessary if we cannot assume uniqueness for this.
[23] See Harris, "Co-occurrence and transformation in linguistic structure," for discussion
of many points related to the notion "degree of grammaticalness."

categories that are not warranted by any empirical evidence. This is unfortunate, and naturally we will try to reduce them to a minimum. But we cannot drop all further investigation into linguistic structure until all problems connected with grammaticalness are completely resolved. One reason why this is impossible is that problems of grammaticalness are not independent of later considerations. The analysis of grammaticalness must be carried out in such a way as to relate correctly to more advanced constructions, and we cannot know how extensive the description of this first step in determining grammaticalness must be until we have some idea about what can be accomplished on higher levels of analysis (cf. Preface). Whenever we make assumptions about the absolute analysis, these can be understood as conditions on the function f. That is, not only will f have to be designed so as to give the correct relative minima, but also so as to give the correct absolute minimum. As is likely with any assumptions, investigation may reveal that these are not valid, i.e., that these conditions on f should be removed. This must be kept in mind when we suggest reliance on absolute categories below. Linguistic theory is a complex system with many interconnections between its parts. It is apparently necessary at this early stage in its development to let speculation outrun available evidence at many points in the theory, so that the data obtainable at other points may fit into some reasonable conceptual framework—these data then supplying conditions of adequacy which the underlying conceptual framework must meet.

40   Throughout this discussion we have been assuming that projection is determined by rules of combination framed in terms of words. But this is certainly a debatable assumption. There is nothing in our formulation of syntactic analysis that explicitly requires that words and not morphemes be considered as the fundamental units for this first, basic step in projection. However, the choice of words seems to me to be the correct one.

We need not require that the projection given by the system $\mathscr{C}$ be final and immutable. If later considerations in terms of higher levels show that adjustment of the boundaries of the set of grammatical sentences eliminates complexities and irregularities, then such adjustment may be permissible. But it is easy to fall into circularity if we build into the theory a possibility for very radical readjustment at later levels. To reduce the danger of emptiness and circularity, we certainly try to choose as the elements categorized in forming the system $\mathscr{C}$ those elements that are least likely to be revised and altered in the light of later syntactic considerations, and that occur as independently as possible in the stream of discourse. It seems apparent that these considerations rule in favor or words rather than morphemes. Morphemes may be continuous or discontinuous, they may undergo complex contextually determined alternation, they are often subject to rather special restrictions on occurrence,[24] and, as we will see below, choice of a morphemic analysis is heavily dependent on considerations of much higher levels. Words are relatively free from these difficulties.

The method of §35 cannot furnish a complete answer to the problem of projecting the corpus to a set of grammatical sentences. For one thing, this method does not generate sentences longer than those of the original corpus. But the class of grammatical sentences is infinite—there is no longest sentence. There are many other grammatical possibilities and restrictions that clearly cannot be adequately characterized in terms of syntactic categories. At best, then, the proposed account of grammaticalness represents only the first stage of projection. But an analysis of this account brings out the general character of each stage in the construction of the set of grammatical sentences. **41.1**

At each stage of this construction we are presented with a set of sentences, and we are required to project this set to a new set, where "projection" is to be understood in the broad sense of Note 1. The process of projection is intimately bound up with the notion of linguistic level. We can picture each new level as being constructed in order to simplify the description of the sentences already generated in terms of the preceding levels (cf. §14.4). At each stage of linguistic analysis, we find that the description of the presented grammatical sentences can be simplified if we project this set to a new set, adding many new sentences and perhaps dropping certain sentences. Thus the generation of new sentences becomes an automatic consequence of the process of describing already given sentences in terms of the descriptive machinery available in the new level. Putting this a little differently, we might say that each level provides a certain point of view from which to investigate the structure of the presented set S of sentences already generated. Investigating S from the new vantage point offered by this higher level, we discover that the structure underlying the set S is only partially realized in this set—there are many gaps, and certain exceptions. By filling in the gaps with new sentences, and dropping the exceptions,

---

[24] Thus investigation of Harris's results ("From phoneme to morpheme") on isolation of tentative segments in terms of independence seems to show that word boundaries are much more clearly indicated than morpheme boundaries, and that it might be possible to determine words directly from the phonemic record. The prospects for morphemes seem much more doubtful. See Hockett, "Problems of morphemic analysis," and Harris, *Methods*, Chapters 12, 13, for discussion of these problems.

we project S to a new set S^*, which serves as the presented set for description in terms of the next level.

In the foregoing discussion of the first stage of projection, the set S of presented sentences was the corpus itself. Introducing the level of syntactic categories (the system $\mathscr{C}$), we find that the corpus can be studied as a set of instances of a relatively small number of sentence forms. But the set of sentence forms is imperfectly realized in the corpus. We discard certain inadequately represented forms (in the manner of §37), and we form new sentences conforming to the adequately represented forms, thus projecting the corpus to a set S^* of sentences of the highest degree (first order) of grammaticalness (and incidentally, we presumably unearth a good deal of further information about lower-degree, partial grammaticalness and absolute grammaticalness). This set S^* serves as the basis for study in terms of higher levels. We need not be concerned about the fact that partially grammatical sentences are not discussed on other levels. They have not been totally excluded from the grammar, and once we have the system $\mathscr{C}$, they can be derived from the set of highest-degree grammatical sentences.

In subsequent chapters, we will investigate this set S^* of highest-degree grammatical sentences from the point of view of phrase structure and transformational structure. In each case, we see that the process of projection outlined above is repeated in terms of the descriptive potentialities of these higher linguistic levels.

41.2 This account of projection emphasizes the implications for the order of descriptive operations of the point of view we have adopted. It suggests that after phonemic analysis, the first step in grammar construction is the placing of word boundaries, and the second step is the limited projection provided by the method of §35 or something similar, i.e., by description in terms of the system $\mathscr{C}$ of syntactic categories of words. We then find that the relation between words and phonemes, as well as between sequences of words and phrase sequences, is simplified tremendously by morphological analysis of words. In this view, then, morphology appears as a higher level of analysis. Morphological representations are provided for grammatical sequences of words in such a way as to simplify the description of these sequences and the statement of their relations to phoneme and phrase sequences.

This outline of an order of descriptive operations should not, however, be taken literally. We are not attempting to present procedures for the grammatical analysis of languages, but only to discuss characteristics of a completed description. See §10.3 for further discussion of this point.

In carrying further the study of grammaticalness and grammatical **41.3** structure, it is necessary to make certain assumptions about this first stage of grammaticalness. Some of these have such strong intuitive support that we can take it to be a criterion of adequacy for any proposed analysis of grammaticalness that these assumptions be verified. As far as possible, we will try to develop our analysis of English in subsequent chapters on the basis of such assumptions.

LOWER LEVELS OF GRAMMATICAL STRUCTURE

VI

Most of the methodological work in modern linguistics has been devoted to problems of phonemic and morphological analysis. We will have little to add to this here; the discussion in this chapter is limited to a brief description of the levels of phonemes, morphemes, words, and syntactic categories in terms of the framework that has been developed above. We can then turn to the higher levels of phrase structure and trans- formational structure that provide the main substance for our inves- tigations.

To characterize a linguistic level $\mathbf{L}$ we must describe the set L of primes of $\mathbf{L}$, the set $\mu^{\mathbf{L}}$ of $\mathbf{L}$-markers, the relations among elements of $\mathbf{L}$, the mapping $\Phi^{\mathbf{L}}$ of $\mathbf{L}$-markers into grammatical utterances, and the conditions of compatibility relating $\mathbf{L}$ to other levels (cf. Chapter III). We begin by considering a corpus of utterance tokens upon which conformity has been defined by the paired utterance test.[1] Conformity

---

[1] See §13.3. We will assume henceforth that conformity is an equivalence relation; i.e., that utterances are partitioned into equivalence classes in such a way that every two members of one class conform, and no members of different classes conform. Actually, of course, conformity as interpreted by the paired utterance test is only a matching relation (reflexive, symmetrical, nontransitive). We are assuming, then, that an equiv- alence relation has been constructed from this. For example, we might take the ancestral of this matching relation, stating now that two tokens conform if they can be connected by a chain of tokens every two of which conform in the old sense of the paired utterance test. There is an important linguistic point involved in this assumption. Phonemic analysis is based on a distinction between relevant and irrelevant physical features. We

can be defined on parts of utterances, if our phonemic theory requires this. In general, in describing **L** it is sufficient to characterize $\Phi^{\mathbf{L}}$ as a mapping of elements of **L** into elements of some intermediate level, rather than directly into the set of utterance tokens.

43   The characterization of the linguistically significant levels is much simplified if we introduce a lowest level of representation whose elements are given a physical description by means of the mapping Φ on this level. We thus establish a phonetic alphabet **Pn** as the lowest level of representation. The primes of **Pn** are phonetic symbols and **Pn** can be taken as an "absolute" level, fixed and available for all linguistic description. For any given language, $\mu^{\mathbf{Pn}}$ will be a set of strings whose membership is largely determined by higher-level constructions. $\Phi^{\mathbf{Pn}}$ will associate these strings with specific utterances by providing a physical description of phones. If X is a string of phones, then "$\Phi^{\mathbf{Pn}}(X)$" will designate the set of utterance tokens which are represented by X on the level **Pn**. $\Phi^{\mathbf{Pn}}$ must have the following properties:

1   (i)   Every string of phonetic symbols is in the domain of $\Phi^{\mathbf{Pn}}$; every utterance of the corpus is in its range.

(ii)   With each prime p of Pn there is associated a certain set of S of defining physical properties. $\Phi^{\mathbf{Pn}}(p)$ is the set of phone tokens characterized by the properties S. Thus application of $\Phi^{\mathbf{Pn}}$ can be thought of as a process of setting up phone types in the corpus.

(iii)   If X and Y are strings in **Pn**, then $\Phi^{\mathbf{Pn}}(X{^\frown}Y)$ is the set of phone token sequences formed by concatenating one of the sequences from $\Phi^{\mathbf{Pn}}(X)$ and one of the sequences from $\Phi^{\mathbf{Pn}}(Y)$, in that order. If S_x and S_y are the physical specifications of $\Phi^{\mathbf{Pn}}(X)$ and $\Phi^{\mathbf{Pn}}(Y)$, respectively, then the physical specification of $\Phi^{\mathbf{Pn}}(X{^\frown}Y)$ is the sequence (S_x, S_y).

(iv)   Two utterances of the corpus conform if and only if they have the same phonetic representation, i.e., the same **Pn**-marker. That is, among the symbols of Pn (the sets of available physical properties) we pick just those that characterize conformity, in the language under analysis, to represent the utterances of this language. The choice is not necessarily unique.

---

might attempt to characterize the relevant features (e.g., voicing, but not rate of speed) as those that distinguish the equivalence classes formed by the ancestral of conformity. See my review of Hockett, *Manual of Phonology*, Section 9, for further discussion.

Thus Φ^{Pn} gives a specification of strings in **Pn** in terms of certain physical properties associated with the alphabet *Pn*. A string X in **Pn** may represent (by Φ^{Pn}) utterances of the corpus (in this case, all of these conform, and any utterance conforming to one of them is represented by X), or it may represent grammatical or nongrammatical utterances which do not happen to be in the corpus. Each such string is essentially a phonetic description of some utterance, recorded or unrecorded, grammatical or ungrammatical. Since all the utterances of the corpus are represented in **Pn**, it is sufficient to relate all higher levels to **Pn**. We will henceforth apply the term "phones" to symbols of **Pn**, as well as to the utterance tokens represented by them.

The first really significant linguistic level is the level **Pm** of phonemes.   **44.1**
The essence of a phonemic theory is contained in the definition of the mapping Φ^{Pm} that carries strings of phonemes into strings of phones. The principles by which phones are "assigned" to phonemes in the procedures of linguistic analysis will appear here as conditions on Φ^{Pm}. We now consider some of the conditions that Φ^{Pm} must meet.

From the general characterization of levels in Chapter III it follows that

2 Φ^{Pm} is single-valued,

that is, the reading of a phonemic representation must be unambiguous. Moreover, we surely want Φ^{Pm} to meet the analogue of 1iii, above. That is,

3   If X and Y are strings in **Pm**, then $\Phi^{Pm}(X^\frown Y) = \Phi^{Pm}(X)^\frown\Phi^{Pm}(Y)$.

But the phonetic shape of a phoneme (i.e., the phone associated with it) may depend on context. Thus if **3** is to be satisfied, Φ^{Pm} cannot in general be defined on phonemes, but only on strings of phonemes that are invariant in their phonetic form. Let I be the set of all such strings. We require that I (which is the domain of Φ^{Pm}) be closed under concatenation; i.e., any string formed by concatenating strings in I is in I. Many of the minimal elements in I will correspond to syllables, but some to syllable sequences.[2] From the general characterization of levels

---

[2] As, e.g., in such words as "water" or "medal," where the form of the medial consonant is determined by the preceding and following syllable. More generally, in the case where medial clusters cannot be assigned to either surrounding syllable (the clusters that Hockett, *ibid.*, calls "interludes"), the syllables in question may be excluded from I. Boundaries between members of I in the decomposition of any utterance should always be syllable boundaries, however. Decomposition of any phonemic representation into a sequence of elements of I should also be unique.

it follows that μ^{Pm} (the set of phonemic representations of grammatical utterances) must be included in I. From **2** above and 1iv of §43, it follows that

4   two utterance tokens of the corpus conform if they have the same phonemic representation.

Some would add the further requirement that no conforming utterance tokens may have distinct phonemic representations, but there seems to be no particular motivation for this requirement, and it can be shown to lead to certain artificialities.[3]

44.2   Let us make the assumption that a string X of I which is n phonemes in length is carried by Φ^{Pm} into a string Y which is n phones in length.[4] In this case we can say that the ith phone of Y is an *allophone* of the ith phoneme of X. For example, if the phoneme sequence /spil/ is carried by Φ^{Pm} into the phone sequence [sp=il],[5] then [p=] is an allophone of /p/. A phoneme is often viewed as the class of its allophones, though we do not take this position, and various conditions are placed upon the set of allophones of one phoneme. Two phones are said to be in *complementary distribution if* there is no context in which both occur.[6] Almost every familiar conception of the phoneme requires that

5   allophones of a single phoneme must be

    (a)   in complementary distribution,[7]
    (b)   phonetically similar.

---

[3] See Harris, *Methods*, for discussion of this condition, often called the "biuniqueness condition." See Chomsky, Halle, and Lukoff, "On accent and juncture in English," Halle, *The Sound Pattern of Russian*, for considerations favoring its rejection. This condition may have some motivation in a linguistic theory that aims to construct a discovery procedure for grammars, but with our weaker goals, it seems superfluous.

[4] This is of course too strong and can be replaced by a weaker and more complex assumption. The points we will make hold, however, for any such elaboration. It is not actually necessary to set up the relation "is an allophone of" between phones and phonemes, but we will do this, in the customary way, to bring out certain points about the logic of phonemic description.

[5] We shall follow the usual practice of giving phonemic transcriptions within slant lines and phonetic transcriptions within brackets, suppressing the concatenation symbol in both cases.

[6] Note that the case of free variation has been eliminated by 1iv, above. See also Note 1. Free variation is not a linguistically significant notion, since the amount of free variation that one chooses to recognize, subphonemically, is quite arbitrary. In a sense, every two utterance tokens display free variation.

[7] Or free variation (cf. Note 6).

The motivation behind **5a** is apparently a desire to ensure non-ambiguity of phonemic representation. It is true that if allophones of a single phoneme are in complementary distribution, then the reading of a phonemic representation will be unambiguous. But it is a mistake to think that **5a** is a necessary condition for nonambiguity. In fact, even the stronger condition of biuniqueness (cf. below **4**) does not require that allophones of a single phoneme be in complementary distribution. The familiar case of partial phonemic overlapping illustrates this.[8] Suppose that the phoneme A has an allophone x in the context P and an allophone y in the context Q. Suppose, at the same time, that the phoneme B has an allophone x in the context Q. This is the situation, e.g., in Danish, where we take A as $/t/$, B as $/d/$, x as [d], y as [t], P as the so-called "weak position," and Q as the "strong position." Then we have

6

	$/t/$	$/d/$	
[d]			weak position
[t]	[d]		strong position

Thus both x and y ([d] and [t]) occur in the context Q (stong position). Hence x and y are not in complementary distribution; there are two phonemically distinct utterances that differ only in that one has x where the other has y. Yet there is an unambiguous reading for each phonemic representation, given by the mapping

7 Φ^{Pm}: $A \to x$ in env. —— P

$A \to y$ in env. —— Q

$B \to x$ in env. —— Q

In fact, Φ^{Pm} may even be one to one in this case. **5a** is thus seen to be an essentially unmotivated requirement. If we accept it, it will in general rule out the possibility of partial overlapping, leading to many complications in phonemic analysis, and offering no advantage in return. **5a** must therefore be rejected as a criterion for phonemic analysis.[9]

[8] For discussion of phonemic overlapping, cf. Bloch, "Phonemic overlapping"; Schatz, "The role of context in the perception of stops." The example used below is taken from Jakobson, Fant, and Halle, *Preliminaries to Speech Analysis*, pp. 4–5, quoted also by Harris, *Methods*, pp. 148–149.

[9] The real motivation for **5a** lies in the attempt to develop discovery procedures for linguistic notions. If we aim to develop a step-by-step mechanical procedure for con-

The case of partial overlapping also sheds light on condition 5b. Since allophones of a single phoneme may (in other contexts) serve to distinguish phonemically distinct utterances, it is evident that absolute phonetic similarity cannot be what is required. Nevertheless, a phonemic theory is unthinkable without some consideration of phonetic similarity. We are therefore led to define "phonetic similarity" not in terms of absolute closeness of match, but in terms of possession of common properties from a given set of properties.[10] This allows much more latitude, since these properties may be relative (e.g., more front, more aspirated, etc.) rather than absolute (labiodental, aspirated to such and such a degree, etc.) and application of these properties may be relativized to context. Thus suppose that phones x and y occur in one context and phones z and w in another, and suppose that x is more aspirated than y and z more aspirated than w, but that y and z are in fact identical. In terms of the property "more aspirated," relativized to context, it will then appear that (x, z) and (y, w) are the phonetically similar pairs, despite the absolute match of (z, y).

Given a set of physical properties (some absolute, some relative), defined in the general theory of linguistic structure and available for the description of any language, we can proceed to develop a phonemic theory in various ways. There are many divergent approaches to phonemic analysis,[11] and there will remain room for disagreement until some objective theory has been shown to meet clear criteria of adequacy. To develop an explicit phonemic theory we would have to define a set of physical features, lay down conditions on the formation of "opposition sets" of phones, relative to which the feature analysis of phones is carried

---

structing phonemes directly from the raw data, it is natural (though not necessary) to make use of such properties as complementary distribution. We see, however, that in the long run this requirement is unacceptable, and there is in fact no real motivation for it in our terms.

It is possible to develop a weaker sense of "complementary distribution" which will not rule out partial overlapping, but in this case the condition is equivalent to 2, and hence no additional requirement on allophones.

[10] What Bloomfield, Jakobson, and others call "distinctive features." See Bloomfield, *Language*; Jakobson, Fant, and Halle, *Preliminaries to Speech Analysis*; Jakobson and Halle, *Fundamentals of Language*.

[11] For exposition of a theory fully compatible with the general framework outlined here, see Halle and Chomsky, "Evaluation procedures in linguistics," in preparation. See Harris, *Methods*, for discussion of many considerations that can be brought to bear in phonemic analysis. See also Bloch "A set of postulates for phonemic analysis," for a careful exposition of one approach. See also Hockett, *Manual*; Jakobson and Halle, *Fundamentals*.

out,[12] and show how any phonemic analysis may be evaluated, presumably in terms of most efficient and symmetrical utilization of the avaliable features.

Essentially, the mapping Φ^{Pm} assigns a physical content to the symbols of the phonemic alphabet. As on every other linguistic level, however, we may find that the grammar is much simplified if this assignment is given in a rather indirect way. That is, there is no need to think of phonemes as literally occurring in sequence, each with its distinctive physical properties, in the stream of speech. Any attempt to maintain such a view will lead to very artificial phonemicization. Consider, for example, the phonemically distinct English words "writer" and "rider," which, for certain dialects, can be transcribed phonetically as

44.3

8 (a) [ráyRɨr]
   (b) [rá:yRɨr]

respectively, where [R] stands for the apico-alveolar tongue flap, and [a:] is the single phone "long a." These words are distinguished only by the phones [a]–[a:]. The view that phonemic representation by Φ^{Pm} is "order-preserving" would require us to set up a phoneme [a:] occurring only in stressed position in the context ——y + voiced consonant;[13] and length would have to be set up as a phonemic feature, functioning distinctively only in this special case. But this a hardly an acceptable phonemic description.

Inquiring into the matter further, we find that except for the consonant [R], [a] and [a:] are contextually determined variants in the context [——yC]. That is, part of the characterization of Φ^{Pm} will be given by the conversions

9 /a/ → {[a] in env. ——y + unvoiced consonant}
          {[a:] in env. ——y + voiced consonant }

This rule is needed so as to account for such forms as [váypɨr] ("viper")–[fá:ybɨr] ("fiber"), [layf] ("life")–[la:yv] ("live"), etc. It is a special case of a much more general rule about the effect of voicing on preceding vowels. We also find that there is no /t/–/d/ contrast in inter-

---

[12] See my review of Jakobson and Halle, *Fundamentals*, for a brief exposition of how this might be done.

[13] Certain phonemic theories would require, as a consequence of this, that the vowel of "rod," "father," etc., also be assigned to /a:/. I am considering here only a dialect in which there is no contrast between, e.g., "balm" and "bomb."

vocalic, post-stress position. That is, there is no distinction between "latter" and "ladder," "metal" and "medal," etc. In this position both appear as [R], which is not found elsewhere. The simplest way to account for these facts is to add to the characterization of Φ^{Pm} the conversions

10 $\begin{Bmatrix} /t/ \\ /d/ \end{Bmatrix} \rightarrow$ [R] in env. N——V, where N is a stressed "syllabic nucleus," i.e., vowel or vowel + semivowel[14]

Rules **9, 10** are needed anyway, irrespective of how we analyze "writer" and "rider." But we now note that if these words are phonemicized /ráytɨr/, /ráydɨr/, respectively, then rules **9** and **10**, applied in that order, will give the phonetic representations 8a, 8b automatically, as required. Thus no new rules are needed to account for these forms, and there is no need to introduce the new phoneme /a:/ and the distinctive feature of length, both of which are of extremely limited and unique distribution. We also find, of course, that this simpler analysis correlates with independent morphological considerations.

On the phonemic level, then, "writer" and "rider" are distinguished by their fourth phonemes /t/–/d/. On the phonetic level, they are distinguished only by the second phones [a]–[a:]. This obviously superior analysis indicates that we cannot think of phonemes as occurring literally in sequence with their assigned physical properties. Even on this lowest level, linguistic representation need not be order-preserving, and considerations of simplicity play a role in the choice among alternative analyses.[15]

Note also that we must describe /d/ as voiced and /t/ as unvoiced, even though certain "allophones" of /t/ (e.g., in 8a) are physically voiced. Otherwise **9** will not apply properly in the case of "writer"–"rider." From this we learn that the characterization of phonemes in terms of a "distinctive feature table"[16] is essentially an abstract system of classification of phonemes, mapped into physical features. By and large, considerations of simplicity will lead us to interpret this characterization directly; that is, the phonemic classification "voiced" will correspond

---

[14] We disregard questions about phonemicization of syllabic nuclei and dialectal differentiation that are interesting, but not relevant here. Note that the biuniqueness condition is violated by **10**. This could be avoided, e.g., by arbitrarily assigning [R] to /d/. The cost would be that the simple analysis of 8 that we describe directly would no longer be avaiable. This need not concern us, however, since we found no particular motivation anyway for this condition.

[15] See Harris, *Methods*, for other similar examples.

[16] See the references of Notes 10 and 12.

to the phonetic fact of voicing, etc., but there is good reason not to require such correspondence as a condition on Φ^{Pm}.

The metaphor of "higher" and "lower" levels can be understood in various ways. If we understand a higher level to be one with primes that are "longer" (in the number of phonetic segments contained by their images under Φ), then the next level above phonemics is the level **M** of morphemes. If we take a higher level to be one which is relatively independent of the construction of lower levels (i.e., we understand the ordering of levels as referring to the rough order of analytic procedure),[17] then the next level above phonemes appears to be the level **W** of words. Following the latter course, we consider next the level **W**. 45

Φ^{W} will be a single-valued mapping of words and strings of words into strings of phonemes, meeting the analogue of **3** (§44.1), on the level **W**. μ^{W} is a set of strings of words which will be defined on higher levels, in part, in terms of syntactic categories. **W** is the only level on which it seems reasonable to insist that the representation relation Φ be order-preserving. Our general theory seems to require that there be a method for determining words from the corpus almost to uniqueness (cf. §40), and the most important problem on this level is to develop such a method.[18]

The mapping Φ^{W} will be a specification of the phonemic shape of words. This can be given as an immense list, but a good deal of simplification and organization is possible through the introduction of morphological and morphophonemic levels. In general, this mapping can be described most effectively and simply by assuming an amalgamation of

[17] We might emphasize again that order of descriptive procedure plays no part in this theory, and that no level is considered to be independent of "higher levels," strictly speaking.

[18] The most reasonable suggestion that I know of is Harris's in "From phoneme to morpheme" (cf. Note 24, Chapter V). Investigation of his data seems to indicate that word boundaries can be placed much more effectively than morpheme boundaries by this method. The problem is whether this can be done on the basis of a corpus of reasonable size, so that we need not introduce "word" as an additional primitive with some elicitation technique as its operational interpretation.

Often in linguistic theorizing it is argued that "word" cannot be defined in general, but that words can be characterized in particular languages by features of stress, juncture, etc. (e.g., Wells, "Immediate constituents"). The familiar ambiguity of the word "define" (defining things *vs.* defining words) then sometimes suggests that these *ad hoc* characterizations replace a definition of "word." As pointed out before (Chapter I), however, formal markers for elements arbitrarily set up in particular languages offer no assistance in the task of constructing a general theory of linguistic structure or in validating grammars of particular languages, and are therefore of no relevance to this study.

the four levels involved, i.e., by the formation of a new system of concatenation with words, morphemes, morphophonemes, and phonemes as primes, concatenation of these elements being freely permitted, and all relations and interconnections of these levels being carried over into this new system. Then the mappings of words to phonemes can be given by a sequence of statements of the form $X \to Y$, so that derivations of phonemic sequences from word sequences can be constructed in the manner of Chapter IV. We can then study the relative simplicity of various proposed morphological and morphophonemic analyses, we can determine the hierarchy of statements within morphology and the degree to which conditions of optimality can be reached (cf. §28), etc.[19]

46   Following the order of relative independence, the next higher level will be the level **C** of syntactic categories. This is the first level in which a string can represent a set of nonconforming utterance tokens. We form **C** by interpreting the system $\mathscr{C}$ of §33.2, as a concatenation algebra, with the C_i^n as primes. Mirroring Chapter V, we characterize the set C of primes of **C** as

11    $C = \{C_{n_i}^n\}$

      where   (i) $1 \leqslant n \leqslant N$
                (ii) $1 \leqslant n_i \leqslant a_n$
                (iii) $a_1 > a_2 > ... > a_N$

We have a relation g of *generation*, holding between strings in **C** and strings in **W**, and meeting the condition

12   (i)   If $C_i^n \in C$ and $g(C_i^n, X)$, then X is a prime of **W** (i.e., $X \in W$).[20]

         (ii)   If Y and Z are strings in **C** $(Y, Z \neq U)$, then $g(Y^\frown Z, X) \Leftrightarrow$ there are strings W_1, W_2 in **W** such that (a) $X = W_1^\frown W_2$ and (b) $g(Y, W_1)$ and $g(Z, W_2)$.

       (iii)   For all $C_i^n \in C$, there is an X such that $g(C_i^n, X)$.

       (iv)   For all $C_i^n, C_j^n \in C$, if $i \neq j$, then there is an X such that $g(C_i^n, X)$ but not $g(C_j^n, X)$.

We define a *grammatical sentence form* of order n as a string $X = C_{\alpha_1}^n {}^\frown C_{\alpha_2}^n {}^\frown ... {}^\frown C_{\alpha_m}^n$ such that some Y generated by X is in the corpus (omitting now, in this oversimplified sketch, the refinements

---

[19] See my *Morphophonemics of Modern Hebrew* for a detailed study of these matters.
[20] That is, g relates categories to single words.

of §37). We now define the first approximation to the set of first-order grammatical sentences in the sense of Chapter V:

13 $Gr_1(W)$ is the set of X's such that for some grammatical sentence form Y of order 1, $g(Y, X)$

We define **C**-markers as follows:

14 K is a **C**-marker if and only if $K = \{C_0, C_1, ..., C_N\}$, where

> (i) C_i is a grammatical sentence form of order i;
> (iii) $\{X \mid g(C_i, X)\} \subset \{X \mid g(C_{i+1}, X\}$ $(0 < i < N)$;
> (iii) C_0 is a string of words; $g(C_1, C_0)$.

Thus a string of words will have more than one **C**-marker just in case at least one of the words is a syntactic homonym of some order (i.e., is in the overlap of several categories). The representing mapping Φ^C associates with each **C**-marker the string of words C_0 of **14**.

In stating **C**, we also specify a certain n_A, $1 \leqslant n_A \leqslant N$, which gives the absolute order of categories, and a basic dichotomy of grammatical and ungrammatical (cf. §39).

In addition to these specifications, we require that **C** be related to the corpus in the manner discussed in Chapter V (see particularly §35). The basic character of **C** is expressed in this set of relations.

The most important contribution of the level **C** is the set $Gr_1(W)$, a first approximation to μ^W, the set of grammatical strings of words. Ultimately the purpose of a grammar is to provide a specification and description of the grammatical utterances of the language, that is, the utterances represented by strings of μ^W on the level **W**. But, as we have seen in §41, we must approach this description in stages. The establishment of $Gr_1(W)$ is the first stage. We have seen in Chapter V that at best $Gr_1(W)$ is a close approximation to the set of grammatical utterances of less than some fixed length, this being the length of the longest (adequately represented—cf. §37) sentence of the corpus. $Gr_1(W)$ is thus a finite projection of the corpus. It plays the same role for higher levels of analysis that the corpus itself played for the lower levels (cf. §41).

The level of morphophonemic representation is introduced to simplify   **47** the statement of the mapping Φ^W from words to phonemes. The systematic motivation for introduction of a level **M** of morphological representation is primarily the resulting simplification in the derivation of word sequences from phrase sequences.[21] Each string of words has a morphemic spelling, and the set μ^M of **M**-markers will thus be a set of strings in **M** correlated by Φ^M to μ^W. Φ^M thus corresponds basically to an operation of putting in word boundaries in morpheme sequences. But this is an oversimplification. The correlation will not in general be direct. Morphemes may be discontinuous, a string of morphemes may correspond to a single word or phoneme sequence even if parts of this morpheme sequence do not correspond to parts of the word or phoneme sequence,[22] morphemes may have null phonemic content, etc.

Since the systematic role of morphological analysis is to simplify the derivation of word sequences from phrase sequences, we can regard **M** as a level intermediate between the level **W** of words and the level **P** of phrase structure. This suggests that it might be useful to consider separately two classes of morphological elements, those that figure in the statement of phrase structure and those whose function is limited to the description of word structure. In the first class (call it $\overline{\mathbf{M}}$), we have what we can call "morphological heads" as well as those affixes that function syntactically (e.g., morphemic long components[23] expressing agreement in gender and number, etc.). In the second class we have such elements as English *ess* (*actress*, etc.) which do not themselves enter into the description of phrase structure, but which enter into the formation of the minimal units that play some role in syntax. $\overline{\mathbf{M}}$ can be pictured (for the time being) as embedded into the level **P**. Derivations in **P** thus lead from the representation *Sentence* to strings in $\overline{\mathbf{M}}$. These derivations are then extended through the levels **M** and **W** by first analyzing the morphological heads into strings of morphemes, and then placing word boundaries (i.e., applying Φ^M).

$\overline{\mathbf{M}}$ can be set up as a subalgebra of **M**. The primes of $\overline{\mathbf{M}}$ are then a set H of morphological heads and a set Af of syntactically functioning affixes. $\overline{\mathbf{M}}$ is the only part of **M** that need be considered on higher levels of syntax. We will have several occasions below to return to the study of $\overline{\mathbf{M}}$, and its relations with **M** and **W**.

The level **M** will add an important contribution to the analysis of

---

[21] There is also a strong extrasystematic motivation for the construction of this level, namely, the desire to lay bare the formal basis for certain strong intuitions about form, i.e., about the placement of morpheme boundaries, identification of morpheme alternants, etc.

[22] As in the case of what Hockett has called "portmanteau" forms. See "Problems of morphemic analysis" for this and other discussions of morphology. See also the relevant sections in Harris, *Methods*, and Nida, *Morphology*.

[23] See Harris, *Methods*, Chapter 17. The distinction we are drawing is essentially that between the morphological processes of inflection and composition. See Bloomfield, *Language*.

grammaticalness. On the one hand, it will surely be the case that he morphology can be simplified by revising the boundaries of $Gr_1(W)$ to some extent. On the other, there are productive morphological processes that can lead to a further extension of $Gr_1(W)$ much in the manner discussed in Chapter V. But exactly how these processes of projection (in the broad sense) are to be characterized is a difficult and intricate problem to which we can offer no solution here.

Appendix: *Morphophonemics of Modern Hebrew* [omitted here; a brief **48** summary follows]. This is a segment of a grammar in the sense of Chapter IV, with an explicit procedure of generation of phoneme strings from word and morpheme strings represented morphophonemically. It appears that a great deal of compression and generalization is possible, using the devices of Chapter IV. A rudimentary syntax, with phrase-structure rules supplemented by extensive use of long components, provides the strings of words and morphemes. Sample derivations are constructed, and it is shown that a partial ordering is imposed on the statements of the grammar by the criterion of simplicity, so that there is a hierarchy of morphological processes. [The depth of ordering demonstrated in this sense is of the order 25–30]. This amounts to a partial validation of the grammar, in the one dimension of ordering (it must also be demonstrated that the elements chosen lead to the simplest grammar, etc.; furthermore, the validation shows only that the simplicity value is a relative maximum in the sense that any interchange of rules related by the partial ordering reduces this value). The grammar apparently meets the conditions of optimality suggested in §28.

PHRASE
STRUCTURE
VII

The first level that we will consider in any detail is the level **P** of phrase structure. In accordance with the general program outlined in Chapter III, this discussion will differ in aim from such treatments of constituent analysis as those of Harris[1] or Wells.[2] There will be no attempt here actually to furnish a practical procedure for discovering the constituents of a language. Instead, attention will be focussed on the problem of stating the general underlying structure to which any proposed analysis must conform, and investigating the logical status of the basic notions of constituent analysis. The goal of this investigation, as on other levels, will be, ultimately, to provide a practical evaluation procedure for any description of constituent structure proposed for a given language.

The motivation behind the construction of the level **P** has already been outlined in §§14 and 24. One further motive has appeared, incidentally, in the discussion of grammaticalness. There we were only partially successful in projecting the set of observed sentences to a set of grammatical sentences. The technique of projection constructed on the level **C** enabled us to determine grammatical sentences of length less than some fixed n, but we were not able to account for the generation of longer and longer sentences—we could not account for the unboundedness of the set of grammatical sentences.

When we turn to the level of phrase structure, we find that certain rules may have a recursive character. Thus *Noun Phrase* (*NP*) might be analyzed in such a way that one of its components may be a *NP*,

---

[1] *Methods in Structural Linguistics.*
[2] "Immediate constituents."

as in such a sentence as "the man who made the discovery is my brother," which might be derived by means of such conversion as

1    $NP \rightarrow NP_1 \smallfrown who \smallfrown VP$
      $VP \rightarrow V \smallfrown NP^3$

Conversions of this sort will permit generation of infinitely many sentences by that part of the grammar that deals with phrase structure, though not without some revision of the form of grammars.

Following the general plan outlined in §41, then, we will construct the level **P** in an abstract manner as a new point of view from which to discuss grammatical sentences, with new descriptive potential. Projection in terms of **C** yields a set $Gr_1(W)$ of sentences of bounded length. It is to be expected that the simplest description of this set in terms of the descriptive apparatus available in **P** will include a recursive characterization of certain elements. If we allow these recursions to run on freely, we will find that new and longer[4] sentences are generated. In this way we may hope to remedy the inadequacy of the analysis of grammaticalness provided by **C**. Our program now is to construct the level of phrase structure and to investigate its adequacy in remedying the deficiencies that led to its construction, in particular, the complexity and intuitive inadequacy of a grammar that does not go beyond word structure and the inability of such a grammar to account for the full set of grammatical sentences.[5]

50.1   The primes of the level **P** will be, for English, such representations of strings of words as *Sentence, Noun Phrase* (*NP*), *Verb Phrase* (*VP*), *Noun* (*N*), *Verb* (*V*), etc., as well as elements corresponding to individual words and the grammatically functioning morphemes of $\overline{\textbf{M}}$. Thus when we actually develop a model of **P** for English, we will expect to find such strings in **P** as $NP \smallfrown is \smallfrown NP$ and $Sentence \smallfrown John \smallfrown ing \smallfrown VP$. The

---

[3] See Chapter IV.
[4] We must be careful about permitting generation of sentences of length $\leqslant n$ by this method. Otherwise the simplest grammar will simply state that all word sequences are grammatical sentences. This absurdity is avoided if we insist that none of the new sentences generated on the level **P** be of length $\leqslant n$, i.e., that these grammatical sentences already be exhausted by the methods of Chapter V. No doubt some weaker condition can be found which will also exclude this absurd result, but it must be remembered that some condition is necessary.
[5] In the appendix to this chapter we study the possibility of remedying the latter inadequacy by incorporating recursive devices of a simpler kind into a grammar that does not go beyond the level of words or morphemes. On this matter, see also my "Three models for the description of language."

fact that the second string represents nonsense will have to be brought out in the grammar of English, but does not prevent this concatenation of elements from being a full-fledged string in **P** for English. We cannot set up a level distinction within **P** such that only words can be concatenated with words, only "first-level" phrases with other "first-level" phrases, etc. This is evident from the recursive character of **P** discussed above. For example, if **P** is constructed in accordance with **1**, *NP* and *VP* cannot be ordered relative to one another. It should be noted that, just as in the case of the level **C**, the names chosen for the elements of **P** in the English model (i.e., *NP*, *V*, etc.) have no significance and are devoid of content in the system developed here. That is, there will be no attempt here to define *Noun Phrase* within general linguistic theory, but only to define "constituent" in such a way that Noun Phrases, Verb Phrases, etc., will turn out to be constituents, and in fact, different constituents (cf. §19).

The level **P** is based on a relation of representation which we will denote by ρ. This is the relation holding, in English, between *NP* and *the⌢old⌢man*, between *Sentence* and *John⌢came⌢home*, between *Sentence* and *NP⌢VP*, between the latter and *John⌢came⌢home*, and between *N* and *John*. Tentatively, the converse of ρ can be read "is a." That is,

50.2

2 ρ (*NP*, *the⌢man*) if and only if *the⌢man* is a *NP*.

The relation ρ has the following properties:

3 ρ is irreflexive, asymmetrical, transitive, and nonconnected.

Thus ρ gives a partial ordering of the strings of **P**. There is a unique prime of **P** which essentially stands "first" in this ordering. This is the prime *Sentence* (*S*). *S* is the unique prime that represents every grammatical string. There are also certain primes that are "last" in this ordering, i.e., that bear the relation ρ to no string. We will call the set containing just these primes and the strings formed from them the set $\bar{P}$. Basically, $\bar{P}$ can be thought of as being the set of strings of morphological heads and syntactically functioning affixes (i.e., the subalgebra $\overline{\mathbf{M}}$ of **M** discussed in §46).[6]

---

[6] It is actually preferable not to insist that $\overline{\mathbf{M}}$ is directly embedded into **P** as $\bar{P}$, but rather a set of elements closely related to $\overline{\mathbf{M}}$. Thus there may be "dummy elements" in $\bar{P}$ which do not appear as morphemes (cf. below, on dummy carriers); there may be a distinction between bearers of long components as elements of $\overline{\mathbf{M}}$ and the long com-

Among the strings of $\bar{P}$, certain ones will correspond (under a mapping related to Φ^P) to grammatical strings of words (i.e., to strings of μ^W). These will be the strings derived from S by derivations of the level $\mathbf{P}$.[7] We will call these *terminal* strings. The correspondence between terminal strings and strings of μ^W may be quite loose. Thus the mapping in question may rearrange the order of elements of terminal strings and may specify their morphemic shape in various ways. The set of terminal strings—grammatical strings in $\bar{P}$—will be designated $Gr(P)$. Thus we want $Gr(P)$ to be mapped onto a set containing $Gr_1(W)$ (cf. §46 and §40).

There are other conditions that must be met by ρ and the set of terminal strings. We will require that the relation ρ be carried over under concatenation. Furthermore, we will require that ρ never relate two strings vacuously, in the sense that the given relation between the two strings plays no part in the description of any terminal string. A string which does appear in the description (derivation) of some terminal string will be called a *normal* string.

Definition 1. X is a *normal string* if and only if one of the following is the case:

   (a) $X = S$
   (b) X is a terminal string ($X \in Gr(P)$)
   (c) $\rho(S, X)$ and there is a terminal string Y such that $\rho(X, Y)$

We cannot require that every string that represents a terminal string be normal.[8] To see that this requirement would be too strong, suppose that

4 $\rho(Adj, young)$
      $\rho(N, men)$
      $\rho(V, like)$
      $\rho(N, sports)$

Thus $N^\frown V^\frown N$ represents the terminal string *men*$^\frown$*like*$^\frown$*sports*. The requirement under investigation provides that $\rho(S, N^\frown V^\frown N)$. But since ρ is transitive and carried over under concatenation, $Adj^\frown S$ represents

---

ponents themselves as minimal elements in $\bar{P}$; and there may be differences of order between the grammatical strings of $\bar{P}$ and the corresponding strings of $\overline{\mathbf{M}}$.

[7] See Chapter IV.

[8] Nor can we require normality of every string represented by S, as we will see in §54.

the terminal string $young^\frown men^\frown like^\frown sports$. If, however, we consider $Adj^\frown S$ to be a grammatical sentence form [i.e., if $\rho(S, Adj^\frown S)$], we will be assigning the constituent structure adjective–sentence to the sentence "young–men like sports,"[9] quite contrary to obvious requirements on any grammar of English. Thus the requirement is untenable, and we see that normality is a significant and restrictive additional condition on strings.

In the remainder of this chapter we will generally drop the super-script "**P**" on "$\rho^\mathbf{P}$," "$\Phi^\mathbf{P}$," etc., it being understood throughout that the elements under discussion belong to the level **P**.

To recapitulate, we are concerned with an algebra **P** in the sense of §18:   51

5     $\mathbf{P} = [P, ^\frown, =, Gr(P), \rho, \mu, \Phi]$

where P is the (finite and nonempty) set of primes. **P** meets the following conditions:

Axiom 1. ρ is irreflexive, asymmetrical, transitive, and nonconnected.

Definition 2. $\bar{P}$ is the set of strings X such that for no Y, $\rho(X, Y)$.

Axiom 2. If p is prime, $p \in \bar{P}$ if and only if there are X, Y such that $X^\frown p^\frown Y \in Gr(P)$.

Axiom 3. $p \in \bar{P}$ or there is an $X \in \bar{P}$ such that $\rho(p, X)$.

Axiom 4. If p_i is prime and $X \neq U \neq Y$, then $\rho(X^\frown Y, p_1^\frown ... ^\frown p_n)$ if and only if there is a $k < n$ such that (i), (ii), or (iii):

$$\begin{array}{lll} \text{(i)} & \rho(X, p_1^\frown ... ^\frown p_k) & \text{and} \quad \rho(Y, p_{k+1}^\frown ... ^\frown p_n) \\ \text{(ii)} & \rho(X, p_1^\frown ... ^\frown p_k) & \text{and} \quad Y = p_{k+1}^\frown ... ^\frown p_n \\ \text{(iii)} & X = p_1^\frown ... ^\frown p_k & \text{and} \quad \rho(Y, p_{k+1}^\frown ... ^\frown p_n) \end{array}$$

Axiom 5. There is a unique prime p such that for all $X \in Gr(P)$, $\rho(p, X)$. This prime is the element *Sentence* (S).

Definition 3. $\rho_1(X, Y)$ if and only if $\rho(X, Y)$ and there is no Z such that $\rho(X, Z)$ and $\rho(Z, Y)$.

---

[9] Analyzed into two constituents as shown by the dash.

Axiom 6.   Where p is prime, if $\rho_1(p, X)$ then there are Y, Z, W such that

(i) Y and Z are normal

(ii) $Y = Z\left[\dfrac{p}{(X, W)}\right]$ [10]

Other conditions on **P** will be discussed below, in particular, the conditions pertaining to Φ and $Gr(P)$.

Note that although there is a good sense in which S is the initial element in the ordering ρ, there may in general be primes $\neq S$ such that for no X, $\rho(X, p)$. For example, in the grammar of English there is no X such that $\rho(X, NP)$. Nor is S distinct from other primes in that there is no X, Y, Z such that $\rho(X, Y^\frown S^\frown Z)$. Again, in the grammar of English we will find that $\rho(NP, that^\frown S)$. S is distinct from all other primes in that we have

Theorem 1.   For all $p \in P$, $p = S$ or there are X, Y such that $\rho(S, X^\frown p^\frown Y)$.

52.1   There are several basic and interrelated notions that must be developed within the level **P**:

(1)   Given that $X \in Gr(P)$ and that Y is a substring of X, we want to know whether Y in some sense occurs "significantly" in X, that is, as a *constituent* of X. And if so, we want to know what kind of constituent Y is, i.e., which strings in P represent it (is it a NP, VP, $Adj^\frown N$, etc.).[11]

(2)   We must develop a set of **P**-markers which characterize grammatical utterances on the level **P**. Along with this, we will have to develop further the restricted relation between S and the strings of $Gr(P)$, which is narrower in general than ρ.

52.2   Perhaps the fundamental notion to be developed in **P** is the relation between *the$^\frown$man* and NP, etc., i.e., the relation which might be read "is a" (*the$^\frown$man* is a NP). This was proposed above as the reading for the converse of ρ, since $\rho(NP, the^\frown man)$. But this must be relativized to a given occurrence of the element in question in a given sentence. Thus "reading books" is a Noun Phrase in "reading books is his chief occu-

---

[10] See Definition 2, §22.
[11] But cf. §50.1.

pation," but not in "he was reading books on agriculture." This leads immediately to the notion of constituent and the first part of question (1) of §52.1.

Given the sentence $X =$ "that young pianist will play a Beethoven sonata," we would like to say that, e.g., "that young pianist," "will play a Beethoven sonata," "a Beethoven sonata," "young," etc., are among its constituents, whereas "pianist will" and "play a Beethoven" are not. A fundamental condition on constituent analysis, without which it would quickly become chaotic, is that within a sentence constituents may not overlap. But we are now faced with the problem that in order to maintain this requirement we must relativize the notion of constituent to a given "interpretation" of a sentence. To see this, consider the crucial case of *constructional homonymity.*[12] Sentences such as "I saw many old men and women," "they are flying planes," or "John kept the car in the garage" seem intuitively to have two interpretations, with conflicting constituent analyses. Among the constituents of the first can be either "old" and "men and women," or "old men" and "women," depending on whether the women are meant to be old or not. In the second, "flying planes" will be the constituent when the sentence is used to identify certain specks near the horizon, but the constituent will be "are flying" in answer to "What are John and Bill doing now?" In the third, the constituents will be "kept" and "the car in the garage" in the context "——but sold the one in the driveway," but certainly not when the sentence is interpreted as similar in structure to "John put the car in the garage."

In order to reflect this ambiguity, it is necessary to relativize the notion of constituent to a given interpretation of a sentence. This is the only way to retain nonoverlap of constituents and still to reach the only intuitively valid description.[13]

In other words, the notion "X is a Y" will have to be doubly relativized, first to a given occurrence of X in some given sentence, and second, to a particular interpretation of that sentence.

What exactly is meant by the phrase "a particular interpretation of a sentence"? This question leads us directly to the construction of

---

[12] See §§14.5, 17.

[13] As an aside, it should be reemphasized that the consideration of intuitive adequacy is perfectly in place here, since we are now trying to determine, presystematically, the form of an adequate system of constituent analysis; but it will have to be avoided, of course, when we consider the problem of selecting, for a given language, a model of the formal structure that we are now trying to develop (i.e., a grammar of this language). The method for discovering or evaluating grammars will have to be so constructed that the cases of constructional homonymity given above will turn out to have two analyses in the highest-valued grammar.

P-markers, for these elements will be the systematic analogues to the idea of an "interpretation" on the level **P**, in accordance with the general conception of levels from which we began.

53.1   To know whether a given occurrence of X in a string Z is a Y it is necessary and sufficient to know which strings in fact represent Z. Suppose that $Z = W_1 {}^\frown X {}^\frown W_2$ and there is a string $Z' = W_1 {}^\frown Y {}^\frown W_2$ that represents Z [i.e., $\rho(Z', Z)$].[14] In this case we say that with reference to Z', X is a Y in Z. For example, let

6 $X = are {}^\frown flying$
       $Y = V$
       $W_1 = they$
       $W_2 = planes$

Then $Z = W_1 {}^\frown X {}^\frown W_2$ is *they* ${}^\frown$ *are* ${}^\frown$ *flying* ${}^\frown$ *planes* and $Z' = W_1 {}^\frown Y {}^\frown W_2$ is *they* ${}^\frown V {}^\frown$ *planes*. If $\rho(V, are {}^\frown flying)$, then we will say that with respect to Z', $are {}^\frown flying$ is a V in *they* ${}^\frown$ *are* ${}^\frown$ *flying* ${}^\frown$ *planes*.

Suppose on the other hand that

7 $\bar{X} = flying {}^\frown planes$
       $\bar{Y} = NP$
       $\bar{W}_1 = they {}^\frown are$
       $[\bar{W}_2 = U]$

Then $\bar{Z} = \bar{W}_1 {}^\frown \bar{X} {}^\frown \bar{W}_2$ is *they* ${}^\frown$ *are* ${}^\frown$ *flying* ${}^\frown$ *planes* ($= Z$ of **6**) and $\bar{Z}' = \bar{W}_1 {}^\frown \bar{Y} {}^\frown \bar{W}_2$ is *they* ${}^\frown$ *are* ${}^\frown NP$. If $\rho(NP, flying {}^\frown planes)$, then we will say that with respect to $\bar{Z}'$, $flying {}^\frown planes$ is a NP in *they* ${}^\frown$ *are* ${}^\frown$ *flying* ${}^\frown$ *planes*. Thus the representing strings Z' and $\bar{Z}'$ give conflicting interpretations of Z ($= \bar{Z}$), since the constituents of Z with respect to Z' and $\bar{Z}'$ overlap.

Consideration of such examples suggests that we define "is a" in terms of a class of representing strings. If K is a class of strings containing Z and Z', where Z' differs from Z only in that it contains a substring Y replacing the substring X of Z, and if furthermore $\rho(Y, X)$ or $X = Y$, then we say that the given occurrence of X is a Y of Z with respect to (wrt) K. In the case of **P**-markers, the class K will have to be chosen so as to give a nonoverlapping interpretation of Z.

---

[14] Note that it follows from Axiom 4 that $\rho(W_1 {}^\frown Y {}^\frown W_2, W_1 {}^\frown X {}^\frown W_2)$ if and only if $\rho(Y, X)$.

Definition 4. $E_0(X, W, Y, Z, K)$ if and only if

    (i) K is a class of strings

    (ii) W is an occurrence of X in Z^{15}

    (iii) K contains the strings Z and $Z\left[\dfrac{Y}{(X, W)}\right]$

    (iv) $\rho(Y, X)$ or $X = Y$

The following immediate consequence of the definition plays a certain role below:

Theorem 2.   If there is an X, Y such that $E_0(X, W, Y, Z, K)$, then $E_0(U, W, U, Z, K)$.

In Chapter IV we developed the notion of a *derivation* of a string X **53.2** generated by a grammar of conversions. We will now concern ourselves more particularly with that fragment of the derivation that appears within the level **P**. In this case, the place of the conversions is taken by the statement of the relation ρ. For reasons which will appear below (§55.2), we will modify the notion of derivation, requiring that its initial string be not *Sentence* but $J^\frown Sentence^\frown J$, where J, indicating sentence boundary, is a prime of $\bar{P}$. For $Z \in \bar{P}$, then, a ρ-derivation of Z is a sequence of strings beginning with $J^\frown Sentence^\frown J$ and ending with $J^\frown Z^\frown J$, and such that each string of the sequence is represented by the string that precedes it in the sequence. More generally, given any two-place irreflexive relation Q between strings, we say that

Definition 5.   The sequence $D = (A_1,..., A_n)$ is a Q-derivation of Z if and only if

    (i) $A_1 = J^\frown S^\frown J;$ $A_n = J^\frown Z^\frown J$

    (ii) $Q(A_i, A_{i+1})$ $(i < n)$

    (iii) there is no Y such that $Q(Z, Y)$

Definition 6.   If D is a Q-derivation of Z, we call Z the *product* of D.

Definition 7.   The Q-derivation D is *restricted* just in case its product is terminal, i.e., in the set $Gr(P)$.

Theorem 3. Z is normal if and only if it is a step in some restricted ρ-derivation.

---

[15] See Definition 1, §20.

Theorem 4. Every string in $Gr(P)$ is the product of a ρ_1-derivation. Thus $Gr(P)$ is exactly the set of products of restricted ρ_1-derivations.

53.3   We can now proceed to construct **P**-markers. A **P**-marker of Z must give us all information about the constituent structure of Z, for a given interpretation . It must provide, with no ambiguity or overlaps, all information about E_0 for Z. The natural approach would thus be to take a certain class of strings representing Z as its **P**-marker.

It is clear that **P**-markers will be closely related to ρ_1-derivations. Since different interpretations of Z will certainly be related to different ρ_1-derivations, we might consider taking the set of steps of a ρ_1-derivation D as a **P**-marker. But the converse of this is not true, i.e., not all different derivations of Z correspond to different interpretations. Consider the ρ_1-derivations D_1 and D_2 of Z.[16]

8    $D_1 = (A_1 , A_2 , A_3 , A_4)$

where
$$A_1 = S$$
$$A_2 = b_1 {}^\frown b_2$$
$$A_3 = c_1 {}^\frown c_2 {}^\frown b_2$$
$$Z = A_4 = c_1 {}^\frown c_2 {}^\frown c_3 {}^\frown c_1$$

9    $D_2 = (A_1', A_2', A_3', A_4')$

where
$$A_1' = S$$
$$A_2' = b_1 {}^\frown b_2$$
$$A_3' = b_1 {}^\frown c_3 {}^\frown c_1$$
$$Z = A_4' = c_1 {}^\frown c_2 {}^\frown c_3 {}^\frown c_1$$

Clearly, these distinct derivations differ only in the order in which the constituents are developed, thus inessentially from the viewpoint of constituent interpretation. They give equivalent interpretations of Z in a certain sense, wheras a different constituent interpretation of Z would be given by D_3 :

10    $D_3 = (A_1'', A_2'', A_3'', A_4'')$

where
$$A_1'' = S$$
$$A_2'' = b_1 {}^\frown b_2$$
$$A_3'' = c_1 {}^\frown c_2 {}^\frown c_3 {}^\frown b_2$$
$$Z = A_4'' = c_1 {}^\frown c_2 {}^\frown c_3 {}^\frown c_1$$

---

[16] To simplify this discussion we neglect the requirement that steps of a Q-derivation must be bounded by J.

This may become clearer if we represent Q-derivations diagrammatically in an obvious way. Thus to D_1, D_2, and D_3 correspond the graphic representations of Figure 1.

D_1 and D_2 are clearly equivalent in a certain sense, while both differ from D_3. This equivalence can be recorded graphically by collapsing the diagrammatic representations, dropping all mere repetitions, as in Figure 2.

Thus D_1 and D_2 reduce to the same collapsed diagram, while D_3 reduces to a different diagram. These collapsed diagrams correspond to what we mean by different interpretations of Z.

It is clear that we could not define a **P**-marker as the set of "steps" of   53.4
a collapsed diagram, since all three collapsed diagrams have the same

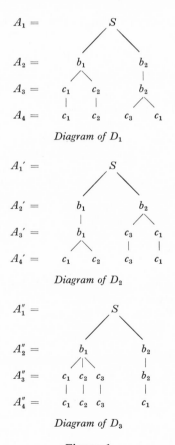

Diagram of D_1

Diagram of D_2

Diagram of D_3

Figure 1

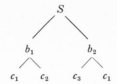

Collapsed diagram of D_1 and of D_2

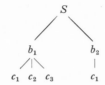

Collapsed diagram of D_3

Figure 2

three steps: S, $b_1 {}^\frown b_2$, $c_1 {}^\frown c_2 {}^\frown c_3 {}^\frown c_1$. We must require that the **P**-marker contain $b_1 {}^\frown c_3 {}^\frown c_1$ and $c_1 {}^\frown c_2 {}^\frown b_2$ in the case corresponding to D_1 and D_2, and contain $b_1 {}^\frown c_1$ and $c_1 {}^\frown c_2 {}^\frown c_3 {}^\frown b_2$ in the case corresponding to D_3, if we are to be able to state the constituent structure correctly in terms of the **P**-marker. In other words, given a **P**-marker M of Z, we will say that an occurrence W of X is a constituent of Z wrt M if M contains the string

11    $$Z\left[\frac{p}{(X,\,W)}\right]$$

for some prime p. In this case, $E_0(X, W, p, Z, M)$.

Looking back at D_1 and D_2, then, we see that the set of all those strings which are steps of D_1 or steps of D_2 can serve as a **P**-marker, but not the set of steps of either of these derivations alone. More generally, we call two derivations equivalent if they have the same collapsed diagram and thus differ only in the order of development of their terms. Then the set of steps of the derivations that constitute an equivalence class of derivations can serve as the **P**-marker of their common product. This equivalence, which has its graphic counterpart in identity of collapsed diagrams, we must now proceed to define carefully.

53.5   [Omitted.] This section gives a precise definition of the notion of equivalence of derivations in the intended sense, namely, correspondence to the same collapsed diagram.

We can now restate formally the notion of **P**-marker proposed in §53.4.   53.6
Suppose that $\{D_1, ..., D_n\}$ is an equivalence class of ρ_1-derivations of Z
and that W is an occurrence of some segment X of Z which is, in the
presystematic sense, a constituent of Z. Then there will be some derivation D_i in which (X, W) is the last constituent to be developed. That is,
at a certain step A_m of D_i, Z will be completely reduced to primes of $\bar{P}$
except for the given instance of X, i.e., for some prime p,

$$12 \qquad A_m = Z\left[\frac{p}{(X, W)}\right]$$

We can therefore define **P**-markers, as suggested in §53.4:

Definition 8. K is a **P**-marker of Z if and only if there is an equivalence
class $\{D_1, ..., D_n\}$ of ρ_1-derivations of Z such that for each i,
$D_i = (A_{i_1}, ..., A_{i_{m(i)}})$, and $K = \{A_{i_j} \mid j \leqslant m(i), i \leqslant n\}$

Theorem 5.   There is a one-to-one correspondence between **P**-
markers and equivalence classes of ρ_1-derivations. Each **P**-marker
K is the **P**-marker of a unique string $Z \in \bar{P}$ which is the product of
each derivation in the equivalence class corresponding to K.

Definition 9.   If K is a **P**-marker of Z, then Z is also called the *product*
of K.

Definition 10. (X, W) is a *constituent* of Z wrt K if and only if W is
an occurrence of X in Z, $Z \in K$, and there is a prime p such that
$$Z\left[\frac{p}{(X, W)}\right] \in K.$$

Theorem 6.   In this case, $E_0(X, W, p, Z, K)$.

Definition 11. $X \leqslant Y$ if and only if there are Z, W such that
$Y = Z{}^\frown X{}^\frown W$; $X < Y$ if and only if $X \leqslant Y$ and $X \neq Y$.

Definition 12.   A class K of strings gives a *consistent analysis* of $Z \in K$
if and only if for all X, W, X', W', if $(X, W{}^\frown X)$ and $(X', W'{}^\frown X')$
are constituents of Z wrt K and $W' < W$, then either $W'{}^\frown X' \leqslant W$
or $W{}^\frown X \leqslant W'{}^\frown X'$.

Put informally, if K gives a consistent analysis of Z then no two
constituents of Z wrt K overlap unless one is included in the other.

Theorem 7. A **P**-marker gives a consistent analysis of its product.

54.1   It has been pointed out above that not all derivations lead to grammatical strings, i.e., strings of $Gr(P)$, even though the product of every derivation must be a string in $\bar{P}$. We must now consider what is involved in the construction of *restricted* derivations that do produce terminal strings (cf. §53.2).

Definition 13. **P** is *restricted* if and only if every ρ-derivation in **P** is restricted.

Theorem 8. If **P** is restricted then

   (i)   if $\rho(Sentence, Z)$ and Z is in $\bar{P}$, then Z is in $Gr(P)$
   (ii) if $\rho(Sentence, Z)$, then Z is normal

Theorem 9. For any language, there is a way of defining ρ such that **P** will be restricted.

   In particular, let ρ hold between *Sentence* and each string Z of $Gr(P)$, and between nothing else. Then P (the set of primes of **P**) contains just S and the primes of $\bar{P}$, and ρ is exactly the same relation as ρ_1, each ρ-derivation containing exactly two steps.
   Why should we not require that **P** be restricted since we know that this requirement can be fulfilled in one or another way? The reason is that this would give a conception of constituent analysis clearly at variance with the intended one, in the case of any sufficiently complex language. This is obviously the case when **P** is restricted in the manner just described, but it must be the case for any restriction of **P**. We might, in fact, rule out systems of the sort just proposed by adding to **P** the natural condition, call it C, that $\{X \mid \rho_1(p, X)\}$ is finite for $p \in P$.
   To see this, suppose that **P** is restricted. Suppose that $\rho(Sentence, ...P_i ...)$, $\rho_1(P_i, Z_j)$, and $\rho_1(P_i, Z_k)$, where P_i is a prime, and ...———... is any context. Suppose furthermore that P_i is the only prime which represents either Z_j or Z_k. Then Z_j and Z_k are completely mutually substitutable as constituents in normal strings. But this is much too strong a requirement to be placed in general on constituents. There will, for instance, be various strings which we would like to say are noun phrases, even though they do not all appear grammatically (with first-order grammaticalness) as subjects of the same verb phrases, although

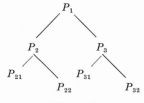

Figure 3

each occurs grammatically with some verb phrase. This is the property of linguistic systems sometimes known as *selection*.[17]

Consider for example the case diagrammed in Figure 3, and corresponding to

13 $\rho(P_1, P_2^{\frown}P_3)$
       $\rho(P_2, P_{21})$, $\rho(P_2, P_{22})$
       $\rho(P_3, P_{31})$, $\rho(P_3, P_{32})$
       $P_{21}^{\frown}P_{31}$ and $P_{22}^{\frown}P_{32}$ are strings of $Gr(P)$
       $P_{21}^{\frown}P_{32}$ and $P_{22}^{\frown}P_{31}$ are not in $Gr(P)$

A model of **13** in English is easily found. Consider the models M_1 and M_2 :

M_1 : $P_1 = S$; $P_2 = NP$; $P_3 = VP$; $P_{21} = John$
       $P_{22} = the^{\frown}rearming^{\frown}of^{\frown}Germany$; $P_{31} = is^{\frown}at^{\frown}dinner$
       $P_{32} = is^{\frown}Western^{\frown}policy$
       $Gr(P)$ contains $John^{\frown}is^{\frown}at^{\frown}dinner$,
            $the^{\frown}rearming^{\frown}of^{\frown}Germany^{\frown}is^{\frown}Western^{\frown}policy$
       $Gr(P)$ does not contain $John^{\frown}is^{\frown}Western^{\frown}policy$,
            $the^{\frown}rearming^{\frown}of^{\frown}Germany^{\frown}is^{\frown}at^{\frown}dinner$

M_2 : $P_1 = Sentence$; $P_2 = NP$; $P_3 = VP$; $P_{21} = a^{\frown}man$
       $P_{31} = is^{\frown}coming^{\frown}today$; $P_{22} = several^{\frown}men$;
            $P_{32} = are^{\frown}coming^{\frown}today$
       $Gr(P)$ contains $a^{\frown}man^{\frown}is^{\frown}coming^{\frown}today$,
            $several^{\frown}men^{\frown}are^{\frown}coming^{\frown}today$
       $Gr(P)$ does not contain $a^{\frown}man^{\frown}are^{\frown}coming^{\frown}today$,
            $several^{\frown}men^{\frown}is^{\frown}coming^{\frown}today$

These are (given **13**) subsytems of a nonrestricted system **P**. For descriptive adequacy, then, we must have a nonrestricted **P** from which

---

[17] See §39. The fact that **P** is nonrestricted will play a certain role in establishing transformations in English; see below.

P-markers and constituent structure can be derived. Thus we will want to say that *John, the⌢rearming⌢of⌢Germany, a⌢man,* and *several⌢men* are all *NP*'s, that there is a general $NP⌢VP$ (i.e., "actor–action") form of sentence, etc. On the other hand, we want to construct a grammar of English that will provide derivations for exactly the members of $Gr(P)$. And we want this grammar to be related to **P** in such a way that given **P**, we can derive the grammar, and given the grammar, we can determine the underlying system of phrase structure **P** on which it is based, and the constituent analysis that this underlying **P** carries along with it.

The problem posed in the last paragraph can be construed as the problem of constructing a relation ρ^r such that all ρ^r-derivations are restricted, and all restricted ρ_1-derivations are ρ^r-derivations. We will define $\rho_1{}^r$ as the relation which holds between successive steps of restricted ρ_1-derivations. That is, suppose that $(A_1, ..., A_k)$ is a restricted ρ_1-derivation. Then it will be the case that $\rho^r(A_1, A_2)$, $\rho_1{}^r(A_2, A_3)$, etc. ρ^r will then be related to $\rho_1{}^r$ as ρ is related to ρ_1. That is, if $(A_1, ..., A_k)$ is a restricted ρ_1-derivation, then it is the case that $\rho^r(A_1, A_2)$, $\rho^r(A_1, A_3)$,..., $\rho^r(A_1, A_k)$, $\rho^r(A_2, A_3)$, $\rho^r(A_2, A_4)$,..., $\rho^r(A_2, A_k)$, etc. Then the $\rho_1{}^r$-derivations are exactly the restricted ρ_1-derivations, and the ρ^r-derivations are exactly the restricted ρ-derivations. Given **P**, we can determine all restricted ρ-derivations in **P**; hence we can determine ρ^r. We will see below that **P** can be axiomatized in such a way that ρ is reconstructible from ρ^r as well. In the simplest case, we will determine ρ from ρ^r in the following manner: suppose that $\rho^r(W_1⌢P_i⌢W_2, W_1⌢X⌢W_2)$, where P_i is a prime. Then we know that there is some restricted ρ_1-derivation which contains the step $A_k = W_1⌢P_i⌢W_2$ and the step $A_{k+1} = W_1⌢X⌢W_2$ which is formed from A_k by replacing P_i in A_k by X. In this case we will say that $\rho_1(P_i, X)$. We will see that, with some qualifications, we will be able to determine the relation ρ completely [that is, we will be able to determine for which strings X and Y it is the case that $\rho(X, Y)$] in this manner. This means that given the grammar of the language (constructed in terms of ρ^r and giving us all ρ^r-derivations, hence all restricted ρ-derivations) we will be able to reconstruct completely the relation ρ and the system of phrase structure **P**. Of the two prerequisites for the level **P** stated at the outset of §52 (§52.1), ρ will satisfy the first and ρ^r the second.

The relation between **P** and the grammar as stated in the last few paragraphs has no content unless we state what we mean by a grammar. We will go into this below, arriving at a conception like that of Chapter IV, except for an extension of the notion of generation. Meanwhile, we assume that whatever a grammar is, it must be related to the relation ρ^r in the sense that ρ^r is uniquely recoverable from the grammar, and a grammar can be constructed (perhaps in various ways) in terms of ρ^r. We then require that **P** be related biuniquely to ρ^r, in the sense that **P** be uniquely recoverable from ρ^r, and ρ^r be uniquely constructible from **P**.

By definition, the set of ρ-derivations is uniquely determined by **P**.   54.2
Thus if ρ^r is defined to uniqueness in terms of ρ, one part of this biunique relation will hold. But the requirement that **P** be recoverable from ρ^r is more troublesome.

We want ρ^r to be a relation f such that

14   the set of f-derivations is exactly the set of restricted ρ-derivations.

From (14) it follows that $f \subset \rho$. It also follows that

15   for normal strings X and Y, $\rho(X, Y) \Leftrightarrow f(X, Y)$.

From Axiom 4 (cf. §51) we know that ρ can be recovered from the statement of ρ for the domain of primes. Furthermore, ρ is simply the ancestral of ρ_1. It is in fact sufficient to know ρ_1, with the domain limited to primes, in order to reconstruct ρ completely. But Axiom 6 tells us that if $\rho_1(P_i, X)$ (for P_i prime), then there are two normal strings Y_j and Y_k differing only in that Y_j contains P_i where Y_k contains X. Then of course $\rho_1(Y_j, Y_k)$, and by 15, $f(Y_j, Y_k)$. In fact, $f_1(Y_j, Y_k)$, where f_1 is defined analogously to ρ_1 (cf. Definition 3, §51).

But it is also the case that if $f_1(Y_j, Y_k)$ then $\rho_1(Y_j, Y_k)$. And clearly this means that Y_k differs from Y_j only in that a single prime P_i of Y_j is replaced by some X in Y_k. In this case, $\rho_1(P_i, X)$.

We see then that if for every two normal strings Y_j, Y_k, we know whether or not $f_1(Y_j, Y_k)$, and if we always know in addition *which* prime of Y_j is replaced by some X in forming Y_k, then we can recover ρ completely from f_1, and hence from f, since f_1 is defined in terms of f. Thus we are very close to being able to meet the second half of the biuniqueness condition. The difficulty is that we cannot always tell, given that $f_1(Y_j, Y_k)$, which prime of Y_j is replaced by some X in forming Y_k.

For instance, suppose it is the case that $\rho_1(P_r, P_r \frown P_s)$ and $\rho_1(P_t, P_s \frown P_t)$. Then given $Y_j = ...P_r \frown P_t...$ we can form $Y_k = ...P_r \frown P_s \frown P_t...$ [where $\rho_1(Y_j, Y_k)$] by converting P_r to $P_r \frown P_s$ or by converting P_t to $P_s \frown P_t$. Thus given $f_1(Y_j, Y_k)$ we could not tell which prime of Y_j was converted in forming Y_k.

The most straightforward way to avoid the problem is simply to exclude recursions such as $\rho_1(P_i, P_i{}^\frown X)$ and $\rho_1(P_i, X{}^\frown P_i)$.

Axiom 7. There are no P_i, X (P_i a prime) such that $\rho_1(P_i, P_i{}^\frown X)$ or $\rho_1(P_i, X{}^\frown P_i)$.

Then given f meeting **14**, we can define ρ_1 by means of

Theorem 10. Where P_i is a prime, $\rho_1(P_i, X)$ if and only if there are strings W, Z such that $f_1(W{}^\frown P_i{}^\frown Z, W{}^\frown X{}^\frown Z)$.

Axiom 7 limits the possibility of recursive statements,[18] while not of course excluding all so-called "endocentric constructions." Less restrictive formulations are possible, but it may be that natural accounts of actual endocentric constructions do not violate this condition. We might proceed somewhat differently, defining ρ_1 in terms of a more complex relation g such that if $g(P_i, X, W_1, W_2)$ then $f_1(W_1{}^\frown P_i{}^\frown W_2, W_1{}^\frown X{}^\frown W_2)$, P_i a prime. In effect, g states that $P_i \rightarrow X$ in env. W_1——W_2 (cf. Definition 1, §27.1). Then $\rho_1(P_i, X)$ if for some W_1, W_2, $g(P_i, X, W_1, W_2)$. The relation g in general contains more information than can be derived from f. An f_1-derivation would suffice to determine a **P**-marker, given g, if instead of Axiom 7 we were to impose the less restrictive condition: if $...P_i{}^\frown P_j...$ is normal (P_i, P_j primes), then there is no X such that $\rho_1(P_i, P_i{}^\frown X)$ and $\rho_1(P_j, X{}^\frown P_j)$. We will continue, however, assuming Axiom 7, disregarding the alternative possibility just sketched.

If we define ρ^r meeting condition **14** to uniqueness in terms of ρ, then we can establish the required biunique relation between **P** and the grammar constructed in terms of ρ^r.

The obvious way to define ρ^r is as the minimal relation meeting condition **14**:

Definition 14. $\rho^r(X, Y)$ if and only if X and Y are normal and $\rho(X, Y)$.

Definition 15. $\rho_1{}^r(X, Y)$ if and only if $\rho^r(X, Y)$ and there is no Z such that $\rho^r(X, Z)$ and $\rho^r(Z, Y)$.

Theorem 11. ρ^r is the minimal relation meeting **14**.

---

[18] That is, it limits the possibility of having the same superscript on both sides of the identity sign in Harris's treatment of phrase structure; cf. *Methods*, Chapter 16. Note that we may still have $\rho(P_i, P_i{}^\frown X)$, $\rho(P_i, X{}^\frown P_i)$, or $\rho_1(P_i, X{}^\frown P_i{}^\frown Y)$.

Theorem 12. By Theorem 10, ρ is definable in terms of ρ^r.

We have thus taken ρ^r to be the relation that connects the steps of restricted ρ-derivations. We can gain some further insight into this relation by asking to what extent the axioms for ρ (cf. §51) can be satisfied by a relation f meeting condition **14** in a nonrestricted system. Such a relation f satisfies all axioms except for Axiom 4. But f, in a nonrestricted **P**, cannot satisfy Axiom 4 generally from left to right. In other words, in a nonrestricted **P** it will be the case that there are compound strings X and Y such that $f(X, Y)$, but this relation cannot be decomposed so that f holds term by term between each prime of X and some part of Y. Thus f carries certain representations into other representations *only in certain contexts*. This is the basic idea behind the restriction of ρ to ρ^r.

The notion of restriction leads directly to the consideration of long components.[19] It might be possible to extend the formal systems which have been considered so as to permit these to be introduced in an effective way. The basic contribution of long components is that they offer a way of restricting **P** without violating the prerequisite of descriptive adequacy, as would be the result if **P** were restricted directly. This can be illustrated clearly by the example diagrammed in Figure 3 (§54.1).

    54.3

Suppose that our notations were extended so that the following would be significant:

16 $P_1 \rightarrow P_2{}^k {}^\frown P_3{}^k$
          $k \rightarrow a$
          $k \rightarrow b$

And suppose further that by convention, all identical superscripts assume the same value in derivations. Then we could interpret $P_2{}^a$ as P_{21}, $P_2{}^b$ as P_{22}, $P_3{}^a$ as P_{31}, and $P_3{}^b$ as P_{32}. The derivations would now work out exactly right, the algebra would be restricted, and the notations NP, VP, etc., would be retained with all essential generality.

This method might in fact be useful for M_2 of §54.1, i.e., in the case of agreement in number. But even if we did extend our formalism so as to admit this possibility, we would still not want to apply it for M_1, because the vast selectional complex involved here would require a tremendous number of components, and a very inelegant characterization.

---

[19] See Harris, *Methods*, and for a detailed example, my *Morphophonemics of Modern Hebrew*.

This is an important question, deserving a much fuller treatment,[20] but it will quickly lead into areas where the present formal apparatus may be inadequate. The difficult question of discontinuity is one such problem.[21] Discontinuities are handled in the present treatment by construction of permutational mappings from **P** to **W**, but it may turn out that they must ultimately be incorporated somehow into **P** itself.

55.1 ρ^r is the relation between steps of a restricted ρ-derivation. Knowing it, we can construct all such derivations, and, by Theorem 10, we can reconstruct the system of phrase structure and the notion of constituent completely. However, the problem of actually bridging the gap between this theory and an actual grammar, or more generally, a fixed form of grammars for which the notion of simplicity has been given some meaning (cf. Chapter IV), is still unsolved.

In Chapter IV, we presented a certain conception of a grammar as a sequence of conversion statements "$\alpha \to \beta$," where α and β are strings, and derivations are constructed mechanically by proceeding down the list of conversions, interpreting "$\alpha \to \beta$" as the instruction "rewrite α as β." In Chapter VI, we have seen how a grammar of this sort might be developed from levels lower than $\bar{\textbf{M}}$, so that derivations of grammatical utterances from strings in $\bar{\textbf{M}}$ can be mechanically constructed. We must now show how the statement of the structure **P** can be converted into a grammar of this form, so that we can derive (in the sense of Chapter IV) strings in $\bar{\textbf{M}}$ from the representation *Sentence*. This will complete (in outline) the statement of how the hierarchy of conventional levels is related to the form of grammars. We know from the biuniqueness relation between **P** and ρ^r that it is sufficient to show how the statement of ρ^r can be converted in general into a sequence of conversions of the form "$\alpha \to \beta$," in such a way that ρ^r can be uniquely recovered from this sequence of conversions.

We can look at this in a slightly different way. One way to give a description of the level **P** is actually to list ρ^r, i.e., to present a list of pairs of strings (X, Y) such that $\rho^r(X, Y)$. But since we would like to make the description of **P** as simple as possible, we would like to discover a more limited relation than ρ^r in terms of which ρ^r can be reconstructed. We will now consider various ways of *reducing* ρ^r. The condition that all such reductions must meet is that the set of derivations remain invariant, that any new technique of providing a description of phrase structure must lead to exactly the set of derivations obtained from ρ^r. We will

---

[20] See my *Morphophonemics of Modern Hebrew* for a specific and fairly complex instance of such a system.

[21] See references of Chapter III, Note 10, for discussion of this problem.

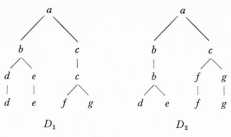

Figure 4

see that the attempt to reduce ρ^r in this manner leads to a sequence of conversion statements of the form "$\alpha \rightarrow \beta$," i.e., to a grammar in the sense of Chapter IV. In this development, we retrace some of the ground covered in Chapter IV, but now building our case on examples drawn from the level **P**.

Reduction 0.   First it is clear that ρ_1 is such a limited relation. Thus   55.2
the grammar might consist of a complete statement of ρ_1^r, i.e., a
characterization of all pairs (α, β) such that $\rho_1^r(\alpha, \beta)$.

But even this list is "redundant" in the sense that a proper sublist would provide all the information necessary to reconstruct **P**. Given a single member of each equivalence class of derivations (see paragraph 1, §53.6), we can mechanically construct all derivations. But complete knowledge of ρ_1^r enables us to construct all derivations directly, and thus contains an overspecification of **P**.

Reduction 1.   Construct R_1, a narrower relation than ρ_1^r, from which
we can reconstruct one derivation from each equivalence class.

To see that R_1 may be narrower than ρ_1^r, consider the simple case we have discussed before, diagrammed in Figure 4. Given just this sytem of derivations, a complete account of ρ_1^r would be the set of pairs[22]

17 (a,bc)
          (bc,dec) (bc,bfg)
          $(dec,defg)$ $(bfg,defg)$

whereas the set of pairs in the left-hand column alone will suffice to give just D_1, and can thus be taken as R_1. Thus the grammar can be shortened (simplified) by dropping the right-hand column, which can be recovered mechanically, given R_1.

---

[22] We will often drop the concatenation sign where there can be no ambiguity.

Reduction 2. Drop from each pair in R_1 the terms which play no role in the derivation, i.e., those which are not developed and do not determine how the development takes place. The relation which consists of just the pairs which play a role in the formation of derivations can be called R_2.

Thus R_1 from **17** can be replaced by

18 (a,bc) (b,de) (c,fg)

which can be taken as R_2 in this instance. Note that if we had performed Reduction 2 directly on $\rho_1{}^r$, we would still have obtained **18**. Thus Reduction 1 was superfluous in this case. Note further that R_2 is exactly ρ_1, limited to its prime domain. This will be the case whenever the system is restricted, as is the system of derivations given in Figure 4.

To take a more significant instance, consider the system D_1, D_2, D_3, where D_1 and D_2 are as in Figure 4, and D_3 is shown in Figure 5. The system D_1, D_2, D_3 is now nonrestricted. $\rho_1{}^r$ for this system is **17** plus

19 (a,bh) $(bh,\delta\epsilon h)$

Applying Reduction 1 to $\rho_1{}^r$ in this case, we obtain as R_1

20 (a,bc) (a,bh)
        (bc,dec) $(bh,\delta\epsilon h)$
        $(dec,defg)$

Applying Reduction 2 to R_1, we obtain as R_2

21 (a,bc) (a,bh)
        (bc,dec) $(bh,\delta\epsilon h)$
        (c,fg)

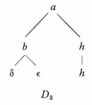

D_3

Figure 5

Figure 6

Applying Reduction 2 to $\rho_1{}^r$ (**17** plus **19**) directly gives **21** plus

22 (bf,def)

Thus Reductions 1 and 2 are independent.

Where there are an infinite number of ρ_1-derivations, $\rho_1{}^r$ and R_1 will be infinite, but R_2 may be finite, and in fact will be finite if we add the natural additional condition that for every prime p, $\{X \mid \rho_1(p, X)\}$ be finite (cf. condition C, §54.1). Thus R_2 will provide a finite specification of ρ, as required for a grammar.

Reduction 2 provides a certain possibility of ambiguity which may make it impossible to reconstruct **P** correctly from R_2. This results from the fact that R_2 relates *parts* of normal strings. Suppose that we have the derivation D_4 as in Figure 6 as our only derivation in **P**. Then R_1 will be given by the set of pairs containing just (a,ab) and (ab,cdb), as will R_2. But our general rule for reconstructing R_1 from R_2 will tell us that if $R_2(X, Y)$ and $W_1{}^\frown X{}^\frown W_2$ is a string in a derivation, then $W_1{}^\frown Y{}^\frown W_2$ can be the next string in the derivation, and $R_1(W_1{}^\frown X{}^\frown W_2, W_1{}^\frown Y{}^\frown W_2)$. But in the case of D_4 as in Figure 6, this rule of reconstruction will allow us to reconstruct $R_1(ab,abb)$, since $R_1(a,ab)$ and ab is a string in a derivation. Hence we can also have the derivation D_5 as in Figure 7 contrary to assumption.

The difficulty here is that we cannot distinguish between the case where a string α can be rewritten as β in a derivation whenever α is part of a line (i.e., in any context) and the case where the rewriting can only take place when α is the whole line (i.e., in the null context). We can best resolve this ambiguity by revising slightly our notion of *derivation*

Figure 7

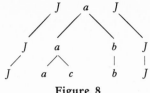

Figure 8

as suggested in §53.2. We have considered a derivation to be a sequence of strings beginning with *Sentence* (*S*) and ending with a string in $\bar{P}$. We now consider a derivation to be a sequence beginning with $J^\frown S^\frown J$ and ending with a string in $\bar{P}$, where J is a prime of $\bar{P}$ indicating utterance initial and utterance final position (i.e., J will be one of the zero elements $\emptyset_i$ of the level **P**). Then D_4 will be rewritten as shown in Figure 8. R_1 will be given by the set of pairs $(JaJ, JabJ)$, $(JabJ, JacbJ)$; and R_1 will be given by the set of pairs (aJ, abJ), (ab, acb). The reconstruction of R_1 from R_2 now gives D_4 as the only derivation on the level **P**, as required in this case.

Clearly, R_2 is the simplest relation in terms of which **P** can be reconstructed (it contains fewest pairs, and each pair is as short as possible). Thus if we wish to construct an even more concise grammar than a listing of R_2, we cannot search for a simpler relation, but must consider features of the listing itself. That is, we must begin a meta-linguistic investigation of grammars. Thus we now investigate the possibility of utilizing the actual form of the presentation of the grammar in terms of R_2 to effect a further reduction.

We have seen that the system of phrase structure for a given language can be recovered from the relation R_2, that is, from a list of the pairs (X, Y) such that $R_2(X, Y)$. Suppose we have such a list. Then if we preserve the order of the listing, and we rewrite "$R_2(X, Y)$" as "$X \to Y$" we have a *linear grammar* of the sort discussed in §28. The linear grammar is a sequence of conversion statements $S_1, ..., S_n$, where each S_i is of the form $X_i \to Y_i$. We can produce derivations from this linear grammar by applying the conversions S_i (interpreted as the instruction "rewrite X_i as Y_i") in sequence. Among the S_i we distinguish between obligatory conversions that must be applied in the production of every derivation, and permissible conversions that may or may not be applied. There are only a finite number of ways to run through the linear grammar, applying all obligatory and some permissible conversions; hence only a finite number of derivations can be produced by the linear grammar $S_1, ..., S_n$. This was not a difficulty on earlier levels, but we know that infinitely many sentences must be generated by some mechanism in the grammar. We can permit this infinite generation on the level **P** by allowing the possibility of running through the linear grammar $S_1,..., S_n$ an indefinite number of times in the production of derivations. If the derivation formed by running through the sequence of conversions does not terminate with a string in $\bar{P}$, then we run through the sequence again. Thus we can understand the linear grammar to be the sequence of conversions $S_1,..., S_n,\ S_1,..., S_n,\ S_1,..., S_n,....$ We then say that a derivation D is *recursively produced* by the linear grammar $S_1,..., S_n$. We define a *proper linear grammar* as a linear grammar which is so constructed that it is impossible to run through it over and over again vacuously. Our final reduction, Reduction 3, then, will be to construct a proper linear grammar from which R_2 can be completely reconstructed. That is, we construct a proper linear grammar which recursively produces just those derivations which are formed by the use of the relation R_2 (i.e., all $\rho_1{}^r$-derivations).

We now proceed with a more careful development of the course sketched   55.3
in the last paragraph. The grammar will be given by a list of statements of the form (α, β), one statement for each (α, β) such that $R_2(\alpha, \beta)$. The significant formal feature of this list of statements is that it can be given in a linear order. It is natural to inquire whether a manipulation of this order can provide a simpler grammar.[23]

Suppose that we have a sequence $S_1,..., S_n$, where S_i is an ordered pair (X_i, Y_i), X_i and Y_i being strings. In accordance with the conception of grammar in Chapter IV, we can interpret such a sequence (or the sequence of statements corresponding to it) as instructions for constructing derivations. That is, we might construct a definition something like this:

23 D is *produced* from $S_1,..., S_n$ if there is a sequence $\alpha_1,..., \alpha_{n+1}$
such that:

(i) $\alpha_1 = X_1$
(ii) for $i \geqslant 1$, α_{i+1} is formed from α_i by replacing X_i in α_i by Y_i (thus $\alpha_{i+1} = \alpha_i$ if X_i does not occur in α_i)
(iii) D is formed from $\alpha_1,..., \alpha_{n+1}$ by dropping each α_i which is identical with α_{i-1}, i.e., all repetitions

---

[23] We have seen some general reasons why this may be the case in §28. In my *Morphophonemics of Modern Hebrew* it is shown that in practice, manipulation of order can effect great reduction on the morphophonemic level. Now we investigate the function of order in simplifying our characterization of **P**, citing later just one of the many ways in which such simplification can come about.

But this formulation is too rigid. First of all, X_i may occur several times in α_i, so that S_i must apply several times in forming α_{i+1}. Secondly, this formulation does not cover the case in which S_i does not apply, even though X_i appears in α_i. That is, it leaves no room for a certain indeterminacy in the production of derivations that should be built into the grammar. In English, for instance, we may have $\rho_1(NP, N)$ and $\rho_1(NP, A^\frown N)$. In listing R_2, then, we will have the pairs

24 (NP, N)
$(NP, A^\frown N)$

But if we defined production as in **23**, and if **24** is part of the grammar, then ...$A^\frown N$... will never occur in a derivation, since NP will always be eliminated by the earlier statement. Thus we must distinguish between statements of the grammar which are obligatory and those which are optional. We can thus prefix to each statement either "B" (obligatory) or "P" (optional), and can formulate the definition of "production" in terms of a sequence of statements of this form. Combining these two inadequacies, we see that we must also provide for the case in which X_i occurs in several places in α_i, but only certain of these occurrences are replaced by Y_i. We must define production, then, so that produced derivations may have any of these various properties.

Suppose in the following that we have a sequence $S = (S_1,..., S_n)$ of ordered triples, where $S_i = (I_i, X_i, Y_i)$, and I_i is either B or P, these being distinct elements of some sort that we can construct in **P**. Then S_i can be understood as the statement "it is obligatory to rewrite X_i as Y_i," if $I_i = B$, or as the statement "it is permitted to rewrite X_i as Y_i," if $I_i = P$.

Preparatory to defining "production," consider certain sequences t, α, and $Z^{(i)}$ which jointly meet the following condition, given the sequence $S = (S_1,..., S_n)$, where $S_i = (I_i, X_i, Y_i)$ as above:

25   (I) t is a sequence of numbers $t = (t_1,..., t_{k+1})$ such that $t_1 = 1$ and $t_i < t_{i+1}$

(II) α is a sequence of strings, $\alpha = (\alpha_1, \alpha_2,..., \alpha_{t_{k+1}})$

(III) $Z^{(i)}$ $(1 \leqslant i \leqslant k)$ is a sequence of strings, $Z^{(i)} = (Z_1^{(i)},..., Z_{m_i}^{(i)})$, where $m_i = t_{i+1} - t_i$, and

(i) $Z_1^{(i)} > Z_2^{(i)} > \cdots > Z_{m_i}^{(i)}$ [24]

---

[24] Where $X < Y$ means that there are strings Z, W such that $Y = ZXW$ and $Z \neq U$ or $W \neq U$, i.e., X is a continuous proper substring of Y. $>$, $\leqslant$, and $\geqslant$ are defined in the obvious way in terms of $<$.

(ii)   if $X_i \leqslant \alpha_{t_i}$ and $S_i = (B, X_i, Y_i)$, then $Z_j^{(i)}(1 \leqslant j \leqslant m_i)$ is an occurrence of X_i in α_{t_i}

(iii) if $Z_j^{(i)}$ is not an occurrence of X_i in α_{t_i}, then $Z_j^{(i)} = U$

(IV)   For each i, $t_{i+1} - t_i \leqslant$ the number of distinct occurrences of X_i in α_{t_i}, if $X_i \leqslant \alpha_{t_i}$; equality holds if $S_i = (B, X_i, Y_i)$

We then take α to be the derivation (when repetitions have been struck out). α_1 will be X_1, and for $i \geqslant 1$, if $t_i < j \leqslant t_{i+1}$, the rule used in forming α_j will be S_i. The effect of this rule will be to replace an instance of X_i in α_{j-1} by Y_i. Because of the way that occurrence has been defined, we must be sure that in the sequence of steps using rule S_i to replace occurrences of X_i by Y_i in α_{t_i}, occurrences to the right (literally, longer occurrences) are replaced first (cf. §20). We see that S_i is applied $m_i = t_{i+1} - t_i$ times in constructing the derivation, where m_i is the number of distinct occurrences of X_i in α_{t_i} if S_i is obligatory and there are such occurrences. If $m_i = 1$, and S_i is optional, then $Z_1^{(i)}$ may be either U or an occurrence of X_i in α_{t_i}. $Z_1^{(i)}$ will always be U when X_i does not occur in α_{t_i}. Note that no matter what a, b, and c are,

$$a \left[\frac{b}{(c,\ U)} \right] = a.$$

Definition 16. D is *produced* from $S = (S_1, ..., S_n)$ if and only if there are sequences t, α, and $Z^{(i)}$ (for $1 \leqslant i \leqslant k$) jointly meeting 25 and such that:

(i) $\alpha_1 = X_1$

(ii)   for j such that $t_i \leqslant j < t_{i+1}$,
$$\alpha_{j+1} = \alpha_j \left[\frac{Y_i}{(X_i,\ Z_{j+1-t_i}^{(i)})} \right]$$

(iii) D is formed from α by dropping any α_j such that $\alpha_j = \alpha_{j-1}$

(iv) $\alpha_{t_{k+1}}$ is a string in $\bar{P}$

In this case, for $i \geqslant 1$, $\alpha_{t_{i+1}}$ is formed from α_{t_i} by successive replacement of the occurrences $Z_1^{(i)}, ..., Z_{m_i}^{(i)}$ of X_i by Y_i in α_{t_i}, where all occurrences of X_i are replaced when $I_i = B$, i.e., S_i is an obligatory rule.

There is still a serious gap in this account of production of derivations from a grammar. Given any grammar $S_1, ..., S_n$, only a finite number of derivations can be produced from it in accordance with Definition 16.

But in fact, **P** will typically contain infinitely many derivations.[25] Suppose, for instance, that $\rho_1{}^r(a,bc)$ and $\rho_1{}^r(bc,dac)$, in a certain system **P**. Then there will be infinitely many derivations in **P**, since we can have $a \to bc \to dac \to dbcc \to ddacc$, etc. This is incidentally, not a far-fetched example. It occurs in English, for instance, with $a = Sentence$, $b = Noun\ Phrase$, $c = Verb\ Phrase$, $d = that$. To cope with this possibility it is necessary to reformulate Definition 16, adding a recursive step, so that infinitely many derivations can be produced by a finite grammar.

Definition 17. D is *recursively produced* from $S = (S_1,..., S_n)$ if and only if, for some $m \geqslant 1$, D is produced in the sense of Definition 16 from $T^m = (T_1,..., T_{mn})$, where, for $i \leqslant n$,

$$T_i = T_{i+n} = T_{i+2n} = ... = T_{i+(m-1)n} = S_i$$

Thus $T_1,..., T_{mn} = G_1,..., G_m$, where $G_i = S_1,..., S_n$. In other words, if we run through $S_1,..., S_n$ and come out with a string X which is not a string in $\bar{P}$ [hence not in $Gr(P)$], then we run through the grammar again with X as the initial term α_1, and so on if the product is again not a string in $\bar{P}$. It is important to recognize that there is a mechanical and terminating procedure for determining whether a given string X is a string in $\bar{P}$, given $S_1,..., S_n$.

Having defined recursive production, we must rephrase the optimality conditions **23** of (§28) replacing (i) by the requirement that every derivation can be recursively produced, i.e., produced by running through the grammar a finite number of times.

One further restriction should be added to the notion of a grammar $S_1,..., S_n$ to eliminate the possibility of running through the grammar over and over again vacuously. This would be a possibility, for instance, if each conversion were optional. To avoid this, we may define a *proper linear grammar*:

Definition 18. $S = (S_1,..., S_n)$ is a *proper linear grammar* if each $S_i = (I_i, X_i, Y_i)$, where X_i and Y_i are strings and I_i is either B or P, and for each X_j ($1 \leqslant j \leqslant n$), there is at least one S_{b_j} in $S_1,..., S_n$ such that $S_{b_j} = (B, X_j, Y_{b_j})$.

Thus each X_j must appear in one obligatory statement, not necessarily the final statement in which X_j is the left-hand term. Given

---

[25] We must assume this now, although below we suggest that this is not the case, and that the burden of infinite projection falls on the next higher level.

a proper linear grammar, we can run through it vacuously a second time only if the product of the first run-through is a string in $\bar{P}$, or contains none of the left-hand terms X_j from the grammar. The same effect could be achieved with a weaker but more complex condition.

It is worth noting one other point in connection with the production of derivations. Suppose that we have a proper linear grammar S and T^1, T^2,... as in Definition 17. If, for some m, D is produced in the sense of Definition 16 by T^m (hence is recursively produced by S), then since the last line of D is a string in $\bar{P}$ [cf. (iv), Definition 16], D is also produced by T^{m+1}. Suppose we introduce a notion of "weak production" which holds between $S = (S_1,..., S_n)$ and a sequence D which meets conditions (i)–(iii) of Definition 16, but may or may not meet condition (iv). Thus if D is produced by S it is weakly produced by S, but if D is weakly produced by S it is not produced by S unless the final string in D is in $\bar{P}$. We then say that

Definition 19. D is a *terminated derivation* of S if D is weakly produced by T^m and T^{m+1}, for some m.

Clearly every derivation produced from S is a terminated derivation of S. But the converse is not true. Certain derivations may simply be "blocked" before they reach a string of $\bar{P}$. They may terminate in strings which, though not in $\bar{P}$, still do not contain any of the terms X_i which are converted into some Y_i by some conversion S_i of S. And in this case no further application of S will carry the derivation any farther. However this need not trouble us, since given any terminated derivation D of S we can immediately determine whether it is recursively produced by S and hence actually qualifies as a derivation by checking the primes of its product. Hence given S and a purported derivation D, we can mechanically determine whether D is in fact a derivation. Given S, we can weakly produce terminated derivations and we can check to see whether or not they are real derivations.

We can now return to the problem of reduction. Given a listing of R_2 55.4 as in §55.2, we perform

Reduction 3. Construct a proper linear grammar $S_1,..., S_n$ which produces exactly those derivations constructible by means of R_2.

We have not yet shown that Reduction 3 actually can give a simpler grammar (but cf. §28). To see how this may be the case, consider a system **P** consisting of the equivalent derivations D_1, D_2, D_3 as sketched

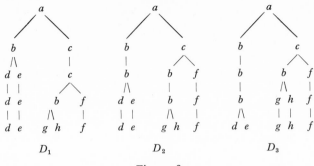

Figure 9

in Figure 9. R_2 will vary, depending on which derivation we choose to construct directly. Choosing D_1, we have, as R_2

26 (a,bc) (bc,dec) (c,bf) (bf,ghf)

It is at once clear that the grammar **26** provides an overspecification, since the following simpler grammar corresponds to **26**, producing exactly D_1, if we require that the order of these "grammatical rules" be preserved in constructing derivations:

27 (a,bc) (b,de) (c,bf) (b,gh)

Thus **27** can be taken as the grammar of this system. In this case all statements of the grammar are obligatory. Naturally, with the more complex cases that one finds in actual languages the reduction is far more significant, as was evident from the appendix to Chapter VI.

As we pointed out in the last paragraph of §55.2, by the process of reduction we can convert a description of the system **P** of phrase structure for a language into a grammar of the type studied in Chapter IV. (We discuss below the domain of applicability of this process of reduction.) Thus the gap between the general theory and this model for grammatical description is bridged completely, on the level **P**, and the characterization of simplicity developed in Chapter IV can be used to evaluate various models of **P** proposed for a given language.

The recursive extension which permits infinite production of derivation might pose a problem for the determination of simplicity. Thus we may ask whether a grammar is simpler if it is necessary to run through it fewer times to set up derivations. There are several possible ways to place conditions on grammars that will eliminate a conflict between this consideration and the criterion of simplicity already established. We will not go into this question any further, since we will find below that there are strong reasons for dropping the notion of recursive production altogether (see §110).

Throughout our discussion of linguistic structure we have made a three-way distinction between what we may briefly call (i) language, (ii) structure of a language, and (iii) grammar of a language. By a "language" we mean here simply a set of utterances. By "the structure of a given language" we mean the particular system of levels which has been assigned to this set of utterances and which, we assert, underlies the set of utterances. By a "grammar" we mean, in general, any system having the properties described in Chapter IV, and above in §55. That is, a grammar is a set of instructions "rewrite α as β," where α and β are strings, and a "proper linear grammar" is a sequence of such instructions, with at least one obligatory instruction for each α which undergoes conversion in some rule. By "the grammar of a given language (with a given structure assigned to it)" we mean, then, a description of this structure, showing exactly how this structure is related to the language, i.e., showing how just this set of utterances can be generated in a mechanical manner in terms of the system of levels. On the level of phrase structure, the structure (ii) will be a particular model of the system **P**, and the grammar will be a proper linear grammar of the form described above.

56.1

We have now reached the point where we can begin to consider certain fundamental questions about the limits of grammatical description, and the adequacy of particular conceptions of linguistic structure. We would like to know the answers to such questions as these: does there exist for every properly constructed grammar a linguistic structure which it describes? Can every linguistic structure be described by some properly constructed grammar? Does every language have a grammar? Is a certain abstract conception of linguistic structure rich enough so that for any language we can find a corresponding linguistic structure (i.e., an appropriate model of the system of levels) which can be described by a grammar? Such questions have no clear meaning until we state what we mean by a linguistic structure (system of levels) and by a grammar. But we have done this on the level of phrase structure. We have given an abstract description of a certain system **P** and have developed a notion of "proper linear grammar," and we have shown how a particular model of **P** may be reduced to a particular grammar which describes this model of **P** in the sense that the model can be reconstructed in a mechanical way from the grammar. We can therefore ask the following questions:

28   Is every proper linear grammar the description of some particular system of phrase structure? If not, can we tell by investigating such a system whether or not it is reduced from some model of **P**.

29   (a)   Is there a system of phrase structure for every language?
(b)   Is there a finite grammar in terms of R_2 for every language?
(c)   Can every system of phrase structure be reduced to a proper linear grammar?
(d)   Is there a proper linear grammar for every language? That is, does every language have some underlying system of phrase structure which can be reduced to a proper linear grammar?

Negative answers to these questions may point the way to inadequacies in our theory, as we will see below.

56.2   Consider first question 28. We ask whether every proper linear grammar is a reduced form of some system **P**. The answer to this is clearly negative. To determine whether a proper linear grammar G does correspond to some model of the system **P** we must investigate the derivations produced from G. There are two kinds of conditions that these derivations must meet if G is reduced from a system of phrase structure.

In the first place, each derivation must have the proper internal construction. Each step must be constructed from the preceding step by developing exactly one prime into a string ($\neq U$). Moreover, no unbroken branch in the diagram of the derivation can pass from a prime P_i back to P_i. That is, no piece of the diagram can be of the form

30

or the requirement of irreflexivity for ρ will be violated. There are several other conditions of this sort.

In the second place, the whole set of derivations must simultaneously meet certain conditions. Thus there can be no two derivations which together cause the asymmetry of ρ to be violated. More interesting is a certain condition of completeness required for the set of derivations corresponding to **P**, a condition which shows how much more powerful and selective the notion of grammar can be in full generality than the notion of grammar reduced from **P**. This condition can be stated as follows:

Theorem 13. Suppose that we have a system **P**, and suppose that D_1 are D_2 are ρ_1-derivations in **P**, where

$$D_1 = A_1, ..., A_j, A_{j+1}, ..., A_m$$
$$D_2 = B_1, ..., B_k, B_{k+1}, ..., B_n$$

Suppose further that $B_k = A_j$. Then there must also be a D_3 such that

$$D_3 = A_1, ..., A_j, B_{k+1}, ..., B_n$$

and D_3 is a ρ_1-derivation in **P**.

Clearly there is no necessity for a grammar $G = (S_1, ..., S_n)$ to have the property that the set of produced derivations meets Theorem 13. One of the conversions of G may be the statement S_i which gives the instruction "rewrite α as β." Suppose that S_i is obligatory. Then we would state S_i as

31   B: $\alpha \rightarrow \beta$

But there may be another statement S_{i+k} which asserts that it is obligatory to rewrite α as γ, and is thus given in the form

32   B: $\alpha \rightarrow \gamma$

S_i (**31**) asserts that all α's appearing *at this point* in the construction of derivations are rewritten as β, and S_{i+k}(**32**) asserts that all α's appearing at this *later* point in the construction of derivations are to be rewritten as γ, the α's appearing at the $(i + k)$th stage having been introduced *after* the change of α to β at the ith stage. But this grammar may well violate Theorem 13, since we may have derivations $D_1 = A_1, ..., \alpha, \beta, ..., A_m$ and $D_2 = B_1, ..., \alpha, \gamma, ..., B_n$, but no derivation $D_3 = A_1, ..., \alpha, \gamma, ..., B_n$.

A historical analogy may clarify the point in question. Our general conception of grammar is formally somewhat analogous to a description of historical change. Each statement "$\alpha \rightarrow \beta$" states that α becomes β. The analogy can be extended if we rewrite "$\alpha \rightarrow \beta$" using Definition 1, Chapter IV (§27.1) as "$b \rightarrow b'$ in env.: a——c," where $\alpha = a \frown b \frown c$ and $\beta = a \frown b' \frown c$. Thus a——c can be understood as the conditioning context for the change of b to b' (if $a = c = U$, this would be analogous to the case of unconditioned sound change). In its full generality, our notion of grammar has the full power of a descriptive statement of historical change. To return to the example of the preceding paragraph, suppose that at a certain historical period (the ith stage) every α becomes β (i.e., where $\alpha = a\frown b\frown c$, every b in the context $:a$——c becomes b'). Suppose that after this change, α's are somehow reintroduced, and that at a later historical period (the $(i + k)$th stage) every α becomes γ. This is a perfectly possible historical statement. What happens at one period has no necessary connection with what happens at another.

But a grammar reduced from **P** does impose an organic connection between the changes introduced at one stage and those introduced at another. If α becomes β at one point, where α and β are in normal strings, then any later α must also be transformable into β. The specific case of grammars reduced from **P** corresponds, then, not to a model of historical change in full generality, but to a model of hostorical change (if this were possible) in terms of universal laws of development, or changes which are universal for a given language throughout its history.

These are certain necessary conditions for a grammar to be a reduced form of some **P**. It would be possible and important to go on to investigate sufficient conditions. At any rate, we see that not every grammar is a reduced form of some system **P**. In particular, the morphophonemic study presented in the appendix to Chapter VI fails both types of tests outlined above, and thus could not be taken, even formally, as a description of some system of phrase structure. This is natural enough. **P** and **M**[26] have certain similarities, and in particular, both may be reducible to a single form of grammatical statement. If this is the case, a single grammar can be given incorporating both **P** and **M**, so that sequences of phonemes can be generated directly from the representation *Sentence*.[27] But they are also formally different, e.g., in that the notion *constituent* has no comparable significance when applied to morphophonemic representations. Another formal difference is that only finitely many derivations are produced by the grammar corresponding to **M**, while infinitely many correspond to **P**. This explains why it was possible to produce all derivations from the morphophonemic statement of Chapter VI by simply running through the sequence once. In this case *produces* is the same relation as *recursively produces*.

Since not every proper linear grammar is a reduced form of a system of phrase structure, it is necessary, when presenting a grammar, not

[26] More properly, $\varPhiM$, because this is what was really analyzed in the morphophonemic study. See §56.5 for the problems involved in analyzing $\varPhiP$.

[27] But cf. §56.5.

only to show that the (finite—cf. §46) set of derivations of first-order grammatical sentences is properly given, but also to prove that the grammar is a reduced form of some model of **P**, i.e., that it actually describes a system of phrase structure. Only if this proof is given can we speak of an evaluation procedure for the grammar in question. This leaves an important theoretical gap, since we would like to have a mechanical evaluation procedure that can be applied directly to any proposed grammar, and there may not be a mechanical method for determining whether or not any given grammar is a reduced form of some system **P**. This leads us back to the second part of question **28** in §56.1. If we cannot provide a general mechanical method for determining whether, given any proper linear grammar, the structure derived from this grammar is actually a system of phrase structure, then our general program of constructing linguistic theory in such a way as to provide an evaluation procedure for any grammar (cf. §10.3) will have failed. If the grammar produced only a finite number of derivations, this problem would not arise. Below we will find many other reasons to question the validity of the extension of the notion of *production* to *recursive production*, and we will finally arrive at the decision to limit production on the level **P** to a finite set of derivations, accounting for the remaining sentences in a different manner.

We turn now to the consideration of question **29**, §56.1. This is essentially   **56.3**
the question of whether our conceptions of phrase structure and of grammar are rich enough so that for any language we can construct a grammar which gives the phrase structure of this language.

A language is a set of utterances. The phrase structure of a language is a particular model of the level **P** associated with this language by a mapping $\Phi^{\mathbf{P}}$ which maps **P**-markers into utterances. Each **P**-marker is a set of strings in **P** containing exactly one "lowest level" string of $Gr(P)$. Thus, in a derivative way, $\Phi^{\mathbf{P}}$ relates strings in $Gr(P)$ to utterances. We will simplify the study of question **29** by breaking it down into two parts. First we ask whether for any choice of $Gr(P)$ there is a phrase structure and a grammar. Then, in §56.4, we ask whether the mapping $\Phi^{\mathbf{P}}$ itself can be represented by a properly constructed grammar.

The only conditions on $Gr(P)$ is that it be a set, finite or infinite, of strings of finite length, and that only a finite number of symbols (primes of $\bar{P}$) appear in strings of $Gr(P)$. Since we are now taking the language to be just $Gr(P)$, question **29**a asks whether for any set $Gr(P)$ there is a corresponding system of phrase structure. The answer to this question is positive, trivially, in that if we allow ρ to hold between *Sentence* and each string Z of $Gr(P)$, and between nothing else, then the axioms for **P** are statisfied trivially. Hence if $Gr(P)$ is the set of strings $\{Z_1, Z_2, ...\}$, we can always assign to $Gr(P)$ the system of phrase structure which contains just the derivations (*Sentence*, Z_1), (*Sentence*, Z_2),... [but cf. condition *C*, §54.1].

Question **29**b asks whether for any set $Gr(P)$ (any language) there is a finite set of instructions "rewrite α as β" from which, for some associated system of phrase structure, we can generate just those ρ_1-derivations which are ρ_1-derivations of strings in $Gr(P)$. That is, does every language have a grammar in the weakest sense of grammar, where no order is imposed on the rules "$\alpha \rightarrow \beta$." The answer to this question is negative, also trivially. It is easy to show that there are more languages than there are grammars; hence some languages cannot have grammars even in this weak sense. Note that this does not contradict our statement in §55.2 that any system of phrase structure can be reduced (by Reduction 2) to a relation R_2. What we have stated now is that in certain cases the relation R_2 will be infinite in extension. In the same way we can show that the answers to **29**c and **29**d are negative; not every system of phrase structure can be reduced to a proper linear grammar, and not every language has some proper linear grammar.

What we have just asserted can be restated as follows:

33   (i)   Reductions 1 and 2 can always be carried out, but the result may not be a finite grammar.

      (ii)   It is not always possible to carry out Reduction 3 (to a proper linear grammar), since a proper linear grammar must, by definition, be finite.

It is also the case that

34   even if Reductions 1 and 2 yield a finite grammar, when applied to a given system of phrase structure, it is not necessarily the case that Reduction 3 can be applied.

Our major effort, from this point on, will be devoted to exploring various consequences of this situation. To anticipate a later development, we will see that while it is probable that Reductions 1 and 2 will always give a finite grammar in the case of actual languages, at the same time there is good reason to believe that this grammar will be so complex as to be almost useless, *if we require that a constituent analysis (i.e., a* **P***-marker) be provided directly for every grammatical utterance*; furthermore, it will appear below that English phrase structure, in particular, is not amenable to Reduction 3 (not reducible to a proper linear grammar) if the italicized condition is met. This state of affairs is indicative of a serious deficiency in our theory of linguistic structure. It will serve as one of many arguments for rejecting the requirement that a **P**-marker must be provided directly[28] for every grammatical utterance. This failure to meet optimality requirements (cf. §§28, 55.3) will thus provide a systematic motivation for the development of transformational analysis as a part of linguistic theory. We return to these questions in the appendix to this chapter and again in the following three chapters.

In the last section we asked whether there is a phrase structure and a grammar for any choice of $Gr(P)$. Now we turn to the second part of question **29**, as this question was broken down in the second paragraph of §56.3. That is, we now ask whether the mapping Φ^P which converts **P**-markers into grammatical utterances (and hence, indirectly, converts strings of $Gr(P)$ into grammatical utterances) can be represented by a proper linear grammar. **56.4**

In §55.1 we posed the problem of developing a method for converting any given model of the structure **P** into a grammar of the form described in Chapter IV, which can be evaluated in terms of its complexity. If this can be done, then we will be able to derive the strings of $Gr(P)$ from the representation *Sentence*. Assuming that we can derive such a grammar from lower levels, in the manner touched on in Chapter VI, we are also able to derive strings of phones from strings in $\overline{\mathbf{M}}$ (cf. §47). But there remains one gap to bridge before we can construct derivations of strings of phones from the representation *Sentence*, thus completing the program of grammar construction laid down in Chapter IV. We must show that the strings of $Gr(P)$ which are derived in **P** can be converted mechanically by a sequence of conversions of the form $\alpha \rightarrow \beta$ into the strings in $\overline{\mathbf{M}}$ from which lower-level derivations begin (i.e., the set $\mu^{\overline{\mathbf{M}}}$). This is essentially the problem of characterizing the mapping Φ^P. If we could define this mapping by a sequence of statements of the form $\alpha \rightarrow \beta$, then this sequence of statements could be placed after the sequence of statements that forms the grammar of **P**, and before the sequence that gives the lower-level grammar, and the program would be completed. But we will find in investigating English syntax that this mapping cannot be so described unless we develop an inordinately complex system of phrase structure. If we try to develop a simple system of phrase structure for the language, we will find that the mapping Φ^P will have to perform certain reorderings of morphemes,

---

[28] We will see later that a constituent analysis is provided indirectly for every grammatical utterance.

and will have to assign specific values to certain nonheads of a string X of $Gr(P)$ in a manner which requires knowledge not only of the actual shape of X, but also of its past "history," i.e., of the manner of its derivation from *Sentence*. As we shall see, this amounts to the requirement that we know the constituent analysis of X in order to convert it from a string of $Gr(P)$ to a string of morphemes. And this is just a way of rephrasing the fact that the domain of $\Phi^{\mathbf{P}}$ (i.e., the set of **P**-markers) cannot be taken as strings of $Gr(P)$, but must be developed in the way we have described above. We will see, then, that if we are to achieve a reasonably simple grammar, then no sequence of rules of the form $\alpha \rightarrow \beta$ will be sufficient to state the mapping $\Phi^{\mathbf{P}}$, because these rules do not take into account the way in which α was developed from *Sentence*.

We see then that our formulation of the structure of a grammar in Chapter IV was incomplete, and that there remains at least the problem of describing $\Phi^{\mathbf{P}}$, that is, of showing how a string of $Gr(P)$ with a given phrase structure can be converted into a grammatical string of morphemes. We discuss this somewhat further in Chapter VIII, but the real solution for this problem will appear as a special case in the development of transformations.

57   To recapitulate, we have developed a process of *reduction* whereby a model of the system **P** (assigned to a given language as its phrase structure) can be transformed into a grammar, which can be evaluated with respect to its simplicity by determining its length under the "notational transformations" of Chapter IV. This reduced grammar will be a sequence of instructions of the form $\alpha \rightarrow \beta$. Given the grammar we can construct one derivation from each equivalence class of derivations. The other derivations can be mechanically recovered, so that we are able to determine the relation $\rho_1{}^r$ which holds between consecutive steps of restricted derivations. Theorem 10 of §54.2 tells us that this determines ρ. Thus given a grammar derived from a system of phrase structure by reduction, the underlying system of phrase structure can be uniquely recovered. A model for grammatical statement and the abstract structure associated with it must be related in this manner. I think that these comments are sufficient to indicate once again that the study of the relation between the general theory of linguistic structure and the particular form in which a grammar is presented is an important one, and that this relation must be given quite a careful analysis, at least if features of the grammar (such as simplicity) are to be taken into consideration in validating grammars.

In §56 we have found that the account given in the preceding paragraph somewhat overstates the case. Several important problems remain unresolved which question seriously the adequacy of the theory in its present form. For one thing, we cannot tell by inspection of a grammar whether or not it is in fact a grammar of phrase structure. Secondly, it is not possible to carry out the reduction to a grammar in the case of any possible language. In fact, we will see below that the reduction to a proper linear grammar (Reduction 3) apparently cannot be carried out successfully in the case of English, and that although reduction to a finite (unordered) grammar may be possible, it will apparently be too complex to be of much interest, if we attempt to cover sentences of other than the simplest construction. Finally, we have asserted (and will see below, in greater detail) that if we hope to find a simple enough system of phrase structure, we will apparently not be able to state the mapping Φ^P in a grammar of the contemplated form, so that there is a gap between phrase structure and lower levels. We return to these questions in the appendix to this chapter, and the greater part of the following three chapters will be devoted to investigating these inadequacies in greater detail and exploring ways to remedy them.

In the light of the connection now revealed between the system **P** and 58 the form of grammars studied in Chapter IV, we can state a final condition on **P**, thus arriving at an evaluation procedure for constituent analysis. Suppose that we have a corpus of utterances which has been analyzed in terms of the system **C** and projected to a set $Gr_1(W)$ of first-order grammatical sentences in the manner discussed in Chapter V.[29] We now construct a system of phrase structure (i.e., a specific model of the system **P**) with the property that every string of $Gr_1(W)$ becomes the image under Φ^P of some **P**-marker, in other words, with the property that each string of $Gr_1(W)$ receives a constituent analysis. We further require that no string shorter than the longest string in $Gr_1(W)$ receives a **P**-marker.[30] In the manner which we have just outlined, we next reduce this system of phrase structure to a grammar, i.e., a sequence of conversion statements of the form "$B(\alpha \rightarrow \beta)$" (read "it is obligatory to rewrite α as β") or "$P(\alpha \rightarrow \beta)$" (read "it is permitted to rewrite α as β"). We then evaluate this grammar in the manner of Chapter IV. That is, we investigate the simplicity of the grammar, understood as the amount of generalization it provides, and measured in terms of

---

[29] We might suppose further that we have analyzed $Gr_1(W)$ in terms of **M**, and that we have projected to a set $Gr_1(M)$ as mentioned (but not discussed) in the last paragraph of §47.

[30] See Note 4 above. Here too, as in the case of **M**, we omit the discussion of the analogue to §37. Acually, here too, just as in applying **C**, we can try to find a method for redrawing the borders of $Gr_1(W)$ so as to exclude strings that are exceptional from the point of view of phrase structure.

the possibility of compression with selected notational devices. The best constituent analysis will be the highest-valued system having the structure of **P** and related in the proper way to $Gr_1(W)$. Each model of **P** proposed for $Gr_1(W)$ projects $Gr_1(W)$ to a new set, and if recursive production is permitted, this projection may be infinite.

This account requires two qualifications. First, the order of descriptive procedures outlined has no theoretical significance in our terms, as we have emphasized above. Second, the system of phrase structure is not evaluated by itself, but conjointly with the partial grammars derived from other levels. That is, complication of **P** may be permitted if this leads to much simpler statements on other levels.

Although this account is schematic in parts and contains serious gaps, it is possible to proceed to investigate its empirical consequences in construction of actual grammars. In fact, the morphophonemic study of the appendix to Chapter VI is an instance of a grammar constructed along these lines, and containing a partial validation. That is, it is shown that no interchange of the order of the statements in the morphophonemic component of that grammar can give a simpler grammar. In Chapter VIII we will consider English phrase structure from this point of view.

To the question: what is ultimately involved in the proper choice of **P**, for a given language, we have given the general answer: the total simplicity of the grammar for which **P** provides the underlying phrase structure. More specifically, the more features of the language can be stated in terms of the elements of **P**, the simpler will be the grammar which **P** underlies, since these features will not have to be independently stated. Thus each such feature can be taken in a loose sense as a criterion for **P**. This is actually a loose sense, because the only ultimate criterion for **P** is the total simplicity of the grammar. Simplicity is a measure for a whole system. If these features appear on other levels than **P**, we have interdependence of levels, with **P** being "validated" in terms of these other levels. We will see below that **P** is not independent of the "higher" level of transformations.

The following features appear to be criteria for **P** in English, in this loose sense. (That is, these features are all statable in terms of roughly the same set of elements, and this set of elements in fact satisfies the axiom system for **P**; hence **P** might as well be taken as having these elements as its "vocabulary.")

1. The rule for conjunction
2. Intrusion of parenthetical expressions
3. Ability to enter into transformations
4. Certain intonational features

We will investigate these and other "criteria" for determining phrase structure in the next chapter. After having developed transformational analysis and applied it to English, we will see that the first two features mentioned, and many others, are special cases of the third, so that of these only three and four remain within our framework.

There are many other notions which must be developed in **P**, and   59.1
although I do not know how to do justice to them, I think it might be profitable to at least suggest how they might fit in to the system which has been presented, if only as a sketch of some of the remaining difficulties. Chief among these are the related set of notions "grammatical relation" (e.g., *actor–action* or *subject–predicate*, *verb–object*, etc.), "head," "modifier," "coordinate construction," "subordinate construction," etc.

The theory of grammatical relations can be based on a set of functions that might be called "selectors." These are functions which, for each prime P_i, select a unique occurrence of some prime P_j in each X directly represented by P_i.

Definition 20. f is a *selector* in **P** if and only if for all P_i, X, there is a unique P_j, Z, such that

$$f(P_i, X) = (P_j, Z)$$

where

(i) Z is an occurrence of P_j in X
(ii) $\rho_1(P_i, X) \Leftrightarrow Z \neq U \neq P_j$

Definition 21. F is a *complete set of selectors* for **P** if and only if

(i) $f \in F \Rightarrow f$ is a selector in **P**
(ii) for all P_i, P_j, Z, X, if $\rho_1(P_i, X)$ and Z is an occurrence of P_j in X, then there is a unique $f \in F$ such that $f(P_i, X) = (P_j, Z)$.

Thus a complete set of selectors would enable us to assign a unique function f to each occurrence of P_j in a string X, if we know to what kind of constituent this occurrence belongs. Given $NP \frown VP$, and $\rho_1(Sentence, NP \frown VP)$, there would be a certain f_s associated with NP, and a certain f_p associated with VP. In terms of F we can investigate the logical status of such notions as subject, object, etc., given a prior account of grammatical relations.

Definition 22. A *grammatical relation* (or *construction*) is an ordered pair (P_i, X) such that $\rho_1(P_i, X)$.

Thus *actor–action* is the grammatical relation (*Sentence*, $NP^\frown VP$), and *verb–object* is the grammatical relation (VP, $V^\frown NP$). Note that under this formulation, a constituent X can enter into various grammatical relations. Another approach would be to define a grammatical relation as an ordered n-tuple of primes that form a constituent, e.g., to define *actor–action* as the grammatical relation (NP, VP). The many unanalyzed problems in this area of syntax make it difficult to find a crucial instance to decide between these formulations, but it seems likely that the extra generality given by Definition 22 will be required for descriptive adequacy.

Assuming *grammatical relation* to be defined as in Definition 22, we can explain each of the notions *subject*, *object*, etc. as an ordered pair of a selector f and a grammatical relation Q. Given the grammatical relation (P_i, X) and the selector f, $f(P_i, X)$ will be a certain prime of X, e.g., the subject of the grammatical relation, if this is the *actor–action* relation and $f = f_s$ [which might, for instance, be the selector that selects the first prime of a two-prime string, or the first head (cf. below), etc.].

To give further content to this area of syntax, it is necessary then to enter into the construction of a set F.

59.2   Given that $\rho_1(P_i, P_{i_1}{}^\frown...{}^\frown P_{i_n})$, we can distinguish three different cases:

35   (i) $P_i = P_{i_j}$, for some $j \leqslant n$
     (ii) $n = 1$
     (iii)   neither (i) nor (ii)

Case (i) is, essentially, the case where in Harris's Morpheme-to-Utterance characterization of constituents[31] the superscripts are not raised. Case (ii) amounts to giving the membership of a class. We might give names to these cases as follows:

Definition 23.   Given a grammatical relation $Q = (P_i, P_{i_1}{}^\frown...{}^\frown P_{i_n})$, if Q is:

     an instance of case **35i**,   then Q is a *recursion* of P_i,
     "   "   "   "   **35ii**,   then Q is a *listing* of P_i,
     "   "   "   "   **35iii**,   then Q is a *partition* of P_i.

Since ρ is irreflexive, (ii) and (i) are exclusive. Hence these are three distinct cases.

---

[31] *Methods*, Chapter 16.

The notion of "head of a construction" is somewhat ambiguous. In one sense, by a head of P_i is meant a prime that appears in every development of P_i. In the case of a recursion, we might say that the head is P_i itself.

Definition 24. $Hd(P_j, P_i)$ if and only if (i) for all X, if (P_i, X) is a grammatical relation but not a recursion, then $P_j \leqslant X$, where P_j is prime,[32] or (ii) there is an X such that (P_i, X) is a recursion and $P_j = P_i$.

In terms of this notion, we might suggest an extension of the axiom system for ρ:

Axiom 8. Every partition has a head. That is, if (P_i, X) is a partition of P_i, then there is a $p \leqslant X$ such that $Hd(p, P_i)$.

This condition would rule out such obviously inadequate interpretations for **P** as that offered below Theorem 9 of §54.1, where P would have contained just *Sentence* and the primes of $\bar{P}$.

Axiom 9. The heads of P_i stand alone in some fixed and unique order in a partition of P_i. That is, the heads of P_i in a partition can be ordered in a fixed and unique way as $p_1, ..., p_n$ such that

$$\rho_1(P_i, p_1 \frown ... \frown p_n)$$

Definition 25. In this case, the grammatical relation $(P_i, p_1 \frown ... \frown p_n)$ is called a *coordinate construction*.

We can now define the kth head of a grammatical relation. There are several ways open, depending on how we interpret "kth head." We might mean simply the kth occurrence of a head in a given partition, or, alternatively, the occurrence of the element in the given partition which is in fact the kth prime in the coordinate construction guaranteed by Axiom 9. In this case, the kth head of one partition of P_i will always be identical with the kth head of another partition of P_i, but this is not necessary in the former case. If we choose the latter formulation, Axiom 9 is crucial; with the former version, we can dispense with this axiom. I see no way to choose between these alternatives. Continuing arbitrarily with the former, we have

---

[32] See Note 24.

Definition 26. $Hd_k(P_i, X) = (P_q, Z)$ if and only if either

(I) $\rho_1(P_i, X)$ and there is a $Z_1, ..., Z_n, p_1, ..., p_n$ such that

(i) $1 \leqslant k \leqslant n$
(i) $Z_1 < Z_2 < ... < Z_n$
(iii) Z_r is an occurrence of p_r in X
(iv) $p_1, ..., p_n$ are exactly the heads of P_i
(v) $P_q = p_k$ and $Z = Z_k$

or

(II) $P_q = Z = U$

Theorem 14. Hd_k is a selector, for $k \geqslant 1$.

Analogously, we can define kth *subordinate* (nonhead) of a grammatical relation:

Definition 27. $Sb_k(P_i, X) = (P_q, Z)$ if and only if either

(I) $\rho_1(P_i, X)$ and there is a $Z_1, ..., Z_n, p_1, ..., p_n$ such that

(i) $1 \leqslant k \leqslant n$
(ii) $Z_1 < Z_2 < ... < Z_n$
(iii) Z_r is an occurrence of p_r in X
(iv) $p_1, ..., p_n$ are exactly the nonhead primes of P_i
(v) $P_q = p_k$ and $Z = Z_k$

or

(II) $P_q = Z = U$

Theorem 15. Sb_k is a selector, for $k \geqslant 1$.

Given any ordered pair (P_i, X), we can find the kth head and kth subordinate of this pair, and these will be units just in case either (P_i, X) is not a grammatical relation, or it is a grammatical relation but contains fewer than k heads or k nonheads, respectively. In terms of Sb_k we should be able to define *subordinate* construction, and perhaps *modifier*. But it is not clear to me when a nonhead is properly called a modifier, and whether the grounds for this are formal.

Finally, we have

Theorem 16. $F = \{Hd_k \mid 1\} \cup \{Sb_k \mid k \leqslant 1\}$ is a complete set of selectors for **P**.

Returning to the end of §59.1, let Q be the grammatical relation *actor–action*. Then Q is the ordered pair (*Sentence, NP⌢VP*). The notion of "subject" can be understood as the ordered pair (Hd_1, Q), and $Hd_1(Q) = NP$ is the subject of the grammatical relation Q.

This discussion only scratches the surface. There are many ways in which it could be generalized or altered completely. In particular, the definitions are fairly arbitrary in that the terms defined are often used in quite different ways. The additional axioms have only the justification that they give a somewhat more organized picture of constituent structure. But of course this is not a sufficient motivation. There are other ways in which the system could have been elaborated. The difficulty here is that not enough detailed work is available on constituent structure of actual languages for us to be able to determine what the effect would be on the grammar of these languages if one or another conception is applied. Hence there must be quite a large element of speculation even in such skeletal theoretical work as this. It can do little more in this instance than suggest problems and gaps toward which empirical study might direct itself.

It is interesting to investigate the various kinds of constructional **60** homonymity that can arise in **P**. We have a real case of constructional homonymity when several **P**-markers are mapped by Φ^P into the same grammatical string in **W**. We cannot quite discuss this case yet, since we have not yet considered the problem of how constituent structure is carried over under mappings. But we can discuss a closely related problem, namely, the case in which several **P**-markers are assigned to a given string in $Gr(P)$, i.e., the case of several **P**-markers with a common product. Two simple cases of homonymity are these:

36   (I)   A string may be broken up into constituents in two different ways.

   (II)   A string may be broken up into parts in only a single way, but these parts may be constituents of different sorts, i.e., they may be represented by different primes.

Examples of both kinds can be found in English. The cases in §52.2 ("old men and women," etc.) are instances of (I). As an instance of (II), consider

37   *Flying planes can be dangerous*

Here "planes" can be the object of "fly," or "flying" can be an adjective modifying "planes."[33] In both cases the constituent analysis is "flying planes–can be dangerous." But in one case the noun phrase subject is an instance of *Adjective⌢Noun* (hence in this case a plural noun phrase), and in the other, an instance of some form of *Verb⌢Noun* (forming, in this case, a singular noun phrase).

In *Two Models*, Hockett utilizes cases of homonymity to demonstrate the independence of various syntactic notions, in particular the independence of construction from form and order. He argues that if our system permitted only case (I) types (difference of constituent boundaries) or case (II) types (difference of construction), it would necessarily be inadequate, as these examples show.[34]

61 In §54 we saw that considerations of descriptive adequacy require that **P** be nonrestricted for English. In particular, nonrestriction is necessary if "John," "the rearming of Germany," "a man," and "several men" are all to be *NP*s. Such considerations can be extended, leading to further requirements on *P*.

The notion of nonrestriction is reminiscent of the notion of degree of grammaticalness of Chapter V. There it was observed that, e.g., "horse" and "justice" are both nouns, although they are rarely or never substitutable. In the case of "horse" and "justice" we have now repeated this observation, pointing out that they are both *NP*s, although perhaps never substitutable as *NP*s. We note then that in certain cases (when the phrases in question consist word by word of members of the same syntactic category), the notions of partial grammaticalness and non-restriction coincide. For such cases we can state the requirement of nonrestriction axiomatically as a condition on **P**, in terms of the notion of *absolute analysis* introduced in §39. This axiom will state a condition of compatibility between **P** and **C**. That is, we require that for each absolute category A_i of **C**, there must be a corresponding prime P_j of **P** such that a word w is in A_i [i.e., $g(A_i, w)$, in terms of §46] just in case on the level **P**, $\rho(P_j, w)$. But the elements of **C** do not literally occur in **P**. Nevertheless, we know that each w in A_i can be analyzed in terms of its morphological heads and affixes, i.e., it is associated with a certain string $m \in \overline{\mathbf{M}}$ such that $\Phi^{\overline{\mathbf{M}}}(m) = w$. Assuming $\overline{\mathbf{M}}$ to be embedded in **P**

---

[33] See Chapter VIII for a further discussion of this case. The analysis given there makes 37 a case of (I), not (II). In Chapter X we return essentially to the conception given here.

[34] The fact that our theory permits both types shows that it *may* be adequate, not that it *is* adequate. To show this it is necessary to establish that the highest-valued interpretation of the system automatically yields this solution. We will investigate this in subsequent chapters.

(cf. §§47, 50.2, and Note 6), we can give this condition of compatibility on **P** and **C** as follows:

Axiom 10. For each category A in the absolute analysis of **C**, there is a prime p in **P** such that $g(A, w)$ if and only if there is an m and a q such that $\rho(p, q)$ and $\Phi\overline{M}(q) = w$.[35]

This requirement and the motivation for it can be rephrased in the terms of Chapter V (cf. §39). Suppose Y and Z are instances of the same structural form, i.e., of a single sequence of categories. Then we would like to require that X and Y are phrases of the same sort. But the difficulty remains that "same structural form" is a notion relative to degree of grammaticalness, and any two strings (of the same length) are of the same structural form at least on the lowest level of grammaticalness. Thus this requirement has no significance unless we fix an absolute sense to "same structural form," as we have in fact done in §39 by defining the absolute analysis. In particular, suppose that *Adjective* and *Noun* are categories in the absolute analysis, but that on the level of first-order grammaticalness, we have subcategories A_1 (containing "green") and A_2 (containing "apparent") of adjectives, and subcategories N_1 (containing "grass") and N_2 (containing "failure") of nouns. Suppose further that in **P** (without Axiom 10) the simplest grammar would have $\rho_1{}^r(NP^\frown..., A_1{}^\frown N_1{}^\frown...)$ and $\rho_1{}^r(NP^\frown..., A_2{}^\frown N_2{}^\frown...)$. Then we would not have the information in **P** that "green grass" and "apparent failure" have the structural similarity that they are both *Adjective^Noun*. It would certainly be a defect in the grammar if we did not know that "green grass" and "apparent failure" have the same phrase structure in a sense in which "green grass" and "the man" do not. This difficulty is avoided by Axiom 10.[36] Note that if the supposition of §39 that the absolute analysis cannot be the highest-level analysis is correct, then **P** must be nonrestricted. Axiom 10, or some similar condition, will play an important role in the development of transformations.

We see that the requirement that **P** must meet Axiom 10 might lead to some complication of the grammar, as in the case just given. This might be avoided by reinterpreting Axiom 10 as a further reduction in **P** (cf. §55). Then given the absolute categories, we can leave the grammar in the simplest form and require that Axiom 10 be met in the

---

[35] Note that this formulation overlooks the problems raised in Note 6.

[36] When we develop the level of transformations, we will see that there is a transformational relation between structures such as *Noun-is-Adjective* and *Adjective-Noun*. It may be, then, that the highest-valued grammar involving transformations will provide the equivalent of Axiom 10 as an empirical generalization about languages.

reconstruction of **P** from the grammar. There does not seem to be any particular problem in giving this formulation, and we omit it here.

We have given no formal requirement on **P** from which it follows in a similar way that the more general case (e.g., of "John" and "the rearming of Germany," etc.) will be satisfactorily dealt with, nor do I see how one could be given. Our expectation is that the requirement of simplicity (cf. §58) will compel the adoption of a system of phrase structure in which this more general case is also handled adequately. If detailed investigation of English syntax show that this is not the case, then some such formal requirement will have to be sought.

62.1   It remains to specify the relation between **P** and **W**, that is, to axiomatize $\Phi^{\mathbf{P}}$. As we shall see, the characterization of $\Phi^{\mathbf{P}}$ raises many problems, and cannot be properly given until we have developed the notion of grammatical transformation in Chapter IX. We give here only a preliminary discussion, sufficient for the attempt in the following chapter to construct a partial grammar for English phrase structure.

Recalling the questions raised in Note 6, let us first define a relation γ, somewhat analogous to g on the level **C** (cf. §46), which relates $\bar{P}$ to $\bar{\mathbf{M}}$. Suppose that γ meets the following condition:

38   (i)   If X is a prime in $\bar{P}$ and $\gamma(X, Y)$, then Y is a prime of $\bar{\mathbf{M}}$, or $Y = U^{\mathbf{M}}$ (i.e., Y is the unit of $\bar{\mathbf{M}}$). [In the latter case, we denote X by "$\emptyset_i$," for some i (cf. §16). These cases are not exclusive. One value for X may be a prime and one a unit.]

       (ii)   If X, Y are strings in $\bar{P}$ ($X, Y \neq U$), then $\gamma(X^\frown Y, Z) \Leftrightarrow$ there are strings W_1, W_2 in $\bar{\mathbf{M}}$ such that

             (a) $Z = W_1^\frown W_2$
             (b) $\gamma(X, W_1)$ and $\gamma(Y, W_2)$

      (iii)   If $X \in \bar{P}$, then $\exists Y$ such that $\gamma(X, Y)$.
      (iv)   If $\gamma(X, Y)$, and Y is a morphological head (cf. §47), then Y is the unique value of γ for X.

Thus only nonheads can be dependent on the context for their morphological "realization" (i.e., can belong to long components). We are taking $\bar{P}$ not as $\bar{\mathbf{M}}$ itself, but as a set of elements closely related to $\bar{\mathbf{M}}$. In particular, it turns out to be more convenient (or even necessary) to specify the exact morphemic shape of long components such as number, gender, etc. (i.e., elements whose domain extends over some syntactic unit longer than a word) not within the level **P** itself, but by means of the mapping which relates **P** to lower levels. Thus we find it expedient to take $\bar{P}$ as the set containing morphological heads and "bearers" of long components as its primes. Strings in $\bar{P}$ will then be mapped into actual strings of morphemes.

γ thus relates a string X of $\bar{P}$ to a string of $\bar{M}$ (or to several strings, since γ is not necessarily single-valued). But note that $\Phi^{\mathbf{P}}$, in a derivative way, can be said to relate a string X of $\bar{P}$ to a string in $\bar{M}$ (this time a unique string, since $\Phi^{\mathbf{P}}$ is a single-valued mapping); namely, where X is the product of the **P**-marker K, $\Phi^{\mathbf{P}}$ associates X with $\Phi^{\mathbf{P}}(K)$, which is a string in $\bar{M}$ which is then mapped into $\mu^{\mathbf{W}}$ as discussed in §47. A major difference between $\Phi^{\mathbf{P}}$ and γ (where $\Phi^{\mathbf{P}}$ is considered derivatively as a mapping of strings in $\bar{P}$ into $\bar{M}$) is that $\Phi^{\mathbf{P}}$ need not be order-preserving while γ (taken as a mapping) is. Thus if $X \in Gr(P)$ and $\gamma(X, Y)$, it is not necessarily the case that Y is grammatical. It may be a permutation of a grammatical string or may fail to be grammatical because the element assigned as a value to some nonmorphological head of X may not fit grammatically into its context in Y.

We now relate $\Phi^{\mathbf{P}}$ to γ and complete, tentatively, the characterization of $\Phi^{\mathbf{P}}$. For expository convenience, we will speak of γ too as a mapping of $\bar{P}$ into $\bar{M}$, with $\gamma(p) = m$ for $\gamma(p, m)$.

The general requirement (cf. §§17–18) is that the mappings of each level carry a certain set of markers of that level into a set of markers of of "lower" levels and thus ultimately into grammatical utterances. We have taken **P**-markers to be sets of strings of equivalent restricted ρ_1-derivations. Recall that $Gr(P)$ is the set of products of restricted ρ_1-derivations. Thus we have, as the essential condition on $\Phi^{\mathbf{P}}$, the following:

Axiom 11. If $X \in Gr(P)$ and X is the product of the **P**-marker K, then $\Phi^{\mathbf{P}}(K)$ is an $\bar{\mathbf{M}}$-marker.

We have seen that a constituent interpretation of a string X in $\bar{P}$ is given by a class K containing X even when K is not a **P**-marker. It seems reasonable, then, to take as the domain of $\Phi^{\mathbf{P}}$ sets K containing a single string in $\bar{P}$, or, putting it differently, ordered pairs of a set K and a string $X \in \bar{P}$ contained in K. Thus we add:

Axiom 12. The domain of $\Phi^{\mathbf{P}}$ is the set of pairs (X, K), where X is a string in $\bar{P}$ and K is a set of strings containing X. $\Phi^{\mathbf{P}}(X, K)$ is a string in $\bar{\mathbf{M}}$.

The simplest way to relate γ and $\Phi^{\mathbf{P}}$ would be to require that $\Phi^{\mathbf{P}}(X, K)$ be one of the values of $\gamma(X)$. But this we cannot do, since $\Phi^{\mathbf{P}}$

is not in general a concatenation-preserving mapping. This complication of the mapping is necessitated, for one reason, by the possibility of discontinuous phrases. For example, if we are to develop anything like a reasonable phrase structure for English, the sentence "I called him up" will contain the same verbal element (the compound verb phrase "called up") as does "I called up my friends." Both sentences will be represented by $NP^\frown V^\frown NP$, where V represents "called up." So if we wish to retain a one-dimensional system of representation, we must pay for it by complicating the mappings, or, alternatively, by a considerable complication in the characterization of ρ (if this would indeed be possible). We will see in the analysis of English in Chap. VIII that there are many other such cases, particularly in the analysis of the auxiliary verb.

We can however, make this weaker requirement:

Axiom 13. $\Phi^P(X, K)$ is a permutation of the primes of one of the values of $\gamma(X)$, where γ meets condition **38**.

62.2   We can further subdivide Φ^P into a series of steps. This is necessary in practice because of the immense complexity of this mapping when it is stated in detail. Thus we regard Φ^P as a compound transformation $\Phi^P_m(\Phi^P_{m-1}(...(\Phi^P_1)))$.

There are a variety of problems left unresolved in this discussion. We have not given an explicit statement of *how* a transformation takes into account the constituent structure of a string. And we have not shown how the actual statement of the mapping can be given in the grammar. We have not explained what a compound transformation might be. In fact, this is an impossible notion in our present formulation, since the argument of a mapping is a pair (X, K), and its value is a string X'. Finally, we have not explained in what sense the result of a mapping, the string which is its value, can be said to have a constituent structure. This elaboration is certainly necessary. We must be able to refer to the noun phrase, verb phrases, etc., of sentences given in words.

We will leave these problems unanswered now. We will be able to characterize Φ^P more explicitly below, when the requisite notions will have been developed for transformations.

63   *Appendix: On the Range of Adequacy of Various Types of Grammars* [omitted here. This section discusses the generative capacity of finite-state grammars, phrase-structure grammars, and proper linear grammars. A revised version of this material appeared as "Three models for the description of language" (1956). Only one section relates directly to subsequent material, namely, the final two paragraphs, which follow the

observation that "certain proper linear grammars may not lead to systems of phrase structure, and that certain systems of phrase structure which can be represented by finite grammars are not representable by proper linear grammars." The text concludes as follows:]

This opens up a new possibility for testing the adequacy of the syntactic theory constructed in outline above. We know that ordering of the statements of the grammar can lead to considerable simplifications; i.e., that it is very useful to assume a hierarchy of syntactic and morphological processes. The condition on a sequence of statements that gives a proper linear grammar (i.e., the requirement that every nonterminated derivation be advanced with each application of the grammar) seems a very natural one, and one that increases the value and utility of the grammar. Since we know that Reduction 3 is not always applicable even to a set of derivations producible from a finite grammar, we may ask whether the set of derivations which we require for some actual languages is in fact reducible to a proper linear grammar. A negative answer to this question will be strong evidence that our conceptions of syntactic structure are still inadequate.

In the next three chapters we will bring evidence in favor of the following thesis: the phrase structure of English cannot be reduced to a proper linear grammar; there is a subset of English sentences, interesting on quite independent grounds, which can be provided with a very simple system of phrase structure which is reducible to a proper linear grammar; each grammatical English sentence can be provided with a constituent analysis derivatively by considering its relation to this subsystem of phrase structure; this approach to syntax provides a much simpler grammar, reveals many underlying regularities of the language, and offers formal explanation for much of the "linguistic intuition" of the native speaker, the traditional practice of grammarians, etc.

DESCRIPTION IN TERMS OF PHRASE STRUCTURE
VIII

Having developed the level **P** abstractly, we can now attempt to determine its effectiveness by applying it to the description of actual language material. The sketch of English phrase structure that follows is presented both for illustration and for later reference. It is obvious that it could not be complete or balanced without far exceeding the scope of this study. Some parts of English phrase structure will be omitted completely, others will be very broadly sketched, and others given in fair detail, the place and degree of detail being determined partly by the desire to determine how satisfactory an analysis of English can result from a rigorous reliance on the conceptions of Chapter VII, and partly by the needs of the theoretical exposition to follow in the next chapter, where we will attempt to develop the means for a more adequate grammatical description. If more detail were given, I think that the points to follow in the next chapter could in fact be made even more strongly, though the detail might obscure the demonstration of their validity.

The notations used here will be those of Chapter IV, with occasional minor and self-explanatory deviations. The primes of **P** will be labeled so as to suggest their customary names (e.g., *NP*, *V*, etc.). A more rational labeling system would permit certain statements to be made more elegantly (if the notational devices were extended in simple and obvious ways, e.g., to permit use of indices). In general, there has been no attempt here to present the grammar in the completely reduced form, but I have attempted to set up the elements just the way they would appear in the most elegant form. In other words, the grammatical statement which we will gradually develop in this chapter, and finally present in §72.2, is, subject to the qualifications given above, an expanded version of the simplest statement I have been able to develop.

65.1   While we cannot give a thorough validation of the particular analysis of phrase structure which will be proposed, at least some of the reasoning involved can be sketched. In §58, four grammatical features were mentioned as criteria, in a loose sense there outlined, for the analysis of English. The first of these is the rule for conjunction.

The rule giving the distribution of "and" can be used as a criterion for constituent analysis in the following way. If we have a context $Z_1 \frown \rule{1cm}{0.4pt} \frown Z_2$, and if both X and Y occur in this context, we can determine whether they occur as constituents by seeing whether $X \frown and \frown Y$ can occur in this context. This is a fairly sensitive criterion for the determination of phrase structure, though considerable qualification is necessary. It is clear that it works effectively in the extreme cases. Thus, given

1   *the men walked down the road*

2   *the boys walked down the road*

3   *the men disappeared into the distance*

we have also

4   *the men and the boys walked down the road*

5   *the men walked down the road and disappeared into the distance*

indicating that "the men," "the boys," "walked down the road," and "disappeared into the distance" are constituents here. But given

6   *the little tug chugged up the river*

7   *the great liner sailed down the river*

we do not have

8   *the little tug chugged up the and great liner sailed down the river*

indicating that "little tug chugged up the" and "great liner sailed down the" are not constituents.

Before applying this criterion, it is important to emphasize again its real status. The rule for conjunction is a criterion for constituent analysis in the sense that if we choose constituents so that only constituents of the same type can be so repeated, we have a very simple and concise rule for conjunction (namely, we can state that if X and Y are constituents of the same type and the same internal structure, in a sense to be specified, in the context $Z_1 \frown \text{——} \frown Z_2$, then $Z_1 \frown X \frown and \frown Y \frown Z_2$ is also a sentence), whereas if we choose them so that this is not the case, the rule for the occurrence of *and* will be exceedingly complex. The examples cited indicate that this criterion coincides with intuition in certain clear cases. But the correspondence with intuition supports this criterion only in a derivative sense. It really gives direct support only to the general policy of applying considerations of simplicity to the determination of constituent structure. Similarly, if we cannot (or, for other reasons, do not) set up as constituents exactly the elements with this property of entering into conjunction, this is not to be understood as a repudiation of the criterion of conjunction. The particular criteria of analysis that we set up have only the function of collecting under one heading certain related ways of simplifying the grammar. The ultimate criterion is total systematic simplicity, and to this there are no exceptions.

We can apply the conjunction criterion directly to the determination of the place of the major constituent break. Given the sentence

9   *my friend enjoyed the book*

we might consider analyzing it in any of the following ways, as a first step:

10   *my friend–enjoyed the book*

11   *my friend enjoyed–the book*

12   *my friend–enjoyed–the book*

But we have

13   *my friend liked the play and enjoyed the book*

This rules out the direct analysis **12** into three immediate constituents (since "enjoyed the book" is repeatable as a unit), and gives **10** as one permissible analysis. That this is the only permissible analysis follows from the nongrammaticalness of

14   *my friend enjoyed and my family liked the book*

which rules out **11**. Application of this criterion thus supports the intuitive analysis

15   ρ (*Sentence, Noun Phrase⌢Verb Phrase*)

as the basic analysis of the sentence. Thus the basic grammatical relation (cf. §59) is *actor–action* (*subject–predicate*).

Further investigation shows the possibility of

16   *my friend enjoyed the book and the play*

17   *my friend read and enjoyed the book*

so that there is a secondary analysis: ρ (*Verb Phrase, Verb⌢Noun Phrase*), and a secondary grammatical relation *verb–object*.

It is worth noting that the decision between **10, 11**, and **12** cannot be made in terms of substitutability, at least in any obvious way. There is little to choose between the alternative sets of substitution classes arising from these analyses in terms of size, freedom, etc.

Consider now the sentence

18   *my friend has been reading the book*

We might consider analyzing the verb phrase in **18** into either **19** or **20**:

19   *has been–reading the book*

20   *has been reading–the book*

The conjunction criterion in this case favors **19**, since we have **21** as a natural English sentence, but not **22**.

21   *my friend has been reading the book and smoking a cigar*

22   *my friend has been reading and has been enjoying the book*

This suggests that the primary analysis of the verb phrase should be into auxiliary phrase and a second type of verb phrase, the latter being analyzable into verb and object. In the reduced form, we have as the beginning of the grammar:

23   *Sentence* $\rightarrow NP \frown VP$

$$VP \rightarrow VP_A \frown VP_1$$
$$VP_1 \rightarrow V \frown NP$$

The conjunction criterion will play an important role in this analysis, and a much more careful investigation of the distribution of "and" is certainly called for. In particular, it is necessary to study the parallel in internal structure required for elements to be joined by "and." Here we have discussed only the external parallel, the fact that they must both be represented by the same element and must play the same role in the sentence. We will see below that this study requires a prior study of transformations.

In carrying out the investigation of conjunction, it will be important to bear in mind that we are only interested in the *systematic* behavior of "and," where "systematic" is defined as in Chapter V.[1] Given a set of first-order grammatical categories, and a linguistic corpus, we have a set of sentences generated. In this set we will find instances that are true, false, humorous, logically contradictory, enlightening, meaningless, etc. Exactly what are the boundaries of this set (which defines systematic behavior in the first approximation to grammaticalness given in Chapter V) depends on the subtlety of our category analysis. We are interested in describing just this set, which will include many sentences that no one would ever say, under normal circumstances. If this set is not inclusive enough to contain sentences of these various types, it will fail to meet presystematic requirements, as we have seen. When we say that **13, 16, 17,** and **21** are grammatical, but not **14** and **22,** what is really asserted is that in an adequate[2] corpus of English, the sentence forms of which the former are instances will be grammatical in the sense of Chapter V, but the sentence forms of which the latter are instances will not. The difference between unnatural (or meaningless) instances of grammatical sentence forms and unnatural (or meaningless) instances of ungrammatical sentence forms is crucial for us.

---

[1] We have also noted that when our theory is sufficiently developed, the notion of "systematic behavior" or "grammaticalness" should become refined with the establishment of **M** and with the establishment of **P** itself.

[2] Naturally, if the corpus does not contain a large number of occurrences of "and" in various positions in normal sentences, then we could not make these distinctions on the basis of the corpus. But this is just the tautology that if we have no data, we have nothing to describe. All of our discussion is based on the assumption that the data have been collected—that the grammar is based on an adequate corpus. We have not discussed the very important linguistic question of *how* a corpus is put together and how the linguist obtains the information about linguistic behavior. See Lounsbury, "Field methods and techniques in linguistics"; Harris and Voegelin, "Eliciting."

65.2 A second criterion is that of intrusion of such parenthetical elements as "in my opinion," "as it turned out," "however," etc., with a special comma intonation. This is a less sensitive criterion than conjunction, since though it selects a set of major constituent breaks where intrusion can occur, it does not differentiate among these as to relative order. But the distinction between those places where parenthetical intrusion can occur and where it cannot can be used as support for an analysis, regarding the points of intrusion as more "major" than the points of no intrusion. The choice of **10** over **11** is thus supported by the existence of **24** but not **25**:

24   *my friend, as you can see, enjoyed the book*

25   *my friend enjoyed, as you can see, the book*

However, this criterion conflicts with conjunction in certain instances. Thus we have

26   *his performance was, in my opinion, very undistinguished*

27   *he should, in my opinion, have done much better*

These are subsidiary breaks by the conjunction criterion. The conflict can be resolved by giving two sources for parenthetical intrusion, first, intrusion at major constituent breaks, and second, intrusion at the points where a certain class of adverbs (e.g., "certainly") occur. Thus we have

28   *his performance was certainly very undistinguished*

29   *he should certainly have done much better*

These sources are both necessary. The second is needed to explain **26** and **27**, the first, to explain

30   *he was killed, so I heard, in an automobile accident*

65.3 The third criterion mentioned in §58 concerned the simplification of transformations. We will return to this below, when the notions involved have been developed. We will see then that a more integrated conception of criteria of analysis, including those of this chapter and a large number of others, will be a by-product of the development of transformational analysis.

The final criterion mentioned in §58 (and one which we can barely **65.4** touch on here, without going far afield) is the position of junctures, more generally, the rules for stress and pitch. There is a striking correspondence between the degree of stress and height of pitch and constituent boundary. To take a simple case, consider

31   *the old man in the corner has been reading the newspaper*

The heaviest stress and highest pitch is normally on "newspaper." The stress and pitch on "corner" are heavier than on "man" or "reading." These in turn have a higher stress and pitch than "old," which in turn exceeds "the," "has," "been," "in."

Suppose we mark constituent boundaries (except word boundaries) by a vertical line at the end of each constituent. Thus a word which is at once the final word of *n* constituents (e.g., "corner" concludes the Noun Phrase and the Prepositional Phrase) will be followed by *n* vertical lines. Then, considering the sentence as a whole as its own largest constituent, we have

32   *the old man | in the corner || has been reading | the newspaper |||*

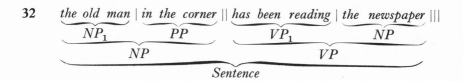

Sentence

The rule that the degree of the major stress of a word and the height of pitch are proportional to the number of vertical bars following the word in question determines the relative stress and pitch of words in the proper way in this instance, when we add the subsidiary rule that certain words ("the," "in," "has," "been," etc.) always have zero stress and pitch. Thus the rules for stress and pitch can be considerably simplified with a proper choice of constituents, or in other words, stress and pitch are criteria for constituent analysis.

The analysis proposed for **32** conflicts with the analysis **23**, and with the choice of **19** over **20**. This conflict of criteria can be resolved by noting that, because of the subsidiary rule concerning "has," "the," "been," "in," etc.,[3] we would have exactly the same statement of relative stress if we had put in the vertical bars in accordance with **23**, since the bars after "been" would have no effect. Thus this criterion is

---

[3] This rule is necessary anyway, to account for such sentences as "John has been" (the answer to "who has been absent?").

neutral with respect to the choice between **19** and **20**, and we could just as well have written **32** in accordance with **23**.

The rule for predicting stress and pitch as sketched above is intended to be suggestive, not definitive. It is greatly oversimplified, and will not account successfully for other cases without elaboration.[4] Recent linguistic work[5] has shown that the study of suprasegmental features such as stress and juncture is a complex one, and the relation between the syntactic structure and suprasegmental patterning requires a careful study. Although it has often been suggested that constituent structure be determined by considerations involving suprasegmentals, I am not acquainted with any attempt at a general and abstract statement as to how this might be accomplished. This is an important question, but once again further discussion and investigation would carry us into areas that have arbitrarily been placed beyond the scope of this study.

65.5   We might consider, as a criterion for syntactic analysis, such a phenomenon as intermittent pause. For example, it might be argued that **9** can be said with a pause at the constituent break suggested in **10**, but not at the break suggested in **11**. There are other cases where a sentence *can* be said so that its interpretation is unmistakable, but is ordinarily said so that its interpretation is ambiguous. But if the datum we are analyzing is normal speech, then it seems preferable to handle such possible readings as derivative from the grammar (rather than as criteria for the grammar), i.e., to explain them as being a reflection of the fact that the speaker knows (on other grounds) the place of the constituent breaks. The task of the linguist, then, becomes the isolation of these other grounds. This is the same problem that we have discussed above in §34.2 and Note 6 of Chapter II.

Other criteria for constituent analysis will appear below, as we investigate the actual formulation of the syntactic description.

---

[4] One interesting fact, in this connection, is that there is a certain subclass K of grammatical sentences that has an independent significance and for which rules of this kind apparently come much closer to being adequate. The importance of this remark will only become clear later, when we see that K, which we will later call the *kernel* of the language, can be isolated by purely syntactic techniques on the higher level of transformational analysis, quite independently of any consideration of suprasegmentals. We will then argue, on independent grounds, that only the elements of K need be assigned a phrase structure.

[5] See, for instance, Pike, *The Intonation of American English*; Newman, "On the stress system of English"; Trager and Smith, *An Outline of English Structure*. For investigation of the relation between constituent structure and suprasegmentals, see Chomsky, Halle, and Lukoff, "On accent and juncture in English."

Since the auxiliary verb phrase VP_A plays a central role in English 66.1
syntax (particularly, as we will see below, in transformational analysis),
we must analyze it in some detail. The forms to be accounted for under
the auxiliary verb are given in Table 1, with "take" as the verb. "will"
has been used as the representative of a class M containing "will,"
"can," "may," "shall," "must," "would," "could," "might," "should."
We can fill the gaps in column II by taking "would," "could," "might,"
"should," "must" as compounds, these being, respectively, the "past
tense" forms of "will," "can," "may," "shall," "must." It turns out that
this analysis does in fact simplify the direct description of the auxiliary
phrase, even though the gaps in column III remain. But its ultimate
acceptability also depends on its effects on the formulation of other
statements of the grammar, such as "sequence of tense" statements,
which I have not investigated.

Column IV can be disregarded for the time being, as involving a
special fact about the morpheme "be," not a feature specific to the
auxiliary phrase. This is evident from the fact that "be" in its use as the
main verb also has the peculiarity that it has a separate form for past
singular and plural.

Rows 14, 15, and 16 contain forms whose status may be in some
doubt. Whether they are to be included or not depends on a gram-

Table 1

	I	II	III	IV
1	takes	took	take	—
2	is taken	was taken	are taken	were taken
3	is taking	was taking	are taking	were taking
4	has taken	had taken	have taken	—
5	will take	—	—	—
6	is being taken	was being taken	are being taken	were being taken
7	has been taken	had been taken	have been taken	—
8	will be taken	—	—	—
9	has been taking	had been taking	have been taking	—
10	will be taking	—	—	—
11	will have taken	—	—	—
12	will have been taken	—	—	—
13	will have been taking	—	—	—
14	has been being taken	had been being taken	have been being taken	—
15	will be being taken	—	—	—
16	will have been being taken	—	—	—

maticalness decision. The analysis of the auxiliary phrase is simpler if they are included, or in other words, they conform to the "structure" of the verb phrase. They certainly have a clear meaning, which can be expressed in no other way, and I have noted several instances of these forms in normal conversational speech. If they are excluded on some grounds, then no doubt such forms as "he has been being very cooperative today" will be excluded on the same grounds. If so, this exclusion will require a special statement, outside the analysis of the auxiliary phrase, since in this latter case the second "be" is the main verb, not the auxiliary.[6] In any event, the decision as to their grammaticalness will apparently not affect the analysis to be given of the auxiliary phrase. If this analysis is the simplest when they are admitted, then this analysis plus the rule excluding them will, apparently, be the simplest analysis if they are excluded.

The words in the auxiliary phrase have the property of containing no major stress (other than contrastive stress, which any word can assume). There are certain other elements which might be considered as belonging to the auxiliary phrase, including "ought to," "used to," "have to," the passivizing "get," "want to," etc. All of these will be discussed below (several, repeatedly) in this chapter and in Chapter X.

66.2   We have in the grammar the statement "$VP \to VP_A{}^\frown VP_1$" (cf. **23**), and we now face the problem of giving the statement "$VP_A \to ...$" in such a way as to include in "..." all the forms of Table 1 and no others.

As the components of VP_A, we may take the elements

33   (i)   *ed, C*
          (ii) *M = will, shall, can, may, must*
          (iii) *have$^\frown$en*
          (iv) *be$^\frown$ing*
          (v)   *be$^\frown$en*

ed is the morpheme of the past tense. *C* is an element of $\bar{P}$ (i.e., a "lowest level" element of the level **P**) which carries the long component of number. The analysis of *C* into morphemes is thus effected by a mapping (cf. §62.1). Given these elements we can analyze the auxiliary phrase as

34 $VP_A \to \begin{Bmatrix} ed \\ C \end{Bmatrix} \langle M \rangle \langle have^\frown en \rangle \langle be^\frown ing \rangle \langle be^\frown en \rangle$

[6] But see below, §67.2, where passives are analyzed as *Verb + Adjective*.

Thus an auxiliary phrase must contain as its initial element either *ed* or *C*, and this initial element can be followed by zero or more of *M*, *have⌐en*, *be⌐ing*, *be⌐en* in that order. *M* can then take any of the forms in 33ii.

But the sequence of morphemes which results from an application of **34** is not in the correct order. Thus to complete the statement we give the following rule:

35   Let *Y* be any one of *ed, C, en, ing* (i.e., *Y* is any affix), and let *Z* be a prime. Then $X^\frown Y^\frown Z^\frown W \to X + Z^\frown Y + W$, where $+$ is the marker of word boundary, i.e., it is the concatenation operation of the level **W**.

When **35** is properly formulated, it will thus appear as a part of the mapping Φ^P which carries the products of derivations in **P** ultimately into strings in **W**. The result of the application of **34** (when *M* is analyzed by 33ii) is thus part of a string of $Gr(P)$, and we have here the first instance in which it is required that Φ^P not be order-preserving (cf. §62).

These two statements, one rule of the grammar, one statement of a mapping, serve to generate exactly the forms in Table 1 (if rows 14, 15, and 16 are to be excluded, then a statement must be added to this effect). As an example of their operation, suppose we have $VP_A{}^\frown take$, and VP_A is analyzed by **34** as

36 $ed^\frown[have^\frown en]^\frown[be^\frown ing]^\frown take = ed^\frown have^\frown en^\frown be^\frown ing^\frown take$

Applying rule **35** to this segment of a string of $Gr(P)$ three times (with $Y = ing$, $Y = en$, $Y = ed$), we derive

37 $have^\frown ed + be^\frown en + take^\frown ing$

which by the morphological rules (i.e., the mappings of **M** into **W** and **Pm**) is carried into

38 $had + been + taking$

Similarly, when **35** is correctly formulated as a mapping, every other element of Table 1 and only these elements, can be generated. Column II results when the initial element of the VP_A is *ed*, columns I and III, when the initial element is *C*.

C will in turn be analyzed by a mapping $\Phi_i{}^P$ (§62.2) whose content will be roughly as follows, where for noun phrases, *S* is taken as the plural morpheme, and $\emptyset$ as the singular morpheme (thus each *NP* becomes either $NP^\frown S$ or $NP^\frown\emptyset$):

39   *C* goes into *S* in the environment $NP^\frown\emptyset$——, and into $\emptyset$ into the environment $NP^\frown S$——.

Thus the long component of number has the peculiar feature that the verb is "singular" when the subject is "plural," and *vice versa.*[7] That the same morpheme *S* is affixed to both the noun and the verb is evident both from the fact that this is a long component, and from the fact that the same morphophonemic statements must be made about both elements (e.g., both are voiced after voiced consonants, etc.).[8] When *C* becomes *S*, we have column I, when it becomes $\emptyset$, we have column III. Note that several rules are required in the morphology to account for the special behavior of *be* and *have* with *S* and $\emptyset$ (just as rules have to be given in the morphology to state the phonemic shapes of particular verbs with *en*, *ed*, and *ing*, as well as *S*) and for the fact that the elements of *M* (cf. **33**ii) do not change their shape with *S*.

In this analysis we have considered the elements *ed*, *S*, $\emptyset$, *en*, *ing* as belonging to the auxiliary phrase, although we saw earlier that the constituent break is, e.g., *John–was–eating*, thus $NP\text{-}VP_A\text{-}VP_1$. These two analyses are not strictly compatible, unless the conjunction criterion can be restricted to apply, somehow, *after* the mapping whose content is **35** has been carried out. Such a condition has no clear meaning in terms of our present theoretical development. See also §62.2. We will proceed as if there were no problem here, and will return to this later with more adequate means.

66.3   Further light is shed on the internal structure of the auxiliary verb phrase by the investigation of infinitive phrases. Consider the constituent analysis of

40   *to prove that theorem was difficult*

Clearly, the major constituent break is after "theorem," making "to prove that theorem" the noun phrase subject. The constituents of this noun phrase are customarily taken to be the infinitive "to prove" and the noun phrase "that theorem." But this analysis is not satisfactory.

---

[7] Note that "I" and "you" are "plural" from the point of view of this rule of "disagreement in number."

[8] That these rules are morphophonemic, not phonemic, is evident from such pairs as "peers"–"pierce," "raisins"–"essence," etc.

It can be preserved only at the cost of duplicating the description of the verb phrase. To show this properly would require a detailed comparison of the alternatives, but note that part of the description of the verb phrase will be a statement of the objects, prepositional phrases, etc., with which each verb can occur, i.e., a statement, for each verb V_i, of the set K_i of conditioning contexts in which *verb* can become V_i. But if our constituent analysis of the noun phrases in question is *Infinitive* $^\frown X$, then this information must be repeated in stating the development of *Infinitive* to $to^\frown V_i$. That is, we will have to give the general analysis of noun phrases of this type by such a statement as **41**:

41 $NP \rightarrow Inf^\frown X$

$$Inf \rightarrow to \begin{Bmatrix} V_1 \\ \vdots \\ V_n \end{Bmatrix} \text{ in env. } \begin{Bmatrix} K_1 \\ \vdots \\ K_n \end{Bmatrix}$$

where X is a statement of everything that can occur after a verb to complete the verb phrase, and each K_i is a detailed specification of the conditioning context for V_i.

But any complete verb phrase can be turned into a noun phrase by prefixation of "to." Thus the most economical description of such noun phrases is simply

42 $NP \rightarrow to^\frown VP$

so that in **40** the constituents are "to" and "prove that theorem." This avoids the superfluous specification of X and the K_i given in **41**. The internal construction of these noun phrases is now given completely by the analysis of the verb phrase, an analysis which will in any case have to be given separately. Various alternative ways of preserving the analysis of NP as $Inf^\frown X$, where $Inf \rightarrow to^\frown V$, also appear to be redundant and complex as compared to **42**. The unreasonableness of taking the infinitive as $to^\frown verb$, rather than $to^\frown Verb\ Phrase$ becomes particularly clear in cases like

43   {*to keep the soldiers under control wasn't easy*
           {*to call these people up is silly*

This analysis requires some elaboration, however. Not every verb phrase can occur after *to*, but only those containing neither C nor *ed*, nor any member of M (cf. **33**). That is, we can have "to take," "to have taken," etc., but not "to took," "to takes," "to can take," etc. The simplest way to handle this situation is to revise **34**, replacing it by

44 $VP_A \rightarrow VP_{A1} \langle VP_{A2} \rangle$

$VP_{A1} \rightarrow \begin{Bmatrix} ed \\ C \end{Bmatrix} \langle M \rangle$

$VP_{A2} \rightarrow \langle have\frown en \rangle \langle be\frown ing \rangle \langle be\frown en \rangle$[9]

Then as a complete specification of infinitive phrases, we have simply

45 $NP \rightarrow to \langle VP_{A2} \rangle VP_1$

66.4   This completes the internal analysis of VP_A, but it is necessary to add statements of certain contextual restrictions on the form of the auxiliary phrase. This is not surprising, since we know that **P** is a nonrestricted system for English. The principal restrictions are these:

46   (i) $be\frown en$ can occur only when the following verb is transitive;

(ii) $be\frown ing$ cannot occur in the environment: ——$\begin{cases} V_m\frown that... \\ V_n ... \end{cases}$

where

$V_m = know,\ believe,\ think,\ ...$
$V_n = own,\ like,\ belong\ to,\ ...$

Thus we cannot have "John is barked," "John is knowing that he will come," "John is owning his house," etc. The first restriction (**46**i) must certainly be recognized if the conception of "systematic behavior" (i.e., "grammaticalness") developed in linguistic theory is to be judged adequate.[10] About the second (**46**ii) there may be more question.

This general account of the auxiliary phrase will underlie much of

----

[9] Note that we cannot have $\rho(X, U)$. Thus a notational convention must be added that in cases like the analysis of VP_{A2}, where all elements appearing in the analysis are "angled," at least one of them must be developed, i.e., only $2^n - 1$ of the 2^n ways of developing such statements permitted by Definition 5, §30, can actually be permitted.

[10] That is, we must assume that the methods of Chapter V (which are stated in terms of words) lead to the construction of a category of intransitive participles ("barked," "slept," etc.), which never occur in the context "John was——," etc., alongside of a category of intransitive "finite" verbs ("bark," "sleep," etc.). The methods of morphological analysis, which we have not discussed, must be such as to lead to the identification of these sets element by element. That is, we must show that the grammar is simplified in certain ways by this identification, or we must develop independent means to reach the same result. Obviously, these problems of morphology deserve very serious study, and failure to undertake this is a serious gap in this theoretical development. We might hope that the correspondence between these two categories need not be one-to-one in order for linguistic method to carry out the identification. This leads into the problem of projection on the level **M**, which we have also not discussed.

the discussion and analysis given below. Later considerations will require that it be slightly recast, but the basic feature of the analysis, rule **35**, will be retained throughout.

Independent support for rule **35** comes from investigation of the noun **66.5** phrase (and, we will see presently, from further investigation of the verb phrase). Alongside of **40** and **43** we have

47 $\begin{cases} \textit{proving that theorem was difficult} \\ \textit{keeping the soldiers under control wasn't easy} \\ \textit{calling these people up is silly} \end{cases}$

It is clear that these are perfectly parallel in their construction to **40** and **43**, and that notions of "verbal noun," etc., are unsatisfactory for the same reasons as is "infinitive." By virtue of **35**, however, we can analyze these as $ing^\frown Verb\ Phrase$, so that "to" and "ing" are elements of exactly the same kind. Thus, where NP_I is a special kind of noun phrase (in fact, a subclass of abstract nouns), we have

48 $\qquad NP_I \rightarrow \begin{Bmatrix} to \\ ing \end{Bmatrix} \langle VP_{A2} \rangle\ VP_1$

replacing **45**. The fact that *ing* occurs as a suffix (not as a preposed word, like *to*) is an automatic consequence of **35**, which, as we have seen, was independently motivated.

One restriction seems necessary here. $be^\frown ing$ cannot occur after *ing* (e.g., there is no "being eating dinner when they arrive would be quite impolite," though there is "to be eating dinner when they arrive would be quite impolite").

It will appear below that **48** plays a crucial role in the analysis of the verb phrase. We note already that **48** might be said to furnish a criterion (in much the same sense as does the rule for conjunction) for the establishment of the major constituent break in the sentence, i.e., for the choice between **10** and **11** as analyses for **9**. Given $N^\frown V^\frown N$, $N^\frown V^\frown PP$ ($PP = Prepositional\ Phrase$), etc., if we set up a prime Q representing $N^\frown V$, and analyze these sentences into $Q^\frown N$, $Q^\frown PP$, etc., in accordance with **11**, then this prime Q will be of no further utility in stating grammatical rules—it will appear nowhere else, and in **48** we will have to list all the forms $V^\frown N$, $V^\frown PP$, etc., as new elements, which have played no previous role in the grammar. But if we analyze these sentences into $N^\frown VP$, with VP representing $V^\frown N$, $V^\frown PP$, etc., in accordance with **10**, then this prime VP can appear again, with no further discussion, in **48**, to be analyzed in the grammar by the same conversion that develops VP into $V \frown N$, $V \frown PP$, etc., when VP occurs in $N \frown VP$. The various forms of VP need not be listed in **48**. In other words, we might say, in a loose sense, that a corollary of the principle of simplicity is that **P** should be constructed in such a way that each prime will appear in many statements of the grammar.

One way to test the adequacy of a formal construction is to compare the analysis to which it leads with our intuitive conception of linguistic form (cf. §15). Correspondence can be taken as a partial corroboration for the abstract underlying conceptions from one viewpoint, or, from another viewpoint, as providing a formal linguistic basis for these intuitions. We have not yet analyzed the verb phrase, but clearly one possible analysis will give the sentence type

49 $NP \frown is \frown NP$

e.g., "John is my friend." But we have seen that one form of the NP is NP_I as in **48**. Thus we should be able to have

50 $NP \frown is \frown NP_I$

e.g., "the important thing is to be happy."

Thus it follows from the analysis to which we have been led that there should be two ways of interpreting a sentence of the form

51 $NP \frown is \frown ing \frown VP_1$

either as a case of **50**, with *is* as the main verb and $ing \frown VP_1$ as the NP_I, or, with $is \frown ing$ as the auxiliary, as a case of

52 $NP \frown VP_A \frown VP_1$

But this is in fact quite in accord with intuition. Clearly we understand **53** and **54** in quite different ways,

53   *the important thing is winning*

54   *our team is winning*

with quite different constituent structure. **53** is an instance of **50**, and **54** is an instance of **52**. Despite some clumsiness, we might consider

55   *his suggestion was becoming famous*

to be a case of presystematic constructional homonymity.

To sum up our major conclusions at this point, the basic structure of **66.6** the English interpretation of **P** can be stated as follows:

56   *Sentence* → $NP \frown VP$
$$VP \rightarrow VP_A \frown VP_1$$
$$VP_A \rightarrow VP_{A1} \langle VP_{A2} \rangle$$
$$VP_{A1} \rightarrow \begin{Bmatrix} ed \\ C \end{Bmatrix} \langle M \rangle$$
$$VP_{A2} \rightarrow \langle have \frown en \rangle \langle be \frown ing \rangle \langle be \frown en \rangle$$

The basic mappings are **35** and **39**.

We have not yet discussed VP_1, except to point out that one analysis **67.1** is as $V \frown NP$. The investigation of the distribution of the infinitive elements *to* and *ing* in the verb phrase provides a further analysis. Consider first the case of *to*-phrases. There are three fundamental patterns for the occurrence of these in the verb phrase. Where "*to*-phrase" denotes any instance of NP_l beginning with *to* (cf. **48**), we have three classes of verbs, V_a, V_b, V_c:

57   (i) $VP_1 \rightarrow V_a \langle NP \rangle$ *to*-phrase
        (ii) $VP_1 \rightarrow V_b \frown NP \frown$*to*-phrase
        (iii) $VP_1 \rightarrow V_c \frown$*to*-phrase

$V_a =$ want, like, ask, beg, . . .
$V_b =$ advise, compel, order, persuade, . . .
$V_c =$ decide, demand, begin, try, fail, . . .

Conforming to **57**i, we have "they want him to come" or "they want to come"; conforming to **57**ii, "they advise him to come"; conforming to **57**iii, "they decided to come."

For *ing*-phrases (where "*ing*-phrase" denotes any NP_l beginning with *ing*) we have a parallel situation, with classes V_α, V_β, V_γ such that

58   (i) $VP_1 \rightarrow V_\alpha \langle NP \rangle$ *ing*-phrase
        (ii) $VP_1 \rightarrow V_\beta \frown NP \frown$*ing*-phrase
        (iii) $VP_1 \rightarrow V_\gamma \frown$*ing*-phrase

$V_\alpha =$ imagine, visualize, . . .
$V_\beta =$ find, catch, . . .
$$V_\gamma = \begin{cases} V_{\gamma_1} = \text{urge, postpone, regret, forget, stop, . . .} \\ V_{\gamma_2} = \text{avoid, begin, try, . . .} \end{cases}$$

Conforming to **58**i we have "I can't imagine him riding a horse" or "I can't imagine riding a horse"; conforming to **58**ii, "I found him smoking"; conforming to **58**iii, "I urged putting it off for a few days."

The distinction between subclasses of V_γ, though not of V_c, is necessitated by the somewhat broader distribution of *ing*-phrases. An NP_I can occur after a possessive adjective ("the man's," "my," etc.), but only if it is an *ing*-phrase. It is thus necessary to distinguish between verbs that can be followed by *ing*-phrases accompanied by possessive adjectives, and those that cannot. Thus we have "I regretted their refusing to come," but not "I avoided their refusing," etc. An analogous distinction might be necessary in V_α, but it appears that all members of V_α can occur with these adjectives. Thus we have "I imagined their being lost in the storm," etc. This distinction seems to vary somewhat from speaker to speaker, as does the distinction between V_α and V_{γ_1}, and it requires much further study. It may be that V_{γ_1} should be treated together with V_α, with the possessive adjective as a variant of the "objective" subject. We return to this later on.

Since *to*-phrases and *ing*-phrases are noun phrases (by **48**), we might regard **57** and **58** as being special cases of transitive verb phrases, with either one or two objects. Thus "they want to come" would be a case of *NP-V-NP*, like "they want a drink," and "they want him to come" would be a case of *NP-V-NP-NP* like "they asked him a question." But this counterintuitive analysis is excluded by a closer consideration of such sentences. We will return to this below, after analyzing the transitive verb.

67.2   There is also a class of verbs V_δ that occurs with *ing*-phrases but not with *to*-phrases:

59 $VP_1 \to V_\delta{^\frown}NP \langle ing \rangle VP_1{}^{11}$
V_δ = see, feel, hear, watch, . . .

Thus we have "I saw him come," "I saw him coming," etc.

V_δ is a class of special interest because it introduces a distinction between *be${^\frown}en$* and the other elements of the auxiliary phrase. Alongside of **59** we also have

---

[11] But note that **59** as it stands is very likely to lead to a violation of Axiom 7, §54.2. We cannot rewrite "VP_1" on the right as "VP_2" because in running through the grammar a second time, this element must itself be subject to **59**, since we can have "I saw him watching them coming down the road," etc. We will continue the analysis overlooking this potential trouble spot, which will be avoided in Chapter X.

60 $VP_1 \rightarrow V_\delta{}^\frown NP \langle ing \rangle\ be^\frown en^\frown VP_1$

giving such sentences as

61   *I don't like to see people* $\begin{Bmatrix} be \\ being \end{Bmatrix}$ *intimidated*

62   *I don't like to see people* $\begin{Bmatrix} be \\ being \end{Bmatrix}$ *accused without evidence*

But we cannot have either **63** or **64**:

63   *I don't like to see people* $\begin{Bmatrix} be \\ being \end{Bmatrix}$ *drinking*[12]

64   *I don't like to see people* $\begin{Bmatrix} have \\ having \end{Bmatrix}$ *drunk*

Thus $be^\frown en$ can occur in this position, but neither $be^\frown ing$ nor $have^\frown en$ (nor, of course, $[have^\frown en]^\frown[be^\frown ing]$, etc.) can occur here.

A way to avoid the necessity of treating **60** as an exception is suggested by the fact that **65** is a grammatical sentence:

65   *I don't like to see people* $\begin{Bmatrix} be \\ being \end{Bmatrix}$ *argumentative without cause*

This is a case of **59** $= V_\delta{}^\frown NP \langle ing \rangle\ VP_1$, where VP_1 becomes $be^\frown adjective^\frown PP$. But "accused" $[= en^\frown accuse]$ (or "intimidated") can also be regarded as an adjective. If it is, then **60** becomes a special case of **59**, paralleling **65**. This suggests that the analysis can be simplified if $be^\frown en$ is dropped from VP_{A2}, so that a passive such as "John was accused" is treated as a special case of $be^\frown adjective$, just like "John was sad" or "John was tired."[13]

---

[12] We must be careful about choice of examples here. Thus we might have $A_1 =$ "I don't like to see people be$\langle ing \rangle$ intimidating," but not $A_2 =$ "I don't like to see people be$\langle ing \rangle$ indimidating others." But the grammaticalness of the former is irrelevant to the point at issue. We know that this is a case of an adjectival, not verbal, use of "intimidating" because if A_1 is acceptable, then so is $A_3 =$ "I don't like to see people be$\langle ing \rangle$ very intimidating." Hence A_1, even if judged grammatical, does not contain an instance of the auxiliary $be^\frown ing$, as does **63**.

[13] But note that "accused" will still be in a different subcategory of adjectives than "sad" or "tired," since it cannot be preceded by "very."

There are other examples of a distinction between $be\frown en$ and the other elements of VP_{A2} that lend further support to the analysis of passives as $be\frown adjective$. For instance, we see that **66** and **67** are acceptable sentences, but not **68**:

66   *it is pleasant to attend meetings and be applauded (by supporters)*

67   *it is pleasant to attend meetings and be friendly (with the delegates)*

68   *it is pleasant to attend meetings and be running for office*

Here again $be\frown en\frown V$ is treated as a VP_1 with the main verb *be* and a predicate adjective $en\frown V$, rather than as $VP_{A2}\frown V$. In this case, the evidence that it is in fact a VP_1 is given by the conjunction criterion, since "attend meetings" is certainly a VP_1 .

We will find additional support for this analysis below. It appears to be the case that this analysis of passives as $be\frown adjective$ is actually forced on us by considerations of simplicity. However, it is not an intuitively acceptable analysis, as it stands, since it fails to account for the fact that in "John was accused," "accuse" has, intuitively, a "verbal force" not shared by "sad" in "John was sad," "tired" (which is also $en\frown verb$) in "John was tired," or "surprising" in "his success seems surprising." The failure of this analysis to account for intuition becomes even clearer in the case of "John was accused by his enemies,"analyzed as *John-was-adjective-PP*, like "John was successful on the stage." Furthermore, the fact that this construction is limited to transitive verbs (cf. **46i**, §66.4) remains unexplained.

There are also systematic difficulties with this analysis, since the subcategory of adjectives consisting of true passives (cf. Note 13) fails to share certain distributional features of predicate adjectives; e.g., they do not occur after "stative" verbs—we do not have "he seems accused." This stands as an unmotivated exception at the present level of analysis. Actually neither of the possible alternative analyses seems quite right on this level, a fact which suggests that our theory is inadequate. This is a conclusion which has already appeared several times, and to which we will be led repeatedly throughout this discussion of phrase structure. We will continue to record these inadequacies and proceed with the analysis, returning to them later with more adequate means.

67.3   The analysis of transitive verbs depends on how fine an analysis is made of nouns, and both questions thus refer back to the grammaticalness considerations of Chapter V. In this analysis of English phrase structure, we assume that, among others, the following distinctions have been established:

69 N_{anim} = John, boy, dog, . . .

N_{inan} = table, book, . . .

N_{ab} = sincerity, truthfulness, justice, companionship, . . .

Certainly many further distinctions must be recognized, but this will suffice for present purposes.

Transitive verbs V_T can be classified by the subjects and objects that they take. We will recognize, for the time being, the following subclasses of V_T :

70 V_{t1} = appoint, feed, sue, scold, . . .

V_{t2} = like, recognize, admire, desire, seek, . . .

V_{t3} = frighten, surprise, bore, entertain, interest, thrill, . . .

V_{t4} = carry, scratch, see, throw, . . .

We can add to the specification of VP_1 a statement based on (71):

71 $$VP_1 \rightarrow \begin{Bmatrix} V_{t1}\frown...N_{anim} \\ V_{t2}\frown NP \\ V_{t4}\frown...\begin{bmatrix} N_{anim} \\ N_{inan} \end{bmatrix} \end{Bmatrix} \text{ in env. } N_{anim}\frown VP_A\text{——}$$
$$VP_1 \rightarrow V_{t3}\frown...N_{anim}$$

Thus we have "John appointed the boy," "John likes sincerity," "John carried the table," "sincerity frightens John," etc.

We can also distinguish among the intransitives V_I , between those that have animate and inanimate subjects, thus recognizing the classes

72 V_{I1} = sleep, run, bark, . . .

V_{I2} = occur, break, . . .

71 And **72** will play a crucial role in the following discussions. Since these rules of the grammar state how the choice of the verb is determined by the nature of the subject and the object, we will refer to them as *rules of verbal selection*. We will extend this name to refer to any form that these rules may take under subsequent formulations of the grammar, and to extension of these rules to cover other positions where V_T and V_I may occur. This account is much oversimplified. Actually, the rules of verbal selection will be much more complex in a detailed and adequate grammar. Note that we are building a system of phrase structure only for first-order grammatical sentences, a category that presumably excludes such semisentences as "sincerity appointed the table" and "John frightens sincerity." Given the grammar, these partially grammatical sequences can be recovered from the system **C**. Note further that the fact that an element is in one class does not, of course, mean that it cannot also be a member of other classes.

If we proceed with the system of **56**, one major qualification must be added to **71**. This rule will hold only if VP_A does not contain *be⌢en*. If *be⌢en* does appear in VP_A, then a transitive verb can occur even with no following noun phrase, and a separate rule of verbal selection must be given, since in the passive, subject and object are interchanged. This is a major distinction between *be⌢en* and the other elements of the auxiliary phrase. This consideration lends support to the proposal of §67.2 that *be⌢en* be dropped from VP_A and that passives be treated as *be⌢adjective*. If this is done, then no qualification need be added to **71**, though it is still necessary, naturally, to give a statement of the contextual conditions on the occurrence of transitive verbs in the context *be⌢en——*. Note further, in this connection, that the major restriction on the development of VP_A, namely **46i**, can also be dropped if we follow this suggestion, though the fact expressed remains unexplained. We will proceed now, accepting this revision. *be⌢en* is dropped from VP_{A2} in **56**, (i) is dropped from **46**, **60** can be dropped from the grammar (becoming now a special case of **59**), and we will find it easier to account for sentences like **66**. We are left with a grammatical statement that is somewhat simpler, but that does not succeed in grounding certain clear intuitions about linguistic form, since the apparent verbal force of the passive is unexplained, as are other anomalies. We will return to the case of the passive form the different point of view which will be developed in the next chapter, where it will appear that one dimension of the analysis has been left out. We must now state, as part of the analysis of the adjective phrase AP,

73 $AP \rightarrow en⌢V_T$

74 Gives a partial analysis of the verb phrase with *be* as the main verb:

74 $VP_1 \rightarrow be \begin{Bmatrix} NP \\ AP \quad \langle PP \rangle \end{Bmatrix}$ (*PP = Prepositional Phrase*)

Having accepted this solution for the passive, we can rephrase **48** somewhat more adequately as

75 $NP_I \rightarrow \left\{ \begin{array}{l} to \ \langle VP_{A2} \rangle \\ ing \ \langle have\frown en \rangle \end{array} \right\} VP_I$

The extra restriction given below **48** is now incorporated into rule **75**.

The further analysis of VP_1 gives such forms as   **67.4**

76 $V_e \ \langle that \rangle$ Sentence   (*I knew* $\langle that \rangle$ *he would come*)

$V_e \frown NP \frown to \frown be \left\{ \begin{array}{l} NP \\ AP \end{array} \right\}$ (*I believe him to be a creative thinker, ... to be hopeless*)

$V_f \frown NP \frown NP$ (*I gave him three books*)
$V_g \frown NP \frown NP$ (*they elected him president*)

$V_h \frown NP \left\{ \begin{array}{l} NP \\ AP \end{array} \right\}$ (*they considered him a creative thinker, ... hopeless*)

V_e = know, believe, think, discover, . . .
V_f = give, ask, refuse, make, . . .
V_g = elect, choose, . . .
V_h = consider, think, make, . . .

V_f and V_g differ in that V_g requires agreement in number between the succeeding noun phrases.

There are still further forms of the verb phrase, but if we were to continue to analyze these we would apparently be led to quite counter-intuitive analyses. We will return to the more complex forms later on, in Chapter X, when English grammar will be examined from a different point of view.

We now return to the investigation of the validity of the proposal of the   **68.1**
last paragraph of §67.1 that "they want to come" be analyzed as NP-V-NP,[14] and "they want him to come" as NP-V-$NP\frown NP$, with the final NP in each case being NP_I of **75**. This proposal then offers as part of the analysis of VP_1

---

[14] Actually, as $NP\frown VP_A\frown V\frown NP$. In discussing various alternative analyses we often will omit mention of the auxiliary phrase, where this plays no role in the choice between them. Major constituent breaks will often be marked by a dash in informal discussion.

$$77 \quad VP_1 \to \left\{ \begin{array}{c} \left\{ \begin{array}{c} V_a \\ V_\alpha \end{array} \right\} \langle NP \rangle \\ \left\{ \begin{array}{c} V_b \\ V_\beta \\ V_f \\ V_g \end{array} \right\} NP \\ \left\{ \begin{array}{c} V_c \\ V_\gamma \\ V_T \end{array} \right\} \end{array} \right\} NP'$$

where $NP' \to NP_1$ when the verb is not V_f, V_g, or V_T. There are two overriding considerations that rule out this analysis. One concerns the rules of verbal selection, and one a certain rule of agreement in number.

We have analyzed sentences like

78   *John wants to read the book*

as though "wants" were the main verb, and "read" part of the succeeding nominal phrase. But alternatively, we might consider "read" to be the main verb, and "wants to" to be a special type of preposed auxiliary. Actually, the latter analysis seems to be necessary at this point. To see this consider the rule of verbal selection given above in **71**. Exactly the same rule applies for the environment **79** as for **80**:

79 $NP^\frown VP_A{}^\frown V_a{}^\frown to\text{——}NP$[15]

80 $NP^\frown VP_A\text{——}NP$

Thus we have **81** but not **82**:

81   (a) *the law covers these cases*
          (b) *the law fails to cover these cases*

82   (a) *the law eats lunch*
          (b) *the law fails to eat lunch*

A more detailed analysis of transitive verbs than the one we have given would also show the possibility of **83** but not **84**:

---

[15] The following discussion applies to both V_a and V_c.

83 $\begin{cases}\text{(a)} & \textit{the law applies to theft} \\ \text{(b)} & \textit{the law fails to apply to theft}\end{cases}$

84 $\begin{cases}\text{(a)} & \textit{John applies to theft} \\ \text{(b)} & \textit{John fails to apply to theft}\end{cases}$

It follows that the simplest way to give this rule is to cover both cases in a single statement, i.e., paralleling **71**, as

85 $VP_1 \rightarrow V_{ti} \frown NP_y$ in env. $NP_x \frown VP_A \langle V_a \frown to \rangle$——, where NP_x and NP_y are specifications of the various relevant types of noun phrases, and $i = 1,..., 4$ (cf. **71**)

or perhaps

86 $V_T \rightarrow V_{ti}$ in env. $NP_x \frown VP_A \langle V_a \frown to \rangle$——$NP_y$

But if we develop the grammar on the basis of **77**, it will be impossible to give the same rule for both the case with $V_a \frown to$ and the case without it. The reason for this is that the rule which converts NP_I into $to \frown VP_1$, i.e., **75**, must apply after **77**, since NP' (which becomes NP_I) is introduced in **77**. Hence the VP_1 within NP_I will not be developed in running through the grammar the first time, since the statement that develops VP_1 is **77**. The result of running through the grammar once will thus be, in the case of **78**,

87   *John-wants-to* $\frown VP_1$

and only by running through the grammar again will VP_1 become *read* $\frown$ *the* $\frown$ *book*. But **85** or **86** will not apply (in the form given) to this VP_1 in running through the grammar the second time, since NP_x in **85** or **86** will have been fully developed in running through the grammar the first time, and the form of NP_x which appears in these rules will thus no longer be present as a conditioning context.[16] Thus if we consider "want" as the main verb in **78**, we must rephrase **85** or **86** with a double characterization of NP_x, once in only partially developed form to

---

[16] Note that it is important to place the rule of verbal selection *before* the rule that gives the full development of *NP* in the sequence of rules that forms the reduced grammar. Otherwise, all the specific forms into which *NP* will be developed will have to be listed as conditioning contexts in the rule of selection, and this is of course a vast list. An optimal grammar gives each rule at the point where the conditioning contexts have been developed just to the degree relevant for correct application of the rule. See §28.

determine the choice of the main verb "read" in such sentences as "John reads the book," and once in fully developed form (with a departure from optimality in this case—cf. Note 16) to determine the choice of the verb in the following *to*-phrase in sentences like **78**. Various attempts to avoid this run aground as long as **77** is retained as the basic analysis.

A second and related difficulty concerns agreement in number. Consider the sentences

88 $\begin{cases}(a) & \textit{John wants to be an officer} \\ (b) & \textit{they want to be officers}\end{cases}$

If "wants" is regarded as the main verb, as in **77**, then the same difficulties will arise in explaining the possibility of **88** alongside of the impossibility of

89 $\begin{cases}(a) & \textit{John wants to be officers} \\ (b) & \textit{they want to be an officer}\end{cases}$

If "be" is considered part of the following noun phrase, it will not be developed until the second run-through of the grammar, necessitating a complex statement of agreement in number for just the reasons we saw above in the case of verbal selection.

The rule which has just been discussed, as well as all subsequent rules of similar type, will be referred to as *rules of agreement in number*. The two major considerations in rejecting **77**, then, are the complications which result for the rules of verbal selection and agreement in number. The effect of the latter is considerably less compelling, however, since agreement in number could be handled by a mapping, somewhat similar in form to **39**.[17] In investigating the further effect of these rules we will concentrate on the problem of selection and show how considerations of number parallel this.

68.2 These considerations lead us to set up a second auxiliary verb phrase VP_B containing V_a. Whatever solution is adopted for V_a will hold as well for V_α, V_c, and V_γ. Thus VP_B will contain these elements as well. The simplest way to accomplish this is to incorporate V_a into V_b and V_c, and V_α into V_β and V_γ, taking V_a as the overlap of V_b and V_c and V_α as the overlap of V_β and V_γ. VP_B will then contain V_c and V_γ, and also sequences $V_c{}^\frown V_c$, $V_c{}^\frown V_\gamma$, etc., since in a sentence like

---

[17] For a different but related possibility for distinguishing between the rules of number and selection in terms of their systematic significance, cf. §54.3.

90 *John wanted to try smoking a different brand*

"smoke" must be treated as the main verb for the reasons that we have seen above.

We have, then, as possible analyses of VP, both $VP_A {}^\frown VP_B {}^\frown VP_1$ and $VP_A {}^\frown VP_1$. The correct way to analyze the first of these strings seems to be as $VP_A\text{-}VP_B {}^\frown VP_1$. As the initial part of the analysis of the verb phrase, then, we will have

91 $VP \rightarrow VP_A {}^\frown VP_1$
$\quad\quad VP_1 \rightarrow \langle VP_B \rangle\, VP_2$

This analysis is necessitated, on the one hand, by the fact that $VP_B {}^\frown VP_2$ occurs in the same positions as VP_2 (e.g., in "I saw him trying to open the door" alongside of "I saw him opening the door"), and, on the other hand, by the conjunction criterion, since we have, e.g.,

92   *they should stop wasting time and get down to serious work*

A complicating factor is that VP_B can be followed by VP_{A2} (where VP_{A2} can be only *have* ${}^\frown$ *en* after *ing*), e.g.,

93   *he wanted to have been introduced*

This possibility, with exactly the correct restriction, would have been taken care of automatically by **75** if the analysis of **93** as *NP-wanted-NP$_I$* had in fact been accepted, but in the solution we have just adopted, it must be given separately. This would seem to shed some doubt on our analysis, but we will see below, in §72.2, when we come to actually sketch the grammar, that these two restrictions can still be stated together, even with our present solution. We will overlook this apparent complication here, omitting sentences like **93**, but in presenting the grammar below we will include them again (cf. statements 10, 21, §72.2).

In the light of this discussion, we amend **56** as follows:

94   *Sentence* $\rightarrow NP {}^\frown VP$
$\quad\quad\quad VP \rightarrow VP_A {}^\frown VP_1$
$\quad\quad\quad VP_1 \rightarrow \langle VP_B \rangle\, VP_2$
$\quad\quad\quad VP_A \rightarrow VP_{A1} \langle VP_{A2} \rangle$
$\quad\quad\quad VP_{A1} \rightarrow \begin{Bmatrix} C \\ ed \end{Bmatrix} \langle M \rangle$

$$VP_{A2} \rightarrow \langle have \frown en \rangle \langle be \frown ing \rangle^{18}$$
$$VP_B \rightarrow Z_1 \langle Z_2 \langle \dots \langle Z_n \rangle \rangle \rangle$$

where each Z_i is one of the forms $V_c \frown to$, $V_y \frown ing^{19}$

Coalescing several steps, we can write the derivation of **78** as

95   *Sentence*
$NP \frown VP$
$NP \frown VP_A \frown VP_1$
$NP \frown VP_A \frown VP_B \frown VP_2$
$NP \frown C \frown VP_B \frown VP_2$
$NP \frown C \frown want \frown to \frown VP_2$
$John \frown C \frown want \frown to \frown read \frown the \frown book$

68.3 The solution embodied in **94** incidentally has a more satisfactory intuitive correspondence than the solution **77**, which we have now rejected, since "John" does seem intuitively to be the subject of "read" in **78**. Further evidence that we are on the right track comes from a closer investigation of V_α and V_y. We find that as these classes are defined in **58** (recall now that we have assigned V_α to both V_β and V_y, as the overlap of these classes), only a part of them is subject to this analysis.

We have seen that such verbs as "want" are properly assigned (in certain of their uses) to an auxiliary phrase VP_B. The criterion applied in this assignment was the following:

96 v is assigned to an auxiliary phrase $v \frown to$, rather than being regarded as the main verb (with object $to \frown VP_1$), if it meets the condition that for each noun phrase np, and for each verb phrase vp, if $np \frown v \frown to \frown vp$ is grammatical, then so is $np \frown vp$.[20]

If this condition is met, we found that the rules of selection and number were simplified significantly by this analysis. In fact, all members of V_a and V_c meet this condition. Investigating V_α and V_y, however, we find that this is not the case. V_y, it will be recalled, is the class of verbs

---

[18] See Note 9.

[19] We have not provided for statements like this in the construction of the form of grammars, but such a recursive extension of the notations could be carried out. There is no need for this however, since, as we will see below, this statement can be eliminated completely.

[20] Failure of the converse case would be treated as a case of selection of the v by the np subject, and need not concern us here.

that occur in the environment ——*ing*⌢VP_1 . For a verb v to fail to meet the analogue for V_y of **96**, it must be the case that

97   there is a noun phrase *np* and a verb phrase *vp* such that *np*⌢*v*⌢*ing*⌢*vp* is grammatical, but *np*⌢*vp* is not.

But **97** is in fact satisfied for certain verbs v in V_y , e.g., $v = forbid$. Thus we have **98** but not **99**:

98   {(a)   *that law forbids eating in the park*
{(b)   *decency forbids mentioning that incident*

99   {(a)   *that law eats in the park*
{(b)   *decency mentions that incident*

The same is true of "prevent," "concern," "cover," etc. This makes it necessary to distinguish between those members of V_y that meet **96** and those that do not. Suppose that we continue to denote by "V_y" those that meet **96**, thus preserving **94**. Those that do not meet **96** we can then extract from V_y and set up as a new subclass V_{t5} of V_T , occurring with "abstract" objects NP_I . Thus we add to **71**

100 $VP_2 \rightarrow V_{t5}⌢...NP_I$[21]

This gives a distinction between the sentence forms **101** and **102**:

101 $NP\text{-}V_{t5}\text{-}NP_I$

102 $NP\text{-}VP_B\text{-}VP_1$

with **98** as instances of the former and

103   {(a)   *John likes eating in the park*
{(b)   *John avoided mentioning that incident*

as examples of **102**. We see then that in pursuing the program of describing grammatical sentences in as simple a way as possible, we are led to assign quite different analyses to **98** on the one hand and **103** on the other, as, intuitively, should be the case.

---

[21] Note that what we denoted by "VP_1" in **71** has now been renamed "VP_2" in **94**.

68.4   Continuing in this manner, we see that, with one qualification which we give below, the solution to which we have been led permits a certain interesting case of constructional homonymity in the case of a verb v which is a member of both V_y and V_{t5}.

Given **101** and **102**, suppose that $NP_1 \to ing^\frown VP_1$ (in **101**), and $VP_B \to V_y^\frown ing$ (in **102**). Suppose further that $V_{t5} \to v$ in **101** and that $V_y \to v$ in the further development of **102**. That is, v is a member of both V_{t5} and V_y. Then we may have a sentence of the form

104 $NP^\frown VP_A^\frown v^\frown ing^\frown VP_1$

analyzed into both **105** (from **101**) and **106** (from **102**):

105 $NP^\frown VP_A\text{--}v\text{--}ing^\frown VP_1$

106 $NP^\frown VP_A\text{--}v^\frown ing\text{--}VP_1$

where "–" marks constituent break.

There are actual instances that, intuitively, are subject to this ambiguity. Thus with $v = stop$, we have

107   *the policemen must stop drinking after midnight*

understood as analogous in construction to **98** or **103**.

There is one difficulty here, however, We have given the criteria for membership in V_y (**96**) and V_{t5} (**97**) as contradictories, and this excludes the possibility of homonymity. Thus we have no basis for putting "stop" into both V_y and V_{t5}. Any verb meeting **97** (as does "stop") is simply in V_{t5}. This difficulty is only apparent. It is due to an insufficient account of grammatical sentences. A more detailed study would reveal that verbs in V_y appear in certain contexts not shared by verbs in V_{t5}, and this will lead us to replace **96** by a fuller characterization which is not the contradictory of **97**. For example, we find that for verbs in V_y, e.g., "try," we have

108   (a)   *John tried reading to himself*
           (b)   *try reading to yourself*

But for verbs such as "forbid," "suggest," etc. in V_{t5} we cannot have the analogous forms

109   (a)   *John forbade reading to himself*
           (b)   *suggest reading to yourself*

The grammatical explanation for this need not concern us here. The grammaticalness of **108** but not **109** shows that for a verb to be in V_γ it must meet the positive criterion that sentences like **108** be grammatical. Verbs which are only in V_{t5} fail to meet this condition. But "stop" is in V_{t5}, because of

110   *this new law will stop drinking*   (but not *"this new law will drink"*)

and it is in V_γ, because of

111 $\begin{cases}\text{(a)} & \textit{John stopped reading to himself} \\ \text{(b)} & \textit{stop reading to yourself}\end{cases}$

Thus if we can establish the grammaticalness of sentences like **108** but not **109**, then **107** does appear as a case of constructional homonymity.

Another such case of constructional homonymity arises from the fact that "is to," as in

112   *John is to come tomorrow*

meets **96**, and hence is assigned to VP_B. But *is* as a main verb can have an NP_I object (cf. §66.5), as in

113   *the important thing is to be happy*

Our analysis thus leads to the possibility of a distinction between these intuitively quite different cases. **114**, like **55**, is a case of constructional homonymity, both intuitively, and by our analysis[22]:

114   *his suggestion was to become famous*

Such intuitive and semantic correspondences cannot be used directly to support the analysis, but they do support the conception of syntax upon which the analysis was grounded by indicating that these grounds lead to intuitively correct results. By the same token, intuitive

---

[22] Note that we have not shown that 112 and 113 are *not* cases of constructional homonymity, and that they in fact have only one interpretation. It may be that this can be shown by a more detailed development of the possibilities for describing grammatical sentences in terms of phrase structure, or it might require the methods of the next chapter, which will enable us to make use, in support of the correct analysis, of the fact that we have, e.g., "to be happy is the important thing," but not "to come tomorrow is John."

inadequacy of the results is an argument against the soundness of the underlying conception. In the case of **98** and **103**, it seems likely that the intuitive correspondence can be demonstrated by a detailed investigation; in the case of **107**, it seems perhaps less so. Cases which we meet below will present strong reasons for doubting the adequacy of our underlying conceptions.

It will be recalled (last paragraph of §66.2) that the adopted analysis of the auxiliary phrase was strictly incompatible with the conjunction criterion, because of the treatment of the affixes "ing," etc. The same difficulty arises here with regard to *ing* and *to*. Thus we have

115   (a)   *John likes reading novels and playing tennis*
          (b)   *John likes to read novels and to play tennis*

although the adopted analysis puts the constituent break after *like⌢ing* and *like⌢to*. We will continue to disregard this difficulty for the moment, returning to it below.

69.1   In §68 we have seen how the rules of verbal selection and agreement of number play a crucial role in determining the structure of the verb phrase. They furnish criteria for the analysis in exactly the same sense as does conjunction. Since at best these rules are quite complex, we set up the analysis in such a way as to avoid compounding this complexity by requiring these rules to be stated twice, once with the conditioning contexts partially developed, to just the relevant forms (i.e., in the case of selection, the forms of **69**; in the case of number, the two primes NP_{plural} and $NP_{singular}$, or something similar), and once with the conditioning contexts fully developed. In fact, the desirability of avoiding the latter formulation alone suggests an important criterion of analysis because of the great complexity of this formulation and the consequent departure from our conditions of "optimality" for grammars, as pointed out in Note 16. We may now investigate the effect of these criteria on the further analysis of the noun phrase.

To simplify the following discussion, we will overlook the distinction brought out above between VP_1 and VP_2.

One form that can be assumed by the noun phrase is given by

116 $NP \rightarrow NP_a{}^\frown ing{}^\frown VP_1$

for example, the noun phrase subject of **117**a, or the object of **117**b:

117   (a)   *the people holding these slips – may enter*
          (b)   *I know – the man standing at the bar*

The expression on the right in **116** is an instance of $NP \frown NP_I$, i.e., of a compound noun phrase, and the subscript a in NP_a is given purely for reference. Although there are certain restrictions on the *NP*s that can occur here, we will not concern ourselves with them for the moment.

Consider now the problem of analyzing such noun phrases, that is, the problem of introducing **116** into the reduced grammar. The conversion statements of the grammar which are relevant in this connection are the following:

118   1.   The statement converting VP_1 into $V_T \frown NP$, $be \frown NP$, etc. We will call this statement the "VP_1-analysis."

2.   The statement converting *NP* into the terms relevant for the rule of verbal selection, i.e., essentially, the analysis into the left-hand terms of **69**. We will call this the "*NP*-analysis" (more specifically, the "selectional *NP*-analysis").

3.   The rule of verbal selection (see, §67.3).

4.   The statement converting *NP* into the terms relevant for the rule of agreement in number, essentially, a statement of the form:

$$NP \rightarrow \begin{cases} NP_{singular} \text{ in env. } \underline{\qquad} \\ NP_{plural} \;\; \text{ in env. } \underline{\qquad} \end{cases}$$

or something similar.

5.   The rule of numerical agreement (see §67.1).

6.   The rule which completes the development of the noun phrase to specific nouns.

Consider now the relative order of **116** and 1, 2, 3, 6 of **118**. It is first of all clear that 1 precedes 2 precedes 3. Otherwise the rule of selection will not apply properly to simple *NP-V-NP* sentences. We must assume further that 6 follows the rule of selection 3, or the conditions of optimality will immediately be violated as pointed out above. We may assume further that both *NP*-analyses, **118**-2 and **118**-4, apply to NP_a from **116** as well as to *NP*, since there is no need here to distinguish between the nouns that do and do not occur in the NP_a position. To simplify the discussion, we refer here only to transitive verbs.

Let us say that a *selectional relation* holds between a certain noun and a certain verb in a given sentence if the choice of the verb by the rule of verbal selection depends on the form of the given noun. This can be given much more precisely as a relation between "positions" in strings, but the notion involved is clear.

If we are to meet the criteria posed by the rule of verbal selection (see first paragraph of this section), then in any case where such a selectional relation holds, the verb must appear as V_T and the noun as N_{anim}, N_{inan}, or N_{ab} (cf. **69**) at the point in the derivation where the rule of verbal selection applies to the verb in question. This is to say that the rule of verbal selection cannot apply to the verb in question before the application of the *NP*-analysis to the *NP* in question, or after the application of **118-6** to the *NP* in question. Let us call this requirement the condition *C*.

We now investigate the selectional relations in sentences of the type **117** with the purpose of determining where **116** must be placed relative to 1, 2, and 3 of **118** in order for condition *C* to be met. Since $NP_a \frown ing \frown VP_1$ can be either subject or object, we have the following selectional relations:

119   (1)   The relation between the NP_a and the main verb V_T, where $NP_a \frown ing \frown VP_1$ is the subject of the V_T (e.g., "the *man* standing at the bar *broke* a glass").

      (2)   The relation between NP_a and the main verb V_T, where $NP_a \frown ing \frown VP_1$ is the object of V_T (e.g., "he *approached the man* standing at the bar").

      (3)   The relation between NP_a and the V^* into which the VP_1 of $NP_a \frown ing \frown VP_1$ is developed (e.g., "he approached the *man stand*ing at the bar").

Suppose that **116** is placed after the *NP*-analysis **118-2**. Then the *NP* analysis will apply to NP_a only in running through the grammar the second time. Suppose that $NP_a \frown ing \frown VP_1$ is the object of the main verb *v*, and that *np* is the subject of *v*, But the rule of verbal selection cannot apply to *v* in running through the grammar the first time, or condition *C* will be violated for the *v-NP_a* relation **119-2**, since NP_a will not yet have been developed by the *NP*-analysis. Nor can this rule apply to *v* in running through the grammar after the first time, or condition *C* will be violated for the *np-v* relation, since *np* will have been fully developed by **118-6**. The same is true if $NP_a \frown ing \frown VP_1$ is the subject of *v*.

Suppose that **116** precedes the VP_1-analysis **118-1**. But suppose again that $NP_a \frown ing \frown VP_1$ is the object of the main verb *v*, and that *np* is its subject. Thus the *NP* which is to become $NP_a \frown ing \frown VP_1$ is introduced by the VP_1-analysis, and hence cannot be developed by **116** until the second run-through of the grammar. But *np* will be developed by **118-6** in the first run-through, so that condition *C* is violated exactly as before.

Suppose then that **116** is placed after **118-1** and before **118-2**. Then the NP_a of $NP_a \frown ing \frown VP_1$ will be developed by the *NP*-analysis **118-2** and by **118-6** in running through the grammar the first time, thus before the VP_1-analysis **118-1** can apply to the VP_1 of the phrase $NP_a \frown ing \frown VP_1$ since this phrase is introduced subsequently to the VP_1-analysis. This contradicts condition *C* for the relation 3 of **119**.

We see then that **116** cannot be introduced into the grammar without conflicting with condition *C* and thus complicating the rule of selection in just the way we have been trying to avoid. We see further that the relations **119-2** and **119-3** are alone sufficient to preclude the introduction of **116**. This is important below.

Exactly the same situation results from the consideration of the rule of numerical agreement, i.e., from the consideration of the relative order of **116**, **118-1**, **118-4**, **118-5**, and **118-6**. In this case we consider that the verb *be* replaces V_T as the main verb of the sentence, and as the verb of the VP_1 of $NP_a \frown ing \frown VP_1$. The selectional relations which now hold between noun phrases, are the following:

120 (1) The relation between NP_a of $NP_a \frown ing \frown VP_1$ and NP^*, where $NP_a \frown ing \frown VP_1$ is the subject, *be* the main verb, and NP^* the predicate noun phrase (e.g., "the *man* standing at the bar is my *friend*").

   (2) The relation between NP_a of $NP_a \frown ing \frown VP_1$ and NP^*, where NP^* is the subject, *be* is the main verb, and $NP_a \frown ing \frown VP_1$ is the predicate (e.g., "*he* is a young *student* working his way through college").

   (3) The relation between NP_a of $NP_a \frown ing \frown VP_1$ and NP^*, where VP_1 becomes $\langle VP_B \rangle \, be \frown NP^*$ (e.g., "he interviewed all *students* expecting to be PhD *candidates* in June").

The order that must be maintained is **118-1–118-2–118-5–118-6**, and considerations analogous to those above show that **116** cannot be introduced without violating the criteria stated in the first paragraph of §63.1.

For clarity, let us now restate the results of this section, concentrating on transitive verbs. We have considered such sentences as

121   *I know the man reading the book*

From our earlier discussion of simpler English sentences, we are led to make, in particular, the following statements about the phrase structure of **121**:

122   (a) *I* is a *NP*
     (b) *I* is a N_{anim}
     (c) *know⌢the⌢man⌢reading⌢the⌢book* is a VP_1
     (d) *know* is a V_T
     (e) *know* is a V_{t2}
     (f) *the⌢man⌢reading⌢the⌢book* is a *NP*
     (g) *the⌢man* is a *NP*
     (h) *read⌢the⌢book* is a VP_1
     (i) *read* is a V_T
     (j) *read* is a V_{t4}
     (k) *the⌢book* is a *NP*
     (l) *man* is a N_{anim}
    (m) *book* is a N_{inan}

In other words, we give, in part, the following analysis of **121**:

123

I N_{anim}	*know* V_{t2}	*the*	*man* N_{anim}	*ing*	*read* V_{t4}	*the*	*book* N_{inan}
NP	V_T	*NP*			V_T	*NP*	
					VP_1		
		NP					
	VP₁						
Sentence							

In detail, this goes slightly beyond the analysis to which we have been led, but not in respects relevant to the present discussion.

    We have also arrived at a certain condition on the associated grammar which we have called the condition *C*. Condition *C* can be restated in the following terms: in that derivation of **121** which is directly provided by the associated proper linear grammar, the string

124 N_{anim}-V_T-*the*⌢N_{anim}-V_T-*the*⌢N_{inan}

must appear as a representing string. This is a way of rephrasing the requirement that the noun phrases relevant to the selection of a given verb must be in parallel (and sufficiently advanced) states of development at the point when the rule of verbal selection applies to the verb in question.

We have seen that **121** and **124** jointly lead to the consequence that the conversion rule **116** cannot be introduced into the grammar. Restating this in a different manner, the consequence is that the VP_1-analysis must be given twice in the grammar. The reason for this can easily be seen from **123**. In fact, the derivation of **121** given by the grammar must be essentially **123**, read from bottom to top. And we see that in forming such a derivation the conversion: $VP_1 \rightarrow V_T{}^\frown NP$ (i.e., the VP_1-analysis) is applied twice before *any* conversion of N_{anim} (into *I*, *John*, *man*, etc.) or condition C will be violated. But this double application is impossible in a proper linear grammar unless the VP_1-analysis is stated twice. By induction, we can show that the VP_1-analysis must be stated infinitely many times, since we must also be able to account for sentences of the type

125   *I know the man watching the man watching the man . . .*

with an obvious extension of **124**, to cover such cases. But a proper linear grammar must be finite. Hence we have here outlined the construction of a set of derivations which cannot be produced by a proper linear grammar. And since **122** and condition C are not cotenable, we have been led to a system of phrase structure which apparently cannot be given by a proper linear grammar (or a grammar of any other type that we have considered) without a departure from optimality.

This is reminiscent of the situation that we faced above in §68 in the case of sentences of the form   **69.2**

126 $NP_x\text{-}V_c{}^\frown to\text{-}v\text{-}NP_y$

Since the selection of v was determined by both NP_x and NP_y, it was necessary that these noun phrases be in parallel states of development when the rule of verbal selection applies. But NP_x is completely developed in running through the grammar the first time, and if the solution of **77** is adopted, v and NP_y will be developed in the second run-through, so that condition C is violated. But here there was the simple solution of taking v as the main verb.

Assuming for the moment that condition C must be maintained, we might try to avoid the problem we now face by dropping the simple linear sequence of conversion statements in the grammar. Thus we might add to the English grammar a requirement that every time VP_1 is introduced into a derivation by some statement of the grammar, then we must return to the VP_1-analysis and proceed from that point down the list of statements. With this revision the present difficulty can be avoided, but the general statement of the form of grammar and the notion "derivable" will become much more complex.

We can achieve the same result without dropping the simple ordering of grammatical rules if we add to every conversion statement following the VP_1-analysis the condition that the statement does not apply if VP_1 appears in the string under consideration, whether in the conditioning context for this conversion or not.[23] It would be sufficient to add this condition to certain rules, e.g., to **118-6**. This would guarantee that all relevant NP's be in parallel states of development when the rule of verbal selection is to apply, by making it impossible to develop any NP^* beyond the relevant form until all verbs to which NP^* might bear a selectional relation have already been selected. (Exactly what secondary effects this will have on the grammar it is difficult to determine without a detailed investigation—let us now assume that there are no complicating effects). One immediate difficulty with this approach is that it requires an infinite specification of conditioning contexts, since we now have to give as the conditioning context for, e.g., **118-6**, a list of everything that can occur as a context for the elements being developed and that does not contain VP_1. However, this is not an insuperable difficulty. We might hope to bypass it by developing further our stock of notations for grammar.[24]

69.3   Before attempting to develop such additional modes of expression for the grammar, let us investigate what their effect will be in related instances. Let us now suppose that we have developed some means of qualifying a certain rule

127 $b \to b'$ in env. a——c

---

[23] Recall that the conditioning context has been reduced to the point where it contains just those elements that determine how the rule in question operates.

[24] We might, incidentally, suspect that the problem of introducing such sentences as **117** could be solved by taking these to be derived from sentences of the form "...*who⌢is*..." by an optional grammatical rule "*who⌢is* → Ø⌢Ø," counting on the word "who" (as opposed to "which" or "that") to carry the selectional information even when NP_a is developed beyond the relevant forms. But the incorrectness of this view becomes quite clear when we note that inanimate and abstract nouns cannot be distinguished in this way, so that, e.g., "the sincerity scratched by John was ...," "the table manifested by John was ...," etc., would have to be admitted as fully grammatical, even though **69** does permit us to exclude such semigrammatical material as "John scatched sincerity," "John manifested the table," etc. We will see later that there are other reasons why this approach is not possible.

so that the conversion of b to b' does not take place if a certain element d appears anywhere in the string in which $a \frown b \frown c$ occurs. Let us refer to this as the qualification Q. In particular, the conversion of N_{anim} ($= b$) to *John* ($= b'$) will not take place if VP_1 ($= d$) appears anywhere in the string in question. We note first that the line of reasoning followed in §68 is no longer valid. That is, given a sentence of the form **121**, NP_x need no longer be developed completely in running through the grammar the first time, and NP_x and NP_y can appear in parallel states of development when the rule of verbal selection applies to v in running through the grammar the second time. Thus we are forced to accept[25] the analysis **77** which analyzes "John wants to come" as $N\text{-}V_T\text{-}NP$ (paralleling *John-wants-a* $\frown$ *book*) and "John wants him to come" as $N\text{-}V_T\text{-}N\text{-}NP$ (like *John-gave-him-a* $\frown$ *book*). Consequently, we lose the intuitive correspondences of §§68.3, 68.4, and we base our analysis on an intuitively invalid formal analogy.

An intuitively much more serious consequence comes from noting that the whole discussion of §68 applies in a perfectly analogous way to sentences of the form

128 $NP_x\text{-}V_v \frown ing\text{-}v\text{-}NP_y$

for instance,

129   *John-likes* $\frown$ *ing-read-the* $\frown$ *book*   ("*John likes reading the book*")

But we can carry this one step further. The discussion of §68 also carries over to sentences of the form

130 $NP_x\text{-}is \frown ing\text{-}v\text{-}NP_y$

for instance,

131   *John-is* $\frown$ *ing-read-the* $\frown$ *book*   ("*John is reading the book*")

which is perfectly analogous to **126** in all relevant respects. It is obvious that the analysis of **131** as a sentence of the form *NP-be-NP*, paralleling

---

[25] Our reasons for not accepting it are now invalid, and in favor of this analysis is the fact that an extra sentence form and an extra element (VP_B) are dropped, and that we have the intuitively unacceptable but formally compelling parallels given in **77**.

132   *John-is-a⌒politician*

with "be" as the main verb and "reading the book" as a predicate noun phrase is completely counterintuitive. The obviously correct solution, which we adopted above, is the analysis with "be" as part of the auxiliary, and "read" as the main verb, but the only considerations militating against the analysis as *NP-be-NP* are those adduced against **77**, e.g., the fact that if we accept this analysis, then NP_x and NP_y of **130** will not be in parallel stages of development when it comes to selecting v. But the qualification Q which we are now assuming to be available bypasses this objection, as we have seen in the first paragraph of §69.3. In fact we are now forced to accept the completely counterintuitive analysis of **131** as *NP-be-NP* (i.e., as a sentence of the same form as **132**) by considerations of simplicity (cf. Note 25). In its favor are the fact that "reading the book" must anyway be assigned to *NP* because of

133   *reading the book will only take a few hours*

and that choosing this analysis, we arrive at the sentence form *NP-be-NP*, which is already familiar on independent grounds. In fact, since the predicate *NP* in the analysis of **131** is now NP_I, we can drop from the analysis of *NP* in the grammar the condition that *NP cannot* become NP_I after N_{anim} ... *be*. If we permit the suggested qualification, then, it appears that we are required to accept a completely counterintuitive analysis of sentences like **131**, at the same time dropping *be⌒ing* from the auxiliary verb phrase, just as earlier we dropped *be⌒en* (and, incidentally, losing the intuitive correspondences pointed out in §68.4, **112-4**).

69.4   Not only does the qualification Q lead to intuitively unacceptable analyses, as we have just seen, but it also has certain systematic consequences for the form of grammars which we may find difficult to accept. We have seen that if we extend the machinery available for grammatical description to the point where qualification Q becomes formulable, what we have really done is equivalent to rejecting the linear ordering of grammatical statements. More exactly, if the context a——c contains all of the information relevant to the conversion of b to b' (instead of to b''), then the qualification Q "holds back" the conversion of b to b' in env. a——c, if there is some element (which may be outside of a——c) to which b bears a certain kind of selectional relation. In other words, it may be the case that (i) there is a rule S_i of the form

$b \rightarrow b'$ in env. a——c[26]; (ii) $a\frown b\frown c$ appears at the stage when S_i is to apply in running through the grammar the first (or nth) time; (ii) S_i does not apply to convert $a\frown b\frown c$ into $a\frown b'\frown c$, because of qualification Q; (iv) in running through the grammar the second time [or $(n+k)$th time], even though a——c has not been changed, S_i does apply to convert $a\frown b\frown c$ into $a\frown b'\frown c$, since Q may no longer apply.

But this situation in itself can be considered a departure from the optimal form of a grammar, since where it arises, we cannot convert a certain element at the point where its entire conditioning context has been developed to the degree relevant to the determination of which of the possible alternative conversions may take place.

We might try to escape the dilemma posed in §69.1 in a different manner, **69.5** by rejecting condition C, i.e., rejecting the requirement that **124** appear as a representing string in the derivation produced by the grammar. We saw that condition C can be disregarded only at the exorbitant cost of adding to the grammar a rule determining the selection of the verb by each particular noun (instead of just the classes N_{anim}, N_{inan}, etc., or whatever classes are taken to be relevant to the selection of verbs). But the reasoning which led to this conclusion will no longer be valid if we revise certain earlier steps in our analysis of English phrase structure.

We have been assuming here a grammar of roughly the following form:

134 (a) *Sentence* $\rightarrow NP\frown VP_1$
     (b) $VP_1 \rightarrow V_T\frown NP$, etc.
     (c) $NP \rightarrow \begin{Bmatrix} N_{anim} \\ N_{inan} \\ N_{ab} \end{Bmatrix}$
     (d) $V_T \rightarrow V_{t1}$ in env. N_{anim}——N_{anim}, etc.

The crucial point here is that the rule of verbal selection **134d** presupposes a prior analysis of the subject and object nouns. If we give the rule of verbal selection in this form, then condition C appears to be an inescapable requirement. But we might reformulate the grammar along the lines of **71**, for example, so that the choice of the verb is determined by the choice of the subject, and the choice of the object is determined by the particular verb that has been selected. That is, instead of **134**, we might have

---

[26] This may even be an obligatory rule. We are not here making the distinction between optimal and obligatory.

135   (a)   *Sentence* $\rightarrow NP^\frown VP_1$

(b) $NP \rightarrow \left\{ \begin{matrix} N_{anim} \\ N_{inan} \\ N_{ab} \end{matrix} \right\}$

(c) $VP_1 \rightarrow V_{t1}^\frown NP$ in env. N_{anim}———, etc.

(d) $NP \rightarrow N_{anim}$ in env. V_{t1}———, etc.

or something of this kind. Such a revision would entail many other alterations in the grammar which we need not discuss here. The crucial point is that the selection of the verb as V_{t1}, etc., no longer presupposes a prior development of the surrounding noun phrases, so that the reasoning which led us to stipulate condition C no longer holds. We can now introduce the conversion rule **116** into the grammar without the unfortunate consequences discussed in §69.1, by ordering the conversions as follows in the proper linear grammar:

136   (i)   **135**a

(ii)   **135**b

(iii)   **135**c

(iv) $N_{anim} \rightarrow I$, *John*, etc.

(v)   **116**

(vi)   **135**d

(vii) $V_{t1} \rightarrow$ *know*, etc.

By means of the grammar **136** we can produce a derivation of the form of **123** (read from bottom to top), not containing the string **124**. This grammar already represents a certain departure from optimality, since the *NP*-analysis must be given in two separate statements (**135**b,d), once for the subject and once for the object, if we are to be able to derive simple *Noun-Verb* and *Noun-Verb-Noun* sentences with no recursions by running through the grammar once. But a closer examination shows even more disturbing consequences.

Suppose that we are generating such sentences as **121** (= "I know the man reading the book") by means of the grammar **136**. The derivation will look something like this:

137   1.   *Sentence*

2. $NP^\frown VP_1$ (136i)

3. $N_{anim}^\frown VP_1$ (136ii)

4. $N_{anim}^\frown V_{t1}^\frown NP$ (136iii)

5. $I^\frown V_{t1}^\frown NP$ (136iv)

6. $I^\frown V_{t1}^\frown NP_a^\frown ing^\frown VP_1$ (136v)

7. $I^\frown V_{t1}^\frown N_{anim}^\frown ing^\frown VP_1$ (**136**vi)
8. $I^\frown know^\frown N_{anim}^\frown ing^\frown VP_1$ (**136**vii)

---

9. $I^\frown know^\frown N_{anim}^\frown ing^\frown V_{t2}^\frown NP$ (**136**iii)
10. $I^\frown know^\frown the^\frown man^\frown ing^\frown V_{t2}^\frown NP$ (**136**iv)
11. $I^\frown know^\frown the^\frown man^\frown ing^\frown V_{t2}^\frown N_{inan}$ (**136**vi)
12. $I^\frown know^\frown the^\frown man^\frown ing^\frown read^\frown N_{inan}$ (**136**vii)

---

13. $I^\frown know^\frown the^\frown man^\frown ing^\frown read^\frown the^\frown book$ (**136**iv)

We note that in this derivation, the conversion of N_{anim} to *the$^\frown$man* (step 10) takes place after the conversion of V_{t1} to *know* (step 8). But note that in certain cases the conversion of N_{anim} is dependent directly on the subject of V_{t1}. For example, if the subject is *I*, as in this case, then the object of *know* in ordinary *Noun-Verb-Noun* sentences could be *myself*, but not *himself*, etc. Hence the rule which applies to form step 10 in **137** must read in part

138 $N_{anim} \to$ *myself* in env. *I know*——, etc.

But in the conditioning context for this conversion it will be necessary to list *every* individual verb along with *know*, since the V_{ti} have already been developed. But this is clearly an intolerable complication. Note that we are now troubled by a difficulty which is a special case of a more general characteristic of the type of grammar under discussion. I refer to the fact, discussed above in §56.2, that the conversions in these grammars do not take into account the past history of the elements undergoing conversion, but only the present shape of these elements. If we could introduce past history into the statement of the conditioning context we could replace the list of all verbs in **138** by the statement that the conversion in question takes place whenever an element derived from an earlier V_T (or V_{ti}, for $i = 1, 2,...$) is present. But we have not yet discussed or developed general means for introducing such statements, or for evaluating grammars in which they appear.

The intolerable elaboration of **138** is a consequence of the fact that the conversion of N_{anim} to *the$^\frown$man* in **137** takes place after the conversion of V_{t1} to *know*. We therefore must inquire into the possibility of reordering the conversion rules in question. But note that the conversion of VP_1 to $V_{t2}^\frown NP$ in **137** (step 9) must precede the conversion of N_{anim} to *the$^\frown$man*, or the rule **136**iii = **135**c will have to list every animate noun instead of just N_{anim} in the conditioning context. Hence if we accept the reordering in question here, the rule **136**iii (the VP_1-analysis) will have to apply twice before **136**vii applies even once, and we know that this is impossible in a proper linear grammar unless the VP_1-analysis is actually stated twice in the grammar. But this is a productive construction. Hence by reasoning analogous to that of the last paragraph of §69.1 we can show that the VP_1-analysis will have to be stated infinitely often if this course is taken. It thus appears that the damage cannot be repaired, and that **135** is not an acceptable alternative.

It is important to note that the argument which we have presented against **135** does not apply with the same force against **134**, the grammar which meets condition C. In **134** subject and object are introduced and developed simultaneously before the conversion of V_T to V_{t1},... to *know*,... We can thus elaborate **134c**, introducing *I, you, myself*, etc. as additional forms of *NP*, and stating the relation between them by means of conversion statements in which only V_T (and not all instances of transitive verbs) must appear. This is of course a rather unhappy solution for this problem. Not only is **134c** further complicated, but it is now necessary to list separately the elements N_{anim}, N_{inan}, *I, you, myself*, etc., in later rules of conversion where previously only N_{anim}, N_{inan}, or N_{ab} had to be listed. But this complication, though undesirable, is still much less objectionable that the elaboration of **138** which would be necessary, as we saw above, if **135** were selected in preference to **134**. It appears, then, that rejection of condition C simply leads to an extension of the difficulties which appeared in §69.1.

69.6 Reviewing the situation, it seems that we are faced with a set of unacceptable alternatives. If we retain the conception of grammars that we have developed, we are apparently unable to incorporate such sentences as **117** and **121** without a serious departure from optimality, i.e., without violating the criteria stated at the outset of §69. (If we try to revise earlier steps in the analysis so that these criteria no longer apply, we are faced with other equally serious difficulties, as we have seen in §69.5.) If we try to alter our present conceptions of the form of grammar so as to make room for such sentences as **117** and **121**, we find that we are led to such completely unacceptable results as those of §69.3 in other cases, where previously we did apparently reach a satisfactory solution, and that in fact, the grammar fails to have certain other desirable properties. It appears then, that when we begin to go beyond sentences of the very simplest structure, the difficulties begin to mount so rapidly that grammars, in the form that we have outlined, become inordinately complex. If we were to continue to investigate more and more complex sentences, the overwhelming difficulty of stating the structure of **P** rigorously and completely would become continually more evident, and the essential clarity of the structure of the simple sentences would be completely obscured.

We will therefore exclude from consideration such sentences as **117** and **121** that are based on **116**. We have no real warrant for this arbitrary limitation from any general considerations that have been developed up to this point. This poses a fundamental theoretical gap to which we will return below.

We note, incidentally, that it is intuitively quite easy to explain why the construction of a system of phrase structure should begin to break down just at the point when we begin to investigate sentences like **117** and **121**. These are our first instances of sentences that seem intuitively to be compounded out of other more simple sentences. That is, given a sentence like "I know the man standing at the bar," we really find that in a certain sense the sentence "the man is standing at the bar" is incorporated within it. And it is not surprising that at just this point the network of selectional relations, which now in a way cross over a kind of "sentence boundary," should become so complex as to make the possibility of an optimal grammar appear remote. But this intuitive reasoning has no analogue in our linguistic theory, as so far developed. This theory approaches "simple" and "complex" sentences in a neutral way, and the notion of one sentence "incorporated" in another has no significance in our terms. This suggests a way of circumventing these problems which we will explore below.

In §63 we initiated an investigation into the limitations of particular types of grammar from a formal, abstract point of view. In this section we have approached the same problem from the other end, investigating the empirical consequences of a strict attempt to construct grammars of the prescribed form for actual language material. In our earlier abstract investigation we noted that certain sets of derivations which are in fact associated with a system of phrase structure may not be producible by any proper linear grammar. In this section we have outlined the construction of a certain set of derivations (to which we were led by a sequence of observations about simple sentences, each of which seemed reasonable in itself) which is in fact not producible by a proper linear grammar. It appeared to be the case, furthermore, that even if we drop the requirement of proper linearity for grammars, we are not able to present a satisfactory description of the system of phrase structure in question, or to find an alternative phrase structure for the sentences under consideration which could be described in a satisfactory way. It is important to remember that we have not literally proved that optimal grammars cannot be constructed to cover these more complex sentences. For one thing, we have obviously not exhausted all possible alternative analyses. For another, our criteria of optimality are much too vaguely stated for any proof to be possible. It would be an important and non-trivial project to rephrase these criteria more precisely and to carry out a much more serious formal investigation of the kinds of selectional relations that lead to violation of optimality, or to the breakdown of some rigorously stated form for grammatical description. Coupled with a much more intensive study of the empirical consequences of applying strictly certain notions of grammar, such an investigation could fill the tremendous gap still remaining between the investigations of §63 and those of §69, and might lead to a conclusive answer to the question of the formal adequacy (the question of intuitive adequacy would still remain open—a grammatical theory must meet conditions of simplicity *and* intuitive adequacy, as we have pointed out in §15 and elsewhere) of description in terms of phrase structure. We have at most suggested an outline for a demonstration of a negative answer to this question. But this discussion does, I think, shed serious doubt on the possibility of describing phrase structure in a way that is both reasonably simple and organized on the one hand, and comprehensive, on the other.

70   In §63 we completed the analysis of sentences like "John wanted wanted to read," hence generally of V_c and V_y (see §67.1). We now consider the adequacy of the proposal, given in **77**, that **139** and **140** be analyzed as instances of **141**.

139   *John-wanted-him-to come*

140   *the guard-caught-him-trying to escape*

141   *NP-V-NP-NP$_I$*

There is of course no possibility here, as there was in §68, of the verb from NP_I being the main verb, since its selection is determined by the second, not the first NP. The selectional relations in sentences of the form **141** are (among others) between the second NP and the verb of NP_I, as we can see from the grammaticalness of **142** but not **143**:

142   (a)   *John wanted Bill to read*
         (b)   *John wanted justice to prevail*

143   *John wanted justice to read*

and between V (the main verb) and the second NP, as we can see from the grammaticalness of **144** but not **145**:

144 $\begin{cases}(a) & \textit{John asked Bill to read} \\ (b) & \textit{John wanted justice to prevail}\end{cases}$

145 *John asked justice to prevail*

But we have seen in §69 that with these selectional relations it is impossible to introduce

146 $VP_1 \rightarrow V_T{}^\frown NP$
$NP \rightarrow NP_a{}^\frown ing{}^\frown VP_1$

into the grammar without serious complications. By exactly the same reasoning it is impossible to introduce

147 $VP_1 \rightarrow V_T{}^\frown NP{}^\frown NP_I$

directly. Hence the analysis of **139** or **140** as **141** cannot be introduced without complication. These sentences must be excluded from consideration just as the sentences based on **116** were excluded.

Actually an even more unpleasant conclusion seems to be forced on us if we attempt to account for these sentences despite the resulting complexity. There seems to be no reason not to consider **140** to be analogous to **117**, i.e., to be a simple sentence of the form $NP\text{-}V_T\text{-}NP^*$, with NP^* converted by **116** into $NP_a{}^\frown ing{}^\frown VP_1$. Thus we may take V_β to be simply a subclass of V_T, and we may have, as a part of the grammar,

148   (i)   *Sentence* $\rightarrow NP{}^\frown VP_1$
         (ii) $VP_1 \rightarrow V_T{}^\frown NP$
         (iii) $NP \rightarrow NP_a{}^\frown ing{}^\frown VP_1$
         (iv) $V_T \rightarrow V_{t1}, ..., V_\beta$

The derivations of both **117** and **140** would be basically

149   *Sentence*
         $NP{}^\frown VP_1$
         $NP{}^\frown V_T{}^\frown NP$
         $NP{}^\frown V_T{}^\frown NP_a{}^\frown ing{}^\frown VP_1$
         etc.

We cannot really show that this is the best analysis, since we do not know how to include **148**iii in the grammar, but, speculating, this seems like the most reasonable approach.

Even with this analysis, V_β will have to be retained as a special subclass of V_T with certain distributional pecularities. For instance, **148**iii operates somewhat differently in the environment V_β—— than in other environments. Thus we have

150   *they caught him trying to escape*   [*catch* a member of V_β]

but not

151 $\begin{cases}(a) & \textit{him trying to escape was a mistake} \\ (b) & \textit{I know him trying to escape}\end{cases}$

[*know* not a member of V_β]

Furthermore, we can have

152   *imagine the dog having jumped over that fence*

[*imagine* a member of V_β]

but not

153   *recognize the dog having jumped over the fence*

[*recognize* not a member of V_β]

Thus the form $ing^\frown have^\frown en^\frown VP$ permitted by **75** can occur only after V_β. Again, all transitive verbs not in V_β can have objects of the form NP as well as the form $NP_a^\frown ing^\frown VP_1$. Thus we have

154   *I know the man*

alongside of **117**, etc. But some verbs in V_β do not have this property. For example, we do not have, alongside of **152**,

155   *imagine the dog*

This does not distinguish V_β from the rest of V_T, however, since many members of V_β also have this property.

Another special statement distinguishing V_β from other members of V_T will be added to the rule of verbal selection for V_T, for the context *en*——. That is, we will have

156 $V_T \rightarrow V_\beta$ in env. *en*——NP_I

This will be one of a number of selectional statements for V_T in this position. It accounts for the possibility of **157** but not **158**:

157   *the man was caught trying to escape*

158   *the man was known trying to escape*

This particular case will turn out to be of special importance later on.

It seems fairly clear that the simplest way to describe this situation will be, essentially, **148**, with a statement of special conditions for the case where the main verb is in V_β. If this is correct, then we have a situation here which contrasts sharply with that of §68. There we saw that the analysis led to certain intuitively appealing results. Sentences that were intuitively different in structure received different analyses, and certain cases of intuitive homonymity were paralleled by constructional homonymity which was a consequence of the application of formal criteria. But in §70 we have found exactly the opposite situation. Certainly **140** differs from "I know the man standing at the bar" (= **117**), and **159** differs from **160** in much the same way that "John likes eating in the park" (= **103**a) differs from "that law forbids eating in the park" (= **98**a):

159   *I can't imagine the dog climbing that tree*

160   *I can't recognize the man climbing that tree*

but in these cases we have been led to a single analysis. Furthermore,

161   *I can't catch the dog climbing that tree*

is intuitively an ambiguous construction (with the analysis of **159** on the one hand, and **160** on the other), just as is "the policemen must stop drinking after midnight" (= **107**). But here we have been led to assign only a single **P**-marker. We will return to this intuitive inadequacy below.

The analysis of **139** poses a somewhat different problem, since there is no analysis of *NP* related to **139** the way **116** is related to **140**. That is, we do not have "I recognize the man to stand at the bar," etc. Nevertheless, the simplest way of handling **139** is probably by an elaboration of **148**iii, continuing along the lines suggested above. In all of these cases an infinitive phrase is involved, so that this elaboration to include **139** may actually have the effect of removing a restriction, rather than adding a condition.

Summing up the discussion of V_b, V_c, V_β, V_γ, then, we see that V_c and V_γ can be successfully incorporated into the grammar without excessive complexity and with intuitively appealing results. But V_b and V_β, which introduce one additional selectional relation, can be incorporated into the grammar only at the cost of a departure from desirable formal properties on the one hand, and a counterintuitive description of phrase structure on the other. Since V_a and V_α have been assigned to V_b, V_c and V_β, V_γ, as their respective overlaps, this concludes, for the time being, the discussion of the elements of **57, 58**. In Chapter X we will be led to give quite a different analysis for these constructions.

The case of V_δ (cf. §67.2) and sentences like "I saw him come⟨ing⟩" should be similar. There is a selectional relation between "him" and "come," but it is difficult to find a clear case, at least on the level of grammaticalness with which we are now working, of a selectional relation between "see" and "him," If the latter cannot be established, then V_δ can actually be introduced. Because of the parallel between this case and the others of this section, however, we will also drop this case from consideration in the grammatical sketch presented below, returning to it later with a different approach.

71.1 We may now survey the cases to which the rule of verbal selection applies, after the restrictions imposed in the preceding section. In running through the grammar the first time, the only selectional relations relevant to this rule are those of subject–verb and verb–object. Considering in this account only V_{t1},..., V_{t4} and V_{I1}, V_{I2} (cf. **70, 72**, §67.3), we have as the relevant parts of the conditioning contexts:

162	*Initial conditioning context*	*Final conditioning context*
V_{t1}	N_{anim}	N_{anim}
V_{t2}	N_{anim}	N_{anim}, N_{inan}, N_{ab}
V_{t3}	N_{anim}, N_{inan}, N_{ab}	N_{anim}
V_{t4}	N_{anim}	N_{anim}, N_{inan}
V_{I1}	N_{anim}	
V_{I2}	N_{anim}, N_{inan}, N_{ab}	

In other words V_{t1} can appear only in env. N_{anim} ...———... N_{anim}, etc. If we treat V_I as the subclass of V_T that occurs when there is no object, then the VP_1-analysis (see **118**-1) will contain a statement $VP_1 \rightarrow V_T \langle NP \rangle$, and the rule of verbal selection will include, for the case of **162**, such statements as

163 $V_T \to V_{t1}$ in env. N_{anim} ...———... N_{anim}
$V_T \to V_{I2}$ in env. N_{inan} ...———
etc.

There are four other major cases to which the rule of verbal selection applies, all having to do with the verb which appears in the development of NP_I (see **75**), hence all occurring in running through the grammar a second (or later) time. First we have the selectional relation between V_T and NP when NP_I is converted, e.g., into $to^\frown V_T^\frown NP$, e.g., "to *write* a *novel* is his ambition." This is the same as the relation between verb and object. Then we have the selectional relation between $NP*$ and V_T where NP_I is, e.g., $ing^\frown V_T^\frown NP$, and NP_I is preceded by a possessive adjective $NP*^\frown S_1$ (e.g., "*John's fly*ing those big planes is something I don't approve of").[27] This is the same as the relation between subject and verb.

Since the possessive adjective may or may not occur, we have

164

	Initial conditioning context	Final conditioning context
V_{t1}	$\langle N_{anim}^\frown S_1 \rangle$	N_{anim}
V_{t2}	$\langle N_{anim}^\frown S_1 \rangle$	N_x [28]
V_{t3}	$\langle N_x^\frown S_1 \rangle$	N_{anim}
V_{t4}	$\langle N_{anim}^\frown S_1 \rangle$	N_{anim} , N_{inan}
V_{I1}	$\langle N_{anim}^\frown S_1 \rangle$	
V_{I2}	$\langle N_x^\frown S_1 \rangle$	

Thus the rule of verbal selection, applying in the second run-through of the grammar, will include, for **164**, such statements as

165 $V_T \to V_{t1}$ in env. $\langle N_{anim}^\frown S_1 \rangle$ ...———... N_{anim}
etc.

The third case comes from a conversion of NP into $NP_1^\frown$ *Prepositional Phrase*, where the prepositional phrase is $of^\frown NP*$. An ordinary example would be "the men of England," etc. If $NP_1 \to NP_I$, we have a phrase

166 $NP_I^\frown of^\frown NP*$

---

[27] The possessive morpheme S_1 cannot be identified with the noun plural and verb singular morpheme S. Despite similar morphophonemic effects, they differ, as we can see from "wives" (plural) but "wife's" (singular possessive).

[28] We use "N_x" when any of the three forms of the noun that we are considering can appear.

In this case, NP_I can only be converted into the special cases $\begin{Bmatrix} to \\ ing \end{Bmatrix} V_T$, and there is a selectional relation between V_T and NP^* (e.g., "the *screech*ing of *brakes*," "*read*ing of good *literature*"). When $V_T \rightarrow V_{t1},..., V_{t4}$, this relation is that of verb–object, when $V_T \rightarrow V_{l1}$, V_{l2}, it is the relation of verb–subject, as is evident from the parenthesized examples.

When $V_T \rightarrow V_{t1},..., V_{t4}$, we have as a fourth case, the possibility of a possessive adjective $NP^{**}\!\frown\! S_1$ preceding the noun phrase **166**, and we then have a selectional relation between NP^{**} and V_T, the same relation as subject–verb (e.g., "*John*'s *read*ing of good literature has convinced him that . . ."). Coalescing these two cases, we have

167   *Initial conditioning*   *Final conditioning*
                            context   *context*

	Initial conditioning context	Final conditioning context
V_{t1}	$\langle N_{anim}\!\frown\! S_1\rangle$	$of\!\frown\! N_{anim}$
V_{t2}	$\langle N_{anim}\!\frown\! S_1\rangle$	$of\!\frown\! N_x$
V_{t3}	$\langle N_x\!\frown\! S_1\rangle$	$of\!\frown\! N_{anim}$
V_{t4}	$\langle N_{anim}\!\frown\! S_1\rangle$	$of\!\frown\! N_{anim},\; of\!\frown\! N_{inan}$
V_{l1}		$of\!\frown\! N_{anim}$
V_{l2}		$of\!\frown\! N_x$

Thus the rule of verbal selection will include, for **167**, such statements as

168 $V_T \rightarrow V_{t1}$ in env. $\langle N_{anim}\!\frown\! S_1\rangle$ ...———... $of\!\frown\! N_{anim}$
        etc.

Clearly **162**, **164**, and **167** can be consolidated into a single generalized form. But the rule of verbal selection will remain quite a complicated statement.

71.2   "Selectional relation" and "same selectional relation" have been used here only as suggestive terms. Actually, all that we know of the relation between noun and verb is given in the charts **162**, **164**, and **167**. We have developed no theory of selectional relations which would permit us to state that the relation of "brakes" to "screech" is the same in "the screeching of brakes" as in "the brakes screech." We could perhaps develop such a theory within **P**. This would give us an important new approach to grammatical relations, different from that of §59, though not unrelated to it.[29] In this discussion we have seen enough examples of the use of the term "selectional relation" to indicate roughly what the content of such a development would be. We see, for one thing, that the notion of selectional relation is relative to a given way of stating the grammar. It may be that there is a string $Z = X_1 \frown X_2 \frown X_3$ in which the choice of X_3 is partially determined by the choice of X_1,[30] but yet it will not necessarily be the case that a selectional relation in the sense in which we have been using the term holds between X_1 and X_3. For a selectional relation in our sense to hold, it is necessary that the *rule* of the grammar that states the analysis of X_3 contain forms of X_1 as a relevant part of the conditioning context. If the simplest grammar states the selection of X_2 in terms of X_1, and of X_3 in terms of X_2, then there is no selectional relation between X_1 and X_3, but only between X_1 and X_2, and between X_2 and X_3.[31] This property is crucial if we wish to develop a significant notion of grammatical relations from selectional considerations. Certainly among the major grammatical relations are subject–verb and verb–object, but we might, on some level of gram- maticalness find that the choice of subject partially determines the choice of the object. We would not want to set up, on the basis of this, a third relation between subject and object, and in our present sense of "selectional relation," this unwelcome possibility would be excluded for the reasons just sketched.

However, there will be certain difficulties in constructing a theory of grammatical relations in selectional terms. Thus on our present level of grammaticalness, there are verbs which occur only in the environment $N_{anim}\cdots \text{------} N_{anim}$. Here the grammatical relations subject–verb and verb–object correspond to the same selectional relation. The relation of noun to verb is the same in both cases. But here, as opposed to the case of $NP \frown V_i$ and $V_i\text{-}of \frown NP$ ("brakes screech" and "screeching of brakes"), we would not want to say that the same gram- matical relation is involved. On the other hand, if certain verbs can take any noun as object, then in selectional terms the verb–object relation would, in such cases, simply not appear. The further development of this theory is thus not obvious.

[29] There are also other approaches which we have not considered. For example, one might approach grammatical relations in terms of the study of the domain of long components, government, etc. These approaches should be integrated into a single theory of grammatical relations.

[30] That is, it may be the case that if $X_1 \rightarrow Y_1$, then X_3 must be converted into W_1, whereas if $X_1 \rightarrow Y_2$, then X_3 becomes W_2.

[31] Of course, we might be able to develop a significant notion of primary and derivative selectional relations.

We will not go on to try to develop such a theory. The results which we might hope to obtain from it will appear as a by-product of the constructions of the next chapter.

72.1   With this much introduction, we can proceed to sketch the outlines of a grammar of English phrase structure in reduced form (but cf. §64), so that derivations can be given and the underlying phrase structure reconstructed. In discussing the form of grammars (cf. §55) it was emphasized that a distinction must be made between statements which are obligatory and those which are merely optional. We can simplify this grammatical sketch considerably by giving a single general rule to determine when a statement of the grammar is obligatory, so that no qualification to this effect need actually be incorporated in the grammar.[32]

The grammar is in the first place a sequence of elementary statements, each of the form $\alpha \rightarrow \beta$. When we apply the "notational transformations" of Chapter IV, we collapse this sequence to a reduced sequence $\Sigma_1, ..., \Sigma_n$ of statements containing brackets and angles, these statements being numbered 1, 2,..., n. Suppose that the ith statement Σ_i, when expanded fully into elementary statements, is

169 $\begin{aligned} S_{i_1}: &\quad \alpha_1 \rightarrow \beta_1 \\ S_{i_2}: &\quad \alpha_2 \rightarrow \beta_2 \\ &\quad \vdots \\ S_{i_m}: &\quad \alpha_m \rightarrow \beta_m \end{aligned}$

$\alpha_1, \alpha_2, ..., \alpha_m$ need not be distinct, and it may be the case that for some $j, k \leqslant m$, α_j contains α_k as a proper substring (i.e., $\alpha_k < \alpha_j$).

The grammar will be presented as the reduced sequence $\Sigma_1, ..., \Sigma_n$ of numbered statements, and each of these numbered statements corresponds, as in **169**, to a certain sequence of elementary statements. The formation of the reduced, generalized grammar $\Sigma_1, ..., \Sigma_n$ thus imposes a grouping on the sequence of elementary statements S_{i_j} of the form $\alpha \rightarrow \beta$. We can make use of this grouping to formulate a general rule for the occurrence of obligatory statements among the S_{i_j}.

Rule 1:   Suppose that the ith statement Σ_i is reduced from (and hence expandable to) **169**. Then S_{i_j} is obligatory if and only if for each k such that $j < k \leqslant m$, $\alpha_k \neq \alpha_j$.

---

[32] Note that it is really illegitimate to simplify a given grammar by a rule of the sort we are about to give unless we are willing to generalize this rule to all grammars, that is, unless we are willing to regard it as a reduction in the sense of §55. But the study of the form of grammars is at such an early stage that it is worthwhile to investigate ways of simplifying given grammars even if we are not yet prepared to generalize. See §26.

In other words, if in **169** there are several conversions S_{i_j} which convert a string α into some string β, then only the last of these is obligatory. This method of utilizing the grouping of conversions in the completely reduced grammar $\Sigma_1, \dots, \Sigma_n$ to determine automatically the place of obligatory conversions in the sequence of conversions is the same as that employed in the morphophonemic study in §48, and is in accord with the general motivation for distinguishing obligatory and optional conversions.

As an example of the functioning of this rule, suppose that Σ_i is

170 $\Sigma_i: \quad \alpha \to \begin{Bmatrix} \beta \\ \gamma \end{Bmatrix}$ in env. ——— $\delta \begin{Bmatrix} \langle \epsilon \rangle \\ U \end{Bmatrix}$

The unique expanded form of **170** is

171 $S_{i_1}: \quad \alpha\delta\epsilon \to \beta\delta\epsilon$
$S_{i_2}: \quad \alpha\delta \to \beta\delta$
$S_{i_3}: \quad \alpha\delta \to \gamma\delta$

Suppose that in constructing derivations D, D', and D'', we arrive, respectively, at the strings Z, Z', and Z'' after having applied $\Sigma_1, \dots, \Sigma_{i-1}$:

172 $Z = \dots\alpha\delta\epsilon\dots$
$Z' = \dots\alpha\delta\eta\dots$
$Z'' = \dots\alpha\eta\dots \quad (\eta \neq \delta, \epsilon)$

By Rule 1, S_{i_1} and S_{i_3} (but not S_{i_2}) are obligatory in **171**. Hence the result of applying Σ_i in the case of the derivation D will be $\dots\beta\delta\epsilon\dots$; in the case of D', it may be either $\dots\beta\delta\eta\dots$ or $\dots\gamma\delta\eta\dots$; in the case of D'' it will be $\dots\alpha\eta\dots$.

Note that the fact that α appears on the left in **170** does not mean that α must be eliminated by application of Σ_i. The rule applies only to the expanded sequence **171**. This rule causes occasional complications (statements 16 and 17, below), but its total effect is a great simplification, since it is no longer necessary to present along with each substatement S_{i_j} an indication as to whether or not it is obligatory. This indication would be difficult to include in the reduced grammar $\Sigma_1, \dots, \Sigma_n$. We will see below that the occasional complications disappear at a higher level of analysis.

Phrase Structure of English. In accordance with the plan of §64, many   **72.2**
statements of restriction and many possible conversions are omitted in this sketch.

1. Sentence $\rightarrow NP \frown VP$

2. $VP \rightarrow VP_A \frown VP_1$

3. $VP_1 \rightarrow \langle D_2 \rangle \langle VP_B \rangle \left\{ \begin{array}{l} \left\{ \begin{matrix} V_f \\ V_g \end{matrix} \right\} NP \frown NP \\ V_e \left\{ \begin{matrix} \langle that \rangle \ Sentence \\ NP \frown to \frown be \frown Predicate \end{matrix} \right\} \\ \left\{ \begin{matrix} be \\ V_h \frown NP \end{matrix} \right\} Predicate \\ V_T \langle NP \rangle \langle PP \rangle \end{array} \right\}$

D_2 is a special class of adverbs containing "certainly," "quickly," etc. $PP = Prepositional\ Phrase.$

4. $NP \rightarrow \left\{ \begin{matrix} NP_s \\ NP_p \end{matrix} \right\}$ except in env. $V_g \frown NP$———[33]

NP_s is the singular noun phrase, NP_p, the plural.

5. $Predicate \rightarrow \left\{ \begin{matrix} NP \\ \langle AP \rangle \langle PP \rangle \end{matrix} \right\}$ [34]

$AP = Adjective\ Phrase.$

6. $NP \rightarrow \left\{ \begin{matrix} NP_s \\ NP_p \end{matrix} \right\}$ in env. $\left\{ \begin{matrix} NP_s \\ NP_p \end{matrix} \right\}$ ... ———,

where ... contains no NP_s, NP_p

7. $\left\{ \begin{matrix} NP_s \\ NP_p \end{matrix} \right\} \rightarrow T \langle AP \rangle \ N \left\{ \begin{matrix} \varnothing \\ S \end{matrix} \right\} \langle PP \rangle$

8. $N \rightarrow \left\{ \begin{array}{l} N_A, \text{ except in env. } ——— \left\{ \begin{matrix} \varnothing \frown S_1 \\ S \end{matrix} \right\} \\ N_{anim} \\ N_{inan} \end{array} \right\}$

The conditioning environment $\varnothing \frown S_1$ in statement 8 will only appear in running through the grammar the second and later times,

---

[33] In this and several other places we give statements in a form that is literally inadmissible, since we have not introduced formally the notions used in formulating the restriction. But in all such cases, the restriction will appear below to be eliminable.
[34] See Note 9.

S_1 being here the possessive suffix introduced in statement 17, below. The context——S appears in running through the first time, where S is the plural morpheme. N_A is a generalized class of abstract nouns, containing N_{ab} and NP_I (see **69** and **75**). Many other restrictions can and should be added here, e.g., we cannot have $N_{anim} ...is... N_A$, only N_{anim} can follow V_f, etc.

Statement 9 gives the information contained in **162**, **164**, and **167**. That is, it is the rule of verbal selection. It is quite a complex statement, though a good deal of generalization is possible.[35] The part of statement 9 corresponding to just **162**, i.e., the statement of the rules for the subject–verb and verb–object relation in simple N-V and N-V-N sentences, can be given as follows:

$$9^*. \quad V_T \rightarrow \left\{\left\{\begin{matrix} V_{t1-4} \\ V_{t2,\,t4} \\ V_{t2} \\ V_{t1-2} \end{matrix}\right\} \begin{matrix} \\ \\ V_{t3} \\ V_{I2} \end{matrix}\right\} \text{ in env. } \left\{\begin{matrix} N_{anim} \\ \\ ... \\ ... \end{matrix}\right\} \left[\begin{matrix} S \\ \varnothing \end{matrix}\right] \langle PP \rangle\, VP_A \langle D_2 \rangle \langle VP_B \rangle$$

$$\underline{}\langle T \rangle \langle AP \rangle \left\{\left\{\begin{matrix} N_{anim} \\ N_{inan} \\ N_A \\ ... \\ N_{anim} \\ ... \end{matrix}\right\}\right\}$$

We will see in Chapter X that statement 9* (with some simplifications) suffices alone for the grammar of English. **164** and **167** will be derived from statement 9* by methods to be developed below. We will therefore not trouble to give statement 9 in full detail here.

$10.^{36}$ $\quad VP_B \rightarrow Z_1 \langle Z_1 \langle ... \langle Z_n \rangle \rangle \rangle$

where Z_i is one of the elements of the form

$$\left\{\begin{matrix} V_c \\ V_\gamma \end{matrix}\right\} Inf \langle VP_{A2} \rangle$$

---

[35] Note that in stating **162**, **164**, and **167** the statement of that part of the conditioning contexts introduced in statements 1–8 was omitted.

[36] See Note 19.

Actually a distinction should be made between subclasses of V_c and V_y in terms of the selection of subject, but we will not go into this refinement.

11. $N_{anim} \rightarrow \begin{Bmatrix} N_{ac} & \langle \text{in env.} \text{——} S \rangle \\ N_p \end{Bmatrix}$

N_p is the class of proper nouns; N_{ac}, animate common nouns. Many further subdivisions and much more detailed restrictions can be stated.

12. $PP \rightarrow P^\frown NP$

13. $P \rightarrow of, in, by, \ldots$

14. $T \rightarrow \begin{Bmatrix} \begin{Bmatrix} \emptyset \\ the \end{Bmatrix} \text{ in env.} \text{——} \begin{bmatrix} \langle AP \rangle \begin{bmatrix} N_{ac} \\ N_{inan} \end{bmatrix} S \\ N_A \begin{bmatrix} J \\ X, & \text{but only sometimes when} \\ & X = of^\frown Y \end{bmatrix} \end{bmatrix} \\ \begin{Bmatrix} \begin{Bmatrix} a \\ the \end{Bmatrix} \\ \emptyset \end{Bmatrix} \text{ in env.} \text{——} \langle AP \rangle \begin{Bmatrix} \begin{bmatrix} N_{ac} \\ N_{inan} \end{bmatrix} \emptyset \\ N_p \end{Bmatrix} \\ \begin{Bmatrix} a \\ the \\ \emptyset \end{Bmatrix} \end{Bmatrix}$

This formulation permits "a sincerity of manner," "a screeching of brakes," and "a certain sincerity," but not "a sincerity," "a screeching" (cf. Note 33). This statement is only partially adequate, but here, too, we will not give the further detail necessary. J signifies sentence boundary (cf. §55.2).

15. $N_A \rightarrow \begin{Bmatrix} N_{ab} \\ Inf \begin{Bmatrix} V_T \\ \langle VP_{A2} \rangle VP_1 \end{Bmatrix} \end{Bmatrix}$, except in env. $\begin{Bmatrix} \text{——} of \\ \begin{Bmatrix} the \\ a \end{Bmatrix} \langle AP \rangle \text{——} \end{Bmatrix}$

Thus *Inf*-phrases as abstract nouns are divided into two types, $Inf^\frown V_T$ and $Inf \langle VP_{A2} \rangle VP_1$. Only the former can occur before *of* or after the article. Thus (with $Inf \rightarrow ing$) we have "screeching of brakes," "the screeching," "an unpleasant screeching," but not "playing the

piano yesterday of . . . ," "the playing the piano yesterday," "an unpleasant playing the piano yesterday," with a full verb phrase. This
analysis may be correct as far as it goes (that is, some detail is omitted),
but it certainly gives little insight into the processes at work here.

$$16. \quad Inf \rightarrow \begin{Bmatrix} to \text{ in env. } \begin{Bmatrix} J \\ V_c \end{Bmatrix}\text{---} \\ ing \langle \text{in env. } J\text{---} \rangle^{37} \end{Bmatrix}$$

$$17. \quad AP \rightarrow \begin{Bmatrix} NP^\frown S_1 \text{ in env. } \begin{bmatrix} \emptyset \\ be \end{bmatrix}\text{---} \langle \begin{Bmatrix} ing \\ \begin{Bmatrix} N_{ac} \\ N_{inan} \end{Bmatrix} \emptyset \end{Bmatrix} \rangle^{37} \\ \begin{Bmatrix} \langle D \rangle \begin{Bmatrix} A \\ ing^\frown V_j \\ en^\frown V_k \end{Bmatrix} \\ \langle D_2 \rangle \begin{Bmatrix} ing^\frown V_{l1,l2} \\ en^\frown V_T \end{Bmatrix} \end{Bmatrix} \langle \text{in env. } \begin{bmatrix} \emptyset \\ be \end{bmatrix}\text{---} \rangle^{37} \end{Bmatrix}$$

The possessive adjective $NP^\frown S_1$ deserves some comment. In a
phrase like "the boy's companions," "the" goes with "boy," not with
"companions." Thus the phrase is not of the same form as "the strange
companions." This is proved by the impossibility of "the boy's and
strange companions," by the possibility of "a man's children" (but not
"a children"), "John's book is . . ." (but not "book is . . ."), etc.[38] All
of these cases show that the possessive suffix is not added to a noun
which appears in the adjective position, between an article and a noun,
but to a noun phrase which appears in the adjective position with a
$\emptyset$ article (or no article, in an alternative treatment). Only certain NP's
can appear in this position (cf. statement 8, above). To determine
whether a noun phrase of the form *Noun^Prepositional Phrase* can
appear in this position it is necessary to make a decision as to the grammaticalness of "the man from Philadelphia's car," etc. I have noted
many such instances in normal conversation, and would thus be inclined
to admit this possibility, which is in fact allowed for in this grammatical
sketch (cf. statement 7, above). A more detailed study than this, taking
into consideration adjective sequence and selection, should result in a
more complete and satisfactory analysis of the character of the possessive
phrase.

---

[37] This is one case where the convention of §72.1 increases the complexity of the statement.
[38] We also have "a children's book," but only with the stress pattern of a compound
noun (like "lighthouse"). These we treat as single words, and so "a children's book"
is a construction like "a lighthouse" or "a tree."

18. A rule of verbal selection suitably restricted to apply only to the V_T introduced in statement 17 (the passive).

This rule is related to statement 9, with initial and final conditioning contexts interchanged, and other alterations. We do not give it in detail, since it is quite complex and subsequent methods will permit its elimination.

A rule of selection should also be given for the V_{I1}, V_{I2} introduced in statement 17. We omit this too.

19. $VP_A \rightarrow VP_{A1} \langle VP_{A2} \rangle$

20. $VP_{A1} \rightarrow \begin{Bmatrix} ed \\ C \end{Bmatrix} \langle M \rangle$

21. $VP_{A2} \rightarrow \langle have\widehat{\ }en \rangle \langle be\widehat{\ }ing$ except in env. *ing* ———$\rangle$[39]

22. $D \rightarrow \begin{Bmatrix} D_1 \\ D_2 \end{Bmatrix}$

23. $D_1 \rightarrow$ very, rather, . . .
$D_2 \rightarrow$ quickly, certainly, . . .
$A \rightarrow$ old, red, . . .
$N_p \rightarrow$ John, . . .
$N_{ab} \rightarrow$ sincerity, truthfulness, . . .
$N_{ac} \rightarrow$ boy, dog, . . .
$N_{inan} \rightarrow$ table, store, . . .
$M \rightarrow$ will, can, shall, may, must
$V_{t1} \rightarrow$ appoint, feed, . . .
$V_{t2} \rightarrow$ recognize, admire, . . .
$V_{t3} \rightarrow$ frighten, surprise, . . .
$V_{t4} \rightarrow$ carry, see, . . .
$V_{I1} \rightarrow$ sleep, laugh, . . .
$V_{I2} \rightarrow$ flourish, occur, . . .
$V_c \rightarrow$ want, decide, . . .
$V_\gamma \rightarrow$ prefer, urge, . . .
$V_e \rightarrow$ know, believe, consider, . . .
$V_f \rightarrow$ give, ask, . . .
$V_g \rightarrow$ elect, choose, . . .
$V_h \rightarrow$ consider, think, make, . . .
$V_j \rightarrow$ interest, surprise, excite, . . .
$V_k \rightarrow$ tire, drink, bore, . . .

[39] See Notes 9, 33.

This gives us an analysis into elements of $\bar{P}$ (cf. §51). It remains to characterize the relation between the level **P** and the level $\overline{\mathbf{M}}$, i.e., to set up the mapping $\Phi^{\mathbf{P}}$, which in §62.2 we have considered to be broken down into components $\Phi_1,..., \Phi_n$. It will be recalled that these are mappings of **P**-markers ultimately into strings in $\overline{\mathbf{M}}$. Hence in stating these mappings we may refer to the constituent structure of the mapped string, i.e., to any stage in its "history," and not just to its present form, as in giving the statements of the grammar. In Chapter VII we did not go into the nature of these mappings very deeply, and here we will simply give an informal characterization of them, to which we will return below. The effect of these mappings will be to convert the products of derivations produced from §72.2 into actual strings of $\overline{\mathbf{M}}$, which will become strings of words by placement of word boundary (cf. §47).

As mappings we have (cf. **35, 39**):

Φ_1 :   To be added in Chapter X.

Φ_2 :   ...$C^{\frown}M$... goes into ...M...

Φ_3 : $\begin{Bmatrix} NP_s \\ NP_p \end{Bmatrix} C$ goes into $\begin{Bmatrix} NP_s{}^{\frown}S \\ NP_p{}^{\frown}\emptyset \end{Bmatrix}$

Φ_4 : $be \rightarrow were$ in env. NP_p——ed

Φ_5 :   Let $K = \{\emptyset, S, ed, en, ing\}$. Suppose that Z is of the form

$$X_1{}^{\frown}k_1{}^{\frown}d_1{}^{\frown}v_1{}^{\frown}X_2{}^{\frown}k_2{}^{\frown}d_2{}^{\frown}v_2{}^{\frown}...X_n{}^{\frown}k_n{}^{\frown}d_n{}^{\frown}v_n{}^{\frown}X_{n+1}$$

where

> X_i is a string not containing $k_j{}^{\frown}d_j{}^{\frown}v_j$
> $k_i \in K$
> d_i is a D or is U
> v_i is a verb, an M, *have*, or *be*

Then

$$\Phi_5(Z) \text{ is } X_1{}^{\frown}d_1{}^{\frown}v_1{}^{\frown}k_1{}^{\frown}X_2{}^{\frown}d_2{}^{\frown}v_2{}^{\frown}k_2{}^{\frown}...X_n{}^{\frown}d_n{}^{\frown}v_n{}^{\frown}k_n{}^{\frown}X_{n+1}$$

> In other words, if k is an affix of K, then $k \langle D \rangle$ *verb* goes into $\langle D \rangle$ *verb*$^{\frown}k$ (where *verb* stands for verbs, modals, auxiliaries).

Φ_6 , Φ_7 :   To be added in Chapter X.

Φ_8 : $\varnothing$ goes into U

$\Phi_8(\Phi_7(...(\Phi_1)))$ maps **P**-markers into strings of $\overline{\mathbf{M}}$, over-looking the problems raised in §62.2. $\Phi\overline{\mathbf{M}}$ then assigns word boundaries (cf. §47), giving strings in **W**, in fact, **W**-markers of grammatical sentences.

$\Phi\overline{\mathbf{M}}$:   Let $Z = X_1 \frown ... \frown X_n$ (where X_i is a prime). Let K be as in the description of Φ_5 . Let $X_{\alpha_1} , ..., X_{\alpha_m}$ $(1 \leqslant \alpha_1 < ... < \alpha_m \leqslant n)$ be all the primes of Z not followed directly by some k of the class K, or by S_1 . Let $X_{\alpha_0} = U$

Then for each i, $1 \leqslant i \leqslant m$, $X_{\alpha_{i-1}+1} \frown ... \frown X_{\alpha_i}$ goes into a single word, i.e., a single prime of $\overset{\frown}{\mathbf{W}}$.

In other words, word boundaries are introduced everywhere except before affixes of K, or before S_1 .

Φ_3 is **39**. Φ_4 takes care of column IV of Table I, §66.1. Φ_5 is **35**. For Φ_8 , cf. §16. It must still be demonstrated that this informal characterization which refers to constituent structure has some clear and precise significance.

72.4   We present two sample derivations to illustrate the functioning of the grammatical sketch. Steps are coalesced where a single rule applies several times (e.g., step 6, derivation 1). The number of the rule used in forming a given line of the derivation appears in brackets to the right of that line. The mappings are added at the end as separate steps. Dashes indicate repetition of the material immediately above the dashes.

Derivation 1

1. *Sentence*
2. $NP⌢VP$ [1]
3. $NP⌢VP_A⌢VP_1$ [2]
4. $NP⌢VP_A⌢V_T⌢NP$ [3]
5. $NP_s⌢VP_A⌢V_T⌢NP_p$ [4]
6. $T⌢N⌢O⌢VP_A⌢V_T⌢T⌢AP⌢N⌢S$ [7]
7. $T⌢N_{anim}⌢O⌢VP_A⌢V_T⌢T⌢AP⌢N_{inan}⌢S$ [8]
8. — — — — V_{t4} — — — —   [9]
9. $T⌢N_p$ — — — — —   [11]
10. $O⌢N_p⌢O ~ VP_A ~ V_{t4}⌢O⌢AP⌢N_{inan}⌢S$ [14]
11. — — — — $D⌢ing⌢V_j⌢N_{inan}⌢S$ [17]
12. — — $VP_{A1}⌢VP_{A2}$ — — — —   [19]
13. — — C — — — — —   [20]
14. — — $C⌢have⌢en$ — — —   [21]
15. — — — — D_1 — — —   [22]
16. $O⌢John⌢O⌢C⌢have⌢en⌢witness⌢O⌢very⌢ing⌢surprise⌢event⌢S$ [23]
17. — — — — — S — — — $[Φ_3]$
18. — — — $have⌢S⌢witness⌢en$ — — — $surprise⌢ing$ — — — $[Φ_5]$
19. $John⌢have⌢S⌢witness⌢en⌢very⌢surprise⌢ing⌢event⌢S$ $[Φ_8]$
20. $John\text{-}have⌢S\text{-}witness⌢en\text{-}very\text{-}surprise⌢ing\text{-}event⌢S$ $[Φ_M]$
21. *John has witnessed very surprising events*   [by morphological rules]

In step 20, hyphens indicate word boundaries.

Derivation 2

1. Sentence
2. $NP \frown VP$ [1]
3. $NP \frown VP_A \frown VP_1$ [2]
4. $NP \frown VP_A \frown D_2 \frown V_T \frown PP$ [3]
5. NP_p — — — —   [4]
6. $T \frown N \frown S \frown VP_A \frown D_2 \frown V_T \frown PP$ [7]
7. $T \frown N_{anim} \frown S$ — — —   [8]
8. — — — V_{I1} — —   [9]
9. $T \frown N_{ac} \frown S$ — — — —   [11]
10. — — — — $P \frown NP$ [12]
11. — — — — $of \frown NP$ [13]
12. the — — — — —   [14]
13. $the \frown N_{ac} \frown S \frown VP_{A1} \frown D_2 \frown V_{I1} \frown of \frown NP$ [19]
14. — — ed — — —   [20]
15. $the \frown voter \frown S \frown ed \frown sincerely \frown approve \frown of \frown NP$ [23]
16. — — — NP_s [4]
17. — — — $T \frown AP \frown N \frown \emptyset$ [7]

18. ————— $N_A \frown \emptyset$ [8]
19. ————— $\emptyset$ ————— [14]
20. ————— $Inf \frown VP_1$ [15]
21. ————— ing ————— [16]
22. ————— $\emptyset \frown NP \frown S_1 \frown ing \frown VP_1$ [17]
23. ————— $be \frown Pred$ [3]
24. ————— $\emptyset \frown NP_s$ ————— [4]
25. ————— AP [5]
26. ————— $\emptyset \frown T \frown N \frown \emptyset \frown S_1 \frown ing \frown be \frown AP$ [7]
27. ————— $N_{anim} \frown \emptyset \frown S_1 \frown ing \frown be \frown AP$ [8]
28. ————— N_p ————— [11]
29. ————— $\emptyset \frown \emptyset$ [14]
30. $the \frown voter \frown S \frown ed \frown sincerely \frown approve \frown of \frown \emptyset \frown N_p \frown \emptyset \frown S_1 \frown ing \frown be \frown en \frown V_T$ [17]
31. ————— V_{t1} [18]
32. ————— $\emptyset \frown John$ ————— [23]
33. ————— $elect$
34. $the \frown voter \frown S \frown sincerely \frown approve \frown ed$ ————— $be \frown ing \frown elect \frown en$ [Φ₅]
35. $the \frown voter \frown S \frown sincerely \frown approve \frown ed \frown of \frown John \frown S_1 \frown be \frown ing \frown elect \frown en$ [Φ₈]
36. *The voters sincerely approved of John's being elected* [Φ_M]

We have taken "of John's being elected" to be a prepositional phrase, but we might consider an alternative analysis with "approve of" as a transitive verb. This has intuitive appeal, particularly in sentences like "I approve of John," but whether or not it would turn out to be the simplest analysis is an involved question. We will see below, however, that from a point of view different than the one developed so far, the latter analysis is in fact dictated by other considerations.

73   In §68.4 we found that (assuming a certain extension of the analysis of grammaticalness) strict application of criteria of simplicity compelled us to assign several **P**-markers to certain utterances which happened simultaneously to be instances of two independently established patterns, so that constructional homonymity resulted in a manner which, in that instance, was in accord with strong intuitive judgment. Investigating the grammatical sketch just presented, we can find several other cases where even our limited account of grammaticalness leads to intuitively correct instances of constructional homonymity.

Statement 17 gives $ing^\frown V_I$ as one analysis of the adjective phrase. Thus with $V_I = bark$, we have

173   *barking dogs never bite*

as an instance of *Adjective Phrase–plural Noun–Verb Phrase* (AP-$N^\frown S$-VP).

Statements 15 and 16 give $ing^\frown VP_1$ as one analysis of the noun phrase. Thus with $VP_1 = play^\frown musical^\frown instruments$, we have

174   *playing musical instruments is his chief joy in life*

as an instance of *abstract Noun–be–Noun Phrase* ($N_A^\frown \emptyset$-be-NP). That the abstract noun is singular is evident from the singular "is." Since the verb is singular, we know that the subject of **174** cannot be an instance of the construction *AP–plural Noun*, as is the case in **173**.

Given a verb that is both transitive and intransitive (e.g., "fly," which can occur in "planes fly" and "they fly planes"), we can therefore construct a sentence which is simultaneously an instance of *AP-Noun-VP* and N_A-*VP* (where $N_A \rightarrow ing^\frown VP_1$), for instance,

175   *flying planes can be dangerous*

which can be understood in the sense of either **176** or **177**:

176   *flying planes is a dangerous sport for an untrained pilot*

177   *flying planes cast strange shadows*[40]

175 is ambiguous, but **176** and **177**, **178** and **179** are not, since the number of the verb is indicated:

178   *flying planes is dangerous*

179   *flying planes are dangerous*

This again is a case where the results of strict application of our criteria correspond to our intuitive judgment about constituent analysis and dual interpretation, and thus where formal considerations of the kind we have adduced suggest a basis for this intuition.

In §68.4 we saw that

180   *the police stopped drinking*

could be analyzed either as "the police–stopped–drinking" (NP-V_T-NP) or "the police–stopped⌒ing–drink" (NP-V_B-VP). A third interpretation is now provided for certain sentences by the possibility of forming an adjective phrase $ing⌒V_j$ (cf. statement 17). Thus we have

181   *rats leave sinking ships*   (NP-V-$AP⌒N$)

182   *John likes reading books*   (NP-$like⌒ing$-VP, i.e., NP-V_B-VP)

Both interpretations are possible in

183   *bombardiers like sinking ships*

There should, then, be three possible ways of construing certain sentences of the form N-V-ing-V-N. It is difficult, however, to discover a clear and natural instance of a triple homonym.[41]

---

[40] These instances are not normally marked by difference in stress, as are "hunting dogs" and "hunting lions" in "hunting lions is a dangerous pastime" and "hunting dogs must be carefully trained."

[41] In fact, it is difficult to find even a double homonym which is natural in the case of N-V-ing-V-N. Thus the interpretation of "the police stopped drinking hard liquor" in the same sense as "the law forbade drinking hard liquor" is forced, though both interpretations are natural when the object of "drink" is dropped, as in **180**.

74.1   One extremely serious deficiency of this grammar, and of the conception of grammar on which it is based, is that we really have no good way to introduce the rule for conjunction as a statement of the grammar. But the simplification of the conjunction rule was one of the fundamental criteria for the determination of constituent structure. Hence if the grammar cannot incorporate this rule, the proposed approach to a demonstration of validity is undermined, and there is considerably less justification for the particular form that the grammar has assumed. Of course, inability to state the conjunction rule is itself a serious defect, irrespective of the fundamental character of this rule as a criterion for the establishment of constituents.

Roughly, the conjunction rule asserts that **184** is an optional conversion:

184 $...X... \rightarrow ...X^{\frown}and^{\frown}X...$,   where X is a prime

But our framework has no place for such a statement as **184**. It will be recalled that each rule of the grammar operates on the forms as they appear in the last step of the derivation in question, at the point when the rule is to be applied. Our characterization of the process of producing derivations from grammars does not provide for the possibility of taking into account the history of the elements that appear in this last step of the derivation in question. But if **184** were introduced into the grammar as a statement, it would be necessary to know the history of the elements that appear in the last step of the derivation at the point where **184** is to be applied. That is, we should have to know which substring is represented by a single prime, i.e., is a constituent, and in fact, what sort of constituent it is. (Alternatively, we should have to introduce one statement of the form **184** for each prime.)

This suggests that **184** be stated as a mapping Φ_i, rather than as a statement of the grammar, since the mappings are defined on **P**-markers, and **P**-markers do give us the constituent structure of a string. But clearly this idea would involve a radical revision of our whole notion of levels as systems of representation. The function of the mappings of **P** into **W**, as this conception of linguistic structure has been developed, is to provide the information that, e.g., the representation of "John was here" on the level **P** is a certain abstract element K (called a **P**-marker) from which the constituent structure of "John was here" can be derived in the manner described in Chapter VII, just as its representation on the level **W** is a certain string of words, namely, *John^was^here*. It makes no sense to say that K is also the representation on the level **P** of "John and Bill were here," as would be the case if the conjunction rule were construed as part of the mapping Φ^P. A further difficulty is that some notion of nonobligatory mapping is implied here, and this has as yet no meaning.

Another approach would be to generalize our conception of the form of grammars so that the history of an element can be utilized in applying a rule to a step of a derivation. This would invalidate a good part of Chapter VII, and seems an unfortunate step to take in view of the simplicity and naturalness of the conception of grammatical form developed there, and in view of the adequacy of this conception of grammar for limited description such as that of §17 (or the appendix to Chapter VI). On the other hand, in the preceding sections we have noted a considerable number of inadequacies in this conception. Some of these might be remedied with a more elaborate development of the conception of grammars.

    We will see that a third approach can be developed which will enable us to construct the conjunction rule in accordance with the suggestion of §74.1 (final paragraph), but avoiding the objections raised there; to resolve the problems which have arisen in applying the conceptions which have been developed without any alteration of these conceptions or any broadening of the basis on which they have been constructed; and finally, to extend the scope of syntactic analysis considerably beyond the bounds imposed by the system of levels so far developed.

74.2

TRANSFORMATIONAL ANALYSIS
IX

In a broad sense, the problem of syntactic analysis is to determine and describe the membership of the class μ^W of grammatical strings of words. The goal of a grammar is to provide a method for constructing exactly this set. There are trivial ways to approach this requirement. For instance, the set of sentences of books in the New York Public Library (with obvious qualifications) might be, so far as experiment would show, a fairly good approximation to the set μ^W. But the purpose of a linguistic grammar is to rebuild the vast complexity of the language more elegantly and systematically by extracting the contribution to this complexity of the various linguistic levels. And in linguistic theory, we face the problem of constructing each level in an abstract manner, so that we can systematically develop a characterization of μ^W for any given language by interpreting the abstract formalism of linguistic theory for the corpus of observed sentences of this language. The system of levels of linguistic theory not only provides the means for giving a simplified description for this enormously complex set of grammatical sentences, but also for determining the bounds of this set in the first place. Thus the New York Public Library contains an approximation not to μ^W itself, but only to that part of it that the linguist might ever come in contact with. But a linguistic grammar must answer further questions which cannot be dealt with by this trivial "grammar," e.g., how can a speaker produce and understand new sentences?

Clear examples of this systematic and piecemeal reconstruction of the complexity of language have appeared in the preceding chapters. For example, we developed a more systematic and workable notion of constituent by requiring nonoverlap of constituents (relative to a given interpretation of a sentence), but we recovered the original complexity by assigning alternative **P**-markers ("interpretations") to certain strings, where special circumstances dictate this multiple assignment. We have seen that when we interpret the abstract levels in the prescribed manner so as to lead to the simplest grammar, there are, in specific instances, correspondences with strong intuition about language structure. This result may be interpreted as giving an explanation, in terms of a theory of linguistic structure, for these intuitions of the native speaker.

In other words, suppose that we had constructed only one syntactic level, namely, **W**. We would then be able to represent utterances only as strings of phonemes, morphemes, and words. The result of attempting to construct a grammar in accordance with this limited theory of linguistic structure would have been an enormously complex grammar of completely unmanageable proportions. Furthermore, we would have found that many strong intuitions of the native speaker would be quite unaccounted for. These considerations would have led us to construct a new and higher level **P**, as a part of linguistic theory.

Having constructed **P**, we must investigate the extent of its success in resolving these two difficulties. That there is a considerable degree of success is evident from all that has been said above. But we have seen in the course of working out the interpretation of **P** for English that both types of inadequacy remain. All but the simplest sentences had to be excluded, at least if we wished to achieve anything near an "optimal" grammar in which each rule applies when just the relevant specification of strings has been given and in which what is essentially a single rule of selection need not be repeated in several different forms for the various cases. We saw that any attempt to introduce more complex sentences not only led to overwhelming complexities (which, incidentally, threatened to distort seriously the simple and adequate picture of the simple sentences) in the formulation of the grammar, because of the tremendous number and involved types of recursions and selectional relations, but also appeared to favor analyses that were in sharp contradiction to strong intuition.

We might, then, seek to amend **P**, perhaps along the lines suggested above in §§71.2, 74.2. Alternatively, for exactly the reasons that led to the establishment of **P** in the first place, we might attempt to construct a new level of linguistic structure in terms of which utterances can be described. An investigation of the specific shortcomings of our present theory will, I think, favor the latter course. We will now proceed to survey some of the major classes of problems that this theory leaves unresolved.

76.1   There are cases where similar strings have intuitively quite different interpretations, but where we can discover no grounds, on any of our present levels, for assigning different markers to them. For instance,

1   *this picture was painted by a real artist*

2   *this picture was painted by a new technique*

are quite different sorts of sentences. **3** lends itself to either interpretation:

3   *John was frightened by the new methods*

This can mean, roughly, "John is a conservative—new methods frighten him." Or it can have the sense of "new methods of frightening people were used to frighten John" (an interpretation which would be the normal one in the case of "John was being frightened by the new methods"). Introspecting, the two interpretations seem to involve a difference of construction. In the first case, "methods" is the "subject" (as is "artist" in **1**); in the second, it seems to be the noun of a prepositional phrase expressing means (as is "technique" in **2**).

4 differs intuitively from **5** in the same way that **1** differs from **2**:

4   *the escaped prisoner was caught by the police*

5    $\begin{Bmatrix}(a)\\(b)\end{Bmatrix}$ *the escaped prisoner was caught* $\begin{Bmatrix}by\ the\ railroad\ tracks\\by\ ten\ o'clock\end{Bmatrix}$

6, much like **3**, is ambiguous, being subject to the interpretations of either **4** or **5**a:

6   *the man was killed by the car*

In the intuitive conception, then, **1** and **4** are classed together as opposed to **2** and **5**, the distinction being some feature of construction. (A subsidiary three-way distinction within the group **2**, **5**a, **5**b apparently has to do with the meaning of "by," and need not concern us in our investigation of the adequacy of a grammatical theory.) **3** and **6** seem intuitively to be cases of constructional homonymity, cases of overlap of opposed structural patterns. Yet **1–6** are all instances of the pattern *NP-was-A-PP* (cf. §§67.2, 67.3 and statements 3, 5, 17, 18, §72.2). A theory of selectional relations might be of some help here. A detailed account of statement 18, §72.2, would reveal that the *PP* in **2** and **5** is of a type that need not be stated as a conditioning context in statement 18,[1] whereas the *PP* of **1** and **4** must be stated there. But even if this distinction can be developed in some systematic way, it will apparently class **3** and **6** along with **2** and **5**, rather than as ambiguous sentences. Furthermore we have seen (cf. §71.2) that there are many potential trouble spots in this approach. Finally, such an approach will provide no explanation for the "verbal force" of "paint," "frighten," catch," "kill" in **1–6**, or of "tire" in

7   *John was tired by the unusually hard work*

as compared with the nonverbal character of "tire" in **8** or of "bore" in **9**:

8   *John was tired by evening*

9   *John was bored by that time*[2]

Note further that such sentences as **10** are intuitively cases of constructional homonymity, in a different way than are **3** and **6**:

10 $\begin{Bmatrix} (a) \\ (b) \\ (c) \end{Bmatrix}$ *John was* $\begin{Bmatrix} frightened \\ surprised \\ bored \end{Bmatrix}$

For example, in **10**a, "frightened" can be "verbal" as in either interpretation of **3** or in "he was once frightened by a mad dog," or it can be "adjectival" as in the intuitive interpretation of "John was obviously very frightened." But in all of these cases, we are compelled simply to classify these $V^{\frown}en$ forms in a single way, as a certain subclass of adjectives.

There is thus a complex of intuitively quite different structural patterns, overlapping in cases of constructional homonymity, but with no counterpart in the rigorous application of our present theory.

There are other instances of intuitively felt difference in structure that are not properly accounted for in the application of the theory of

---

[1] Further investigation of grammaticalness might wipe out even this distinction if, e.g., such sentences as "the factory was owned by a new technique," "... by the railroad tracks," are excluded as not fully grammatical.

[2] We know that "tire" and "bore" are in a different subclass of verbs from "paint," etc. (cf. Note 13, Chapter VIII, and statement 17, §72.2), but the *en* forms of both are adjectives, as we have seen in §§67.2, 67.3 and neither of these subclasses of adjectives is, for any formal reason that we have yet established, more "verbal" than the other.

syntactic structure as so far developed. Consider the difference in our feeling for the structure of 11 and 12:

11 *the growling of lions . . .*

12 *the reading of good literature . . .*

Or, with either interpretation,

13 *the rearming of Germany . . .*

14 *the shooting of the hunters . . .*

In the case of 11, "lions" is intuitively the subject. In the case of 12, "literature" is intuitively the object. In the case of 13 and 14, the noun of the *PP* can be understood as either the subject or the object. But these comments, although intuitively obvious, are beyond the range of our theoretical development. The phrases in 11–14 are all similarly constructed in our terms. All are instances of *NP-PP* (cf. the discussion relating to 167, §71.1). In terms of the grammatical sketch of §72.2, 13 and 14 are in fact cases of constructional homonymity, since the verbs "rearm," "shoot" can be either V_{t1} or V_{t1}. But the relevant distinction is not this, but is rather in the relation between the verb and the noun of the following prepositional phrase.[3] For some cases, an elaboration of the notion of selectional relation might give a basis for this felt difference, but for others (including 13 and 14, on the present level of grammaticalness), it would not, unless the difficulties cited in §71.2 are somehow resolved.

In §70, we came across another example of unexplained dual interpretation (159–161). We saw there that, e.g.,

15 *I found the boy studying in the library*

can be interpreted as having the same construction as

16 *I know the boy studying in the library*

but that it can also be interpreted, even more naturally, in quite a different way, as having the same construction as

[3] If we had analyzed verbs differently into three classes, wholly transitive, wholly intransitive, and those that are either transitive or intransitive, then 13 and 14 would in fact have only single P-markers.

17   *I found him studying in the library*

This distinction is an obvious and clear one, as we can see by adding, e.g., "not running around in the streets" to these three sentences. In the case of **16** and one interpretation of **15**, "the boy studying in the library" is the complex noun phrase object of the main verb. In the case of **17**, and a second interpretation of **15**, it seems more natural to regard "found ... studying in the library" as being, somehow, a complex discontinuous verbal element with "the boy" and "him" as its "objects" (though even this is not satisfactory, since "the boy" and "him" appear at the same time to be "subjects" of "study"). In any event, we have no grounds for establishing or describing the difference in construction between **16** and **17**, or the ambiguity of **15**. In our analysis, the phrase structure of all of these sentences seems to be identical.

Another fairly subtle but nonetheless real case of dual interpretation arises in sentences such as

18   *I don't approve of his drinking*[4]

In one sense, this might be paraphrased roughly by "I don't think he ought to drink" (i.e., he's too young), in another sense, by "I don't like the way he drinks." Similarly

19   *I don't approve of his cooking*

may indicate that I think his wife should cook, or that I think he uses too much garlic.

Introspecting, the difference between the two interpretations in both cases seems to depend on the extent to which we regard "his" as the "subject" of "drink" (and "cook"), or as an adjective modifying "drinking" (and "cooking"). But we can find no grounds for a dual interpretation within the study of phrase structure.

The cases cited in this section exemplify one type of intuitive inadequacy of our present theoretical framework. That is, these are examples of sentences with dual interpretations, but where we have no grounds for establishing constructional homonymity in the intuitively relevant manner.

---

[4] Or, since some speakers require "him" with one of these interpretations in this position, consider "his drinking is something I don't approve of."

The opposite deficiency would occur if we were sometimes led to assign   76.2
several **P**-markers to sentences that have, intuitively, only one analysis.
We can also find cases of this kind. Consider the sentence

20   *the dog is barking*

In accordance with the analysis presented in Chapter VIII, we
analyze **20** as

21   *the⌢dog–is⌢ing–bark*,   i.e., $NP\text{-}VP_A\text{-}V_I$

as is intuitively correct. But "barking" is also an adjective (cf. statement
17, §72.2), as in

22   *barking dogs never bite*

and there is a sentence form $NP\text{-}be\text{-}A$ (cf. statements 3, 5, 17, §72.2),
as in

23   *the dog is mangy*

Thus by a completely different route we arrive at the analysis of
20 as

24   *the⌢dog–is–barking*,   i.e., $NP\text{-}is\text{-}A$

making **20** analogous in construction to **23**. But this analysis has no
intuitive support.

This, then, is a case where we have too much constructional
homonymity.[5]

We have come across cases where the distinction between what are   76.3
intuitively quite differently constructed sentences is not properly marked,
and where distinctions are characterized that are not intuitively felt.
A third problem arises when the correct number of **P**-markers are
assigned, but where the considerations so far available lead to the
assignment of what is intuitively the wrong marker. The analysis of **17**
as *I–found–him⌢studying⌢in⌢the⌢library* (i.e., $NP\text{-}V\text{-}NP_I$) is one such
case. In §69.3, we found that if we were to attempt to present a descrip-

---

[5] If we analyze **20** in the counterintuitive manner rejected in §69.3 and discussed below
in §76.3, the difficulty remains. We still have two analyses, now both intuitively incorrect, where only one should appear.

tion of phrase structure that would cover all grammatical sentences, then there would be another and more serious case of this nature.

To recapitulate briefly, it seems intuitively clear that in a sentence such as

25   *John was eating a sandwich*

"was eating a sandwich" is a verb phrase, analyzable either into the auxiliary "was" and the verb phrase "eating a sandwich" (the latter being further analyzable into the verb "eating" and the noun phrase "a sandwich"), or into the verb phrase "was eating" and the noun phrase "a sandwich." But under one assumption (which we will state directly), the grounds available to us at this point apparently necessitate the different and counterintuitive analysis into the main verb "was" and the noun phrase "eating a sandwich," so that the sentence **25** is of the form *NP-was-NP*, like

26   *John was a politician*

The reason for this analysis is formal similarity and simplicity. Since we must anyway assign some occurrences of "eating a sandwich" to *NP* because of

27   *eating a sandwich takes only a few minutes*

it is clearly more economical to assign it to *NP* in this instance too, particularly since we arrive at a sentence form *NP-was-NP*, which is already familiar on independent gounds because of **26**. We actually manage to drop one restriction now in the analysis of this form, i.e., the requirement that *NP* cannot become $ing^\frown VP_1$ in the context $N_{anim}\text{-}be$—.

The assumption under which this counterintuitive analysis follows is that we add to the language of grammar certain notational devices which permit us to adjoin to certain statements of the grammar a restriction which in §69.3 we called the qualification Q. But we saw in §69.3 that we could not provide an analysis for certain sentences (without serious departures from certain desirable properties that we would like a grammar to have) unless these notational devices were available. Hence if we construct linguistic theory in such a way that the grammar can present a phrase structure for every sentence directly, within the segment of the grammar which is reduced (in the sense of §55) from the level **P**, then this counterintuitive analysis of **25** as analogous to **26** will follow. Thus we must either arbitrarily limit the grammatical description to only the simplest sentences (in a sense which cannot be independently characterized, at this point), or we must accept a strongly counterintuitive analysis of phrase structure.

Summing up this discussion, then, we see that one type of difficulty is that rigorous application of the methods we have so far sketched apparently leads us to analyses that are either too many, too few, or simply incorrect.

A second class of difficulties concerns the distinction between various different kinds of sentences. It would be hard to disagree with the judgment that "John!," "come here!," "John was here," "was John here?" are in some sense sentences of quite different kinds. Are there, in our terms, general formal grounds for this distinction?[6] **77.1**

In Chapter VIII we found that the rule for conjunction serves as a criterion for determining sameness or difference of structure. If X and Y are sentences of different "types," then we would expect that $X^\frown and^\frown Y$ should be ungrammatical, just as instances of $Sentence^\frown and^\frown NP$, $...VP^\frown and^\frown PP...$ are ungrammatical. This is in fact the case. We have "I saw him yesterday and I lent him a book," but not "I saw him yesterday and can you come?" or "John! and I saw him yesterday." This indicates that the component sentences in these compounds must be considered as different "constituents," i.e., in this case, as different kinds of sentences, since they are the maximal constituents of themselves. In other words, had we given a more complete grammar in §72.2, the first statement of this grammar would have had to be

$$
28 \quad Sentence \rightarrow \begin{Bmatrix} Imperative\ Sentence \\ Interrogative\ Sentence \\ Declarative\ Sentence \\ \vdots \end{Bmatrix}
$$

However, the conjunction criterion is not entirely satisfactory as a basis for setting up sentence types. We have not discussed the conjunction rule in anywhere near sufficient detail, but in our present

---

[6] It has been pointed out correctly (Trager and Smith, Fries) that intonation cannot serve as a ground for this distinction. Different intonational patterns can appear fairly freely with the various sentence types. Fries has carried out certain exploratory investigations of sentence types on the basis of the linguistic and situational context in which the sentence occurs. This approach goes beyond the basis that we have assumed. What we are trying to determine here is whether this distinction can be made by further theoretical constructions on the same limited basis as earlier theoretical constructions, that is, assuming no new kinds of data.

context we can easily see that any formulation of it will fail to make exactly the distinction that we require. We can formulate this criterion so that X and Y are sentences of the same type if *either* $X^\frown and^\frown Y$ or $Y^\frown and^\frown X$ is grammatical, or only if *both* $X^\frown and^\frown Y$ and $Y^\frown and^\frown X$ are grammatical. If we choose the first alternative, then imperatives and future declaratives are not distinguished from one another, since we have

29   *come here and I will tell you a secret*

If, noting that **30** is not grammatical, we choose the second alternative, then we will not be able to set up a class of declarative sentences, since **31** (without contrastive stress) is no more grammatical than **30**:

30   *I will tell you the secret and come here*

31   *I will tell you the secret and I am here*

77.2   Furthermore, there are subtypes of sentences within these basic types, and these naturally cannot be distinguished by the conjunction criterion if the main types can be distinguished in this way. Within the general type of interrogatives we must distinguish such subclasses as those to which **32** and **33** belong:

32   *was he here?*

33   *who was here?*

If we decide that such sentences as

34   *did he come and who saw him?*

are grammatical, then we have no way of distinguishing **32** and **33** as separate subtypes. If, on the other hand, **34** is considered ungrammatical, then we cannot set up interrogatives as a sentence type. Either way, the result is unsatisfactory, since **32** and **33** are clearly more similar to one another than are declaratives to interrogatives, but less similar than, e.g., two sentences of the "form" **32**.

There is also an intuitively clear subclassification of declaratives. Most grammars of English set up passives as a special sentence type. But there seems to be no compelling formal reason to do this.[7] Why

---

[7] The necessity of a separate selectional statement for passives (statement 18, §72.2) and

is "John was seen at the lunch counter" more different in form from "John stopped at the lunch counter" than is "John was eating at the lunch counter " or "John was tired in the morning"? Why does "John was seen at the lunch counter," alone among these sentences, require special treatment in the grammar? Such sentences seem intuitively to hold an intermediate position between "John was here" and "was John here." While they have the basic subject–predicate form, we are nonetheless inclined to treat them separately. We have as yet provided no motivation for this special treatment.

We have a classification of sentences into

$$
35 \quad
\begin{cases}
\text{Declarative} & \begin{cases} \text{active} \\ \text{passive} \end{cases} \\
\text{Interrogative} & \begin{cases} \textbf{32, etc.} \\ \textbf{33, etc.} \end{cases} \\
\text{Imperative}
\end{cases}
$$

This is not an exhaustive classification. It has good intuitive support (as well as support in the traditional practice of grammatians), but, as yet, no formal grounds in terms of the system we have constructed. It appears that to distinguish sentence types properly, some criterion additional to conjunction and other criteria of the level **P**, some completely new approach, is required.[8]

In the same connection, it seems that certain sentences of presumably different types are related to one another. Thus "he was here" and "was he here," or "John hit Bill" and "Bill was hit by John" seem related in a way in which such pairs as "John hit Bill" and "Bill hit John," "John hit Bill" and "John was hit by Bill," "he was here" and "he will be here," or "John hit Bill" and "John was hitting Bill" are not. Exactly what this relation is not clear. It certainly has some connection with meaning. On the other hand, it is not synonymy or logical equivalence. This is clear enough in the case of question and answer, but

77.3

---

other special properties of passives that we have noted indicate that passives are somehow distinct, but we require a systematic explanation for this distinction.

[8] There are other criteria on the level **P** for making some of the distinctions that we require. For example, declaratives are formally distinct from nondeclaratives in that they occur after *that*. This is an important distinguishing feature, and it would lend support to a separate analysis of declaratives, but it does not permit us to distinguish among the various types of nondeclaratives, or among the subclasses of declaratives. Nor is there any systematic justification of selecting this environment as "diagnostic."

it is also true in the case of active and passive. We have at present no way of explaining such relations.

77.4   A related phenomenon is that in each of these pairs of related sentences, one seems somehow more basic than the other and more central as far as the structure of the language is concerned. A study of the arrangement of English words in sentences will normally treat first such "basic" patterns as subject–predicate (actor–action), using as examples such simple declarative sentences as "John was here" or "I like John," and will discuss passives, questions, imperatives, sentences with relative clauses, etc., only as subsidiary and derived phenomena.

There seems to be no obvious formal justification for this procedure, though if it were not to be followed, the results of grammatical analysis might prove to be quite strange. Suppose, for instance, that the investigation of the phrase structure of English were initiated on the basis of such examples as

36   *whom have they nominated*

Investigating various analyses of **36** into two parts, etc., in accordance with the procedures of constituent analysis, it seems that we would not arrive at such conceptions as that of a basic actor–action relation at all. In fact, there seems to be no reasonable way to even begin to construct an intuitively satisfactory **P**-marker for this sentence. Nevertheless, the subject–verb relation does, clearly, appear in **36**, with "they" as the *NP* subject, and "whom have . . . nominated" as the verb phrase, with the object "whom" and the verb "have . . . nominated." But the search for general formal grounds in **P** for such an analysis seems futile and formally unmotivated. It seems reasonable to consider the possibility of denying any **P**-marker to **36**, and of somehow deriving a partial constituent analysis for **36** by considering its relation to some more "basic" sentence which does have a **P**-marker, e.g., "they have nominated John."

The significance of this class of basic sentences, the manner of its construction, and the nature of the relations between basic sentences and "derived" sentences of noncentral sentence types remain to be explored. The process of construction of derived sentences is not an unfamiliar one. It makes intuitive sense to form the passive of a given active sentence, or to construct a question corresponding to a given declarative, active or passive. But we see at once that these processes of derivation cannot be commuted or compounded freely. Thus there is no clear sense to the notion of "the passive of a question."

The study of these relations and processes has no place within the framework of linguistic theory as we have so far outlined its development (though these notions are discussed in traditional grammar). The considerations of this section thus suggest that this theory is too limited in scope to reconstruct completely and adequately our presystematic conception of linguistic form.

A third class of difficulties has to do with the complexity of the gram-   78
matical statement when this is unlimited in scope. We discovered in investigating English grammar with the tools so far available that when declarative sentences of other than the simplest type are considered, the grammar becomes unwieldy and loses its "optimal" character (cf. in particular §§69, 70). And the application of criteria of simplicity, though still formally possible, ceases to have much meaning. The difficulties become even more extreme if we try to state the structure of other sentence types, e.g., the full range of interrogatives, within the same grammatical framework (and there is no systematic justification for not doing this). Although it is clear that the same selectional relations hold for these sentences as for the simple declaratives, the inversions make a single statement of verbal selection quite involved. We have already observed a departure from optimality in the case of statement 18, §72.2; and in statements 4, 6, 8, 10, 14, 15, 21 we were forced to use devices which are really unwarranted (cf. Notes 19, 33, 37, Chapter VIII). Furthermore, we saw in §74 that even the fundamental rule on which much of the validation of the grammar was based could not be introduced into the grammar. We noted in §71.1 (see also statement 9*, §72.2) that the rule of verbal selection becomes extremely complex even if we limit ourselves to declarative statements, and that we are as yet unable to make use of some striking similarities in selectional relations to simplify it.

Several other theoretical gaps have been exposed incidentally in the course of our discussion. Thus in the final paragraphs of §66.2 and §68.4 we noted that many affixes are apparently associated with the wrong elements, with consequent difficulties, for example, in stating the rule for conjunction. A more far-reaching inadequacy is that we have no means for stating the mapping Φ which carries **P**-markers into strings of words (cf. §62, Chapter VII, and §72.3). The fundamental unresolved difficulty in stating Φ is that we have no way to take into account the "history" (i.e., constituent structure) of a string in converting it further. We noted several times that this same difficulty recurs within the description of English phrase structure. This suggests that the difficulty of describing English phrase structure completely and our inability to characterize Φ may have the same (or a similar) source. It will be noted, incidentally, that our inability to state the mapping Φ in sufficient generality leaves the status of discontinuous constituents in doubt, since these cannot be introduced in the sequence of conversions that gives the internal structure of **P**.

In the grammatical sketch developed in Chapter VIII, and presented in §72.2, we avoided the enormous number of recursions and the excessive complication of formulation caused by more complex sentences (and by different types of sentences) by simply excluding all but the simplest sentences from consideration. In this way we were able to develop a fairly simple and intuitively adequate picture of phrase structure for a limited class of sentences. But we have no real warrant for this arbitrary limitation.

79   In the abstract development of the level **P** of phrase structure we left open the possibility that images of **P**-markers under the mapping $\Phi^{\mathbf{P}}$ will not exhaust the set of grammatical strings of words. That is, we left open the possibility that certain grammatical strings of words will not be generated by the sequence of conversions corresponding to the level **P** and will thus not be provided with a constituent analysis by this segment of the grammar. The reason for this was to avoid making the level **P** overcomplicated. Thus it was intended that derivations and constituent analysis be provided for sentences only where it is profitable to do so, where an organized and simple system of phrase structure results. If we do deny **P**-markers to certain strings, then we must provide some other way for generating and characterizing these un-marked sentences, In the light of all that has been said, it seems most natural to characterize these sentences in terms of some notion of grammatical transformation, regarding these sentences as transforms of certain sentences which are derived on the level **P**.

We are thus led to develop a new level of syntactic analysis, the level **T** of transformations, and to assign **T**-markers to strings of words as markers of their "transformational history." That is, the **T**-markers of a string of words will tell us how this string is derived from a certain *kernel* of sentences which have ρ_1-derivations and **P**-markers. In terms of previous levels we can represent each sentence as a string of phonemes, words, syntactic categories, and, in various ways, as strings of phrases. Now we will be able to represent a sentence as a sequence of operations by which this sentence is derived from the kernel of basic sentences, each such sequence of operations corresponding to a **T**-marker.

We will try to construct the level **T** in such a way that cases of constructional homonymity and difference of interpretation will have their formal analogue in the assignment of different **T**-markers, i.e., different sequences of operations originating from the same or different kernel sentences, and resulting in a given string. The notion of "relation between sentences" may also find an explanation in transformational terms. Thus we may say that a sentence X is related in the sense in question to a sentence Y if, under some transformation set up for the language, X is a transform of Y or Y is a transform of X. Centrality of structure can be explained wherever we can show that certain trans-formations have no inverses in the grammar, i.e., that although X can be derived from Y, Y cannot be derived from X. We can identify sentence types and subtypes with particular transformations and subsidiary transformations of transforms. Finally, we may hope that the residual complexity of the level **P**, caused essentially by the com-plicated network of selectional relations in a complex sentence and by the inversions, etc., characteristic of different sentence types, can be eliminated by adjoining this new level, which will enable us to construct new sentences out of already existing sentences with the selectional relations already "built in."

These are the goals of transformational analysis. In the remainder of this chapter and in the following chapter, I will try to show that a theory of transformations can provide a unified and quite natural approach to all of the problems mentioned in §§76–78, and that it can result in syntactic description which is considerably more economical and revealing. Furthermore, it will appear that this theory can be developed on the same basis as is already required for the familiar levels. That is, no new notions, semantic or otherwise, need be introduced to establish the level of transformations and the procedures of transforma-tional analysis. The motivation, the form, and the basis for the level of transformational analysis are those which are familiar from the levels that we have already established.

The problem before us is to develop a set of grammatical transformations **80** which will apply in a certain set of cases (e.g., those of which instances were given in §§76–78) in an interesting way. This dual program of constructing a certain potentiality of description and then demonstrating that it applies in just the right cases is by now a familiar one. On each level **L** we have tried to state the general structure of **L**, and to give a rigorous account of the central notions of **L**, and have then tried to develop a procedure whereby, for a given language, various interpretations of this formal structure can be evaluated, and the best of them selected.

We turn first to the technical problem of developing an adequate abstract notion of grammatical transformation. This technical discussion must make a certain set of transformations available for grammatical description. Before actually presenting the construction, I will try to give a fairly thorough account of the reasoning behind the particular formulation which will be adopted. That is, I will try to show how certain conditions are imposed on this construction by the nature of the linguistic material, by our general conception of linguistic theory and of linguistic levels, and by systematic considerations of simplicity and convenience. It is important to show just how the construction is motivated (particularly, in this very early stage in the discussion of transformational analysis) so that if further research shows its inadequacy to linguistic material, it will be clear at what points the construction can best be modified or recast. As elsewhere, the construction of transformations must be regarded as tentative—as an attempt to generalize from the problems that have arisen in limited investigation of linguistic materials (such as those reported on in Chapter X).

§§81, 82 will be devoted to a step-by-step development of the notion of transformation which we will finally adopt, along with a statement of the motivation for each step. In §84, we present a more concise and systematic account of this development, with some further refinement. In §§84, 85 we discuss some particular transformations of special interest for transformational analysis, and show that in a certain sense these serve as a basis for the whole system. This discussion is carried further in §§86, 87, where we investigate the problem of assigning constituent structure to transforms. In §88 we apply the notions that have been developed to clarification of the status of the mapping Φ^P. In §§89 and 91 we develop transformations as a linguistic level of the form discussed in Chapter III, and we generalize these notions so that transformations can apply to sets of strings. This whole development is necessarily somewhat technical and detailed. We summarize it in §93, the first section of Chapter X, which is devoted in full to application of transformational analysis. The reader who wishes to bypass the technical discussion might then proceed directly to §93, taking it for granted that there are reasons for the fact that the description of transformations, as presented there, is so involved.

81.1 We are concerned with the level **W** of words, the level **P** of phrase structure, and the level **T** of transformations. Suppose that for the sake of simplifying this informal exposition we assume that **W** is actually embedded in **P**. That is, we assume that strings of words are also strings in **P**, in fact, strings in $\bar{P}$, which, it will be recalled, is the set of "lowest-level" strings in **P**, strings which bear ρ to no string.

We are concerned with certain large classes of sentences such as "answers" and questions, or actives and passives, which are paired in the sense that sentence by sentence, there is a constant formal difference between them; i.e., there is a fixed formal property such that to each sentence X of one class, there is a sentence Y of the other class differing from X in just this formal property. The formal property may be a difference in word order, a fixed added element, the deletion of a certain element, regrouping, or some combination of these. Thus passives are formed from actives by interchanging subject and object, and placing *be⌢en* before the main verb, and *by* after it, so that *John⌢S⌢love⌢Mary* (= "John loves Mary") becomes *Mary⌢S⌢be⌢en⌢love⌢by⌢John* (= "Mary is loved by John").

The first requirement for grammatical transformations is that the result of a transformation must be unambiguous. Each transformation must be a single-valued mapping of certain strings in $\bar{P}$ into $\bar{P}$. The reasons for this condition are just those behind the requirement that the product of a **P**-marker be unique. The purpose of transformational analysis, from one point of view, is to provide a substitute analysis for sentences which are not provided with derivations in **P**, i.e., which are not the products of restricted ρ_1-derivations. Given an analysis (a **P**-marker or a **T**-marker), we must know of what sentence it is an analysis.

Suppose that a certain transformation **T** is basically a permutation which carries a_1-a_2-a_3 into a_3-a_2-a_1, for any strings a_1, a_2, a_3. Suppose that T is to be applied to

37   *my friend hit Bill*

This is ambiguous. If we interpret **37** as "my friend–hit–Bill," the result of applying T will be

38   *Bill–hit–my friend*

If we interpret **37** as "my–friend hit–Bill," the result of applying T will be

39   *Bill–friend hit–my*

Clearly these grammatical transformations cannot be taken simply as permutations on strings and the like. There must be a qualification specifying the analysis of the string to which the transformation is applied. This qualification could be given as part of the definition of the transformation. That is, we could define a certain permutational transformation as applying only, say, to strings of the form $NP\text{-}V\text{-}NP$, so that in the instance discussed above, only **38** is possible. Alternatively, we can take the domain of a transformation to be the set of ordered pairs (X, K), where X is a string and K is an analysis of the string and we can allow transformations to be applied freely to such ordered pairs. For the case discussed above, either limitation would be adequate, but we will see that both of these restrictions are necessary for other reasons.

We note first of all that transformations must be limited by definition to certain kinds of strings. The transformation which turns an answer into a question will be based (in part) on a permutation of $a_1\text{-}a_2\text{-}a_3$ into $a_2\text{-}a_1\text{-}a_3$, since it will convert "John can come" into "can John come." But certainly it will not be the case that in general a string which is an $X\text{-}Y\text{-}Z$ can be transformed significantly into $Y\text{-}X\text{-}Z$. This will be the case only, e.g., when $X = NP$, Y is an auxiliary verb of some sort, etc. So we cannot allow transformations to be unrestricted mappings of (X, K) into Y, where K gives the analysis of X. Transformations must be limited by definition to certain kinds of strings.

But this limitation alone is not sufficient, in general. We cannot define transformations with a qualification as to domain and then allow them to apply freely to strings in $\bar{P}$, for how will we know whether a given string X in $\bar{P}$ has the analysis required by the transformation? To determine this, we must be provided with a **P**-marker of X. But X may have several **P**-markers (and these different **P**-markers may in fact have one or more steps in common[9]). That is, we may have a string Z in $\bar{P}$ with the **P**-markers K_1 and K_2, and it may be the case that there is a string $X^\frown Y$ which is a member of both K_1 and K_2. And this string $X^\frown Y$ may in fact correspond to two conflicting analyses of Z into constituents. Suppose, for instance, that we have the following situation:

40 $\rho_1(Sentence,\ X^\frown Y)$
        $\rho_1(X,\ a^\frown b),\ \rho_1(X,\ a)$
        $\rho_1(Y,\ b^\frown c),\ \rho_1(Y,\ c)$
        $a^\frown b^\frown c$ is a grammatical string of words

Then we have two different **P**-markers of $a^\frown b^\frown c$, which can be diagrammed as shown in Figure 1. Suppose that T is limited in application to strings of the form $X\text{-}Y$. Then $T(a^\frown b^\frown c)$ is ambiguous if the **P**-marker is not specified.

---

[9] Although **P**-markers are based on equivalence classes of derivations, this does not imply that distinct **P**-markers are disjoint classes of strings. In fact, every two **P**-markers overlap at least in the element *Sentence* and perhaps elsewhere.

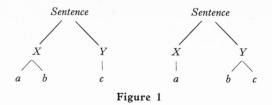

Figure 1

If T is in general to be a single-valued mapping, then, it must apply to pairs (Z, K), where K gives the analysis of Z. If the analysis K were always to be a **P**-marker, we could define T as a mapping of **P**-markers into strings in $\bar{P}$, since the product of a **P**-marker is unique. But there is actually a quite general sense in which a class K of strings may give an analysis of Z, even if K is not a **P**-marker. Thus E_0 has been defined in terms of a class K which may or may not be a **P**-marker (cf. §53.1). This generality will be useful below, since we will also want to apply transformations to strings which are themselves products of transformations, and which do not have **P**-markers although they do have associated with them a unique class K of strings that provides them with a derived analysis. Actually, each such class K will, as we shall see, contain only one string in $\bar{P}$. But for perspicuity of presentation (and to leave the general question tentatively open) we will define transformations not on K alone, but on the pair (Z, K), where Z is a member of K.

Summing up these considerations, we have the following conditions on the set of grammatical transformations: **81.2**

C1   A grammatical transformation T is defined on ordered pairs (Z, K), where

       (a) Z and $T(Z, K)$ are strings in $\bar{P}$

       (b) K is a set of strings in **P**, and Z is a member of K

   Thus T operates on a string Z of $\bar{P}$, with the analysis given by K, and produces a new string of $\bar{P}$ which we denote by "$T(Z, K)$."

C2 $T(Z, K)$ is unique. That is, T is a single-valued mapping.

C3   The domain of each T is limited to strings of a certain structure. This limitation can be effected by associating with each T a finite *restricting class* Q of sequences of strings. Suppose that the sequence $(W_1, ..., W_r)$ [where W_i is a string] is a member of Q. Then T can be applied to (Z, K) only if Z is analyzed by K into a W_1 concatenated with a W_2 ... concatenated with a W_r.

These conditions are fundamental. Condition **C1** gives the elements which qualify for inclusion in the domain and range of some transformation. Condition **C3** requires that each transformation apply only to a certain subpart of this potential domain. Condition **C2** prescribes that only certain of the mappings from the set of ordered pairs (Z, K) to $\bar{P}$ be admissible into the set of grammatical transformations, namely single-valued (functional) mappings which determine a unique string of the range for each ordered pair (Z, K) in the domain.

Each transformation T in the sense of conditions **C1–C3** can be represented as a set of ordered triples (Z, K, Z'), where $Z' = T(Z, K)$. Conditions **C1–C3** set up certain requirements that a set of ordered triples must meet in order to quality as a transformation. We now go on to investigate further requirements.

81.3   If we are to be able to use transformations in grammatical description they must be finitely characterizable. In particular, we must be able to characterize the domain of the transformation in a finite manner. **C3** gives a necessary condition that a set of pairs (Z, K) must meet in order to qualify as the domain of some transformation. It is now necessary to add a sufficient condition.

We cannot simply replace the "only if" of **C3** by "if and only if." The reason for this is that for certain choices of Z, K, Q, it will be the case that Z can be analyzed by K in various ways into a sequence of strings that correspond, term by term, to the terms of some sequence in Q. The case discussed in **40** provides an example of this possibility:

41   Assume **40**.   Let $Z = a\frown b \frown c$
$$K = \{Z, X\frown c, X\frown b \frown c\}$$
$$Q = \{(X, Y)\}$$

Then Z is analyzed by K into $a\text{-}b\frown c$ or $a\frown b\text{-}c$, each of which is an instance of $X\text{-}Y$.

But suppose that T is defined as, e.g., the permutation that carries $X\text{-}Y$ into $Y\text{-}X$. And suppose that (Z, K) is a member of the domain of T. Then in the case of **41**, the result of the transformation will be either $b\frown c\text{-}a$ or $c\text{-}a\frown b$, depending on whether Z is analyzed by K into $a\text{-}b\frown c$ or $a\frown b\text{-}c$ (each of which is an $X\text{-}Y$), thus contradicting **C2**.

We might suspect that the difficulty here is due to the fact that in **41**, K is an inconsistent analysis of Z (cf. §53.6). But the same difficulty can arise even in the case of a consistent analysis, as we can see from **42**:

42   Suppose that $Z = a⌢b⌢c⌢d$
$K = \{X⌢c⌢d, a⌢b⌢Y, Z\}$
$Q = \{(X, c, d), (a, b, Y)\}$
$\rho(X, a⌢b)$
$\rho(Y, c⌢d)$

Then Z can by analyzed by K into $a⌢b$-c-d or a-b-$c⌢d$, each of which corresponds term by term to a sequence in Q.

The simplest way to resolve the difficulty is to require that for (Z, K) to be in the domain of T (with restricting class Q) it is necessary that there be exactly *one* way of analyzing Z by K so as to conform term by term to some sequence of Q. Preparatory to giving this conditions a **C4**, we define the notion of "proper analysis."

Definition 1.   Let Q be a set of sequences of strings. Then $(Y_1, ..., Y_r)$ is a *proper analysis* of Z with respect to (wrt) K, Q if and only if

   (i) $Z = Y_1⌢...⌢Y_r$
   (ii)   there is a $(W_1, ..., W_r) \in Q$ such that for each $j \geqslant 1$, Y_j is a W_j of Z wrt K [i.e., such that $E_0(Y_j, Y_1⌢...⌢Y_j, W_j, Z, K)$].[10]

For example, suppose that $Q = \{(NP, verb, NP)\}$; $Z =$ "John caught a fish"; and K is a **P**-marker of Z with respect to which one constituent analysis of Z is *John–caught–a⌢fish*. Suppose further that *John* and *a⌢fish* are *NP*'s, and that *caught* is a *verb*. Then in this case the sequence (*John, caught, a⌢fish*) is a proper analysis of Z wrt K, Q.
We can now state **C4**:

C4   With each T there is associated a finite restricting class Q such that (Z, K) is in the domain of T[11] if and only if there is a unique proper analysis of Z wrt K, Q.

One particular type of restricting class contains only sequences r terms in length, for some fixed r.

Definition 2. Q is an *r-termed restricting class* if and only if Q is a finite set of *r*-ads of strings. That is,

$$Q = \{(W_1^{(i)}, ..., W_r^{(i)}) \mid 1 \leqslant i \leqslant N_Q\}$$

---

[10] See §53.1 for the definition of E_0.
[11] That is, such that for some Z', $(Z, K, Z') \in T$, where T is taken (as in the last paragraph of §81.2) as a set of ordered triples.

From the fact that the unit element U can appear as $W_j^{(i)}$, and from Theorem 2, Chapter VII, §53.1, it follows that any domain defined by a finite restricting class (as in **C4**) is also defined by some r-termed restricting class. Hence there is no loss in generality if we replace "finite restricting class" by "r-termed restricting class" in **C4**. These terms are not freely interchangeable, however, in all later contexts. From now on we will consider only r-termed restricting classes. A transformation is essentially a certain fixed way of rearranging and otherwise reconstructing a sequence of r terms of a given kind. It seems natural, then, to require that for each grammatical transformation the number of terms on which it operates be fixed.

We can then add as an amendment to **C4**,

C5   A restricting class Q is said to be associated with a transformation T only if Q is an r-termed restricting class, and Q characterizes the domain of T in the sense of **C4**.

C5 poses a condition for the definition of "associated restricting class." **C4** states the existence of an associated restricting class for each T.

We can now specify the domain of a transformation in terms of a finite set of sequences of strings, each r terms in length. It remains to find some fixed and finite way to characterize T so that knowing Z and K, we can determine $T(Z, K)$.

81.4   Consider now the converse of the requirement **C2** that every grammatical transformation be a single-valued mapping. A little reflection shows that we must limit the set of grammatical transformations to exclude all but a very limited kind of functional mapping. One reason for this conclusion is that not every such mapping is finitely characterizable. But we can reach the same conclusion from another approach.

Suppose that K_J is the **P**-marker of "John came home," K_B of "Bill came home," K_M of "Mary came home," etc. There is a perfectly good functional mapping φ that carries $(John^\frown came^\frown home, K_J)$ into "a police car was cruising around the neighborhood," $(Bill^\frown came^\frown home, K_B)$ into "have you seen today's paper?," $(Mary^\frown came^\frown home, K_M)$ into "I think so," etc. But such a mapping as φ would clearly be of no interest, and we will certainly want to exclude it from the grammatical description of English. In fact, we *must* exclude such mappings somehow from the set of grammatical transformations in the general theory, or there will be no hope of applying transformational analysis to any language in an interesting way, since all (functional) relations between classes of sentences will appear as special cases of some transformation. We might hope to exclude φ on the grounds of simplicity of the grammar, since clearly the description of φ for English will be extremely complex. But this will not succeed, within our present framework, for the reason that the strings in English can be enumerated, and such mappings as φ can be defined in completely general terms in linguistic theory in terms of an arbitrary enumeration of strings. Though the definition of φ in general linguistic theory may be extremely complex, its application to a particular grammar, once it is defined abstractly, will not add to the complexity of this grammar, given an enumeration. And we have no way to include complexity of linguistic theory as a factor in the evaluation of particular grammars. Thus φ and similar mappings must be excluded from the set of grammatical transformations from the start, by an appropriate abstractly formulated condition.

The point here is roughly this. We do not want a transformation to depend on the "content" of the particular strings into which Z is decomposed for the purposes of transformation, but only on the number and order of these substrings. Only such transformations will reflect general structural relations between classes of strings. Once we have settled on some fixed way of characterizing grammatical transformations in terms of certain structural properties, it will be possible to take the complexity of this fixed form of characterization into account as a feature in the evaluation of given grammars.

We can give this condition a more precise formulation. From **C1, C4**, we know that a transformation T converts a string Z analyzed in a certain way (say, into $Y_1\text{-}...\text{-}Y_r$) into a second string. The particular $(Y_1,..., Y_r)$ into which Z is analyzed for the purpose of applying T is determined by the relation between the restricting class Q associated with T and the class K which gives the analysis of Z. This sequence $(Y_1,..., Y_r)$ we have called the *proper analysis* of Z wrt K, Q. Thus a proper analysis of Z is a sequence of terms of Z which figure in some way in the transformation, which are rearranged, dropped, or developed somehow in the application of T.

We can characterize a transformation by stating how the terms of the proper analysis are embedded in the transform. We require that for each T, there be a fixed manner of embedding these terms into a constant and fixed context of strings:

C6   Suppose that T is a grammatical transformation. Then there is a sequence of strings $C = (Z_1,..., Z_{k+1})$ and a sequence of integers $A = (a_0,..., a_k)$ such that

(i) $k \geqslant 0$; $a_0 = 0$; $1 \leqslant a_j \leqslant r$ for $1 \leqslant j \leqslant k$

(ii) there is an r-termed restricting class Q associated with T such that for all Z, K, if $(Y_1 ,..., Y_r)$ is the unique proper analysis of Z wrt K, Q, then

$$T(Z, K) = Y_{a_0} {}^\frown Z_1 {}^\frown Y_{a_1} {}^\frown Z_2 {}^\frown Y_{a_2} {}^\frown ... {}^\frown Y_{a_k} {}^\frown Z_{k+1}$$

where $Y_{a_j} = U$ if and only if $a_j = 0$.

We now add a further condition on the notion of "associated restricting class":

C7   A restricting class Q is said to be *associated with* a transformation T only if for some C and A, Q characterizes T in the sense of **C6**.

C7, like **C5**, is a condition on the notion "associated restricting class." **C6**, like **C4**, thus states the existence of an associated restricting class for each T.

We will call the sequence $C = (Z_1 ,..., Z_{k+1})$ a *constant part* of T [or of $T(Z, K)$], and we will call the sequence $A = (a_0 ,..., a_k)$ a *term arrangement* of T [or of $T(Z, K)$]. If $k = 0$, then no term of the proper analysis occurs in the transform, except possibly, for certain Z's, in the constant part.

It follows that each transformation is completely and uniquely determined by a triple (Q, C, A), where Q is an r-termed restricting class, C is a sequence of strings (the constant part), and A is a sequence of integers (the term arrangement). A is a rearrangement (not necessarily a permutation—thus terms may be dropped or repeated) of the indices of the terms of the proper analysis, whatever these terms may be. Distinct triples (Q, C, A) may determine the same transformation (i.e., the same set $\{(Z, K, Z')\}$—see last paragraph of §81.2).

Note that not every triple (Q, C, A) determines a transformation. Certain triples may fail to meet condition **C6**.

43   Let

$$Q = \{(W_1^{(i)},..., W_r^{(i)}) \mid 1 \leqslant i \leqslant N_0\}, \ W_j^{(i)} \text{ a string}$$
$$C = (Z_1 ,..., Z_s), \ Z_j \text{ a string}$$
$$A = (a_0 ,..., a_t), \ a_j \text{ an integer}$$

Then a necessary and sufficient condition for (Q, C, A) to define a transformation with Q as its associated restricting class, C as its constant part, and A as its term arrangement, is that

(i) $s = t + 1 > 0$

(ii) $a_0 = 0$

(iii) $1 \leqslant a_j \leqslant r$ for $1 \leqslant j \leqslant t$

(iv)   for $i \leqslant N_O$, $1 \leqslant j \leqslant t$, it is the case that $W_{a_j}^{(i)} \neq U$

43 is correct only when we take one of the transformations to be a null transformation, i.e., the null set of triples $(Z, K, T(Z, K))$. This null transformation will turn out to be a sort of "identity" transformation under an extension to be introduced below in §84.2. To say that a triple (Q, C, A) defines the null transformation is not the same as to say that it defines no transformation at all.

Suppose, for example, that we have a transformation T with an associated restricting class Q whose sole member is $(W_1, ..., W_5)$. Suppose that the associated term arrangement is $(0, 3, 5, 3)$, and that the corresponding constant part is (Z_1, Z_2, Z_3, Z_4). Suppose that the unique proper analysis of Z wrt K, Q is $(Y_1, ..., Y_5)$. Then

$$T(Z, K) = Z_1 \frown Y_3 \frown Z_2 \frown Y_5 \frown Z_3 \frown Y_3 \frown Z_4$$

Suppose that we have a second string Z' whose unique proper analysis wrt K', Q is $(Y_1', ..., Y_5')$. Then

$$T(Z', K') = Z_1 \frown Y_3' \frown Z_2 \frown Y_5' \frown Z_3 \frown Y_3' \frown Z_4$$

Thus although Z and Z' may be completely distinct from one another in "content," there is a clear sense in which the structural relation of Z to $T(Z, K)$ is the same as the structural relation of Z' to $T(Z', K')$. This seems to be a natural way to approach the problems posed at the outset of this section.

The conditions **C1–C7** delimit a certain set $\mathcal{T}_1$ of transformations.   **81.5** Each $T \in \mathcal{T}_1$ is a single-valued mapping on a subset of $\{(Z, K)\}$, where Z is a string in $\bar{P}$ and K is a class of strings, one of which is Z. T carries the elements of its domain into strings of $\bar{P}$ which differ from one another and from their preimages in the sense of condition **C6**. That is, $T(Z, K)$ differs from Z in some structural characteristic which is fixed for T. A subset S of $\{(Z, K)\}$ qualifies as the domain of some transformation if there is a set $Q = \{(W_1^{(i)}, ..., W_r^{(i)}) \mid 1 \leqslant i \leqslant N_0\}$ such that $(Z, K) \in S$ if and only if there is exactly one sequence $(Y_1, ..., Y_r)$ such that $Z = Y_1 ... Y_r$ and for some i, it is the case that for each $j \leqslant r$, Y_j is a $W_j^{(i)}$ of Z wrt K. $\mathcal{T}_1$ is thus a set of sets of ordered triples $(Z, K, T(Z, K))$ meeting these conditions, and each $T \in \mathscr{T}_1$ can be characterized in a finite manner as a triple (Q, C, A), appropriately related as in **43**.

81.6 A further requirement for grammatical transformations is suggested by an investigation of the restrictions imposed on the proper analysis of a string by the conditions we have laid down above. **C2** and **C6** jointly impose the following condition on grammatical transformations:

44   Suppose that T is a grammatical transformation with Q and Q' as associated restricting classes, for a given constant part C. Suppose that $A_Q = (a_0, a_1, ..., a_k)$ and $A_{Q'} = (a_0, a'_1, ..., a'_k)$ are the respective term arrangements. Suppose further that for some Z, K, the unique proper analysis of Z wrt K, Q is $(Y_1, ..., Y_r)$, and the unique proper analysis of Z wrt K, Q' is $(Y_1, ..., Y_s)$. Then $Y_{a_1} = Y'_{a_1}; ...; Y_{a_k} = Y'_{a_k'}$.

We define the proper analysis of a string with respect to a transformation in the obvious way:

Definition 3. $(Y_1, ..., Y_r)$ is a proper analysis of Z wrt K, T if and only if for some Q which is an associated restricting class of T, $(Y_1, ..., Y_r)$ is the proper analysis of Z wrt K, Q.

From **44** we see that if (Z, K) is in the domain of T, then the proper analysis of Z wrt K, T is uniquely determined up to a certain point. In particular, if, for a given constant part C, all terms of some proper analysis of Z wrt K, T appear in $T(Z, K)$ outside of the constant part, then the nonunit terms of every proper analysis of Z wrt K, T are uniquely determined. That is, the actual break-up of Z into terms is unique, given K, T, C. This, for instance, is the case if T is a permutational transformation. But clearly uniqueness of the nonunit terms is not the case in general, even with a fixed constant part, as we can see from the following example:

45   Suppose that

$\rho(X, a^\frown b)$ and if $\rho(X, Y)$, then $Y = a^\frown b$
$Z = a^\frown b^\frown c$
$K = \{Z, X^\frown c\}$
Z, Z_1 are strings in $\bar{P}$

Let T be the transformation whose single member is $(Z, K, Z_1 \frown c)$. That is, $Z_1 \frown c = T(Z, K)$. Then both Q and Q' are associated restricting classes of T:

$$Q = \{(X, c)\}$$
$$Q' = \{(a, b, c)\}$$

and T is defined by (Q, C, A_Q) and by $(Q', C, A_{Q'})$, where $C = (Z_1, U)$, $A_Q = (0, 2)$, and $A_{Q'} = (0, 3)$. But in the first case $(a \frown b, c)$ is the proper analysis, and in the second case (a, b, c) is the proper analysis.

As an example to show that even if all the terms of some proper analysis appear in the nonconstant part of the transform (where the constant part is fixed), the proper analysis of Z wrt K, T is still not uniquely determined in full, consider the following:

46   Suppose that

$$Q = \{(W_1)\}$$
$C = (Z_1, Z_2)$, Z_1 and Z_2 being strings in $\bar{P}$
$A = (0, 1)$
T is the transformation defined by (Q, C, A)

Suppose that

$$Q' = \{(W_1, U)\}$$
T' is the transformation defined by (Q', C, A)

But in this case, $T = T'$. For suppose that (Z, K) is in the domain of T. Then $E_0(Z, Z, W_1, Z, K)$; the one-termed sequence (Z) is a proper analysis of Z wrt K, T; and $T(Z, K) = Z_1 \frown Z \frown Z_2$.

But then it is also the case that $E_0(U, Z \frown U, U, Z, K)$ (cf. Theorem 2, Chapter VII, §53.1). Hence we can analyze Z into the proper analysis (Z, U) wrt K, T', and $(Z \frown U, K) = (Z, K)$ is in the domain of T', with $T'(Z, K) = Z_1 \frown Z \frown Z_2$.

Similarly every member of T' is a member of T. Thus $T = T'$, and both (Z) and (Z, U) are proper analyses of Z wrt K, T.

There are good reasons for requiring that the constant part of a transformation be unique; distinct constant parts correspond to distinct analyses of those terms of the transformed string that do figure in the transformation. However, there does not seem to be any compelling motivation in the linguistic material for requiring that the proper analysis be uniquely determined beyond those terms that actually appear in $T(Z, K)$ in the nonconstant part. Nor is there any apparent gain in the extra freedom that results from dropping the uniqueness requirement. Since the terms that appear in the transform should certainly be uniquely determined (and are, in fact, if the constant part is fixed—cf. **44**), and since is a certain resulting systematic simplification (along with an increase in the power of the system), as we will see in §82, we will go on to require

C8   The proper analysis of Z wrt K, T is unique (if it exists).

It follows from **C8** that for any transformation which is sufficiently diversified in application to be of any interest, the constant part is unique. This condition of "sufficiently diversified application" is given below, in §82.3, as **C12**. Theorem 9, §86.5, indicates that for independent reasons we must limit ourselves to transformations that meet **C12**.

Conditions **C1–C8** delimit a set of elements which we may call $\mathcal{T}_2$. Each $T^2 \in \mathcal{T}_2$ can be represented as a set of ordered quadruples $\{(Z, K, Z', Pr)\}$, where the set $\{(Z, K, Z')\} = T^1 \in \mathcal{T}_1$, and for some fixed Q which is an associated restricting class of T^1, Pr is the proper analysis of Z wrt K, Q. Pr is thus uniquely determined for each (Z, K) in the domain of T^2. $\mathcal{T}_2$ is more specific than $\mathcal{T}_1$. That is, each $T^1 \in \mathcal{T}_1$ corresponds to a subclass of $\mathcal{T}_2$ consisting of transformations which produce the same transformational effect as T_1, but which differ in the way proper analyses are assigned to strings. Clearly each $T^2 \in \mathcal{T}_2$ is also uniquely determined by a triple (Q, C, A) meeting **43**, just as is each $T^1 \in \mathcal{T}_1$. In other words, a triple (Q, C, A) provides more information than is necessary to specify a $T \in \mathcal{T}_1$; distinct triples may determine the same $T \in \mathcal{T}_1$. Some of this extra information is utilized in constructing $\mathcal{T}_2$.[12] While **C6** restricted the set of grammatical transformations by eliminating all but a special kind of functional mappings, **C8** in a sense enlarges the set by giving us several transformations, each imposing a different proper analysis, where before we had only one.

82.1   This still does not exhaust the requirements for grammatical transformations. It is necessary to study the internal effects of these transformations on strings in greater detail than we have done so far. The basic reason for this is that we must provide a *derived* constituent structure for transforms, for one thing, so that transformations can be compounded.

---

[12] In fact, almost all of it is utilized. It is possible for distinct triples to determine the same $T^2 \in \mathcal{T}_2$, but only under very special circumstances which might perhaps be excluded for other independent reasons by a more complete axiomatization of **P**.

From **C1**, §81.2, it follows that transformations can be applied only to analyzed strings. Compounding of transformations will permit the formation. e.g., of a question "was the game won by John?" from the passive "the game was won by John," which in turn is derived from the active "John won the game" (cf. §77.4).

To provide a constituent structure for $T(Z, K)$, it is necessary to mark off constituent boundaries, and then to state how E_0 holds for the marked-off segments. There are various sources from which this kind of information can be drawn.

Certain relevant information can be supplied by our previous knowledge about the level **P**. That is, it may be the case that one of the segments of the transform is in fact a P_i, for some prime P_i of **P** (i.e, P_i bears ρ to this segment). Suppose, for instance, that passives are dropped from the kernel of basic sentences for which **P**-markers are provided by ρ-derivations. Passives must then be introduced by transformation of actives which are derived on the level **P** in the normal way. Thus

47   *the game was won by John*

is formed from "John won the game" by inverting subject and object, and adding several morphemes, in particular, adding "by" before the former subject to form "by John." But we know from **P** itself that "by John" is a prepositional phrase. Hence "by John" in **47** can be regarded as a *PP*. This approach to the structural analysis of transforms merits a much fuller discussion, and we return to it below in §§86–87, where we develop the notion of "derived constituent structure" in greater detail.

Another source for information about constituent structure is in the definition of the transformation itself. Transformations can be defined in such a way as to impose a certain constituent structure on the transformed string, and this is the approach to derived structure that concerns us directly now.

It is in fact possible to define transformations in so detailed a fashion that *all* information about the constituent structure of the transform is provided by the transformation itself, and that any constituent hierarchy can be imposed on any transform by an appropriate transformation. On the other hand, there are reasons for limiting the contribution of this source of information. For one thing, such a conception would make the definition of transformations extremely cumbersome. For another, it would not permit the fact that a constituent of $T(Z, K)$ is a well-known phrase (as in the example cited above) to be used in support of a transformation. Yet this does seem to be a relevant support. But fundamentally, this conception of derived structure would be inadequate for the same kind of reason that led to the framing of condition **C6** in §81.4. Just as we do not want every functional relation to serve as a grammatical transformation, similarly, given Z, K, and $T(Z, K)$, we do not want any arbitrary derived analysis of $T(Z, K)$ to be the result of some transformation on Z, K. This would be extremely *ad hoc*, and we would never be able to justify the assignment of one derived analysis or another (i.e., the choice of a transformation giving one analysis or a transformation giving another) if all were equally available. The question is, then, to what extent should derived constituent structure be provided by the transformation itself.

Information about E_0 can be brought to bear on the analysis of the transform only after segments have been marked off in this string. Hence at least the initial marking off of segments must be provided by the transformation itself.

There is a natural way in which an initial segmentation of the transform can be provided by the operation of the transformation itself In developing the elements of $\mathcal{T}_1$, we found it necessary to consider the transformed string Z to be analyzed into a proper analysis $(Y_1, ..., Y_r)$ such that $Z = Y_1 {}^\frown ... {}^\frown Y_r$ and the Y_i are the segments of Z which actually figure in the transformation, i.e., which are moved, dropped, or to which elements are adjoined. We can characterize any transformation which imposes an r-termed proper analysis by stating what effect this transformation has on each of the r terms of the proper analysis of the string Z to which it is applied. That is, we can associate with each transformation T an *elementary transformation* t such that if $(Y_1, ..., Y_r)$ is the proper analysis of Z wrt K, T, then $T(Z, K) = t(Y_1) {}^\frown ... {}^\frown t(Y_r)$. This leads us to define the *proper analysis of the transform* as the sequence of terms $t(Y_1), ..., t(Y_r)$.

For the same reasons that led to condition **C2**, we stipulate that the proper analysis of $T(Z, K)$ must be unique. Just as we want the product of a ρ_1-derivation to have a unique analysis associated with it, given the derivation, we would like the analysis of each $T(Z, K)$ to be unique, given Z, K, T. The terms of the proper analysis of $T(Z, K)$ can be taken as providing the basic constituent segmentation for $T(Z, K)$

Summing up these remarks, we have the following informal condition on grammatical transformations:

C9   Underlying each T there is an elementary transformation t. If $(Y_1, ..., Y_r)$ is the proper analysis of Z wrt K, T, then there is a unique sequence $(\bar{Y}_1, ..., \bar{Y}_r)$, called the *proper analysis* of

$T(Z, K)$ wrt Z, K, T, such that $\overline{Y}_i$ is the transform under t of Y_i, and $T(Z, K) = \overline{Y}_1{}^\frown...{}^\frown\overline{Y}_r$.

The requirement that the proper analysis of $T(Z, K)$ must have the same number of terms as the proper analysis of Z might seem at first glance to be an overly severe limitation. But actually this is not so. We can add indefinitely many units to either sequence and choose t so that it converts units into nonunit strings, or nonunit strings into units. Since Z and $T(Z, K)$ are the concatenations of their proper analyses, the effect is that Z and $T(Z, K)$ are not necessarily divided into the same number of (nonunit) terms even if their proper analyses are of the same length. This same possibility permits us, by revision of the restricting class Q, to change the position of the constituent breaks in $T(Z, K)$ freely, even if the term arrangement and constant part of T are fixed. Thus under the interpretation of transformational analysis that we have selected, one set of constituent boundaries for $T(Z, K)$ is determined by T, and T can be chosen so as to permit these constituent breaks to be put in anywhere in a fixed $T(Z, K)$.

This freedom is important. For example one of the effects of the passive transformation that converts $Z = $ "most people–like–summer" into "summer–is liked–by most people" is to introduce the element $en{}^\frown by$ between "like" and "summer,"[13] both of which are terms of the proper analysis of Z. But it is crucial that the transformation be framed in such a way that en go with "like", and by with "most people."

Such a construction of transformations tells us something about the constituent boundaries in $T(Z, K)$, but nothing about how E_0 holds for these constituents. But we need not require that all of the information about E_0 be provided by the already known algebra $\mathbf{P}$ (as suggested in the third paragraph of §82.1). Below, in §87, we will discuss certain general conditions under which constituent structure can be automatically carried over under transformation.

There is one asymmetry here that should be noted. The product of a ρ_1-derivation not only has a unique analysis, given the derivation, but a consistent analysis. But a transform $T(Z, K)$ does not necessarily have a consistent analysis (though it has a nonoverlapping proper analysis), since the proper analysis may be "completed" in various ways. To require a consistent analysis it would be necessary either to add some condition on $\mathbf{P}$, or to extend the sense in which the constituent analysis is determined by T beyond the proper analysis. I do not know whether the consequences of this discrepancy are serious or fortunate.

---

[13] This is not quite correct (cf. §98); but the principle remains.

82.2   To give condition **C9** a precise content, we must define the set of elementary transformations. The specific motivation for this definition is much the same as that behind the definition of grammatical transformations, so that this definition is modeled closely on the statement of condition **C6**.

Suppose now that we have a system S which is a level or a sum of levels.[14]

Definition 4. $\mathcal{T}_{el} = \{t_i \mid i \geqslant 1\}$ is a set of *elementary transformations* defined by the following property: for each pair of integers n and r such that $n \leqslant r$, there is a unique sequence of integers, $(a_0, a_1, ..., a_k)$, and a unique sequence of strings in S, $(Z_1, ..., Z_{k+1})$, such that

(i) $a_0 = 0$; $k \geqslant 0$; $1 \leqslant a_j \leqslant r$ for $1 \leqslant j \leqslant k$
(ii)   for each $Y_1, ..., Y_r$,

$$t_i(Y_1, ..., Y_n ; Y_n, ..., Y_r) = Z_1 {}^\frown Y_{a_1} {}^\frown Z_2 {}^\frown Y_{a_2} {}^\frown ... {}^\frown Y_{a_k} {}^\frown Z_{k+1}$$

That is, the domain of t_i is the set of ordered pairs (P_1, P_2), where P_1 is an n-ad of strings, P_2 is an $(r - n + 1)$-ad of strings, and the last element in P_1 is the first element in P_2. Thus t_i will be understood as converting the occurrence of Y_n in the context

$$Y_1 {}^\frown ... {}^\frown Y_{n-1} {}^\frown \text{\_\_\_\_} {}^\frown Y_{n+1} {}^\frown ... {}^\frown Y_r$$

into a certain string which is unique, given the sequence of terms into which $Y_1 {}^\frown ... {}^\frown Y_r$ is divided, but which may vary for different divisions into r terms, or divisions into different numbers of terms.

We say that two elementary transformations are *r-equivalent* if they have the same effect, term by term, on all strings which are broken up into r terms:

Definition 5.   Suppose that $t_i, t_j \in \mathcal{T}_{el}$. Then t_i and t_j are *r-equivalent* if and only if for all n and r such that $n \leqslant r$,

$$t_i(Y_1, ..., Y_n ; Y_n, ..., Y_r) = t_j(Y_1, ..., Y_n ; Y_n, ..., Y_r)$$

Given $t_i \in \mathcal{T}_{el}$, we define the *derived transformation* of t_i.

Definition 6. t_i^* is the *derived transformation* of t_i if and only if for all $Y_1, ..., Y_r$,

$$t_i^*(Y_1, ..., Y_r)$$
$$= t_i(Y_1 ; Y_1, ..., Y_r) {}^\frown t_i(Y_1, Y_2 ; Y_2, ..., Y_r) {}^\frown ... {}^\frown t_i(Y_1, ..., Y_r ; Y_r)$$

[14] See below, §84.1, for a more exact formulation.

Thus the domain of a derived transformation t_i^* is an r-ad of strings, and this is carried into a unique string by t_i^*.

We can give a simple example to illustrate the effect of **C9**, given these definitions for "underlying elementary transformations." Suppose that we have an elementary transformation t such that

48 $\quad t(Y_1 ; Y_1 , Y_2) = Z_1 {}^\frown Y_2 {}^\frown Z_2 {}^\frown Y_1$
$\quad\quad t(Y_1 , Y_2 ; Y_2) = Y_1$

We can obviously carry over the terms *constant part* and *term arrangement* for elementary transformations, from the analogous use for grammatical transformations in §81.4. Thus from Definition 4 we see that for each n and r such that $n \leqslant r$, t has a unique constant part and a unique term arrangement. In the case of **48**, for $n = 1$, $r = 2$, the term arrangement of t is $(0, 2, 1)$, and the constant part is (Z_1 , Z_2 , U). For $n = 2$, $r = 2$, the term arrangement is $(0, 1)$, and the constant part is (U, U). The derived transformation t^* will have the property that

49 $\quad t^*(Y_1, Y_2) = t(Y_1 ; Y_1, Y_2){}^\frown t(Y_1, Y_2 ; Y_2) = Z_1 {}^\frown Y_2 {}^\frown Z_2 {}^\frown Y_1 {}^\frown Y_1$

Suppose that we have Q, Z, K as follows

50 $\quad Q = \{(X, c)\}$
$\quad\quad Z = a {}^\frown b {}^\frown c$
$\quad\quad K = \{Z, X {}^\frown c\}$ $\quad$ where $\rho(X, a {}^\frown b)$

Then Q and t together define a transformation T which, as we know from **C9** has the following effect on (Z, K):

51 $\quad$ The proper analysis of Z wrt K, T is $(a {}^\frown b, c)$.

$$T(Z,K) = t^*(a {}^\frown b, c) = Z_1 {}^\frown c {}^\frown Z_2 {}^\frown a {}^\frown b {}^\frown a {}^\frown b$$

The proper analysis of $T(Z, K)$ wrt Z, K, T is the sequence

$$(t(a {}^\frown b; a {}^\frown b, c), t(a {}^\frown b, c; c)) = (Z_1 {}^\frown c {}^\frown Z_2 {}^\frown a {}^\frown b, a {}^\frown b)$$

Thus $a {}^\frown b$ plays the role of Y_1 and c the role of Y_2 from **48** and **49**. The term arrangement of T is $(0, 2, 1, 1)$, and the constant part is (Z_1 , Z_2 , U, U). In this case the term arrangement of T is formed by running together the term arrangements of t for $n = 1$, $r = 2$, and for $n = 2$, $r = 2$ (dropping the second 0), and the same is true of the constant parts. But this is not necessarily the case, as we can see from the following example, formed from **50** by taking $c = U$:

52   Suppose **48, 49**. Suppose that

$$Q' = \{(X, U)\}$$
$$Z' = a^\frown b$$
$$K' = \{Z', X\} \qquad \text{where } \rho(X, a^\frown b)$$

Then Q' and t define a transformation T', with Q' as associated restricting class and t again as underlying elementary transformation. T' has the following effect for (Z', K'):

53   The proper analysis of Z' wrt K', I' is $(a^\frown b, U)$.

$$I'(Z, K) = t^*(a^\frown b, U) = Z_1^\frown U^\frown Z_2^\frown a^\frown b^\frown a^\frown b$$
$$= Z_1^\frown Z_2^\frown ab^\frown a^\frown b$$

The proper analysis of $I'(Z, K)$ wrt Z, K, I' is the sequence

$$(t(a^\frown b;\ a^\frown b,\ U),\ t(a^\frown b,\ U;\ U)) = (Z_1^\frown U^\frown Z_2^\frown a^\frown b,\ a^\frown b)$$
$$= (Z_1^\frown Z_2^\frown a^\frown b,\ a^\frown b)$$

Here $a^\frown b$ again plays the role of Y_1 of **48** and **49**, and U plays the role of Y_2. But now (cf. **C6**ii, §81.4—note that $Y_{a_j} \neq U$) the term arrangement of T' is $(0, 1, 1)$ and the constant part is $(Z_1^\frown Z_2,\ U,\ U)$.

82.3   We can now rephrase **C9** more precisely, in several steps:

C10   Underlying each T there is a $t \in \mathcal{T}_{el}$ such that if $(Y_1, ..., Y_r)$ is the proper analysis of Z wrt K, T, then $T(Z, K) = t^*(Y_1, ..., Y_r)$, where t^* is the derived transformation of t.

Definition 7.   Suppose that t underlies T in the sense of **C10**. Suppose that $(Y_1, ..., Y_r)$ is the proper analysis of Z wrt K, T. Then the *proper analysis* of $T(Z, K)$ wrt Z, K, t is the sequence of terms $(t(Y_1;\ Y_1, ..., Y_r), t(Y_1, Y_2;\ Y_2, ..., Y_r), ..., t(Y_1, Y_2, ..., Y_r;\ Y_r))$.

Definition 8.   A sequence S is a proper analysis of $T(Z, K)$ wrt Z, K, T if and only if for some t underlying T in the sense of **C10**, S is the proper analysis of $T(Z, K)$ wrt Z, K, t.

As things now stand, although the proper analysis of $T(Z, K)$ wrt Z, K, t is clearly unique, the proper analysis of $T(Z, K)$ wrt Z, K, T is not, since various elementary transformations may underlie T. That the proper analysis of the transform is not necessarily unique can be seem from a simple example:

54   Let t_1 be an elementary transformation such that

$$t_1(Y_1 ; Y_1, Y_2) = c^\frown d$$
$$t_1(Y_1, Y_2 ; Y_2) = U$$

Let t_2 be an elementary transformation such that

$$t_2(Y_1 ; Y_1, Y_2) = c$$
$$t_2(Y_1, Y_2 ; Y_2) = d$$

Suppose that c, $d \in \bar{P}$. But now let T be any transformation with a two-termed associated restricting class, and suppose that T maps every pair (Z, K) in its domain into $c^\frown d$. Then both t_1 and t_2 underlie T in the sense of **C10**. But the proper analysis of each $T(Z, K)$ wrt Z, K, t_1 is $(c^\frown d, U)$, and the proper analysis of each $T(Z, K)$ wrt Z, K, t_2 is (c, d).

But uniqueness of the proper analysis of the transform is called for by **C9**. Thus we must add the further condition:

C11   The proper analysis of $T(Z, K)$ wrt Z, K, T is unique.

The conditions **C1–C11** are met by a set of elements which we call $\mathcal{T}_3$. Each $T^3 \in \mathcal{T}_3$ is a set of ordered quintuples $\{(Z, K, Z', Pr^{(1)}, Pr^{(2)})\}$, where $\{(Z, K, Z', Pr^{(1)})\} \in \mathcal{T}_2$ (cf. final paragraph of §81). $Pr^{(2)}$ is uniquely determined for each $(Z, K, Pr^{(1)})$. Furthermore, there is a $t \in \mathcal{T}_{el}$ associated with T^3 such that if $(Z, K, Z', Pr^{(1)}, Pr^{(2)}) \in T^3$, and $Pr^{(1)} = (Y_1, ..., Y_r)$, then $Z' = t^*(Y_1, ..., Y_r)$ and $Pr^{(2)} = (t(Y_1 ; Y_1, ..., Y_r), ..., t(Y_1, ..., Y_r ; Y_r))$. Thus if we know the set of elements $\{(Z, K, Pr^{(1)})\}$ associated with a given T^3, then knowledge of t will complete the determination of T^3. But the associated restricting class Q determines the set of triples $\{(Z, K, Pr^{(1)})\}$. Hence a pair (Q, t) of an associated restricting class and an underlying elementary transformation will suffice to determine an element of T^3.

C11 can be interpreted as a condition on the set of elementary transformations that can underlie a given $T \in \mathcal{T}_3$. Let $PA_1(T)$ be the set of proper analyses of Z wrt K, T, for all Z, K. That is, $PA_1(T)$ is the set $\{Pr_j^{(1)}\}$ of elements that occur in the fourth place of the quintuples that belong to T. Suppose that t_1 and t_2 underlie T. Then for each $(Y_1, ..., Y_r) \in PA_1(T)$, and for each $n \leqslant r$, $t_1(Y_1, ..., Y_n ; Y_n, ..., Y_r) = t_2(Y_1, ..., Y_n ; Y_n, ..., Y_r)$. This is close to the definition of r-equivalence (cf. Definition 5, §82.2). In fact, for any sufficiently interesting T, it will always be the case that

C12   If t_1 and t_2 underlie T, where T is determined by an r-termed associated restricting class, then t_1 and t_2 are r-equivalent.

If T meets **C12**, we say that it is *determinate*. A necessary and sufficient condition for determinateness is that the term arrangement of T be unique, and uniqueness of the term arrangement can fail only when the membership of $PA_1(T)$ is severely restricted. Below, in §86.5, we will see that there are good reasons for limiting ourselves to determinate transformations. But for the time being, we do not make this restriction.

Clearly $\mathcal{T}_3$ is related to $\mathcal{T}_2$ just as $\mathcal{T}_2$ is related to $\mathcal{T}_1$. That is, each $T^2 \in \mathcal{T}_2$ corresponds to a subclass of $\mathcal{T}_3$ consisting of elements which differ only in the proper analysis assigned to the transform. We have seen that each element of $\mathcal{T}_2$ is determined (even overdetermined) by a triple (Q, C, A), where Q is an associated restricting class, C is a constant part, and A is a term arrangement. But such a triple does not give enough information to specify an element of $\mathcal{T}_3$, as we can see from an elaboration of example **54**:

54a   Suppose that t_1, t_2, c, and d are as in **54**. Suppose that

$$a, b \in \bar{P}$$
$$Z = a^\frown b$$
$$K = \{a^\frown b\}$$
$$Q = \{(a, b)\}$$

Then $(Q, (c^\frown d), (0))$ is an ordered triple of a restricting class Q, a constant part $(c^\frown d)$, and a term arrangement (0), which defines an element of $\mathcal{T}_2$, in fact the element T^2 whose sole member is $(Z, K, c^\frown d, (a, b))$. But two elements of $\mathcal{T}_3$ correspond to $(Q, (c^\frown d), (0))$, since either $(c^\frown d, U)$ or (c, d) can be the proper analysis of the transform $c^\frown d$, depending on whether t_1 or t_2 (which are not 2-equivalent) is chosen as the underlying elementary transformation.

We see, then, that an element of $\mathcal{T}_3$ is determined not by an ordered triple (Q, C, A), but by an ordered pair (Q, t), where Q is an associated restricting class, and t is an underlying elementary transformation. t, in turn, is determined, for each n, t such that $n \leqslant r$, by a constant part and a term arrangement (cf. Definition 4). Each element of $\mathcal{T}_3$ is uniquely determined by some such (Q, t).

Not every (Q, t) defines a transformation $T \in \mathcal{T}_3$, however. We can arrive at a necessary and sufficient condition for (Q, t) to define some T by noting that for each $t \in \mathcal{T}_{el}$, and for each r and n such that $n \leqslant r$, there is a unique term arrangement $(a_0, a_1, ..., a_k)$. Since t^* is formed by concatenating elementary transforms under t, for fixed r and for $n = 1, ..., n = r$ (in this order), we can define a unique term arrangement of t^*, for fixed r, in an obvious way:

Definition 9. Let t^* be the derived transformation of $t \in \mathcal{T}_{el}$. Suppose that for each $n \leqslant r$, the (unique) term arrangement of t for n, r is $(0, a_1^{(n)}, ..., a_{k_n}^{(n)})$. Then the *term arrangement* of t^* *for* r is the sequence $(0, a_1^{(1)}, ..., a_{k_1}^{(1)}, a_1^{(2)}, ..., a_{k_2}^{(2)}, ..., a_1^{(r)}, ..., a_{k_r}^{(r)})$

Analogously, we can define the *constant part of* t^* *for* r.

Note that the term arrangement of t^* may not be the same as the term arrangement of the transformation T defined in terms of t, although the latter term arrangement must be a subsequence of the former (cf. **52**, **53**, §82.2).

We can now characterize the set of pairs (Q, t) that define some transformation.

55   Suppose that Q is the r-termed restricting class $\{(W_1^{(i)}, ..., W_r^{(i)}) \mid 1 \leqslant i \leqslant N_Q\}$. Suppose further that $t \in \mathcal{T}_{el}$, t^* is the derived transformation of t, and $(0, b_1, ..., b_m)$ is the term arrangement of t^* for r, with $(Z_1, ..., Z_{m+1})$ being the constant part of t^* for r.

Then a sufficient condition for (Q, t) to define some transformation is that

   (i)   for each $k \leqslant m$, either for all i, $W_{b_k}^{(i)} = U$, or for all i, $W_{b_k}^{(i)} \neq U$.
   (ii) Z_i is a string in $\bar{P}$.

This is also a necessary condition if we assume Q to be *minimal*, in the sense that if for some i, $(W_1^{(i)}, ..., W_r^{(i)})$ is deleted from Q, then the resulting restricting class defines (in the sense of **C4**, §81.2) a different domain than does Q. We could in fact define restricting classes in such a way that they must be minimal, relative to a given system **P**. In practice we usually deal only with minimal Q's, since the length of the description of Q is a factor in the evaluation of the grammar, and a minimal Q can very often be more simply described. In any event, **55** will suffice for the practical purpose of deciding whether a given (Q, t) legitimately determines a transformation, even if we do not define restricting classes as necessarily minimal.

We can now proceed to construct the set of grammatical transformations **83.1** somewhat more systematically, summing up the remarks of §§81, 82.

Suppose we have a system S which is a level or a sum of levels. S must include **P**. $\bar{P}$ was taken as the set of all element of **P** that bear ρ to no element. We now extend $\bar{P}$ to include all elements of S that bear ρ to no element. Since only elements of **P** can bear ρ, this means that $\bar{P}$ includes all strings of S that belong to levels other than **P**, as well as $\bar{P}$ in the old sense. In practice, this means that transformations can be defined on strings of words and morphemes (and into such strings). In other words, we regard **W** and $\bar{\mathbf{M}}$ as embedded into **P** as "lowest-level" elements of **P**.

Definition 10*. Let Q be an r-termed restricting class and t an elementary transformation with the derived transformation t^*. Suppose that (Q, t) meets **55**. Then (Q, t) *determines the set of ordered quintuples $T = \{(Z, K, Z', Pr^{(1)}, Pr^{(2)})\}$, where

  (i) Z, Z' are strings in $\bar{P}$
  (ii) $Pr^{(1)}$ is the unique sequence $(Y_1, ..., Y_r)$ such that
    (a) $Z = Y_1 \frown ... \frown Y_r$
    (b) there is a $(W_1^{(i)}, ..., W_r^{(i)}) \in Q$ such that for each $n \leqslant r$, $E_0(Y_n, Y_1 \frown ... \frown Y_n, W_n^{(i)}, Z, K), Z' = t^*(Y_1, ..., Y_r)$, and $Pr^{(2)} = (t(Y_1 ; Y_1, ..., Y_r), ..., t(Y_1, ..., Y_r ; Y_r))$
  (iii) if any quintuple q meets (i) and (ii), then $q \in T$.

Definition 11*. In this case,

  $Pr^{(1)}$ is the *proper analysis* of Z wrt K, Q
  $Pr^{(2)}$ is the *proper analysis* of Z' wrt Z, K, T
  Q is *associated* with T
  t underlies T
  Z' is denoted "$T(Z, K)$"

We will continue to use the term "domain" to cover the set $\{(Z, K)\}$, and the term "transform" for $Z' = T(Z, K)$, just as if T were a simple mapping of (Z, K) to Z', as in the case of $\mathscr{T}_1$.

Definition 12*. T is a *grammatical transformation* if and only if there is a Q and a t meeting the premises of Definition 10* and such that (Q, t) *determines T. The set of grammatical transformations we denote by "$\mathscr{T}$."

$\mathscr{T}$ is the set denoted "$\mathscr{T}_3$" in §82.3.

Definition 13. $\mathscr{T}_2$ is the set of sets of quadruples $\{(Z, K, Z', Pr^{(1)})\}$ such that for some $Pr^{(2)}$, $\{(Z, K, Z', Pr^{(1)}, Pr^{(2)})\} \in \mathscr{T}$. $\mathscr{T}_1$ is the set of sets of triples $\{(Z, K, Z')\}$ such that for some $Pr^{(1)}$, $\{(Z, K, Z', Pr^{(1)})\} \in \mathcal{T}_2$.

Theorem 1. *Determination, in the sense of Definition 10*, is unique, and the terms defined above meet the conditions laid down in §§81, 82.

One emendation of this system of transformations will be quite useful **83.2** below. We have limited the domain of each grammatical transformation T to a subset of $\{(Z, K)\}$, but we will find it convenient to extend the domain of each T to cover the whole set of pairs (Z, K) such that Z is a string in $\bar{P}$, and K a class of strings. This means that we must add to each $T \in \mathcal{T}$ a quintuple $(Z, K, Z', Pr^{(1)}, Pr^{(2)})$ for each such (Z, K) which is not already in the domain of T, in the sense of Definition 10*. The simplest and most convenient way to do this is by taking Z' as Z, and both $Pr^{(1)}$ and $Pr^{(2)}$ as the one-termed sequence (Z), in all such cases. Then T applies to all pairs (Z, K) of a string in $\bar{P}$ and a class of strings, but it applies only trivially to pairs which are not in the domain of T in the sense of §83.1. Note that the null transformation of $\mathcal{T}$, in the sense of §83.1 (i.e., the null class of quintuples), is converted by this extension into an "identity" transformation I having the property that $I(Z, K) = Z$, and that the proper analysis of $I(Z, K)$ wrt Z, K, I is identical with the proper analysis of Z wrt K, I.

Definitions 10*, 11*, and 12* are now superseded by Definitions 10, 11, and 12, as follows:

Definition 10. Let Q and t be as in Definition 10*. Then (Q, t) *determines* the set of ordered quintuples $T = \{(Z, K, Z', Pr^{(1)}, Pr^{(2)})\}$ where Z, Z' are strings in $\bar{P}$ and K is a class of strings, and either: (I) there is exactly one sequence $(Y_1, ..., Y_r)$ such that

    (a) $Z = Y_1 \frown ... \frown Y_r$
    (b) there is a $(W_1^{(i)}, ..., W_r^{(i)}) \in Q$ such that for $n \leqslant r$, $E_0(Y_n, Y_1 \frown ... \frown Y_n, W_n^{(i)}, Z_j, K_j)$, in which case

$$Z' = t^*(Y_1, ..., Y_r)$$
$$Pr^{(1)} = (Y_1, ..., Y_r)$$
$$Pr^{(2)} = (t(Y_1; Y_1, ..., Y_r), ..., t(Y_1, ..., Y_r; Y_r))$$

or (II) it is not the case that there is exactly one sequence $(Y_1, ..., Y_r)$ meeting (a) and (b), in which case

$$Z' = Z$$
$$Pr^{(1)} = Pr^{(2)} = (Z)$$

Definition 11. In this case,... etc. as in Definition 11*.

Definition 12. Exactly as Definition 12*, with *determine* now in the sense of Definition 10, not Definition 10*.

Whenever we speak of "determination," transformation," "proper analysis," etc., below, we use these terms in the sense of Definitions 10–12 of this subsection.

This is by no means all that there is to say in this connection, but instead of pursuing this line of investigation further, we will turn to the further development of the theory. The major points to be kept in mind are that each transformation has fixed structural properties, in the sense of **C6** and Definition 4; that each transformation imposes a proper analysis on the transform; and that each transformation can be characterized in a fixed way in terms of a pair (Q, t) of an r-termed restricting class and an elementary transformation. An elementary transformation t, in turn, can be characterized, for each $n \leqslant r$, by giving the constant part and the term arrangement. Since we need never characterize t beyond the number of terms of the restricting class, we have a finite way to specify any grammatical transformation.

84.1 There are certain special kinds of transformations that seem to have a particular relevance to syntactic description. We will turn now to a discussion of these.

One kind of transformation that is of interest consists in the addition of certain elements to a string in a fixed syntactic position, or the deletion of certain elements in fixed position. Thus in converting such verb phrases as "eat lunch" into noun phrases such as "eating lunch" ($= ing\frown eat\frown lunch$) or "to eat lunch," we affix the element *ing* or the element *to* to the verb phrase in a fixed position. Or in forming the passive, we affix the element *en* to the verb, and add the proper form of *be* before the verb (along with other changes). And there seems to be no reason to exclude by definition the converse process of, e.g., forming an active from a passive by dropping these elements.[15] Addition and

[15] Later we will see that considerations specific to English syntactic structure require that the passive be derived from the active, and not *vice versa*. If we did not permit both possibilities in the theory, we would not be able to make the interesting discovery that, almost without exception, conditions inherent in the language under analysis require that transformations be irreversible, i.e., that there is a preferred direction. In general it is wise to make the theory as nonspecific as possible (consistent with the demands that motivated its construction), so that the observations that we make in applying the theory will not be mere tautologies about the manner in which we have chosen to describe data, but will be statements with empirical content.

deletion of elements can be included in the same kind of transformation. Deletion can be effected by adding a "minus" element (essentially, an element which is a left inverse to every element) before the element in question. The transformations which involve just addition and deletion of elements will be called *deformations*. Combination of deletion of one element and addition of another in its place amounts to substitution. We can construct the set of deformations in the following series of steps.

We have assumed a system S which is a level or a sum of levels. Let us suppose that S has a single unit element and concatenation is permitted freely among the elements of the various component levels. Let X_1, X_2, be some enumeration of the strings in S. We adjoin to S a new prime σ, and consider the set

56 X_0, X_1, X_2, ...

where $X_0 = \sigma$. Let O be an enumeration of finite sequences of strings of **56**. We omit detailed specification of particular enumerations, which is straightforward.

57   Let A_{jk} be the jth sequence of $2k$ elements in terms of the ordering O such that

> (i) $A_{jk} = (X_{j_1}, ..., X_{j_{2k}})$
> (ii) $j_i \neq 0$ for $i = 2n$

That is, the even elements X_{j_2}, X_{j_4}, ..., $X_{j_{2k}}$ are not σ.

Definition 14. Suppose that A_{jk} is as in **57**. To A_{jk} we associate the elementary transformation δ_{jk} such that

> (i)   if $k = r$, then $\delta_{jk}(Y_1, ..., Y_n ; Y_n, ..., Y_r) = W_n$, where
>
> > (a) $W_n = X_{j_{2n}}$, if $X_{j_{2n-1}} = \sigma$
> > (b) $W_n = X_{j_{2n-1}} \frown Y_n \frown X_{j_{2n}}$, if $X_{j_{2n-1}} \neq \sigma$
>
> (ii) if $k \neq r$, then $\delta_{jk}(Y_1, ..., Y_n ; Y_n, ..., Y_r) = Y_n$

Inadmissibly, but suggestively, we might say that in case (i), $W_n = (X_{j_{2n-1}} \frown Y_n) \frown X_{j_{2n}}$, and for any i, $\sigma \frown X_i = U$, assuming now that the operation inside the parantheses is carried out before the operation outside the parentheses, i.e., that associativity of concatenation is nullified.

δ_{jk} is an elementary transformation. That is, $\delta_{jk} \in \mathcal{T}_{el}$, for each j, k.

Where δ_{jk}^* is the derived transformation of δ_{jk}, and A_{jk} is as in **57**, we have

58 $\delta_{jk}^*(Y_1,\ldots,Y_k) = W_1{}^{\frown}\ldots{}^{\frown}W_k$

where $W_i = Z_i{}^{\frown}X_{j_{2i}}$, and $\begin{cases} Z_i = X_{j_{2i-1}}{}^{\frown}Y_i \text{ if } X_{j_{2i-1}} \neq \sigma \\ Z_i = U \text{ if } X_{j_{2i-1}} = \sigma \end{cases}$

Definition 15.   Let $\varDelta$ be the set of grammatical transformations for which some δ_{jk} is the underlying elementary transformation. The members of $\varDelta$ will be called *deformations*.

Thus given a transformation based on **57** and **58**, W_i is the ith term of the proper analysis of the transform, and Y_i is the ith term of the proper analysis of the transformed string $Y_1{}^{\frown}\ldots{}^{\frown}Y_k$.

Suppose for example that A_{j2} (the jth sequence of four elements) is (σ, a, b, c) Then δ_{j2} will be the elementary transformation such that

59 $\delta_{j2}(Y_1 ; Y_1, Y_2) = a$
$\delta_{j2}(Y_1, Y_2 ; Y_2) = b{}^{\frown}Y_2{}^{\frown}c$
$\delta_{j2}^*(Y_1, Y_2) = a{}^{\frown}b{}^{\frown}Y_2{}^{\frown}c$

That is, if T is based on δ_{j2}, and (Y_1, Y_2) is the proper analysis of Z wrt K, T, then T deletes the first term of the proper analysis of Z, replacing it by a, and T replaces the second term Y_2 of the proper analysis of Z by $b{}^{\frown}Y_2{}^{\frown}c$; T carries Y_1–Y_2 into a–$b{}^{\frown}Y_2{}^{\frown}c$.

84.2   Deformations are transformations whose term arrangements are a subsequence (not necessarily a proper subsequence—thus every index is included if the element σ does not occur in the sequence A_{jk} which defines the deformation) of the sequence of indices of the terms of the proper analysis. That is, the order of these terms is never changed by a deformation. Another class of transformations that can be expected to play a major role in syntax is the class based on permutations, or, more generally, rearrangements of the indices of the terms of the proper analysis.

Suppose that we have an ordering O' of finite sequences of integers. Let B_{jk} be the jth sequence, in terms of O', of k integers $(a_1,\ldots,a_k)$, not necessarily distinct, with $a_i \leqslant k$ for $i \leqslant k$.

Definition 16.   To each B_{jk} we make correspond β_{jk} such that
$\beta_{jk}(Y_1,\ldots,Y_n ; Y_n,\ldots,Y_r) = Y_{q_n}$, where

if $k = r$, then $q_n = a_n$
if $k \neq r$, then $q_n = n$

β_{jk} is an elementary transformation. Where β_{jk}^* is its derived transformation, we have

60 $\qquad \beta_{jk}^*(Y_1,\dots,\ Y_k) = Y_{a_1}\frown\dots\frown Y_{a_k}$

Definition 17. Let B be the set of transformations based on some β_{jk}. The members of B will be called *rearrangements*.

Given $T \in B$, where T is based on the underlying transformation β_{jk}, we see that if the proper analysis of Z wrt K, T is $(Y_1,\dots,\ Y_k)$, then $T(Z, K) = Y_{a_1}\frown\dots\frown Y_{a_k}$, and Y_{a_n} is the nth term of the proper analysis of $T(Z, K)$ wrt Z, K, T.

Suppose, for example, that $B_{j3} = (1, 2, 1)$. Then β_{j3} is the elementary transformation such that

61 $\qquad \beta_{j3}(Y_1\ ;\ Y_1\ ,\ Y_2\ ,\ Y_3) = Y_1$
$\qquad \beta_{j3}(Y_1\ ,\ Y_2\ ;\ Y_2\ ,\ Y_3) = Y_2$
$\qquad \beta_{j3}(Y_1\ ,\ Y_2\ ,\ Y_3\ ;\ Y_3) = Y_1$
$\qquad \beta_{j3}^*(Y_1\ ,\ Y_2\ ,\ Y_3) = Y_1\frown Y_2\frown Y_1$

Suppose that $(Y_1\ ,\ Y_2\ ,\ Y_3)$ is the proper analysis of Z wrt K, T, where T is based on β_{j3}. Then $T(Z, K) = Y_1\frown Y_2\frown Y_1$, and the proper analysis of $T(Z, K)$ wrt Z, K, T is $(Y_1\ ,\ Y_2\ ,\ Y_1)$.

We arrive at deformations by concentrating on the constant part of the transformation. Deformations do not affect the arrangement of terms of the proper analysis, except, perhaps by dropping terms. Rearrangements, on the other hand, are transformations which have a null constant part, but which do affect the order of terms of the proper analysis. That is, we arrive at rearrangements by considering the term arrangement of the transformation exclusively. There is one ("identity") transformation which is both a deformation and a rearrangement.

If B_{jk} contains each $a_i \leqslant k$ exactly once, then we will call any transformation based on the corresponding β_{jk} a *permutation*.

Definition 18. Let Π be the set of transformations based on an elementary transformation π_{jk} whose defining sequence B_{jk} is a permutation of the integers $(1,\dots,k)$. The members of Π will be called *permutations*.

Deformations and permutations will be the basic elements in the transformational analysis of English.

We will use the terms "deformation" and "permutation" to denote the grammatical transformation as well as the elementary transformation that underlies it. We will use "Δ_{el}," "B_{el}," and "Π_{el}" to denote the sets of elementary deformations, rearrangements, and permutations, respectively.

85.1   If we had a technique for compounding grammatical transformations, we could investigate the possibility of generating all members of $\mathcal{T}$ from such subsets as Δ and Π by compounding. A grammatical transformation T applies to a pair (Z, K), i.e., to a string with a given constituent analysis. Hence to apply a transformation T_2 to the product of a transformation T_1, it would be necessary to have associated with the transform $T_1(Z, K)$ a fixed class $\overline{K}$ which provides the string $T_1(Z, K)$ with a derived constituent structure. But we have not yet succeeded in developing the notion of "derived analysis" in this sense, although we have developed transformations in such a way as to impose on the transform a partial analysis into terms.

We can, however, investigate the generative adequacy of such subsets as Δ and B in an indirect manner, by developing a method for compounding elementary transformations. We can then determine whether some subset of the elementary transformations (e.g., Δ_{el}, B_{el}, etc.) will provide, by compounding, a set t of elementary transformations which is extensive enough so that all of $\mathcal{T}$ (or all of some interesting subpart of $\mathcal{T}$) is determined by pairs (Q, τ), where $\tau \in t$.

The interest of this investigation extends beyond the fact that it gives us more insight into the abstract structure of the system of grammatical transformations which we hope to apply in syntactic analysis. We will see below, in studying derived constituent structure, that the crucial notions of this study can be defined readily and naturally for deformations, rearrangements, and certain similar transformations, but not for transformations in general. Hence if we can show that these subsets of $\mathcal{T}$ are adequate to generate all of $\mathcal{T}$, or all that we need for some purpose, by compounding, then we can define such notions directly only for the cases where the definition is natural and motivated, and we can carry these notions over indirectly for the elements of $\mathcal{T}$ which are generated by compounding.

A further motivation for the study of compounding comes from an analysis of the reasoning involved in the development of a system of transformations in the first place, in §§81, 82. We noted there that if grammatical transformations are to be available for the actual construction of grammars, and if the complexity of the characterization of transformations is to be a factor in the evaluation of these grammars, then there must be a fixed and finite way to characterize transformations (just as in Chapters IV and VII we found it necessary to develop a fixed form for grammars on lower levels). In §83 we saw that any transformation can be determined by a pair (Q, t), where Q is a finite set of finite sequences of strings. But not every elementary transformation can be represented in a fixed and finite manner. However, any deformation δ_{jk} can be so characterized by stating A_{jk}, and any rearrangement β_{jk}, by stating B_{jk}, both A_{jk} and B_{jk} being finite sequences. And the same will be true of the η-transformations that we introduce below. Thus, in particular, any finite compound of these elementary transformations is available for grammatical analysis.

Given two elementary transformations t_1 and t_2 we can form a compound $t_3 = t_2(t_1)$ which is also an elementary transformation. t_3 is defined (cf. Definition 4, §82.2) by stating its term arrangement and constant part for each n, r such that $n \leqslant r$, and stating these in terms of the term arrangements and constant parts of t_2 and t_1. The obvious way to do this is as follows: **85.2**

Definition 19. Given $t_1, t_2 \in \mathcal{T}_{el}$. Then $t_2(t_1)$ is the elementary transformation t_3 such that for all r, and all $n \leqslant r$,

$$t_3(Y_1, ..., Y_n ; Y_n, ..., Y_r) = t_2(W_1, ..., W_n ; W_n, ..., W_r)$$

where $W_m = t_1(Y_1, ..., Y_m ; Y_m, ..., Y_r)$ (for $m \leqslant r$)

Theorem 2. $t_2(t_1)$ as thus defined is in fact an elementary transformation of $\mathcal{T}_{el}$.

By virtue of Theorem 2, we see that Definition 19 enables us to speak of all finite compounds $t_n(t_{n-1}(...(t_1)))$, where $t_i \in \mathcal{T}_{el}$ for $1 \leqslant i \leqslant n$ Any such compound is itself an elementary transformation.

Suppose, for example, that t_1 and t_2 are elementary transformations such that

62
$$t_1(Y_1 ; Y_1, Y_2, Y_3) = Y_3 \qquad t_2(Y_1 ; Y_1, Y_2, Y_3) = Z_1$$
$$t_1(Y_1, Y_2 ; Y_2, Y_3) = Y_2 \qquad t_2(Y_1, Y_2 ; Y_2, Y_3) = Y_2{}^\frown Z_2$$
$$t_1(Y_1, Y_2, Y_3 ; Y_3) = Y_1 \qquad t_2(Y_1, Y_2, Y_3 ; Y_3) = Z_3{}^\frown Y_3{}^\frown Z_4$$

Thus t_1 is a permutation and t_2 is a deformation. Where $(t_i(t_j))^*$ is the derived transformation of $t_i(t_j)$, we have, in the case of **62**,

63 $(t_1(t_1))^* (Y_1 , Y_2 , Y_3) = t_1^*(Y_3 , Y_2 , Y_1)$
$$= Y_1{}^\frown Y_2{}^\frown Y_3$$
$(t_1(t_2))^* (Y_1 , Y_2 , Y_3) = t_1^*(Z_1 , Y_2{}^\frown Z_2 , Z_3{}^\frown Y_3{}^\frown Z_4)$
$$= Z_3{}^\frown Y_3{}^\frown Z_4{}^\frown Y_2{}^\frown Z_2{}^\frown Z_1$$
$(t_2(t_1))^* (Y_1 , Y_2 , Y_3) = t_2^*(Y_3 , Y_2 , Y_1)$
$$= Z_1{}^\frown Y_2{}^\frown Z_2{}^\frown Z_3{}^\frown Y_1{}^\frown Z_4$$
$(t_2(t_2))^* (Y_1 , Y_2 , Y_3) = t_2^*(Z_1 , Y_2{}^\frown Z_2 , Z_3{}^\frown Y_3{}^\frown Z_4)$
$$= Z_1{}^\frown Y_2{}^\frown Z_2{}^\frown Z_2{}^\frown Z_3{}^\frown Z_3{}^\frown Y_3{}^\frown Z_4{}^\frown Z_4$$

If it is furthermore the case that for $r \neq 3$, $n \leqslant r$, $t_1(Y_1 ,..., Y_n ;$ $Y_n ,..., Y_r) = Y_n$, then $t_1(t_1)$ is the identity elementary transformation.

In §84 we developed two major sets of elementary transformations, the set Δ of deformations, and the set B of rearrangements. We see at once that not every elementary transformation can be represented as a finite compound of deformations and rearrangements. Suppose that we call an elementary transformation *finitary* if there is an s such that for all $r > s$, and for all $n \leqslant r$, $t(Y_1 ,..., Y_n ; Y_n ,..., Y_r) = Y_n$. Then clearly only a finitary elementary transformation can be represented as a finite compound of deformations and rearrangements. On the other hand, finitary elementary transformations are sufficient to enable us to reconstruct completely the set $\mathscr{T}$ of grammatical transformations. That is, every $T \in \mathscr{T}$ is determined (in the sense of Definition 10, §83.2) by some (Q, t), where t is finitary. For if Q is an r-termed restricting class, then the effect of t on proper analyses of more than r terms is irrelevant to the determination of T by (Q, t).

But Δ and B do not even suffice to generate all of the finitary transformations needed to determine $\mathscr{T}$. The strongest statement that we can make, limiting ourselves to deformations and rearrangements is

Theorem 3.   The set $\mathscr{T}_1$ is generated by compounding from Δ and B. That is, if $T^1 \in \mathscr{T}_1$, then there is a Q and a t such that (Q, t) determines T^1 and $t = t_n(t_{n-1}(...(t_1)))$, where each t_i $(1 \leqslant i \leqslant n)$ is a deformation or a rearrangement.

$\mathscr{T}_1$, it will be recalled, is the set whose members are sets of ordered triples $\{(Z, K, T(Z, K))\}$. Each $T^1 \in \mathscr{T}_1$ becomes a grammatical transformation of $\mathscr{T}$ when a proper analysis of Z and a proper analysis of $T(Z, K)$ are associated in the correct manner with each $(Z, K, T(Z, K)) \in T^1$. Theorem 3 follows directly from the fact that the unit U can appear as a term of the proper analysis and the restricting class.

85.3   To obtain a stronger result we consider a third class of elementary transformations that combine certain features of Δ and B in that they have a null constant part, but that the rearrangement of terms is effected by "attaching" terms to some fixed term of the proper analysis, as in a deformation.

We suppose once again that we have an ordering O' of finite sequences of integers. Let C_{jk} be the jth sequence, under the ordering O', of $2k$ integers $(a_1 ,..., a_{2k})$ such that for each $i \leqslant 2k$, $0 \leqslant a_i \leqslant k$.

Definition 20. To C_{jk} we associate the elementary transformation η_{jk} such that

$$\eta_{jk}(Y_1 ,..., Y_n ; Y_n ,..., Y_r) = W_n$$

where

$$W_n = Y_{a_{2n-1}} {}^\frown Y_n {}^\frown Y_{a_{2n}} , \text{ if } k = r; \text{ and } Y_0 = U$$

$$W_n = Y_n , \text{ if } k \neq r$$

η_{jk} is an elementary transformation.

Definition 21. Let H be the set of transformations for which some η_{jk} is the underlying elementary transformation. The members of H will be called adjunctions.

Suppose, for example, that C_{j2} (the jth sequence of four elements) is $(2, 0, 1, 1)$. Then η_{j2} is the elementary transformation such that

64
$$\eta_{j2}(Y_1 ; Y_1 , Y_2) = Y_2 {}^\frown Y_1 {}^\frown Y_0 = Y_2 {}^\frown Y_1$$
$$\eta_{j2}(Y_1 , Y_2 ; Y_2) = Y_1 {}^\frown Y_2 {}^\frown Y_1$$
$$\eta_{j2}(Y_1 , Y_2) = Y_2 {}^\frown Y_1 {}^\frown Y_1 {}^\frown Y_2 {}^\frown Y_1$$

It is still not the case that $\mathscr{T}$ can be recovered from $\varDelta$, B, and H. But we do have a result that appears to be just as effective for the purposes of syntactic description.

Actually, the only terms of interest in the proper analysis of a string are the nonunits. If two proper analyses differ only by units, then they yield the same constituent breaks. Recognizing this, suppose that we define a relation E holding between X and Y if Y is a sequence of strings, and X is formed from Y either by adding unit terms on to the end of Y or deleting unit terms from the end of Y. Thus the string formed by concatenating the elements of X is identical with the string formed by concatenating the elements of Y, and one of the sequence X, Y contains the other as an initial subsequence. E is an equivalence relation.

A transformation T is a set of quintuples $\{(Z, K, Z', Pr^{(1)}, Pr^{(2)})\}$. We say that two transformations T_1 and T_2 are *E-related* if there is a one-to-one relation between T_1 and T_2 that carries each $(Z, K, Z', Pr_i^{(1)}, Pr_i^{(2)}) \in T_1$ into $(Z, K, Z', Pr_j^{(1)}, Pr_j^{(2)}) \in T_2$, where E holds between $Pr_i^{(1)}$ and $Pr_j^{(1)}$, and between $Pr_i^{(2)}$ and $Pr_j^{(2)}$. Then for each Z, K, E-related transformations carry (Z, K) into the same string Z', and they give the same constituent breaks in Z'.

We can now state

Theorem 4. For any $T_1 \in \mathcal{T}$, there is a T_2 E-related to T_1 such that T_2 is determined by a pair (Q, t), where t is a finite compound of deformations and adjunctions.

It seems reasonable to assume, in the light of this observation, that the purposes of syntactic description will be adequately served by that part of $\mathcal{T}$ which is generated by compounding from $\varDelta$, B, and H. All the transformations that we will actually require in the analysis of English which will be presented below, in Chapter X, are in fact determined directly by compounds of elementary transformations drawn from $\varDelta_{el}$, B_{el}, and H_{el}.

86.1   We can now return to the important topic (introduced above in §82.1) of the effect of transformations on constituent structure. The central idea behind transformational analysis is that it will be profitable to select among grammatical sentences a certain *kernel* of basic sentences for which a simple phrase structure can be described, and in which all grammatical relations and selectional relations can be discovered. Only the kernel sentences are derived in the grammar by ρ_1-derivations; hence only these sentences have **P**-markers conferred on them in that part of the grammatical statement that corresponds to the level **P**. But even though we need not attempt to find **P**-markers for such sentences as

65   *whom have they nominated*

66   *the game was won by John*

67   *I know the man standing at the bar*

which are deleted from the kernel, we must still assign some constituent analysis to them. The major systematic motivation for the development of the notion of "derived constituent structure" lies in the fact that transformations must be compoundable. Thus from the transform **66** we must be able to form the second transform "was the game won by John." But a transformation can apply only to a string with an assigned constituent analysis. Hence we must somehow assign constituent structure to such sentences as **66**, and in general, to all transforms.

There are two sources from which information about this derived constituent analysis can be drawn. We can determine the place of constituent breaks, the selectional relations, and the content of E_0 for a derived sentence by (i) investigating the sentence (or sentences) from which it is derived and the manner of its derivation from these sentences; or, as we have noted in §82.1, by (ii) applying information already available in the statement of the level **P**. Our present concern is to investigate in some detail just how these sources can be exploited.

Until now the development of the theory of transformational analysis has been fairly straightforward. The presystematic demands imposed on the construction of this theory by the nature of the linguistic material and by the purposes of such analysis were fairly clear, and we were able to meet them in what seemed to be a natural manner. The constructions of §§86, 87 appear, by comparison, somewhat makeshift and arbitrary. In large measure this is due to the fact that the presystematic demands on this construction are not too clear. That is, it is difficult to determine just what is an intuitively adequate derived constituent structure for nonkernel sentences. But there is also little doubt that a more careful study of the formal structure of the system of transformations could lead to a more satisfactory and natural conception of derived constituent structure. We will concentrate now on developing a conception which will be adequate for the needs of the transformational analysis of English to be undertaken in Chapter X, and we will make no systematic attempt to generalize much beyond this goal.

The proper analysis of Z wrt K, T is the sequence of terms into which   **86.2** Z is divided for the purpose of applying T. We can begin the discussion of derived constituent structure by noting that a term of the proper analysis of Z is either carried over unaltered by transformation (as in a rearrangement), dropped completely (as in deformations with the element σ), or else it has adjoined to it either other terms of the proper analysis (as in adjunctions) or constant terms (as in deformations). But it can undergo no internal changes. If a term is carried over unaltered, it is natural to require that the constituent structure of its contained segments be invariant under the transformation. Thus in transforming

68   *your friend–will–bring the book tomorrow*

into

69   *will–your friend–bring the book tomorrow*

the initial noun phrase "your friend" and the final verb phrase "bring the book tomorrow" (with its contained NP "the book") are carried over intact. We would certainly like to say that "your friend" and "the book" are still NP's in **69**. To permit such statements in general, we must associate with each term of the proper analysis of $T(Z, K)$ a unique term of the proper analysis of Z which is in a certain sense its *root* under T. This notion will play a central role in the discussion of derived structure.

  If the order of terms is not changed by the transformation T (e.g., if T is a deformation), then the root of a term of the proper analysis of $T(Z, K)$ will be just its preimage under the elementary transformation t that underlies T. That is, if $t(Y_1, ..., Y_n; Y_n, ..., Y_r) = Z_1 \frown Y_n \frown Z_2$, then the root of $Z_1 \frown Y_n \frown Z_2$ is Y_n. Similarly, if terms of the proper analysis of Z are adjoined to some Y_i of the proper analysis of Z, as in an adjunction, then it seems natural to take Y_i as the root of the resulting term of the proper analysis of $T(Z, K)$. If T is a rearrangement, then the root of the ith term of the proper analysis of $T(Z, K)$ will naturally be the jth term of the proper analysis of the transformed string Z, where i corresponds to j under the rearrangement. For example, if $Z = Y_1 \text{-} Y_2 \text{-} Y_3$ goes into $T(Z, K) = Y_3 \text{-} Y_2 \text{-} Y_1$, then the occurrence Y_1 of Y_1 in Z is the root of the occurrence $Y_3 \frown Y_2 \frown Y_1$ of Y_1 in $T(Z, K)$. In the case of a rearrangement, then, each term is identical with its root.

Definition 22. (Y_j, Z_j^Y) is the *root*$_1$ of (W_i, Z_i^W) wrt $(Y_1, ..., Y_r)$, t if and only if

        (i) $i, j \leqslant r$
        (ii) $Z_j^Y = Y_1 \frown ... \frown Y_j$
        (iii) $W_i = t(Y_1, ..., Y_i; Y_i, ..., Y_r)$
        (iv) $Z_i^W = t(Y_1; Y_1, ..., Y_r) \frown ... \frown t(Y_1, ..., Y_i; Y_i, ..., Y_r)$

and either (v) or (vi)

        (v) $t \in \Delta_{el}$ or $t \in H_{el}$, and $i = j$

        (vi) t is a B_{el} based on $B = (a_1, ..., a_k)$, and $\begin{cases} j = a_i, & \text{if } k = 2r \\ j = i, & \text{if } k \neq 2r \end{cases}$

We can then define the root$_1$ of (W_i, Z_i^W) wrt Z, K, T as

70   the root$_1$ of (W_i, Z_i^W) wrt $(Y_1, ..., Y_r)$, t, where $(Y_1, ..., Y_r)$ is the proper analysis of Z wrt K, T and t underlies T.

There is thus a natural way to define "root" for Δ, B, and H, though there is no obvious way to define it for transformations in general. But we can extend the notion to compound elementary transformations, which, as we have seen, provide us with all the transformations needed for grammatical analysis. Thus we can define a relation "root*" as the ancestral of "$root_1$."

Definition 23. (Y_j, Z_j^Y) is the $root_1$* of (W_i, Z_i^W) wrt $(Y_1, ..., Y_r)$, t if and only if either

    (i) (Y_j, Z_j^Y) is the $root_1$ of (W_i, Z_i^W) wrt $(Y_1, ..., Y_r)$, t

or

    (ii)   there is a t_1, t_2, (X_m, Z_m^X) such that

        (a) $t = t_2(t_1)$
        (b) (Y_j, Z_j^Y) is the $root_1$* of (X_m, Z_m^X) wrt $(Y_1, ..., Y_r)$, t_1
        (c) (X_m, Z_m^X) is the $root_1$ of (W_i, Z_i^W) wrt
             $(t_1(Y_1 ; Y_1, ..., Y_r), ..., t_1(Y_1, ..., Y_r ; Y_r))$, t_2

We can now define the $root_1$* of (W_i, Z_i^W) wrt Z, K, T, for any T that we need for grammatical analysis, as **70** with "$root_1$*" replacing "$root_1$."

But now we face the new difficulty that in terms of this definition, the $root_1$* is not unique. The reason for this is that an elementary transformation can often be derived by compounding in several different ways from elements of $\varDelta$, B, and H, and as we have defined roots, these alternatives may assign different roots to a given occurrence of a term in the proper analysis of the final transform. In particular, any rearrangement β which is not a permutation is identical with a compound of elementary transformations which assigns to some term of the proper analysis of the transform $\beta^*(Y_1, ..., Y_r)$ a different root than is assigned when β is simply taken as a rearrangement. To demonstrate this, it is sufficient to prove

86.3

Theorem 5.   Any nonpermutational elementary rearrangement is identical with a compound of elements of $\varDelta_{el}$ and H_{el}.

A nonpermutational rearrangement assigns (Y_i, Z_i^Y) as a root to (W_j, Z_j^W) for some j and some $i \neq j$, where the proper analysis of the transformed string is $(Y_1, ..., Y_r)$ and the proper analysis of the transform is $(W_1, ..., W_r)$, and where Z_i^Y and Z_j^W are as in Definition 22. But deformations and attachments can assign (Y_i, Z_i^Y) as a root to (W_j, Z_j^W)

under these circumstances, only if $i = j$ [cf. (v), Definition 22], so the nonuniqueness of the root follows from Theorem 5.

To see that Theorem 5 is true, consider a rearrangement β based on

71 $B = (a_1, ..., a_k)$, where $1 \leqslant a_i \leqslant k$, and for a certain $m \leqslant k$, m does not appear as one of the a_i.

This is a necessary and sufficient condition for β to be a nonpermutation.

For each $i \leqslant k$, let δ_i be the elementary transformation such that

72 $\begin{cases} \delta_i(Y_1, ..., Y_i \,;\, Y_i, ..., Y_k) = U \\ \delta_i(Y_1, ..., Y_n \,;\, Y_n, ..., Y_r) = Y_n, \text{ for } n \neq i \text{ or } r \neq k \end{cases}$

Thus δ_i is a deformation, and δ_i^* deletes the ith term of $(Y_1, ..., Y_k)$. That is, $\delta_i^*(Y_1, ..., Y_k) = Y_1 \frown ... \frown Y_{i-1} \frown U \frown Y_{i+1} \frown ... \frown Y_k = Y_1 \frown ... Y_{i-1} \frown Y_{i+1} ... \frown Y_k$.

For each $i, j \leqslant k$, let η_{ij} be the elementary transformation such that

73 $\begin{cases} \eta_{ij}(Y_1, ..., Y_i \,;\, Y_i, ..., Y_k) = Y_i \frown Y_j \\ \eta_{ij}(Y_1, ..., Y_n \,;\, Y_n, ..., Y_r) = Y_n, \text{ for } n \neq i \text{ or } r \neq k \end{cases}$

Thus each η_{ij} is an adjunction, and $\eta_{ij}^*(Y_1, ..., Y_k) = Y_1 \frown ... \frown Y_{i-1} \frown (Y_i \frown Y_j) \frown Y_{i+1} \frown ... \frown Y_k$. Note that the compound $\eta_{ij}(\delta_i)$ essentially replaces the ith term by the jth term. That is,

74   Let $\sigma_{ij} = \eta_{ij}(\delta_i)$. Then $\sigma_{ij}^*(Y_1, ..., Y_k) = Y_1 \frown ... \frown Y_{i-1} \frown Y_j \frown Y_{i+1} \frown ... \frown Y_k$.

Let ι be the identity elementary transformation such that for all n, r such that $n \leqslant r$,

75 $\iota(Y_1, ..., Y_n \,;\, Y_n, ..., Y_r) = Y_n$

We can now easily construct a finite sequence of elementary transformations $t_1, ..., t_k$ such that $t_k(...(t_1)) = \beta$ and each t_i is a compound of σ_{ij}'s as in **74** or is ι as in **75**—hence each t_i is a compound of deformations and adjunctions. The construction is by induction.

We know that $\beta^*(Y_1, ..., Y_k) = Y_{a_1} \frown ... \frown Y_{a_k}$. We construct $t_1, ..., t_k$ such that, where $\bar{t}_i = t_i(...(t_1))$, then for all $Y_1, ..., Y_k$,

76 $\bar{t}_i^*(Y_1, ..., Y_k) = Y_{a_1} \frown ... \frown Y_{a_i} \frown Y_{b_1} \frown ... \frown Y_{b_{k-i}}$, where for each $j \leqslant k$, Y_{a_j} is one of $Y_{a_1}, ..., Y_{a_i}, Y_{b_1}, ..., Y_{b_{k-i}}$

Step 1

Case I. Suppose $m = 1$ (where m is as in **71**). Then $t_1 = \sigma_{1a_1}$. But $\sigma_{1a_1}^*(Y_1, ..., Y_k) = Y_{a_1} \frown Y_2 \frown ... \frown Y_k$, and for each $j \leqslant k$, Y_{a_j} is one of Y_{a_1}, $Y_2, ..., Y_k$, since only Y_m has been deleted, and m, by assumption is not one of the terms of $B = (a_1, ..., a_k)$.

Case II. Suppose $m \neq 1$.

      (a) Suppose $a_1 = 1$; then $t_1 = \iota$
      (b) Suppose $a_1 \neq 1$; then $t_1 = \sigma_{1a_1}(\sigma_{m1})$

In Case IIa, no term is deleted by t_1^*. But in Case IIb,

$$t_1^*(Y_1, ..., Y_k) = \sigma_{1a_1}^*(Y_1, ..., Y_{m-1}, Y_1, Y_{m+1}, ..., Y_k)$$
$$= Y_{a_1} \frown Y_2 \frown ... \frown Y_{m-1} \frown Y_1 \frown Y_{m+1} \frown ... \frown Y_k$$

Hence in Case IIb, only Y_m is deleted.

Hence in either Case I or Case II, $t_1^* = \bar{t}_1^*$ meets **76**.

Step 2

Suppose that for some $i < k$ we have constructed $t_1, ..., t_i$ such that $\bar{t}^*$ meets **76**, where $\bar{t}_i = t_i(...(t_1))$. We rename $Y_{a_1}, ..., Y_{a_i}$, $Y_{b_1}, ..., Y_{b_{k-i}}$ as $Z_1, ..., Z_k$, respectively. By the inductive hypothesis, we know that $Y_{a_{i+1}}$ appears as one of the strings $Z_1, ..., Z_k$. And since, by hypothesis, **76** holds for all choices of $Y_1, ..., Y_k$, we know that a_{i+1} actually appears as one of the indices $a_1, ..., a_i$, $b_1, ..., b_{k-i}$. Suppose that a_{i+1} corresponds to q under the renaming which we have just carried out, so that $Y_{a_{i+1}}$ has been renamed Z_q.

We know that m does not appear in the sequence $B = (a_1, ..., a_k)$ and that $m, a_1, ..., a_k \leqslant k$. Hence there are at most $k - 1$ distinct numbers among $a_1, ..., a_k$. But the sequence $B^* = (a_1, ..., a_i, b_1, ..., b_{k-i})$ is a sequence of k terms containing each term of B. Hence there must be at least one term Q of B^* for which either (i) or (ii) of **77** is the case:

77   (i) Q is not a term of B
        (ii) Q is identical with an earlier term of B^*

If a term of B^* has this property, we say that it is *redundant* with respect to B. Suppose that the nth term of B^* is the *last* term of B^* which is redundant with respect to B. Then we know that no matter how $Y_1, ..., Y_k$ were originally chosen, either Z_n is distinct from all of $Y_{a_1}, ..., Y_{a_k}$ or there is an $\bar{n} \neq n$ $(\bar{n} \leqslant k)$ such that for some $j \leqslant k$, $Z_n = Z_{\bar{n}} = Y_{a_j}$ (i.e., to put it loosely, Z_n is not the only instance of Y_{a_j} in $Z_1, ..., Z_k$). Clearly, then, even if the nth term of the sequence $Z_1, ..., Z_k$ is deleted, each of $Y_{a_1}, ..., Y_{a_k}$ appears in the remaining sequence $Z_1, ..., Z_{n-1}, Z_{n+1}, ..., Z_k$. We can therefore proceed, analogously to Step 1, with n now taking the place of m in Step 1.

We have selected n so that the nth term in the sequence $B^* = (a_1, ..., a_i, b_1, ..., b_{k-i})$ is either not from B or is identical with an earlier number in this sequence.

Case I. Suppose that the nth term in this sequence is not from B. Then $n \geqslant i + 1$ (i.e., the nth term is one of $b_1, ..., b_{k-i}$).

Ia: Suppose $n = i + 1$. Then $t_{i+1} = \sigma_{i+1,q}$ (where q corresponds to a_{i+1}, as above). But

$$\sigma^*_{i+1,q}(Z_1, ..., Z_k) = Z_1 {}^\frown ... {}^\frown Z_i {}^\frown Z_q {}^\frown Z_{i+2} {}^\frown ... {}^\frown Z_k$$

$$= Y_{a_1} {}^\frown ... {}^\frown Y_{a_i} {}^\frown Y_{a_{i+1}} {}^\frown Y_{b_2} {}^\frown ... {}^\frown Y_{b_{k-1}}$$

and only Z_n has been deleted, so that t^*_{i+1} meets **76**.

Ib: Suppose $n > i + 1$.

     (a)   Suppose $b_1 = a_{i+1}$; then $t_{i+1} = \iota$
     (b)   Suppose $b_1 \neq a_{i+1}$; then $t_{i+1} = \sigma_{i+1,q}(\sigma_{n,i+1})$

     But then

$$t^*_{i+1}(Z_1, ..., Z_k)$$
$$= Z_1 {}^\frown ... {}^\frown Z_i {}^\frown Z_q {}^\frown Z_{i+2} {}^\frown ... {}^\frown Z_{n-1} {}^\frown ... {}^\frown Z_{i+1} {}^\frown Z_{n+1} {}^\frown ... {}^\frown Z_k$$
$$= Y_{a_1} {}^\frown ... {}^\frown Y_{a_i} {}^\frown Y_{a_{i+1}} {}^\frown Z_{i+2} {}^\frown ... {}^\frown Z_{n-1} {}^\frown Z_{i+1} {}^\frown Z_{n+1} {}^\frown ... {}^\frown Z_k$$

     But only Z_n has been deleted without reappearing, so that $\bar{t}^*_{i+1}$ meets **76**.

Case II. Suppose that the nth term in the sequence $B^* = (a_1, ..., a_i, b_1, ..., b_{k-i})$ is from B. But this term has been chosen so as to be redundant with respect to B. Hence **77ii** must hold for this term—there must be an $\bar{n} < n$ such that the $\bar{n}$th term of B^* is identical with the nth term and in consequence, $Z_{\bar{n}} = Z_n = Y_{a_j}$, for some $j \leqslant k$.

IIa: Suppose $n \geqslant i + 1$. Then proceed as in Case I. [In the case analogous to Case Ib(b) we must be careful to choose

$q \neq n$. But this is always possible. q must be chosen so that a_{i+1} is the qth term of B^*. If a_{i+1} is the nth term of B^*, it is also the $\bar{n}$th term (where $\bar{n} < n$), and q can be taken as $\bar{n}$.] Since only Z_n is deleted by this procedure, and since $Z_{\bar{n}} = Z_n$ remains, it follows that $\bar{t}_{i+1}^*$ meets **76**.

IIb: Suppose $b_1 = a_{i+1}$. Then set $t_{i+1} = \iota$, as in Case Ib(a).

IIc: Suppose $n \leqslant i$ and $b_1 \neq a_{i+1}$. Then $Z_{\bar{n}} = Y_{a_{\bar{n}}} = Z_n = Y_{a_n}$, and $q \neq i + 1$.

(i) Suppose furthermore that $q > i + 1$, Then set $t_{i+1} = \sigma_{n\bar{n}}(\sigma_{qn}(\sigma_{i+1,q}(\sigma_{n,i+1})))$. But in this case, $t_{i+1}^*(Z_1, ..., Z_k) = Z_1 \frown ... \frown Z_{n-1} \frown Z_{\bar{n}} \frown Z_{n+1} \frown ... \frown Z_i \frown Z_q \frown Z_{i+2} \frown ... \frown Z_{q-1} \frown Z_{i+1} \frown Z_{q+1} \frown ... \frown Z_k = Y_{a_1} \frown ... \frown Y_{a_{n-1}} \frown Y_{a_n} \frown ... \frown Y_{a_i} \frown Y_{a_{i+1}} \frown Z_{i+2} \frown ... \frown Z_{q-1} \frown Z_{i+1} \frown Z_{q+1} \frown ... \frown Z_k$. In other words, the effect of t_{i+1}^* is simply to interchange Z_q $(= Y_{a_{i+1}})$ with Z_{i+1}. No terms are deleted, so that t_{i+1}^* meets **76**.

(ii) Suppose that $q \leqslant i$. Suppose that there are p distinct terms among $a_1, ..., a_i$. But since $q \leqslant i$, it must be the case that $a_{i+1} = a_j$ for some $j \leqslant i$. Therefore there are p distinct terms among $a_1, ..., a_{i+1}$. Therefore there are at most $p + k - i - 1$ distinct terms among $a_1, ..., a_k$, i.e., less than $p + k - i$ terms.

By assumption, $n \leqslant i$ and n is the last term of B^* which is redundant with respect to B. Therefore all the terms $b_1, ..., b_{k-i}$ of B^* are terms of B and are distinct from one another and from all the terms $a_1, ..., a_i$ (which are the initial terms of B^* as well as B). But since $a_1, ..., a_i$ are p distinct terms, the sequence B must contain $p + k - i$ distinct terms, since $a_1, ..., a_i$, $b_1, ..., b_{k-i}$ are all terms of B.

Thus the assumption that n, $q \leqslant i$ leads to a contradiction, and this case is ruled out.

Hence in Case I or Case II, $\bar{t}_{i+1}^*$ meets **76**. It follows that we can construct $\bar{t}_k = \beta$ in this manner out of elementary deformations and adjunctions, thus establishing Theorem 5.

The elementary transformations σ_{ij} which figure so heavily in this demonstration will play an important role below.

Suppose that we call an elementary transformation *equivocal* wrt a set L of elementary transformations if it can be compounded in various ways from members of L giving various different root$_1$* assignments to some transformation that it underlies. We have just seen that nonpermutational rearrangements are equivocal wrt $L' = \Delta_{el} + B_{el} + H_{el}$. But nonpermutational rearrangements are not equivocal wrt $L = \Delta_{el} + \Pi_{el} + H_{el}$. Hence a simple way to avoid this particular difficulty is to limit (vi), Definition 22, to permutations. Thus we now consider L, instead of L', as our basic set of elementary transformations. Nonpermutational rearrangements are still derivable from L, but they are not equivocal wrt L.

86.4   The decision to restrict the set of basic elementary transformations in terms of which "root" is defined to Δ_{el}, Π_{el}, and H_{el}, excluding the rest of B_{el}, has consequences that require more explicit statement

Suppose, for example, that we have an elementary transformation t such that

78 $t^*(Y_1, Y_2, Y_3) = Y_1\text{-}Y_1\text{-}Y_3$

with the proper analysis as indicated by the dashes.

If t were treated as a rearrangement, then the root of the second term of $t^*(Y_1, Y_2, Y_3)$ would be the first term of $Y_1 \frown Y_2 \frown Y_3$, i.e., it would be (Y_1, Y_1). But if we treat t in the manner of the proof of Theorem 5, as a compound of deformations and adjunctions, then the root of the second term of $t^*(Y_1, Y_2, Y_3)$ is the second term of $Y_1 \frown Y_2 \frown Y_3$, i.e., it is $(Y_2, Y_1 \frown Y_2)$. If the root of each term of the proper analysis of the transform is to be unique, then one of these analyses of t must be rejected. But there is enough independent motivation to each root assignment to suggest that it would be profitable to retain each analysis, with two distinct senses of the notion of "root."

We were originally led to the notion of "root" in §86.2 by noting that we clearly must be able to say that both "your friend" and "the book" are *NP*'s in

79   *will–your friend–bring the book tomorrow*   (= **69**)

which is derived by permutation from

80   *your friend–will–bring the book tomorrow*   (= **68**)

But there is an important difference between the case of "your friend" and that of "the book." The analysis of "the book" as a *NP* is a matter purely internal to one of the terms of the proper analysis. But the analysis of "your friend" as a *NP* is a matter that might affect the total constituent structure of the transform **79** since "your friend" is a complete term of the proper analysis, and to call it a *NP* determines the role that this term of the proper analysis may play in the constituent structure of the sentence as a whole. The fact that a given term of the proper analysis of the transform is a *NP* may affect the analysis of other terms of the proper analysis, and the analysis of strings of these terms, as we will see below. Given a term of the proper analysis of the transform then, we can distinguish between its internal structure, which is immaterial to the determination of the derived analysis of the rest of the transform, and its external structure, including its own constituent assignment, and the assignment of strings of which it is a part. In the case of **79–80**, this distinction is of no particular importance, but in the case of such transformations as *t* in **78**, it may become important.

The motivation for considering *t* of **78** to be a rearrangement comes from the consideration of internal constituent structure. The internal structure of the second term of the transform is the same as that of the first term of the transformed string. Thus from this point of view, we would like to consider (Y_1, Y_1) to be the root of $(Y_1, Y_1 {}^\frown Y_1)$, as in the treatment of *t* as a rearrangement.

The motivation for considering *t* to be a compound $\eta(\delta)$, where

81 $\delta^*(Y_1, Y_2, Y_3) = Y_1\text{-}U\text{-}Y_3$
$\eta^*(Y_1, U, Y_3) = Y_1\text{-}(U {}^\frown Y_1)\text{-}Y_3 = Y_1\text{-}Y_1\text{-}Y_3$

comes from the consideration of the external constituent structure of the second term of the transform. When *t* is analyzed as in **81**, it is the elementary transformation σ_{21}, as this is defined in **73**, **74**, in §86.3. That is, it amounts to a substitution of Y_1 for Y_2 in $Y_1\text{-}Y_2\text{-}Y_3$. We would naturally expect the substituend Y_1 to play the same role in the overall structure of the sentence as did the term Y_2 for which it is substituted. From this point of view, then, we are led to consider $(Y_2, Y_1 {}^\frown Y_2)$ to be the root of $(Y_1, Y_1 {}^\frown Y_1)$.

In the last paragraph of §86.3, we chose the latter analysis. Thus the notion of "root" as we are developing it here will have particular relevance to external constituent structure. In actually defining derived constituent structure, we will have to account for the purely internal structure of terms of the proper analysis of the transform in at least partially independent terms.

The real significance of the distinction that we have drawn between external and internal constituent structure will become clearer when we study generalized transformations, below, in §91. There we will see that **78** serves as an instance of a very important type of transformation. It will prove convenient to derive such sentences as

82   *that he was unhappy–was quite obvious*

from

83   *that he was unhappy–it–was quite obvious*[16]

taken as Y_1-Y_2-Y_3 . But now t as in **78** will convert this into

84   *that he was unhappy–that he was unhappy–was quite obvious*

and a further deformation which carries Y_1-Y_2-Y_3 into U-Y_2-Y_3 (δ_1 of **72**, where $k = 3$), will carry **84** into **82**. But now the internal structure of the second term of **84** ($=$ the first nonunit term of **82**) is the same as that of the first term of **83** (ultimately, it is that of the sentence "he was unhappy," from which this first term is derived). The external constituent structure of the second term of **84**, however, is that of the second term of **83**. That is, "that he was unhappy" in **82** is the noun phrase subject of **82**, just as "it" is the *NP* subject of "it was quite obvious."

We have already seen in §86.3 that by combining adjunctions and certain deformations, we can achieve the effect of a substitution of one term of the proper analysis for another, with the substituend having the same external structure as the term for which it is substituted. Such compound transformations as these appear often enough and significantly enough to receive a special name. Generalizing somewhat over **73, 74,** we define the class of *substitutions*, as follows:

Definition 24. t is a *substitution* if and only if there is a $t_1,..., t_n$ such that $t = t_n(...(t_1))$, and for each $i \leqslant n$,

   (i) t_i is either a deformation or an adjunction, and $t_1 \in \Delta_{el}$.
   (ii)   if $t_i \in \Delta_{el}$, and A is its defining sequence, then the terms of A are either σ or U (cf. §84.1).
   (iii)   if t_i is an adjunction, and its defining sequence is $C =$
   $(a_1,..., a_{2k})$, then for each $j \leqslant k$,
   (a) $a_{2j-1} = 0$
   (b) $a_{2j} = 0$ or $\bar{t}_{i-1}(Y_1,..., Y_j ; Y_j,..., Y_r) = U$, where
   $\bar{t}_{i-1} = t_{i-1}(...(t_1))$
   (iv) $t \notin \Delta_{el}$.

---

[16] The details of this analysis will be somewhat different in respects that are not now relevant.

The class of elementary substitutions will be denoted by "Σ_{el}," and the class of grammatical transformations based on them, by "Σ."

Theorem 6. For each sustitution t_s there is a sequence $D = (a_1, ..., a_{2k})$ such that

(i) $a_{2j-1} = 0$ or σ

(ii) if $a_{2j-1} = 0$, then $a_{2j} = 0$

(iii) if $a_{2j-1} = \sigma$, then a_{2j} is an integer m such that $0 \leqslant m \leqslant k$

(iv) there is an m such that $1 \leqslant m \leqslant k$, $a_{2m-1} = \sigma$, and for all $i \leqslant 2k$, $a_i \neq m$

(v) there is a $j \leqslant k$ such that $a_{2j} \neq 0$, $a_{2j} \neq j$

(vi) $t_s(Y_1, ..., Y_n ; Y_n, ..., Y_r) = \begin{cases} Y_{a_{2n}} \text{ if } r = k \text{ and } a_{2n-1} = \sigma, \\ \text{where } Y_0 = U \\ Y_n \text{ if } r \neq k, \text{ or } a_{2n-1} = 0 \end{cases}$

and each sequence D such that (i)–(v) determines some substitution t_s such that (vi).

Thus D as in Theorem 6 determines the substitution t_s that carries Y_n of Y_1-...-Y_n-...-Y_k into a string W_n which is identical with Y_n if $a_{2n-1} = 0$ and is identical with $Y_{a_{2n}}$ (where $Y_0 = U$) if $a_{2n-1} = \sigma$. Condition (iv) ensures the deletion of some term Y_m which is not reintroduced elsewhere by t_s (hence t_s is certainly not a permutation). Condition (v) guarantees that there is at least one term Y_j which displaces some other term. By means of the sequence D, substitutions can be characterized in much the same way as deformations and adjunctions.

Suppose, for instance, that $D = (\sigma, 0, \sigma, 1, 0, 0)$. Then the associated t_s is the elementary transformation such that

85     $t_s(Y_1 ; Y_1, Y_2, Y_3) = U$
$t_s(Y_1, Y_2 ; Y_2, Y_3) = Y_1$
$t_s(Y_1, Y_2, Y_3 ; Y_3) = Y_3$
$t_s{}^*(Y_1, Y_2, Y_3) = U^\frown Y_1^\frown Y_3 = Y_1^\frown Y_3$

That is, t_s is the elementary transformation that carries **84** into **82**.

With this clarification, we can return to the discussion of §§86.2, 86.3.   86.5 We found in §86.3 that the requirement of uniqueness for the root led us to exclude nonpermutational rearrangements from the class of basic elementary transformations for which the root is directly defined. But even when we define the basic set of elementary transformations as $L = \Delta + \Pi + H$, there remain elementary transformations that are equivocal wrt L, even in the set L itself. In fact, we can show that a deformation whose defining sequence contains σ at any point is equivocal wrt L. That is, there is an analysis of this deformation which contains exactly one permutation (distinct from the identity ι). We have seen in §86.4 that in the case of nonpermutational rearrangements, the equivocation revealed a real equivocation in the notion of root, but in the case of these deformations, and in certain other cases, the alternative analysis in which a permutation figures seems to have no independent motivation.

One simple way to eliminate all further equivocation and to guarantee uniqueness of the root, is to restrict the occurrence of permutations in compounds. We can define a *compoundable* sequence of elementary transformations as a sequence which contains permutations only if there is no way to achieve the effect of the compound formed from this sequence without using permutations:

Definition 25. $(t_1,\ldots, t_n)$ is *compoundable* if and only if for all $i \leqslant n$, $t_i \in \varDelta_{el} + \varPi_{el} = H_{el}$, and either (i) or (ii):

   (i)   for all $i \leqslant n$, $t_i \in \varDelta_{el} + H_{el}$
   (ii) there is no $t_1{}',\ldots, t_m{}'$ such that

        (a) $t_m{}'(\ldots(t_1{}')) = t_n(\ldots(t_1))$
        (b)   for all $j \leqslant m$, $t_j{}' \in \varDelta_{el} + H_{el}$

If in the general definition of "root" for compounds, we limit ourselves to compoundable sequences, then there can be no equivocation, and, at the same time, there is no restriction on the generative power of compounding. That is, every elementary transformation t that can be derived by compounding from rearrangements, deformations, and adjunctions will assign a unique term of the proper analysis as a root to each term $t(Y_1,\ldots, Y_n ; Y_n,\ldots, Y_r)$ of the transform. A less stringent and more flexible requirement than compoundability in this sense might also be devised.

We thus arrive, finally, at the definition of "root," combining the definitions of "$root_1$" and "$root_1*$" (Definitions 22, 23), with the emendations of the intervening discussion:

Definition 26. $(Y_j , Z_j{}^Y)$ is the $root_{el}$ of $(W_i , Z_i{}^W)$ wrt $(Y_1,\ldots, Y_r)$, t if and only if either (I)

    (i) $i, j \leqslant r$
    (ii) $Z_j{}^Y = Y_1{}^\frown \ldots {}^\frown Y_j$

(iii) $W_i = t(Y_1 ,..., Y_i ; Y_i ,..., Y_r)$

(iv) $Z_i^W = t(Y_1 ; Y_1 ,..., Y_r)^\frown...^\frown t(Y_1 ,..., Y_i ; Y_i ,..., Y_r)$

and either (v) or (vi)

(v) $t \in \Delta_{el} + H_{el}$, and $i = j$

(vi) $t \in \Pi_{el}$, and t is based on $B = (a_1 ,..., a_k)$,

and $\begin{cases} \text{if } k = r, \text{ then } j = a_i \\ \text{if } k \neq r, \text{ then } j = i \end{cases}$

or (II) there is a compoundable sequence $t_1 ,..., t_n$ and a pair (X_m , Z_m^X) such that

(i) $t = t_n(\bar{t})$, where $\bar{t} = t_{n-1}(...(t_1))$

(ii) (Y_j , Z_j^Y) is the root_{el} of (X_m , Z_m^X) wrt $(Y_1 ,..., Y_r)$, $\bar{t}$

(iii) (X_m , Z_m^X) is the root_{el} of (W_i , Z_i^W) wrt $\bar{t}(Y_1 ; Y_1 ,..., Y_r)$, ..., $\bar{t}(Y_1 ,..., Y_r ; Y_r)$, t_n

Theorem 7. Suppose

(i) $t_1 ,..., t_n$ are elementary transformations of $L = \Delta + \Pi + H$

(ii) $t = t_n(...(t_1))$

(iii) for $Y_1 ,..., Y_r$, and all $n \leqslant r$, $t(Y_1 ,..., Y_n ; Y_n ,..., Y_r) = W_n$

Then there is a unique pair $(Y_j , Y_1^\frown...^\frown Y_j)$ such that $(Y_j , Y_1^\frown...^\frown Y_j)$ is the root_{el} of $(W_n , W_1^\frown...^\frown W_n)$ wrt $(Y_1 ,..., Y_r)$, t where $j, n \leqslant r$.

Definition 27. (Y, Z^Y) is the *root* of (W, Z^W) wrt Z, K, T if and only if there is a $Y_1 ,..., Y_r$, t such that

(i) $(Y_1 ,..., Y_r)$ is the proper analysis of Z wrt K, T

(ii) t underlies T

(iii) (Y, Z^Y) is the root_{el} of (W, Z^W) wrt $(Y_1 ,..., Y_r)$, t

Theorem 8. Suppose that some elementary transformation underlying T is a finite compound of permutations, deformations, and adjunctions. Then for each Z, K, every term of the proper analysis of $T(Z, K)$ wrt Z, K, T (and only such terms) has a term of the proper analysis of Z wrt K, T as its root.

We require further that this root must be unique. Theorem 7 assures us that for each underlying t, the root of each term is unique (since the proper analysis of Z wrt K, T is unique). But there may be various underlying transformations. In §82.3, we proposed a condition **C12** which defined a set of *determinate* transformations. We noted that determinate transformations are those with a unique term arrangement. It is in fact the case that

Theorem 9. If T meets the condition of Theorem 8, and T is determinate, then every term of the proper analysis of the transform has a unique root with respect to T.

Any transformation that is general enough in its application to be of interest in syntactic analysis is determinate. Henceforth, we will always assume that the grammatical transformations under discussion are determinate. That is, we restrict ourselves to that part of $\mathcal{T}$ which meets **C12**, §82.3, as well as **C1–C11**, and we can thus assume uniqueness of root assignment.

Theorem 4, §85.3 and Theorem 5, §86.3 give us some reason to believe that the condition of Theorem 8 is not too restrictive for syntactic analysis, since we can construct a transformation E-related to any grammatical transformation, within the limits of this condition. The condition of compoundability does however impose a restriction on root assignment which may turn out not to be desirable, in view of the role of the notion of "root" in the determination of derived constituent structure. There is good reason to be somewhat suspicious about the maneuvers that have been carried through here to ensure the existence and uniqueness of the root. But they do leave intact the transformations that we will find useful in the transformational analysis of English, and, as we have seen, they have systematic motivation as well as some linguistic motivation.

Note in particular that a pair π, δ or δ, π (where $\pi \in \Pi_{el}$, $\delta \in \Delta_{el}$) are compoundable only if[17] δ does not delete any terms of the proper analysis, i.e., if its defining sequence does not contain σ as a term. We have already seen the utility of defining substitutional elementary transformations composed of δ, η where the defining sequence of δ contains *only* σ (and U), i.e., where δ only deletes terms, adding nothing. In fact, outside of the elements of Δ_{el}, Π_{el}, and H_{el} themselves, the only elementary transformations that appear in the analysis of English that we will present below are substitutions and π–δ transformations of the type just described. Thus the machinery that we have developed

---

[17] "Only if" can be replaced by "if and only if" in this statement if we add the condition that $\pi(\delta) \neq \iota$.

will be adequate for the analysis to be presented in Chapter X, in this respect.[18] The fact that the only deformations that actually appear in compounds are those with no deletions or those with only deletions (i.e., with only null constant part) suggests an alternative approach from which it might be useful to study the basic structure of the system $\mathscr{T}_{el}$.

We began the discussion of the constituent structure of transforms by proposing that to each term W_i of the proper analysis of the transform there be assigned a term Y_j of the proper analysis of the transformed string as the unique root of W_i. Having provided the means for this assignment, we can go on to investigate derived constituent structure.   **87.1**

Suppose, throughout this discussion, that Z is a string, and that K is a class of strings which provides the analysis of Z (thus a **P**-marker, if Z is directly derived by a ρ_1-derivation on the level of phrase structure). Suppose further that we have a transformation T, with $(Y_1,..., Y_r)$ being the proper analysis of Z wrt K, T, and $(W_1,..., W_r)$ being the proper analysis of $T(Z, K)$ wrt Z, K, T. We know that for each i, there is a unique j such that the occurrence $Y_1{}^\frown...{}^\frown Y_j$ of Y_j is the root of the occurrence $W_1{}^\frown...{}^\frown W_i$ of W_i.

The problem that we now face is analogous to a problem to which much of Chapter VII was devoted. We were interested there in developing the notion "X is a Y of Z" which was to hold whenever X is a "significant" segment of Z (i.e., a constituent), and when the given occurrence of X in fact functions as a Y. Thus we wanted to be able to say that *the⁀man* is a *NP* in *the⁀man⁀was⁀here*; that *called⁀up* is a *Verb* in *John⁀called⁀up⁀his⁀friends*, though not in *John⁀called⁀ up⁀the⁀stairs*, etc. This problem was solved in a general and apparently effective manner by the development of **P**-markers (which always give a consistent analysis; cf. Theorem 7, §53.6) and the relation E_0 (cf. §53.1, Definition 4). But now we are assuming that the algebra **P** and the relation ρ are limited so that only certain sentences have **P**-markers, namely, the kernel sentences. And we are interested in constructing notions for nonkernel sentences (i.e., transforms) that will fulfill the function served for kernel sentences by **P**-markers and E_0.

The optimal solution to this problem would be to construct a notion of *derived interpretation* in such a way that the derived interpretation K' of $T(Z, K)$ is a set of strings uniquely determined by Z, K, T and giving an analysis of $T(Z, K)$, just as K gives an analysis of Z. Then E_0 could hold without alteration for $T(Z, K)$, K'.

---

[18] There would be certain exceptions to this if the analysis were carried far enough (cf. §87.5). But even these exceptions appear to be of a very restricted type, and do not seem to falsify the concluding sentence of this paragraph.

There are many difficulties in this course, and we have not managed to achieve a completely satisfactory solution to the problems that arise. We will approach the construction of "derived interpretation" indirectly, by means of a relation E more general than E_0. This construction will not ensure that the derived interpretation will provide a consistent analysis (cf. last paragraph of §82.1), and in its details it is rather too closely tied down to the specific requirements of the transformational analysis of English. Hence this construction should at most be regarded as providing a partial set of conditions that will have to be met by some more general and revealing construction of the concepts of derived constituent structure. It is possible to generalize these conditions in various ways. My own impression is that we are again at a point where reasonable theoretical construction must be deferred until the actual empirical consequences of various approaches are more thoroughly explored.

87.2 In §82.1 we noted that our previous knowledge about the level **P** can automatically provide us with a certain amount of information about derived constituent structure. It may be the case that a term W_i of the proper analysis of $T(Z, K)$, or a string of terms $W_i \frown ... \frown W_{i+j}$ is represented by some prime P_i of **P** (i.e., P_i bears ρ to this term or string of terms). For example, we know from **P** that "by John" is a *Prepositional Phrase* (*PP*). That is, from the fragment of the grammar associated with the level **P** in English we can reconstruct the following partial specification of ρ:

86 $\rho(PP, P \frown NP)$, $\rho(P, by)$, $\rho(NP, John)$

Hence $\rho(PP, by \frown John)$. Thus when we form the passive

87   *Bill–was–accused–by–John*

from "John accused Bill," with the proper analysis as indicated by the dashes, then we know automatically that $by \frown John$ is a *PP* in **87**.

It is very important to note that it is not necessary here that "by John" actually occur in some kernel sentence as a *PP*. We know (cf. §54) that the algebra **P** is *nonrestricted*. Hence even if a certain phrase (e.g., "by John") never occurs as a P_i in the restricted part of **P** (i.e., in a restricted ρ-derivation), it may still be a P_i for reasons inherent in the construction of the phrase structure of kernel sentences and having nothing to do with transformational analysis. Thus as long as **86** is required by considerations of simplicity internal to the system of phrase structure developed for the kernel grammar, the analysis of "by John" in **87** as a *PP* will be forthcoming.

Note in particular the significance of Axiom 10, Chapter VII, §61, in this connection. This axiom requires that the classes of the absolute analysis (cf. §39) be carried over into **P**, thus increasing greatly the degree to which **P** is nonrestricted. Let us consider for a moment the effect of this requirement on the derived analysis of the passive. The absolute categories, it will be recalled, are intended to be those broad categories such as Noun, Verb, Adjective, etc. that mark the major distributions and that establish an overall dichotomy between grammatical and ungrammatical.

It will certainly be the case that "by" and "from," for instance, belong to the same absolute category. Similarly, it would seem reasonable to assume that the differences in distribution between two subclasses of adjectives A_1 and A_2 will not be marked on the absolute level, where A_1 is the class containing "tired," etc., adjectives that can occur after "very," and A_2 contains those elements, such as "accused," that cannot.[19] Hence there will be a prime *Prep* in **P** such that $\rho(Prep, by)$ and $\rho(Prep, from)$, and a prime A such that $\rho(A, en^\frown tire)$ and $\rho(A, en^\frown accuse)$. Suppose further that $\rho(NP, John)$ and $\rho(NP, the^\frown trip)$. It would seem that all of these assumptions must turn out to be the case in any adequate statement of the level **P**, if the notions of phrase structure are to have their intended significance.

Suppose now that **87** is deleted from the kernel, to be reintroduced by transformation, but that

88   *Bill was tired from the trip*

is retained in the kernel. We will see in Chapter X that there are good reasons why this should be the case.[20] But in the statement of phrase structure for kernel sentences, **88** is analyzed as an instance of

89   *NP-was-A-PP*

Hence, under the assumptions we have just made, it follows that **87** also receives this analysis, automatically. But this was just the analysis of

---

[19] Thus A_1 contains $en^\frown V_k$ (cf. statements 17, 23, §72.2, and Note 13, Chapter VIII). A_2 contains $en^\frown V_T$ for all members of V_T not in V_k, e.g., "accuse." We have "very tired," but not "very accused."

[20] These reasons turn on the fact that such expressions as "very" can precede "tired" in **88**, but cannot precede "accused" in **87**. The statement of this distribution would be complicated if **88** were dropped from the kernel. Furthermore there are positive gains from dropping **87**, but not from dropping **88**.

passives to which we were led in §67.3. This is important, because it means that even if passives are dropped from the kernel, their derived constituent structure is that of a kernel sentence. This is not in general true of transforms, and it can account for the intuitively intermediate status of passives commented on in §77.2. In discussing this analysis of passives as **89** in §67.3, we noted that it was intuitively inadequate in that the "verbal force" of, e.g., "accused" in **87** (as opposed to the really "adjectival" status of "tired" in **88**) was unexplained. But this inadequacy is now eliminated (once we show that passives must be deleted from the kernel and derived transformationally, cf. §98), since the verbal force of "accused" is explained by the fact that **87** is derived from a sentence where "accuse" is actually a transitive verb. It is thus explained on a higher level than the level **P** of phrase structure.

We can state the condition on derived constituent structure that has been implicit in this discussion as the definition of a notion E_1, related to E_0, but including T as an extra "parameter."

Definition 28. $E_1(X, V, S, Z, K, T)$ if and only if there is a $W_1,..., W_r$, i, j such that

    (i) $(W_1,..., W_r)$ is the proper analysis of $T(Z, K)$ wrt Z, K, T

    (ii) $1 \leqslant i \leqslant j \leqslant r$

    (iii) $X = W_i {}^{\frown}...{}^{\frown}W_j$

    (iv) $V = W_1 {}^{\frown}...{}^{\frown}W_j$

    (v) Suppose (R_k, S_k) is the root of $(W_k, W_1 {}^{\frown}...{}^{\frown}W_k)$ and for each k, $i \leqslant k < j$, $S_{k+1} = S_k {}^{\frown}R_{k+1}$. Then for some k such that $i \leqslant k \leqslant j$, $W_k \neq R_k$

    (vi) S is a prime

    (vii) $\rho(S, X)$[21]

Thus the occurrence V of X is an S of $T(Z, K)$ if S is a prime that represents X in the kernel grammar, where X is a string of one or more terms of the proper analysis of $T(Z, K)$, and X has in fact been formed by application of the transformation T, not simply carried over intact from Z. Case (v) is necessary in Definition 28 (and Definition 29) to preclude the assignment of a new and irrelevant analysis to a constituent that does not change at all under the transformation.

Note that since **87** has the analysis **89**, it also has the analysis *NP-VP*, since $\rho(VP, was{}^{\frown}A{}^{\frown}PP)$ must be the case on the level **P** to account for **88**. The fact that $was{}^{\frown}accused{}^{\frown}by{}^{\frown}John$ is a *VP* of **87** thus

---

[21] Note that S here is a variable over primes, not to be confused with the symbol S used earlier as an abbreviation for *Sentence*.

follows from Definition 28, taking as X a string of three terms of the proper analysis of **87** (namely, *was, accused, by^John*). This conclusion then follows on the same assumptions about **P** that were made above to show that the transform **87** has the analysis **89**. Similarly we can show that **87** is a *Sentence*. Thus the passive **87** has the full constituent structure of a kernel sentence, by virtue of Definition 28. This is so far true only of the external structure of terms of the proper analysis (cf. §86.4). In Definitions 31 and 33 below we add further conditions on internal structure from which it will follow finally that passives actually have ρ-derivations and **P**-markers, even when deleted from the kernel, although not, of course, restricted ρ-derivations.

We can weaken the assumption about absolute categories upon which these comments about the status of passives have been based. We assumed that the distinction between A_1 (containing "tired" = *en^tire*) and A_2 (containing "accused" = *en^accuse*) would not be marked on the absolute level of analysis. But even this reasonable assumption can be dropped if we generalize E_1 to a relation E_2 which will assert that X is an S if there is an X' with some representing string in common with X and such that $\rho(S, X')$.

Definition 29. $E_2(X, V, S, Z, K, T)$ if and only if

   (i) X is a string of terms of the proper analysis of $T(Z, K)$ wrt Z, K, T

  (ii) V is an occurrence of X in $T(Z, K)$

 (iii)   there is an X', W such that

        (a) $\rho(S, X')$
        (b) $\rho(W, X')$
        (c) $\rho(W, X)$

  (iv) S is a prime
   (v)   = (v), Definition 28, where $X = W_i^\frown...^\frown W_j$

E_1 is a special case of E_2, where $S = W$ and $X = X'$.

But we have seen in Chapter VIII that there is a prime V_T such that $\rho(V_T, tire)$ and $\rho(V_T, accuse)$. That is, both "tire" and "accuse" are transitive verbs, though they belong to different subclasses of V_T. The decision to set up such an element V_T is unaffected by the deletion of passives from the kernel. But now, whether or not A_1 and A_2 are distinguished on the absolute level, it follows that *accused* is an A, if $\rho(A, tired)$. For "accused" within the level **P** appears as *en^accuse*, and "tired" as *en⌢tire*.[22] Hence both *en⌢accuse* and *en⌢tire* are represented by *en⌢V_T*. Taking *en⌢accuse* as X, *en⌢tire* as X', *en⌢V_T* as W, and A as S, we have the conclusion that *en⌢accuse* is an A if $\rho(A, en⌢tire)$, by Definition 29, where T is the passive transformation, and $Z =$ "John accused Bill." That is, in this case, E_2 (*en⌢accuse*, *Bill⌢was⌢en⌢accuse*, A, Z, K, T).

It appears, however, that Definition 29 is too strong in certain other cases (cf. §43.2).

87.3   We see, then, that a good deal of useful information about derived constituent structure can be drawn from the system of phrase structure that is constructed for kernel sentences. But naturally, this source of information will not suffice to determine derived structure completely. It will be recalled that the grammar constructed for kernel sentences was based on a restricted relation ρ^r from which ρ could be mechanically reconstructed (cf. §55). But as sentences are withdrawn from the kernel the relation ρ^r will become more limited in application. In fact, the primary systematic goal of transformational analysis is to delete from the kernel a sufficient number of sentences so that a simple characterization of ρ^r (i.e., an "optimal" grammar) can be presented. Hence the relation ρ as it is reconstructed from the kernel grammar will not be sufficiently rich and diversified to account for the total constituent structure of transforms.

But even though transforms may not have **P**-markers, they do have constituent structure, and this must be stateable in terms of the level **P**. Thus we must construct a relation ρ^T which will supplement ρ^r, and we must revise the requirement of §55, requiring now that ρ be mechanically recoverable from ρ^r and ρ^T.

We will have to characterize ρ^T somehow on the level of transformational analysis. If ρ^T were known, then the problem of defining "X is an S in $T(Z, K)$" would be considerably simplified. If $\rho(S, X)$ in the kernel grammar, then E_1, E_2, or some elaboration of them may prove sufficient. If it is not the case, in terms of the kernel grammar, that $\rho(S, X)$, then we can use the fact that $\rho^T(S, X)$ in a definition perfectly analogous to Definition 28. On the other hand, if the relation "X is an S in $T(Z, K)$" is known completely, then the characterization of ρ^T will pose no problem. We can simply define ρ^T as the relation holding between S and X where for some transform $T(Z, K)$, X is an S of

---

[22] That is, Φ^P carries *en⌢accuse* into *accuse⌢en*, which by morphological rules (i.e., Φ^M) becomes "accused" (cf. §§66, 67.3, 72.3).

$T(Z, K)$. Thus the dual problem of determining ρ^T and the relation "is a" for transforms can be approached in various ways.

Suppose that we choose the first approach of characterizing ρ^T independently, then defining "X is an S of $T(Z, K)$" in terms of it. The grammar for ρ^T can be constructed in the same manner as the grammatical statement based on ρ^r. We would develop this grammar so as to give the simplest characterization of a relation ρ^T that will suffice to give all the derived constituent structure necessary for compounding of transformations, wherever this is called for.

This is a possible course, but one which it would be preferable to avoid. The systematic motivation for transformational analysis is the desire to eliminate the immense complexity of a full statement of constituent structure. There is no point in simply transplanting a vast segment of this complexity to a new level. Furthermore, this procedure has an unpleasantly *ad hoc* flavor. We will find that by a further study of the roots of the terms of transforms, and the manner in which a transform is derived, we can eliminate the necessity for characterizing derived structure in this *ad hoc* and cumbersome fashion, by stating general conditions under which a derived constituent structure is assigned. Each step that we take in defining derived constituent structure is designed to eliminate the need for a part of the listing ρ^T in the actual grammar of English. It will appear to be the case that ρ^T can be eliminated without residue, at least to the extent that we have experimented with transformational analysis in English in Chapter X. But it should be kept in mind that if a certain transformational analysis requires an assignment of constituent structure to a transform in a way that cannot be derived from knowledge of **P** and knowledge of the transformation T, then it is possible to save this analysis by listing the requisite ρ^T, if this results in an overall simplification of the grammar.

We now proceed with the second course of defining derived constituent structure in a general way, leading to a partial or (we hope) complete specification of ρ^T in terms of the notion "X is a Y of $T(Z, K)$."

Suppose that   87.4

90   *I–called–my friend–up*

is dropped from the kernel to be reintroduced by transformation from

91   *I–called–up–my friend*

In **91**, "called up my friend" is a *VP* with the subject "I," and in **90** we should like to say that "called my friend up" is a *VP* as well.

In fact, the conjunction criterion that we found so useful in Chapter VIII necessitates this analysis, since we have

92   *I called my friend up and invited him*

and "invited him" is clearly a *VP*.

The motive for dropping such sentences as **90** from the kernel is obvious, when we bear in mind the general inadequacy of the system of phrase structure developed in Chapter VII for the case of discontinuous elements. We return to the transformational analysis of such sentences in §100, Chapter X.

If we follow the first approach suggested in §87.3, we might supply the required information by adding to the grammar statements expressing the relationship

93 $\rho^T(VP,\ called\frown my\frown friend\frown up)$

But it is clearly both possible and preferable to state in linguistic theory general conditions under which such results as **93** will be derivable, so that no special statement at all need be added to the grammar of English to provide the constituent analysis.

90 is formed from **91** by a permutation that carries Y_1-Y_2-Y_3-Y_4 into Y_1-Y_2-Y_4-Y_3. The rule that we would like to construct should tell us that in such cases, if Y_2-Y_3-Y_4 is an *S*, then Y_2-Y_4-Y_3 is an *S* as well.

The general requirement can be given as a definition of E_3 :

Definition 30. $E_3(X, V, S, Z, K, T)$ if and only if there is a $Y_1,...,\ Y_r$, $W_1,...,\ W_r$, i, j such that

     (i) $(Y_1,...,\ Y_r)$ is the proper analysis of Z wrt K, T
    (ii) $(W_1,...,\ W_r)$ is the proper analysis of $T(Z, K)$ wrt Z, K, T
   (iii) $1 \leqslant i \leqslant r; 0 \leqslant j \leqslant r - i$
   (iv) $X = W_i\frown...\frown W_{i+j}$
    (v) $V = W_1\frown...\frown W_{i+j}$
   (vi)   for each $k, 0 \leqslant k \leqslant j$, there is an $m, 0 \leqslant m \leqslant j$, such that

        (a) $(Y_{i+m},\ Y_1\frown...\frown Y_{i+m})$ is the root of
                          $(W_{i+k},\ W_1\frown...\frown W_{i+k})$ wrt Z, K, T
        (b) $E_0(Y_i\frown...\frown Y_{i+j},\ Y_1\frown...\frown Y_{i+j},\ S, Z, K)$

   (vii)   *S* is a prime of **P**

If T is the permutation that converts Y_1-Y_2-Y_3-Y_4 into Y_1-Y_2-Y_4-Y_3, **87.5**
then Definition 30 will account for the fact that "called my friend up"
is a *VP* in **90** if "called up my friend" is a *VP* in **91**.

But Definition 30 does not require that T be taken as a permutation.
If T is not a permutation, then $k = m$ in (vi), Definition 30. There are
at least three interesting cases that are correctly dealt with in terms of E_3
as defined here, where T is not a permutation.

(i) Suppose that T is a substitution based on an elementary
transformation $t_s \in \Sigma_{el}$ (cf. Definition 24, §86.4). In §86.4 we noted that
the substituend must have the same external constituent structure as
the term for which it is substituted. Thus "it" is the *NP* subject of
"it–was quite obvious." But we form

94   *that he was unhappy–was quite obvious* $(= 82)$

by substituting "that he was unhappy" for this occurrence of "it."
Hence "that he was unhappy" must be the *NP* subject of **94**.

Definition 30 tells us that if the effect of T is to replace Y_i in $Z =$
$...Y_i...$ by Y_j, then this occurrence of Y_j is an S if the given occurrence
of Y_i was an S (and any string of terms of the proper analysis of $T(Z, K)$
containing this occurrence of Y_j is an S only if the corresponding string
of roots containing Y_i is an S). Hence **94** will be correctly analyzed,
where **94** $(= 82)$ is derived from **84** in the manner of §86.4; "that he
was unhappy" will be a *NP*, and **94** will be a *Sentence* of the form *NP-VP*.

(ii) Suppose that T is a deformation having the effect of **95**, where
hyphens mark terms of the proper analyses, as throughout this discussion:

95 T: Y_1-Y_2-$Y_3 \rightarrow Y_1$-$W_1 \frown Y_2 \frown W_2$-$Y_3$

In this case, T can be regarded as substituting $W_1 \frown Y_2 \frown W_2$ for Y_2
in $Z = Y_1$-Y_2-Y_3, and it seems reasonable to require that $W_1 \frown Y_2 \frown W_2$
play the same role in $T(Z, K)$ that Y_2 played in Z, for reasons similar
to those that arose in the case of substitutions.

As an instance, suppose that we were to introduce "very" transformationally, modifying adjective phrases (*AP*). Thus, where $W_1 = very$
$Y_2 = old$, $W_2 = U$, T converts

96 Y_1-*old*-Y_3

into Y_1-*very* $\frown$ *old*-Y_3. But "very old" is an *AP* in the transform, where
"old" is an *AP* in **96**. And if "old" in **96** is part of an *NP* "old men,"

then "very old" in the transform is part of an NP "very old men." This is provided for by Definition 30.

We will see that there are reasons for not introducing "very" transformationally. But there are many instances similar to the one just sketched, where transformational treatment seems to be in order. Suppose, for example, that in **95**, Y_2 is one of the M's, i.e., Y_2 is one "can," "will," .... Suppose that $W_1 = U$, and W_2 is the element n't which, suffixed to an M, gives "can't," "won't," etc. But these negatives must be analyzed as M's, because they are subject to the same further transformations as "can," "will," etc. For example, from "he can't come" we can form "can't he come?" just as we can form "can he come?" from "he can come," etc. But again, that "can't" is an M if "can" is an M follows from Definition 30, where the negative element is introduced by transformation as here outlined. Similarly, if "can come" is a VP, then "can't come" is a VP in the transform.

(iii) If W_1 or W_2 in **95** is one of Y_1, Y_2, or Y_3, then T is an adjunction. As an instance, consider the mapping Φ^P (cf. §72.3 and **35**, §66.2), which, in particular converts **97** into **98**:

97   *...ing⌢eat⌢lunch...*

98   *...eat⌢ing⌢lunch...*

We might treat this as a permutational mapping, but it is also possible, with much superior results, to treat it as based on an adjunction η such that

99 η: $...Y_1\text{-}Y_2\text{-}Y_3... \rightarrow ...Y_1\text{-}Y_2{}^\frown Y_1\text{-}Y_3...$

followed by a deformation δ such that

100 δ: $...Z_1\text{-}Z_2\text{-}Z_3... \rightarrow ...U\text{-}Z_2\text{-}Z_3...$

Neglecting now the surrounding context indicated by the dots, $\delta(\eta)$ will be the elementary transformation such that

101 $\delta(\eta)$: $Y_1\text{-}Y_2\text{-}Y_3 \rightarrow Y_1\text{-}Y_2{}^\frown Y_1\text{-}Y_3 \rightarrow U\text{-}Y_2{}^\frown Y_1\text{-}Y_3 = Y_2{}^\frown Y_1\text{-}Y_3$

or, in particular,

102   *ing-eat-lunch → ing-eat⌢ing-lunch → U-eat⌢ing-lunch = eat⌢ing-lunch*

The advantage of this analysis with $\delta(\eta)$ is that by virtue of Definition 30, $Y_2 \frown Y_1$ is an S in the transform in **99** and **101** if Y_2 is an S in $...Y_1$-Y_2-$Y_3...$; and $Y_2 \frown Y_1$-Y_3 is an S in the transform if Y_2-Y_3 is an S in $...Y_1$-Y_2-$Y_3...$ In particular, it follows from Definition 30 that "eating" is a transitive verb V_T, and "eating lunch" is a VP_1. This shows us the way out of one of the recurrent difficulties in Chapter VIII. We noted (cf., for instance, last paragraph of §66.2) that the conjunction criterion requires that

103   *John–is–eating lunch*

be analyzed, with the constituent breaks given by the dashes, as *NP– auxiliary phrase–VP*$_1$. But at the same time, we found that the most effective analysis of the verb phrase is achieved by considering *"is$\frown$ing"* to be an auxiliary, with "eat lunch" the VP_1, and a mapping Φ^P converting *is$\frown$ing$\frown$eat$\frown$lunch* into *is$\frown$eat$\frown$ing$\frown$lunch*. In Chapter VIII, the analyses did not seem to be compatible. But we see now that if the mapping in question is based on the elementary transformation $\delta(\eta)$ (as in **101**), then these two analyses are in fact perfectly compatible, by virtue of Definition 30.

In §86.4 we noted a distinction between external and internal constituent structure. We have discussed the former in §§87.4, 87.5, and we can now turn to a discussion of the internal structure of terms of the proper analysis. **87.6**

Suppose that X is a part (or the whole) of Y_i, and Y_i is the root of W_j. Suppose further that Y_i is not deleted in forming W_j. Thus $W_j = Z_1 \frown Y_i \frown Z_2$ (where $Z_1 = Z_2 = U$, if the transformation is a permutation). Then, since X is unaffected by the transformation, we would naturally be led to insist that the matched occurrence of X in W_j is an S if the given occurrence of X in Y_i is an S. For example, "the other team" is a NP in "the game–was–won–by the other team," as is "the game" (in the latter case, $X = Y_i = W_j$). Similarly, both "your friend" and "the book" are NP's in **69** as in **68** (§86.2).

We give this requirement as a definition of E_4:

Definition 31. $E_4(X, V, S, Z, K, T)$ if and only if there is a $Y_1, ..., Y_r$, $W_1, ..., W_r$, a, b, c, d, i, j such that

     (i) $(Y_1, ..., Y_r)$ is the proper analysis of Z wrt K, T
     (ii) $(W_1, ..., W_r)$ is the proper analysis of $T(Z, K)$ wrt Z, K, T
     (iii) $1 \leqslant i, j \leqslant r$

(iv) $V = \bar{V}{}^\frown c {}^\frown a {}^\frown X$, where $\bar{V} = \begin{Bmatrix} U, \text{ if } i = 1 \\ W_1{}^\frown ... {}^\frown W_{i-1}, \text{ if } i > 1 \end{Bmatrix}$

(v) $W_i = c {}^\frown a {}^\frown X {}^\frown b {}^\frown d$

(vi) $Y_j = a {}^\frown X {}^\frown b$

(vii) $(Y_j, Y_1{}^\frown ... {}^\frown Y_j)$ is the root of $(W_i, W_1{}^\frown ... {}^\frown W_i)$ wrt Z, K, T

(viii) $E_0(X, \bar{Y}{}^\frown a {}^\frown X, S, Z, K)$,

where $\bar{Y} = \begin{Bmatrix} U, \text{ if } j = 1 \\ Y_1{}^\frown ... {}^\frown Y_{j-1}, \text{ if } j > 1 \end{Bmatrix}$

The model behind this is the following:

104 $Z = Y_1{}^\frown ... {}^\frown Y_j{}^\frown ... {}^\frown Y_r$,
$T(Z, K) = W_1{}^\frown ... {}^\frown W_i{}^\frown ... {}^\frown W_r$
$Y_j = a {}^\frown X {}^\frown b$ is the root of $W_i = c {}^\frown a {}^\frown X {}^\frown b {}^\frown d$, and V is the relevant occurrence of X in $T(Z, K)$

If $T \in \Pi$, then $c = d = U$. Definition 31 tells us that if X is an S in Z, then it is an S in $T(Z, K)$.

This definition serves the required purpose for T's based on permutations, deformations, and elementary compounds of these, but it clearly is not adequate for the affixed term of an adjunction. For example, consider the adjunction T based on η with the defining sequence $(0, 0, 1, 0)$. Thus

105 $\eta(Y_1 ; Y_1, Y_2) = Y_1$
$\eta(Y_1, Y_2 ; Y_2) = Y_1{}^\frown Y_2$
$\eta*(Y_1, Y_2) = Y_1\text{-}Y_1{}^\frown Y_2$

Thus T carries $Y_1\text{-}Y_2$ into $Y_1\text{-}Y_1{}^\frown Y_2$. But the root of the second term $Y_1{}^\frown Y_2$ of the proper analysis of the transform is Y_2. For occurrences of X in Y_2, E_4 will be adequate, but not for occurrences of X in the first part Y_1 of Y_2. Instead of defining E_5 so as to remedy this deficiency in general, we will define it only for the special case of substitutions (cf. §86.4), since the definition is simplest for these cases, and these are the only cases needed for our analysis of English.

Definition 34. $E_5(X, V, S, Z, K, T)$ if and only if there is a $Y_1, ..., Y_r$, $W_1, ..., W_r$, a, b, i, j such that

(i) $(Y_1, ..., Y_r)$ is the proper analysis of Z wrt K, T

(ii) $(W_1, ..., W_r)$ is the proper analysis of $T(Z, K)$ wrt Z, K, T

(iii) $1 \leqslant i, j \leqslant r$

(iv) $V = \bar{V}\frown a\frown X$, where $\bar{V} = \begin{cases} U, \text{ if } i = 1 \\ W_1\frown...\frown W_{i-1}, \text{ if } i > 1 \end{cases}$

(v) $W_i = Y_j = a\frown X\frown b$

(vi) T is based on the elementary transformation $t_s \in \Sigma_{el}$, with the defining sequence $D = (a_1,..., a_{2i-2}, \sigma, j, a_{2i+1},..., a_{2r})$ [cf. Theorem 6, §86.4]

(vii) $E_0(X, \bar{Y}\frown a\frown X, S, Z, K)$,

$$\text{where } \bar{Y} = \begin{cases} U, \text{ if } j = 1 \\ Y_1\frown...\frown Y_{j-1}, \text{ if } j > 1 \end{cases}$$

The model behind this is the following (the order of i and j is irrelevant):

106 $Z = Y_1\frown...\frown Y_j\frown...\frown Y_i\frown...\frown Y_r$
$T(Z, K) = W_1\frown...\frown W_j\frown...\frown W_i\frown...\frown W_r$
where $Y_j = a\frown X\frown b = W_i$ and Y_i is the root of W_i;
$W_i = (\sigma\frown Y_i)\frown Y_j = Y_j$ (where the operation within parentheses is carried out first)

In this case the root of W_i is not Y_j, but Y_i. But the internal constituent structure of W_i is that of Y_j. The fact that we cannot use the root in giving this definition is connected with the distinction between the two senses of "root" discussed in §86.4.

One further requirement for derived constituent structure is that if   **87.7**
$T(Z, K) = ...X...$, then X is an X in $T(Z, K)$. This is needed to complete the parallel between the derived notion of "is a" and E_0 (cf. Definition 4, §53.1).

Definition 33. $E_6(X, V, S, Z, K, T)$ if and only if

(i) V is an occurrence of X in $T(Z, K)$
(ii) $X = S$

In §87.1 we set ourselves the task of constructing a notion for transforms analogous to E_0 for kernel sentences. We can now define a relation E which meets this requirement (subject to the qualifications suggested in §87.1):

Definition 34. $E(X, V, S, Z, K, T)$ if and only if (I)

(i)   there is an i such that $E_i(X, V, S, Z, K, T)$
(ii) $X = U$ if and only if $S = U$

or (II) there is an X_1, X_2, V_1, S_1, S_2 such that

(i) $E(X_1, V_1 {}^{\frown} X_1, S_1, Z, K, T)$
(ii) $E(X_2, V, S_2, Z, K, T)$
(iii) $V = V_1 {}^{\frown} X_1 {}^{\frown} X_2 = V_1 {}^{\frown} X$
(iv) $S = S_1 {}^{\frown} S_2$

The inductive condition, (II), states that if X_1 is an S_1 and X_2 is an S_2 in Z, where $Z = ...X_1 {}^{\frown} X_2...$, then $X = X_1 {}^{\frown} X_2$ is an $S_1 {}^{\frown} S_2$ in Z. The analogous property holds for E_0. (Iii) is added to preclude the assignment of constituent structure to unit terms of the proper analysis of $T(Z, K)$. This restriction is necessary to ensure that the axiom system for ρ will be met, where ρ is recovered partially from ρ^T which is defined in terms of E, as suggested in §87.3.

Now that we have at least partially developed the notion of derived structure, in the form of a definition of E, we can proceed to state the condition on ρ^T as proposed in §87.3:

107   If $E(X, V, S, Z, K, T)$ and $X \neq S$, then $\rho^T(S, X)$

This can be reconstructed as a necessary and sufficient condition (i.e., a definition) for ρ^T if we are prepared to accept the conclusion that ρ^T never need be independently stated, even in part (cf. §87.3). If we are willing to allow a certain amount of independent specification of ρ^T under the condition of overall simplification of the grammar, then **107** will be an axiom to be met on the level of transformational analysis by the independent notions E_{1-6} and ρ^T.

The form of Definition 34 is intended to suggest that we have not completed the characterization of E, and that further conditions can be added as additional relations E_i. But its incompleteness is only one respect in which the characterization of E is inadequate. As we have developed E here, it is not sufficiently restrictive in its assignment of derived constituent structure. That is, it undoubtedly assigns constituent structure in certain ways that we would not like to accept. In particular, it does not in general provide a consistent analysis for transforms, a fact which may indicate a serious formal inadequacy.

Suppose that I is an identity transformation that carries Z with the proper analysis (Z) into $I(Z, K) = Z$ with the proper analysis (Z) (cf. Case II, Definition 10, §83.2). Then

Theorem 10. $E_0(X, V, S, Z, K)$ if and only if $E(X, V, S, Z, K, I)$

Thus E_0 can be regarded as one of the special cases of E, with T in this case the identity transformation I.

The second goal proposed in §87.1 was the construction for each $T(Z, K)$ of a set K' of strings to be assigned to $T(Z, K)$ as its *derived interpretation*, just as a **P**-marker is a set of strings giving the constituent interpretation of a kernel string. K' must clearly be taken as the set of strings that provides exactly the constituent structure carried over from (Z, K) under T. Thus we have

Definition 35. K' is the *derived interpretation* of $T(Z, K)$ wrt Z, K, T if and only if K' is a minimal set of strings such that for all X, V, S, $E_0(X, V, S, T(Z, K), K')$ if and only if $E(X, V, S, Z, K, T)$.

Theorem 11.   Suppose that Z is a string in $\bar{P}$, K a set of strings containing Z, and T a grammatical transformation based on an elementary transformation t which is a finite compound of deformations, permutations, and adjunctions. Then there exists a unique set of strings K' such that K' is the derived interpretation of $T(Z, K)$ wrt Z, K, T. If $T = I$ (as in Theorem 10), then $K' \subset K$.

We cannot in general state that $K' = K$ if $T = I$, because K may contain irrelevant material, while K' is minimal.

Theorem 11 permits us to characterize a great many transformations (including, apparently, all those in which we are interested) as sets $T = \{(Z, K, Z', K')\}$, where Z, Z' are strings in $\bar{P}$ belonging to the sets K, K' respectively, and $Z' = T(Z, K)$ differs from Z in some structural feature constant for T. Thus T maps a string Z with the interpretation K into a new string Z' with the derived interpretation K'. This is the fundamental feature of transformational analysis.

Now that we have supplied a precise (though no doubt incomplete) sense for the notions of derived constituent structure and "derived interpretation," we can proceed to develop a technique for compounding transformations. The problem in defining "$T_2(T_1(Z, K))$" was that $T_1(Z, K)$ is a string Z', while T_2 must operate on a pair (Z', K'). But now we do have a unique set K' associated with $T(Z, K)$ and providing its constituent structure. We can therefore define a compound transformation $[T_2(T_1)]$ by the following condition:

108   Suppose that $T_1, T_2 \in \mathcal{T}$. Then

$$[T_2(T_1)]\,(Z, K) = T_2(T_1(Z, K), K')$$

87.8

87.9

where K' is the derived interpretation of $T_1(Z, K)$ wrt Z, K, T. $[T_2(T_1)]$ (Z, K) is denoted "$T_2(T_1(Z, K))$." The derived interpretation of $T_2(T_1(Z, K))$ wrt $T_1(Z, K)$, K', T_2 is called "the derived interpretation of $T_2(T_1(Z, K))$ wrt Z, K, $[T_2, T_1]$."

By assigning to $[T_2(T_1)]$ proper analyses of the transformed string and of the transform, we could regard $[T_2(T_1)]$ as a transformation, i.e., as a set of ordered quintuples $\{(Z, K, Z', Pr^{(1)}, Pr^{(2)})\}$ (cf. §82.3). We could then ask whether $\mathscr{T}$ is closed under compounding, i.e., whether $[T_2(T_1)]$ is necessarily in $\mathscr{T}$ if T_1 and T_2 are. The answer to this is clearly in the negative. Thus we have to define a compound of more than two elements by an inductive definition more general than **108**.

Definition 36.   Suppose $T_1 ,..., T_n \in \mathscr{T}$, and T_i is based on t, which is a finite compound of deformations, permutations, and adjunctions. Suppose $n = 1$. Then:

    (I) $[T_1]$ $(Z, K) = T_1(Z, K)$
    (II) "The derived interpretation of $T_1(Z, K)$ wrt Z, K, $[T_1]$" is defined as "the derived interpretation of $T_1(Z, K)$ wrt Z, K, T_1 ."

Suppose $n > 1$. Then:

    (I) $[T_n ,..., T_1]$ $(Z, K) = T_n(Z^{n-1}, K^{n-1})$
    where $\begin{cases} Z^{n-1} = [T_{n-1} ,..., T_1](Z, K). \\ K^{n-1} \text{ is the derived interpretation of } Z^{n-1} \\ \quad \text{wrt } Z, K, [T_{n-1} ,..., T_1]. \end{cases}$

    (II) "The derived interpretation of $T_n(Z^{n-1}, K^{n-1})$ wrt Z, K, $[T_n ,..., T_1]$" is defined as "the derived interpretation of $T_n(Z^{n-1}, K^{n-1})$ wrt Z^{n-1}, K^{n-1}, T_n ."

Definition 37. $[T_n ,..., T_1]$ (Z, K) is denoted "$T_n(...T_1(Z, K))$."

We know from §81.5 and Definition 13, §83.1, that each grammatical transformation T is associated with a set of ordered triples $T^1 = \{(Z, K, Z')\}$, where $Z' = T(Z, K)$. Similarly, each compound transformation $[T_n ,..., T_1]$ is associated with a set of ordered triples $T_n^1 = \{(Z, K, Z^n)\}$, where $Z^n = T_n(...T_1(Z, K))$. T^1 meets conditions **C1**–**C7**, §81 (with the emendation of §83.2). But T_n^1 may fail condition **C6**. That is, the undesirable transformations of the type described in §81.4, and excluded by **C6**, are readmitted by compounding. But the difficulty in §81.4 was not the availability of these transformations, but the fact that they were no more complex than the transformations of the type admitted by **C6**, so that the latter set of intuitively much simpler transformations was in no way preferred. Now, however, the situation is quite different. The transformations excluded by **C6** can only be reintroduced by compounding; that is, they must be described by a sequence of transformations of the type admitted by **C6**. Hence their characterization is considerably more complex, the complexity depending on how flagrantly they violate **C6**, i.e., how long a sequence must be given to describe them. This result seems satisfactory. The descriptive potential of the theory is not reduced by **C6**, but we can rank the transformations available for syntactic analysis by complexity (i.e., length of description) in what seems to be an intuitively acceptable way, with those that meet **C6** ranking above those that do not. Thus the transformations that meet **C6** will be preferred in grammars which are evaluated in terms of the standard of simplicity.

Before leaving the topic of compound transformations we will extend the notation "$[T_n, ..., T_1]$" to cover the case where the T_i themselves may be compound transformations:

Definition 38. Suppose that for each i such that $1 \leqslant i \leqslant n$, T_i is the compound transformation $[T_{i_{m_i}}, ..., T_{i_1}]$, where the T_{i_j} are each based on a finite compound of elementary deformations, permutations, and adjunctions. Then $[T_n, ..., T_1]$ is the compound transformation

$$[T_{n_{m_n}}, ..., T_{n_1}, T_{n-1_{m_{n-1}}}, ..., T_{n-1_1}, ..., T_{1_{m_1}}, ..., T_{1_1}]$$

It remains to define a notion of equivalence among transformations, so that such expression as "$T_m = [T_n, ..., T_1]$" or "$[T_{a_m}, ..., T_{a_1}] = [T_{b_n}, ..., T_{b_1}]$" are provided with a clear sense:

Definition 39. T_1 and T_2 are equivalent if and only if (i), (ii), (iii), (iv), or (v):

    (i) T_1 and T_2 are grammatical transformations of $\mathscr{T}$, and they are identical.

    (ii) T_1 is the compound transformation $[T_2]$, where $T_2 \in \mathscr{T}$, or T_2 is $[T_1]$, where $T_1 \in \mathscr{T}$.

    (iii) T_1 is the compound transformation $[T_{1_m}, ..., T_{1_1}]$, and T_2 is the compound transformation $[T_{2_n}, ..., T_{2_1}]$, where $T_{1_j}, T_{2_k} \in \mathscr{T}$, and for all Z, K:

          (a) $[T_{1_m}, ..., T_{1_1}](Z, K) = [T_{2_n}, ..., T_{2_1}](Z, K)$.

          (b) the derived interpretations are identical in case (iiia).

(iv) T_1 and T_2 are compound transformations in the extended sense of Definition 38 and their expanded forms meet (a), (b) of (iii).

(v)   There is a T_3 equivalent to both T_1 and T_2.

In all cases we write: $T_1 = T_2$ or $T_2 = T_1$ (interchangeably).

Thus in all cases, if $T_1 = T_2$, then T_1 and T_2 give the same transforms and derived analyses. This is a notion that deserves a good deal more study.

88.1   We can now return to the consideration of the mappings of **P** into **W** which was broken off at the conclusion of Chapter VII. Incidentally to the construction of transformations, we have developed machinery which will enable us to complete the characterization of the level of phrase structure. It will be recalled that the development of **P** was broken off at the point (§62.2) where it became necessary to state just how the mappings Φ_1^P, Φ_2^P,... of **P**-markers into strings in $\overline{\mathbf{M}}$ [and, by $\Phi^{\overline{M}}$, into $Gr_1(W)$] take constituent structure into account, what sense should be attached to a compound mapping, how a mapping can be actually described in the grammar, and how E_0 holds of the strings of words which are produced by the mappings. But now it is clear that each of these problems is solved in terms of the development that we have just outlined if we formulate each mapping as a transformation. Although the construction of transformations was motivated by quite different considerations (cf. §§76–78), we see that these constructions would have been necessary anyway, if only to complete the discussion of phrase structure.

88.2   It will be useful for later discussions to elaborate slightly the notations for describing mappings.

Definition 40.   Suppose that $\Phi^P = [\Phi_m^P ,..., \Phi_1^P]$. Then we designate $\Phi^{\overline{M}}$ as Φ_{m+1}^P and define $\psi_k = [\Phi_k^P ,..., \Phi_1^P]$, for $1 \leqslant k \leqslant m + 1$.

It follows from Axiom 11, §62.1, that $\psi_m(Z, K)$ is a string in $\overline{\mathbf{M}}$, if K is a **P**-marker of Z, and in this case, $\psi_{m+1}(Z, K)$ is a string in **W**. These statements may also be true if K is not a **P**-marker of Z. In fact, we will formulate the level of transformations in such a way that they will be true when K is the derived interpretation of Z.

Suppose that we define the *complement* of ψ_k as follows:

Definition 41. $\psi_k{}'$ is the *complement* of ψ_k , for $1 \leqslant k \leqslant m + 1$, under the assumption of Definition 40, where $\psi_k{}' = [\Phi^{\mathbf{P}}_{m+1} ,..., \Phi^{\mathbf{P}}_{k+1}]$.

Theorem 12. $[\psi_k{}' , \psi_k] = \Phi^{\mathbf{P}}$, where $\Phi^{\mathbf{P}}$ is taken now as a mapping of P-markers into grammatical strings of words.

This treatment of mappings as transformations enables us to clarify an important feature of transformational analysis. A given transformation may apply to (Z, K), where Z is a string in $\bar{P}$ (i.e., where Z is composed of "lowest-level" elements of **P**, e.g., it is the product of a ρ-derivation), or it may apply only when Z has already been partially developed by mappings, or when Z has been totally developed into a string in **W**. The fact that a transformation T may apply when Z is partially developed by mappings is a major reason for analyzing $\Phi^{\mathbf{P}}$ as a compound of many transformations. We can now make sense of this condition by requiring that T be compounded with just that ψ_k which is required for T to apply properly. 88.3

This of course implies that a compound transformation can in general be formed from two transformations only if these apply to strings which are developed by mappings to the same point, or if the second applies to a string developed beyond the point of application of the first member of the compound. This is a limitation which it might be possible and worthwhile to avoid. In certain cases it can be avoided by special devices, but it cannot be avoided in general unless each $\Phi_i{}^{\mathbf{P}}$ is a one-to-one transformation. This suggests a possible extension of our general framework to include somehow the notion of an inverse of a transformation. Exactly how such an extension might be carried out (or whether the one-to-one assumption for $\Phi^{\mathbf{P}}$ is a correct one, in fact) is not clear. In the transformational system for English there seems to be no particular need for such an extension. But this point must be kept in mind as a possible defect in the system being developed here.

Having constructed the set of grammatical transformations which are to be available for syntactic description, we can proceed with the program outlined in §80, that is, we can turn to the construction of the level **T** of transformational analysis as a linguistic level, and to the determination of the criteria that are to apply in the evaluation of a grammar containing a transformational level. We can construe transformational analysis as a new level, having the same status and the same formal structure as other levels, and introduced for the same general systematic purpose, to simplify the generation of grammatical sentences. Since this is a syntactic level, our purpose is to simplify the description of the set $Gr_1(W)$ of 89.1

grammatical strings of words. We must then construct a set of **T**-markers which are mapped into a certain subset of $Gr_1(W)$ by a mapping Φ^T, just as on the level **P** we constructed **P**-markers some of which are mapped into a certain subset of $Gr_1(W)$. Between them, **P**-markers and **T**-markers must exhaust (under the respective mappings) the set $Gr_1(W)$. More generally, the combined range of Φ^P and Φ^T must be exactly the set μ^W of **W**-markers.[23]

Consider the level **T** defined as follows:

109 $\mathbf{T} = [\tau, \frown, =, \rho^T, \mu^T, \Phi^T]$,   where τ is the set of primes of **T**, ρ^T is the relation discussed in §§87.3, 87.7, μ^T is the set of **T**-markers, and Φ^T is the mapping that carries these into strings of words.

If **107**, §87.7, is strengthened to a definition of "ρ^T," as suggested there, then ρ^T can be dropped as an independent element.

It has been evident throughout our development of transformations that the level **T** is intimately related to the level **P**, and as we axiomatize **T**, this relationship will become explicit in that will have a set of conditions of compatibility holding between **P** and **T**. To begin with, strings in $Gr(P)$ (the set of products of restricted ρ-derivations) and **P**-markers of these strings must be taken as primes of **T**. More generally, we proceed with the assumption of §83.1 and §84.1 that: we have a system S including **P**, $\overline{\mathbf{M}}$, and **W** and containing a single unit U (which serves for all subalgebras of S) and a single concatenation operation, so that elements of the various subsystems of S can be freely concatenated (in other words, $\overline{\mathbf{M}}$ and **W** can be regarded as being embedded in **P**); $\overline{P}$ is extended to include all elements not bearing ρ, i.e., $\overline{P}$ in the old sense as well as all strings in $\overline{\mathbf{M}}$ and **W**; the formal properties of **P**, $\overline{\mathbf{M}}$, and **W** are carried over into S, for these subsystems. We can thus analyze the set τ of primes of **T** as follows:

---

[23] $Gr_1(W)$ is the (finite) set of strings of words which are first-order grammatical in terms of syntactic category analysis. μ^W is the (infinite) set of grammatical strings of words, i.e., the set of **W**-markers. We have suggested a way in which $Gr_1(W)$ can be extended to μ^W by means of the descriptive potential of the level **P**. Below we will suggest rather that the major source of this extension lies in the descriptive potential of the level **T**. Recall that in terms of **P** and **T** we may not only extend $Gr_1(W)$, but also drop certain parts of it, in forming μ^W. Hence the statement in the text is not quite correct. We will omit this possibility and the attendant conceptual complications here for the sake of simplifying the exposition (though I do not wish to imply that there are no problems here).

Axiom 1. $\tau = \tau_1 + \tau_2 + \tau_3 + \tau_4$, where

$\tau_1 = \{Z \mid Z$ is a string in $\bar{P}\} + \{\sigma\}$ (cf. §84.1)
$\tau_2 = \{K \mid K$ is a set of strings in $S\}$
$\tau_3 = \{T \mid T$ is a grammatical transformation$\} = \mathscr{T}$
$\tau_4 = \{T \mid T$ is a compound transformation$\}$ (cf. §87.9)

Note that τ_2 contains **P**-markers, and τ_3 contains the mappings $\Phi_i{}^{\mathbf{P}}$, as we have seen in §88. Other special instances of τ_3 are the "identity" transformations which carry each (Z, K) into Z. We will select a single one of these, name it "I," and refer to it henceforth as *the* identity transformation. I can be taken as the transformation with the identity permutation ι as its underlying elementary transformation, and with $Q = \{(U)\}$ as its restricting class. For any $Z \neq U$, $I(Z, K)$ is thus an instance of case II, Definition 10, §83.2. Thus it is always the case that $I(Z, K) = Z$, and that the proper analysis of Z wrt K, $I =$ the proper analysis of $I(Z, K)$ wrt $Z, K, I = (Z)$. I must not be confused with the unit element of **T**. I is a real transformation, which simply has no effect on any pair (Z, K).

In developing the level of phrase structure we were able to begin at once with its algebraic formulation, but before constructing **T** as a level we found ourselves involved in a long discussion of transformations. The reason for this is obvious when we compare the primes of **T** with the primes of **P**. It was pointed out repeatedly in Chapter VII that the primes of **P** have no real content, as we have developed the level **P**. Although we used the notation "Noun Phrase" (*NP*), we had not really defined "Noun Phrase" but only "constituent"; and we decided to label one of the constituents *NP*, though we did not succeed in giving systematic significance to this labeling. But in the preceding discussion we have in a sense actually given the content of the sets τ_3 and τ_4 of primes of **T**. In fact, given an ordering of the strings in S for a particular language, we can, in constructing the transformational level for this language, actually choose from an already given stock of transformations. Thus we know a good deal more about the transformational level than about the phrase level. Here we can, for instance, compare different languages with respect to the actual content of their transformational levels, not only with respect to their formal structure on this level, just as on the phonemic level we can compare phonemic structures in substantial terms (e.g., languages A and B both have voiced stops, etc.). On the phrase level, we must be content with formal comparisons only (e.g., languages A and B have **P**-markers with similar diagrams, in the sense of §53.3ff, etc.).

89.2   Strings in **T** are formed by concatenating the primes of **T**. The question is: how are we to interpret such concatenations? We will interpret strings in **T** in terms of the following correspondence:

110 $Z^\frown K^\frown T$ corresponds to $T(Z, K)$

$T_1^\frown...^\frown T_n$ corresponds to $[T_n ,..., T_1]$ (cf. Definitions 36, 38)

We can now define:

Definition 42. A is a *normal string* of **T** if and only if $A = Z^\frown K^\frown T_1^\frown...^\frown T_n$, where $Z \in \tau_1$, $K \in \tau_2$, $T_i \in \tau_3$ or τ_4.[24]

110 explains how we may understand any normal string, and we may take normal strings to be the only significant strings in **T** (for the moment—we generalize this below, in §91). In particular, then, the **T**-markers will be normal strings. Φ^T is the mapping which assigns **T**-markers to grammatical strings in **W**. Hence Φ^T is defined by **110**. Thus we have

Axiom 2.   Suppose that A is the normal string $Z^\frown K^\frown T_1^\frown...^\frown T_n$. Then $\Phi^T(A) = T_n(...T_1(Z, K))$ (cf. Definition 37).

It is clear that concatenation of transformations is the same as compounding, and that $\Phi^T(A)$ does not depend on the ultimate grammatical transformations into which the terms of the transformational part of A are analyzed. That is,

Theorem 13.   Suppose that $A = Z^\frown K^\frown T_{i_1}^\frown...^\frown T_{i_n}$ and $B = Z^\frown K^\frown T_{j_1}^\frown...^\frown T_{j_m}$, where A and B are normal, and $[T_{i_n},..., T_{i_1}] = [T_{j_m},..., T_{j_1}]$ (cf. Definition 39). Then $\Phi^T(A) = \Phi^T(B)$.

Thus we can set up equivalence classes of **T**-markers differing inessentially, in that the transformational part of one corresponds to the same compound transformation as does the transformational part of the other.

---

[24] We might drop the distinction between τ_3 and τ_4 by interpreting each grammatical transformation T as identical with the one-termed compound $[T]$, thus incorporating τ_3 into τ_4.

Definition 43. Suppose that A and B are normal strings in **T** such that

$$A = Z^\frown K^\frown T_{i_1}{}^\frown ... {}^\frown T_{i_n}$$
$$B = Z^\frown K^\frown T_{j_1}{}^\frown ... {}^\frown T_{j_m}$$

Suppose further that $[T_{i_n}, ..., T_{i_1}] = [T_{j_m}, ..., T_{j_1}]$. Then A and B are *equivalent*.

Equivalent normal strings will then be mapped into the same string in **W** by $\Phi^{\mathbf{T}}$, with the same derived interpretation. However, certain nonequivalent **T**-markers may be mapped into the same string in **W**. Only in the case of identically-mapped nonequivalent **T**-markers is there a real case of structural ambiguity. It is not necessary to distinguish between equivalent **T**-markers in syntactic analysis.

The level **P** is characterized in part by a set $Gr(P)$ of strings in $\bar{P}$. This is exactly the set of products of restricted ρ-derivations (cf. Theorem 4, §53.2), that is, the set of strings which are generated in the grammar reduced (in the sense of §55) from the level **P**.[25] We can define the *kernel* of a language as the subset of grammatical strings of words which is the image of $Gr(P)$ under $\Phi^{\mathbf{P}}$:

89.3

Definition 46. The *kernel* is the set KR of strings such that $Y \in KR$ if and only if there is a Z and a K such that

    (i) $Z \in Gr(P)$
   (ii) K is a **P**-marker of Z
  (iii) $Y = \Phi^{\mathbf{P}}(Z, K)$

Thus the kernel is included in $\mu^{\mathbf{W}}$, but does not in general exhaust $\mu^{\mathbf{W}}$. Our intention in constructing transformational analysis was to limit the kernel to a subset of $\mu^{\mathbf{W}}$, in fact to just that subset for which a simple, systematic, and "optimal" syntactic description can be provided, deriving the other members of $\mu^{\mathbf{W}}$ from the kernel by transformation. Thus for every string in $\mu^{\mathbf{W}}$ but not in the kernel, we must provide a **T**-marker based on a kernel string. We thus place the following condition on the set $\mu^{\mathbf{T}}$ of **T**-markers:

---

[25] Note that a string outside of $Gr(P)$ may still have a **P**-marker, for **P**-markers are based on equivalence classes of ρ-derivations which need not be restricted ρ-derivations. This is important, because it means that some transformationally derived strings may have **P**-markers, i.e., they may be closer structurally to kernel strings than are other derived strings. The case of the passive, discussed above in §87.2, is one important instance of this.

Axiom 3. $\mu^{\mathbf{T}}$ is a set of strings $\{A_i\}$ such that

(i) A_i is a normal string of **T**.
(ii) $A_i = Z^\frown K^\frown...$, where $Z \in Gr(P)$, and K is a **P**-marker of Z.
(iii) If Z is not in the kernel, then $Z \in \mu^{\mathbf{W}}$ if and only if there is an $A_i \in \mu^{\mathbf{T}}$ such that $\Phi^{\mathbf{T}}(A_i) = Z$.

For every Z in the kernel, there is in fact a string A_i meeting (i) and (ii) and such that $\Phi^{\mathbf{T}}(A_i) = Z$, namely,

111 $A_i = \bar{Z}^\frown K^\frown \Phi^{\mathbf{P}}$, for some $\bar{Z}$ and K

Hence we might alternatively drop the antecedent of (ii) in Axiom 3 and add all strings **111** (with a proper choice of $\bar{Z}$, K) to $\mu^{\mathbf{T}}$.

In order for Axiom 3 to be met, it will be necessary to give an extremely complicated characterization of $\mu^{\mathbf{T}}$ as matters now stand. Below, in §91, we will generalize the algebra of **T** in such a way as to permit Axiom 3 to be met significantly.

89.4 In §88.3 we noted that each transformation T applies to the ψ_k-transform, for some k, of a string Z. And the transformation operation is completed by continuing to apply the mappings $\Phi^{\mathbf{P}}_{k+1}$, $\Phi^{\mathbf{P}}_{k+2}$,... until the result is a string in **W**. Thus the typical **T**-marker will be of the form

112 $Z^\frown K^\frown \psi_k^\frown T^\frown \psi_k'$

if T is a transformation applying to ψ_k-transforms. Suppose now that T_1 applies to ψ_k-transforms, and T_2 applies to ψ_{k+j}-transforms, and that we wish to apply T_2 after T_1 to form a compound transformation. The corresponding **T**-marker will be

113 $Z^\frown K^\frown \psi_k^\frown T_1^\frown \Phi^{\mathbf{P}}_{k+1}{}^\frown...^\frown \Phi^{\mathbf{P}}_{k+j}{}^\frown T_2^\frown \psi_{k+j}'$

Continuing to more general cases, it certainly seems reasonable to impose further conditions on normal strings in terms of the distribution of mappings $\Phi_i^{\mathbf{P}}$ in these strings. Because of the potential trouble spot mentioned in §88.3, any condition we set is somewhat suspect. But it will be inconvenient to carry out an actual description of transformational structure without setting some condition. We will impose, tentatively, the strong condition that the segments of $\Phi^{\mathbf{P}}$ must be found as a unique substring of a normal string.

The notations ψ_k and ψ_k' introduced in §88.2 are significant only in terms of a fixed decomposition of Φ^P into $[\Phi^P_{m+1},\dots,\Phi_1^P]$. Hence any use of these notations presupposes a fixed decomposition. In practice, there will for any language be only a single decomposition of Φ^P to which reference will ever be made in constructing the grammar, since if alternative decompositions are utilized, they must be independently stated, thus increasing the complexity of the grammar. Though this is not absolutely necessary, it would be quite possible to propose the uniqueness of this decomposition as a condition on that part of the grammar of phrase structure that deals with mappings. (It will be recalled that there was a gap in our formulation of the requirements for grammars just at this point—cf. §56.5.) In any event, we assume here a fixed decomposition of Φ^P into $[\Phi^P_{m+1},\dots,\Phi_1^P]$, where $\Phi^P_{m+1} = \Phi\overline{\mathbf{M}}$ (cf. §88.2), and the discussion is relative to this assumption.

Definition 45. T is a *component* of Φ^P if and only if for some i, j such that $1 \leqslant i \leqslant i + j \leqslant m + 1$, $T = [\Phi^P_{i+j},\dots,\Phi_i^P]$.

In particular, given an analysis of Φ^P as assumed, ψ_k and ψ_k' are components of Φ^P. We see that components of Φ^P play a special role in **T** in that they provide, in a sense, a certain skeletal structure for **T** markers.

Definition 46. Suppose that A is a string in **T**. Then $(T_1,\dots,T_k)$ is a *Φ^P-skeleton* of A if and only if

    (i) $\Phi^P = [T_k,\dots,T_1]$.

    (ii) Each T_i is a component of Φ^P.

    (iii) There are strings $X_1,\dots,X_{k+1}$ in **T** such that $A = X_1 ^\frown T_1 ^\frown X_2 ^\frown \dots ^\frown X_k ^\frown T_k ^\frown X_{k+1}$.

Axiom 4. A string of μ^T has a unique Φ^P-skeleton.

The definitions and axioms of §89 will be generalized and elaborated below in §91.

The level **T** is established primarily in order to enable us to avoid the vast complexity and inelegance which is the necessary consequence of any attempt to state μ^W directly and exhaustively in terms of phrase structure. The grammatical statement of **T** for a given language will contain a specification of the strings in **T** which are **T**-markers of strings of μ^W, and the characterization of those transformations that appear in these strings. The latter will be effected by stating, for each transformation, its underlying elementary transformation t and its restricting class Q. We have discussed the form of this characterization above. If the transformation in question is compound, we describe it in terms of a sequence of its noncompound components of $\mathscr{T}$. A grammar containing a level **P** and a level **T** is thus evaluated by considering its total simplicity. In practice this means that for each class of strings of μ^{W}, we must decide whether or not the strings in question belong to the kernel by determining the relative complexity of deriving them by ρ-derivation in **P**, or by a transformational analysis. Again, we have at best an evaluation procedure, since simplicity is a measure that applies to a complete grammar. For this evaluation procedure to be significant, it is necessary, actually, to prescribe a fixed form of grammatical statement for the level **T**, just as we did for **P**. We will not go into this in detail, though certain reductions will be described in the next two sections. To do so would duplicate a large portion of the discussion already given, and at this early stage of the study of transformational analysis, there are many tasks that seem more immediately important. In actually applying transformational analysis to English, as a test case, we will drop sentences from the kernel only when it is quite clear that with any reasonable definition of the form of grammatical statement for **T**, the transformational analysis is simpler. See also §93, below, in this connection.

89.6   We have interpreted transformational analysis as adding a new level of linguistic structure, having the same status as other levels. There are arguments for and against such an interpretation. As levels are characterized abstractly in Chapter III, transformational analysis can be put into the form of a linguistic level, as we have just seen. The level **T** is clearly quite different, however, in many respects, from the lower levels that we have described. For one thing, there is no relation between "left-to-right" order in strings in **T** and temporal order of sounds in the represented utterance. On the other hand, as we have seen, this is too strong a requirement even for other levels. But it is true that on no other level is there so little relation between order of representation and temporal order.

There are several considerations in favor of considering transformational structure to constitute a linguistic level, beyond the trivial and purely formal fact that it can be considered to have the basic form of a concatenation algebra. For one thing, this treatment adds considerably to the unity of linguistic theory. Just as we can represent each utterance by a sequence of phonemes, morphemes, words, and phrases, we can represent each utterance by a sequence of operations by which it is derived from a kernel sentence (more correctly, from a string in $Gr(P)$ which is mapped by Φ^P into a kernel sentence). The most convincing support for the treatment of transformational analysis in this manner lies in the extension of the notion of constructional homonymity that results automatically from this treatment. Just as we have the possibility of multiple representation on every other level, we have, on the level **T**, the possibility of assigning several **T**-markers to a given sentence. We will see below that assignment of multiple analyses on the level **T** has the same effect as constructional homonymity on any other level, namely, ambiguity of interpretation of the sentences which fall in the overlap of the distinct structural patterns provided by distinct markers. Finally, we will see below, in §91, that the interpretation of **T** as a concatenation algebra leads to a quite natural and effective generalization of transformations, with little extra machinery needed.

This theory of transformations has been based on a conception of 90.1 transformations as single-valued mappings. There are, however, many cases in which any one of a certain set of elements in a sentence is a sentence is subject to what is essentially the same transformation. Thus any constituent C can be replaced by $C^\frown and^\frown C$ (with certain qualifications). Or, more narrowly, any Noun Phrase in a sentence (again with certain qualifications) can be replaced by the element "who" (or "what," depending on what sort of Noun Phrase it is) which is placed at the beginning of the sentence to form a question. For example, given "I saw John reading a book," we have "whom did I see reading a book," "what did I see John reading," etc. We will find it quite useful to have at hand a method for indicating briefly that a certain transformation applies, in some sense, to all elements of a certain kind in a sentence. As matters now stand, the uniqueness condition on transformations requires that to convey this we must construct a whole set of transformations separately, one for each occurrence of the element in question (constituents in the first example, Noun Phrases in the second). The inconvenience of this (and the complexity to which it leads in the statement of the grammatical strings in **T**) leads us to the notion of a family of transformations. By a family of transformations we will mean a set of grammatical transformations, all with the same underlying transformation, and all having restricting classes meeting some fixed condition.

Definition 47. A *family F* of transformations is defined by an ordered pair (C, t), where C is a condition on r elements (i.e., a schema $C(\alpha_1, ..., \alpha_r)$ with $\alpha_1, ..., \alpha_r$ as its only free variables), and t is an elementary transformation. T is a member of the family F if and only if

(i) T is a grammatical transformation;

(ii) t is the elementary transformation underlying T;

(iii) if $Q = \{(W_1^{(i)},..., W_n^{(i)}) \mid 1 \leqslant i \leqslant N_Q\}$ is the restricting class for T, then $n = r$ and for each i, $C(W_1^{(i)},..., W_r^{(i)})$ (i.e., the terms of the restricting class, in the given order meet the condition C).

Thus C is a condition that the restricting classes of a transformation must meet to belong to F. Since a transformation is determined by an ordered pair (Q, t), it is thus also determined by a properly chosen (C, t) (though in this case, of course, determination is not in general unique).

Since it will in general be much simpler to give the condition C than to spell out in detail what the restricting class must be so as both to meet C and at the same time to define a grammatical transformation, this notion can lead to an essential simplification in the statement of the grammar of **T**, whenever it is the case that there is a set of **T**-markers that differ from one another only by members of a family F. In such a case, we can simply state the pair (C, t) corresponding to F and assert that any string containing a $T_i \in F$ in the proper position is a **T**-marker, without having to actually state these transformations T_i separately and explicitly. We have not developed a rigid form of grammatical statement for the transformational level. If we were to go on to do so, we would introduce a notational convention permitting us to list "...F...," where F is a family of transformations, in the list of **T**-markers in place of the set of statements "...T_i...," where $T_i \in F$. Naturally, this simplification permits many more transformations to appear in this position than would be permitted by an exhaustive list, since many transformations that it would have been unnecessary to define will meet the condition C. But this is a harmless duplication. No new sentences will be generated if C is properly chosen.

The introduction of the concept of "family" plays the same role on the level **T** that the reductions of §55 played on the level **P**. By permitting us merely to give the conditions that transformations must meet to appear in **T**-markers, this development leads to a considerable simplification of the statement of the grammar of **T**.

90.2   Axiom 3 requires that each **T**-marker be a string of the form $Z^\frown K^\frown...,$ where $Z \in Gr(P)$, i.e., where Z is actually derived on the level **P**. It is possible to develop another reduction of the grammar of **T** which will enable us to include in the list of **T**-markers strings in **T** that begin with a string $Z \notin Gr(P)$, it being understood that Z must be derived by one of the other transformational statements. This could always be avoided by giving a compound transformation instead, but only at the cost of some complexity. We will give this reduction in a more detailed and satisfactory form as a part of a more generalized characterization of μ^{T} below (as condition 4, §91.4).

A grammatical transformation, as we have defined it, converts a string 91.1 interpreted in a certain way into a second string with a derived interpretation. An investigation of the problems that motivated transformational analysis reveals certain inadequacies in this conception. Such sentences as

114   (a)   *that John was unhappy was quite obvious*
       (b)   *the men who lost their jobs were bitter*
       (c)   *since John liked the book, I decided to give it to him*
       (d)   *John read the book and enjoyed it thoroughly*

are evidently instances of sentences constructed transformationally from a pair of kernel sentences. This suggests the need for a generalization of the notion of transformation to include transformations defined on n-ads of sentences (more correctly, n-ads of pairs of a string Z and an interpretation K).

It may be that the best approach to this problem would be a direct and independent definition of generalized transformations; we will approach the problem, however, in a different way, extending the notions developed above. We will do this by stating a set of conditions which can be regarded as an extension of the axiom system for **P** and **T**. This extension actually necessitates some minor readjustments in the axioms that have already been given. These are fairly obvious, and we will not trouble to indicate them.

One way to generate a transform from two given sentences, within our present framework, is to run the two sentences together into a single long sentence and apply a transformation to this new compounded sentence. Given (Z_1, K_1) and (Z_2, K_2), we can form (Z_3, K_3), where Z is $Z_1 \frown Z_2$, and K_3 is essentially the Cartesian product of K_1 and K_2 (i.e., it is the set of strings that contains $X_1 \frown X_2$, wherever $X_1 \in K_1$, $X_2 \in K_2$). To avoid ambiguity, however, we must indicate in Z_3 and in the strings that make up K_3 exactly where the break between the two sentences lies. Thus we add to the set of primes of the system S (cf.

§89.1) an element #, indicating sentence boundary, and we extend the set $Gr(P)$ to include complex strings containing #.[26]

Condition 1. There is an element $\# \in \bar{P}$. There are no strings X_1, X_2, X_3 such that X_1 is a prime of **P** and $\rho(X_1, X_2 \frown \# \frown X_3)$.

Condition 2. If Z_1, $Z_2 \in Gr(P)$, then $Z_1 \frown \# \frown Z_2 \in Gr(P)$.

Definition 47. $Z_1 \frown \# \frown Z_2$ is a *complex string*.

Since Condition 2 is recursive, $Gr(P)$ can include strings with any number of occurrences of #. Thus $Gr(P)$ consists of strings with restricted ρ_1-derivations, and complex strings whose ultimate components are the products of such derivations.

Given this extension, we can find transformations which will give **114** when applied to complex strings in $Gr(P)$, and we can construct normal strings as **T**-markers of these sentences. The strings of $Gr(P)$ from which **114** are derived might be

115   (a)   *John was unhappy # it was quite obvious*
        (b)   *the men were bitter # the men lost their jobs*
        (c)   *John liked the book # I decided to give it to him*
        (d)   *John read the book # John enjoyed it*[27] *thoroughly*

In all cases but (c), the transformation will presumably drop the element #. In case (c) this can be retained as an intonation marker. We have pointed out several times that a major deficiency of our constructions is their failure to cover suprasegmental features such as pitch, stress, and juncture. If these constructions were somehow extended to cover this aspect of grammar, then # would be one of a set of juncture elements of a considerably wider distribution and playing a much more central role in the grammatical description, and the element # would thus lose its special and unique character.[28]

Since generalized transformations are, in terms of this construction, simply special cases of grammatical transformations, the notions of derived constituent structure, family of transformations, etc., carry over without special comment.

---

[26] The new prime # is what was designated J in §55.2.

[27] Or we may have "the book" in place of "it," as we shall see below.

[28] For a study of the grammatical role of junctures, see Chomsky, Halle, and Lukoff, "On accent and juncture in English."

We can now account for such sentences as **114**a with a transformation   91.2
T_{th} which carries any instance of **116** into the corresponding case of **117**:

116   *Sentence–#–it–was$^\frown$quite$^\frown$obvious*

117   *that$^\frown$Sentence–was$^\frown$quite$^\frown$obvious*

We then have a single statement to the effect that any string of the
form **118** is a **T**-marker:

118 $Z^\frown K^\frown T_{th}$, where the $\Phi^\mathbf{P}$-skeleton is to be properly inserted.

This is oversimplified, and a good deal more generalization is
possible. But the improvement brought about by the development of
generalized transformations should be clear.

Note that T_{th} here has the restricting class **116** (which can obviously
be generalized beyond "was quite obvious") and at the present stage
of development of the theory, it appears to be based on an elementary
transformation which is the compound of a substitution t_s and a deformation δ, where

119 $\delta:\quad Y_1-Y_2-Y_3-Y_4 \rightarrow that^\frown Y_1-Y_2-Y_3-Y_4$
$\qquad t_s:\quad Z_1-Z_2-Z_3-Z_4 \rightarrow U-U-Z_1-Z_4 = Z_1-Z_4$
$\qquad t_s(\delta):\quad Y_1-Y_2-Y_3-Y_4 \rightarrow U-U-that^\frown Y_1-Y_4 = that^\frown Y_1-Y_4$

In the case of **115**a, $Y_1 =$ "John was unhappy," $Y_2 = \#$, $Y_3 =$ "it,"
and "$Y_4 =$ "was quite obvious."

We have discussed the derived constituent structure of such
sentences above in §87.5, (i), pointing out that "that John was unhappy"
is the *NP*-subject of **114**a since it substitutes for "it" of "it was quite
obvious."

Even though generalized transformations offer a considerable improve-   91.3
ment, certain artificialities in the treatment of more complicated cases
still remain and indicate the need for a further development.

Before going on to discuss these inadequacies, we define more
carefully what we mean by the interpretation of a complex string.

Definition 48. If K_1 and K_2 are classes of strings, then $K_1 * K_2$ is
the class of strings $Y^\frown \#^\frown Z$, where $Y \in K_1$ and $Z \in K_2$.

Thus $K_1 * K_2$ is the interpretation of the complex string $Z_1 \frown \# \frown Z_2$, where K_1 is the interpretation of Z_1, and K_2 is the interpretation of Z_2.

The remaining deficiencies in our conception of generalized tranformations become most clear when compounding of transformations is required. We illustrate this by an example:

120   Suppose that

> $Z_1 =$ "they had found John"; K_1 is the **P**-marker of Z_1;
> $Z_2 =$ "it was quite obvious"; K_2 is the **P**-marker of Z_2;
> T_{th} is the transformation described above with **116** as restricting class, and $t_s(\delta)$ of **119** as underlying transformation.

> Suppose further that we have a transformation T such that $Z_3 = T(Z_1, K_1) =$ "John had been found"; K_3 is the derived interpretation of Z_3 wrt Z_1, K_1, T.

It should clearly be the case that

121   *that they had found John was obvious*

122   *that John had been found was obvious*

are derived in essentially the same way, by **T**-markers of the form **118**. That is, the **T**-marker of **121** should be

123 $(Z_1 \frown \# \frown Z_2) \frown (K_1 * K_2) \frown T_{th}{}^{29}$

and the **T**-marker of **122**, analogously, should be

124 $(Z_3 \frown \# \frown Z_2) \frown (K_3 * K_2) \frown T_{th}$

But $Z_3 \frown \# \frown Z_2 \notin Gr(P)$, since Z_3 is derived by the transformation T. Thus **124** does not qualify as a **T**-marker (cf. Axiom 3, §89.3). This

---

[29] We must be careful to distinguish concatenation in **P** from concatenation in **T**. Within the parentheses we have concatenation in **P** (more generally, in the system S which incorporates **P**, $\overline{\mathbf{M}}$, and **W**). The parenthesized terms are primes of **T**, and concatenation between parenthesized expressions in **123** and **124** is concatenation in **T**. Thus these parentheses cannot be dropped, since different concatenation operations (which could be differently symbolized) are involved. We omit the Φ^P-skeleton, as in **118**.

means that we must construct a new and distinct transformation T' which combines features of T_{th} and T of **120**, and then we must derive **122** by a **T**-marker:

125 $(Z_1 \frown \# \frown Z_2) \frown (K_1 * K_2) \frown T'$

But this is obviously unsatisfactory. This treatment fails to indicate the intuitively obvious fact that **121** is derived from Z_1 in the same way that **122** is derived from Z_3. It should be possible to give a uniform treatment of **121** and **122** in terms of the transformations T and T_{th} which are independently necessary, thus dispensing with the new and *ad hoc* transformation T'.

This difficulty might be avoided in the manner of §90.2 by defining an appropriate reduction in the grammar which would allow us to state **124** in the list of **T**-markers, it being understood that Z_3 is derived by another transformation. Alternatively, the difficulty can be avoided by extending the class of normal strings to include strings of the form

126 $Z_1 \frown K_1 \frown T - Z_2 \frown K_2 - T_{th}$

which in the case of **120** will be interpreted as applying T_{th} to the string $T(Z_1, K_1) \frown \# \frown Z_2$ with the interpretation $K_3 * K_2$. We will first exploit this approach, returning to the suggestion of §90.2 below.

We now proceed to extend Definition 42, §89.2, permitting "T_i" in this definition to be replaced by "$Z_i \frown K_i \frown T_i$." Definition 42 is now superseded by

Definition 49. *A* is a *normal* string in **T** if and only if $A = S_1 \frown ... \frown S_n$ ($n \geqslant 1$), where

(i) $S_1 = Z_1 \frown K_1 \frown T_1$
(ii) $S_1 = Z_i \frown K_i \frown T_i$ or $S_i = T_i$, where $Z_i \in \tau_1$, $K_i \in \tau_2$, $T_i \in \tau_3 + \tau_4$[30]

Thus **126** must be rewritten with the identity transformation I as

127 $Z_1 \frown K_1 \frown T \frown Z_2 \frown K_2 \frown I \frown T_{th}$

and interpreted as applying T_{th} to $T(Z_1, K_1) \frown \# \frown I(Z_2, K_2) = T(Z_1, K_1) \frown \# \frown Z_2$, just as before. The normal strings of Definition 42

[30] See Axiom 1, §89.1, and Note 24.

are special cases of the normal strings of Definition 49, with each $S_i = T_i$, for $i > 1$.

We must now replace Axiom 2, §89.2, by a more general statement covering normal strings as defined in Definition 49, and supplying the interpretation for **126** and **127** that we have informally described. Before rephrasing Axiom 2 for the more general case, we define the *value* of a normal string:

Definition 50. Let $A_n = S_1 \frown ... \frown S_n$ be a normal string, where $S_1 ,..., S_n$ are as in (i), (ii), Definition 49. For $m \leqslant n$, we define the *value* of $S_1 \frown ... \frown S_m$ $[= Val(S_1 \frown ... \frown S_m)]$ as the ordered pair $(Z_m{}' , K_m{}')$, where

> *Case I:* $m = 1$
>> $Z_m{}' = T_1(Z_1 , K_1)$
>> $K_m{}'$ is the derived interpretation of $Z_m{}'$ wrt Z_1, K_1, T_1 (cf. Definition 35, Theorem 11, §87.8)

> *Case II:* $m > 1, S_m = T_m$
>> $Z_m{}' = T_m(Z'_{m-1} , K'_{m-1})$
>> $K_m{}'$ is the derived interpretation of $Z_m{}'$ wrt Z'_{m-1}, K'_{m-1}, T_m

> *Case III:* $m > 1, S_m = Z_m \frown K_m \frown T_m$
>> $Z_m{}' = Z'_{m-1} \frown \# \frown T_m(Z_m , K_m)$
>> $K_m{}' = K'_{m-1} * \overline{K}_m$, where $\overline{K}_m$ is the derived interpretation of $T_m(Z_m , K_m)$ wrt Z_m, K_m, T_m

In all cases, we denote $Z_m{}'$ by "$Val_1(S_1 \frown ... \frown S_m)$" and $K_m{}'$ by "$Val_2(S_1 \frown ... \frown S_m)$."

Replacing Axiom 2, §89.2, we have

Condition 3.   If A_n is a normal string, then $\Phi^T(A_n) = Val_1(A_n)$.

We regard Φ^T as undefined for nonnormal strings in **T**. Since a normal string can be analyzed in only one way as $S_1 \frown ... \frown S_n$ such that (i), (ii), Definition 49, it follows that $\Phi^T(A_n)$ is unambiguous.

As an example of Definition 50 and Condition 3, let $A_n = $ **127**. Then $n = 3$, and $A_n = S_1 \frown S_2 \frown S_3$, where

128 $S_1 = Z_1 \frown K_1 \frown T$
    $S_2 = Z_2 \frown K_2 \frown I$
    $S_3 = T_{th}$

Then we have the following set of values:

129　　$Val_1(S_1) = T(Z_1, K_1) = Z_3$　　(cf. **120**)
　　　　$Val_2(S_1) = K_3$　　　　　　　(cf. **120**)

Thus $Val(S_1) = (Z_3, K_3)$

$Val_1(S_1 \frown S_2) = Z_3 \frown \# \frown I(Z_2, K_2) = Z_3 \frown \# \frown Z_2$
$Val_2(S_1 \frown S_2) = K_3 * K_4$ (where $K_4 \subset K_2$ is just the relevant part of K_2—cf. Theorem 11, §87.8).

Thus $Val(S_1 \frown S_2) = (Z_3 \frown \# \frown Z_2, K_3 * K_4)$

$Val_1(A_n) = Val_1(S_1 \frown S_2 \frown S_3) = T_{th}(Z_3 \frown \# \frown Z_2, K_3 * K_4)$.

Therefore $\Phi^T(A_n) = T_{th}(Z_3 \frown \# \frown Z_2, K_3 * K_4)$, just as in the informal account given above.

Condition 3 contains Axiom 2 as a special case.

In §89.2, after defining Φ^T implicitly by Axiom 2, we went on (Definition 43) to define equivalence classes of **T**-markers with equivalent transformational parts. This was important, since it is necessary to state that we have constructional homonymity on the level **T** only when we have *nonequivalent* **T**-markers A and B such that $\Phi^T(A) = \Phi^T(B)$. Definition 50 permits new cases of normal strings that are mapped into the same string in **W** by Φ^T for reasons inherent in the construction of these strings in **T** and having nothing to do with the language under analysis. The discussion of equivalence of **T**-markers is facilitated when we note that each normal string A has a substring $Z_1 \frown K_1 \frown ... \frown Z_2 \frown K_2 \frown ... \frown Z_n \frown K_n$ consisting of the strings in $\bar{P}$ on which it is based and their interpretations, and a substring $...Y_1...Y_2...Y_n$ consisting of the transformations that appear in A.

Definition 51. Let A be a normal string in **T**. Then the **P**-*basis* of A is the maximal sequence $((Z_1, K_1),..., (Z_n, K_n))$ such that

    (i) $Z_i \in \tau_1$　　(i.e., Z_i is a string in $\bar{P}$);
    (ii) $K_i \in \tau_2$　　(i.e., K_i is a set of strings);
    (iii) there is a $Y_1,..., Y_n$ such that $A = Z_1 \frown K_1 \frown Y_1 \frown Z_2 \frown K_2 \frown Y_2 \frown ... \frown Z_n \frown K_n \frown Y_n$. In this case, $(Y_1,..., Y_n)$ is called the *transformational part* of A.

Theorem 14. The **P**-basis and the transformational part of a normal string exist and are unique.

In a direct generalization of Definition 43, §89.2, we might say that two normal strings with the same **P**-basis are equivalent if, term by term, their transformational parts correspond to equivalent transformations (in the sense of Definition 41, §88.2). But this characterization of equivalence will still permit cases of nonequivalent multiple **T**-markers which, because of their universality, do not mark genuine homonymity.

Suppose that

130 $Z = Z_1 {}^\frown \# {}^\frown Z_2 \,; Z_1 \,, Z_2 \in Gr(P)$
K_1 is the interpretation of Z_1, and K_2 of Z_2
$K = K_1 * K_2$
$T(Z, K)$ is a string of words

As **T**-markers of $T(Z, K)$ we may have, among others

131   (i) $Z {}^\frown K {}^\frown T$
(ii) $Z_1 {}^\frown K_1 {}^\frown I {}^\frown Z_2 {}^\frown K_2 {}^\frown I {}^\frown T$

(i) is an instance of the normal string $A_1 = S_1$; (ii) is an instance of $A_3 = S_1 {}^\frown S_2 {}^\frown S_3$, where $S_1 = Z_1 {}^\frown K_1 {}^\frown I$, $S_2 = Z_2 {}^\frown K_2 {}^\frown I$, and $S_3 = T$. In general then, two **T**-markers present a legitimate case of constructional homonymity only if under all substitutions of strings and interpretations for the noncomplex components of these **T**-markers, the same string in **W** results by Φ^T. We could go on to formalize this condition. Though fairly obvious, it is involved; we will bypass this construction, merely noting that in practice, considerations of simplicity of grammar will generally militate against the admission of equivalent **T**-markers into μ^T.

91.4   The extension of the class of normal strings by Definition 49 enables us to give a more elegant characterization of μ^T in particular cases, by extending the possibilities of transformational treatment in what seems a natural way. We can, in terms of it, give a more adequate condition on μ^T. Axiom 3, §89.3, will be replaced by Condition 4, which incorporates generalized transformations and certain other simplifications (e.g., §90.2).

The most direct way to generalize Axiom 3 would be to require that each term $(Z_i \,, K_i)$ of the **P**-basis of a **T**-marker must meet (ii), Axiom 3; i.e., that each Z_i be in $Gr(P)$ with K_i as its **P**-marker. But this condition (call it "condition C") would lead to certain artificialities and complications that are not resolved by the generalization carried through by Definition 49.

Suppose that we have a normal string $A = S_1 ^\frown ... ^\frown S_n$, with $S_j = Z_i ^\frown K_i ^\frown T_i$ and $S_{i+1} = T_{i+1}$ for a certain $i < n$. Thus T_{i+1} is a generalized transformation operating on the string

132 $\quad Val_1(S_1 ^\frown ... ^\frown S_{i-1}) ^\frown \# ^\frown T_i(Z_i, K_i)$ (cf. Case III, Definition 50)

The suggested generalization of Axiom 3 would require that Z_i, in this case, must be in $Gr(P)$, thus that T_i be a compound transformation incorporating the changes that (Z_i, K_i) undergoes before T_{i+1} applies to it. For each of the possible transformational developments of (Z_i, K_i), a different T_i must be given.

Suppose further that there are transformations $V_1, ..., V_r$ such that all combinations $V_1(Z_i, K_i)$, $V_2(Z_i, K_i), ..., V_r(Z_i, K_i)$, $V_2(V_1(Z_i, K_i))$, $V_3(V_1(Z_i, K_i)), ..., V_r(V_1(Z_i, K_i))$, etc., can occur significantly on the level **T**. In other words, in stating the grammar of **T** we will provide that any string of the form

133 $\quad Z_i ^\frown K_i \langle V_1 \rangle \langle V_2 \rangle ... \langle V_r \rangle$

is in μ^T, where the angle notation is carried over from earlier chapters (cf. §§27, 30), with the emendation that at least one of $V_1, ..., V_r$ must occur.[31]

Suppose now that T_{i+1} can apply not only to **132**, but to any string

134 $\quad Val_1(S_1 ^\frown ... ^\frown S_{i-1}) ^\frown \# ^\frown X_i$

where X_i is given by one of the strings generated by **133**. Then we will be forced to state, alongside of A, a large number (in this case, $2^r - 1$) of **T**-markers differing only in that in place of T_i they have some transformation corresponding to one of the cases of **133**. This is not only overly complicated, but also repetitious in a way we would like to avoid, since all of **133** will essentially be repeated, case by case, in describing this set of **T**-markers.

But this case is actually the rule. Very often a generalized transformation will apply when various transforms appear as components of the complex string to which it applies. This suggests that we relax condition C, and require merely that each Z_i in the **P**-basis be either a string in $Gr(P)$ or be $\Phi^T(X)$, for some **T**-marker X. This relaxation of condition C gives §90.2 as a special case.

---

[31] The same emendation was made in Chapter VIII (cf. Note 9, Chapter VIII).

There are reasons for relaxing condition C still further. Typically, a **T**-marker $A = S_1 \frown ... \frown S_n$ will have $S_n = \psi_k'$. That is, its final term will be the remainder of the mapping Φ^P (see §88). We have not found it necessary to state this as a special case, since ψ_k' is itself a transformation. But it is clear from investigation of the motives for transformational analysis that this is typical, and that S_n will fail to be ψ_k' (for some k) only if the mapping Φ^P has been completed before S_n is applied, i.e., if the transformation S_n applies to strings of words.[32] We might say then that the correct ψ_k' is automatically added on to each **T**-marker, to convert the transform into a string in **W**. When a term (Z, K) appears in the **P**-basis of a **T**-marker, we expect Z to be not $\Phi^T(X)$, for some **T**-marker X, but rather $\Phi^T(Y)$, where $X = Y \frown \psi_k'$ is a **T**-marker. In other words, the components of a complex string will not ordinarily be mapped completely into words. In this case we will call Y the *reduced correlate* of the **T**-marker X.

Definition 52. If $A = S_1 \frown ... \frown S_n$ is a normal string, and for some k, $S_n = \psi_k'$, then we define the *reduced correlate* of A as $A^{\text{red}} = S_1 \frown ... \frown S_{n-1}$.

Replacing Axiom 3 §89.3, we now have

Condition 4. μ^T is a set of strings $\{X_i\}$ in **T** such that

(i) X_i is normal;
(ii) for each i, if $((Z_1, K_1),..., (Z_m, K_m))$ is the **P**-basis of X_i, then for each $j \leqslant m$, either

        (a) $Z_j \in Gr(P)$, and K_j is a **P**-marker of Z_j

or

        (b) $(Z_j, K_j) = Val(Z^{\text{red}})$, where Z^{red} is the reduced correlate of some $Z \in \mu^T$;

(iii) $Y \in \mu^W$ if and only if there is an $X_i \in \mu^T$ such that $\Phi^T(X_i) = Y$.

Note that with this construction, a nonkernel string of μ^W need not have a **T**-marker based on kernel strings,[33] though it will always have a **T**-marker with a **P**-basis the elements of which derive ultimately

---

[32] Note that **T**-markers will normally end with $S_n = T_n$, although we have not required this. If they fail to, then the result given by the **T**-marker in question will be a complex string containing # rather than a string of words. Note also (cf. §89.4) that we assume throughout a fixed decomposition of Φ^P into $\Phi^P_{m+1},..., \Phi_1^P$.

[33] Literally, based on the preimages under Φ^P of kernel strings.

from strings of $Gr(P)$. Every string in $\mu^{\mathbf{W}}$ has a **T**-marker, kernel strings having the **T**-marker $Z^\frown K^\frown \Phi^{\mathbf{P}}$, where $Z \in Gr(P)$. We might proceed now to define the class of branched structures—which in an obvious way can be represented in linear form—that give the complete record of the derivation of a string ultimately from strings of $Gr(P)$, and we might take these structures to be the **T**-markers. We will not take this course here, limiting our attention rather to the elements defined by Condition 4.

The set of **T**-markers may be infinite; as we shall see, there are even reasons for *limiting* the recursive property of the grammar to the level **T**. Therefore we still face the problem, analogous to the problem of reduction discussed in §55 in connection with the level **P**, of giving a finite characterization of the set of **T**-markers. Consider the set of strings derived from normal strings by replacing terms of the **P**-basis by appropriate variables. Then a finite set of these strings may characterize an infinite set of **T**-markers, where these are defined as in Condition 4; this remains true even when $Gr(P)$ is finite, as we will later assume. We will make the assumption that the level **T** can be finitely characterized in this way, that is, that along these lines we can establish the required relation between the level **T** and a finite grammar.

The structural characterization of normal strings begun in §89.4 must **91.5** be generalized to include the new cases of normal strings permitted by Definition 49, with Axiom 4 retained as a special case in this extension. Partly because of the difficulties pointed out in §88.3, I am not quite sure how this extension should be carried out. Unless some such condition is laid down, however, the definition of $\mu^{\mathbf{T}}$ given above will be too broad—far too many strings will be permitted to enter $\mu^{\mathbf{T}}$ and an important feature of abstract transformational structure will be omitted.

There are two ways of proceeding at this point. We may simply apply this system as given above to language without laying down further restricting conditions on normal strings, using *ad hoc* measures in each particular case to make sure that no complication arises. Since $\mu^{\mathbf{T}}$ as characterized above is too broad, we can be sure that nothing will be left out by this procedure. Or we may attempt to lay down a restricting condition on normal strings in the manner of §89.4, but generalized, and we may then apply the system within the limits of this restriction. We can thus determine, for any particular suggested restriction on normal strings, just what is the cost, for a particular grammar, of setting up this restriction in the general theory. Since ultimately some such restriction will be necessary, I think that the latter course will be more interesting. We will thus go on to develop what seems to be the most natural generalization of Axiom 4.

Condition 5. Suppose that

    (i) $A = S_1 \frown ... \frown S_n$ is a normal string in **T**, where the S_i are such that (i), (ii), Definition 49, §91.3

    (ii) $A \in \mu^{\mathbf{T}}$

    (iii) $S_{n+1} = U$

    (iv) $Y_1, ..., Y_{r+1}$ is a subsequence of $S_1, ..., S_n, S_{n+1}$ such that

        (a) S_i is one of $Y_1, ..., Y_r$ if and only if S_i is a component of $\Phi^{\mathbf{P}}$

        (b) $Y_{r+1} = S_{n+1} = U$

    (v) $S_t \frown S_{t+1} \frown ... \frown S_{t+j}$ is a segment of A, where for some $k \leqslant r + 1$

        (a) $S_{t+j} = Y_k$

        (b) $1 \leqslant t < t + j \leqslant n + 1$

        (c) If $t > 1$, then $S_{t-1} = Y_{k-1}$

        (d) $S_{t+i} = T_{t+i}$ or $Z_{t+i} \frown K_{t+i} \frown T_{t+i}$ for $0 \leqslant i < j$

Then for each i such that $S_{t+i} = Z_{t+i} \frown K_{t+i} \frown T_{t+i}$, either (I) or (II):

    (I) $Z_{t+i} \in Gr(P)$, and $T_{t+i} \frown Y_k \frown Y_{k+1} \frown ... \frown Y_{r+1}$ contains a $\Phi^{\mathbf{P}}$-skeleton (cf. Definition 46, §89.4)

    (II) $Z_{t+i} = Val_1(Z^{\mathrm{red}})$, where Z^{red} is the reduced correlate of some $Z \in \mu^{\mathbf{T}}$, and $Z^{\mathrm{red}} \frown T_{t+i} \frown Y_k \frown Y_{k+1} \frown ... \frown Y_{r+1}$ contains a unique $\Phi^{\mathbf{P}}$-skeleton [34]

Thus $S_t \frown ... \frown S_{t+j-1}$ is a segment of A enclosed between Y_{k-1} and Y_k, if $t > 1$; between U and Y_1, if $t = 1$. In particular, $S_1 \frown Y_1 \frown ... \frown Y_{r+1}$ contains a unique $\Phi^{\mathbf{P}}$-skeleton. Axiom 4 now holds as a special case, when each $S_i = T_i$ $(i > 1)$. It also follows that when a generalized transformation applies to a complex string, each elementary component of the complex string must be mapped to the same stage, the stage required by the transformation. Essentially, this condition means that if we analyze a generalized transformation into its several branches, each one originating in a single kernel string (cf. §91.4), then each such branch contains a unique $\Phi^{\mathbf{P}}$-skeleton, i.e., each mapping $\Phi_i^{\mathbf{P}}$ is applied once and only once to each kernel string in the process of deriving the ultimate string in **W** that results from this generalized transformation.

    There are certain complications in applying transformational analysis when this condition is incorporated. Consider for example the transformation T that carries **135** into **136**:

135   *John–knew–it–#–Sentence*

[34] This notion is not precise, and should be replaced by an appropriate inductive definition.

136 *John–knew–that⌢Sentence*

Suppose that *T* applies before any part of the mapping Φ^P. Then the **T**-marker for **136** will be

137 "John knew it" $⌢K_1⌢I\text{–}Sentence⌢K_2⌢I\text{–}T\text{–}\Phi^P$

where in place of *Sentence* we have some particular sentence. Φ^P thus applies to the whole string **136**. But this means that Φ^P must actually apply twice to **136**, once to the string as a whole, and once to the *that*-clause, which has the internal construction of a sentence.

Suppose that in place of *Sentence* in **136** we choose the sentence **136**, thus deriving

138 *John–knew–that⌢John⌢knew⌢that⌢Sentence*

in essentially·the same way as we derived **136**—i.e., by a **T**-marker

139 "John knew it"$⌢K_1⌢I\text{–}$"John knew that *Sentence*"$⌢K_3⌢$
$I\text{–}T\text{–}\Phi^P$

Then Φ^P must essentially apply three times to **138**. And since there is no limit to this process, the mapping Φ^P will have to be formulated in such a way that it can apply indefinitely many times. It is possible to do this within our present framework. Each submapping Φ_i^P will be given as an infinite family of transformations (characterized, of course, by a finitely stable condition), and the transformations will have to be carefully formulated with just the right derived constituent structure given so that each mapping will apply correctly to each part of any sentence.

This is the major difficulty associated with the structural characterization proposed for normal strings in Condition 5. This effect of Condition 5 indicates that very likely this condition is not the correct one. It seems that it should be possible to have the proper mappings apply to each transform *X* before it enters into a further transformation, and still to have these mappings reapply in the correct way to any further transform *Y* including *X*, without disturbing *X* internally. I have, however, found no good general formulation that meets these requirements. We will continue the investigation of transformations, then, accepting Condition 5 as a tentative and not completely satisfactory formulation. In investigating transformational structure, we will come across several instances of this and related difficulties, and we will see in detail the effects of accepting Condition 5. This detailed investigation can be regarded as offering data for some future investigation of a preferable alternative to Condition 5.

91.6 With these qualifications, the system of generalized transformations that has been developed in §91 seems adequate for the cases cited in §91.1 and many others. It is interesting to see how it applies to cases like

140   *that John was unhappy was quite obvious*   (= **114**a)

in greater detail.

The **T**-marker of **140** can be taken as

141 $Z_1 \frown K_1 \frown \Phi^{\mathbf{P}} \frown T_{that} \frown Z_2 \frown K_2 \frown \Phi^{\mathbf{P}} \frown T_x$, where

(i) Z_1 is a string of $Gr(P)$ such that $\Phi^{\mathbf{P}}(Z_1, K_1) =$ "John was unhappy"

(ii) Z_2 is a string of $Gr(P)$ such that $\Phi^{\mathbf{P}}(Z_2, K_2) =$ "it was quite obvious"

(iii) T_{that} is the deformation that converts Y into $that\frown Y$.

(iv) T_x is the transformation determined by (Q, t_s), where $Q = \{(that\frown Sentence, \#, it, VP)\}$, t_s is the elementary substitution such that

$$t_s: \quad Y_1 - Y_2 - Y_3 - Y_4 \rightarrow U - U - Y_1 - Y_4 = Y_1 - Y_4$$

Thus T_x converts anything of the form $that\frown Sentence\text{–}\#\text{–}it\text{–}VP$ into the corresponding string of the form $that\frown Sentence\text{–}VP$.

141 is a normal string $S_1 \frown S_2 \frown S_3 \frown S_4$, where $S_1 = Z_1 \frown K_1 \frown \Phi^{\mathbf{P}}$, $S_2 = T_{that}$, $S_3 = Z_2 \frown K_2 \frown \Phi^{\mathbf{P}}$, and $S_4 = T_x$. We can trace the operation of **141** in several steps by determining Val_1 of its initial substrings (cf. Definition 50, §91.3).

142 $Val_1(S_1) = \Phi^{\mathbf{P}}(Z_1, K_1) = John\frown was\frown unhappy$
Let $Val_2(S_1) = K_3$
$Val_1(S_1 \frown S_2) = T_{that}(John\frown was\frown unhappy, K_3) = that\frown John\frown was\frown unhappy$
$Val_1(S_1 \frown S_2 \frown S_3)$
$\quad = (that\frown John\frown was\frown unhappy)\frown \#\frown \Phi^{\mathbf{P}}(Z_2, K_2)$
$\quad = (that\frown John\frown was\frown unhappy)\frown \#\frown (it\frown was\frown quite\frown obvious)^{35}$
$Val_1(S_1 \frown S_2 \frown S_3 \frown S_4) = T_x(Val_1(S_1 \frown S_2 \frown S_3), K_4) = $ **140**
$\quad$ [where $K_4 = Val_2(S_1 \frown S_2 \frown S_3)$]

---

[35] See Note 29.

Other strings of the same form as **140** can be obtained by changing the **P**-basis $((Z_1, K_1), (Z_2, K_2))$ of **141**. Note that it is not necessary to take Z_1 and Z_2 as strings of $Gr(P)$ (cf. Condition 4). In the grammar corresponding to the level **T**, then, we can state **141** with variables replacing the terms of the **P**-basis, and perhaps a condition on the values that these variables can take, instead of listing all the **T**-markers that differ from **141** only in their **P**-basis.

A sufficiently detailed grammatical statement will of course have to indicate that there is a restriction on the distribution of "that John was unhappy" in grammatical sentences. This restriction can be given either as a part of the definition of the restricting class of T_x, or, if this is simpler, as a condition on the strings that can form the **P**-basis in the **T**-marker schema formed from **141**, as suggested above, by taking "Z_1," "K_1," "Z_2," and "K_2" as variables.

In the case we have just discussed, the sentence **140** was formed by substituting the transform "that John was unhappy" for the noun phrase subject of "it was quite clear," which is itself a kernel sentence. It may be that there is no kernel sentence of which the generalized transform is a substitution instance in this sense. In this case a dummy carrier can be added to the set of primes of **P**, and its distribution given as a part of the kernel grammar. Then the transformation in question can be very simply defined as applying only to sentences containing this dummy carrier. Thus in the case of **140**, if there were no kernel sentence $NP\frown was\frown quite\frown clear$, we could adjoin to **P** a prime p, and give the distribution of p completely in the phrase grammar. This might be the simplest procedure even if there is a kernel element (e.g., "it") occurring in every position where "that John was nervous," etc., can appear. Of course if we take this approach, we must account for the case where the transformation T is not applied, perhaps relaxing the condition that the product of a **P**-marker must itself map into μ^{W}, in the case of such dummy carriers.

In one way or another, then, the distribution of "that John was unhappy" will be given in the description of phrase structure as the distribution of a simple noun phrase (with possible modification in terms of conditions on the **P**-basis of **T**-marker schemata), and the internal structure of this simple noun phrase will be given by a transformation. Thus we can describe the distribution of a complex element on the level **P**, where this is most easily done, and we can describe its internal construction transformationally, instead of complicating the level **P** by requiring that this too be given directly. It will be recalled that a good many of the complications that arose in the attempt to construct a grammar of phrase structure in Chapter VIII were due to the many recursions which were necessary, and to the difficulty of properly ordering the rules in which complex phrases played a role (cf. §§69, 70). These difficulties can be avoided now by generalized transformations.

The general class of **T**-markers of which **141** is an instance operate by converting a string Y_1 into $\overline{Y}_1$, and then substituting $\overline{Y}_1$ for some element X of a second string Y_2. In the case of **141**, $Y_1 = \Phi^P(Z_1, K_1) =$ "John was unhappy," $\overline{Y}_1 = $ "that John was unhappy," $Y_2 = \Phi^P(Z_2, K_2) = $ "it was quite obvious," and $X = $ "it." The result, then, is a string $...\overline{Y}...$—in the case of **141**, it is **140**. The derived constituent structure of $...\overline{Y}_1...$ is determined in the following way:

(i)   The internal structure of $\overline{Y}_1$ is just that carried over by the transformation from Y_1 to $\overline{Y}_1$ (cf. especially §87.6).

(ii) The external constituent role of $\overline{Y}_1$ is just that of the element X for which it was substituted. If X is a Z in Y_2, then $\overline{Y}_1$ is a Z in $...\overline{Y}_1....$ If some segment containing X is a Z in Y_2, then this segment, with $\overline{Y}_1$ replacing X, is a Z in $...\overline{Y}_1....$ [cf. §86.4, §87.5(i)].

Thus in the case of the derivation of **140**, above, the internal structure of "John was unhappy" is that of a sentence, and the external structure of "that John was unhappy" is that of the noun phrase "it" for which it substitutes.

92   A grammar corresponding to the level **T** for a given language is basically a statement of the set μ^T of **T**-markers for this language. The simplest way to present such a grammar is to list **T**-markers with variables for the elements of the **P**-basis, and to set various conditions on these variables to determine which pairs (Z, K) can actually occur in the **P**-basis of such a schematic **T**-marker. In general, we can expect to find that an order of application is defined on these schematic **T**-markers, and we may be able to utilize this fact, as we did in the construction of grammars on lower levels, to simplify the statement of conditions on **P**-bases of **T**-markers. For instance, we might be able to order **T**-marker schemata in such a way that the **P**-basis of each schema can be occupied by any strings of $Gr(P)$ (and their **P**-markers) or by any strings derived by earlier **T**-markers (and their derived interpretations). We have not investigated the problem of developing a form of grammatical statement for the transformational level and relating this statement to the grammar corresponding to lower levels. A more urgent task is to investigate the range and power of transformational analysis, and this is the problem to which we turn in the next chapter.

In the course of these constructions, we have incidentally come across potential solutions for a number of the difficulties that originally suggested the desirability of establishing a new and higher level of syntactic analysis. Thus we have pointed out that generalized transformations will enable us to avoid much of the complexity caused by recursions in the grammar of phrase structure. As another instance, note that the conjunction rule, which we saw could not be incorporated into the grammar of phrase structure (cf. §74), can now be stated as a generalized transformation (actually, a family of generalized transformations, cf. §90.1). Thus we can avoid transformationally a difficulty that actually undercut much of the reasoning that led to the particular form of the interpretation of **P** for English, i.e., much of the validation of the statement of English phrase structure. We will now go on to a more detailed study of the transformational structure of English, and the effectiveness of transformational analysis in remedying the descriptive inadequacies of the previously established levels.

TRANSFORMATIONAL
ANALYSIS OF
ENGLISH X

In the preceding chapter, we developed an abstract theory of trans- 93.1
formational analysis and formulated a corresponding linguistic level **T**.
This development was motivated by a series of difficulties which arose
when we tried to describe English sentence structure exhaustively in
terms of the theoretical devices available on lower levels. Certain
inadequacies of our earlier constructions were summarized in §§76–78,
and in §79 we pointed out that some notion of "grammatical transformation" might provide means for resolving these not inconsiderable
problems. We must now investigate this claim, applying these new
conceptions of transformational analysis to English just as we applied
the notions of the level **P** to English in Chapter VIII. Before proceeding
with this empirical investigation, however, we will briefly summarize
the central ideas and technical devices which have been developed in
§§81–91 and which will be taken for granted in the remainder of this
chapter.

In Chapter VII we showed how the phrase structure of a language
can be reconstructed from a grammar which has the form of a sequence
of conversions $\alpha \rightarrow \beta$, where β is formed from α by replacing a single
prime of α by some string. By running through this sequence of con-
versions over and over, interpreting each as the instruction "rewrite α
as β," we can construct a *derivation* of a *terminal string* Z to which
none of the conversions applies further. Thus $Z \in \bar{P}$, the set of "lowest
level" strings of **P**. We have since extended $\bar{P}$ to include also words and
morphemes (thus "embedding" **W** and **M**—actually $\bar{\mathbf{M}}$—into **P**).
This derivation of Z is a sequence of strings with the string *Sentence*

401

as its first term and the string Z as its final term, and such that each term in the sequence is formed from the preceding term by the application of some conversion to this preceding term. The set of strings of $\bar{P}$ which were derived in this way we denoted "$Gr(P)$." We noted that a string Z will in general have various derivations which are equivalent from the point of view of constituent structure. Given a set $\{D_1, D_2, ...\}$ of equivalent derivations of Z, we define a **P**-marker of Z as the set of strings each of which appears as a term in one of the derivations $D_1, D_2, ...$. Given a **P**-marker of Z, we found that we were able to reconstruct completely the constituent structure of Z. We noted further that any set K of strings such that Z is a member of K (whether or not K is a **P**-marker of Z) can be said to provide an "interpretation" of Z, i.e., a certain constituent analysis of Z. The grammar of phrase structure for a given language is then completed by the statement of a mapping $\Phi^{\mathbf{P}}$ which converts every string Z of $\bar{P}$ which is the product of some derivation into a string of words.

We now propose to limit derivability on the level **P** to a certain subset of the grammatical strings in $\bar{P}$. That is, we no longer require that every grammatical string of words be the result of application of $\Phi^{\mathbf{P}}$ to some string of $Gr(P)$, i.e., some string which is actually derived on the level **P** and to which, therefore, phrase structure is assigned directly. The set of strings which do result from $Gr(P)$ by application of $\Phi^{\mathbf{P}}$ we call the *kernel* of the language, and we require that all other grammatical strings of words be derived ultimately from kernel strings [more correctly, from the strings in $Gr(P)$ which underlie kernel strings] by grammatical transformations.

Each grammatical transformation T operates on a string Z with the constituent interpretation K (which may or may not be a **P**-marker) and converts it into a new string Z' with the derived interpretation K'. Z' will be denoted "$T(Z, K)$," and K', which gives the constituent structure of Z', is called "the derived interpretation of $T(Z, K)$ with respect to (wrt) Z, K, T." Both Z' [$= T(Z, K)$] and K' are uniquely determined for each (Z, K). Thus, given a string Z with the constituent interpretation given by K, we know unambiguously, for each transformation T, just what string results by application of T to (Z, K) and what is the constituent structure of this new string $T(Z, K)$. Furthermore, each grammatical transformation T has fixed structural properties; for every pair (Z, K), the corresponding transform (Z', K') differs from (Z, K) in a fixed way (if it differs at all).

Each T operates significantly only on a certain restricted set of pairs (Z, K). This set is determined by a *restricting class* Q which is associated with T. Q is a set of sequences $(W_1, ..., W_r)$ (with r fixed for Q), where each W_i is a string in **P**. Suppose that $(W_1,..., W_r)$ is a member of Q. Then T applies to (Z, K) significantly in case Z is analyzed by K into a W_1 followed by a W_2 ... followed by a W_r. For example, suppose one of the sequences in Q is (τ, A, N, saw, NP). Then the associated transformation will apply significantly to a string Z with the interpretation K if Z is analyzed by K into an article (τ) followed by an adjective followed by a noun followed by *saw* followed by a noun phrase. For example, it will apply to $Z = a$–*single–witness–saw–the⌒accident*, with its appropriate **P**-marker K. Note that a transformation may apply to a string with one interpretation, but not with another; i.e., it may apply to (Z, K_1) but not (Z, K_2). If Z is not analyzed by K into some sequence of terms which corresponds to a member of the restricting class Q associated with T, then T converts (Z, K) into (Z, K) itself. [More accurately, it converts it into (Z, K'), where K' is that part of K relevant to determining the original constituent structure of Z]. In particular, the transformation with the restricting class whose sole member is (U) is an *identity transformation I* which converts every string into itself, leaving constituent structure unchanged.

To characterize an transformation T completely we must determine the class of pairs (Z, K) to which it applies significantly (by stating the constitution of the associated restricting class Q) and we must state the fixed structural change that T effects on each (Z, K) to which it significantly applies. The latter information is provided by an *elementary transformation t* associated with T. The elementary transformations that interest us are each limited in significant application to sequences of strings n terms in length, where n is fixed for t. t will have no effect on sequences of terms of length different from n. Given a sequence of strings $(Y_1,..., Y_n)$, t converts Y_1 into W_1, Y_2 into $W_2,..., Y_n$ into W_n, where the form of W_i depends not only on Y_i but also, perhaps, on $Y_1,..., Y_n$. We express this by writing

I $t(Y_1,..., Y_i ; Y_i,..., Y_n) = W_i$

for each i. Thus t essentially converts the string Y_1-Y_2-...-Y_{n-1}-Y_n into W_1-W_2-...-W_{n-1}-W_n. We express this more precisely by associating with t a *derived transformation t** such that

II $t^*(Y_1,..., Y_n) = W_1⌒...⌒W_n$

For each i, the form of W_i has a fixed relation to the form of Y_i, $(Y_1,..., Y_n)$. That is, if

III $t(Y_1,..., Y_i ; Y_i,..., Y_n) = W_i$
$t(\overline{Y}_1,..., \overline{Y}_i ; \overline{Y}_i,..., \overline{Y}_n) = \overline{W}_i$

then W_1-...-W_n differs from Y_1-...-Y_n in the same way as $\overline{W}_1$-...-$\overline{W}_n$ differs from $\overline{Y}_1$-...-$\overline{Y}_n$.

A grammatical transformation T is completely determined by its restricting class Q and its underlying elementary transformation t. Q tells us to which strings T applies, and t tells us what effect it has on these strings. We can state Q as a finite set of finite sequences; we discuss the method of describing t directly below. The notions of restricting class and elementary transformation are more carefully developed in §§81–83. Very frequently we find that there are many transformations all with the same underlying elementary transformation t, and with restricting classes all of which are characterized by some fixed condition C. We then say that the pair (C, t) determines a *family F* of transformations T_1, T_2,..., where each T_i in F is determined by a pair (Q_i, t), where Q_i meets the condition C. This generalization, given more carafully in §90.1, leads to considerable simplification of the grammatical statement of the level of transformations.

In §§84, 85, we study certain particularly interesting elementary transformations, including, in particular, all those which will appear in this chapter. We define a *deformation* δ as an elementary transformation whose only effect on a string Y_1-...-Y_n is to delete terms or to add some constant string to certain terms. Thus for each i, either

IV $\delta(Y_1,..., Y_i ; Y_i,..., Y_n) = U$

in case δ deletes the ith term of Y_1-...-Y_n, or

V $\delta(Y_1,..., Y_i ; Y_i,..., Y_n) = W_i \frown Y_i \frown \overline{W}_i$

where W_i or $\overline{W}_i$ (or both) may be U or may be certain constant strings. If we know W_i, $\overline{W}_i$ for each $i \leqslant n$, then we know everything about δ. We assume that we have an element σ such that if $W_i = \sigma$, then $\overline{W}_i = U$ and $W_i \frown Y_i \frown \overline{W}_i = U$. Thus σ is a kind of "deleting" element. We can then characterize δ completely by a sequence

VI $A = (W_1, \overline{W}_1,..., W_n, \overline{W}_n)$

where $\overline{W}_i = U$ if $W_i = \sigma$. In this case, δ will convert any string Y_1-...-Y_n into the string $W_1 \frown Y_1 \frown \overline{W}_1$-...-$W_n \frown Y_n \frown \overline{W}_n$, where if $W_i = \sigma$, then $W_i \frown Y_i \frown \overline{W}_i = U$.

For example, let the sequence $A = (U, in\frown the\frown window, U, U, \sigma, U)$. Then applied to any string $Y_1\text{-}Y_2\text{-}Y_3$, the corresponding δ yields the transform $U\frown Y_1\frown in\frown the\frown window\text{-}U\frown Y_2\frown U\text{-}U = Y_1\frown in\frown the\frown window\text{-}Y_2$. For example, applied to the string *the$\frown$book–was$\frown$sold–to$\frown$a$\frown$student*, it yields the transform *the$\frown$book$\frown$in$\frown$the$\frown$window–was$\frown$sold*.

We define a *permutation* π as an elementary transformation whose only effect on a string $Y_1\text{-}...\text{-}Y_n$ is to permute the terms of this string. Thus

VII $\qquad \pi^*(Y_1,..., Y_n) = Y_{a_1}\frown...\frown Y_{a_n}$

where $(a_1,..., a_n)$ is a permutation of the integers $(1,..., n)$; and for each i,

VIII $\qquad (Y_1,..., Y_i ; Y_i,..., Y_n) = Y_{a_i}$

π is thus completely characterized by the sequence of integers $B = (a_1,..., a_n)$.

For example, let $B = (2, 1, 3)$. Then π converts $Y_1\text{-}Y_2\text{-}Y_3$ into $Y_2\text{-}Y_1\text{-}Y_3$; e.g., it converts *he–can–come* into *can–he–come*.

We define an *adjunction* η as an elementary transformation whose sole effect is to "attach" certain terms to other terms. For example, the elementary transformation that converts $Y_1\text{-}Y_2\text{-}Y_2$ into $Y_1\text{-}Y_1\frown Y_2\text{-}Y_3$ (prefixing Y_1 to Y_2) would be an adjunction. This particular adjunction can be characterized in an obvious way by the sequence of integers $(0, 0, 1, 0, 0, 0)$, indicating that it prefixes nothing to the first term, suffixes nothing to the first term, prefixes the first term to the second term, suffixes nothing to the second term, prefixes nothing to the third term, and suffixes nothing to the third term. In general, an adjunction η is characterized by a sequence of nonnegative integers $C = (a_1,..., a_{2n})$, where each a_i is less than or equal to n. Then η converts $Y_1\text{-}...\text{-}Y_n$ into $Y_{a_1}\frown Y_1\frown Y_{a_2}\text{-}...\text{-}Y_{a_{2n-1}}\frown Y_n\frown Y_{2n}$, where $Y_0 = U$. In this case,

IX $\qquad \eta(Y_1,..., Y_i ; Y_i,..., Y_n) = Y_{a_{2i-1}}\frown Y_i\frown Y_{a_{2i}}$

For example, let $C = (0, 3, 0, 0, 0, 0)$. Then the associated adjunction carries $Y_1\text{-}Y_2\text{-}Y_3$ into $Y_1\frown Y_3\text{-}Y_2\text{-}Y_3$. For example, it carries **X** into **XI**:

X $\qquad$ *the$\frown$man–was$\frown$coming$\frown$this$\frown$way–in$\frown$the$\frown$dark$\frown$suit*

XI $\qquad$ *the$\frown$man$\frown$in$\frown$the$\frown$dark$\frown$suit–was$\frown$coming$\frown$this$\frown$way–in$\frown$the$\frown$dark$\frown$suit*

We can form new elementary transformations from given elementary transformations by compounding. Suppose t_1 and t_2 are elementary transformations. Then we define $t_2(t_1)$ as the elementary transformation whose effect on Y_1-...-Y_n is that obtained by application of t_1 followed by application of t_2 to the result. More carefully, suppose that

XII $t_1{}^*(Y_1,..., Y_n) = W_1 {}^\frown ... {}^\frown W_n$ [where $W_i = t_1(Y_1,..., Y_i ;$
$Y_i,..., Y_n)$]

$t_2{}^*(W_1,..., W_n) = Z_1 {}^\frown ... {}^\frown Z_n$ [where $Z_i = t_2(W_1,..., W_i ;$
$W_i,..., W_n)$]

Then $t_2(t_1)$ carries Y_1-...-Y_n into Z_1-...-Z_n . That is,

XIII $[t_2(t_1)]^*(Y_1,..., Y_n) = Z_1 {}^\frown ... {}^\frown Z_n$
$[t_2(t_1)](Y_1,..., Y_i ; Y_i,..., Y_n) = Z_i$

For example, let δ be the deformation which carries Y_1-Y_2-Y_3 into Y_1-*is*${}^\frown Y_2 {}^\frown$*en-by*${}^\frown Y_3$ [where *en* is the morpheme which, e.g., added to *take* gives *taken*—cf. §66]. Thus δ is defined by the sequence

XIV $A = (U,\ U,\ is,\ en,\ by,\ U)$

Let π be the permutation that carries Y_1-Y_2-Y_3 into Y_3-Y_2-Y_1 . Thus π is defined by the sequence

XV $B = (3, 2, 1)$

Then $\delta(\pi)$ is the elementary transformation that carries Y_1-Y_2-Y_3 into Y_3-Y_2-Y_1 and then into Y_3-*is*${}^\frown Y_2 {}^\frown$*en-by*${}^\frown Y_1$; it carries **XVI** into **XVII**:

XVI   *the*${}^\frown$*students–take–the*${}^\frown$*book*

XVII   *the*${}^\frown$*book–is*${}^\frown$*taken–by*${}^\frown$*the*${}^\frown$*students*

By compounding the deformation which deletes the *i*th term with the adjunction that attaches the *j*th term to the *i*th term (now deleted), we can achieve the effect of a substitution of the *j*th term for the *i*th term.

More generally, in §86.4 we defined a substitution as an elementary transformation t_s whose effect is to delete terms or to substitute certain terms for other terms (thus t_s is a compound of deformations and adjunctions). Combining the methods for characterizing deformations and adjunctions, we characterize t_s by a sequence $D = (a_1,..., a_{2n})$, where a_{2i-1} may be σ, and otherwise, $0 \leqslant a_j \leqslant n$ (but $a_{2i} = 0$ if $a_{2i-1} = 0$). Then

XVIII $t_s(Y_1 ,..., Y_i ; Y_i ,..., Y_n) = W_i$

$$\text{where } W_i = Y_{a_{2i}} \qquad\qquad \text{if } a_{2i-1} = \sigma$$
$$W_i = Y_{a_{2i-1}} {}^\frown W_i {}^\frown Y_{a_{2i}} \quad \text{if } a_{2i-1} \neq \sigma$$
$$[\text{and } Y_0 = U]$$

For example, let $D = (\sigma, 0, \sigma, 1, 0, 0)$. Then the corresponding t_s carries Y_1-Y_2-Y_3 into U-Y_1-$Y_3 = Y_1$-Y_3 , since

XIX $t_s(Y_1 ; Y_1 , Y_2 , Y_3) = \sigma {}^\frown Y_1 {}^\frown Y_0 = U$
$t_s(Y_1 , Y_2 ; Y_2 , Y_3) = ((\sigma {}^\frown Y_2) {}^\frown Y_1) = Y_1$
[repressing associativity of concatenation]
$t_s(Y_1 , Y_2 , Y_3 ; Y_3) = Y_0 {}^\frown Y_3 {}^\frown Y_0 = U {}^\frown Y_3 {}^\frown U = Y_3$

Thus t_s has the same effect as the deformation that carries Y_1-Y_2-Y_3 into Y_1-U-$Y_3 = Y_1 {}^\frown Y_3$. However, we will see directly that the derived constituent structure of Y_1-Y_3 is different in this case.

These elementary transformations and their compounds are the only ones that will concern us below. Theorem 4 (§85.3), Theorem 5 (§86.3), and Theorems 8 and 9 (§86.5) give certain grounds for the assumption that deformations, permutations, adjunctions, and their compounds may in general be adequate for transformational analysis.

In §86.3 we studied the problem of assigning derived constituent structure to transforms. We note first of all that if t carries Y_1-...-Y_n into W_1-...-W_n and t is a deformation, permutation, or adjunction, there is an obvious sense in which each W_i has a certain Y_i as its *root*. If t is a deformation or adjunction, we say that Y_i is the root of W_i . If t is a permutation which carries the ith term of Y_1-...-Y_n into the jth term of W_1-...-W_n (in this case, $W_j = Y_i$), then we say that the ith term of Y_1-...-Y_n is the root of the jth term of W_1-...-W_n [in this case, if $\pi \leftrightarrow (a_1 ,..., a_n)$, then $a_i = j$]. The notion of root carries over under compounding. Thus if t is the π–δ transformation discussed above that carries **XVI** into **XVII**, then *the* {}^\frown *students* in **XVI** is the root of *by* {}^\frown *the* {}^\frown *students* in **XVII**, *take* in **XVI** is the root of *is* {}^\frown *taken* in **XVII**, and *the* {}^\frown *book* in **XVI** is the root of *the* {}^\frown *book* in **XVII**. Note that in the case of a substitution t_s , the root of W_i is Y_i , where t_s carries Y_1-...-Y_n into W_1-...-W_n , since substitutions are compounds of deformations and adjunctions. Hence if a transformation replaces X by Y, then X is the root of Y. We define "root" in such a way that the root of each term of the transform is uniquely determined as a term of the transformed string.

We then went on to lay down various conditions on derived constituent structure. Suppose that a transformation T carries Y_1-...-Y_n into W_1-...-W_n.

XX (i) Suppose that within the level **P** it is the case that W_i is an S, for some prime S [i.e., $\rho(S, W_i)$]. Then we say that W_i is an S in W_1-...-W_n. For example, even when passives are deleted from the kernel, the kernel grammar will tell us that $by\frown NP$ is a *PP*. Hence $by\frown the\frown students$ in **XVII** is a Prepositional Phrase. Passives have ρ-derivations, but not ρ^r-derivations, in this case.

(ii) Suppose that $Y_i\frown...\frown Y_{i+j}$ contains all the roots of $W_i\frown...\frown W_{i+j}$ (whether or not in the same order), and $Y_i\frown...\frown Y_{i+j}$ is an S, for some prime S. Then $W_i\frown...\frown W_{i+j}$ is also an S. For example, if T carries $Z = I$–$called$–up–$my\frown friend$ into $Z' = I$–$called$–$my\frown friend$–up, and if $called\frown up\frown my\frown friend$ is a *VP* in Z, then $called\frown my\frown friend\frown up$ is a *VP* in Z'. See §87.5 for several other important cases.

(iii) If part (or all) of W_i is carried over unaltered from its root Y_j, then the internal constituent structure of this part of W_i is unchanged. For example, $the\frown book$ and $the\frown students$ are *NP*'s in **XVII**, just as they are in the kernel string **XVI**.

(iv) If T is a substitution replacing Y_i by Y_j, then Y_j keeps its original internal constituent structure. Thus if T is based on the substitution t_s in **XIX**, carrying, e.g., $that\frown he\frown was\frown unhappy$–$it$–$was\frown quite\frown obvious$ into U–$that\frown he\frown was\frown unhappy$–$was\frown quite\frown obvious$, then the internal structure of $that\frown he\frown was\frown unhappy$ in the transform is that of the same phrase in the transformed string. Note that in this case the external constituent structure of $that\frown he\frown was\frown unhappy$ in the transform is that of *it*, the term for which it was substituted, by virtue of (ii). Thus $that\frown he\frown was\frown unhappy$ is a Noun Phrase in the transform (as is its root *it*), while $he\frown was\frown unhappy$ is a *Sentence*, *he* is a Noun Phrase, etc., as they are in the original string to which T was applied.

(v) If X is part of $T(Z, K)$, then X is an X.

(vi) If X_1 is an S_1 in $T(Z, K)$ and X_2 is an S_2 in $T(Z, K)$, then $X_1 {}^\frown X_2$ is an $S_1 {}^\frown S_2$ in $T(Z, K)$.

We then (in §87.8) defined the derived interpretation K' as the set of strings which gives just that constituent interpretation carried over for $T(Z, K)$ from (Z, K).

Note that since a transformation T carries a string Z with an interpretation K into a string Z' with the unique derived interpretation K', we can compound transformations freely. We define $[T_1, T_2]$ as the transformation which, when applied to (Z, K), gives $T_2(Z', K')$, where $Z' = T_1(Z, K)$ and K' is the derived interpretation of $T_1(Z, K)$ wrt Z, K, T_1. Thus $[T_1, T_2](Z, K)$ is the string which is derived by first applying T_1 to (Z, K) and then applying T_2 to the result; i.e., $[T_1, T_2](Z, K) = T_2(T_1(Z, K), K')$, where K' is as above. Since $[T_1, T_2]$ also gives a unique derived interpretation K'', we can go on to define $[T_1, T_2, T_3]$ and, in general, $[T_1, ..., T_n]$. Thus $[T_1, ..., T_n](Z, K)$ is the string which is derived by applying T_1 to (Z, K), applying T_2 to the result (Z', K'), ..., and finally applying T_n to the result (Z^{n-1}, K^{n-1}).

In §88 we made use of the notions of transformational analysis to clear up the unresolved formal problems connected with the level of phrase structure. In developing **P**, we were able to determine the constituent structure of strings in $Gr(P)$ by deriving them from the string *Sentence* by the use of a sequence of instruction formulas $\alpha \rightarrow \beta$; but we found that the mapping $\Phi^{\mathbf{P}}$ which converts strings of $Gr(P)$ into strings of words could not be characterized in this way. The fundamental difficulty is that to apply $\Phi^{\mathbf{P}}$ correctly to a string Z of $Gr(P)$ it is necessary in general to know the derivation (i.e., the constituent structure) of Z, not just the shape of Z itself. But a conversion of the form $\alpha \rightarrow \beta$ (i.e., "rewrite α as β") applies or fails to apply to Z irrespective of its "history of derivation." Since transformations apply to a string with a constituent structure, this limitation no longer holds if we interpret $\Phi^{\mathbf{P}}$ as a transformation which converts a string of $Gr(P)$ with its **P**-marker K into a string Z' of words with the derived interpretation K'. Though a string of words is not derived directly from *Sentence*, we see that it still has a constituent structure by virtue of the fact that transformations impose a derived interpretation on the strings which they yield.

In constructing the grammar of English in §72.3, we found it extremely useful to break up $\Phi^{\mathbf{P}}$ into successive components $\Phi_1{}^{\mathbf{P}}, ..., \Phi_m{}^{\mathbf{P}}, \Phi^{\overline{\mathbf{M}}}$, which are applied successively to a string of $Gr(P)$. The result of applying $\Phi_1{}^{\mathbf{P}}, ..., \Phi_m{}^{\mathbf{P}}$ is a string of morphemes in $\overline{\mathbf{M}}$, and $\Phi^{\overline{\mathbf{M}}}$ converts this into a string of words by inserting word boundaries in the proper places. Let us relabel $\Phi^{\overline{\mathbf{M}}}$, calling it "$\Phi_{m+1}{}^{\mathbf{P}}$." Transformational analysis of $\Phi^{\mathbf{P}}$ provides a clear interpretation for this fragmentation of $\Phi^{\mathbf{P}}$. We develop each $\Phi_i^{\mathbf{P}}$ as a transformation, and we define $\Phi^{\mathbf{P}}$ as the compound transformation

XXI $\Phi^{\mathbf{P}} = [\Phi_1^{\mathbf{P}},..., \Phi_m^{\mathbf{P}}, \Phi_{m+1}^{\mathbf{P}}]$

It is very important to observe that this development allows us great freedom in determining the point of application of a grammatical transformation T. It is not necessary that T be limited in application to either a string of $Gr(P)$ or a string of words. Since each $\Phi_i^{\mathbf{P}}$ is itself a transformation, T can apply anywhere in the sequence $\Phi_1^{\mathbf{P}},..., \Phi_{m+1}^{\mathbf{P}}$. Suppose that we define Ψ_1 as $\Phi_1^{\mathbf{P}}$, Ψ_2 as $[\Phi_1^{\mathbf{P}}, \Phi_2^{\mathbf{P}}],..., \Psi_{m+1}$ as $[\Phi_1^{\mathbf{P}},..., \Phi_{m+1}^{\mathbf{P}}]$. Thus in general, for $1 \leqslant i \leqslant m + 1$,

XXII $\Psi_i = [\Phi_1^{\mathbf{P}},..., \Phi_i^{\mathbf{P}}]$

In particular, $\Psi_{m+1} = \Phi^{\mathbf{P}}$. Then a transformation T can apply after Ψ_i, for any i. In this case, T will be followed by the remainder of $\Phi^{\mathbf{P}}$ so that the end result is a string of words. Let us define

XXIII $\Psi_i' = [\Phi_{i+1}^{\mathbf{P}},..., \Phi_{m+1}^{\mathbf{P}}]$

for each $i \leqslant m$. Thus $\Phi^{\mathbf{P}} = [\Psi_i, \Psi_i']$, for each $i \leqslant m$. For each specific transformation T, we will now select an i such that T applies after Ψ_i and before Ψ_i'. We will see below that specific transformations in English differ widely in their point of application within $\Phi^{\mathbf{P}}$.

The analysis of $\Phi^{\mathbf{P}}$ is carried out more fully in §88.

Up to this point in the development of transformational analysis we seem to have adopted a point of view radically different from that of our earlier discussion of linguistic structure. In §§89, 91, however, we attempted to show that in a natural way, we can interpret the theory of transformational analysis as a new linguistic level having the same status and fundamental properties as other levels. Just as an utterance can be represented by a sequence of phonemes or a sequence of words, it can be represented by the sequence of operations by which it is derived from a kernel sentence.

To characterize transformational analysis as a linguistic level **T**, we must present a set of primes of **T**, an interpretation for the concatenation operation $\frown$, a set $\mu^{\mathbf{T}}$ of **T**-markers, and a mapping $\Phi^{\mathbf{T}}$ that assigns **T**-markers to utterances as their representations or "spellings" on the level **T**. Among the primes of **T** will be included, first of all, all transformations T and compound transformations

$[T_1,..., T_n]$. Thus in particular, Φ^P and its components (including Ψ_i and $\Psi_i{}'$, for each i) are primes of the level **T**.

We extend the set $\bar{P}$ of "lowest level" elements of **P** to include also all strings of words and morphemes, and mixed strings containing such elements indiscriminately. Then any string Z of $\bar{P}$, in this extended sense, is also a prime of **T**. In particular, then, the strings of $Gr(P)$ and of μ^W (grammatical strings of words) are primes of **T**.

Finally, we include among the primes of **T** any set K whose members are strings in **P** or in $\bar{P}$ in this extended sense. Thus, in particular, all **P**-markers are primes of **T**.

We interpret only certain strings of these primes as possessing significance on the level **T**. In particular, any string $Z {}^\frown K {}^\frown T$ (where Z is a string of $\bar{P}$, K is a set of strings, and T is a transformation—Z, K, T thus are primes of **T**) is interpreted as T applied to Z with the interpretation K. More precisely, we define the mapping Φ^T in such a way that

XXIV $\qquad \Phi^T(Z {}^\frown K {}^\frown T) = T(Z, K)$

That is, Φ^T applied to the string $Z {}^\frown K {}^\frown T$ gives the string $T(Z, K)$, just as Φ^P applied to a certain set of strings (a **P**-marker) gives a string of words, and Φ^{Pn} applied to a string of phonemes gives a string of phones.

More generally,

XXV $\qquad \Phi^T(Z {}^\frown K {}^\frown T_1 {}^\frown ... {}^\frown T_n) = [T_1,..., T_n](Z, K)$

also a string in $\bar{P}$ (in fact, a string of words, if the compound transformation $[T_1,..., T_n]$ includes Φ^P), as we have seen above. Thus $T_1 {}^\frown ... {}^\frown T_n$ (a string in **T**) is interpreted as the compound transformation $[T_1,... T_n]$.

Certain of the strings $Z {}^\frown K {}^\frown T_1 {}^\frown ... {}^\frown T_n$ for which we have provided an interpretation will be **T**-markers of grammatical strings of words. We place certain additional conditions on such strings. For one thing, we must be able to extract Φ^P in a unique manner from any **T**-marker. Thus such strings in **T** as

XXVI $\qquad Z {}^\frown K {}^\frown \Psi_3 {}^\frown T {}^\frown \Psi_3{}'$
$\qquad\qquad Z {}^\frown K {}^\frown T_i {}^\frown \Psi_3 {}^\frown T_j {}^\frown \Phi_4{}^P {}^\frown T_k {}^\frown \Psi_4{}'$ [where T_i, T_j, T_k are transformations, and Ψ_3, $\Psi_3{}'$, $\Psi_4{}'$ are as in **XXII, XXIII**]

etc., qualify for admission into the set μ^T of **T**-markers, since the first contains the sequence Ψ_3, $\Psi_3{}'$ and the second contains the sequence

Ψ_3, $\Phi_4{}^P$, Ψ_4', and both $[\Psi_3', \Psi_3]$ and $[\Psi_4', \Phi_4{}^P, \Psi_3]$ are equivalent to Φ^P, as we have seen above. On the other hand, such strings as

XXVII $Z^\frown K^\frown T$
$Z^\frown K^\frown \Phi_1{}^P{}^\frown T$
$Z^\frown K^\frown T_i{}^\frown \Psi_3{}^\frown T_j$ [where $\Psi_3 \neq \Phi^P$]

etc., are not in general members of the set μ^T of **T**-markers.

We restate this condition on **T**-markers in the following terms: each **T**-marker must contain a unique Φ^P-skeleton. The reason for this requirement is evident when we consider the role that **T**-markers play in the grammar. This requirement guarantees that nonkernel strings which are generated by **T**-markers will be properly mapped into strings of words. Note that the minimal **T**-marker will be

XXVIII $Z^\frown K^\frown \Phi^P$

where Z is in $Gr(P)$ and K is a **P**-marker of Z. In this case (and only in this case), the string $\Phi^P(Z, K) = \Phi^T(Z^\frown K^\frown \Phi^P)$ belongs to the kernel.

In §91 we extended the class of potential **T**-markers to enable us to construct new strings from a set of already generated strings. Suppose that

XXIX Z_1 is the string of $Gr(P)$ underlying "John was unhappy"
Z_2 is the string of $Gr(P)$ underlying "it was quite obvious"

Then

XXX $\Phi^P(Z_1, K_1) = John^\frown was^\frown unhappy$
$\Phi^P(Z_2, K_2) = it^\frown was^\frown quite^\frown obvious$

where K_1 and K_2 are properly chosen **P**-markers. Let T_{that} be the transformation that converts Z_1 into $that^\frown Z_1$. Let T_x be the transformation that converts

XXXI $Y_1\text{-}Y_2\text{-}Y_3\text{-}Y_4$

into

XXXII $U\text{-}U\text{-}Y_1\text{-}Y_4 = Y_1\text{-}Y_4$

Then we interpret the string

XXXIII $Z_1 \frown K_1 \frown \Phi^P \frown T_{that} \frown Z_2 \frown K_2 \frown \Phi^P \frown T_x$

in the following series of steps:

XXXIV   (1)   Apply Φ^P to (Z_1, K_1) forming *John* $\frown$ *was* $\frown$ *un-happy* $= Z_3$. Let K_3 be the derived interpretation of Z_3.

(2)   Apply T_{that} to (Z_3, K_3) forming *that* $\frown$ *John* $\frown$ *was* $\frown$ *unhappy* $= Z_4$.

(3)   Apply Φ^P to (Z_2, K_2) forming *it* $\frown$ *was* $\frown$ *quite* $\frown$ *obvious* $= Z_5$.

(4)   Form the *complex* string $Z_4 - \# - Z_5 =$ *that* $\frown$ *John* $\frown$ *was* $\frown$ *unhappy* $- \# - it \frown was \frown quite \frown obvious$ (where $\#$ is a juncture element, i.e., a particular prime of $\bar{P}$).

(5)   Apply T_x to $Z_4 - \# - Z_5$ broken up into the segments

$$\underbrace{that \frown John \frown was \frown unhappy -}_{Y_1} \underbrace{\# - it}_{-Y_2 - Y_3 -} \underbrace{-was \frown quite \frown obvious}_{Y_4}$$

(6)   By the definition of T_x (see **XXXI, XXXII**, above), the result of step (5) is

$$that \frown John \frown was \frown unhappy - was \frown quite \frown obvious$$

This resulting sentence is the result of applying Φ^T to **XXXIII**, which is taken as the **T**-marker of this sentence. This example is studied more carefully in §91.6, where the constituent structure of the resulting sentence is also discussed.

In general, we attach significance within the level **T** to any string

XXXV $S_1 \frown S_2 \frown S_3 \frown ... \frown S_m$

where $S_1 = Z_1 \frown K_1 \frown T_1$ and each S_i is either T_i or is $Z_i \frown K_i \frown T_i$. Thus **XXXIII** is "broken up" into the segments

XXXVI $$\underbrace{Z_1 \frown K_1 \frown \Phi^P - T_{that}}_{S_1} \underbrace{-Z_2 \frown K_2 \frown \Phi^P - T_x}_{S_2 \quad S_3 \quad S_4}$$

We can now state, by induction how Φ^T maps any significant string of the level **T** into a string of $\bar{P}$. Suppose that **XXXV** is a string in **T**.

Case I.   Let $m = 1$. Then $\Phi^{\mathrm{T}}(S_1) = \Phi^{\mathrm{T}}(Z_1 \frown K_1 \frown T_1) = T_1(Z, K)$.

Case II.   Suppose that Φ^{T} has been defined for $m - 1$ terms, and that $\Phi^{\mathrm{T}}(S_1 \frown S_2 \frown ... \frown S_{m-1}) = Z$, with the derived interpretation K.

   Case IIa.   Suppose that $S_m = T_m$. Then $\Phi^{\mathrm{T}}(S_1 \frown S_2 \frown ... \frown S_m) = T_m(Z, K)$.

   Case IIb.   Suppose that $S_m = Z_m \frown K_m \frown T_m$. Then $\Phi^{\mathrm{T}}(S_1 \frown S_2 \frown ... \frown S_m) = Z \frown \# \frown T_m(Z_m, K_m)$.

Note that Case I and Case IIa are treated just as in **XXIV, XXV**, above, and that Case IIb is the only innovation. Furthermore, the old **T**-markers of the form **XXVI** (or as in **XXIV, XXV**) are special cases of **XXXV** with each $S_i = T_i$ for $i > 1$.

   This inductive characterization enables us to apply Φ^{T} to any string of the form **XXXV**. Note that each such string can be broken up into

XXXVII $Z_1 \frown K_1 \frown ... \frown Z_2 \frown K_2 \frown ... \frown Z_n \frown K_n \frown ...$

where ... contains only transformations. The Z_i in this case are the strings which underlie the resulting tansform. Thus in the example **XXXIV** given above the strings which underlie the sentence "that John was unhappy was quite obvious" are Z_1 (which underlies "John was unhappy") and Z_2 (which underlies "it was quite obvious"). This generalization of **T**-markers makes it possible to develop sentences of a high degree of complexity from very simple parts.

   We have pointed out that every kernel string has a **T**-marker **XXVIII**. We now require that the set μ^{T} of **T**-markers be extensive enough to allow us to generate all nonkernel strings as well. A finite number of **T**-marker schemata will suffice for this purpose, since we can choose already formed transforms as Z_1, Z_2, etc. in the **T**-markers **XXXV** (including **XXVI, XXVIII**, etc., as special cases). Thus every grammatical string of words is represented one way or another on the level **T**.

   We will see that representation on the level **T** has the same general character as representation on lower levels. In particular, many cases of ambiguity will be marked by dual representation on this level, and many sentences that intuitively seem "similar in structure" (are "understood similarly," etc.) will be shown to have partially identical **T**-markers. These facts, along with the simplicity of the generalization to more complex **T**-markers shown above, speak in favor of regarding **T** as simply a new linguistic level, differing from the other levels only in the abstract character of representation on this level.

We can now turn to the task of developing a transformational grammar for English. As was pointed out in §89.5, the problem we face is that of determining which strings to assign to the kernel, and which to derive transformationally from kernel strings. The criterion that we employ in making this choice is simplicity. We investigate, for each particular set of strings, the effect on the grammar of assigning this set to the kernel, or, alternatively, excluding it and treating the strings as transforms.

    93.2

   In a broad sense, we refer by "simplicity" to the whole mass of formal requirements placed on the statement of grammars. In particular, we defined "simplicity" in Chapter IV as "maximal degree of generalization" (in a special and extended sense of "generalization"), measured by length under certain notational transformations designed to convert considerations relating to the similarity of statements into considerations of length. But as was noted in §29, this concept of simplicity cannot be applied directly to determining the relative complexity of distinct levels. The elementary statements of one level may be intrinsically longer than the elementary statements of another. The list of phrases (including words) will be incomparably longer that the list of phonemes. We will not be willing to, say, double the number of phonemes, in order to drop some thirty phrases from the analysis. Thus while this conception of simplicity (though itself undoubtedly oversimplified and incomplete) is fairly successful within a level, in order to apply it in considerations affecting two levels it is necessary to weight the symbols of each level in a certain way, so that increasing the complexity of one level may considerably outweigh an identical reduction on another level. This weighting must of course be established in the general theory; otherwise all sorts of *ad hoc* solutions will be possible in particular cases.

   How is this weighting to be determined? Clearly, the basis for this decision is the same as the basis for every other construction made in the general theory. Our purpose is to construct an integrated and systematic theory, which, when applied rigorously to linguistic material, gives the correct analysis for the cases where intuition (or experiment, under more desirable circumstances) makes a clear decision. We assign the weighting so that this will turn out to be the case, just as we define "word" or "phrase" so that, in application, this will turn out to be the case. In practice, this means that we must investigate the characteristics of correct solutions in great detail, and then formulate abstractly conditions that lead to these correct solutions. There are several levels on which theory may be successful. On the one hand, it is successful if such abstract and effective formulation is possible. But for real success, of course, this formulation must be motivated in some manner which is not too easy to characterize, and is often disguised by the word "natural."

In our present context, we meet a specific form of this problem. A deformation of n terms will have $2n$ elements in its defining sequence (cf. Definition 14, §84.1). Hence the definition of what is conceptually a very simple transformation may contain more symbols than the statement of an intricate and involved construction on the level **P**, with special restrictions and special cases. If the transformational solution is preferable, on extrasystematic grounds, we must so weight statements on the two levels that it is in fact simpler [or equivalently, we must define reductions on the levels **P** and **T** (cf. §55) in such a way as to make it come out simpler]. As long as this is done in the general theory, this is no more *ad hoc* than is our attempt to define "word" so that "writer" and not "ter" is a word in English. What is important is that there be a sharp boundary in terms of total simplicity between the cases where we choose a transformational solution and the cases where we reject it. The only way that the validity of this approach can be determined is by attempting transformational analysis of actual language material. In the following pages, we apply the notions of the preceding chapter to English, and we will attempt to show that in the cases where transformational analysis does give revealing and intuitively satisfactory results, it is also the case that it leads to extensive simplification of the grammar, so that the transformational solution can be formally justified by this fact within linguistic theory.

In general, we introduce an element or a sentence form transformationally only when by so doing we manage to eliminate special restrictions from the grammar, and to incorporate many special cases into a single generalization. As a kind of standard of reference for the ensuing discussion, we might consider certain cases where transformational analysis would not be in place, because no such simplification results.

We might, for instance, drop the word "very" from the kernel and introduce it by a certain family of deformational transformations. If we did this, we would see that the kernel grammar would be simplified in no way other than by the fact that "very" is dropped from it, i.e., that a certain list is shorter by one. Similarly if we drop the perfective element *have⌢en* from the auxiliary verb phrase we can shorten the kernel grammar in §72.2 to the extent that "⟨*have⌢en*⟩" can be dropped from statement 21, but in no other way. Since one transformation is added to the transformational part of the grammar, there has been no saving in this case. If, on the other hand, we drop the progressive element *be⌢ing* from the kernel, we drop from statement 21 of §72.2 both "⟨*be⌢ing*⟩" and a restriction, namely, "except in env. *ing——*." But even this is no saving, since this restriction will have to be put right back into the transformational analysis as a special limitation. It does not become an automatic consequence of some more general structural feature revealed by transformational analysis, as will often be the case below with apparent special restrictions of the kernel grammar. Hence in this case, too, there is no gain in transformational analysis. On the other hand, when we drop out the passive element *be⌢en* from the kernel, not only is a line dropped from statement 17, §72.2 (i.e., "*en⌢V_T*," the final line of this statement, is dropped), but one extra and complex statement, statement 18, the rule of verbal selection for passives, can be eliminated from the kernel grammar. This rule is essentially an inversion of statement 9, since only objects of actives can be subjects of the corresponding passives, etc. And this rule will not have to be reintroduced in some form into the transformational part of the grammar, since the proper verbal selection in passives is provided automatically by the permutational part of the passive transformation. Dropping statement 18, then, is really a significant saving, and this leads us to introduce passives, though not perfectives or progressives, by transformation.

To develop this reasoning formally, within the framework of our scheme of evaluation, we would have to determine a weighting for statements on the levels **P** and **T** in such a way that elimination of passives, but not progressives, will lead to a total simplification. The reasoning we have sketched suggests that this can be done. One might propose a different relative evaluation, which would include both cases, or exclude both from transformational analysis. A different weighting would lead to a different delimitation of the kernel. This question can be resolved in the same way as all similar questions about the definition of elements in linguistic theory, in the way that we have often described above, i.e., by exploring the empirical implications of the various abstract formulations. It seems to me that the decision outlined in the preceding paragraph is the correct one, in the sense that it is most amenable to natural and systematic formulation in the general theory, and that it is consistent with a characterization of transformational analysis that gives a good deal of insight into linguistic structure and the source of linguistic intuition.

It would be possible at this point to assign a weighting by a formal definition, and to give a precise account of the form that the statement of the grammar of the transformational level must assume, and do this in such a way that all of the conclusions of the following pages will be validated.[1] But this seems to me premature. It is much more important, for the present, to investigate informally the potentialities of transformational analysis, the kinds of simplification that it effects, and the kinds of insights that it can reveal. We will therefore make no attempt to present the characterization of transformations in the most concise possible form, but we will point out in detail the kind of simplification that results from each transformational analysis.

Note that the length of the grammar, relative to a fixed set of available notations, is not the only formal feature that can be studied and varied in an attempt to provide an evaluation procedure in terms of what can be broadly understood as "simplicity of grammar." Below, in §110, we will see that there are good reasons for imposing a condition of "finite generation" as a formal requirement on the kernel grammar. And we will see that the problem of evaluating alternative solutions is very much reduced by this condition.

The grammatical sketch of §§72.2, 72.3 will be used as a basis for this investigation. The notations of earlier chapters can be readily adapted for use here, and we will employ them without further comment.

94.1   The simplest class of sentences not included in our grammatical sketch in §§72.2, 72.3 is the class of interrogative sentences taking a yes-or-no answer. For any sentence of the form $NP\text{-}VP_A\text{-}VP_1$ (hence any sentence derived in §72.2), we can form a corresponding question by inverting the NP and an initial segment of the VP_A (auxiliary verb phrase). Thus such a question will be of the form

1     $X^\frown NP^\frown Y^\frown VP_1$

where $X^\frown Y$ is the VP_A of the corresponding declarative. Recall that at the conclusion of a derivation in **P**, VP_A can be any string of one of the forms

2     $\begin{Bmatrix} C \\ ed \end{Bmatrix} \langle M \rangle \langle have^\frown en \rangle \langle be^\frown ing \rangle$

where C becomes either S or $\emptyset$ (by $\Phi_3{}^{\text{P}}$) and M may be "will," "can," etc.

---

[1] In fact, the major conclusions follow from a direct comparison of the alternative solutions, with no weighting.

The X's of 1 can be any of

3   (i) $\begin{Bmatrix} do \\ does \\ did \end{Bmatrix}$ when $Y = U$

(ii) $\begin{Bmatrix} C \\ ed \end{Bmatrix}$ *will*   (*will* being used as the representative of M)

(iii) $\begin{Bmatrix} C \\ ed \end{Bmatrix}$ *have*

(iv) $\begin{Bmatrix} C \\ ed \end{Bmatrix}$ *be*

Thus we have "does John like it," "would John like it" (where "would" comes from $ed^\frown will$—cf. §66.1), "has John seen it" (where "has" comes from $S^\frown have$ by Φ_5^P, S coming from C by Φ_3^P), etc., but not "does John have seen it," etc. Aside from 3i, it is correct that $X^\frown Y$ is the VP_A, as asserted directly below 1. But in the morphology we have a statement to the effect that

4 $do^\frown S \rightarrow does$
    $do^\frown ed \rightarrow did$

This statement is needed to account for the forms of the verb "do" in its appearance as a main verb, as, e.g., in "I did him a favor." Thus we can rephrase 1 and 3i slightly, stating that if $Y \neq U$, then $X^\frown Y$ is the VP_A, and if $Y = U$, then $X = \emptyset$, S, or ed, and $do^\frown X^\frown Y$ is the VP_A. "do" can thus be described as the bearer of $\emptyset$, S, ed when these elements are not affixed to a verb. This idea will appear in a slightly different form below, where do will be introduced by a mapping Φ_6^P, and further support for it will appear from different sources. It turns out finally that the treatment of "do" as an element automatically introduced to carry an unaffixed affix will have a considerable simplifying effect on the grammar. This effect was the determining factor in the decision of §66.2 to analyze C into two morphemes of number $\emptyset$ and S, with the requirement that C must occur in VP_A, rather than to have as the first element of VP_A only the element S, which may or may not occur. The former treatment, with a zero morpheme, permits a uniform treatment of "do," "does," and "did," as the bearer of a displaced affix.

Before investigating the transformational analysis of yes-or-no questions, **94.2** we must determine the effect of introducing them into the grammar of the kernel (§72.2) directly. Actually they can be introduced without essential modification of this grammatical sketch. To incorporate these interrogatives into §§72.2, 72.3, it is necessary to make the following changes and additions:

5   (i)   *Sentence* → $\langle X \rangle$ $NP \frown VP$ (replacing statement 1)

(ii) $X \rightarrow \left\{ \begin{array}{c} do \left\{ \begin{array}{c} C \\ ed \end{array} \right\} \\ \left\{ \begin{array}{c} C \\ ed \end{array} \right\} \left[\begin{array}{c} M \\ have \\ be \end{array} \right] \end{array} \right\}$ (occurring between statements 1 and 2)

(iii) $VP \rightarrow \left\{ \begin{array}{c} U \\ en \langle be \frown ing \rangle \\ ing \\ VP_{A2} \\ VP_A \end{array} \right\}$ VP_1 in env. $\left\{ \begin{array}{c} \left\{ \begin{array}{c} C \\ ed \end{array} \right\} \\ have \\ be \\ M \\ \text{—} \end{array} \right\}$ NP——

(replacing statement 2)

(iv)   The forms in the left-hand bracket of (iii) replace "VP_A" in statement 9*, and a similar adjustment is made in statement 18.

It is necessary to add one new component to the mapping $\Phi^\mathbf{P}$, following $\Phi_2^{\mathbf{P}}$. Thus to §72.3 we add

6 Φ_2': C goes into $\left\{ \begin{array}{c} S \\ \varnothing \end{array} \right\}$ in env.—— $\left\langle \left[\begin{array}{c} have \\ be \end{array} \right] \right\rangle \left\{ \begin{array}{c} NP_s \\ NP_p \end{array} \right\}$

94.3   For the transformational analysis of yes-or-no questions, the underlying elementary transformation is the permutation π_q such that

7 $\pi_q(Y_1 ; Y_1 , Y_2 , Y_3) = Y_2$
$\pi_q(Y_1 , Y_2 ; Y_2 , Y_3) = Y_1$
$\pi_q(Y_1 , Y_2 , Y_3 ; Y_3) = Y_3$

Thus $\pi_q{}^*$ carries Y_1-Y_2-Y_3 into Y_2-Y_1-Y_3 . The restricting class for the transformation in question will be, in accordance with Definition 2, §81.3, a set of triples of strings $\{(W_1^{(i)}, W_2^{(i)}, W_3^{(i)}) \mid 1 \leqslant i \leqslant m\}$. We can characterize this set Q_q as the set of all such triples meeting the following condition:

8   (i) $W_1^{(i)} = NP$

(ii) $W_2^{(i)} = \left\{ \left\{ \begin{matrix} S \\ \varnothing \\ ed \end{matrix} \right\} \left\langle \left[\begin{matrix} have \\ be \end{matrix} \right] \right\rangle \right\}$
$\quad\quad\quad\quad\quad\quad M$

(iii)   if $W_2^{(i)} = \left\{ \begin{matrix} S \\ \varnothing \\ ed \end{matrix} \right\}$, then $W_3^{(i)} = VP_1$

Let T_q be the grammatical transformation determined by the pair (π_q, Q_q) (cf. Definition 10, §83.2). Thus T_q carries any string of the form $NP\text{-}W_2^{(i)}W_3^{(i)}$ into the corresponding string of the form $W_2^{(i)}\text{-}NP\text{-}W_3^{(i)}$, where $W_2^{(i)}$ and $W_3^{(i)}$ jointly meet (ii), (iii) of **8**. We could specify $W_2^{(i)}$ more closely, but this is not necessary. The notations in **8** have the obvious sense carried over from earlier usages. Thus $W_2^{(i)}$ can be any of the forms S, $S\frown have$, $S\frown be$, $\varnothing$, $\varnothing\frown have$, $\varnothing\frown be$, ed, $ed\frown have$, $ed\frown be$, M.

We must now provide for the introduction of "do" by a mapping Φ_6^{P} which must appear between Φ_5^{P} and Φ_8^{P}.

9 Φ_6^{P}: U goes into *do* in env. $\#\!\!-\!\!-\!\!-\left\{ \begin{matrix} \varnothing \\ S \\ ed \end{matrix} \right\}$

We will replace **9** by a more general characterization below.

Each transformation requires that the strings to which it applies be mapped out to a certain stage. T_q must clearly apply after Φ_3^{P} to ensure that C will have the proper form (otherwise we will have to add the mapping Φ_2' of **6** even in the transformational analysis). Thus as a **T**-marker we have

10 $Z\frown K\frown\psi_3\frown T_q\frown\psi_3'$

To determine the effect of **10** for a given choice of Z and K, we first apply ψ_3 to the string Z with the interpretation K, then apply T_q to the string $\psi_3(Z, K)$ with its derived interpretation, and finally apply in turn the remaining components Φ_4^{P}, Φ_5^{P},... of Φ^{P} to the transform under T_q, with its derived interpretation. Suppose that $\psi_3(Z, K)$ does not have the analysis prescribed by the restricting class for T_q, i.e., that it is not analyzable into $W_1^{(i)}\text{-}W_2^{(i)}\text{-}W_3^{(i)}$ meeting **8**. Then we have an instance of case II, Definition 10, §83.2, so that T_q leaves the string

$\psi_3(Z, K)$ and its derived interpretation unaltered. In other words, the effect of **10** on such a pair (Z, K) is to apply the mapping Φ^P to Z, K. As instances of a significant operation of **10**, we have

11 $\emptyset^\frown John^\frown \emptyset - C - come^\frown from^\frown Boston \rightarrow \emptyset^\frown John^\frown \emptyset - S - come^\frown$
$from^\frown Boston$
(by ψ_3)
$S - \emptyset^\frown John^\frown \emptyset - come^\frown$
$from^\frown Boston$
(by T_q)
$do^\frown S - \emptyset^\frown John^\frown \emptyset -$
$come^\frown from^\frown Boston^2$
(by $\Phi_6{}^P$)
$do^\frown S - John - come^\frown$
$from^\frown Boston$
(by $\Phi_8{}^P$)
$does^\frown John^\frown come^\frown from^\frown$
$Boston$
(by $\Phi_{m+1}^P = \Phi^{\overline{M}}$;
morphological rules)

$\emptyset^\frown John^\frown \emptyset - C^\frown have - en^\frown be^\frown ing^\frown read \rightarrow \emptyset^\frown John^\frown \emptyset - S^\frown have -$
$en^\frown be^\frown ing^\frown read$
(by ψ_3)
$S^\frown have - \emptyset^\frown John^\frown$
$\emptyset - en^\frown be^\frown ing^\frown read$
(by T_q)
$has^\frown John^\frown been^\frown$
$reading$
(by ψ_3')

The transformational analysis given by **8**, **9**, and **10** is clearly somewhat simpler than the extension of the kernel grammar of **5** and **6**, even in absolute terms as these analyses now stand. Thus we must accept the transformational analysis of yes-or-no questions, and drop them from the kernel. The difference in complexity between these two analyses

---

[2] Note that in actually formulating $\Phi_5{}^P$ as a grammatical transformation we must be careful to indicate that the element K (cf. definition of $\Phi_5{}^P$ in §72.3) and the following verb are not permuted when K belongs to the preceding noun phrase, as in this case. This is easily done in terms of the notions of derived constituent structure. We simply require that the element K, if it is S or $\emptyset$, must be a C, and this is easily stated in the restricting class for $\Phi_5{}^P$. This refinement is necessary whether or not we accept the transformational analysis for interrogatives.

would become more compelling if we could show that **8** and **9** are needed anyway, for other transformations. But this is in fact the case.

Consider the sentences **94.4**

12 *I saw the play and so did he*
I will see the play and so will he
I have seen the play and so has he
I have been seeing the play and so has he

Since no noun can appear as the final element in **12** unless it can also appear before "saw," we see that there is a selectional relation between the main verb of the first conjunct and the noun phrase of the second. Assuming for the moment that the *and*-transformation has been given as a generalized transformation, the sentences of **12** are most simply derived from pairs of kernel sentences

13 *I saw the play; he saw the play*

as **P**-basis. By the *and*-transformation, **13** is carried into

14 *I saw the play and he saw the play*

There is a selectional relation between the auxiliary phrases of the two conjuncts in **12**. Thus we do not have

15 *I will see the play and so did he*
etc.

The simplest way to provide for this selectional relation, to a first approximation, is to require that the auxiliary phrases must be *identical* in the two conjuncts of **14** for the transformation that gives **12** from **14**, call it "T_{so}," to apply. But investigating the grammatical cases further, we find that excluded along with **15** are such sentences as

16 *I have been reading the book and so has been he*
etc.

We find that T_{so} changes a sentence of the form

17 *NP-Z-W-and-NP-Z-W*

into

18 NP-Z-W-and-so-X-NP

where X can be any of the forms listed in **3**, i.e., any of the initial segments $W_2^{(i)}$ of questions, as in **8**. But this means that we can use **8** and **9** to state this transformation.

Let T_{so} be the grammatical transformation determined by (Q_{so}, t_{so}), where

19 $Q_{so} = \{(W_1^{(i)} {}^\frown W_2^{(i)} {}^\frown W_3^{(i)} {}^\frown and,\ W_1^{(i)},\ W_2^{(i)},\ W_3^{(i)})\}$

where $W_1^{(i)}$, $W_2^{(i)}$, $W_3^{(i)}$ meet **8**[3]

$t_{so} = \delta_{so}(\pi_{so})$, where

(i) π_{so} is the permutation that carries Y_1-Y_2-Y_3-Y_4 into Y_1-Y_4-Y_3-Y_2

(ii) δ_{so} is the deformation that carries Z_1-Z_2-Z_3-Z_4 into Z_1-so-Z_3-Z_4

Thus t_{so} carries Y_1-Y_2-Y_3-Y_4 into Y_1-so-Y_3-Y_2, and T_{so} carries a string of the form $NP_x {}^\frown W_2^{(i)} {}^\frown W_3^{(i)} {}^\frown and$-$NP_y$-$W_2^{(i)}$-$W_3^{(i)}$ into the corresponding string of the form $NP_x {}^\frown W_2^{(i)} {}^\frown W_3^{(i)} {}^\frown and$-$so$-$W_2^{(i)}$-$NP_y$. We now extend **9**, giving "so——" alongside of "$\#$——" as an initial conditioning context for the introduction of "do" by the mapping. (This will be further generalized below.)

Sentences like **12** are thus derived by applying the generalized transformation T_{and} followed by T_{so} as defined above. Thus we add to $\mu^{\mathbf{T}}$ the generalized **T**-marker schema

20 $Z_1 {}^\frown K_1 {}^\frown I$-$Z_2 {}^\frown K_2 {}^\frown I$-$T_{and}$-$\psi_3$-$T_{so}$-$\psi_3'$

But I is the identity, so that the value$_1$ of $Z_1 {}^\frown K_1 {}^\frown I$-$Z_2 {}^\frown K_2 {}^\frown I$ is the complex string $Z_1 {}^\frown \# {}^\frown Z_2$ (cf. Definition 50, §91.3). Thus the first sentence of **12** is derived from the kernel by **20** in essentially the following steps:

21   1. $Z_1 = I {}^\frown ed {}^\frown see {}^\frown the {}^\frown play$
         $Z_2 = he {}^\frown ed {}^\frown see {}^\frown the {}^\frown play$ (Z_1 and Z_2 being two sentences of $Gr(P)$ with K_1 and K_2 as respective **P**-markers)

---

[3] We may add a further specification of $W_1^{(i)}$ to guarantee that the selectional relation of the verb of the first conjunct of **12** and the noun of the second is maintained. But this is irrelevant to the point at issue here.

2. $I{\frown}ed{\frown}see{\frown}the{\frown}play{\frown}\#{\frown}he{\frown}ed{\frown}see{\frown}the{\frown}play$
   $(= \mathrm{Val}_1(Z_1{\frown}K_1{\frown}I{\frown}Z_2{\frown}K_2{\frown}I))$

3. $I{\frown}ed{\frown}see{\frown}the{\frown}play{\frown}and{\frown}he{\frown}ed{\frown}see{\frown}the{\frown}play$ (by T_{and})

3. $----------------see{\frown}the{\frown}play\text{-}ed\text{-}he$ (by π_{so}; ψ_3 applies vacuously)

5. $---------------so\text{-}ed\text{-}he$ (by δ_{so})

6. $--------------so\text{-}do{\frown}ed\text{-}he$ (by Φ_6^P; **9**, as extended above)

7. $I{\frown}saw{\frown}the{\frown}play{\frown}and{\frown}so{\frown}did{\frown}he$ (by the component mappings of Φ^P and the morphological rules)

In a similar way, all other forms of **12** (and only these) can be derived.

The important thing in this context is that the transformation T_{so} makes use of **8** and **9**. Hence given the transformational analysis of yes-or-no questions, sentences of the form **12** can be introduced transformationally in a very simple way, with no independent characterization necessary. If, on the other hand, we had followed the path of §94.2 and retained yes-or-no questions in the kernel with the modifications of **5** and **6**, then **8** and **9** would not be available for the formulation of T_{so}, and we would be compelled to choose between a transformational analysis which restates **8** and **9**, or the equally complex alternative of introducing sentences of the form **12** directly into the kernel. In other words, we have found that two phenomena which on the level of phrase structure are distinct and complex become, in transformational terms, instances of a single generalization. But this naturally leads us to choose the transformational analysis in this case and, in particular, to drop yes-or-no questions from the kernel.

Investigation of sentences like

22   *I saw the play and he did too*

etc., gives additional support to this analysis. These are not quite like **12**, since we can have both

23   *I have been reading the book and he has too*
      I have been reading the book and he has been too

but the simplest characterization of **22**, **23**, etc. is also in terms of **8** and **9**, with a certain emendation.

The transformation T_{so} (and, similarly, T_{too}, had we developed it properly) provides the first instance in our analysis of a "pro-element"—a class of elements of which pronouns will later appear as a special case. *So* (and *too*) is an element which takes the place of a verb phrase ("see the play," etc.). This seems quite in accord with our intuitive understanding of **12** and **22**.

Another case of a transformation that makes use of **8** and **9**, and thus supports the transformational analysis of yes-or-no questions, will be discussed below, in §96.

94.5   The consideration of questions has an effect on our analysis of sentences with *be* as the main verb, i.e., sentences of the form

24 $NP–VP_A–be–Pred$

e.g., "John–will–be–the candidate."
There are several important respects in which *be* behaves quite differently from other main verbs. The first is with respect to the formation of questions. With all other main verbs, the question is formed by inverting the subject and a certain initial segment of the auxiliary verb, as we have just seen, thus giving, e.g., "can John come" from "John can come." But when the main verb is *be*, and the VP_A is minimal (i.e., VP_A is either $\emptyset$, S, or ed), then the question is formed by inverting the subject and $VP_A^\frown be$. Thus the question formed from "John is your friend" is not **25** (as it would be if the verb were *see*), but **26**:

25   *does John be your friend*

26   *is John your friend*

In other words, *be* in **24** is treated exactly as if it were a part of the auxiliary phrase, as it is in "John is eating lunch."
Another respect in which *be* in **24** is treated as an auxiliary is in the placing of *not*, a problem which we will discuss in more detail in §96. The word *not* is usually placed after the first word of the auxiliary phrase, as in

27   *John has not (hasn't) come here*

It certainly never appears after the main verb—we cannot have

28   *John came not (camen't) here*

But when the main verb is *be*, this is exactly what happens. Thus we have

29   *John was not (wasn't) here*

If only the first case, that of questions, is considered there are two ways of handling this anomaly:

1. We can continue to treat *be* as the main verb, and formulate **8** so that $W_2^{(i)}$, the preposed element in the question transformation, covers any instance of "was," "is," etc., whether the instance of *be* in question is the main verb or the auxiliary.
2. We can consider *be* to be an auxiliary always, and we can regard **24** as a certain kind of "nominal sentence," with no main verb.

The difficulty with the second solution is, first, that a special statement is necessary to account for the fact that the element *ing* of the auxiliary *be⌢ing* is missing in **24**, and, second, that it will be difficult to account properly for such sentences as

30   *John is being nice about it*

where the second *be* is clearly the main verb. Nevertheless, this approach may be possible with some juggling.

The first solution can be carried through quite readily. We revise **8**, leaving (i) and (ii) unaltered, and replacing (iii) by

31   If $W_2^{(i)} = \left\{ \begin{array}{c} S \\ \varnothing \\ ed \end{array} \right\}$, then $W_3^{(i)} = V_x\frown...$

where a notational convention will indicate that V_x denotes any of the subclasses of V listed in §72.2, statement 23.

Before continuing with the discussion of *be*, it is worth noting that this replacement of 8iii by **31** is actually necessary for independent reasons. One of the forms of VP_1 is $D_2\frown V_x$ (cf. §72.2, statement 3), as in "John will certainly object." But we cannot form questions such as "will John certainly object" from such sentences. But such transforms would be permitted by 8iii, though excluded by **31** (they could easily be readmitted in **31** by replacing V_x by $\langle D_2 \rangle\, V_x$).

Since *be* is not in any of the subclasses of V (*be* is introduced directly as a main verb in §72.2, statement 3, for quite independent reasons), *be* is not represented by V_x ; and thus **31** indicates that no sequence

(NP, $W_2^{(i)}$, *be*) can be in the restricting class Q_q of T_q, where $W_2^{(i)}$ is $\emptyset$, S, or *ed*. But this excludes the possibility of **25**, etc. The correct form **26** results automatically from 8ii as formulated above, since there was no requirement given in stating 8ii that the element *be* in question be the auxiliary. To have required this, would have led to an additional and special restriction on **8**. We thus note the interesting fact that this apparently irregular behavior of *be* actually *simplifies* the grammar. If we had **25** but not **26** as a grammatical sentence, then a special condition would have to be added to 8ii to indicate that the *be* involved in that statement is *not* the main verb *be*. In addition, it would be necessary to replace V_x in **31** (which, we have seen, must replace 8iii for independent reasons) by $\left\{ \begin{array}{c} V_x \\ be \end{array} \right\}$. But to say that *be* behaves in such a way as to simplify the grammar is to say that its behavior is not irregular but systematic. This gives an important and unexpected justification for the trans-formational approach. If we had continued to analyze English structure on the basis of the devices presented in Chapter VII, the behavior of *be* would have been exceptional, and would have required special statement in the grammar, as can easily be determined by attempting to revise §72.2 and **5** to cope with this phenomenon. If what is exceptional from one point of view becomes systematic and regular from a second, then this may be interpreted as giving some indication that the latter is more fundamental.

Before continuing, it is important to note that the considerations of this section give further support to the transformational analysis of yes-or-no questions, since these considerations fall into place auto-matically in the transformational treatment, but they create further difficulties for the approach of §94.2.

One potential trouble spot remains, however. Just as the main verb *be* is not excluded in 8ii, neither is the main verb *have*. And *have* is also not excluded in the reformulation **31** of 8iii, since *have*, being a transitive verb, is a V_x. Thus if we add no further qualifications, it will follow from the simplest formulation of the question transformation (namely, 8i, 8ii, and **31**) that *have* as a main verb should share the normal characteristics of transitive verbs on the one hand, and the "peculiarities" of *be* on the other. But in fact, this is exactly the case. Though we cannot have **25**, we do have

32   *does John have a ticket*

paralleling the normal "does John play the piano." But it is an interesting fact that *have*, alone among transitive verbs, shares both of the special features of *be* mentioned above. Thus we can have **33** and **34**, but not **35** or **36**[4]:

33   *has he a chance to live*

34   *he hasn't a chance to live*

35   *plays he the piano*

36   *he playsn't the piano*

We see then that two apparent anomalies, the irregular behavior of *be* and the irregular (and different) behavior of *have* as main verbs, turn out to be higher-level regularities. That is, they turn out to be direct consequences of the simplest way of stating the facts for the "regular" main verbs.

Another special feature which appears relevant here is the peculiar behavior of the word *got* in colloquial English. We will not attempt to give a serious account of this—for one thing, such an attempt would lead at once into the study of special dialects—but we note the following facts. First, we have **37** but not **38**:

37   *has John got a chance to live*

38   *will John have got a chance to live*

Second, "got" is not the participial form of "get" (this being "gotten," as we can tell from the normal uses of "get" as a main verb) or any other verb. It appears from this that the simplest way to describe "got" is as a dummy verb that occurs in the normal main verb position when "have" is treated by transformation as an auxiliary (i.e., by 8ii), though it is actually the main verb of the kernel sentence. In transforming

39   *John has a chance to live*

into "has John a chance to live," "have" is treated as an auxiliary, but in transforming

40   *John will have a chance to live*

---

[4] There are many cases where the forms **33** and **34** are strained and unnatural. But the important thing is that if the grammar is detailed and sensitive enough to distinguish the natural cases like **33** and **34** from the unnatural ones, then it is no simpler to add the natural ones to the grammar by special rules than to strike off the unnatural ones. Thus this further consideration does not affect our conclusions here.

into "will John have a chance to live" it is not, since here the element "will" is inverted. Hence in **39**, but not **40**, the main verb position is left open and can be filled by a second transformation by the element "got." This accounts for the possibility of **37**, but not **38**.

But we have seen that both 8ii and **31** cover the case of "have" as a main verb. If we transform **39** by **31**, rather than by 8ii, the result is

41   *does John have a chance to live*

just as with any other transitive verb. Hence **37** and **41** are essentially in a relation of free variation—the question transformation permits either one or the other, freely. But it is a striking intuitive fact that we interpret **37** as meaning roughly the same thing as **41**, not as having the same structure as, say,

42   *has John found a place to live*

If the suggested interpretation of "got" carries through, then the explanation for this will be simply that **37** and **41** are alternative transforms of the same sentence **39**, under the question transformation, while **42** is a transform of the quite different sentence

43   *John has found a place to live*

in which "has" is in fact the auxiliary.

The VP_A of **39** is simply S, while the VP_A of **43** is $S\frown have\frown en$. This accounts for the fact that **37** and **41** are "present" in meaning, while **42** is "present perfect," although **37** superficially appears to be present perfect in form.

A technical requirement that must be met here is that a transformation must be single-valued, and T_q as we have stated it in **8** and **31** is ambiguous in the case of *have*, as we have just seen. This can be settled quickly by regarding T_q as a family of transformations (cf. §80). We specify this family by stating a pair (C, t), where C is a condition on the restricting class and t is an elementary transformation:

44   Let F_q be the family of transformations defined by the pair (C_q, π_q), where

      (i) π_q is the elementary permutation that carries $Y_1\text{-}Y_2\text{-}Y_3$ into $Y_2\text{-}Y_1\text{-}Y_3$ (cf. **7**)

(ii) $C_q(\alpha_1, \alpha_2, \alpha_3)$ is the schema: (I) and either (II) or (III), where

(I) $\alpha_1 = NP$

(II) $\alpha_2 = \left\{ \left\{ \begin{matrix} C \\ ed \\ M \end{matrix} \right\} \left[\begin{matrix} have \\ be \end{matrix} \right] \right\}$ (as in 8ii—note that S is a C and $\emptyset$ is a C, where S and $\emptyset$ are the auxiliaries given by $\Phi_3{}^{\mathrm{P}}$)

(III) $\alpha_2 = \left\{ \begin{matrix} C \\ ed \end{matrix} \right\}$ and $\alpha_3 = V_x \cap ...$ (as in 31)

The **T**-marker schema **10** for yes-or-no questions can now be rewritten:

45 $Z \cap K \cap \psi_3 \cap F_q \cap \psi_3'$

It is important to note that the transformation T_q is irreversible in the sense that we could not have chosen questions as the kernel and considered declaratives to be transforms of them. There are a variety of reasons for this, all turning on the relative complexity of the two alternatives. For one thing, the kernel grammar is more simply stated for declaratives than for questions, as can easily be seen by comparing **5** with the replaced statements of §72.2—particularly, by comparing **5**ii and **5**iii with statements **20** and **21**, which are essentially their parallels for declaratives. It is always easier to describe a continuous element than a discontinuous one, and in interrogatives, the auxiliary phrase is discontinuous. Second, almost all other transforms are derived from declaratives, not questions. Thus if questions are taken as the kernel, most transformations will have to be compound transformations, with resulting complication in the formulation of the level **T**. Third, and most important, we have seen in Chapter VIII fundamental reasons for assigning the constituent structure of §72.2 (or something very similar) to declaratives. But if we choose interrogatives as the kernel sentences and derive declaratives from them by transformation, we will find that this constituent interpretation will not be carried over by the interrogative-to-declarative transformation, from the constituent structure which will be assigned to interrogatives as the new kernel. In fact, even the basic *NP-VP* division would not be established. On the other hand, the reasons adduced in Chapter VIII for assigning a systematic constituent structure to declaratives do not hold in general for questions, and in fact, T_q does not assign a complete derived structure to questions.

94.6

That is, questions will not have **P**-markers conferred on them by trans-formation, as will, e.g., passives (cf. §§87.2, 98, below). From these few remarks it is easy to see that a detailed study would show that there is a considerable gain in overall simplicity of the grammar if declaratives are taken as the kernel sentences and interrogatives derived from them, as opposed to the alternative possibility of choosing interrogatives as the kernel and deriving declaratives by transformation. Thus there is a clear and forceful systematic motivation for the feeling that declaratives are "more basic" and questions a "derived" phenomenon, from the point of view of sentence structure, as well as for the fact that a syntactic study of English would normally discuss simple declarative sentences, the actor–action form, etc., as providing the fundamental sentence types and grammatical relations of the language.[5] We can offer as a reason for this the fact that the simplest grammar takes declaratives as the kernel and derives questions from them by transformation.

It is also important to observe that we made no appeal here to semantic or other nondistributional considerations, nor, for that matter, to detailed selectional relations which are within the realm of distri-butional study. Even the most rudimentary level of grammaticalness would have sufficed to establish T_q. We can regard this transformation, then, as being quite firmly grounded in distributional terms. Con-siderably fewer assumptions about grammaticalness were required here than for the establishment of the system of phrase structure in Chapter VIII.

95.1 A second class of sentences not included in §72.2 is the class of interro-gatives receiving other than a yes-or-no answer, i.e., interrogatives of the form

46   *whom did he see*
      whom has he seen

47   *who saw him*
      who has seen him

On the surface, there seems no special structural reason at all for calling these "interrogatives," thus classifying them along with the sentences investigated in §94, though intuitively, this is a correct classi-

---

[5] In fact, such a careful and detailed study of English structure as Nida's *A Synopsis of English Syntax* does not even include a discussion of questions. But clearly the opposite procedure of sketching English syntax including only questions, excluding declaratives, would be unthinkable.

fication. Furthermore, the sentences of **46** and **47** seem to be of quite different formal types, **46** containing inversions, **47** none; and there seems little formal reason to classify **46** and **47** as belonging to a single subclass of interrogatives, though again this is intuitively quite obviously the case. But in transformational terms, it will appear that both of these intuitions are formally well grounded.

Investigating sentences of the form **46**, we see immediately that the relation between the subject and the auxiliary phrase is exactly that of yes-or-no questions, i.e., the subject is inverted with an initial segment of the auxiliary in exactly the same way. Hence the simplest way to describe sentences of the form **46** is as double transforms of kernel sentences, as transforms of yes-or-no questions where this inversion is already "built in." The kernel sentences leading to **46** are thus

48   *he⌢ed⌢see⌢him*
       he⌢C⌢have⌢en⌢see⌢him

T_q (preceded by ψ_3, cf. **45**) applied to **48** gives

49   *ed⌢he⌢see⌢him*
       S⌢have⌢he⌢en⌢see⌢him

46 is formed by applying to this result the new transformation T_w, which permutes the final noun phrase "him" with the preceding string, then replacing this noun phrase with "whom," thus giving

50   *whom⌢ed⌢he⌢see*
       whom⌢S⌢have⌢he⌢en⌢see

This becomes **46** by applying the remaining mappings ψ_3', with a further generalization of the mapping Φ_6^P that introduces "do."

Investigating T_w in more detail, we note first that its underlying elementary transformation is a compound of a permutation and a deformation. Since the permuted noun phrase may be nonfinal, as in the transformation of "he saw him yesterday" to "whom did he see yesterday," we see that the underlying permutation is again π_q, as in **44i**. We can choose the underlying deformation in various ways. The simplest way, perhaps, is to assume that "whom" is analyzed into a morpheme wh^6 plus *him*, and that "who" is analyzed into *wh* plus *he*. That is, we add morphological rules to the effect that

51 $wh^\frown he \to who$
$wh^\frown him \to whom$

We accordingly revise $\Phi^P_{m+1} = \Phi^{\overline{M}}$ so that the word boundary does not fall after *wh*.

As the underlying deformation we now select δ_q such that

52 $\delta_q: \quad Y_1\text{-}Y_2\text{-}Y_3 \to wh^\frown Y_1\text{-}Y_2\text{-}Y_3$

The defining sequence for δ_q is thus $(wh, U, U, U, U, U,)$. Thus $\delta_q(\pi_q)$ will be the elementary transformation such that

53 $\delta_q(\pi_q): \quad Y_1\text{-}Y_2\text{-}Y_3 \to wh^\frown Y_2\text{-}Y_1\text{-}Y_3$

If $Y_1 = ed^\frown he^\frown see$, $Y_2 = him$, and $Y_3 = U$, then $t_w{}^*(Y_1, Y_2, Y_3) =$ the first sentence of **50**, where $t_w = \delta_q(\pi_q)$.

In §72.2 we did not trouble to make the distinction between *he* and *him*, but this is a trivial matter of added detail. The simplest way would be with a mapping which may precede Φ_1^P. We can then limit the application of T_w to the noun phrase *he*. That is, we can take T_w as the transformation which carries $X_1\text{-}he\text{-}X_3$ into $wh^\frown he\text{-}X_1\text{-}X_3$. As the restricting class for T_w, then, we might consider Q_w defined as the set of triples

54 $\left\{\left(X_1^{(i)}, he \left\{ {\varnothing \atop S} \right\}, X_3^{(i)}\right)\right\}$, where $X_1^{(i)}$ and $X_3^{(i)}$ are strings (or U)

But in this case we have not defined a grammatical transformation, since *he* may occur several times in a string (e.g., **46**), and thus (Q_w, t_w) does not determine a single-valued transformation. To limit T_w to exactly the cases **46** we would have to specify $X_1^{(i)}$ further. But if we take **54** as a condition C_w on restricting classes, then (C_w, t_w) does define a family of transformations F_w. A grammatical transformation belongs to this family just in case its elementary transformation is $t_w = \delta_q(\pi_q)$ and its

---

[6] See Harris, *Methods*, for a discussion of the morphemic treatment of *wh* and *th*, Appendices to §§12.22, 12.41. In this discussion we omit consideration of the other personal pronouns. This is simply a matter of added detail, and need not concern us. For example, we will have to add, as a morphological rule (a part of Φ^M) that $he^\frown S \to they$, $him^\frown S \to them$, etc.

restricting class contains only strings meeting **54**. If it were the case that any transformation beloning to F_w could be applied wherever T_w can be applied (i.e., if T_w can be applied to any occurrence of *he* in a sentence), then we would not need to specify T_w any further, and in stating the grammar of the level **T** could simply state a **T**-marker with F_w . But we will see directly that (within certain limitations—cf. §95.3) this is in fact the case.

Assuming then that we have a family F_w defined by (C_w , t_w), where C_w is **54** and t_w is the elementary transformation **53**, we can construct a **T**-marker schema containing F_w. We have seen that T_w is best construed as applying after the application of T_q. The **T**-marker schema for T_q was given in **45**. We can now generalize **45**, replacing it by the statement that any string of the form **55** is a **T**-marker:

55 $Z^\frown K^\frown \psi_3 {}^\frown F_q \langle F_w \rangle \; \psi_3'$

We have seen that one of the members of the family F_w is the trans- **95.2** formation T_w which carries **49** into **50**, permuting the second occurrence of *him* in **49** with the preceding string. We now turn to other grammatical transformations in F_w , and determine their effects on strings to which F_q has been applied, i.e., strings of the form **49**. Consider now the transformation T_{w_1} that applies to the first occurrence of *he* in **49**.

T_{w_1} analyzes **49** into the proper analysis

56   *ed–he–see$^\frown$him*
         S$^\frown$have–he–en$^\frown$see$^\frown$him
         etc.

Applying t_w , the underlying elementary transformation, to **56**, we derive first **57** (by applying π_q) and then **58** (applying δ_q to the result of applying π_q):

57   *he–ed–see him*
         he–S have–en see him

58   *wh$^\frown$he–ed–see$^\frown$him*
         wh$^\frown$he–S$^\frown$have–en$^\frown$see$^\frown$him

Applying the remaining mappings, we derive

59   *who$^\frown$saw$^\frown$him*
         who$^\frown$has$^\frown$seen$^\frown$him

in the usual fashion. But **59** is exactly **47**. We see then that when we apply T_w to **49** we derive **46**, and when we apply T_{w_1} (another member of F_w) to **49**, we derive **47**. Hence despite their apparent structural differences, **46** and **47** (one set with inversions, and one without) are instances of the same structural type in transformational terms, both having instances of **55** as their **T**-markers. Hence there is formal support, on the level **T**, for the fact that intuitively these sentence types seem to have the same form. An apparent difference in formal structure between two types of sentence once more turns out to be the effect of an underlying regularity, in the sense that the simplest description of one of the types automatically describes the other as well. We found, in constructing the level **P**, that we were able to account for the intuitive fact that sentences distinct in terms of lower levels seemed similar in structure, by showing that these distinct sentences had similar **P**-markers (e.g., "John read the book" and "I saw him," though completely distinct in terms of words, have **P**-markers with very similar construction, are both represented by $NP^\frown VP$, etc.). The case of **46** and **47** is quite analogous, on the level **T**. The similarity of **T**-markers (both being instances of **55**) provides a formal justification for the classification of **46** and **47** into the same subclass of interrogatives. The only difference between the two cases is that in one case the transformation is applied to the subject, and in the other, to the object.

The reason why we do not have any inversion in **47** while we have a complex inversion in **46** becomes evident when we examine the details of the derivation of these sentences. Reducing this to essentials, we see that the transformational derivation of **55** is based on a permutation π_q from T_q which is repeated a second time (from F_w) and then followed by a deformation δ_q (from F_w). The development of the first sentence of **46** and the first sentence of **47** can be compared by the following chart:

60	$T_w(T_q)$	$T_{w_1}(T_q)$
The kernel structure:	$he^\frown ed^\frown see^\frown him$	$he^\frown ed^\frown see^\frown him$
is transformed by π_q of T_q into:	$ed^\frown he^\frown see^\frown him$	$ed^\frown he^\frown see^\frown him$
which is transformed by π_q of F_w into:	$him^\frown ed^\frown he^\frown see$	$he^\frown ed^\frown see^\frown him$

	$T_w(T_q)$	$T_{w_1}(T_q)$
which is transformed by δ_q of F_w into:	$wh \frown him \frown ed \frown he \frown see$	$wh \frown he \frown ed \frown see \frown him$
transformed by $\Phi_5{}^P$ into:	$wh \frown him \frown ed \frown he \frown see$	$wh \frown he \frown see \frown ed \frown him$
transformed by $\Phi_6{}^P$ into:	$wh \frown him \frown do \frown ed \frown he \frown see$	$wh \frown he \frown see \frown ed \frown him$
transformed by the remaining rules into:	$whom \frown did \frown he \frown see$	$who \frown saw \frown him$

The case of the kernel sentence $he \frown S \frown have \frown en \frown see \frown him$ is perfectly analogous. In the case of T_{w_1}, the second application of π_q cancels out the first, i.e., row 3 is identical with row 1. This accounts for the fact that there is no inversion in the derived string of words.

We have seen that two transformations in F_w as defined by (C_w, t_w) **95.3** (**54** and **53**, respectively) give grammatical strings. There will be a distinct transformation in F_w for every position in which *he* can occur. But there are certain occurrences of *he* which cannot be transformed into *who*-questions, and restrictions must be placed on **54** to rule out the possibility of transformation in these cases. Thus we have **61** but not **62**:

61   *your interest in him seemed to me rather strange*

62   *whom did your interest in seem to me rather strange*

On the other hand, we have both cases of **63**, and both cases of **64**:

63   *you lost interest in him ⟨this year⟩*

64   *whom did you lose interest in ⟨this year⟩*

We might account for this by adding to **54** the following condition on $X_1^{(i)}$ and $X_3^{(i)}$:

65 $X_1^{(i)} \neq Z \frown Prep$ unless $X_3^{(i)} = \begin{cases} U \\ Prep\ Phrase \\ Adverbial\ Phrase \end{cases}$

It is interesting to note in this connection that though **62** is not grammatical, **66** is:

66   *in whom did you lose interest*

This possibility can be accommodated quite neatly in our framework by taking *Prep⌢he* as one of the permitted forms of the second term of the restricting class in **54**, and adding to $\Phi_5{}^P$ the requirement that

67   *wh⌢Prep → Prep⌢wh*

95.4   Alongside of the *who*-transformation discussed in §§95.1–95.3, we have an exactly parallel case of *what*-transformations, giving

68   *what did you see*
          what has he seen
          what hit him
          what has hit him

These *what*-questions can be introduced quite readily by noting that just as an occurrence of *he* (or *him*) can be preposed and prefixed by *wh* to give a grammatical sentence of the form **46** or **47**, an occurrence of *it* can be preposed and prefixed by *wh*, by exactly the same transformation, to give a sentence of the form **68**. To account for *what*-questions, then, it is only necessary to add to **54** the condition that the second term of the restricting class may be *it*, and to add to **51** the rule

69   *wh⌢it → what*

This statement is correct for the uses of *it* as an inanimate pronoun, but a sufficiently sensitive analysis of grammaticalness might show that *what*-questions cannot be formed in cases where *it* is used as an animate pronoun (i.e., where it is the subject of a verb that takes only N_{anim} as subject, etc.), e.g., for animals, babies, etc. In this case we would have to add a condition (cf. condition K_A, **138–139**, below) that *it* be inanimate in the **P**-basis of the given **T**-marker. There is an analogous problem for inanimate uses of *he, she,* etc., if *who*-questions cannot be formed in these cases.

95.5   We might continue this analysis with the investigation of such *wh*-questions as

70   *what plane did he take*
what plane arrived today
whose book is that
where was it
when did he come
etc.

This would necessitate adding to **54** the condition that the second (preposed) term of the restricting class be *the* $\langle AP \rangle N \begin{Bmatrix} \varnothing \\ S \end{Bmatrix} \langle PP \rangle$, $he^\frown S_1{}^\frown NP$ (cf. statement 17 and following discussion, §72.2), there,[7] *then*, etc., and to **51** and **69** the further rules

71 $wh^\frown the \rightarrow what$
$wh^\frown there \rightarrow where$
$wh^\frown then \rightarrow when$
etc.

No serious modification seems to be necessary to accommodate these further sentences, though certain further restrictions are necessary on **54**. This requires a detailed study, and we will go into it no further here.

In **9**, §94, we introduced the element *do* by the mapping $\Phi_6{}^P$ as the bearer of a displaced affix at the beginning of a sentence. In §94.4, we extended this to cover also the environment *so*——, and in §95.1 we saw that this must be extended to cover the contexts $wh^\frown he$——, $wh^\frown him$——. It is apparent then that this is quite a general phenomenon —that *do* appears as a dummy verb bearing the affix when no verbal carrier appears for the affix in question. We can take this statement as the informal definition of $\Phi_6{}^P$. It can obviously be given in the proper form as the definition of a grammatical transformation.   **95.6**

In §95.1 we mentioned that we had as yet found no formal grounds for the intuitive classification of **46** and **47** as interrogatives, along with the yes-or-no questions of the type "did he come," etc., investigated in §94, or for the feeling that **46** and **47** constitute a single subclass of interrogatives. We have already seen that the second intuitive judgment   **95.7**

---

[7] This may require making a distinction in the kernel grammar between *there* in "I saw him there" and in "there is a possibility that he will be present," since we do not have "where is a possibility that he will be present," etc. Or a restriction on **56** might cover this.

can be explained on the formal grounds that **46** and **47** are in fact derived from the kernel by the same family of transformations. As a support for the notion that all of these sentences constitute a single class of interrogatives, we note the fact that **46** and **47** are derived from yes-or-no questions by a further transformation. Hence if we define sentence types and subtypes in terms of the sequence of transformations by which sentences are derived from the kernel, it will follow that **46** and **47** are a subtype of the general type to which these and yes-or-no questions together belong; i.e., the first step in deriving all of these sentences is the same, although later steps are different. This suggested formal explanation for the intuitive classification would acquire further plausibility if we could discover a case where F_w is applied directly to kernel structures, with no intervening T_q, and if in this case we did not intuitively consider the result to be a class of interrogatives. Relative clauses are just such a case. In such sentences as

72   *the man whom I visited was ill*
       the people who visited me were pleasant
       etc.

the *who*-clause is derived by F_w directly from a kernel structure, with no intervening interrogative transformation (as we see from the fact that there is no inversion of the auxiliary phrase), and the resulting sentence has, of course, no intuitive interrogative status. Thus it seems correct to explain the feeling that **46** and **47** are a kind of question on the grounds that T_q actually appears in their **T**-markers, i.e., that they are in fact constructed from yes-or-no questions.

We will return to sentences of the form **72** below.

95.8   Since F_q was determined to be "irreversible" (cf. §94.6) then *a fortiori* **46** and **47**, which are secondary transforms of F_q, cannot be kernel sentences. An independent investigation of the possibility of taking these as the kernel sentences instead of declaratives would give clearly negative results, even more strongly than in §94.6. In fact, it is impossible to derive all declarative sentences by a single family of transformations from sentences of this type, since a different transformation will be needed for each noun phrase that can replace "who" in the corresponding declarative. We conclude, then, that declarative sentences constitute the kernel, and that interrogatives of both the types discussed in §§94, 95 are derived from them by transformation.

The distribution of the word *not* was not given in §72.2 in the description **96.1** of phrase structure. This word occurs, in auxiliaries, in exactly the position marked by the definition of the restricting class for T_q , that is, it occurs at the α_2–α_3 break as this is stated in **44**. This break, it will be recalled, has two cases. When the auxiliary phrase consists of just the single morpheme $\emptyset$, S, or *ed*, then *not* occurs after the auxiliary (as in **44ii-III**). If the auxiliary phrase consists of M or any several-morpheme form (as in **44ii-II**), then *not* occurs after the first word of the auxiliary, i.e., after α_2 of **44ii**. For instance, we have

73 *John did not come*   (from *John-ed-not-come*, by $\Phi_6{}^P$)
   John has not come
   John has not been coming
   etc.

This distributional statement could have been detailed in §72.2 for the kernel grammar, but only as a unique and complex phenomenon. Even if questions had been introduced by **5**, the position where *not* occurs would not be marked. But once we have stated the definition of T_q , as in **44**, it is very easy to state the occurrence of *not* transformationally. T_{not} will be based on a deformation introducing the word *not* and a restricting class meeting condition C_q , **44ii**. Thus we have a family of transformations F_N , just as in the case of questions. The fact that **44** appears once more as a condition on transformations lends further support to the position taken in §94 that yes-or-no questions require a transformational analysis.

The deformation which underlies T_{not} introduces the word *not* at this break, but we have a choice as to whether to assign the *not* to α_2 or to α_3 . Thus we have a choice between (U, U, U, not, U, U) and (U, U, U, U, not, U) as the sequence defining the deformation. The choice is resolved in favor of the former alternative by noting that T_q applied to **74** gives **75**:[8]

74 *I can not see it*

75 *can't I see it*

---

[8] If such sentences as "can I not see it" are also considered grammatical, then we must set up two transformations, one based on the latter defining sequence, to account for this sentence, and one based on the former, to account for **75**. We have not troubled to make the distinction between *not* and *n't*. We will disregard this distinction, and rule out "can I not see it," etc.

Thus *can⌢not* must be an *M* in **74**, since T_q carries *NP-M* into *M-NP*, and in general, *not* must be assigned to α_2, as in **44**ii. This result is achieved by basing F_N on a deformation

76 $\delta_{not} \leftrightarrow U, U, U, not, U, U$

which carries $Y_1\text{-}Y_2\text{-}Y_3$ into $U⌢Y_1⌢U\text{-}U⌢Y_2⌢not\text{-}U⌢Y_3⌢U = Y_1\text{-}Y_2⌢not\text{-}Y_3$. The restricting class for F_N is given exactly by **44**ii. The proper derived constituent structure is assigned, as we see from the discussion of §87.5, (ii). There is no particular reason for F_N to apply after ψ_3, as does F_q, and in order to have other transformations apply freely to negative sentences, we give the **T**-marker schema for F_N as[9]

77 $Z⌢K⌢I⌢F_N⌢\Phi^{\mathbf{P}}$

96.2   In §94.5 we discussed the apparent irregularity of *be* and *have* as main verbs in questions, with *be* being treated as if it were the auxiliary *be* and *have* sharing the features of *be* and transitive verbs. Since the restricting class for T_q has been carried over unchanged in the *not*-transformation, it follows that *be* and *have* should behave similarly with respect to the position of *not*. And in fact we do have **78** but not **79**:

78   *John wasn't here*
       John hasn't a chance
       John doesn't have a chance
       John doesn't live here

79   *John doesn't be here*
       John livesn't here

---

[9] There is actually a good reason for F_N to apply before $\Phi_3^{\mathbf{P}}$, the mapping that converts *C* into Ø or *S*. If F_N applies after $\Phi_3^{\mathbf{P}}$, then *not* will be affixed to *S* or Ø. Hence it will be the case that *S⌢not* is an *S*, and *Ø⌢not* is a *Ø* (though this does not change the fact that *S⌢not* is a *C* and *Ø⌢not* is a *C*—this following from the fact that *S* is a *C* and *Ø* is a *C*). But $\Phi_5^{\mathbf{P}}$ converts, e.g., *S⌢V* into *V⌢S*, so that if *S⌢not* is an *S*, then $\Phi_5^{\mathbf{P}}$ will carry *S⌢not⌢V* into *V⌢S⌢not*, giving such impossible sentences as "John livesn't here," etc., unless some special condition is added. If *not* is inserted before $\Phi_3^{\mathbf{P}}$, then *C⌢not* is a *C*, and when *C* → *S* (by $\Phi_3^{\mathbf{P}}$), *S⌢not* is still a *C*, but is not an *S*, so that $\Phi_5^{\mathbf{P}}$ does not convert *S⌢not⌢V* into *V⌢S⌢not*.

Note that if F_N applies before $\Phi_2^{\mathbf{P}}$, then *M* in **44**ii-II must be replaced by ⟨*C*⟩*M* so as to make **44** available for both T_{not} and T_q. Hence $Z⌢K⌢\psi_2⌢F_N⌢\psi_2'$ might be a better choice for a **T**-marker than **77**. But the further transforms of negative sentences may lead to a violation of condition 5, §91.5, if this change is made. A good deal of further investigation is needed here.

Exactly as in the case of questions, this situation turns out to be a consequence of the simplest statement of the rules for the "regular" verbs *live*, etc., hence to be in actuality a higher-level regularity.

Φ_5^P is the mapping that carries $Af\langle D\rangle\ V$ into $\langle D\rangle\ V^\frown Af$, where *Af* stands for any of the affixes Ø, *S*, *ed*, *en*, and *ing*, *D* is an adverb, and *V* a verb, and where angles co-occur. Thus $S^\frown have \rightarrow have^\frown S$ (ultimately, *has*), $S^\frown certainly^\frown have \rightarrow certainly^\frown have^\frown S$ (ultimately, *certainly*$^\frown has$), etc., in such contexts as *John——a$^\frown$chance*. But *not* is not a member of *D*. Hence Φ_5^P does not apply to the string

80   *John$^\frown$S$^\frown$not$^\frown$have$^\frown$a$^\frown$chance*

But this means that *S* is a displaced affix in **80**, so that Φ_3^P carries **80** into

81   *John$^\frown$do$^\frown$S$^\frown$not$^\frown$have$^\frown$a$^\frown$chance*   [→ *John$^\frown$does$^\frown$not$^\frown$(doesn't)*
         have$^\frown$a$^\frown$chance]

Thus no further specification of the mappings is necessary to give the correct forms of negative sentences. See also note 9.

In the case of T_q and T_{not}, then, the apparent irregularities of *be* and *have* disappear. We have given one further transformation based on **44**, namely T_{so} (cf. §96.4). In this case too, we would expect to find that the main verb *be* is treated as an auxiliary, and that the main verb *have* is treated either as an auxiliary or a main verb. And in fact this is exactly the situation that we do find. We have **82** but not **83** as grammatical sentences, just as we have **78** but not **79** in the case of *not*, and **84** but not **85** in the case of questions:

82   *I am here and so is he*
         I have an appointment and so has he
         I have an appointment and so does he
         I kept the appointment and so did he

83   *I am here and so does he*
         I kept the appointment and so kept he

84   *is he here*
         has he a chance
         does he have a chance
         does he live here

85   *does he be here*
         lives he here

We see that in all three cases (the same is true of T_{too}—cf. §94.4), the apparently irregular behavior is actually systematic. These three superficially quite different cases all turn out to be instances of the same general formulation (i.e., **44**), and in fact, they turn out to be consequences of the simplest statement of the rules for regular verbs.

96.3 The statement we have given does not account for all occurrences of *not*. The word *not* also occurs with certain noun phrases, as in

86   (a)   *not a person was there*
         (b)   *not many people were there*
         (c)   *not coming was a mistake*

The third case does not intuitively seem parallel to the first two, but as things stand now there is no reason not to account for all such cases by a statement in the kernel grammar to the effect that $NP \rightarrow not^\frown NP$ under certain circumstances. However, we will see below, in §99.10, that there are grounds for the distinction between (a) and (b) on the one hand and (c) on the other.

Another difficulty in the placing of *not* appears in sentences like

87   *he tried not to fail*

We have not yet accounted for this. Intuitively, there seems to be a constituent break after "tried," and "not to fail" seems to be a noun phrase of the same type as the subject of **86c**, but we have no real basis for this analysis as yet. In fact, the analysis of *V-to-V* expressions to which we were led in Chapter VIII, §68 (which had, it will be recalled, a certain intuitive correspondence), would preclude this intuitively correct analysis, since "try to" was treated there as being a single constituent, i.e., the auxiliary verb V_B. We will see below that this difficulty, too, is resolved when a better analysis of *V-to-V* constructions results from transformational analysis.

However sentences like **86** are analyzed, they clearly associate *not* with the noun phrase, not the VP_A. **86c** thus provides a case of constructional homonymity for sentences of the form

88 $NP^\frown is^\frown not^\frown ing^\frown VP_1{}^{10}$

There are three sources for such sentences. They can be derived from

[10] In §65.5 we discovered two sources for sentences of the form $NP^\frown is^\frown ing^\frown VP_1$.

89   (a) $NP_1\text{-}is\text{-}NP_2$,   with $NP_2 = not^\frown ing^\frown VP_1$
        (b) $NP_1\text{-}is^\frown not\text{-}NP_2$,   with $NP_2 = ing^\frown VP_1$
        (c) $NP_1\text{-}is^\frown not\text{-}ing\text{-}VP_1$,   where $is^\frown ing = VP_A$

89b results from the application of T_{not} to $NP_1\text{-}is\text{-}NP_2$. **89c** results from the application of T_{not} to $NP_1\text{-}VP_A\text{-}VP_1$, where $VP_A = is^\frown ing$ (in the case of **89b**, $VP_A = S$). As examples of these three constructions, we have, respectively,

90   (a)   *the important thing is–not answering the questions (that are unfairly put)*
        (b)   *the important thing is not–answering the questions (so much as knowing the answers)*
        (c)   *John is not answering the questions*

Our analysis of questions paired questions and declaratives in the following way: 97

91   *he comes*   — *does he come*
       he came   — *did he come*
       he will come   — *will he come*
       he has been coming — *has he been coming*
       etc.   etc.

This is intuitively correct, and our theoretical conceptions are supported if they lead to this analysis. However, there is another analysis that we have not considered, but which, superficially, seems at least as a simple as **91**. We are led to consider this alternative by noting that our analysis of declaratives in §72.2 left one form of the declarative sentence out of consideration, namely,

92   *he did come,   he does come,   they do come*

If we bring **92** into consideration, as of course we must in a complete grammar, then **93** seems to be a possible analysis of the declarative–question transformation, in place of **91**:

93   *he does come*   — *does he come*
       he did come   — *did he come*
       he will come   — *will he come*
       he has been coming — *has he been coming*
       etc.   etc.

93 leaves "he comes," etc., unpaired; but 91 leaves 92 unpaired. If 93 is taken as the analysis of F_q, then 44ii-III can be dropped from the characterization of F_q, and "do" will be added to 44ii-II along with "have" and "be." In this case, Φ_6^P will not have to apply to questions. These alterations constitute no real saving, however. Φ_6^P and 44ii-III must still be stated in the grammar for T_{not} and T_{so}. On the other hand, we have not yet shown that 93 is a distinctly less simple analysis.

One argument against the analysis 93 is just this fact that it disturbs the uniformity of the analysis of T_q, T_{so}, and T_{not}, thus leading to certain additional complexity in the statement of the grammar. However, the transformational analysis would be more compelling if we could show that this uniformity is a consequence of what is independently the best analysis, instead of appealing to the resulting uniformity as the criterion for the analysis. And there are indeed independent arguments for the inadequacy of the analysis 93.

For one thing, we note that if "do" is regarded as an auxiliary, it will be subject to certain distributional limitations of a special and unique nature. As distinct from the elements M, "do" does not occur freely with other auxiliary verbs. Thus we do not have

94   *they did have come*, etc.

Similarly, "do" is distinct in distribution from the other elements of the auxiliary phrase. Hence the description of the auxiliary phrase in the kernel grammar will become more complex if "do" is treated as an auxiliary. Furthermore, "do" as an auxiliary cannot occur with the main verb "be"—we cannot have "he did be here," etc.—and this too requires a special restricting statement.

Investigation of 92 shows that these sentences have certain other peculiarities. For one thing, "do" in 92 must occur with heavy stress, whereas "do" in other positions (as an auxiliary) always[11] occurs unstressed. Secondly, all other auxiliaries appearing in the position of "do" in 92 are always[11] unstressed. A complete description of the structure of declaratives would have to account for this with a special statement. The only way to avoid an excessively complicated statement to this effect in the morphology, is to set up an element Ac of *accentuation*

---

[11] Except under contrastive stress, which can occur with almost any word. Exactly what is the status of contrastive stress is unclear, but we will proceed as if the problem of determining this had been solved, and sentences containing it will be set aside. It is worth noting, in this connection, that when sentences which are only partially grammatical do occur, they often contain contrastive stress. Hence one of the functions of this element is to mark the breaking of a grammatical rule.

as a prime of **P** (i.e., a morpheme, in this case), occurring along with "do" in sentences like **92**. As one of the forms of the auxiliary phrase, then, we have

$$
\mathbf{95} \qquad \begin{Bmatrix} S \\ \varnothing \\ ed \end{Bmatrix} {}^{\frown}do{}^{\frown}Ac
$$

And in the morphological rules, i.e., the mapping which carries word and morpheme strings into strings of phonemes, we will have a statement

96 $...V...Ac \rightarrow ...V...$, where V is the vowel just preceding Ac[12]

But this solution in fact rules out **93** as an analysis of the question transformation, since in questions "does" does occur without heavy stress.

    Perhaps an even stronger argument against **93** comes from noting that "do" is also a main verb, as in

97   *he does the crossword puzzle every day*

If "do" also appears as an auxiliary, then "do" will have the same status as "have," and thus the special distributional features noted above in the case of "have" will have to hold as well for "do." But in fact, this is not the case. We do not have

98   *does he the crossword puzzle every day*
       he doesn't the crossword puzzle every day

though we do have the parallel forms **33** and **34** in the case of "have."[13] Thus if **95** is admitted into the kernel grammar as a form of the auxiliary, we will have to add a set of special conditions to **44**.

    89 is thus clearly established as the correct analysis. The considerations adduced above suggest that $do{}^{\frown}Ac$ be analyzed in transformational terms, so that these various complications can be avoided in the kernel grammar.

---

[12] See my *Morphophonemics of Modern Hebrew* for a similar phenomenon.

[13] The third case, that of T_{so}, is inconclusive here, since given "he does the crossword puzzle and so do I," we cannot determine whether the "do" after "so" is the main verb or the bearer of the affix introduced by $\Phi_6 \mathbf{P}$. Note that the revision of **44** which is sketched above for the case where "do" is treated as an auxiliary in the kernel does not affect this situation.

We note at once that only Ac need be introduced by a special transformation. Then the appearance of *do* will be accounted for automatically by Φ_6^P. For suppose that Ac is introduced into the string $C^\frown V$ (or $ed^\frown V$), where V is any verb, giving $C^\frown Ac^\frown V$. But Ac is not an adverb of D. Thus $S^\frown Ac^\frown V$ (or $\emptyset^\frown Ac^\frown V$, both of which result from $C^\frown Ac^\frown V$ by Φ_3^P) will not be converted by Φ_5^P into $Ac^\frown V^\frown S$ (or $V^\frown Ac^\frown S$—see Note 9). But this means that S (or $\emptyset$ or ed) is a displaced affix in $...S^\frown Ac^\frown V...$, and Φ_6^P will thus introduce *do* as a bearer of the affix. This reasoning is perfectly analogous to the case of *not* discussed in §96.2. Thus we see that the forms **95** result automatically when Ac is introduced transformationally in the position where *not* occurs.

We have seen above that Ac and *not* share the further property that neither occurs before *be*, though both occur before all other verbs. The final indication that Ac and *not* are elements of the same type comes from noting that either one or the other may occur, but not both. That is, we do not have

99   *he díd not come*

Clearly the simplest way to handle the forms **92**, then, is to leave both the kernel grammar and T_q unchanged, and to define a transformation T_{Ac} differing from T_{not} only in that Ac appears in the underlying deformation instead of *not*.[14]

This parallel treatment of Ac and *not* certainly has intuitive appeal. It assigns to the paired sentences of **100** the same phrase structure and a parallel transformational structure, the only difference between them being that in one the element Ac appears and in the other the element *not*. And in fact these sentences do seem paired intuitively:

100   *he díd come*   —   *he did not come*
          he hás come   —   *he has not come*

The systematic effect of this analysis is that all asymmetry in the auxiliary verb phrase and in the pairing of questions and declaratives disappears.

[14] This is the simplest way to give the transformational analysis for Ac. An alternative would be to give only 44ii-I, III as the definition of the restricting class for T_{Ac}. This would limit the appearance of Ac to **92**. As we have given T_{Ac}, the element Ac also appears in questions (e.g., "dóes he come") and in the other positions of *not* in declaratives (e.g., "he hás been here"). These cases could be treated as instances of contrastive stress, since they also occur without stress in this position. But the given simpler and more general statement seems reasonable, since "he hás not come" is not grammatical, just as **99** is not (see Note 11).

So far we have investigated methods of extending the grammatical sketch $\quad$ 98.1
of §72.2 transformationally with the ultimate goal of covering the set
$\mu^{\mathbf{w}}$ of grammatical strings of words. It is also necessary to examine
§72.2 itself, to determine whether some of its complexities can be
removed by dropping some of the sentences there generated from the
kernel, and reintroducing them transformationally. We have a hint that
transformational analysis might be called for wherever two distinct
statements are required in the grammar for what is essentially the same
selectional relation. Since selectional relations can be preserved under
a suitable transformation, there is always the possibility of avoiding the
duplication by considering one of the classes of sentences for which the
selectional relation holds to be made up of transforms of the other
class.

The most obvious trouble spot of this kind in §72.2 is statement 18,
the rule of verbal selection for the transitive verbs which appear as
adjectives in the form $en^\frown V_T$, i.e., the passives. Statement 18, had
we given it, would have been at least as complex as statement 9, since
every selectional relation in statement 9 must be restated for passives
in statement 18. Every active has a corresponding passive. In fact,
statement 18 would be considerably more complex than statement 9,
since many prepositional phrases (e.g., "by a new method"—cf. §76.1)
do not function as conditioning contexts for the choice of the verb V_T,
and this will have to be stated.

The passive transformation T_p is based on an underlying elementary
transformation t_p which is the product of a permutation and a deformation. That is, we form a passive by interchanging subject and object
(by a permutation) and adding $be^\frown en$ between the auxiliary and the verb,
and by after the verb. T_p will be applied to any string of the form
NP_1-VP_A-$\langle D \rangle$ V_T-NP_2[15] and will convert it into a string of the form
NP_2-VP_A-$be^\frown en$-$\langle D \rangle$ V_T-$by^\frown NP_1$. Thus it will pair sentences in the
following way:

---

[15] There are other possible variations with more or differently placed adverbs, but we
have not given these other sentence forms in the sketch of the kernel grammar in §72.2.
Any complication needed to state adequately the restricting class for T_p would be
compounded in an alternative nontransformational analysis, since it would appear
once in the description of the active and once in the description of the passive. But it is
necessary to study these variations in detail to see what effect they have on the transformational analysis of passives—i.e., do they necessitate certain special rules, etc. I have
not investigated this question.

101	$Z = NP_1\text{-}VP_A\text{-}V_T\text{-}NP_2$	—	$T_p(Z, K) = NP_2\text{-}VP_A\text{-}be^\frown en\text{-}V_T\text{-}by^\frown NP_1$
	John-ed-meet-Mary (*John met Mary*)	—	*Mary-ed-be⌢en-meet-by⌢John* (*Mary was met by John*)
	John-will⌢have⌢en-meet-Mary (*John will have met Mary*)	—	*Mary-will⌢have⌢en-be⌢en-meet-by⌢John* (*Mary will have been met by John*)

etc.

The permutation that underlies the passive transformation is

102 $\pi_p : \quad Y_1\text{-}Y_2\text{-}Y_3\text{-}Y_4 \to Y_4\text{-}Y_2\text{-}Y_3\text{-}Y_1$

We may select the underlying deformation so as to assign *be*, *en*, and *by* in various ways to the root elements NP, VP_A, V_T, NP. This assignment will determine the derived constituent structure of passives (since it will determine the place of the constituent breaks in the transform), and it will thus determine which further transformations can be applied to passives.

Since we have

103   *he was seen by John and by Mary*

we see that *by⌢John* is a constituent in **103** (by the conjunction criterion), so that *by* must be assigned to the following *NP*, not to the preceding V_T. In §§67.2, 67.3, we noted several reasons for assigning *be⌢en* to the verb phrase, rather than the auxiliary phrase (thus treating *be* as the main verb). Several inadequacies were noted in this analysis, but we will see below that all of them disappear under further transformational analysis. It follows that the underlying deformation δ_p must be

104 $\delta_p : \quad Y_1\text{-}Y_2\text{-}Y_3\text{-}Y_4 \to Y_1\text{-}Y_2\text{-}be^\frown en^\frown Y_3\text{-}by^\frown Y_4$

Thus the defining sequence for δ_p is $(U, U, U, U, be^\frown en, U, by, U)$. Summing up, the passive transformation is defined as follows

105 T_p is determined by (Q_p, t_p), where

$$t_p = \delta_p(\pi_p) \quad \text{(as in **102**, **104**)}$$
$$Q_p = (NP, VP_A, \langle D \rangle V_T, NP)$$

Thus T_p carries any string of the form NP_1-VP_A-V_T-NP_2 into the corresponding string NP_2-VP_A-V_T-NP_1 (by π_p), and finally into NP_2-VP_A-$be\frown en\frown V_T$-$by\frown NP_1$ (by δ_p).

We must now state a **T**-marker schema for T_p. This means that we must determine where T_p applies in the sequence of mappings $\Phi_i^{\mathbf{P}}$. The only requirement here is that T_p must precede the mapping $\Phi_3^{\mathbf{P}}$ which carries C (from the auxiliary verb) into S after a singular noun phrase, and into $\emptyset$ after a plural noun phrase. The reason for this order of application is that the subject must agree in number with the verb in passives. Thus as a **T**-marker schema we can state

106 $Z\frown K\frown T_p\frown\Phi^{\mathbf{P}}$

No further conditions need be placed on the restricting classes of the interrogative and negative transformations to cover the case where T_p applies before them. That is, questions and negatives can be formed freely from passives. In fact, any transformation that applies to declaratives in general will apply to passives as well, since, as we noted in §86.7, passives have the full constituent structure of declaratives conferred on them by transformation, even to the extent that their derived interpretations are actually **P**-markers. As already noted, when passives are deleted from the kernel [from $Gr(P)$], it is still the case that they have ρ-derivations, though not restricted ρ-derivations.

One simplification resulting from the transformational analysis is, **98.2** naturally, that $en\frown V_T$ can be dropped from statement 17, §72.2. This becomes important when we find, below, that $ing\frown V_{I1,2}$ can also be introduced transformationally. Thus the entire third part of the analysis of the adjective phrase in the kernel grammar (statement 17) can be eliminated. These were the adjectives which were marked in the grammar of phrase structure as a separate subclass by virtue of the fact that they could not occur freely with adverbs such as "very," but only with the special subclass of adverbs D_2 containing "certainly," "soon," etc. Thus we can have "the mistakes were soon found," but not "the mistakes were very found." But when passives (and adjectives of the form $ing\frown V_{I1,2}$—e.g., "barking") are introduced transformationally from declaratives, this result will be an automatic consequence of the analysis, since only D_2 can occur with verbs. That is, we have "he soon found the mistakes" but not "he very found the mistakes." Thus one support for the transformational analysis is that this special restriction on certain adjectives need not be separately stated. Furthermore, the restriction of this category of adjectives to transitive verbs is now explained.

The main motivation for the transformational analysis of passives, however, is the desirability of avoiding the complex statement 18, §72.2, the rule of verbal selection for passives. As our analysis becomes more detailed, and our level of grammaticalness becomes more refined, this statement, along with statement 9, will become more complex. Thus the support for the transformational analysis grows with increasing refinement of the notion of grammaticalness. It is interesting and important to determine what is the crudest possible degree of grammaticalness that would support the transformational analysis of passives. This transformational analysis will be called for on any level of grammaticalness for which it is the case that for some choice of noun phrases NP_x and NP_y and verbs V, **107** is grammatical, but **108** is not:

107 $NP_x\text{-}V\text{-}NP_y$
$NP_y\text{-}is\frown Ven\text{-}by\frown NP_x$

108 $NP_y\text{-}V\text{-}NP_x$
$NP_x\text{-}is\frown Ven\text{-}by\frown NP_y$

Given a distinction between abstract and proper nouns, we have **109** but not **110** as highest-degree grammatical sentences:[16]

109   *John appreciates sincerity* — *sincerity frightens John*
sincerity is appreciated by — *John is frightened by sincerity*
John

110   *sincerity appreciates John* — *John frightens sincerity*
John is appreciated by — *sincerity is frightened by John*
sincerity

Thus the distinction between abstract and proper nouns (and the subclasses of verbs that occur with them in first-degree grammatical

---

[16] See Chapter V for discussion of the question of degree of grammaticalness. Recall that the purpose of a grammar, as we have formulated it in Chapter V, is to state the highest-degree grammatical sentences, not those that "can occur" (whatever this may mean). Given a grammatical statement for first-degree grammatical sentences (like **109** but not **110**), and given the system $\mathscr{C}$ of syntactic categories, as in §33.2 (i.e., the level **C** of §46), we will be able to determine that **110** are partially grammatical sentences, hence more grammatical than "John of from," etc. In fact, they may even be "absolutely grammatical" in the sense of the basic dichotomy discussed in §39. But none of this has any bearing on the argument of this section.

sentences) would suffice to establish this transformation. We will see below (§101.2) that the distinction between singular and plural is actually sufficient to establish it.

The passive transformation is irreversible in the same sense as is the question transformation (cf. §94.6). If we were to choose passives as the kernel sentences, and were to derive actives from them by a transformation T_a, it would require a great many fairly complex conditions to establish the fact that T_a applies to 111 but not 112: **98.3**

111 *the wine was drunk by the guests*

112 *John was drunk by midnight*

If passives are derived from actives, there is no analogous complication. Thus passives and not actives must be deleted from the kernel and reintroduced by transformation. We are left with active declarative sentences as our kernel of basic sentences.

The transformational analysis of the passive provides us with an excellent criterion for constituent analysis. Since every passive must be derived from a sentence of a form $NP\text{-}VP_A\text{-}V_T\text{-}NP$, we can determine that an active sentence is of this form by noting the existence of a passive presupposing that the corresponding active have this analysis. This criterion has the immediate effect of ruling out the counter-intuitive possibility suggested in §69.3 (and §76.3) that **98.4**

113 *John–is eating–lunch*

be analyzed as a case of *NP-is-NP*, like "John is a politician." The correct analysis is now dictated by the existence of

114 *lunch is being eaten by John*

which requires the analysis $NP\text{-}VP_A\text{-}V_T\text{-}NP$ for its corresponding active **113**. The passive transformation thus gives us our first really convincing reason for considering **113** to be of the same form as "John ate lunch," the only difference being in the choice of the auxiliary verb (*be⌢ing* in the case of **113**, *ed* in the case of "John ate lunch").

Another effect of this criterion is that it solves correctly the difficulty discussed in §§69, 70 and recapitulated in §76.1, where it was pointed out that there are no grounds for distinguishing **115** and **116** as strings with distinct constituent structure:

115   *I knew the boy studying in the library*

116   *I found the boy studying in the library*

But now we note that **117** are grammatical, but **118** is not:

117   (a)   *the boy studying in the library was known (by the teacher)*
       (b)   *the boy studying in the library was found (by the teacher)*
       (c)   *the boy was found studying in the library (by the teacher)*

118   *the boy was known studying in the library (by the teacher)*

Hence it must be the case that **115** is an instance of

119 $NP_1\text{-}VP_A\text{-}V_T\text{-}NP_2$

with a compound object $NP_2 \rightarrow NP_3\frown ing \frown VP_1$, while **116** must be a case of constructional homonymity, having **119** as one analysis (as in "I found the boy studying in the library, but not the one in the gym"), and **120** as an alternative analysis,

120 $NP_1\text{-}VP_A\text{-}V_T\text{-}NP_2\text{-}ing\frown VP_1$

with NP_2 the object, and $V_T\frown ing\frown VP_1$ a discontinuous compound verb. This would be the analysis, e.g., in "I found the boy studying in the library, not running around in the streets." We have not yet shown that the passive transformation, as it now stands, carries **116** into **117c**. This will be shown below, when a more serious study of sentences of the form **120** is undertaken.

The analysis of **115** as an instance of **119**, and of **116** as a case of constructional homonymity in the overlap of the patterns **119** and **120** is the intuitively correct analysis of these sentences, but there is apparently no support for it except in transformational terms.

In both the case of **113** and the case of **115** and **116**, the passive transformation furnishes a criterion of analysis in the sense of §§58, 65.1. If what happens to be the intuitively correct analysis of constituent structure is given for **113**, **115**, and **116**, then **114** and **117** are generated automatically, i.e., the grammar automatically produces grammatical sentences. If a different constituent analysis is provided for **113**, **114**, and **115**, then **114** and **117c** remain as kernel sentences of a unique structure, and special added statements are required to provide for them, with resulting complexity of the grammar. Thus the criterion of simplicity of grammar leads to (and formally grounds) the intuitively correct analysis, by way of the passive criterion.

It will appear below that this criterion has a rather wide application in determining constituent structure.

Given any passive, e.g., "Mary was met by John," we have a sentence without the *by*-phrase, in this case   98.5

121   *Mary was met*

We account for this possibility with a transformation T_{pd} defined by

122 T_{pd} is determined by (δ_{pd}, Q_{pd}), where

$$\delta_{pd}: \quad Y_1\text{-}Y_2 \rightarrow Y_1\text{-}U = Y_1$$
$$Q_{pd} = \{(X_i{}^\frown en{}^\frown V, by{}^\frown NP)\}, \text{ where } X_i \text{ is any string}$$

Thus the defining sequence for δ_{pd} is (U, U, σ, U), and T_{pd} converts $X{}^\frown en{}^\frown V\text{-}by{}^\frown NP$ into $X{}^\frown en{}^\frown V$, e.g., "Mary was met by John" ($= Mary{}^\frown was{}^\frown en{}^\frown meet\text{-}by{}^\frown John$) into **121** ($= Mary{}^\frown was{}^\frown en{}^\frown meet$). Since this transformation follows T_p, we can state the corresponding **T**-marker schema together with the **T**-marker schema for passives. Thus in the grammar of the level **T**, we replace **106** by

123 $Z{}^\frown K{}^\frown T_p \langle T_{pd} \rangle \, \Phi^{\mathbf{P}}$

This will be revised below in §103.2.

There are other forms similar to the passive that should be discussed at this point. Thus there are "passives" with "with" instead of "by," and with "get" instead of "be," as in   98.6

124   (a) *he was laid up with the grippe*
         (b) *he has been occupied with this problem*
         (c) *all of his time has been taken up with their complaints*
              etc.

125   (a) *he got thrown by the horse*
         (b) *he got recommended for the job*
              etc.

A detailed study of the passive and related forms should prove quite interesting. Many further problems could be cited at this point. But our present purpose is not to present a complete picture of any one transformation, but rather to explore the general scope of this kind of analysis.

98.7   We cannot simultaneously retain the following four requirements, each of which might be considered a desideratum for constituent and transformational analysis:

126   (i)   Nonoverlap of constituents, for a given **P**-marker (i.e., consistency of **P**-markers—cf. §52.2 and §53.6, Definition 12, Theorem 7).

(ii)   The passive transformation T_p

(iii)   The question transformation T_q

(iv)   Every term of the proper analysis of a transformed sentence is an elementary constituent (i.e., a constituent represented by a prime of **P**, as NP, VP, etc.)

This is clear from the fact that the passive and question transformations analyze the auxiliary verb phrase in different ways. Our analysis of VP_A allows (iv) to be satisfied for T_p. An alternative analysis allowing it to be satisfied for T_q, would make it impossible to satisfy it for T_p. We have retained (i)–(iii) in our construction of transformations. If we had retained (iv), transformational analysis would produce a direct and powerful criterion for constituent analysis, but the cost is far too great since many transformations which greatly simplify the grammar would be impossible. Thus transformational analysis can provide only various indirect criteria for constituent analysis (e.g., the passive criterion discussed in §98.4). Nevertheless, we will see that these are the major criteria for constituent analysis.

99.1   The decision to drop passives from the kernel compels us to delete certain other sentences as well. The noun phrase subject of

127   *being elected certainly surprised John*

for instance, was formed in §72.2 by running through the grammar twice (cf. §55.3, Definition 17) in the following series of steps:

128 $N_A \rightarrow Inf^\frown VP_1$ (by statement 15)
$\rightarrow ing^\frown VP_1$ (by statement 16)
$\rightarrow ing^\frown be^\frown Predicate$ (by statement 3)
$\rightarrow ing^\frown be^\frown AP$ (by statement 5)
$\rightarrow ing^\frown be^\frown en^\frown V_T$ (by statement 17)
$\rightarrow ing^\frown be^\frown en^\frown elect$ (by statement 23)
$\rightarrow being^\frown elected$ (by $\Phi_5{}^P$ and morphological rules)

But this path of development is excluded now, since the substatement "$AP \rightarrow en^\frown V_T$" has been dropped from statement 17 of the kernel grammar.

Since at least **127** must be derived by transformation, it is simplest to delete all cases of $Inf^\frown VP_1$ (i.e., all noun phrases of the form "proving that theorem," "to prove that theorem," etc.) from the kernel and to introduce them transformationally. It turns out that this treatment will effect various other simplifications in the kernel grammar, and finally, a condition on the kernel grammar suggested in §**110** below will make the transformational treatment absolutely necessary, apart from all questions of relative simplicity.

We thus have two transformations T_{ing} and T_{to}. T_{ing} is based on a deformation δ_{ing} with the defining sequence (σ, U, ing, U). Thus

129 $\delta_{ing} : \quad Y_1\text{-}Y_2 \rightarrow (\sigma^\frown Y_1^\frown U)\text{-}(ing^\frown Y_2^\frown U) = U\text{-}ing^\frown Y_2 = ing^\frown Y_2$

The restricting class for T_{ing} is

130 $Q_{ing} = \{(NP^\frown VP_{A1}, \langle have^\frown en \rangle \, VP_1)\}$

where VP_{A1}, it will be recalled, is any string of one of the forms $\begin{Bmatrix} S \\ \emptyset \\ ed \end{Bmatrix} \langle M \rangle$. See the final remarks of §**66.3** and the first few paragraphs of §**66.5** for further discussion of *ing*-phrases, connected with this characterization of the restricting class.

Thus T_{ing} as determined by (Q_{ing}, δ_{ing}) carries a string of the form $NP^\frown VP_{A1}\text{-}VP_1$ (e.g., $John^\frown S\text{-}prove^\frown that^\frown theorem$) into the corresponding string of the form $ing^\frown VP_1$ (e.g., $ing^\frown prove^\frown that^\frown theorem$) which becomes, by $\Phi_5{}^P$, $prove^\frown ing^\frown that^\frown theorem$, ultimately "proving that theorem"); and T_{ing} carries a string of the form $NP^\frown VP_{A1}\text{-}have^\frown en^\frown VP_1$ (e.g., $John^\frown S\text{-}have^\frown en^\frown prove^\frown that^\frown theorem$) into $ing^\frown have^\frown en^\frown VP_1$ (e.g., ultimately, "having proved that theorem").

The result of applying T_{ing} to a sentence is not another sentence, but rather a noun phrase $ing\frown VP_1$. Hence T_{ing} must be combined with a second transformation that substitutes this noun phrase $T_{ing}(Z, K)$ for some noun phrase of a second sentence. For example, $T_{ing}(John\frown proves\frown that\frown theorem, K) = proving\frown that\frown theorem$, and we may follow T_{ing} by a transformation T_x that substitutes "proving that theorem" for "it" in "it was difficult," yielding "proving that theorem was difficult." We thus have our first instance of a generalized transformation (cf. §91). In fact, the case of T_{ing} is exactly like the case of the sentence "that John was unhappy was quite obvious" ($= 114a$, Chapter IX), so that the pattern of its construction is just that described in detail in §81.6.

T_{ing} must apply before Φ_5^P, and it is simplest to have it apply before Φ^P altogether. Hence the T-marker for T_{ing} will differ from 141, §91.6, in that "Φ^P" of 141 is replaced by "I." The T-marker schema for T_{ing} will thus be

131    $Z_1\frown K_1\frown I\frown T_{ing}\frown Z_2\frown K_2\frown I\frown T_x\frown \Phi^P$

The effect of 131 is to apply T_{ing} to $I(Z_1, K_1) = Z_1$; and to apply T_x to $Z_3\frown\#\frown Z_2$, where Z_3 is the ing-phrase resulting from the application of T_{ing} and $Z_2 = I(Z_2, K_2)$ (since I is the identity transformation). Letting $Z_1 = John\frown proves\frown that\frown theorem$ and $Z_2 = it\frown was\frown difficult$ (and assuming K_1, K_2, K_3, K_4 to be properly chosen), we can trace the operation of 131 in the following series of steps, which match 142, §91.6:

132    $I(Z_1, K_1) = Z_1$
　　　　$T_{ing}(Z_1, K_3) = proving\frown that\frown theorem$　　　(note that $K_3 \subset K_1$)
　　　　$I(Z_2, K_2) = Z_2 = it\frown was\frown difficult$
　　　　$T_x(proving\frown that\frown theorem \# it\frown was\frown difficult, K_4) = proving\frown$
　　　　　　$that\frown theorem\frown was\frown difficult$　　　(note that $K_4 = K_3{}^*K_2$—
　　　　　　cf. Definition 48, §91.3)

T_x is the as yet unspecified transformation that substitutes $T_{ing}(Z_1, K_1)$ for some noun phrase of Z_2. On the level of grammaticalness assumed in §72.2, ing-phrases are abstract nouns and hence have a distribution similar to N_{ab}. Ing-phrases as abstract nouns are introduced in §72.2 in statement 15. There we saw that there are two types of ing-phrases, $ing\frown V_T$ ("reading") and $ing\langle VP_{A2}\rangle VP_1$ ("reading books," "having read books"); and in statement 21 we saw that VP_{A2} becomes $have\frown en$ in this position. The transformation T_{ing} that we have constructed produces instances only of the second type. We see that these *ing*-phrases with a full VP_1 are excluded from certain environments, namely, before "of" and after the article. There is in fact one abstract noun that is also excluded from these environments. namely "it." "It" is a N_{ab}, since it occurs in all the contexts of N_{ab} and in contexts where only N_{ab} can occur, but we do not have "it of," "the it," etc. In this case, then, we are forced to choose "it" as the element of Z_2 which is replaced by the generalized transformation T_x.

There is one apparent difficulty in the choice of "it" as the element for which *ing*-phrases are substituted. *Ing*-phrases can occur after the possessive adjective phrase $NP^\frown S_1$(cf. statement 17, §72.2), as in "John's flying planes is something I don't approve of," but "it" cannot occur here—we do not have "John's it." But we will see below that this discrepancy is only apparent, since $NP^\frown S_1^\frown ing^\frown VP_1$ will also be deleted from the kernel and introduced transformationally as a unit.

T_x, then, is the transformation that replaces *it* in $Z_2 = ...it...$ by $T_{ing}(Z_1, K_1)$, where *it* is a N_{ab}. Since any such *it* can be replaced (on the level of grammaticalness we are now assuming), we have to do here with a family of transformations F_A. The transformations of this family convert

133 $ing\langle have^\frown en\rangle\ VP_1\text{-}\#\text{-}X_1\text{-}N_{ab}\text{-}X_2$

(where dashes separate elements of the proper analysis) into

134 $U\text{-}U\text{-}X_1\text{-}ing\langle have^\frown en\rangle\ VP_1\text{-}X_2 = X_1\text{-}ing\langle have^\frown en\rangle\ VP_1\text{-}X_2$

T_x must then be based on an elementary substitution t_A such that

135 $t_A: \quad Y_1\text{-}Y_2\text{-}Y_3\text{-}Y_4\text{-}Y_5 \rightarrow U\text{-}U\text{-}Y_3\text{-}Y_1\text{-}Y_5 = Y_3\text{-}Y_1\text{-}Y_5$

The defining sequence for t_A is thus $(\sigma, 0, \sigma, 0, 0, 0, \sigma, 1, 0, 0)$ (cf. Theorem 6 and **85** of §86.4); the derived constituent structure of Y_1 is internally that of Y_1 of the transformed string, and externally that of Y_4, the element for which it substitutes (cf. §91.6). Thus the *ing*-phrase in **134** (or "proving that theorem" in "proving that theorem was difficult") is a N_{ab} with the internal structure of a verb phrase.

The restricting class for any transformation in F_A must meet the following condition:

136 $C_A(\alpha_1, \alpha_2, \alpha_3, \alpha_4, \alpha_5)$ if and only if

$$\alpha_1 = ing\langle have^\frown en \rangle \; VP_1$$
$$\alpha_2 = \#$$
$$\alpha_3 = X_i \qquad [X_i \text{ any string (including } U)]$$
$$\alpha_4 = N_{ab}$$
$$\alpha_5 = X_j \qquad [X_j \text{ any string (including } U)]$$

Thus a transformation of F_A can be applied only to a string of the form **133**, and t_A will convert this string into the corresponding string of the form **134**. But C_A does not yet require that the replaced element α_4 be *it*. We will have to construct this requirement as a condition on **T**-markers, since our presently available theory does not allow us to impose two conditions simultaneously on the terms of the proper analysis of the transformed string. We now define F_A as the family of transformations determined by (C_A, t_A), and we construct the **T**-marker schema

137 $Z_1^\frown K_1^\frown I^\frown T_{ing}^\frown Z_2^\frown K_2^\frown I^\frown F_A^\frown \Phi^{\mathbf{P}}$

We add to the grammar of the level **T** the requirement that for Z_1 and Z_2 to appear in the **P**-basis (cf. Definition 51, §91.3) of **137**, they must meet the condition K_A:

138   Condition K_A: there is a Y and a W such that $Z_2 = Y^\frown it^\frown W$ and the result of applying F_A to $T_{ing}(Z_1, K_1)^\frown \#^\frown Z_2$ is $Y^\frown T_{ing}(Z_1, K_1)^\frown W$.

In other words, for Z_1 and Z_2 to appear in **137**, it is necessary that F_A replace an occurrence of *it* in Z_2 by the *ing*-phrase formed from Z_1. We know from **136** that this occurrence of *it* must be a N_{ab}.

Condition K_A can be phrased more precisely in terms of the notion of "reduced correlate" (Definition 52, §91.4). The reduced correlate of a **T**-marker is obtained by dropping from it the final component of the mapping in the **T**-marker. In the case of **137**, the reduced correlate is formed by dropping $\Phi^{\mathbf{P}}$. Let Z be any actual **T**-marker containing a transformation belonging to F_A and of the form **137**. Let Z^{red} be the reduced correlate of Z. Then

139   Condition K_A: There is a Y and a W such that $Z_2 = Y^\frown it^\frown W$ and $Val_1(Z^{red}) = Y^\frown T_{ing}(Z_1, K_1)^\frown W$ (cf. Definition 50, §91.3).

The necessity for giving a separate statement of the condition that the replaced element of Z_2 be *it* suggests that it might be worthwhile to generalize our conception of transformations to allow several conditions to be imposed simultaneously on the constituent structure of a term of the proper analysis of a transformed string.

As matters now stand, questions and passives can be formed from sentences containing transformationally introduced *ing*-phrases, and *ing*-phrases can be formed from passives, but not questions, as Z_1 in **137**. This result follows from the manner in which derived constituent structure is assigned in these cases, and from condition 4, §91.4, which permits transforms to appear in the **P**-basis of a **T**-marker (i.e., it permits compounding of separately established transformations). In §91.5 we laid down condition 5, which limits the possibilities of compounding by imposing certain conditions on the Φ^P-skeletons of the **T**-markers figuring in the compound. But in the case of the transformations so far established, condition 5 does not restrict the possibility of compounding in any undesirable way. The potential difficulties envisaged in §91.5 do not arise at this point.

In a perfectly analogous way we can provide for the introduction of *to*-phrases such as "to prove that theorem," etc. We construct T_{to} such that

99.2

140 T_{to} is determined by (Q_{to}, δ_{to}), where

$$Q_{to} = (NP^\frown VP_{A1}, \langle VP_{A2} \rangle VP_1)$$
$$\delta_{to} \leftrightarrow (\sigma, U, to, U)$$

Thus δ_{to} carries Y_1-Y_2 into $to^\frown Y_2$. It differs from δ_{ing} only in that *to* replaces *ing* (cf. **129**). Q_{to} differs from Q_{ing} (cf. **130**) only in that it permits T_{to} to apply to strings of the form $NP^\frown VP_{A1}$-$be^\frown ing^\frown VP_1$, whereas T_{ing} cannot. Thus we have "to be eating dinner when they arrive would be quite impolite," but not "being eating dinner when they arrive would be quite impolite" (cf. §66.5).

The distribution of *to*-phrases is more limited than that of *ing*-phrases, however. Only sentence-initial N_{ab} can be replaced by a *to*-phrase (though in a larger class of grammatical sentences than we are now considering, further emendation would be necessary). Hence in the case of *to*-phrases there is no need to set up a family of generalized substitutional transformations, as in the case of *ing*-phrases. As the substitutional transformation which follows T_{to}, we construct T_A, where

141 T_A is determined by (Q_A, t_A), where

t_A is as in **135**
$$Q_A = \{(to\langle VP_{A2}\rangle\ VP_1, \#, U, N_{ab}, X_2)\}$$

Thus with the revision that *to* replaces *ing* and VP_{A2} replaces *have⌒en*, Q_A meets C_A of **136** with $\alpha_3 = U$. The **T**-marker for *to*-phrases can be stated together with the **T**-marker for *ing*-phrases. Thus replacing **137** we have

142 $$Z_1 {}^\frown K_1 {}^\frown I \begin{Bmatrix} T_{to} \\ T_{ing} \end{Bmatrix} Z_2 {}^\frown K_2 {}^\frown I \begin{Bmatrix} T_A \\ F_A \end{Bmatrix} \Phi^{\mathbf{P}}$$

We extend condition K_A **139** in the obvious manner to apply to the **P**-basis of both of the **T**-marker schemata in **142**.[17]

In §§99.1, 99.2 we have accounted only for such *ing*-phrases and *to*-phrases as are noun phrases, i.e., for *Inf* as it appears in statement 15, §72.2. But *Inf* is also introduced in statement 10, §72.2, in sentences like "he wants to read," "he likes reading," in which (as we saw in §68) the *ing*-phrases and *to*-phrases are not to be treated as noun phrases. We will return to the analysis of these sentences below, supplying a transformational analysis which will dispense with the element *Inf* along with statements 15 and 16 completely. Meanwhile we note that the passive criterion gives a further support, now on the transformational level, for the decision of §68 that these *to*-phrases and *ing*-phrases cannot be regarded as noun phrases. Thus we do not have "to read is wanted by him" from "he wants to read." But this situation is complicated by the homonymity pointed out in §68.4

99.3   As an example of the functioning of these transformations, we can derive the sequence

143   *being elected certainly surprised John*   (= **127**)

This is derived by several transformations from the kernel structures

144 $Z_1 = they{}^\frown ed{}^\frown elect{}^\frown John$ (with the **P**-marker K_1)
$Z_2 = it{}^\frown ed{}^\frown certainly{}^\frown surprise{}^\frown John$ (with the **P**-marker K_2)

---

[17] Note that we are not actually presenting **T**-markers, but rather **T**-marker schemata. A **T**-marker contains fixed strings. Hence to turn these schemata into **T**-markers, it is necessary to choose fixed strings and interpretations for the variables "Z," "K," etc., and to select a given transformation from the families listed in the schemata (cf. §92).

Applying the transformations T_p and T_{pd} (as in **123**) to (Z_1, K_1), we derive

145 $T_p(Z_1, K_1) = Z_3 =$ *John-ed-be⌒en⌒elect-by⌒them*, with K_3 as
       its derived interpretation (in this case, a **P**-marker)
       $T_{pd}(Z_3, K_3) = Z_4 =$ *John⌒ed⌒be⌒en⌒elect*, with K_4 as derived
       interpretation

We do not apply Φ^P to (Z_4, K_4), as required by **123**, since by condition 4, §91.4, we know that only the value of the reduced correlate figures in further transformations. We now construct the **T**-marker

146 $Z_4 ⌒ K_4 ⌒ I ⌒ T_{ing} ⌒ Z_2 ⌒ K_2 ⌒ I ⌒ T_x ⌒ \Phi^P$

conforming to the bottom line of **142**, where T_x is a member of the family F_A, having the restricting class $(\alpha_1, \alpha_2, U, \alpha_4, VP_1)$, meeting **136**.
     To determine the value of **146**, we apply T_{ing} to $I(Z_4, K_4) = Z_4$ with the derived interpretation K_4 (literally, $K_4' \subset K_4$):

147 $T_{ing}(Z_4, K_4) = Z_5 =$ *ing⌒be⌒en⌒elect*, with derived inter-
       pretation K_5

$I(Z_2, K_2) = Z_2$ with K_2 as derived interpretation. Hence the next step in determining the value of **146** is to apply T_x to the complex string $Z_5 ⌒ \# ⌒ Z_2$:

148 $T_x(Z_5 ⌒ \# ⌒ Z_2, K_5 * K_2) = T_x(Z_5$-$\#$-$U$-$it$-$ed⌒certainly⌒$
           surprise⌒John, $K_5 * K_2)$
         $= Z_5$-*ed⌒certainly⌒surprise⌒John*
         $=$ *ing⌒be⌒en⌒elect-ed⌒certainly⌒*
           surprise⌒John

Applying Φ^P, we derive **143**, with $\Phi_5{}^P$ applying in three places, i.e., to the affixes *ing*, *en*, and *ed*.
     Closer investigation of grammatical sentences shows that there are restrictions on Z_1 and Z_2 in **142**, beyond that stated in condition K_A. Thus we do not have

149   *being elected tomorrow certainly surprised John*

Apparently, a relation of tense holds between Z_1 and Z_2. Furthermore, the object of Z_1 and the object of Z_2 are related. Since **150** is not grammatical, we also do not have **151**:

150   *they built John*

151   *being built surprised John*

The simplest way to state these limitations in general seems to be to require that Z_1 and Z_2 have the same auxiliary verb phrase (though this may be too strict) and the same object. This condition, if correct, would be added as a condition on the **P**-basis of **142**, alongside of condition K_A, in a detailed grammar.

If this reasoning stands in a detailed study, it will provide us with a structural analogue to the intuition that **143** is related in content to **152**, and not, e.g., to **153**, from which it might also be derived, given only its morphemic constitution:

152   *They elected John. It certainly surprised John.*

153   *They will elect me. It certainly surprised John.*

There are a variety of other limitations on the **T**-markers of the type **142** which should be investigated in detail with a view toward determining structural grounds for the intuitive interpretation of these sentences.

99.4   In §71.1 we noted that the selectional relation between a possessive adjective $NP^\frown S_1$ and the verb in a following *ing*-phrase, as in **154**, is just that between subject and verb:

154   *John's flying is something I don't approve of*

Because of this selectional relation, we can, using a transformation closely related to T_{ing}, delete sentences like **154** from the kernel, thus avoiding some of the complexities which would have appeared in statement 9, §72.2, had we given this statement in detail. (It will be recalled that we gave only a subpart of statement 9, namely 9*, so as to avoid some of these complexities, having noted there that 9* would be shown to be sufficient for the kernel.)

Flying is derived from *John*$^\frown$*flies* by deleting the subject with the deformation δ_{ing} defined by (σ, U, ing, U). Similarly, *John's*$^\frown$*flying* is derived from *John‸flies* by a deformation $\delta_{s\text{-}ing}$ which instead of deleting *John* and the initial part of the auxiliary verb (in the case of *John‸flies*, the element S), deletes only the segment of the auxiliary and affixes S_1 to *John*. The transformation in question (call it "$T_{s\text{-}ing}$") is more precisely defined as follows:

155 $T_{s\text{-}ing}$ is determined by $(\delta_{s\text{-}ing}, Q_{s\text{-}ing})$, where

$$\delta_{s\text{-}ing}: \quad Y_1\text{-}Y_2\text{-}Y_3 \to Y_1{}^\frown S_1\text{-}U\text{-}ing{}^\frown Y_3 = Y_1{}^\frown S_1\text{-}ing{}^\frown Y_3$$
$$Q_{s\text{-}ing} = (NP, VP_{A1}, \langle have{}^\frown en \rangle \, VP_1)$$

Thus $T_{s\text{-}ing}$ converts a sentence of the form $NP\text{-}VP_{A1}\text{-}$ $\langle have{}^\frown en \rangle \, VP_1$ into the corresponding sentence of the form $NP{}^\frown S_1\text{-}ing$ $\langle have{}^\frown en \rangle \, VP_1$. The defining sequence of $\delta_{s\text{-}ing}$ is $(U, S_1, \sigma, U, ing, U)$. Just as in the case of *ing*-phrases, the transform substitutes for abstract nouns, but with the distributional limitations of *it*. Thus we do not have "real John's flying" or "the John's flying," though we have "real sincerity" and "the sincerity." We thus take *it* as the element for which these transforms are substituted, just as in the case of the simple *ing*-phrases. No further statement about the distribution of $T_{s\text{-}ing}$ transforms is necessary. In place of **142**, then, we now state

156 $Z_1{}^\frown K_1{}^\frown I \begin{bmatrix} T_{to} \\ \{T_{ing}\} \\ \{T_{s\text{-}ing}\} \end{bmatrix} Z_2{}^\frown K_2{}^\frown I \begin{bmatrix} T_A \\ F_A \end{bmatrix} \Phi^{\mathbf{P}}$ (with condition K_A)

where F_A is revised to include $T_{s\text{-}ing}$ transforms; i.e., $NP{}^\frown S_1{}^\frown ing$ $\langle have{}^\frown en \rangle \, VP_1$ is given as one of the forms of α_1 in **136**. We can now revise the definitions of T_{to} and T_{ing} to bring out the parallel with $T_{s\text{-}ing}$. Summing up, we replace **129, 130, 140,** and **155** by

157 T_{ing} is determined by (δ_{ing}, Q_{ing})
          $T_{s\text{-}ing}$ is determined by $(\delta_{s\text{-}ing}, Q_{ing})$
          T_{to} is determined by (δ_{to}, Q_{to})

where

$$\begin{Bmatrix} Q_{ing} \\ Q_{to} \end{Bmatrix} = \left\{ \left(NP, VP_{A1}, \begin{Bmatrix} \langle have{}^\frown en \rangle \\ \langle VP_{A2} \rangle \end{Bmatrix} VP_1 \right) \right\}$$

$$\begin{Bmatrix} \delta_{ing} \\ \delta_{to} \\ \delta_{s\text{-}ing} \end{Bmatrix} \leftrightarrow \begin{Bmatrix} \sigma, U \\ \sigma, U \\ U, S_1 \end{Bmatrix}, \sigma, U, \begin{Bmatrix} ing \\ to \\ ing \end{Bmatrix}, U$$

156 now gives the complete set of **T**-markers of this type, where F_A of **136** is revised as mentioned below **156**.

We can now avoid any reference in statement 9, §72.2, to the selection of verbs by NP in $NP^\frown S_1$. We can also drop the conditioning context "$\underline{\quad}ing^\frown VP_1$" in the first line of statement 17. We will see below that this entire first third of statement 17 can be dropped (just as the third third of this statement is dropped; cf. first paragraph of §98.2). We also omit the section of statement 15 that introduces $Inf\langle VP_{A2}\rangle VP_1$, with its restricting contexts, and we omit all restrictions in statement 16 except "$V_c\underline{\quad}$." We will see below that statements 15 and 16 can be dropped completely. The element N_A which is introduced in statement 8 and developed in statement 15 can also be eliminated, being replaced by N_{ab} wherever it occurs. Thus the first line of statement 15 is also dropped, and only "$N_{ab} \to Inf^\frown V_T$" remains for the moment. Finally we eliminate the restriction in statement 21. The elimination of the restrictions in statements 15 and 21 is important, since actually we had no way to state them simply within the framework of the grammar corresponding to **P**, as this had been formulated in Chapter VII and Chapter IV (cf. Note 33, Chapter VIII). If we had attempted to state these restrictions formally, in terms of the available notations, the complexity of the grammatical statement would have risen considerably.

The length of ρ_1-derivations now also drops considerably. For instance, Derivation 2 of §72.4 formerly required running through the grammar three times in 32 steps. Now we apply one of the generalized transformations of **156** to the pair of kernel sentences "John was elected," "the voters sincerely approved of it." The second of these sentences requires the first 15 steps of Derivation 2, with $NP \to N_{ab} \to it$. The order of statements can be rearranged in such a way that no recursions are necessary in the derivation of this sentence. The significance of this fact becomes clear in §110, below.

99.5   In the concluding paragraphs of §77.1, in discussing **18, 19** of that section, we noted that the noun phrases "John's drinking" and "John's cooking" as in

158   *I don't approve of* $\begin{Bmatrix} John's\ drinking \\ John's\ cooking \end{Bmatrix}$

can be viewed in two ways. On the one hand, these phrases are single units, transforms of "John drinks" and "John cooks"; and being transforms of sentences, they are represented by the prime *Sentence* (cf. Definition 30, §87.4). But if we investigate their derived constituent structure in greater detail, we see that since "John's" is an AP in the kernel grammar (by statement 17, §72.2), these phrases are instances of AP-N, like "John's book" (cf. Definition 28, §87.2). The dual interpretation of **158** discussed in the final paragraphs of §76.1 seems to correlate with this dual structural picture. This is not, then, a case of constructional homonymity, since only one **T**-marker is involved, but a case of an overspecified derived constituent structure (i.e., a derived interpretation which contains too much information to qualify as a **P**-marker). Thus the derived interpretation of **158** assigns "John's drinking," "John's cooking" to the pattern AP-N (hence NP) on the one hand; and it sets off the transform as a single unit, having the structure *Sentence*, on the other.

We still have not accounted for the noun phrases of the type $Inf^\frown V_T$ **99.6** (cf. statement 15, §77.2). Actually, $Inf^\frown V_T$ is a special case of $Inf^\frown VP_1$, with $VP_1 \rightarrow V_T$, so we need only account for these $Inf^\frown V_T$ phrases in the positions where $Inf^\frown VP_1$ in general cannot occur, i.e., before *of*, and after the article. In the position before *of* we have cases like

159   *grow*ling *of lions*

160   *read*ing *of good literature*

These cases caused a good deal of trouble in the system of phrase structure discussed in Chapter VIII, since in **159** we find the selectional relation verb–subject, and in **160**, the selectional relation verb–object holding between the italicized parts (cf. the third case discussed in §71.1). Because of these selectional relations, we see that we must derive $Inf^\frown V_T$ from sentences of the form NP-V on the one hand (for **159**) and from the V-N part of NP-V-N on the other (for **160**). Accordingly we set up the transformations T_{sub} (for **159**, where the selectional relation is verb–subject, i.e., subject–verb inverted) and T_{ob} (for **160**, where the selectional relation is verb–object). First we define the elementary transformations π_p, $\delta_{ing\text{-}of}$:

161 $\pi_p :\ Y_1\text{-}Y_2\text{-}Y_3\text{-}Y_4 \rightarrow Y_4\text{-}Y_2\text{-}Y_3\text{-}Y_1$ $(= \mathbf{102})$
$\delta_{ing\text{-}of} :\ Y_1\text{-}Y_2\text{-}Y_3\text{-}Y_4 \rightarrow U\text{-}U\text{-}ing^\frown Y_3\text{-}of^\frown Y_4 = ing^\frown Y_3\text{-}$
$$of^\frown Y_4$$

Thus the defining sequence for π_p is (4, 2, 3, 1) and the defining sequence for $\delta_{ing\text{-}of}$ is (σ, U, σ, U, *ing*, U, *of*, U). The compound elementary transformation $\delta_{ing\text{-}of}(\pi_p)$ thus carries $Y_1\text{-}Y_2\text{-}Y_3\text{-}Y_4$ into $ing^\frown Y_3\text{-}of^\frown Y_1$. T_{sub} and T_{ob} are defined as follows:

162 T_{sub} is determined by $(Q_{sub}, \delta_{ing\text{-}of}(\pi_p))$
T_{ob} is determined by $(Q_{ob}, \delta_{ing\text{-}of})$

where the elementary transformations are as in **161** and

$$Q_{sub} = (NP, VP_A, V_T, U)$$
$$Q_{ob} = (NP, VP_A, V_T, NP)$$

162 can obviously be abbreviated, and coalesced with the very similar **157** to the advantage of both.

T_{ob} thus converts a sentence of the form $NP_1\text{-}VP_A\text{-}V_T\text{-}NP_2$ into the corresponding phrase of the form $U\text{-}U\text{-}ing^\frown V_T\text{-}of^\frown NP_2$. For instance, it converts *he–S–read–good^literature* into *ing^read–of^good^literature*, which becomes **160** by $\Phi_5{}^P$. T_{sub} converts a sentence of the form $NP_1\text{-}VP_A\text{-}V_T\text{-}U$ into the corresponding phrase of the form $U\text{-}U\text{-}ing^\frown V_T\text{-}of^\frown NP_1 = ing^\frown V_T\text{-}of^\frown NP_1$. Thus it converts *lions-Ø-growl-U* into *ing^growl-of^lions*, which becomes **159** by $\Phi_5{}^P$. We define Q_{sub} with the vacuous term U, imposing a four-term proper analysis, so as to be able to use the same underlying transformations in stating T_{sub} and T_{ob}.

Alongside of T_{ob} we have the transformation $T_{s\text{-}ob}$ which has the same relation to T_{ob} as $T_{s\text{-}ing}$ (cf. **155**) has to T_{ing}. Thus $T_{s\text{-}ob}$ carries "he reads good literature" into "his reading of good literature." $T_{s\text{-}ob}$ is thus defined by

163 $T_{s\text{-}ob}$ is determined by $(Q_{ob}, \delta_{s\text{-}ing\text{-}of})$ where Q_{ob} is as in **162** and

$$\delta_{s\text{-}ing\text{-}of}: \quad Y_1\text{-}Y_2\text{-}Y_3\text{-}Y_4 \rightarrow Y_1{}^\frown S_1\text{-}U\text{-}ing^\frown Y_3\text{-}of^\frown Y_4$$
$$= Y_1{}^\frown S_1\text{-}ing^\frown Y_3\text{-}of\text{-}Y_4$$

Thus the defining sequence of $\delta_{s\text{-}ing\text{-}of}$ is $(U, S_1, \sigma, U, ing, U, of, U)$, and $T_{s\text{-}ob}$ converts a sentence of the form $NP_1\text{-}VP_A\text{-}V_T\text{-}NP_2$ into the corresponding phrase of the form $NP_1{}^\frown S_1\text{-}ing^\frown V_T\text{-}of^\frown NP_2$; e.g., it carries *John-S-read-good^literature* into *John^S_1-ing^read-of^good^literature*, which becomes "John's reading of good literature" by further mappings, from Φ^P. **163** too can be assimilated to **162** and **157**.

These three transformations T_{sub}, T_{ob}, and $T_{s\text{-}ob}$ produce noun phrases which substitute for abstract nouns, just as in the case of T_{ing} and T_{to}. Thus we must extend the condition **136** on F_A so that the products of these transformations can appear as α_1. **156** need be expanded only to the extent of adding T_{sub}, T_{ob} and $T_{s\text{-}ob}$ to the bracket containing T_{ing} and $T_{s\text{-}ing}$. Condition K_A (cf. **139**) must be extended to cover $T_{s\text{-}ob}$, since we do not have "the John's reading of good literature," etc., but T_{sub} and T_{ob} are not limited in this way, since we have "the growling of lions," "the reading of good literature," etc., so that condition K_A does not apply to these transformations. We will sum up these revisions in §99.8, below.

Given this transformational analysis, we can drop from statement 9, §77.2, all references to "of" and all statements about the distribution of transitive and intransitive verbs with respect to the nouns of following *of*-phrases, and preceding possessive adjectives. This permits a considerable simplification of statement 9, since the information briefly diagrammed in **153** and **156**, §71.1, need not be built into statement 9 in all its detail. We see then, that statement 9*, §72.1, suffices for the kernel grammar, given the transformational analysis of these phrases. We will see below that statement 9* can be somewhat simplified. It will also appear below that the simplification introduced by these transformations grows even greater as more complicated verb phrases are considered. It stands to reason that the transformational apparatus should remain fairly constant in complexity as more detail is added (or as a higher level of grammaticalness is discussed), whereas the system of phrase structure should increase sharply in complexity, since transformational analysis permits the stepwise formation of complex phrases from already constructed simple phrases, while in terms of phrase structure, simple and complex phrases must in general be constructed simultaneously by a single set of rules.

In §76.1 we noted that **159** and **160** (= **11, 12**, §76.1) have intuitively different interpretations, though both have the same structure *NP-PP*, where *NP* is the abstract $ing^\frown V$. The reason can now be clearly stated in transformational terms. Though they have the same structure on the level **P**, they have different transformational structures. That is, they are differently represented in terms of the operations by which they are derived from the kernel, and in terms of the kernel sentences from which they are derived. **159** is derived from the kernel sentence "lions growl," and **160** from the kernel sentence "he reads good literature," or the like. This provides a systematic explanation in the terms of linguistic theory for the fact that "lions" seems to be the subject of "growling" in **159**, and "good literature" the object of "reading" in **160**. These interpretations are determined by the fact that we do not have "he growled lions" or "good literature reads," so that the alternative interpretation is impossible in each of these cases. However, such sentences as "the rearming of Germany" (= **13**, §76.1) and "the shooting of the hunters"

(= **14**, §76.1) are subject to either interpretation, since we have both "Germany rearms" and "the West rearms Germany," both "the hunters shoot" and "they shoot the hunters," as kernel sentences. These are thus real cases of constructional homonymity on the level **T**, with different **T**-markers, and a different **P**-basis in the kernel. These ambiguous phrases have the same status on the level **T** that "old men and women" has on the level **P**. Just as "old men and women" can be represented in two conflicting ways in terms of phrase structure, and has associated with it two **P**-markers in the simplest grammar of phrase structure (assuming now that it is derived in the kernel grammar—cf. §115), so "the rearming of Germany" and "the shooting of the hunters" are represented in two different ways on the level **T**, as an automatic consequence of the attempt to construct the simplest transformational analysis. The phrase "our rearming of Germany," on the other hand, is unambiguous. It must be derived from "we rearm Germany" by $T_{s\text{-}ob}$.

99.7 It remains to account for the fact that we have "the growling," but not "the playing the piano." The latter is excluded by condition K_A (cf. **139**). The simplest way to account for the possibility of the former seems to be to set up another transformation related to T_{ing} and T_{sub} . We thus define T_I ,

164 T_I is determined by $(Q_{sub}, \delta_{ing_1})$, where

Q_{sub} is as in **162**
$$\delta_{ing_1}:\quad Y_1\text{-}Y_2\text{-}Y_3\text{-}Y_4 \to U\text{-}U\text{-}ing^\frown Y_3\text{-}Y_4 = ing^\frown Y_3\text{-}Y_4$$

Thus the defining sequence for δ_{ing_1} is $(\sigma, U, \sigma, U, ing, U, U, U)$, and T_I carries $NP\text{-}VP_A\text{-}V_T\text{-}U$ into $ing^\frown V_T$; e.g., it carries *lions-Ø-growl-U* into $ing^\frown growl$, which is carried by $\Phi_5{}^P$ into "growling." δ_{ing_1} is very similar to δ_{ing} of **157**.

We now extend **156** so as to include T_I . The family of substitutions F_A is already defined in such a way as to include $ing^\frown V_T$ as one possible case of α_1 in **136**. Condition K_A does not apply to T_I , i.e., $T_I(Z, K) = ing^\frown V_T$ can freely replace abstract nouns, even in such contexts as *the——*.

One bad feature of this analysis is that it assigns two **T**-markers to such sentences as

165   *reading is fun*

"reading" can be derived by T_{ing} or T_I from "they read." But there is no dual interpretation of **165**. This was the case in §72.2, where **165** was derived from $Inf^\frown V_T$ or $Inf^\frown VP_1$. This case of constructional homonymity with no intuitive correlate suggests that something may be amiss in this analysis, and that further investigation of this matter is necessary.

This winds up the discussion of *ing*-phrases and *to*-phrases occurring as abstract nouns. We can sum up the constructions of §§99.1–99.7 as follows.

99.8

As **T**-markers we have all strings Z in **T** such that Z is formed from **166** by choosing strings and interpretations for the variables Z_1, K_1, Z_2, K_2 and by selecting one of the grammatical transformations belonging to F_A, and such that the strings and interpretations chosen in constructing Z meet condition K_A :

$$166 \qquad Z_1^\frown K_1^\frown I \begin{bmatrix} T_{to} \\ \begin{pmatrix} T_{ing} \\ T_{s\text{-}ing} \\ T_{sub} \\ T_{ob} \\ T_{s\text{-}ob} \\ T_I \end{pmatrix} \end{bmatrix} Z_2^\frown K_2^\frown I \begin{bmatrix} T_A \\ F_A \end{bmatrix} \varPhi^{\mathbf{P}}$$

Condition K_A : Where W is one of $T_{to}(Z_1, K_1)$, $T_{ing}(Z_1, K_1)$, $T_{s\text{-}ing}(Z_1, K_1)$, $T_{s\text{-}ob}(Z_1, K_1)$, there is an X and a Y such that

(i) $Z_2 = X^\frown it^\frown Y$

(ii) $\mathrm{Val}_1(Z^{red}) = X^\frown W^\frown Y$, where Z^{red} is the reduced correlate of Z

The elements of **166** are analyzed as follows:

167

$$
\begin{array}{llll}
T_{to} & \text{is determined by} & & (Q_{to}, \delta_{to}) \\
T_{ing} & \text{''} & \text{''} & \text{''} \ (Q_{ing}, \delta_{ing}) \\
T_{s\text{-}ing} & \text{''} & \text{''} & \text{''} \ (Q_{ing}, \delta_{s\text{-}ing}) \\
T_{sub} & \text{''} & \text{''} & \text{''} \ (Q_{sub}, \delta_{ing\text{-}of}(\pi_p)) \\
T_{ob} & \text{''} & \text{''} & \text{''} \ (Q_{ob}, \delta_{ing\text{-}of}) \\
T_{I\text{-}ob} & \text{''} & \text{''} & \text{''} \ (Q_{ob}, \delta_{s\text{-}ing\text{-}of}) \\
T_I & \text{''} & \text{''} & \text{''} \ (Q_{sub}, \delta_{ing_1}) \\
T_A & \text{''} & \text{''} & \text{''} \ (Q_A, t_A) \\
F_A & \text{''} & \text{''} & \text{''} \ (C_A, t_A)
\end{array}
$$

The description of the underlying deformations can be simplified by a notational convention. Given the number of terms in the restricting class of a deformation we know automatically how many terms there are in the defining sequence of its underlying deformation, under the single condition that the deformation in question is not the identity, i.e., that it is not insignificant in the sense that every case to which it applies is an instance of case II, Definition 10, §83.2. Hence assuming significance for all stated transformations, we can unambiguously state that a defining sequence $(a_1 ,..., a_k , U, U, U,...)$, where a_k is the last nonunit term, can be taken as defining any elementary deformation whose defining sequence is any initial part of this sequence, excluding only unit terms. Thus the defining sequence for δ_{ing_1}, which is $(\sigma, U, \sigma, U, ing, U, U, U)$, can simultaneously be taken as the defining sequence for δ_{ing}, which formerly had the defining sequence $(\sigma, U, \sigma, U, ing, U)$.

We can now define the elements of **167** as follows:

168

$$\begin{Bmatrix} \begin{Bmatrix} Q_{to} \\ Q_{ing} \end{Bmatrix} \\ \begin{Bmatrix} Q_{sub} \\ Q_{ob} \end{Bmatrix} \end{Bmatrix} = NP, \begin{Bmatrix} VP_{A1} , \begin{Bmatrix} \langle VP_{A2} \rangle \\ \langle have^\frown en \rangle \end{Bmatrix} VP_1 \\ VP_A, V_T, \begin{Bmatrix} U \\ NP \end{Bmatrix} \end{Bmatrix}$$

$$Q_A = (to\langle VP_{A2} \rangle VP_1 , \#, U, N_{ab} , X)$$

$C_A(\alpha_1 , \alpha_2 , \alpha_3 , \alpha_4 , \alpha_5)$ if and only if

(i) $\alpha_1 = \langle NP^\frown S_1 \rangle ing\langle have^\frown en \rangle VP_1$
(ii) $\alpha_2 = \#$
(iii) $\alpha_3 = X$
(iv) $\alpha_4 = N_{ab}$
(v) $\alpha_5 = Y$

$$t_A \leftrightarrow (\sigma, 0, \sigma, 0, 0, 0, \sigma, 1, 0, 0)$$
$$\pi_p \leftrightarrow (4, 2, 3, 1)$$

$$\begin{Bmatrix} \begin{Bmatrix} \delta_{to} \\ \begin{Bmatrix} \delta_{ing} \\ \delta_{ing1} \end{Bmatrix} \\ \delta_{ing\text{-}of} \\ \begin{Bmatrix} \delta_{s\text{-}ing} \\ \delta_{s\text{-}ing\text{-}of} \end{Bmatrix} \end{Bmatrix} \end{Bmatrix} \leftrightarrow \begin{Bmatrix} \sigma, U \\ U, S_1 \end{Bmatrix}, \sigma, U, \begin{Bmatrix} \begin{Bmatrix} to \\ ing \end{Bmatrix} \\ ing \\ ing \end{Bmatrix}, U, \begin{Bmatrix} U \\ of \\ \begin{Bmatrix} U \\ of \end{Bmatrix} \end{Bmatrix}, U$$

If we had defined reductions for the level **T**, as we did for **P** in §55, we could simplify this statement in various ways. For example, the entire list **167** can be eliminated, and the right-hand side introduced directly into the proper place in **166**. Further coalescence is also possible.

The element *Inf* has been eliminated from the analysis of noun phrases, **99.9** but it is still introduced by statement 10, §72.2, to account for the *V-to-V* (e.g., "want to come") and *V-ing-V* (e.g., "like reading") constructions discussed in §68. But now statement 15 has been dropped completely, so that statement 16 applies only to the element *Inf* introduced in statement 10. We can thus drop the element *Inf* completely from the system of phrase structure, and with it, the remaining parts of statement 16; and we can then reformulate statement 10 as

169 $VP_B \rightarrow Z_1 \langle Z_2 \langle ... \langle Z_n \rangle \rangle \rangle$, where Z_i is one of the elements of the form

$$\begin{Bmatrix} V_c \frown to \langle VP_{A2} \rangle \\ V_v \frown ing \langle have \frown en \rangle \end{Bmatrix}$$

In §72.2 we were able to give a single statement (viz., the restriction in statement 21) covering the distinction between *to* and *ing* with respect to the following auxiliary phrase. But now we have found it necessary to present this distinction once for the *ing*-phrases and *to*-phrases introduced transformationally as noun phrases, in **168**, and once for the elements *to* and *ing* occurring in VP_B, in **169**. We cannot compare the simplicity of the analysis in **P** and the analysis in **T** in this respect, since the restriction in statement 21 was not literally admissible into the grammar of phrase structure (cf. Note 33, Chapter VIII). But in any event, it appears that transformational analysis is not efficient in this respect. But we will see that this inadequacy will be remedied with a deeper analysis of VP_B.

We are still left with a statement that is not literally admissible into the kernel grammar, since in developing the form of grammatical statement in Chapters IV and VII, no allowance was made for recursive statements of the form of **169** or of statement 10 which it replaces. But we will see below that this statement can be eliminated altogether.

With this alteration, then, statements 15 and 16 are dropped completely from the kernel grammar.

The set of transformations that we have discussed in §99 provide a **99.10** criterion for the assignment of a string to VP_1. Whenever we have a phrase $ing \langle have \frown en \rangle$ W, $to \langle VP_{A2} \rangle$ W, etc., functioning as a noun phrase, the statement of the transformations that appear in **166** will be simplified if W is analyzed as a VP_1. Otherwise the definitions of Q_A and C_A in **168** will have to be modified to include W as a new form. This criterion will be of some use below.

99.11   We have not yet accounted for such *ing*-phrases as

170   (a)   *not to see him*
           (b)   *not seeing him*
           (c)   *John's not seeing him*

It is possible to include them, by slight revisions of **166** and **168**. Considering only the case of **170**a, suppose that we restate δ_{to} , Q_{to} as

171 $\delta_{to}: \quad Y_1\text{-}Y_2\text{-}Y_3\text{-}Y_4 \to U\text{-}U\text{-}Y_3\text{-}to\frown Y_4 = Y_3\text{-}to\frown Y_4$

$$Q_{to} = \left(NP,\ VP_{A1}\ ,\ \left\{ \begin{matrix} U \\ not \end{matrix} \right\},\ \langle VP_{A2} \rangle\ VP_1 \right)$$

Thus the defining sequence for δ_{to} is now $(\sigma,\ U,\ \sigma,\ U,\ U,\ U,\ to,\ U)$. T_{to} has exactly the same effect as before on strings without *not*, and it will carry, e.g., *John–will–not–see him* into **170**a. **166** will then fit the resulting phrase **170**a properly into sentences.

Analogous alterations of T_{ing} and $T_{s\text{-}ing}$ will give **170**b–c. This is quite a simple emendation. It seems intuitively adequate, and in particular, it accounts for the feeling noted in §96.3 that **86**c is not a parallel form to **86**a, b, as well as for the homonymity mentioned in §96.3.

There is, however, one difficulty connected with this extension. All phrases such as **170** will have to be derived from negative sentences where the VP_{A1} entirely precedes *not*, i.e., where $VP_A = M$, $\varnothing$, S, or *ed*. And when the main verb is *be*, only $VP_{A1} = M$ will qualify. These restrictions can be understood by noting that *not* in all other cases falls after *have*, *be*, etc., so that the sentences in question will not be of the proper form for T_{to} to apply, i.e., they will not be analyzed in such a way as to meet Q_{to} . This is likely to cause difficulty in a more refined analysis than ours, when certain considerations concerning the conditions on the auxiliary phrases of Z_1 and Z_2 in **166** are introduced (cf. §99.3). Because of this possible difficulty, we have not included this revision above. It may be that some alternative analysis may ultimately prove to be preferable.

100.1   In Chapter VII we used as examples sentences of the form

172   (a)   *the detective brought in the suspect*
           (b)   *the detective brought the suspect in*

but we did not include these in the analysis of English syntax in Chapter VIII, since it did not seem possible to arrive at any adequate analysis of these sentences at that point. On the basis of the criteria of analysis which were then established there seemed to be no reason to relate these sentences, and even no way to express the relationship between them. The only way to analyze sentences such as **172** would have been as instances of a new type of VP_1, namely,

173 $VP_1 \to V^\frown NP^\frown P$

Had we adjoined **173** to statement 3, §72.2 (the analysis of VP_1), we would have discovered in stating the restrictions on occurrence for this position that V_i and P_j appear together in the construction $V_i{}^\frown NP^\frown P_j$ just in case $V_i{}^\frown P_j$ also appears in the construction NP-$V_i{}^\frown P_j$-NP(e.g., **172a**).[18] Thus the whole set of restrictions that must be stated for constructions of the latter type would have to be repeated for verb phrases of the form **173**. This suggests that we relate these constructions transformationally, either deriving **172a** from **172b** or *vice versa*. There are a variety of reasons for choosing to derive **172b** from **172a**, rather than the other way around.

Note first that if **172b** is taken as the kernel sentence, then we need one new sentence form, namely, **173**. However there is good reason for analyzing **172a** as an instance of the already familiar form NP-V-NP with a compound verb "bring in." For one thing, the conjunction criterion favors this analysis. We have "they brought in and questioned the suspect," but not "they brought in the suspect and in his accomplice." The impossibility of the latter rules out the analysis NP-V-PP, with the verb "brought." The existence of the former requires that "brought in" be in the same class as "questioned," or in the same class as "questioned the suspect." But we do not have "they brought in" as a sentence, and we do have "they brought in the suspect." Hence we cannot analyze this sentence as an instance of $(NP^\frown VP)^\frown$ $and^\frown(NP^\frown VP)$ with the first conjunct $NP^\frown VP = they^\frown brought^\frown in$; but we can analyze it as an instance of NP-$(V^\frown and^\frown V)$-NP, with "brought in" the first V and "questioned" the second. Hence the conjunction criterion favors the analysis of "brought in" as an instance of V_T, along with "questioned" (actually, "bring in" and "question" receive this analysis, with *ed* being the affixed auxiliary phrase in this instance).

Further support for this analysis appears from the criterion of parenthetical intrusion (cf. §65.2). We have "he looked, as you can see, in every possible place," but not "he looked, as you can see, up the case

---

[18] The converse is not the case. Certain "compound verbs" of the form $V^\frown P$ do not have separable prepositions as do "bring in," "call up," etc. (cf. §116).

in the records." Hence the latter case must have the constituent break after "look up," not after "look." That is, it cannot be an instance of $NP \frown V \frown PP$, like "he looked in every possible place." The fact that "he looked up, as you can see, the case in the records" is impossible is irrelevant here, since, as we noted in §65.2, parenthetical intrusion can in general not occur between verb and object.

A further reason for the analysis of such sentences as **172a** as instances of $NP\text{-}V\text{-}NP$ with a compound verb is given by the passive criterion. This analysis is necessary in order to provide for the generation of such sentences as

174   *the suspect was brought in by the detective*

Application of the *ing*-phrase criterion discussed in §99.10 leads to the same conclusion. Since we have the phrase

175   *ing-be $\frown$ brought $\frown$ in*   (= *being brought in*)

we see that "be brought in" (= $be \frown en \frown bring \frown in$) is a VP_1, so that $bring \frown in$ must be a V_T. All of these criteria thus converge on the analysis $NP\text{-}V\text{-}NP$ for **172a**.

But if **172b** is selected for the kernel with the analysis **173**, **172a** being derived from it by transformation, then the analysis $NP\text{-}V\text{-}NP$ will not be conferred on **172a** as its derived constituent structure, and it will be necessary to provide for this by some special condition. If **172a** is given in the kernel, then it is only necessary to list "bring in" in statement 23, §72.2, as a V_T, along with all other transitive verbs, for the proper constituent structure to be assigned.

Applied to **172b**, the conjunction criterion determines that "brought the suspect in" must be a VP_1, since we have "the detective brought the suspect in and questioned him," where "questioned him" is a VP_1. But this analysis of **172b** will be provided as its derived constituent structure if it is transformationally derived from **172a**, as we saw in §87.4 (we found in §87.5 that the condition on derived constituent structure under which this analysis is assigned to **172b** is a very general one, which is needed for many other cases as well). Thus all considerations lead us to derive **172b** from the sentence **172a** which has the form $NP\text{-}V\text{-}NP$, "bring in" being the compound transitive verb.

We must therefore add to statement 23, §72.2, a set of statements of the form

176 $V_T \rightarrow V_{sep} \frown P$, where...

where V_{sep} is a certain subclass of verbs, and ... gives the restricting conditions on the choice of P_1 given an element of V_{sep}. We then construct the transformation T_{sep} such that

177 T_{sep} is determined by (Q_{sep}, π_{sep}), where

$$Q_{sep} = (NP, VP_A, V_{sep}, P, NP)$$
$$\pi_{sep}: \quad Y_1\text{-}Y_2\text{-}Y_3\text{-}Y_4\text{-}Y_5 \rightarrow Y_1\text{-}Y_2\text{-}Y_3\text{-}Y_5\text{-}Y_4$$

π_{sep} is thus the permutation with the defining sequence $(1, 2, 3, 5, 4)$, and T_{sep} converts a string of the form $NP\text{-}VP_A\text{-}V_{sep}\text{-}P\text{-}NP$ into the corresponding string of the form $NP\text{-}VP_A\text{-}V_{sep}\text{-}NP\text{-}P$. In particular, it converts 172a into 172b. As a **T**-marker schema we have

178 $Z^\frown K^\frown T_{sep}{}^\frown \Phi^\mathbf{P}$

By Definition 30, §87.4, we see that $V_{sep}\text{-}NP\text{-}P$ is a VP_1 in the transform, and that $VP_A\text{-}V_{sep}\text{-}NP\text{-}P$ is a VP. This accords perfectly with the conjunction criterion and with the *ing*-phrase criterion, since we have "they brought him in and questioned him" and "bringing him in."

There is one feature of the usage of sentences of the form 172 that is not   100.2
brought out by our analysis, and that may indicate a limitation of our whole approach. While in the case of 172 both (a) and (b) are grammatical, in general the separability of the preposition is determined by the complexity of the NP object. Thus we could scarcely have

179   *the detective brought the man who was accused of having stolen the automobile in*

It is interesting to note that it is apparently not the length in words of the object that determines the naturalness of the transformation, but rather, in some sense, its complexity. Thus "they brought all the leaders of the riot in" seems more natural than "they brought the man I saw in." The latter, though shorter, is more complex on the transformational level since it has the infixed sentence "I saw." We will see below that this is a transformational construction. A good deal of further study is needed here to determine the nature of this process and to define properly the relevant sense of complexity of the object.

As the object becomes more complex, then, the naturalness of the transform decreases. This is systematic behavior, and we might expect that a grammar should be able to state it. But it may turn out to involve probabilistic considerations for which our system has no place as it now stands. This is of course not the only case where a grammatical rule, if applied over the full scope of its domain, leads to certain unacceptable results. But it is a particularly clear instance of a phenomenon which may prove to be importance in a more general treatment of linguistic structure.

100.3   The separation of the preposition is obligatory when the object is a pronoun. Thus we have

180   *the detective brought him in*

but not "the detective brought in him." There are two ways in which this situation might be handled. Either we can require that $V_{sep}{}^\frown P$ never occur with pronominal objects, and can add $V_{sep}{}^\frown Pronoun{}^\frown P$ as a new sentence form, or we can add a new mapping $\Phi_i{}^\mathbf{P}$ which operates exactly like T_{sep}. Independently of how we choose to analyze **172** we must choose the second alternative, because of the passive criterion. Since we have

181   *he was brought in by the detective*

we must have the active "the detective–brought in–him" as the product of a derivation in the kernel grammar, i.e., as the product of a **P**-marker, with **180** derived by a mapping. Note that we cannot rely on the transformational analysis with T_{sep} in this case, since the inversion is obligatory. We give this mapping as $\Phi_1{}^\mathbf{P}$:

182 $\Phi_1{}^\mathbf{P}$ is determined by (Q'_{sep}, π_{sep}), where

$$Q'_{sep} = (NP, VP_A, V_{sep}, P, Pronoun)$$
$$\pi_{sep} \text{ is as in } \mathbf{177}$$

We will see below that $\Phi_1{}^\mathbf{P}$ must precede $\Phi_5{}^\mathbf{P}$.

We noted in §100.2 that as the object becomes longer and more complex, the naturalness of the transform decreases. Conversely, as the object becomes shorter, its naturalness increases. There is a certain sense in which pronouns are the "shortest" objects, namely, they never carry stress (except the contrastive stress which can occur quite freely with almost any element). The fact that the transformation is obligatory for pronouns might be considered as the limiting case of the increase in naturalness with decrease in length. Thus the treatment of T_{sep} and $\Phi_1{}^P$ might somehow be unified. We will discover further suggestions to this effect below.

We have seen that the grammatical sketch of §72.2 must be extended   101.1
to include statements of the form **176**. By the same reasoning as in §80.0, we will now see that there are a great many other instances of "compound verbs" with separable elements.

We saw that one form of the verb phrase, namely **173**, can be struck out of the kernel grammar by transformational analysis. Consider now the VP_1 of the form

183 $V_h{}^\frown NP{}^\frown Predicate$

as introduced in statement 3, §77.2. An instance is

184   *they–consider–John–a fool* $(NP_1–V_h–NP_2–Predicate)$

We must analyze this sentence in such a way as to admit the possibility of the passive

185   *John is considered a fool by them*

There seem to be three alternative solutions available for this problem:

I.   We may add a new transformation $\bar{T}_p$ which converts NP_1-V_h-NP_2-*Predicate* into NP_2-*is*${}^\frown$*en*-V_h-*Predicate-by*${}^\frown NP_1$. $\bar{T}_p$ is related to, but distinct from, the passive transformation T_p . We must then revise T_{pd} (§98.5) so that it can apply to $X_i{}^\frown en{}^\frown V{}^\frown Predicate\text{-}by{}^\frown NP$ (cf. **122**) as well as to $X_i{}^\frown en{}^\frown V\text{-}by{}^\frown NP$, since we must account for "John was considered a fool."

II.   We may leave the passive transformation unchanged (i.e., NP_1-VP_A-V-$NP_2 \rightarrow NP_2$-VP_A-*be*${}^\frown$*en*-V-*by*${}^\frown NP_1$) and consider $NP_2{}^\frown$*Predicate* to be the complex object of V_h . The result of applying T_p will then be "John a fool is considered by them" ($NP_2{}^\frown Predicate$-*is*${}^\frown$*en*-V_h-*by*${}^\frown NP_1$). We can then add a mapping $\Phi_\alpha{}^P$ which carries this expression into **185**.

III.   We may leave T_p as is and consider **184** to be formed by application of a mapping $\Phi_\beta{}^P$ from

186   *they–consider a fool–John*

186 is then the product of a **P**-marker, i.e., a sentence derived in the kernel grammar. Then "consider–a fool" is a compound verb like "bring in," and 183 is struck from the VP_1-analysis, statement 3, §77.2. T_p now applies directly to 186, analyzed as *NP-V-NP*, giving 185. We have already seen that T_p applies prior to any mapping.

The first alternative adds two new transformations. The second and third each add a single new mapping.

Alternative II is ruled out immediately by the *ing*-phrase criterion of §99.10. Since we have

187   *being considered a fool* $(= ing \frown be \frown en \frown consider \frown a \frown fool)$

we know that $be \frown en \frown consider \frown a \frown fool$ must be a VP_1. Hence *consider* and $a \frown fool$ must constitute a single verbal element in 185. Now it is possible to formulate Φ_α^P so that "a fool" in the intermediate form "John a fool is considered by them" is adjoined by the mapping to "consider"; then the derived constituent structure of "consider a fool" assigns this phrase to V_T, just as "consider" is a V_T ("consider" being the root of "consider a fool"—cf. Definition 30, §87.4). This would be a case almost exactly like case (iii), §87.5. But T_{ing}, which gives 187, must apply before Φ_5^P and after Φ_α^P; hence Φ_α^P must apply before Φ_5^P. Hence if the result of Φ_α^P is that "consider a fool" is a V_T (like its root "consider"), then Φ_5^P will carry $ing \frown consider \frown a \frown fool$ into $consider \frown a \frown fool \frown ing$, $ed \frown consider \frown a \frown fool$ into $consider \frown a \frown fool \frown ed$, etc. Thus if we choose alternative II we are either forced to complicate Φ_5^P somehow so as to exclude this possibility, or else to formulate Φ_α^P in such a way that 187 will not be forthcoming. Neither of these difficulties arises in alternative III, so that III at least is simpler than II.

The choice between I and III is resolved in favor of III when we note the parallel between the solution of III and the consideration of §100. Φ_β^P as introduced in III is a slight extension of Φ_1^P as defined in §100.3. We thus replace 182 by

188 Φ_1^P is determined by (Q'_{sep}, π_{sep}), where

$$Q'_{sep} = \left\{ \left(NP, VP_A, \begin{Bmatrix} V_{sep}, P, Pronoun \\ V_h, Predicate, NP \end{Bmatrix} \right) \right\}$$

Thus Φ_1^P carries $NP\text{-}VP_A\text{-}V_{sep}\text{-}P\text{-}Pronoun$ into $NP\text{-}VP_A\text{-}V_{sep}\text{-}Pronoun\text{-}P$ and it carries $NP\text{-}VP_A\text{-}V_h\text{-}Predicate\text{-}NP$ into $NP\text{-}VP_A\text{-}V_h\text{-}NP\text{-}Predicate$. In the first case, it carries "they–brought in–him" $(= they\text{-}ed\text{-}bring\text{-}in\text{-}him)$ into "they brought him in" $(= they\text{-}ed\text{-}bring\text{-}$

him-in); in the second case, it carries **186** into **184**. T_p and T_{pd} remain unchanged, and no new mappings or transformations are added. We note as an additional argument for III over II that the mapping $\Phi_\alpha{}^{\mathbf{P}}$ introduced in II is new, while the mapping $\Phi_\beta{}^{\mathbf{P}}$ introduced by III already appears, in part, in **182**.

The total effect of alternative III on the complexity of the grammar, then, is to replace **182** by **188**, and to delete **183** from the kernel grammar. Alternative II requires that we add to the set of grammatical transformations two new transformations, $\overline{T}_p$ and $\overline{T}_{pd}$. But no matter how $\overline{T}_p$ is formulated it will face the same difficulties that made a simple formulation of $\Phi_\alpha{}^{\mathbf{P}}$ impossible. As we saw in discussing alternative II, *be$^\frown$en$^\frown$ consider$^\frown$a$^\frown$fool* must be considered a VP_1, so that *en$^\frown$consider$^\frown$a$^\frown$fool* must be an element of the form *en$^\frown V_T$* (since we have no other forms of VP_1 beginning with *be$^\frown$en*...). Further support for this analysis of *en$^\frown$consider$^\frown$a$^\frown$fool* comes from the conjunction criterion. Since we have

189   *John was mistreated and considered a fool*

we know that "considered a fool" (= *en$^\frown$consider$^\frown$a$^\frown$fool*) must be the same type of element as "mistreated," i.e., an *en$^\frown V_T$*. But the only way to achieve this result in terms of $\overline{T}_p$, just as in the case of $\Phi_\alpha{}^{\mathbf{P}}$, is to formulate $\overline{T}_p$ so that it attaches "a fool" to "consider" as the root term, with the result that "consider a fool" is an X wherever "consider" is an X. Thus $\overline{T}_p$ will be the transformation such that, under $\overline{T}_p$,

190 NP_1–VP_A–V_h–NP_2–*Predicate* $\rightarrow$ NP_2–VP_A–*be$^\frown$en$^\frown V_h{}^\frown$*
                                                     Predicate–by$^\frown NP_1$–U

where dashes indicate the terms of the proper analysis. Thus $\overline{T}_p$ will be a complex transformation of a new type, with a deformation, an adjunction, and a permutation figuring in the definition of its underlying elementary transformation. Furthermore, the difficulties faced by $\Phi_\alpha{}^{\mathbf{P}}$ now reappear. Since *Predicate* has been attached to V_h by an adjunction, it follows that $V_h{}^\frown$*Predicate* is a V_h, so that *en$^\frown V_h{}^\frown$Predicate* is carried by $\Phi_5{}^{\mathbf{P}}$ into $V_h{}^\frown$*Predicate$^\frown$en* (i.e., *en$^\frown$consider$^\frown$a$^\frown$fool* $\rightarrow$ *consider$^\frown$a$^\frown$ fool$^\frown$en*).

This difficulty is avoided only by alternative III. Here $V_h{}^\frown$*Predicate* is listed (along with V_{t1}, $V_{sep}{}^\frown P$, etc.) in statement 23, §72.2 as a V_T. Since "consider a fool" is not formed by attaching "a fool" to "consider," "consider a fool" is not a V_h, though it is a V_T, just as "eat," "bring in," etc. are V_T's. The passive transformation T_p is formulated to apply to V_T, and $\Phi_5{}^P$ is formulated so as to apply to all initial subclasses V_{t1}, V_{sep}, V_h, etc. of V_T.

Thus various considerations lead to III as the correct solution. This seems to be intuitively correct. **185** does appear to be a passive, intuitively, in the same sense as "John is mistreated by them." In **184** and **185**, "a fool" seems intuitively closely related both to "consider" and to "John." Its relation to "consider" is explained by the fact that "consider a fool" is in both cases the verbal element. The formal reason for the relation to "John" will appear below.

As a result of this transformational analysis, certain changes are necessary in the kernel grammar §72.2 (e.g., statement 6 must be revised). But as these alterations will themselves be superseded below, we will not construct them here. We will see that compound verbs of the form $V_h{}^\frown Predicate$ are themselves formed transformationally, so that they need not actually be listed in statement 23.

101.2   In §98.2 we considered the problem of determining the crudest possible grammaticalness assumptions from which it will follow that the passive transformation, in its correct form, must appear as a grammatical transformation in English. We saw there that the distinction between abstract and proper nouns would be sufficient to establish this transformation. But now we find that the distinction between singular and plural is actually sufficient.

We noted, in §98.2, that the passive transformation in the form we have given will be necessary[19] if it is the case that for certain choices of NP_x, NP_y, and V, **191** ($= 107$) is grammatical, but **192** ($= 108$) is not:

191   (a) $NP_x\text{--}V\text{--}NP_y$
          (b) $NP_y\text{--}is^\frown en^\frown V\text{--}by^\frown NP_x$

192   (a) $NP_y\text{--}V\text{--}NP_x$
          (b) $NP_x\text{--}is^\frown en^\frown V\text{--}by^\frown NP_y$

As instances of **191** and **192**, we have, respectively,

193   (a)   *they   consider   John   a   fool*   ($=$ *they--consider$^\frown$a$^\frown$fool--John*)

---

[19] Of course this is nowhere near a sufficient characterization of the conditions under which the passive transformation would be necessary. If such a set of conditions can be given at all, it will be extremely complex. We are reducing the problem here to its bare essentials, and assuming that there are no further instances of sentences that serve as counterexamples to the passive transformation. This is a fair statement of the problem for English (cf. §117).

(b) *John is considered a fool by them* $(= John\text{-}is^\frown en^\frown con\text{-}sider^\frown a^\frown fool\text{-}by^\frown them)$

194 (a) *John considered them a fool*
   (b) *they were considered a fool by John*

with $NP_x = they$, $NP_y = John$, and $V = consider^\frown a^\frown fool$. Since the passive transformation applies before any mapping, it applies in particular before the mapping $\Phi_1{}^P$ which carries the parenthesized forms of **193** into the nonparenthesized forms. Hence it operates on the parenthesized form of **193a**. Since **193a,b** are grammatical and **194a,b** are not, the transformational analysis of passives is required. The point here really is that we have found a case of numerical agreement between the verb and the object. The verb contains an element (*a fool*) which must agree in number with the object (*John*). This verb–object relation is carried over into the passive. The subject of the passive (= the object of the underlying form) must agree in number with the verbal form which was the main verb of the underlying active.

We can put this somewhat differently. One might ask: how can we tell that the passive carries $NP_1\text{-}V\text{-}NP_2$ into $NP_2\text{-}is^\frown Ven\text{-}by^\frown NP_1$, and not into $NP_1\text{-}is^\frown Ven^\frown by^\frown NP_2$. We could not tell this from cases like "John loves Mary," since we have both "John is loved by Mary" and "Mary is loved by John." Harris has pointed out[20] that we have "Casals plays the cello," "the cello is played by Casals," but not "Casals is played by the cello." This will clearly be the case if our analysis of grammaticalness is at all adequate—if it is, then the third sentence will be shown to be only partially grammatical (cf. Chapter V) and will thus not be generated by the grammar (cf. Note 16, this chapter). But now we see that we have **193a,b** but not **194b** as grammatical sentences. Thus any grammar powerful enough to recognize the distinction between singular and plural would correctly solve the problem of stating the passive transformation. This transformation, then, can be considered very firmly established on syntactic grounds.

This argument appears circular in one sense. We relied in part on the passive transformation for the analysis of such sentences as **183**, and we have now used the resulting analysis of such sentences to indicate how limited are the assumptions required by the correct version of the passive transformation. But in this case we have precisely the kind of "circularity" that marks a correct analysis. This is a case where various parts of the analysis support one another—what is the simplest solution for one

[20] "Discourse analysis," *Language* 1952, p. 19.

problem turns out at the same time to be the simplest solution for another. The correct analysis of all the interdependent cases of passives, *ing*-phrases, and sentences of the form **183** follows, with no circularity, from the criterion of simplicity applied to grammar construction. In §110 we will consider a formal condition on grammars from which this support for the passive transformation will be derived in a more direct manner.

102 Exactly the same line of reasoning that we applied in the case of sentences of the form **183** leads us to strike out **195** and **196** from the VP_1-analysis in statement 3, §77.2:

195 $V_e{}^\frown NP_1{}^\frown to{}^\frown be{}^\frown Predicate$ *(they know him to be a fool)*

196 $V_g{}^\frown NP_1{}^\frown NP_2$ *(they elected him an officer)*

Since we have

197   *he is known to be a fool*

198   *he was elected an officer*

we must add "know–to be a fool," "elect–an officer," etc., to the list of compound verbs. **195** and **196** are thus reduced to the general form *NP-V-NP*, with NP_1 being the object in both cases. This explains, incidentally, why the pronoun appears as "him," "her," "them," in this position.

Instead of adding still further qualifications on Q'_{sep} (cf. **188**), we can recognize a subdivision $V^\frown Complement$ of V_T,[21] and, replacing **188**, we can define $\Phi_1{}^P$ as

199 $\Phi_1{}^P$ is determined by (Q'_{sep}, π_{sep}), where

$$Q'_{sep} = \left\{ \left(NP, VP_A, V, \begin{Bmatrix} P,\ Pronoun \\ Complement,\ NP \end{Bmatrix} \right) \right\}$$

In the analysis of V_T we will then indicate, by the necessary restricting statement, that if $V \rightarrow V_h$, *Complement* $\rightarrow$ *Predicate*; if $V \rightarrow V_e$,

[21] More correctly, there will be such a subdivision for each subclass of V_T. We will not go into the details of this statement, since much of it will be introduced transformationally below. For the same reason, we will not go into certain reformulations in the rules of numerical agreement (statements 4, 6, §72.2) which are necessitated by these revisions.

Complement → *to⌢be⌢Predicate*; if *V* → V_g , *Complement* → *NP*; etc. In introducing further instances of this pattern, it will not be necessary to extend the transformational analysis, but only to expand the subdivision *V⌢Complement*.

These developments permit an important distinction, which could not have been made previously among sentences of the form

103.1

200   *NP₁-V-NP₃-PP*

In §77.2. there was no reason to analyze sentences of this kind other than as *NP₁-V-NP₂* , with *NP₂* → *NP₃⌢PP*. But it is intuitively clear that while this analysis fits such sentences as

201   *the police suspect the man behind the counter*

it is not proper for either **202** or **203**:

202   *the police put the man behind bars*

203   *the police questioned the man behind closed doors*

The same distinctions can easily be found with different prepositions.

The distinction between these three types of cases can be made in terms of the passive transformation. The passives corresponding to **201–203** are, respectively,

204   *the man behind the counter was suspected by the police*

205   *the man was put behind bars by the police*

206   *the man was questioned by the police behind closed doors*

The fact that "the man was questioned behind closed doors by the police" also occurs as a grammatical sentence is irrelevant here. **202** and **203** are distinguished by the fact that **206** is permissible, while "the man was put by the police behind bars" is not. There is another distinguishing transformation which we have not discussed. From **203** we can form "behind closed doors, the police questioned the man," but there are no comparable forms for **201–202**. It is interesting to note that the *where*-transformation forms "where did they $\begin{Bmatrix} \text{put} \\ \text{question} \end{Bmatrix}$ the man" from

202–203, but it does not apply to **201**. It is clear that we have only begun to scratch the surface in the analysis of these forms.

From comparing **201–203** with the passives **204–206**, it follows that **201** is of the form $NP_1\text{-}V\text{-}NP_2$, with $NP_2 =$ "the man behind the counter," and that **202** is another instance of a compound verb $V^\frown Comple$-*ment*, with the complement, in this case, being the prepositional phrase *behind*$^\frown$*bars*. Thus the verb in **202** is "put–behind bars." **203** requires an extension of the analysis of §72.2 to include prepositional phrases added to VP_1 as a whole. It might appear that the PP's could just as well be added to the whole sentence, i.e., that "$\langle PP \rangle$" could be added to statement 1, §72.2, instead of statement 3. But the *ing*-phrase criterion for VP_1 rules this out, since we have "questioning him behind closed doors." The conjunction criterion leads to the same conclusion.

With this alteration, and with the various deletions that have taken place until now, statement 3, §72.2, appears as

$$207 \qquad VP_1 \rightarrow \langle D_2 \rangle \langle VP_B \rangle \begin{Bmatrix} V_f{}^\frown NP{}^\frown NP \\ V_e \langle that \rangle\ Sentence \\ be^\frown Predicate \\ V_T \langle NP \rangle \end{Bmatrix} \langle PP_\alpha \rangle$$

where PP_α is a certain class of prepositional phrases that are "detached" from the verb.

The constituent structure of **201**, **202** is thus basically $NP_1\text{-}V\text{-}NP_2$, with NP_2 in **201** being "the man behind the counter," and V in **202** being "put–behind bars"; and the analysis of **203** is $NP\text{-}V\text{-}NP\text{-}PP$. This seems to be in accord with the intuitive analysis of these sentences.

103.2 It is now necessary to revise the passive transformation T_p to account for sentences of the type **203**. It seems that any such sentence can have either a form like **205** or **206** in the passive, as we noted for **203** directly below **206**. This fact leads us to replace T_p by a family of transformations F_p. The underlying elementary transformation for F_p is $t_p{}'$, where

$$208 \qquad t_p{}' = \delta_p{}'(\pi_p{}'),\ \text{where}$$

$$\pi_p{}': \quad Y_1\text{-}Y_2\text{-}Y_3\text{-}Y_4\text{-}Y_5\text{-}Y_6 \rightarrow Y_4\text{-}Y_2\text{-}Y_3\text{-}Y_5\text{-}Y_1\text{-}Y_6$$
$$\delta_p{}': \quad Z_1\text{-}Z_2\text{-}Z_3\text{-}Z_4\text{-}Z_5\text{-}Z_6 \rightarrow Z_1\text{-}Z_2\text{-}be^\frown en^\frown Z_3\text{-}Z_4\text{-}by^\frown Z_5\text{-}Z_6$$

Thus the defining sequence for $\pi_p{}'$ is $(4, 2, 3, 5, 1, 6)$, and the defining sequence for $\delta_p{}'$ is $(U, U, U, U, be^\frown en, U, U, U, by, U, U, U)$, and $t_p{}'$

carries Y_1-Y_2-Y_3-Y_4-Y_5-Y_6 into Y_4-Y_2-$be^\frown en^\frown Y_3$-Y_5-$by^\frown Y_1$-Y_6. We can then define F_p as follows:

209 F_p is determined by (C_p, t_p'), where

       t_p' is as in **208**
       $C_p(\alpha_1, \alpha_2, \alpha_3, \alpha_4, \alpha_5, \alpha_6)$ if and only if

$$\begin{aligned} \alpha_1 &= NP & \alpha_4 &= NP \\ \alpha_2 &= VP_A & \alpha_5 &= U\langle PP_\alpha \rangle \\ \alpha_3 &= \langle D \rangle V_T & \alpha_6 &= U\langle PP_\alpha \rangle \end{aligned}$$

This replaces **105**. For sentences with no PP_α, the effect of a transformation from F_p with $\alpha_5 = \alpha_6 = U$ is exactly that of T_p of **105**. If PP_α does occur, then we can choose a transformation of F_p with $\alpha_5 = PP_\alpha$ and $\alpha_6 = U$, giving a passive of the form of "the man was questioned behind closed doors by the police"; or we can choose a transformation of F_p with $\alpha_5 = U$ and $\alpha_6 = PP_\alpha$, in which case we derive a passive of the form **206**.

We must revise T_{pd} (cf. **122**) correspondingly. By "T_{pd}" we will henceforth understand the transformation defined as follows:

210 T_{pd} is determined by (Q'_{pd}, δ'_{pd}), where

$$Q'_{pd} = \{(X_i{}^\frown en^\frown V, by^\frown NP, U\langle PP_\alpha \rangle)\}$$

$$\delta'_{pd}: \quad Y_1\text{-}Y_2\text{-}Y_3 \to Y_1\text{-}U\text{-}Y_3 = Y_1\text{-}Y_3$$

When we choose U as the third term of Q'_{pd}, we have the case covered by **122**. Sentences like "the man was questioned behind closed doors" are derived from the corresponding sentence of the form **206**. This is the simplest way to cover all cases. Such sentences as "the man was questioned behind closed doors by the police" do not fall within the domain of T_{pd}. Hence **206** appears to be the basic form of the passive for such sentences as **203**. **210** now replaces **122**.

As the **T**-marker schema for passives we now have, instead of **123**, the schema

211 $Z^\frown K^\frown F_p \langle T_{pd} \rangle \Phi^{\mathbf{P}}$

Note that **201** is not really of the form NP_1-V-$NP_3{}^\frown PP$, as we have been rather loosely describing it in our informal exposition. In **201** the only parts that are actually NP's are "the police" and "the man behind the counter," but not "the man" (though this is an NP in other sentences). If this distinction is not kept clear, then T_p and T_{pd} will not apply in the intended way to **201**. The grammatical sketch of the kernel grammar in §72.2 gives a correct account of this situation. In the kernel grammar, the basic steps in the derivation of **201** are

212 1. *Sentence*
      2. $NP\text{-}VP_A\text{-}VP_1$ (statements 1, 2)
      3. $NP\text{-}VP_A\text{-}V_T\text{-}NP$ (statement 3)
      4. $NP\text{-}VP_A\text{-}V_T\text{-}T^\frown N^\frown \emptyset^\frown PP$ (statement 7)
      5. *the police————Ø–suspect–the$^\frown$man$^\frown$behind$^\frown$the$^\frown$counter*

Thus "the man behind the counter" is a *NP*, but "the man" is not, in this sentence. The most that we can say about "the man" is that it is a $T^\frown N^\frown \emptyset$, in terms of §72.2. It is important to remember that the prepositional phrase in **201** is introduced by statement 7; in **202**, by statement 23 (extended to include $V^\frown Complement$); in **203**, by **207** (replacing statement 3).

In §72.2 we did not go into the distribution and restrictions on prepositional phrases (and in fact, we could not have, without a more thorough investigation of grammaticalness). But these restrictions are certainly real enough, and it is apparent that a considerable simplification in any such distributional statement is effected by the transformational analysis, under which the restrictions need be stated only for the kernel sentences.

Just as we must revise the passive transformation to account for the element PP_α, we must revise the definition of T_{sep} and the mapping $\Phi_1{}^P$. **177** is replaced by **213**, and **199** by **214**:

213 T_{sep} is determined by (Q''_{sep}, π'_{sep}), where

$$Q''_{sep} = \{(NP, VP_A, V_{sep}, P, NP, U\langle PP_\alpha\rangle)\}$$
$$\pi'_{sep} \leftrightarrow (1, 2.\ 3, 5, 4, 6)$$

214 $\Phi_1{}^P$ is determined by (Q'''_{sep}, π'_{sep}), where

$$Q'''_{sep} = \left\{\left(NP, VP_A, V, \begin{Bmatrix} P,\ Pronoun \\ Complement,\ NP \end{Bmatrix}, U\langle PP_\alpha\rangle\right)\right\}$$

Obviously, these statements can be coalesced.

103.3   We now have a formal explanation for the intuitively felt difference between the sentences "this picture was painted by a real artist" and "this picture was painted by a new technique," which were discussed in

§76.1 (these are, respectively, 1 and 2 of §76.1). In the kernel we have the sentences **215**a,b but not **216**:

215 (a) *a real artist painted the picture*
(b) *the artist painted the picture by a new technique*

216 *a new technique painted the picture*

The passives corresponding to **215**a,b are

217 (a) *the picture was painted by a real artist*
(b) *the picture was painted by the artist by a new technique*

Because of the possibility of **217**b, we see that **215**b is a case of $NP\text{-}V\text{-}NP\text{-}PP_\alpha$, like **203**. T_{pd} (as reformulated in **210**) applied to **217**b gives

218 *the picture was painted by a new technique*

The distinction between **217**a and **218** (1 and 2, Chapter IX, respectively) is thus a real difference of transformational history, i.e., a difference of structure on the level **T**. Both are instances of $NP\text{-}was\text{-}en\frown V\text{-}PP$, in terms of phrase structure, but the **T**-marker of **217**a is **219**, and the **T**-marker of **218** is **220**:

219 $\quad 215a \frown K_1 \frown T_p \frown \Phi^\mathbf{P}$

220 $\quad 215b \frown K_2 \frown T_p \frown T_{pd} \frown \Phi^\mathbf{P}$

where K_1 and K_2 are the respective **P**-markers. The problems raised in §76.1 concerning sentences **3–9** of that section are solved transformationally in much the same way. Similarly, the sentences

221 $\quad$ *John was* $\begin{Bmatrix} frightened \\ surprised \\ bored \end{Bmatrix}$ $\quad (= \mathbf{10}, \S76.1)$

automatically receive the intuitively correct analysis as homonyms. Their "nonverbal" sense arises from the fact that these expressions all belong to the kernel, as instances of the $en\frown V_k$ form of the adjective phrase (cf. statement 17, §72.2), as we know from the fact that they can be preceded by "very." Their "verbal" sense derives from their transformational derivation by T_p and T_{pd} from "... frightened John," etc.

In § §98.4, 99.5, and 99.6, we have seen that the remaining intuitive inadequacies pointed out in §76.1 and §76.3 have been remedied by transformational analysis. This, along with the many similar cases that we have come across where transformational analysis gives results that correspond to strong intuitive judgments (e.g., the priority of actives over passives and declaratives over questions), and where behavior that appears irregular on the level **P** is shown to be systematic on the level **T** (e.g., the behavior of "be," "have" in question, negatives, and *so*-phrases, discussed in § §94.5, 96.2), indicate that we are well on our way to resolving, in transformational terms, the problems that originally suggested the need for a higher level of syntactic analysis.

103.4   The distinctions made in §103.2 permit certain cases of constructional homonymity. A given sentence of the form $NP\text{-}V\text{-}NP_3\text{-}PP$ ($= 200$) may turn out to be in the overlap of the pattern $NP_1\text{-}V\text{-}NP_2$ (with $NP_2 \to NP_3 {}^\frown PP$), as **201**, and the pattern $NP_1\text{-}V\text{-}NP_3\text{-}PP$, like **203**. For instance,

222   *the police questioned the man in the other room*

is subject to either interpretation, since we have passives of the forms **204** and **206**, respectively:

223    $\begin{cases} \text{(a)} & \textit{the man in the other room was questioned by the police} \\ \text{(b)} & \textit{the man was questioned by the police in the other room} \end{cases}$

This dual interpretation for **222** certainly has intuitive support.

The analysis to which we have come above also permits concatenation of different types of *PP*'s. We may have a sentence Z of the form $NP {}^\frown VP$, where

224    $VP \to VP_A {}^\frown V_T {}^\frown NP {}^\frown PP_\alpha$
$V_T \to Verb {}^\frown Complement$
$Complement \to PP_x$

Thus Z is of the form

225    $NP\text{-}VP_A\text{-}Verb\text{-}PP_x\text{-}NP\text{-}PP_\alpha$

$\Phi_1{}^P$ will carry this into

226    $NP\text{-}VP_A\text{-}Verb\text{-}NP\text{-}PP_x\text{-}PP_\alpha$

As an instance of **226**, we have, e.g.,

227   *they–will–name–him–after⌢his⌢grandfather–after⌢his⌢first⌢ birthday*

In **227**, the V_T is "name–after his grandfather." **228** seems a good deal less acceptable:

228   *they–will–name–him–after⌢his⌢first⌢birthday–after⌢his⌢ grandfather*

The *who*-transformation of §95 applied to **227** (with *him* replacing the *NP* "his grandfather") gives **229**, and applied to **228** (with the same change) it would give **230**:

229   *whom will they name him after after his first birthday*

230   *whom will they name him after his first birthday after*

229 is acceptable, but the ungrammaticalness of **230** supports the exclusion of **228**.

The revision of $\Phi_1{}^P$ given above in **214** accounts for the possibility of **227** (hence **229**), and excludes **228** (hence **230**). If **228** is admitted as grammatical, we will have to define $\Phi_1{}^P$ as a family of transformations, as in **209**.

In §98.4, in discussing the effects of the passive criterion for constituent analysis, we discussed a case just like those of §103.1. We noted there that all cases of **231** are grammatical, though **232** is not: **103.5**

231 $\Bigg\{$
(a)   *I knew the boy studying in the library*   ($=$ **115**)
(b)   *I found the boy studying in the library*   ($=$ **116**)
(c)   *the boy studying in the library was known (by the teacher)*   ($=$ **117a**)
(d)   *the boy studying in the library was found (by the teacher)*   ($=$ **117b**)
(e)   *the boy was found studying in the library (by the teacher)*   ($=$ **117c**)

232   *the boy was known studying in the library (by the teacher)*   ($=$ **118**)

It follows that **231a** has a compound object of the form $NP⌢ing⌢VP_1$, as we noted in §98.4, just as **201** with the passive **204** has a compound object $NP⌢PP$. Since we have the passive **231d** of

231b, we know that **231**b also has this analysis, under one interpretation. But from the passive **231**e, we see that **231**b has an alternative interpretation as the image under $\Phi_1{}^{P}$ of "I–found studying in the library–the boy," an instance of $NP\text{-}V_T\text{-}NP$ with the verb "found–studying in the library." In this interpretation, it is analogous to **202**, which has the passive **205**. We see then that **231**b is an instance of constructional homonymity, and that we must add **233** to the construction *Verb–Complement*:

233 $V\text{-}ing^\frown VP_1$ (*find–studying in the library*)

This leads us one step closer to the solution of one of the problems that arose in the attempt to present a comprehensive system of phrase structure for English. In §69 we found (i) that phrases of the form $NP\text{-}ing^\frown VP_1$ could not be admitted into the grammar of phrase structure (i.e., into the kernel) without great complication, and (ii) that if they were admitted, we would not be able to distinguish such obviously distinct forms as **231**a and **231**b in structural terms. We now have a solution for (ii). We can make the distinction, if we can introduce these phrases. But we still have not indicated how these phrases are to be introduced. We return to this problem below, in §§108.2, 109.5.

The same situation holds for the case of the verbs V_δ discussed in the last paragraph of §70. We add to the *Verb–Complement* construction the forms

234 $V_\delta\text{-}\langle ing\rangle\, VP_1$

Once again, when means for introducing these sentences (e.g., "I saw him come," "I saw him coming," etc.) have been developed, the correct distinctions will be forthcoming.

104.1 Since we managed to delete $V_g{}^\frown NP_1{}^\frown NP_2$ from the VP_1-analysis (in §102), we should expect the analysis of $V_f{}^\frown NP_1{}^\frown NP_2$ to follow fairly smoothly. But these verb phrases pose a somewhat different problem.

V_f is formally distinct from V_g on the level **P** in that NP_1 and NP_2 do not necessarily have the same number after V_f, as they must after V_g. We have

235 $\begin{cases}(a) & \textit{the teacher gave him several books} \\ (b) & \textit{the teacher asked him several questions}\end{cases}$

but not

236   *they elected him officers*

On the transformational level, other differences appear. The only passive formed from "they elected him an officer" (= **196**) is "he was elected an officer by them," *elect* being a V_g. But from $V_f \frown NP \frown NP$ we can have two passives. Thus from **235**a we have

237 (a) *he was given several books by the teacher*
     (b) *several books were given him by the teacher*

and the same is true of **235**b.

The *wh*-transformations also apply differently to **235** and **196**. From **196** we have, for instance, both **238**a,b, as we would expect:

238 $\Big\{$(a) *whom did they elect an officer*
       (b) *what did they elect him*

But from **235**a we have only **239**b, not **239**a.[22]

239 $\Big\{$(a) *whom did the teacher give the books*
       (b) *what did the teacher give him*

Instead of **239**a, we have

240 $\Big\{$(a) *whom did the teacher give the books to*
       (b) *to whom did the teacher give the books*

This suggests that there is a sentence more elementary than **235**a, namely,

241 *the teacher gave several books to him*

and that **235**a is derived from **241** by a transformation T_α. It seems to be true in general that for sentences of the form $NP_1\text{-}V\text{-}NP_2\text{-}\genfrac{\{}{\}}{0pt}{}{to}{for}\text{-}NP_3$, there is a related form $NP_1\text{-}V\text{-}NP_3\text{-}NP_2$. Thus we have "they offered him the job" ("they offered the job to him"), "they found him a job" ("they found a job for him"), etc. We must then require that the *who*-question transformation not apply to any T_α-transform, in order to eliminate **239**a.

---

[22] It should be recalled that we are making no attempt to account for the considerable dialectal variation in this and other cases that are under discussion.

Consider now the sentence **241**. Its passive is

242   *several books were given to him by the teacher*

But the passive **243** and the form **244** also appear permissible:

243   *several books were given by the teacher to John*

244   *to John, the teacher gave several books*

From the possibility of **243** and **244** it follows that **241**, like **203** in §103.1, is an instance of $NP\text{-}V\text{-}NP\text{-}PP_\alpha$.

104.2   One way to describe this situation is in the following series of steps:

1.   To the construction *Verb–Complement* we add the form

245 $V_f {}^\frown PP_\alpha$

one instance of which is "give–to him," with "to him" being the PP_α .

2.   We construct the transformation T_α which carries $X^\frown to^\frown Y$ into $X^\frown Y$, for any strings X, Y.

3.   We allow for the following strings of transformations:

246 $\begin{cases} \text{(a)} \\ \text{(b)} \\ \text{(c)} \end{cases} \begin{Bmatrix} T_p{}^\frown T_\alpha \\ T_p \\ T_\alpha \end{Bmatrix} \Phi^\mathbf{P}$

Applying (a) to the sentence

247   *the teacher–gave to him–several books*

we derive **237b**. Applying **246b** to **247**, we derive **242**. Applying **246c** to **247**, we derive **235a**. Applying $\Phi_1^\mathbf{P}$ directly to **247**, with no intervening transformation, we derive **241**. This leaves **237a** and **243** still unaccounted for.

4.   We can account for the remaining sentences by permitting the strings **248** in **T**-markers:

248   (a) $\Phi_1^\mathbf{P}{}^\frown T_p{}^\frown \psi_1'$
            (b) $\Phi_1^\mathbf{P}{}^\frown T_\alpha{}^\frown T_p{}^\frown \psi_1'$

Applying **248a** to **247**, we derive first **241**, by Φ_1^P, this being a sentence of the form $NP\text{-}V\text{-}NP\text{-}PP_\alpha$. Applying T_p as reformulated in **209**, we derive **243**, with "him" for "John." Applying **248b** to **247**, we derive first **241**, then "the teacher–gave–several books–him" by T_α. But this derived sentence has the same form as the kernel sentence

249   *they–elected–an officer–him*

Hence application of T_p to "the teacher–gave–several books–him" will give **237a**, just as it gives "he was elected an officer by them" from **249**.

5.   We place the condition on **T**-markers that the *who*-question cannot follow T_α, thus eliminating **239a**.

Note that if steps 1–3 of this solution are adopted, then it follows that Φ_1^P must precede the question transformation, so that **240** is generated properly. But we have seen above that the question transformation must apply before Φ_5^P. Hence Φ_1^P must apply before Φ_5^P. If step 4 is accepted as well, then Φ_1^P must precede Φ_3^P, since T_p must precede Φ_3^P.

There are certain potential trouble spots in the derivation of **237a** as outlined in step 4, above. It is necessary that the kernel grammar be carefully formulated so that the proper derived constituent structure is conferred on "the teacher–gave–several books–him" (by analogy to **249**). Later, in fact, we will see that **249** is itself derived by transformation. Hence to carry through step 4 it will be necessary to extend our conception of derived constituent structure in such a way that constituent structure can be conferred on a transform by virtue of an analogic form which is itself derived. Because of this difficulty, and because of the *ad hoc* nature of step 5, above, we see that the reduction of $V_f \frown NP \frown NP$ to the basic form $V_T \frown NP$ is only partially satisfactory.

Note that if **248** is accepted, then it will not be necessary to formulate the passive transformation as a family of transformations, as in **209**. It is possible to construct the passive as a single transformation, and to achieve the necessary variety by applying it either before Φ_1^P (as before) or after Φ_1^P (as in **248a**). There are further implications to this course that we have not studied.

The passive criterion shows us that sentences of the form   105.1

250 $NP\text{-}V_e\text{-}that \frown Sentence$ (*"everyone knew that the play would be a success"*) are also of the form $NP_1\text{-}V\text{-}NP_2$, with $NP_2 = that\frown Sentence$. This follows from the fact that we have such sentences as

251   *that the play would be a success was known by everyone*

These sentences, too, must thus be dropped from the VP_1-analysis. Since *Sentence* in **250** may be a passive or a transform of some other type, we see in fact that **250** must be dropped from the kernel grammar and reintroduced transformationally.

From this point on, the analysis of *that*-phrases is just a simpler version of the discussion in §99 of *ing*-phrases. To **166**, §99.8, we add

252 $Z_1\frown K_1\frown T_{that}\frown Z_2\frown K_2\frown I\frown T_{IN}\frown \Phi^P$

with condition K_A extended to include $T_{that}(Z_1, K_1)$ as one of the forms of W.

T_{that} is based on a deformation that inserts *that* before a sentence. Not every sentence can appear here. For instance, questions are sentences in terms of their derived constituent structure, but they cannot appear after *that*. Questions, however, are not represented by $NP\frown VP$; and closer investigation shows that we can use the representation $NP\frown VP$ to define the set of elements that can follow *that* (i.e., kernel sentences, passives, sentences with *ing*-phrase nouns, etc., are included—questions and, as we will see below, imperatives are excluded). We thus define T_{that} as

253 T_{that} is determined by $(Q_{that}, \delta_{that})$, where

$$Q_{that} = (NP\frown VP)$$
$$\delta_{that} \leftrightarrow (that, U)$$

The transformation T_{IN} in **252** is defined as

254 T_{IN} is determined by (Q_{IN}, t_A), where

$$Q_{IN} = \{(that\frown NP\frown VP, \#, X\frown V_e, N_{inan}, Y\}$$
$$t_A \leftrightarrow (\sigma, 0, \sigma, 0, 0, 0, \sigma, 1, 0, 0) \quad \text{(as in **168**)}$$

Thus in particular T_{IN} converts a string of the form $that\frown NP_1\frown VP\text{-}\#\text{-}NP_2\frown VP_A\frown V_e\text{-}N_{inan}\text{-}U$, where $N_{inan} = it$ (by the extension of condition K_A), into the corresponding string $NP_2\frown VP_A\frown V_e\text{-}that\frown NP_1\frown VP$. The **P**-basis for **250**, then, is

255   (*the play would be a success, everyone knew it*)

with their respective interpretations.

T_{IN} differs from T_A in **166** mainly in that the replaced *it* is inanimate. The choice of *it* as the bearer of the *that*-clause is determined by the same factors that operated in the case of *ing*-phrases (cf. §99.1). A closer analysis of T_{that} would show that there is an internal effect on the sentence, because of sequence of tense restrictions (alternatively, these could be given as added conditions along with K_A). The similarity between **252–254** and **166–168** naturally stands in favor of both of these transformational analyses, since considerable coalescence is possible. We know that the *that*-clause in the transform is an inanimate noun.[23]

Such sentences as **251** are subject to a further transformation. From **251** we can form

105.2

256   *it was known by everyone that the play would be a success*

The transformation $T_{th\text{-}it}$ that gives **256** from **251** can be applied more generally when we have any adjective, not just a passive $en^\frown V$, as in **251**. Thus we have

257   *it was clear to everyone that the play would be a success*

This, incidentally, lends further support to the decision originally reached in §67.3 to consider the $en^\frown V$ forms to be adjectives, rather than to include $be^\frown en$ (alongside of $be^\frown ing$) as an element of the auxiliary verb phrase. We thus have

258 $T_{th\text{-}it}$ is determined by $(Q_{th\text{-}it}, t_{th\text{-}it})$, where

$$Q_{th\text{-}it} = (that^\frown NP^\frown VP, \; VP_A, \; be, \; AP, \; U)$$
$$t_{th\text{-}it} = \delta_{th\text{-}it}(\eta_{th\text{-}it})$$

where $\eta_{th\text{-}it} \leftrightarrow (0, 0, 0, 0, 0, 0, 0, 0, 0, 1)$
$\delta_{th\text{-}it} \leftrightarrow (\sigma, \; it, \; U, \; U, \; U, \; U, \; U, \; U, \; U, \; U)$

The transformational analysis of *that*-clauses enables us to drop one recursion from the kernel grammar, thus effecting a shortening of derivations. We will see in the course of the investigation that all recursions drop from the kernel grammar.

---

[23] Actually, as we have constructed the kernel grammar, in both **168** and **254** the generalized transformations should have $\emptyset^\frown N^\frown C$ as the replaced terms, not just N, and we should thus say that the *that*-phrase is a $\emptyset^\frown N_{inan}^\frown C$. But a more far-reaching analysis of the kernel, and an explicit analysis of pronouns, either transformationally or as part of the kernel, might alter this in detail. See **395**, §113.1.

106   In the last few sections we have managed (with the reservations of
§104.2) to drop out of the VP_1-analysis all forms except $be{}^\frown Predicate$
and $V_T{}^\frown NP$, reducing all other forms to special cases of V_T-NP. We
have also seen in §100 and §103.5 that other forms not included in
§72.2 also fall under this general pattern. The VP_1-analysis given
above as **207** (replacing §77.2, statement 3), thus reduces to

$$259 \qquad VP_1 \rightarrow \langle D_2 \rangle \langle VP_B \rangle \begin{Bmatrix} be{}^\frown Predicate^{24} \\ V_T \langle NP \rangle \end{Bmatrix} PP_\alpha$$

This is actually a significant reduction. In §72.2, the forms in **259**
appeared as part of a list of many forms of the verb phrase (of which
statement 3, §72.2, gives only part). They had no particular systematic
importance. But it is intuitively clear that they are in some sense basic.
Any English grammar will assign primary importance to the grammatical
relations of "predication" and "actor–action." But transformational
analysis of the verb phrase shows that these are in fact fundamental
relations. The forms of **259** are the *only* two forms of VP_1; as we
defined "grammatical relation" in §59, the relations of predication and
actor–action are basic. Later, in §109 we will see that of all the compound
verbs, only the construction *Verb–Preposition* remains in the kernel.

   In connection with the VP_1-analysis, it is interesting to note that
the possibility of analyzing intransitive verbs as transitives with zero
objects is ruled out. If this analysis were accepted, the passive transformation would yield such nonsense as

260    $\emptyset$–was–en${}^\frown$sleep–by${}^\frown$John   (= "*was slept by John*")

107   We have seen (§99.6) that "growling of lions" and "reading of good
literature" can be derived respectively from "lions growl" and "they
read good literature." There are many cases of similar constructions with
a noun related to a verb, but not so simply related as are "growling"
and "reading" to "growl" and "read." Consider, for instance, the noun
phrase subjects of

---

[24] This pattern should be extended to cover the stative verbs "seem," "become," "act,"
etc. These differ from one another somewhat, and they differ from "be" in several
important formal respects (e.g., more limited occurrence with following *NP*, nonoccurrence with following *PP*, etc.). Since these verbs are not also auxiliaries, as is
"be," they do not share the features of the auxiliaries manifested by "be" and discussed
in §§94.5, 96.2.

261   (a)   *the sight of men working in the fields made him sad*
         (b)   *the flight of the birds signaled the coming of spring*
         (c)   *his refusal to come was taken as an insult*
             etc.[25]

These can be derived by generalized transformations in the familiar way from

262   (a)   *he saw men working in the fields # it made him sad*
         (b)   *the birds flew # it signaled the coming of spring*
         (c)   *he refused to come # it was taken as an insult*

The added element is not *ing*, but a certain nominalizing morpheme ν which can be taken as a prime of $\bar{P}$. In the morphology, we have such rules as

263   (a)   *see$^\frown\nu$ = sight*
         (b)   *fly$^\frown\nu$ = flight*
         (c)   *refuse$^\frown\nu$ = refusal*
             etc.

Whether one such nominalizing morpheme will suffice is a matter that requires more elaborate study. Furthermore, the distribution of this morpheme will be limited, since some verbs (e.g., "follow") do not appear with it. It seems evident that a considerable simplification should result from this analysis, since otherwise the heavy distributional restrictions in 261 will have to be separately stated, duplicating much of the analysis of the verb phrase. The transformational analysis is much like that of §99.6, a fact which stands in favor of both of these analyses.

The considerations of §66.2 indicated that the level of morphology is not independent of the level of phrase structure, since only on this level did the criteria for a correct morphological analysis appear. If the preceding paragraphs are correct, then morphology is not independent of the level of transformations for the very same reasons. The distributional relations between "sight" and "see," etc., could not, apparently be recognized on any lower level. Since these words are in fact in different classes, they are never substitutable for one another. And purely distributional morphological analysis, if motivated at all in this case, might well identify "see" with "seat," "sigh" with "sight," etc. But purely distributional analysis on the transformational level does bring out the

[25] See Harris, *Methods*, footnote, p. 8.

distributional relation between these forms, and requires that they be related on the morphological level.

In Chapters V and VI we discussed the problem of constructional homonymity on the level of syntactic categories (ordinary homonymity) and noted that among the homonyms relevant to syntax there were, intuitively, two types. Thus in the overlap of *Noun* and *Verb* we have both "walk" and /riyd/, but these are clearly different kinds of homonyms. In terms of the nominalizing morpheme v, now required by transformational analysis, we can offer a purely syntactic explanation for this intuitively felt distinction. The noun "walk" will be analyzed as "walk⁀v" (where *walk* is the verb) if it is the case that many contexts of this noun are transforms of the contexts of the verb "walk." In other words, one of the variants of v is zero (i.e., in certain contexts, the morpheme v is carried into the phonemic unit). /riyd/ naturally will not be amenable to such analysis. If detailed investigation supports this conclusion, as appears likely, we will have a transformational explanation for the feeling, noted in the final paragraph of §34.4, that "walk" is a single word, in two classes, while /riyd/ is basically two words with the same phonemic shape, i.e., a real homonym.

108.1   Sentences with relative clauses were not included in the grammatical sketch of §72.2. In fact, the discussion of §69 showed that they could not be included without seriously disturbing the grammar. But we can now introduce them quite simply by generalized transformations.

Consider the sentence

264   *all the students watched the man who was lecturing*

We note first of all that this is a sentence of the form $NP_1\text{-}V\text{-}NP_2$, with $NP_2 =$ "the man who was lecturing." This analysis is determined by the passive criterion, since we have **265** but not **266**:

265   *the man who was lecturing was watched by all the students*

266   *the man was watched by all the students who was lecturing*

Investigating other *who*-phrases that can occur in this position, we determine that "who was lecturing" is a transform of a sentence, which can be taken as "he was lecturing." Since we have also

267   *I noticed the man whom I had met yesterday*

we see that the transformation that carries a sentence into a *who*-phrase can operate on a string X_1-*he*-X_2, carrying it into $wh^\frown he$-X_1-X_2, even when $X_1 \neq U$. Hence we have here exactly the family of transformations F_w constructed in §95.1. As was mentioned in §95.7, *wh*-questions are simply F_w-transforms of questions, and relative clauses are F_w-transforms of declaratives.

The generalized transformation T_R which carries *who*-phrase– $\#$–X_i–NP–X_j into X_i–$NP^\frown who$-phrase–X_j will produce **264** and **267**, respectively, from

268   (a)   *who was lecturing $\#$ the students watched the man*

            (b)   *whom I had met yesterday $\#$ I noticed the man*

But we have seen above that the resulting $NP^\frown who$-phrase is itself a *NP*. Hence T_R must be formulated as an adjunction which attaches the *who*-phrase to *NP* as its root. This generalized transformation can apply to many *NP*'s in a sentence. Thus we must construct a family of transformations F_R. Thus we have

269 F_R is determined by (C_R, t_R), where $C_R(\alpha_1, \alpha_2, \alpha_3, \alpha_4, \alpha_5)$ if and only if

        (i) $\alpha_1 = wh^\frown...$

       (ii) $\alpha_2 = \#$

      (iii) $\alpha_3 = X_i$

      (iv) $\alpha_4 = NP$

       (v) $\alpha_5 = X_j$

and $t_R \leftrightarrow (\sigma, 0, \sigma, 0, 0, 0, 0, 1, 0, 0)$.

t_R thus differs from t_A of **168** in only one place, and $NP^\frown wh^\frown...$, a single term of the proper analysis of the transform, is a *NP*.

As **T**-markers we have strings in **T** of the form

270 $Z_1^\frown K_1^\frown I$-F_w-$Z_2^\frown K_2^\frown I$-F_R-$\Phi^\mathbf{P}$

Actually, we have not given anywhere near sufficient detail in the specification of this transformation, and considerable qualification is necessary. For one thing, it must be possible for the *NP* of Z_2 to which the *who*-phrase is added to appear in the position of the replaced noun of the *who*-phrase. For example, we must exclude such sentences as "the man who were lecturing," or, on a higher level of grammaticalness, "the man whom I prevented," etc. The simplest way to account for all such cases is to add a condition K_R on **T**-markers of the form **270**, requiring that the *NP* of α_4 , **269**, be *identical* with the *NP* of Z_1 which is replaced by "who" under F_w . Thus the **P**-basis of **264** would be

271   (*the man was lecturing, the students watched the man*)

But in §95.1, F_w was developed in such a way that only "he," not any *NP*, can be the root of the term "who," "whom." We have not discussed pronouns, but there are actually good reasons for introducing them transformationally as substituends for *NP*'s of the proper kind. Thus the definition of F_w can be made compatible with the condition K_R by replacing the first I in **270** by the transformation that replaces an animate *NP* by "he."

There are several other conditions and revisions that would be necessary in a really accurate and complete analysis. Not every *NP* in Z_2 can have a relative clause affixed to it, so that certain restrictions must be placed on X_i and X_j in **269**. Furthermore, a more detailed study of pronouns will probably lead to the conclusion that "him" is derived from "he" by a mapping which may precede all other components of Φ^P. But this necessitates a slight revision of **270**, since F_w must naturally apply after this mapping.

Just as we have *what*-questions paralleling *who*-questions (cf. §95.4), we have *which*-phrases and *that*-phrases added to inanimate nouns. When these are constructed, along the lines sketched above, we will add still further conditions of compatibility on Z_1 and Z_2 of **270**. We will not investigate these phrases here, nor will we consider the other occurrences of "relative clauses" (i.e., F_w-transforms of declaratives), as in "I know who saw him,", etc.

108.2   Extension of this transformational analysis of relative clauses serves to integrate §108 with earlier discussions. From

272   *I know the boy who is studying in the library*

we can derive, by an additional transformation T_β , the sentence

273   *I know the boy studying in the library*

From this instance, it appears that T_β converts X-*who*$^\frown$*is*-Y into X-Y, but closer investigation shows that sentences like **273** can occur even when the auxiliary verb *be*$^\frown$*ing* cannot appear in the corresponding *who*-phrase. Thus we have **274** and **275**, but not **276**:

274   (a)   *people owning property should pay higher taxes*
         (b)   *everyone knowing the answer may leave*

275   (a)   *people ⟨who⟩ own property*
         (b)   *everyone ⟨who⟩ knows the answer*

276   (a)   *people ⟨who⟩ are owning propery*
         (b)   *everyone ⟨who⟩ is knowing the answer*

From this we see that *ing* in **273** is added by T_β ; it is not the *ing* of **272** carried over under the transformation. We thus set up a family of transformations F_β such that

277 F_β is determined by (C_β , δ_β), where $C_\beta(\alpha_1 , \alpha_2 , \alpha_3)$ if and only if

(i) $\alpha_1 = X$;   (ii) $\alpha_2 = who^\frown VP_A$; $\alpha_3 = Y$
$\delta_\beta \leftrightarrow (U, U, \sigma, U, ing, U)$

A member of F_β thus carries a string $X\text{-}who^\frown VP_A\text{-}Y$ into $X\text{-}U\text{-}ing^\frown Y = X\text{-}ing^\frown Y$. We now add "$\langle F_\beta \rangle$" to **270** following "$F_R$." In this way we derive all those phrases $NP^\frown ing^\frown VP_1$ which are noun phrases as determined by the passive criterion (cf. §98.4, §103.5). This gives us one source for the $NP^\frown ing^\frown VP_1$ phrases which caused so much trouble in §69. The difficulties raised in §69 are now undercut, since **273** is derived from the two kernel sentences "I know the boy," "the boy is studying in the library," neither of which poses any of the problems of §69. We saw in §103.5 that there is also a second source for $NP^\frown ing^\frown VP_1$ phrases. In §109.5, below, we arrive at the second source.

There are a variety of other transformations similar to those of F_β . Thus relative pronouns can be dropped in many positions, as can *that* in *that*-clauses (cf. §105), etc. One such transformation can be used to derive the noun phrases $NP^\frown PP$ discussed in §103.1, e.g., "the man behind the counter" in   **108.3**

278   *the police suspect the man behind the counter*   (= **201**)

$NP^\frown PP$ can be derived from a noun phrase $NP^\frown who^\frown is^\frown PP$. For example, **278** can be derived from

279   *the police suspect the man who is behind the counter*

by a transformation very similar to T_β .

Such analysis should effect quite a considerable simplification in the kernel grammar. A more careful grammar than ours would recognize many restrictions on the selection by noun phrases of a modifying *PP*. These restrictions need now only be given for the occurrence of *PP* as a predicate in sentences *NP-be-PP*. They will be carried over automatically to the *NP⌒PP* position by transformation.

Investigation of the *NP⌒PP* noun phrase construction shows that not all such instances are covered by the transformation from *NP-be-PP*. For instance, we have **280** but not **281**:

280   (a)   *the man with the felt hat*
            (b)   *the men of great wealth*

281   (a)   *the man is with the felt hat*
            (b)   *the men are of great wealth*

We do, however, have

282   (a)   *the man has the felt hat*
            (b)   *the men have great wealth*

and **280** and similar sentences might be derived from these by a second transformation much like T_β. Thus **280**a will have a **P**-basis and transformational history somewhat different from that of "the man with John." "The men with friends" would then be a case of constructional homonymity, deriving either from "the men are with friends" or "the men have friends." Other modifying prepositional phrases have still different origins in the kernel. Thus "the forerunners of modern mathematics" might be derived from "modern mathematics has forerunners," etc. A detailed study of this construction should be interesting.

109.1   The object Noun Phrase of **278** (= **201**) is now eliminated from the kernel in favor of a sentence *NP-be-Predicate*. In discussing **278** in §103.1, we compared it structurally with

283   *the police put the man behind bars*   (= **202**)

This sentence has been shown to be an instance of the very productive construction

284 $V_T \rightarrow V⌒Complement$

of which many other instances were found in §§100–102. But $NP^\frown PP$ in **283** can also be regarded as derived from a sentence of the form *NP-be-Predicate*, namely,

285   *the man is behind bars*

In fact, we have *NP-put-NP_x-PP_y* only for such NP_x and PP_y as occur as *NP_x-is-PP_y*. Investigation of other instances of **284** shows that these too can be transformationally derived. We have already noted in §101.2 that certain verbs given by **284** must agree in number with their objects as well as their subjects (more precisely, the complement part must agree with the object, and the verb part, with the subject), and we have used this fact to support the formulation of the passive transformation with inversion of *NP*'s. But it is more generally the case in the *Verb–Complement* construction that the complement and the object of the compound verb have heavy selectional restrictions which suggest transformational analysis. We will see that all cases except those of §100 (e.g., "call up") can be dropped from the kernel with profit. Transformational analysis is suggested wherever the complement and the object have the same selectional relation as appears in some simple kernel sentence Z. In this case, the verb phrase *Verb–Complement–object* can be derived transformationally from *Verb-Z*. In particular, if the complement contains a noun phrase NP_c which agrees in number with the object NP_o, we may be able to derive the verb phrase from *Verb-Z*, where Z is $NP_o^\frown is^\frown NP_c$.

We must be careful to assure that the result of such a transformation will be a verb phrase *Verb$^\frown$Complement–object*. All such transformations of *Verb-Z* into *Verb$^\frown$Complement$^\frown$object* will thus have to precede the application of Φ_1^P, which converts this phrase into *Verb–object–Complement*. If these requirements are not met, the analysis of §§100–103, with the simplifications there introduced, will not stand.

To simplify this discussion, we may consider only one of the subclasses of transitive verbs. Let us assume, for this discussion, that V_T has only the subconstructions V_t and V_I. The addition of other subclasses will only lead to duplication of the detailed development that we give below. Similarly, in Chapter VIII and in §§100–103 we have not distinguished subclasses of these compound verbs that differ in terms of their selection of subject and object. We consider now only the selectional relation between the complement of the complex verb and the object.

Consider first verb phrases of the form **286** as discussed in §101:   109.2

286 $V_h^\frown NP_o^\frown Predicate$ (*"consider John incompetent"*)

We note that NP_o⌢$Predicate$ can occur in this position only if NP_o-is-$Predicate$ is a sentence.[26] Thus we can have "kindness is a virtue," "I consider kindness a virtue," "John is a good pianist," "I consider John a good pianist," but not "kindness is a good pianist," "I consider kindness a good pianist," "John is a virtue," "I consider John a virtue," etc. The selectional relation between NP_o and $Predicate$ (and, in particular, the numerical agreement between NP_o and NP of the predicate) motivate transformational analysis in the case of **286**.

There are several ways to carry out this analysis. Since each member of V_h can apparently occur with a simple object, we can consider such simple sentences as "he considered it" to be part of the **P**-basis. To ensure the correct derived structure for transform **286** we can, in the kernel grammar, analyze the simple occurrences of V_h as compounds V_h⌢$\emptyset$, where $\emptyset$ is the complement. This seems to be the simplest overall solution.

We have to do here with a generalized transformation, since there are two kernel sentences involved. As **T**-markers we have strings of the form

287 Z_1⌢K_1⌢I–Z_2⌢K_2⌢I–T_{cmp}–$\Phi^{\mathbf{P}}$

where the generalized transformation is analyzed as

288 T_{cmp} is determined by (Q_{cmp}, t_{cmp}), where

$$Q_{cmp} = (NP, VP_A\text{⌢}be, Predicate, \#, NP, VP_A, V_h, \emptyset, NP)$$
$$t_{cmp} \leftrightarrow (\sigma, 0, \sigma, 0, \sigma, 0, \sigma, 0, 0, 0, 0, 0, 0, 0, \sigma, 3, \sigma, 1)$$

T_{cmp} will thus carry a string of the form **289** into the corresponding string of the form **290**:

289 NP_1-VP_A⌢be-$Predicate$-$\#$-NP_2-VP_A-V_h-$\emptyset$-NP_3

290 U- U - U -U-NP_2-VP_A-V_h-$Predicate$-NP_1

where $Predicate$, replacing the complement $\emptyset$, is a complement in the transform, so that V_h⌢$Predicate$ is a V_T (since its root V_h⌢$\emptyset$ is a V_T)

---

[26] The converse is not the case. We did not give the restrictions on the construction **286** in the kernel grammar in §72.2 (except for the restriction to agreement in number), but there clearly are restrictions. For example, $Predicate$ cannot ordinarily be PP after V_h. In a nontransformational treatment, these further conditions will be added to the **P**-grammar; in a transformational analysis, they will be given as a condition on the **P**-basis of the **T**-markers involved.

with the object NP_1, replacing NP_3. Application of $\Phi_1{}^P$ to **290** gives a sentence with the verb phrase **286**, as previously. The **P**-basis of "I consider John a good pianist," then, is

291   *John is a good pianist; I consider it* $(= I\text{--}consider^\frown \mathcal{O}\text{--}it)$

As far as V_h is concerned, then, we can drop the restriction in statement 6, §72.2, as well as the selectional restrictions which we had not given there. This is an important saving, since, as we noted in Note 33, Chapter VIII, this restriction was not really formulable in terms of the notational devices then available.

Note that the passive transformation forms sentences of the form *NP-is-Predicate* (cf. §86.7). Hence T_{cmp} can form verb phrases from passives as well. In fact we do have such sentences as

292   *I consider the issue completely closed*

from "the issue is completely closed" $\#$ "I consider it"—ultimately, from the kernel sentences "this completely closes the issue," "I consider it."

In §102 we saw that V_e and V_g can be analyzed in the same way as V_h.   **109.3**
It is quite clear that the further reduction of §109.2 can be carried over for these elements too. In the case of V_e and V_g we also find the selectional relations and agreement in number characteristic of *NP-is-Predicate, NP-is-NP*, respectively. A further support for the analysis in the case of V_g is the fact that there are special forms of the noun phrase which occur only in the predicate position and after V_g-*NP*, e. g., "president" without the article, as in "he is president," "they elected him president."

We can account for V_g by revising **288**, redefining Q_{cmp} as

293 $Q_{cmp} = \left\{ \left(NP, VP_A\, be, \begin{Bmatrix} Predicate \\ NP \end{Bmatrix}, \#, NP, VP_A, \begin{Bmatrix} V_h \\ V_g \end{Bmatrix}, \mathcal{O}, NP \right) \right\}$

V_e is a slightly different case, since *be* is not dropped here, and *to* is prefixed to it. V_e appears in

294 $NP\text{--}V_e\text{--}NP\text{--}to^\frown be^\frown Predicate$ (*"they know John to be honest"*)

The **P**-basis of this sentence will consist of the kernel sentences "John is honest," "they know $\mathcal{O}$ it." And we see from **294** that $\mathcal{O}$ is replaced not by *Predicate*, but by *to⌒be⌒Predicate*. In other words, another transformation applies to the first component of the complex string $Z_1⌒\#⌒Z_2$ to which T_{cmp} is to apply, before the application of T_{cmp}. The **T**-markers by which V_e is introduced will thus be of the form

295 $Z_1⌒K_1⌒T_\gamma\text{-}Z_2⌒K_2⌒I\text{-}T'_{cmp}\text{-}\Phi^\mathbf{P}$

The transformations in **295** are defined as follows:

296 T_γ is determined by $(Q_\gamma, \delta_\gamma)$, where

$$Q_\gamma = \{NP, VP_{A1}, \langle VP_{A2}\rangle\ be⌒Predicate)\}^{27}$$
$$\delta_\gamma \leftrightarrow (U, U, U, U, to, U)$$

297 T'_{cmp} is determined by (Q'_{cmp}, t_{cmp}), where

$$Q'_{cmp} = \{(NP, VP_{A1}, to\langle VP_{A2}\rangle\ be⌒Predicate, \#, NP, VP_A,$$
$$V_e, \varnothing, NP)\}$$
t_{cmp} is as in **288**

Suppose that Z_1 in **295** is "John is honest" $(= John\text{--}S\text{--}be\text{--}honest)$ and $Z_2 =$ "they know it." Then $T_\gamma(Z_1, K_1) = John\text{--}S\text{--}to\ be\ honest.$ Just as T_{cmp} carries **289** into **290**, T'_{cmp} carries $T_\gamma(Z_1, K_1)⌒\#⌒Z_2$ into **294**.

Dropping $V_g⌒NP⌒NP$ from the kernel enables us to eliminate the exception in statement 4, §72.2. For V_g and V_e, as well as V_h, the special condition in statement 6 is now unnecessary, and thus can be dropped, since these are the only forms to which it applies. This simplification is now possible because all cases of agreement in number have been reduced to the predicative sentence form $NP\text{-}is\text{-}NP$.

109.4   The same analysis carries over for **283** $(= \mathbf{202}, §103.1)$ and like cases. We can extend the brackets in **293** to include a class of verbs V_J, writing "V_J" below "V_g" in **293**, and "PP" below "NP" in the first bracket of **293**. Thus with *put* in V_J, **283** will have the **P**-basis

298   (*the man is behind bars, they put it*)[28]

---

[27] The split between VP_{A1} and VP_{A2} here, as in other *to*-phrases that we have discussed, permits "I consider John to be trying his best," "I know him to have been honest," etc.

[28] The latter sentence is quite unnatural. We might remedy this by extending the transformation so as to take, e.g., "they put it here," as the root. Or we may consider this to be a case of the type discussed in §81.6, with "it" as a dummy carrier.

Here we find the same problem as was discussed in §108.3. Certain prepositional phrases appearing as complements may not be derived from $NP_1\text{-}isPP_x$, but rather from $NP_1\text{-}has\text{-}NP_2$ (where PP_x is $P_x \frown NP_2$), or perhaps from some other kernel sentence. This is a complex problem in itself, and we will not go into it here.

In §103.1 we discussed three types of $NP\text{-}PP$ construction (**201**–**203**). In §108.3 we dropped **201** (= **278**) from the kernel, and now we have dropped **202** (= **283**). This leaves only **203** (= "they questioned the man behind closed doors") as a kernel sentence. This is the only case where intuitively the prepositional phrase seems to be added on to the sentence, and not bound up with either the verb or the object.

In §103.4 we discussed cases of constructional homonymity falling in the overlap of the patterns of which **201** and **203** are instances. Now, comparison of §108.3 and §109.4 suggests that we should be able to find overlaps of **201** and **202**, i.e., sentences of the form $NP_1\text{-}V\text{-}NP_2\text{-}PP$ with $NP_2\text{-}PP$ as the object or $V\text{-}PP$ as the verb. An instance of this is

299   *John kept the car in the garage*

Since we have "the car was kept in the garage by John," this must be an instance of $NP_1\text{-}Verb \frown Complement\text{-}NP_2$, with "in the garage" being the complement.[29] Since we can have "the car in the garage was kept by John" ("but he gave away the one in the lot"), this is also a case of $NP_1\text{-}V\text{-}NP_2$, with $V = kept$, and $NP_2 = the \frown car \frown in \frown the \frown garage$.

This case has a certain interest, if the constructional homonymity described here is accepted as a correct analysis. In both cases, the **P**-basis is the pair of kernel sentences

300   (*the car is in the garage, John kept it*)

and the structural ambiguity of **299** arises from the fact that this sentence can be produced from **300** by two transformational routes, either in the manner of §108.3 or §109.4. But this raises some interesting questions about the relation between transformations and meaning. It is fairly clear from all the examples that we have discussed in this chapter that in some sense meaning is preserved under transformation. Naturally we could not hold that transform and transformed string are synonymous, since a transformation may add or subtract morphemes. But we might have proposed that transform and pre-image differ in meaning only in

---

[29] If "in the garage, John kept the car" and "the car was kept by John in the garage" are accepted as grammatical sentences, an alternative analysis of **299** will be as $NP\text{-}V\text{-}NP\text{-}PP_\alpha$, i.e., as a sentence of the same form as **203**.

the meanings of the morphemes dropped or added. For example, "John is not here" differs semantically from "John is here" in the meaning of *not*. But **299**, as analyzed above, indicates that this cannot be the case, because we have here a case of two distinct sequences of transformations with exactly the same starting point in unambiguous kernel sentences, and with exactly the same end point, but with different meanings associated with this final transform. While transformations have semantic correlation, it is not obvious just how this is to be described.

109.5   In §103.5 we took up, from a transformational point of view, the problem posed in §69 by the construction $NP\text{-}ing\text{-}VP_1$. It appeared in §103.5 that if these phrases can be introduced into the grammar, they can be properly distinguished. In §108.2 we saw how these phrases can be introduced when they are noun phrases. Now, extending the analysis of §§109.1–109.4, we can account for the occurrence of these phrases as instances of the general construction *Verb–Complement*.

In §67.1, we distinguished the following subclasses of verbs:

301
$$\begin{cases} V_a = want,\ like,\ \text{etc.} \quad (\text{"}I\ want\ him\ to\ come,\text{"}\ \text{"}I\ want\ to\ come\text{"}) \\ V_b = persuade,\ advise,\ \text{etc.} \quad (\text{"}I\ persuaded\ him\ to\ come,\text{"}\ \text{not} \\ \qquad \text{"}I\ persuaded\ to\ come\text{"}) \\ V_c = try,\ decide,\ \text{etc.} \quad (\text{"}I\ tried\ to\ come,\text{"}\ \text{not}\ \text{"}I\ tried\ him\ to \\ \qquad come\text{"}) \end{cases}$$

302
$$\begin{cases} V_\alpha = imagine,\ prefer,\ \text{etc.} \quad (\text{"}I\ imagined\ him\ coming,\text{"}\ \text{"}I \\ \qquad imagined\ coming\text{"}) \\ V_\beta = find,\ catch,\ \text{etc.} \quad (\text{"}I\ found\ him\ reading,\text{"}\ \text{not}\ \text{"}I\ found \\ \qquad reading\text{"}) \\ V_\gamma = avoid,\ begin,\ \text{etc.} \quad (\text{"}I\ avoid\ arguing,\text{"}\ \text{not}\ \text{"}I\ avoid\ him \\ \qquad arguing\text{"}) \end{cases}$$

In §68.2 we suggested incorporating V_a into V_b and V_c as the overlap of these classes, and V_α into V_β and V_γ as their overlap. Following this suggestion, we can regard $V_\beta\text{-}ing\ VP_1$ as another form of the *Verb–Complement* construction, thus deriving sentences of the form $NP_1\text{-}V_\beta{}^\frown ing{}^\frown VP_1\text{-}NP_2$ which, by $\Phi_1{}^P$, is carried into $NP_1\text{-}V_\beta\text{-}NP_2\text{-}ing{}^\frown VP_1$. This is the analysis *at* which we arrived in §103.5 for such sentences as "I found the boy studying in the library." But in §109.3 we saw that the very similar construction $V_e\text{-}to{}^\frown VP_1$ (appearing in "they know John to be honest," etc.) can be introduced transformationally as a form of *Verb–Complement* (VP_1 in this case being limited to the form $be{}^\frown Predicate$). A very similar transformational analysis will provide for the introduction of $V\text{-}ing^\frown VP_1$ as a form of *Verb–Complement*, thus giving (by $\Phi_1{}^P$) the second source for the $NP\text{-}ing^\frown VP_1$ phrases. Thus alongside of **295** we have **T**-markers

303 $Z_1{}^\frown K_1{}^\frown T_\gamma{}' \text{-} Z_2{}^\frown K_2{}^\frown I \text{-} T''_{cmp} \text{-} \Phi^P$

The transformations of **303** are analyzed as follows:

304 $T_\gamma{}'$ is determined by $(Q_\gamma{}', \delta_\gamma{}')$, where

$$Q_\gamma{}' = \{(NP, VP_{A1}, \langle have^\frown en \rangle \, VP_1)\}^{30}$$
$$\delta_\gamma{}' \leftrightarrow (U, U, U, U, ing, U)$$

305 T''_{cmp} is determined by (Q''_{cmp}, t_{cmp}), where

$$Q''_{cmp} = \{(NP, VP_{A1}, ing \, \langle have^\frown en \rangle \, VP_1, \#, NP, VP_A,$$
$$V_\beta, \emptyset, NP)\}$$
$$t_{cmp} \text{ is as in } \textbf{288, 297}$$

Suppose that Z_1 in **303** is "the dog climbs that tree" ($= the^\frown dog\text{-}S\text{-}climb^\frown that^\frown tree$) and Z_2 is "I can imagine $\emptyset$ it." $T_\gamma{}'$ carries Z_1 into *the dog–S–ing$^\frown$climb$^\frown$that$^\frown$tree*. T''_{cmp} then replaces "it" in $Z_2 = I^\frown can^\frown imagine^\frown \emptyset^\frown it$ by "the dog," and "$\emptyset$" by "ing climb that tree," yielding

306   *I–can–imagine–climbing that tree–the dog*

which becomes

307   *I can imagine the dog climbing that tree*

by $\Phi_1{}^P$. Thus the operation of T''_{cmp} is just like that of T_{cmp} and T'_{cmp} (in fact, the three can obviously be combined into a single transformation, with Q_{cmp}, Q'_{cmp}, Q''_{cmp} coalesced into a single restricting class). Note that $\delta_\gamma{}'$ differs from δ_γ only in that *ing* replaces *to*. Q_γ and $Q_\gamma{}'$ are also very similar. Note further that $Q_\gamma{}'$ is exactly Q_{ing} of **168**, and $\delta_\gamma{}'$, δ_γ are very close to δ_{ing}, δ_{to} of **168**, respectively.

This concludes the discussion of the complex of problems around $NP^\frown ing^\frown VP_1$, originally begun in §§69–70. The sentences **307** and

308   *I can recognize the man climbing that tree*

---

[30] This permits "I can't imagine the dog having climbed that tree," etc. (cf. Note 27). This is the distinction between *ing*-phrases and *to*-phrases that we have frequently noted above.

now have different transformational histories. **307** is based on the kernel sentences "the dog climbs that tree," "I can imagine it" and **308** is based on the kernel sentences "the man climbs that tree," "I can recognize the man." But the transformational routes by which these sentences are derived are quite different. **307** is derived by way of **306**, which is a sentence of the form

309 $NP_1\text{-}V_T\text{-}NP_2$

with NP_2 being *the dog*, and V_T being the compound verb *imagine–climbing⌒that⌒tree* of the *Verb–Complement* type. **308** is derived by way of "I can recognize the man who climbs (or: who is climbing) that tree," which is also a sentence of the form **309**, but with "the man who climbs that tree" as NP_2 and *recognize* as the simple verb.

In §103.5 we noted that

310   *I found the boy studying in the library*   (= **231**b)

is a case of constructional homonymity (similarly, "I can't catch the dog climbing that tree"). The passive criterion shows that it is subject to both the analysis of **307** and that of **308**, and, intuitively, this is a clear case of structural ambiguity with a correlated meaning difference. But under both interpretations, the kernel sentences from which **310** is derived (i.e., the **P**-basis of the alternative **T**-markers) are the sentences "the boy studies in the library," "I found the boy."[31] It is the transformational histories that are distinct. In one case, **310** derives from the intermediate sentence "I–found studying in the library–the boy" (analogous to **307**). In the second case, the intermediate sentence is "I–found–the boy who studies in the library" (or "I–found–the boy who is studying in the library," if "the boy is studying in the library" is taken as the kernel sentence of the **P**-basis; cf. Note 31). Hence the meaning difference under the two structural interpretations of **310** cannot be due to the kernel sentences from which **310** is derivable, or to the morphemes added or deleted by the transformations that produce

---

[31] However, under the interpretation of **310** as analogous to **308**, the **P**-basis can be taken as "the boy is studying in the library," "I found the boy." But under the alternative interpretation, this **P**-basis is not available as we have formulated T_{γ}' in **304**. If this distinction stands, with further and more detailed study, then the argument in the text in this paragraph must be carried somewhat further, but the main point still holds. The difference in meaning under these two interpretations cannot be attributed to the **P**-basis, but only to the intermediate sentences that underlie **310** in the two transformational developments.

310. This supports the conclusion of the last paragraph of §109.4 that a transform does not differ in meaning from its preimage only in the meanings of the morphemes deleted or added.

We have still not discussed

109.6

311   *John wanted him to come*

and similar sentences involving V_b instead of V_β (cf. **301–302**). Clearly **311** can be handled in the same way as **307**. Alongside of **303** we add **T**-markers

312 $Z_1 \frown K_1 \frown T_\nu'' - Z_2 \frown K_2 \frown I - T_{cmp}''' - \Phi^P$

with the transformations analyzed as in **313–314**:

313 T_ν'' is determined by (Q_ν'', δ_ν''), where

$$Q_\nu'' = \{(NP, VP_{A1}, \langle VP_{A2} \rangle VP_1)\}$$
$$\delta'' \leftrightarrow (U, U, U, U, to, U)$$

314 T_{cmp}''' is determined by (Q_{cmp}''', t_{cmp}), where

$$Q_{cmp}''' = \{(NP, VP_{A1}, to \langle VP_{A2} \rangle VP_1, \#, NP, VP_A, V_b, \varnothing, NP)\}$$
t_{cmp} is as in **288, 297, 305**

Note that δ_ν'' is exactly δ_ν of **296**, and Q_ν'' is exactly Q_{to} of **168**. T_{cmp}''' can be combined along with T_{cmp}, T_{cmp}', and T_{cmp}'' into a single transformation. **311** is derived from the kernel sentences "he comes," "I wanted it," just as **307** was derived by **303**.

There is no homonymity here, as there was in the case of $V_\beta \frown ing \frown VP_1$, since *to*-phrases, unlike *ing*-phrases, do not appear as noun modifiers.

A peculiarity of this construction is that the transforms **311**, etc., are not subject to the passive transformation. That is, we cannot have "I was wanted to come." Similarly, the question transform "whom did John want to come" is at best unnatural. Actually, it is not V_b as a whole that is subject to this limitation, but only the subclass V_a which (cf. paragraph below **302**) has been incorporated into V_b. That is, "I was persuaded to come" and "whom did John persuade to come" are grammatical. We can provide for this with a restriction in the **T**-grammar, or we can perhaps reformulate **313–314** so that the transform does not have the form required by the passive and question transformations.

Neither solution seems particularly good. We return to sentences of the form 311 below, in §111.

109.7   We can now readily introduce the verb class V_δ (cf. §§67.2, 103.5) containing "see," "watch," "hear," etc. and giving such sentences as

315   *I saw him come⟨ing⟩*

The forms without *ing* can be given by **T**-markers

316    $Z_1\!\frown\!K_1\!\frown\!I\text{-}Z_2\!\frown\!K_2\!\frown\!I\text{-}T_{cmp}^{\mathrm{iv}}\text{-}\varPhi^{\mathbf{P}}$

where

317   T_{cmp}^{iv} is determined by $(Q_{cmp}^{\mathrm{iv}}\,,\,t_{cmp})$, where

$Q_{cmp}^{\mathrm{iv}} = (NP,\ VP_A\,,\ VP_1\,,\ \#,\ NP,\ VP_A\,,\ V_\delta\,,\ \varnothing,\ NP)$
t_{cmp} is as in 288, etc.

The forms with *ing* require a preliminary transformation, like T_γ, etc., in place of the first I of 316 to introduce the element *ing* into the kernel sentence "he comes" (in the case of 315, etc.). We might use T_γ' for this purpose, then extending T_{cmp}'' (of 305) to include V_δ along with V_β, were it not for the fact that "I saw John having been coming" is impossible, though "imagine the dog having climbed the tree" is possible, and is permitted by 303–305. This fact leads us to introduce these sentences with **T**-markers

318    $Z_1\!\frown\!K_1\!\frown\!T_\gamma'''\text{-}Z_2\!\frown\!K_2\!\frown\!I\text{-}T_{cmp}^{\mathrm{iv}}\text{-}\varPhi^{\mathbf{P}}$

where T_{cmp}^{iv} is as in 317, and

319   T_γ''' is determined by $(Q_\gamma''',\ \delta_\gamma')$, where

$Q_\gamma''' = (NP,\ VP_A\,,\ VP_1)$
δ_γ' is as in 304

T_{cmp}^{iv} does not have to be extended to include the case where T_γ''' applies to the first component of the complex string to which T_{cmp}^{iv} applies, since $ing\!\frown\!VP_1$, as produced by T_γ''', is a VP_1, as is its root VP_1. Actually, we could have formulated T_{cmp}^{iv} in such a way that T_γ' of 304 could have been utilized here, instead of the new transformation T_γ'''.

The derivation of sentences of the form 315 follows the familiar pattern, and requires no special comment.

Summing up the constructions of §109, we add to μ^T the **T**-marker 109.8
schemata:

320
$$Z_1 {}^\frown K_1 \begin{Bmatrix} I \\ T_\gamma \\ T_\gamma{}' \\ T_\gamma{}'' \\ \begin{Bmatrix} I \\ T_\gamma{}''' \end{Bmatrix} \end{Bmatrix} -Z_2{}^\frown K_2{}^\frown I- \begin{Bmatrix} T_{cmp}^0 \\ T_{cmp}' \\ T_{cmp}'' \\ T_{cmp}''' \\ T_{cmp}^{\mathrm{iv}} \end{Bmatrix} -\Phi^P$$

where

321
T_γ is determined by $(Q_\gamma, \delta_\gamma)$
$T_\gamma{}'$ is determined by $(Q_{ing}, \delta_\gamma{}')$ (Q_{ing} as in **168**)
$T_\gamma{}''$ is determined by (Q_{to}, δ_γ) (Q_{to} as in **168**)
$T_\gamma{}'''$ is determined by $(Q_\gamma''', \delta_\gamma{}')$

and

322
$$\begin{Bmatrix} \delta_\gamma \\ \delta_\gamma{}' \end{Bmatrix} \leftrightarrow \left(U, U, U, U, \begin{Bmatrix} to \\ ing \end{Bmatrix}, U \right)$$

$$\begin{Bmatrix} Q_\gamma \\ Q_\gamma''' \end{Bmatrix} = \left(NP, \begin{Bmatrix} VP_{A1}, & \langle VP_{A2} \rangle \, be^\frown Predicate \\ VP_A, & VP_1 \end{Bmatrix} \right)$$

323 T_{cmp}^k is determined by $(Q_{cmp}^k, t_{cmp})(k = 0,...,4)$, where

$$\begin{Bmatrix} Q_{cmp}^0 \\ Q_{cmp}' \\ Q_{cmp}'' \\ Q_{cmp}''' \\ Q_{cmp}^{\mathrm{iv}} \end{Bmatrix} = \left[\begin{pmatrix} NP, VP_A, be \begin{Bmatrix} PP \\ Predicate \\ NP \end{Bmatrix} \\ Q_\gamma{}^{32} \\ Q_{ing} \\ Q_{to} \\ Q_\gamma''' \end{pmatrix}, \right.$$

$$\left. \#, NP, VP_A, \begin{Bmatrix} V_J \\ V_h \\ V_g \\ V_e \\ V_\beta \\ V_b \\ V_\delta \end{Bmatrix}, \emptyset, NP \right]$$

$$t_{cmp} \leftrightarrow (\sigma, 0, \sigma, 0, \sigma, 0, \sigma, 0, 0, 0, 0, 0, 0, 0, \sigma, 3, \sigma, 1)$$

---

[32] Actually, $Q_\gamma = \{(NP, VP_{A1}, \langle VP_{A2} \rangle be^\frown Predicate)\}$ and Q_{cmp}' begins $(NP, VP_{A1}, to\langle VP_{A2} \rangle be^\frown Predicate, ...)$. But $to^\frown be^\frown Predicate$ is a $be^\frown Predicate$, and $to^\frown VP_{A2}{}^\frown be^\frown Predicate$ is a $VP_{A2}{}^\frown be^\frown Predicate$, in their derived constituent structure (cf. Definition 31, §87.6). Hence we can give the beginning of Q_{cmp}' exactly as Q_γ. The same is true of $Q_{cmp}'', Q_{cmp}''', Q_{cmp}^{\mathrm{iv}}$.

This is quite similar to the set of transformations summarized in §99.8, **166–168**. These analyses can be reformulated so as to bring out further similarities. There are various ways of simplifying **320–323**. For one thing, there is no need to set up $T_{cmp}^0 - T_{cmp}^{iv}$ as five separate transformations. Since the restricting class for a transformation can be defined as a set of sequences $(W_1^{(i)}, ..., W_n^{(i)})$, we can regard **323** as the characterization of the restricting class of a single transformation $\overline{T}_{cmp}$, and we can rewrite **320** as

324   **320** with the second set of brackets (and the contained terms) replaced by "$\overline{T}_{cmp}$"

The similarities with previous constructions (e.g., **166–168**) can also be more fully exploited.

In §§100–103 we discovered that the complex verb phrases that had appeared in the grammar of phrase structure all reduced to the simple verb–object construction, when we set up a subconstruction *Verb–Complement* under transitive verbs. This analysis was forced upon us by the necessity of accounting for the behavior of these verb phrases under transformations which had been set up for the simple verb phrases. Now we see that the construction *Verb–Complement* can itself largely be eliminated by generalized transformations in favor of kernel sentences with simple verb phrases. The motive for this transformational analysis lies in the heavy selectional restrictions (including, as a special case, agreement in number) that hold between the object and the complement, duplicating the selection of subject and predicate in the simple cases. In other words, if we were to define grammatical relations in terms of selectional relations, as suggested briefly in §71.2, we would find, e.g., that the grammatical relation subject–verb in simple sentences is closely related to (cf. Note 26) the grammatical relation object–complement in sentences of the form $NP_1\text{-}V_T\text{-}NP_2$, where $V_T \rightarrow Verb^\frown Complement$ (the sentence becoming $NP_1\text{-}Verb\text{-}NP_2\text{-}Complement$ by Φ_1^P). The only instance of the *Verb–Complement* construction that resists this analysis is the case of $V_{sep}\text{-}P$, discussed in §100, e.g., "call up," etc. These might more properly be called cases of $V_{sep}\text{-}Particle$, since many nonprepositions occur as the complement in such constructions. In §109 we have seen that one of the particles in this construction is Ø, which occurs as the complement when the *Verb* is any of V_h, V_g, V_e, V_β, V_b, V_δ.

110   In the course of this analysis we have found that much of the recursive part of the grammar of phrase structure in §72.2 has been cut away. It seems reasonable to place the formal requirement that no recursions appear in the kernel grammar. Specifically, we rule out such statements as 10,[33] §72.2, and we drop the constructions of §§55.3–55.4 that permit running through the grammar indefinitely many times. As far as I can determine, this formal requirement on **P** does not exclude anything that we would like to retain in **P**; nor does it impose any artificial or clumsy limitation on the actual statement of the grammar corresponding to **P**, now that transformational analysis presents an alternative way of generating sentences. On the other hand, this requirement almost trivializes the problem of validating those transformations which we would like to set up as elements in **T** for the extrasystematic reasons which we have noted throughout this analysis of English structure. Given this requirement on **P**, there is no alternative to transformational analysis in many of these cases. The case of the passive transformation can serve to show how effective this criterion can be in avoiding the necessity for detailed and laborious validation based on total simplicity. Given this nonrecursion requirement, there is no alternative to transformational analysis in the case of *ing*-phrases. By the argument of §101.1 it then follows that "consider–a fool," etc., must be verbal elements, and from this it follows, as we saw in §101.2, that the passive transformation must be constructed with inversion of noun phrases. In §101.2, we had to appeal to overall simplicity of the grammar in putting this argument forward, since the transformational analysis of *ing*-phrases was partially supported by the fact that passives had been deleted from the kernel.

Naturally, much more study is needed to verify this, but it seems at this point that this requirement on **P** meets the conditions discussed in §93.2. That is, it is a simple and natural requirement that, by and large, makes transformational analysis necessary in just those cases where it leads to intuitively satisfactory results.

There are also purely systematic motivations for this formal requirement on the level **P**. It follows from the nonrecursion requirement that the kernel must be finite. In §§55.3–55.4, in developing the general relation between the algebra **P** and actual grammars, we were forced to consider the problem of recursive production of sentences by the grammar, since we know that the set μ^w of grammatical strings of words must be infinite. This led to the artificiality of running through the grammar indefinitely many times (a procedure which, as we saw in Chapter VIII, may lead to considerable complication in the formulation of the grammar). It also produced a serious theoretical gap in our program of devising a mechanical evaluation procedure for grammars.

---

[33] Actually, we have not provided the technical means for the introduction of such statements as 10 into the grammar.

In the last paragraph of §56.2, we noted that it is necessary to prove that a given grammar is a reduced form of some system **P**. This might not be an easy task in particular cases. In fact, it may even be the case that there is no general mechanical procedure for determining by inspection of the grammar that it is a reduced form of some system **P**, if the set of generated strings is infinite. But we can determine in a mechanical way whether or not a given finite set of derivations leads (in the manner discussed in §55) to an underlying algebra satisfying the axiom system for **P**. Hence if the kernel is finite, we do have a mechanical way of determining whether a given grammar is a reduced form of some system **P**.

Now that the higher level of transformational analysis has been established, it is no longer necessary to require that generation by the grammar of phrase structure be infinite. As the level **T** has been formulated, the process of transformational derivation is recursive, since the product of a **T**-marker can itself appear in the **P**-basis of a **T**-marker (cf. condition 4, §91.4). For example, from a sentence we can form a *that*-clause which replaces a noun in a second sentence, giving a more complex sentence from which we can form a *that*-clause, etc. Similarly, the family of generalized transformations that plays the role of the conjunction rule will indefinitely construct longer and more complex sentences.

In §41.1 (cf. also §§49, 58), we sketched the general lines of a definition of grammaticalness, noting that each linguistic level provides a certain descriptive apparatus in terms of which a given set of sentences can be characterized. New sentences are automatically added to this set when we utilize this descriptive machinery to give the simplest characterization of the given sentences. Applying the methods of Chapter V to a linguistic corpus, we construct a finite set $Gr_1(W)$ containing the highest-degree grammatical sentences of a length less than or equal to some fixed length. We construct a system of phrase structure for some subset of $Gr_1(W)$, producing, perhaps, a finite extension of this subset to a kernel K. K is the set of strings of words corresponding (under Φ^P) to the set $Gr(P)$ of products of restricted ρ-derivations. We then construct a set of **T**-markers that generate the rest of $Gr_1(W)$ from the kernel. Allowing these constructed transformations to run on freely, applying to transforms, we generate the infinite set μ^W of grammatical strings of words. We have noted that not all of the corpus of data need be included in $Gr_1(W)$. Similarly, we may be able to construct the systems **P** and **T** in a much more simple way if a limited part of $Gr_1(W)$ is not regenerated. This is a schematic picture, which must be filled in with detailed construction. It may be that along these lines we will be able to develop an adequate explication of the notion of "grammatical sentence" in the infinite sense, and an explanation for the general process of projection by which speakers extend their limited linguistic experience to new and immediately acceptable forms.

Statement 10, §72.2 (now reformulated as **169**, §99.9), is the only instance in §72.2 of a recursive statement. To meet the nonrecursion requirement of §110, this statement must be eliminated in favor of a transformational analysis. However, there are independent reasons, quite apart from this nonrecursion requirement, for making this move.

    In §109.6 we found that such sentences as "John wanted him to come" (= **311**) are introduced by transformation. If we investigate these sentences in more detail, we discover that there are certain restrictions on the occurrence of pronouns. Alongside of **311** we have **325** but not **326**:

111.1

325   (a) *I wanted him to try*
        (b) *I wanted you to try*
        (c) *I wanted to try*

326   *I wanted me to try*

    The only way to avoid a special restricting statement on the level **P** is to add a mapping Φ_x^P that carries **326** into **325**c:

327 Φ_x^P carries *I–want–I–to⌢try* into *I–want–to⌢try*

    We must determine how extensive is the range of application of Φ_x^P. First of all, it is clear that the analogous restriction holds for "you." The case of "he" is more difficult. We have both **328a** and **328b**:

328   (a) *he wanted him to try*
        (b) *he wanted to try*

    The simplest way to handle this situation appears to be to set up two distinct elements *he* and *he** corresponding to the element *he*W of **W**, *he* being an element just like *I* and *you* (which accounts for **328b**), and *he** being an ordinary proper noun (which accounts for **328a**, just as we have "he wanted John to try"). The establishment of this pair of homonyms on the level **P** is further supported by its usefulness for other purposes, as we will see below. We thus replace **327** by the more general characterization

329 $\Phi_x{}^P$ carries $\begin{Bmatrix} I \\ you \\ he \end{Bmatrix}$-*want*-$\begin{Bmatrix} I \\ you \\ he \end{Bmatrix}$-*to*⌢*try*   into

$\begin{Bmatrix} I \\ you \\ he \end{Bmatrix}$-*want-to*⌢*try*

As elsewhere in the discussion of pronouns, we will here leave out the plural pronouns.

We also have

330   (a)   *John wanted him to try*
      (b)   *John wanted to try*
      (c)   *John wanted me to try*

The simplest way to account for this is to revise $\Phi_x{}^P$, replacing **329** by

331 $\Phi_x{}^P$ carries $\begin{Bmatrix} I \\ you \\ NP_y \end{Bmatrix}$-*want*-$\begin{Bmatrix} I \\ you \\ he \end{Bmatrix}$-*to*⌢*try*   into

$\begin{Bmatrix} I \\ you \\ NP_y \end{Bmatrix}$-*want-to*⌢*try* $(NP_y \neq I, you)$

$\Phi_x{}^P$ applied to "John wanted him* to try" gives **330a**; i.e., it does not apply. Applied to "John wanted him to try," $\Phi_x{}^P$ gives **330b**.

Next we note that $\Phi_x{}^P$ applies generally for the class V_a (cf. **301**, §109.5), and we note further that in place of "try" in **331**, we may have any instance of *to* $\langle VP_{A2}\rangle$ VP_1. We thus replace **331** by

332 $\Phi_x{}^P$: $\begin{Bmatrix} I \\ you \\ he \end{Bmatrix}$ becomes Ø in env.:

$\begin{Bmatrix} I \\ you \\ NP_y \end{Bmatrix}$ VP_A⌢V_a⌢——⌢$to\langle VP_{A2}\rangle$ VP_1

111.2   Suppose that VP_1 is itself of the form V_a⌢NP⌢$to\langle VP_{A2}\rangle$ VP_1 as in the sentence

333   *I expect you to want him to try*

This would be derived in several steps by **312–314**, §109.6, from the kernel sentences

334   (a) *he tries*
           (b) *you want it*
           (c) *I expect it*

From the first two we derive, in the usual way,

335   *you want him to try*   (= *you–want–to⌢try–him*)

an instance of the same pattern as, e.g., **330a**. But we can now take **335** as Z_1 in **312**, and **334c** as Z_2, thus deriving **333** from **335**, **334c** just as we derive **335** from **334a**, **334b**. Thus **333** will be an instance of the pattern NP_1-V_T-NP_2, with NP_1 being *I*, V_T being the compound verb *expect–to⌢want⌢him⌢to⌢try* (an instance of *Verb–Complement*), and NP_2 being *you*; **333** is derived from "I–expect–to want him to try–you" by $\Phi_1{}^P$. Investigating various other cases of the same type, we find that we can have **336** but not **337**:

336   (a) *I expect you to want to try*
           (b) *I expect you to want me to try*
           (c) *I expect to want to try*
           (d) *I expect to want you to try*
               etc.

337   (a) *I expect you to want you to try*
           (b) *I expect me to want to try*
           (c) *I expect to want me to try*
           (d) *I expect me to want you to try*
               etc.

Obviously, $\Phi_x{}^P$ applies exactly as in **332** to each "stage" in the transformational history of sentences like **333**. That is, it applies to the intermediate sentence **335**, and then to **333** as a whole. There is no ambiguity in the way it applies to **333** as a whole, since there is only one way to analyze this sentence as an instance of *NP-VP$_A$-V$_a$-NP-to* $\langle VP_{A2} \rangle VP_1$, no matter what the analysis of VP_1 may be. This suggests that we regard $\Phi_x{}^P$ not as a mapping (since, by condition 5, §91.5, a mapping cannot apply more than once in the derivation of a string), but as a transformation T_δ that always follows the transformation T'''_{cmp} (cf. **314**) that carries **334a**, **334b** into **335** and **335**, **334c** into **333**.

But T_δ must precede the mapping Φ_1^P that carries *Verb-Complement-NP* into *Verb-NP-Complement*. We must therefore rephrase **332** slightly in formulating T_δ :

338 T_δ is determined by $(Q_\delta, \delta_\delta)$, where

$$Q_\delta = \left\{\left(\left\{\begin{matrix} I \\ you \\ NP \end{matrix}\right\} VP_A{}^\frown V_a{}^\frown to{}^\frown X, \left\{\begin{matrix} I \\ you \\ he \end{matrix}\right\}\right)\right\}$$

(X any string; $NP \neq I, you$)
$\delta_\delta \leftrightarrow (U, U, \sigma, \emptyset)$

338 is thus **332** revised to apply before Φ^P and given in the proper transformational form. It is the transformation that carries, e.g., "I–want–to come–I" into "I–want–to come–$\emptyset$," which is carried by Φ_1^P into "I–want–$\emptyset$–to come," and by Φ_8^P into "I–want–to come."

312 gives the **T**-markers in which T_{cmp}''' occurs. We must therefore rewrite **312**, replacing T_{cmp}''' in **312** by $T_{cmp}'''{}^\frown T_\delta$. But in **324** we dropped T_{cmp}''' and the set of related transformations in favor of a single transformation $\bar{T}_{cmp}$. Thus T_δ must be added in **324** after $\bar{T}_{cmp}$. This causes no problem when $\bar{T}_{cmp}$ is taken as some transformation of **320** other than T_{cmp}'''. In this case, T_δ will simply not be applicable. Note that V_a (in the restricting class of T_δ) is a subclass of V_b (in the restricting class of T_{cmp}'''). We thus replace **320** not by **324**, but by

339   **320** with the second set of brackets (and the contained terms) replaced by $\bar{T}_{cmp}$-T_δ

Investigating in detail the history of **336a**, we find the following stages:

340   I.   From the kernel sentences "you try," "you want $\emptyset$ it," we derive by **320**, fourth line, the reduced correlate[34] "you–want to try–you."

II.   By T_δ, which now must follow T_{cmp}''' in **320** (as revised in **339**), we derive "you–want to try–$\emptyset$" (which would be carried by Φ_1^P into "you–want–$\emptyset$–to try").

[34] The "reduced correlate," it will be recalled, is the string which results from a **T**-marker before the component of Φ^P which concludes the **T**-marker is applied. Note that further transformations are always applied to the reduced correlate, and not to the transform fully mapped out into a string of words. See §91.4 for details.

III. From the reduced correlate "you–want to try–$\emptyset$" and the kernel sentence "I expect $\emptyset$ it," we derive by **320**, fourth line, the sentence "I–expect to want to try $\emptyset$–you," to which $T\delta$ does not apply. But the sentence "I–expect to want to try $\emptyset$–you" contains the *Verb-Complement-NP* construction twice. Hence in mapping this sentence by Φ^P, Φ_1^P must apply twice,[35] once to "want–to⌢try–$\emptyset$," giving "want–$\emptyset$–to⌢try," and once to "expect–to⌢want⌢to⌢try⌢$\emptyset$–you," giving "expect–you–to⌢want⌢to⌢try⌢$\emptyset$." Applying the remaining mappings we derive **336**a.

In a similar way, the other instances of **336** are derived, while those of **337** are excluded. Investigation of sentences with "he" shows that these follow automatically in the correct way, now that we have the two elements *he* and *he**. The extension to longer and longer strings $V_a...V_a...$ also follows automatically, so that the recursive formulation of **169** (originally, statement 10, §77.2) can be dropped in the case of *to*-phrases. Of course, statement 10 did not account for the full range of sentences of the form **336**. To give a rule which produces **336**, and excludes **337**, directly in terms of phrase structure would be quite difficult. But we see that the correct forms result automatically from the transformational analysis for the simple sentences **325**, etc. This complex of sentences is another example of behavior which is simple and systematic from the point of view of transformational structure, though it appears quite complex in terms of lower levels.

In §91.5, in connection with condition 5, we discussed the problem of repeated application of mappings, and the conditions under which it arises. In step III of **340** we have an instance of the general problem discussed in §91.5. If we construe the **T**-marker in this analysis as **339**, then the reduced correlate will exclude all mappings, and Φ_1^P, in particular, will apply only at the conclusion of the derivation of complex sentences, as in **340**, necessitating repeated application. A much neater solution in this case would be to rewrite **339** as

341   **320**, with "{...} Φ^P" replaced by "$\bar{T}_{cmp}⌢T_\delta⌢\Phi_1^P⌢\psi_1$'"
where "{...}" stands for the second set of brackets in **320**

---

[35] Note that this formulation is not quite accurate. There is no question of literal re-application of mappings. Condition 5 precludes this. Rather, the question is one of formulating the mappings in a complex way as a family of transformations, perhaps an infinite family, each member of which applies to certain instances. Such formulation is possible (if we permit the condition that defines a family to be a condition on infinitely many elements) but it is inelegant, and should be avoidable. See §91.5.

Now the reduced correlate will exclude only the mappings *after* $\Phi_1{}^P$ (cf. Definition 52, §91.5). But if we accept condition 5, §91.5, we will not be able to reapply **341**, substituting a reduced correlate from **341** for Z_1 (a term of the **P**-basis) in **341**, since in this case $\Phi_1{}^P$ will appear twice, once in the reduced correlate and once in the **T**-marker itself, thus violating II, condition 5. If we drop condition 5 and accept **341**, then in place of **340** we will have

342   I.   From the kernel sentences "you try," "you want $\emptyset$ it," we derive by **320**, fourth line, the reduced correlate "you–want to try–you."

II.   By $T\delta$, which now must follow T'''_{cmp} in **320** (as revised now in **341**), we derive "you–want to try–$\emptyset$."

III.   By $\Phi_1{}^P$ we derive "you–want–$\emptyset$–to try."

IV.   From "you–want–$\emptyset$–to try" and the kernel sentence "I expect $\emptyset$ it," we derive by $\overline{T}_{cmp}$ (in this case T'''_{cmp} of **320**) the sentence "I–expect to want $\emptyset$ to try–you" to which $T\delta$ is inapplicable. Applying $\Phi_1{}^P$ to this, we derive "I–expect–you–to want $\emptyset$ to try," which becomes **336a** by ψ_1'.

This approach, with $\Phi_1{}^P$ "sealed in" to the transformation, is considerably neater in application, and will simplify the definition of $\Phi_1{}^P$, since at least for this case, $\Phi_1{}^P$ need apply only once to each stage of the development of **336a**, etc., rather than indefinitely often at the end of this development.

111.3   To sum up the discussion of §§111.1, 111.2, we have made the following points.

1.   There are two elements *he* and *he**, with *he** a proper noun, and *he* a pronoun just like *I, you.*

2.   **320** of §109.8 is replaced finally by **343** or **344**, depending on whether or not condition 5, §91.5, is retained.

343 $$Z_1{}^\frown K_1{}^\frown \begin{Bmatrix} I \\ T_\gamma \\ T_\gamma{}' \\ T_\gamma{}'' \\ T_\gamma{}''' \end{Bmatrix} {}^\frown Z_2{}^\frown K_2{}^\frown I^\frown \overline{T}_{cmp}{}^\frown T_\delta{}^\frown \Phi^P$$

344   **343** with "Φ^P" replaced by "$\Phi_1{}^P {}^\frown \psi_1'$"

$\overline{T}_{cmp}$ is as in **324**, §109.8, and $T\delta$ is as in **338**.

It follows that the simpler sentences **325, 328, 330**, etc., as well as the more complex forms **336**, etc., are correctly generated in a simple and uniform way, while **326, 337**, etc. are rejected. Thus a description which would be quite complex in terms of lower levels can be given with extreme simplicity in transformational terms, with more complex sentences produced from simpler ones. In particular, "I want to try" is derived from "I try," "I want it" just as "I want him to try" is derived from "he tries," "I want it"; and in the very same way, "I expect to want to try" is derived from "I want to try," "I expect it," and "I expect him to want to try" from "he wants to try," "I expect it," ultimately from the kernel sentences "he tries," "he wants it," "I expect it." In all cases, there seems to be good intuitive and semantic support for the resulting analysis. The setting up of two elements *he* and *he** also has support in the referential use of these words. Whereas *I* and *you* have an unambiguous reference in sentences like "John said that I would come," "John said that you would come," in "John said that he would come" the reference is ambiguous. In our terms, if "he" in this sentence is derived from the syntactic element *he* (the pronoun), the reference is to John, as it is in **330b**, where *he* becomes $\emptyset$; if it is derived from the syntactic element *he** (the proper noun), the reference is to a second person, as in **330a**. While the results of our grammatical analysis naturally tell us nothing about reference, this syntactic discussion does provide the means for an adequate description of reference in some semantic description of English.

The analysis at which we have arrived is supported systematically by the following considerations.

1. It eliminates the need for special restrictions on the occurrence of pronouns in the context $NP^\frown V_a{-}to^\frown VP_1$, as well as in longer sentences of the form **336**. These sentences are correctly generated in a simple way. **169** of §99.9 (the revision of statement 10, §72.2) would not correctly account for these forms without complex emendation. This problem did not arise in Chapter VIII, because we could not handle sentences of the form **325a**, etc., at that point.

2. This analysis eliminates **325c** as a special sentence type, reducing it to 325a, b. This will lead to the elimination of the element VP_B, with consequent simplification of several statements of the kernel grammar, and elimination of statement 10 (**169** of §99.9).

3. It is not necessary to repeat the fact that *to* occurs with VP_{A2} (and *ing* with *have*$^\frown$*en*, as we will see directly), since VP_B is eliminated in favor of the standard forms $NP\text{-}V\text{-}NP\text{-}to\text{-}VP_1$, where this fact is anyway stated. This eliminates a difficulty noted in §99.9.

4. In the final paragraph of §68 we pointed out that one difficulty

in analyzing "want to," etc., as auxiliaries is that, under conjunction, the "to" belongs with the following verb, so that in V_1-*to*-V_2 constructions, the constituent break falls after V_1. It now follows automatically that the break is at this point.

5. Sentences such as

345   *he tried not to fail*   ($= 87$)

are now automatically constructed in the correct way from "he ed not fail" (which is mapped into "he did not fail") and "he tried it" (cf. §96.3). Note that the intuitive shortcomings of our earlier analysis noted in §96.3 are now eliminated by this transformational analysis of V-*to*-V constructions.

6. This analysis eliminates a recursive statement in the kernel grammar, namely, statement 10, §72.2 (since rephrased as **169**, §99.9).

In view of §110, the final consideration is alone a sufficient validation for the transformational analysis we have adopted. But I think it is important to note that just as in each of the earlier cases that we have considered, there are strong independent reasons for eliminating the recursive statement. This adds weight to the conclusion of §110 that the nonrecursion requirement should be regarded as a formal condition on grammars (hence a condition of "simplicity," in the broad sense of Chapter IV and §93); i.e., the conclusion that the kernel should be finite, and that the process of generation of new and longer sentences is transformational.

Note incidentally that we can now arrive at an intuitively adequate explanation for the difference between **345** and

346   *he did not try to fail*   (from *he⌒ed⌒not⌒try⌒to⌒fail*)

346 is derived by T_{not} (cf. §96—i.e., by negation) from "he tried to fail," which in turn is derived transformationally from the kernel sentences

347   (a) *he fails*
            (b) *he tried it*

345 is derived, as we have seen, from the kernel sentences **347**, where **347**a is subject to the earlier transformation T_{not} that carries it into "*he⌒S⌒not⌒fail.*" Both **345** and **346** thus originate from **347** (i.e., **347**a, b form their **P**-basis). They differ in that in forming **345**, **347**a is negated, while in forming **346**, **347**b is negated.

This gives in outline the reasoning involved in the elimination of VP_B **111.4**
and some of the consequences of this step. It remains to carry out this
elimination in detail. In Chapter VIII, we limited the discussion to
certain classes of verbs that avoided the pitfalls uncovered there. In the
establishment of a kernel in Chapters IX and X we have found a rationale
for this limitation. But we must now extend the discussion to include
verbs of the types that cannot be adequately described in terms of the
level of phrase structure.

In §67.1, Chapter VIII, we set up three types of verbs that occur
with *to*-phrases (cf. **301**, §109.5). $V_a = \{want, like,...\}$ occurs with
to-phrase or *NP-to-phrase* (e.g., "I want to come," "I want him him
to come"). $V_b = \{persuade, advise,...\}$ occurs only with *NP-to*-phrase
(e.g., "I persuaded him to come," not "I persuaded to come"). $V_c =$
$\{try, decide,...\}$ occurs only with *to*-phrase (e.g., "I tried to come," not
"I tried him to come"). In §68.2, we dropped V_a, considering it as the
overlap of V_b and V_c. We then excluded V_b from consideration, because
of the difficulties that appeared in §§69–70. In §111 we have reversed
the order of precedence and have given V_a as the basic subclass of verbs,
and we must now state the special restrictions that mark V_b and V_c.[36]
Furthermore, we must give the analogous constructions for V_α, V_β,
and V_γ (cf. **302**), which parallel V_a, V_b, V_c, respectively, for the case
of *ing*-phrases.

V_α is readily introduced. Since it shares all the features of V_a
discussed above, we need only revise the definition of T_δ, replacing
338 by

348 T_δ is determined by $(Q_\delta, \delta_\gamma)$, where

$$Q_\delta = \left\{ \left(\left\{ \begin{matrix} I \\ you \\ NP \end{matrix} \right\} VP_A \begin{bmatrix} V_a {}^\frown to \\ V_\alpha {}^\frown ing \end{bmatrix} X, \left\{ \begin{matrix} I \\ you \\ he \end{matrix} \right\} \right) \right\} \quad (NP \neq I, you)$$

$$\delta_\delta \leftrightarrow (U, U, \sigma, \emptyset)$$

This formulation permits the construction of longer strings $V_a {}^\frown$
$to {}^\frown V_\alpha {}^\frown ing {}^\frown V_a {}^\frown to {}^\frown...$, etc., as did the recursive definition of VP_B,
since transformations can be freely compounded.

We can regard V_c and V_γ as subclasses of V_a and V_α, respectively,
with a special restriction on their occurrence in **T**-markers (in the
P-basis). We thus add to the grammar of the level **T** the condition

---

[36] The necessity for treating V_a and V_b as distinct subclasses has already been noted in
§109.6.

349   Condition INF_1 : If Z_2 is a string of the form $\begin{Bmatrix} I \\ you \\ NP \end{Bmatrix} VP_A \begin{bmatrix} V_c \\ V_\gamma \end{bmatrix}...,$

then Z_1 is a string of the form $\begin{Bmatrix} I \\ you \\ he \end{Bmatrix}...$

In other words, we require that a verb of V_c or V_γ be followed by "I" if its subject is "I," by "you" if its subject is "you," and by "he" if its subject is NP as in **338**.

Condition INF_1 is a condition on **T**-markers of the form **343**. Alternatively, we could dispense with **349** and revise **348** to the same effect.

This leaves only V_b and V_β to be described. The obvious suggestion is to supply for these elements a condition differing from condition INF_1 only in that "$\begin{bmatrix} V_c \\ V_\gamma \end{bmatrix}$" is replaced by "$\begin{bmatrix} V_b \\ V_\beta \end{bmatrix}$," and "$Z_1$ is a string of the form ..." is replaced by "Z_1 is not a string of the form ...." This would be a condition that V_b and V_β are *never* followed by "I" if their subject is "I," etc. But this approach is not quite correct. Before suggesting an analysis for V_b , V_β , we turn to the consideration of another transformation.

111.5   Consider the following sentences:

350   (a) *I persuaded him to try*
        (b) *I persuaded you to try*
        (c) *I persuaded myself to try*
        (d) *he persuaded him to try*
        (e) *he persuaded himself to try*
        (f) *John persuaded him to try*
        (g) *John persuaded himself to try*
        (h) *John persuaded me to try*

These sentences are exactly parallel to **325**, **328**, and **330** of §117.1. *Persuade* is a V_b , and the sentences of **350** differ from the sentences of **325**, **328**, and **330** only in that where the pronoun X would be dropped after *want* (a V_a), it becomes *X-self* after V_b .

Consider now the more complex forms discussed in §111.2. If in **336** we replace the V_a's "expect" and "want" by the V_b's "persuade" and "force," and if we replace the deleted pronoun X of **336** by *X-self*, then we derive exactly the set **351** of grammatical sentences with these V_b's:

351 (a) *I persuade you to force yourself to try*
(b) *I persuade you to force me to try*
(c) *I persuade myself to force myself to try*
(d) *I persuade myself to force you to try*
etc.

We see then that we have a transformation T_{self} which applies to V_b exactly as T_δ applies to V_a. The effect of T_{self} is to replace a pronoun X by *X-self* after V_b', wherever T_δ would have replaced it by $\emptyset$ (i.e., essentially, deleted it) after V_a. Investigation of V_β shows exactly the same phenomenon. Thus we have

352 T_{self} is determined by $(Q_{self}, \delta_{self})$, where

$$Q_{self} = \left\{ \left(\begin{Bmatrix} I \\ you \\ NP \end{Bmatrix} VP_A \begin{bmatrix} V_b{}^\frown to \\ V_\beta{}^\frown ing \end{bmatrix} X, \begin{Bmatrix} I \\ you \\ he \end{Bmatrix} \right) \right\}$$

where X is any string and NP is the subclass of noun phrases excluding I and *you*, as in **338**
$\delta_{self} \leftrightarrow (U, U, U, self)$

This explains why V_b and V_β cannot be introduced directly as subclasses of V_a and V_α, respectively, subject to a condition which is the contrary of **349**. In fact the constructions *I-V_b-to*-phrase-*I*, etc., do occur, but T_{self} rather than T_δ applies to them. A simple way to give just as much information about T_{self} as we have developed so far would be simply to revise the **T**-marker schema **343** as

353 $Z_1{}^\frown K_1{}^\frown \{$as in **343**$\}$-$Z_2{}^\frown K_2{}^\frown I$-$\bar{T}_{cmp}$-$T_\delta$-$T_{self}$-$\varPhi^\mathbf{P}$

Since T_δ by definition applies only to V_a and V_α, and T_{self} only to V_b and V_β, this will give the correct forms in all cases. But Z_1 and Z_2 in **353** can be transforms, even transforms produced by **353** itself. Hence just as we can derive stepwise a string $V_a{}^\frown to{}^\frown V_\alpha{}^\frown ing{}^\frown$... of any length, we can also derive strings in which $V_b{}^\frown$*X-self*, etc., are interspersed freely. This permits, e.g.,

354 *John visualized me forcing myself to expect him to try*

which derives ultimately from the kernel strings "he tries," "I expect it," "I force it," "John visualized it." Thus quite a complicated network of sentences is generated by continued application of very simple transformations.

Further examination of the distribution of "self," however, reveals that T_{self} as we have stated it is only a special case of a quite general transformation. Note that "him," "you," etc. in **351** are each the object of the complex verb "persuade–to try" (an instance of *Verb–Complement*). But it is true in general that the object of a verb undergoes the transformation T_{self}, even in kernel sentences. Thus we have [37]

355   *he saw himself*, etc.

The transformation T_{self} must be reformulated, then, to hold more generally of NP-V_T-NP, and it must be given as a mapping, since it is obligatory even for kernel sentences. We replace **352** by **356**, defining the component $\Phi_0{}^P$ of Φ^P

356 $\Phi_0{}^P$ is determined by $(Q_{self}, \delta_{self})$, where

$$Q_{self} = \left\{ \left(\begin{Bmatrix} I \\ you \\ NP \end{Bmatrix} VP_A{}^\frown V_T, \begin{Bmatrix} I \\ you \\ he \end{Bmatrix} \right) \right\} \qquad (NP \neq I, you)$$

$$\delta_{self} \leftrightarrow (U, U, U, self)$$

The application of $\Phi_0{}^P$ to transitive verbs of the form V_b–*to*-phrase, as above, is thus just a special case of its application to all transitive verbs. In particular, it also applies to V_α. Thus alongside **350c** we have

357   *I can't imagine myself acting that way*   (*imagine* a V_α)

Whether it applies to V_α or not depends on a decision as to the grammaticalness of such sentences as

358   *I want myself to act that way*[38]

---

[37] A pronoun in a prepositional phrase that agrees either with the subject or object also undergoes this transformation, even in kernel sentences. Thus we have "I bought a book for myself," "they warned me about myself," etc. The construction of such sentences poses a variety of problems that we have not gone into. For the purpose of this discussion we will omit such constructions (as well as other occurrences of "self," as, e.g., "he saw the President himself") and concentrate on the case of the direct object.

[38] We have "he wanted himself to be elected," "he imagined himself to be president," etc., with the verb "to be," but this is not compelling, because these sentences can be regarded as containing the verb phrase $V_e{}^\frown to{}^\frown be{}^\frown Predicate$, with *imagine, want* as V_e's.

If such sentences are considered grammatical, then no special statement is needed. If not, then a qualification must be added stating that $\Phi_0{}^P$ does not apply to V_a. This will not be the first instance of a special transformational restriction on V_a. We noted above (in §109.6) that the passive transformation does not apply to it. If the exceptions in the case of V_a are in fact not merely sporadic, this may be an indication that a deeper analysis should be sought.

In any event, we see that for V_α, and perhaps for V_a as well, T_δ is not obligatory as was stated in §§111.2, 111.3. It may not apply, in which case $\Phi_0{}^P$ will automatically give 357, 358, etc. We thus might consider reformulating 343 as

359 $Z_1{}^\frown K_1{}^\frown \{\text{as in } 343\}\text{–}Z_2{}^\frown K_2{}^\frown I\text{–}\bar{T}_{cmp} \langle T_\delta \rangle \Phi^P$

But 359 poses certain problems relating once more to condition 5, §91.5. Suppose that we accept condition 5, and with it, 343 (cf. §§111.2, 111.3). Consider now the sentence

360   *I expect you to force yourself to try*

From the kernel sentences "you try," "you force Ø it," we derive, from the reduced correlate of 359,

361   *you–force to try–you*

since T_δ is inapplicable here, *force* being a V_b. Application of Φ^P to 361, as prescribed by 359, would give the correct form

362   *you force yourself to try*

But in forming 360 we take as Z_1 in 359 the reduced form 361, not the fully mapped form 362 (cf. condition 4, §91.4). And as Z_2 of 359 we select "I expect Ø it." With these choices of Z_1 and Z_2 in 359 we derive from the reduced correlate

363   *I–expect to force to try you–you*

But $\Phi_0{}^P$ does not apply to 363, since the pronominal object "you" is distinct from the subject "I." Hence application of Φ^P to 363 will yield

364   *I expect you to force you to try*

instead of **360**. This shows that if we accept condition 5, we must set up both T_{self} *and* $\Phi_0{}^P$ as distinct and separate elements, and we must replace **359** by

365   **359** with "Φ^P" replaced by "$T_{self}{}^\frown\Phi^P$"

Now the derivation of **360** proceeds smoothly. Since T_{self} figures in the reduced correlate (which drops only the final component of the mapping Φ^P, in this case Φ^P itself), we have, instead of **361**,

366   *you–force to try–yourself*

And from this, **360** follows by reapplication of **365** with **366** as Z_1 .

But this is an unfortunate solution, since it means that we cannot regard T_{self} as simply a special case of $\Phi_0{}^P$, but must give it separate status.

If we drop condition 5 and accept **344** (cf. §§111.2, 111.3), then we simply "seal in" $\Phi_0{}^P$ along with $\Phi_1{}^P$. Thus instead of **365** we have

367 $Z_1{}^\frown K_1{}^\frown\{\text{as in }\textbf{343}\}\text{-}Z_2{}^\frown K_2{}^\frown I\text{-}\overline{T}_{cmp}\langle T_\delta\rangle\,\psi_1{}^\frown\psi_1{}'$

[where ψ_1 is the compound $\Phi_1{}^P(\Phi_0{}^P)$]. With this, T_{self} is dropped as a separate element.

There is a related problem which does not, apparently, further affect the discussion pertaining to condition 5. Consider the sentence

368   *John wanted to better himself*

This comes from the kernel sentences "he bettered himself," "John wanted Ø it." But the first of these is a sentence to which $\Phi_0{}^P$ has already applied. Thus whether we accept **365** or **367**, it is necessary to reformulate the **T**-marker so that $\Phi_0{}^P$ applies independently to (Z_1, K_1) and (Z_2, K_2). Thus instead of **365**, we have

369 $Z_1{}^\frown K_1{}^\frown\Phi_0{}^P\text{-}\{\text{as in }\textbf{343}\}\text{-}Z_2{}^\frown K_2{}^\frown\Phi_0{}^P\text{-}\overline{T}_{cmp}\text{-}\langle T_\delta\rangle\text{-}T_{self}\text{-}\psi_0{}'$

and instead of **367**, we have

370 $Z_1{}^\frown K_1{}^\frown\Phi_0{}^P\text{-}\{\text{as in }\textbf{343}\}\text{-}Z_2{}^\frown K_2{}^\frown\Phi_0{}^P\text{-}\overline{T}_{cmp}\text{-}T_\delta\text{-}\psi_1\text{-}\psi_1{}'$

369 still meets condition 5, and **370** now violates it in two respects.

To recapitulate, we have either **369** or **370** as a **T**-marker schema, **111.6** depending on whether or not condition 5, §91.5, is adopted. V_a contains a subclass V_c (and V_α a subclass V_γ) appearing only in **T**-markers meeting condition INF_1 (**349**). That is, if the verb of Z_2 in the **T**-marker is V_c or V_γ, then the subjects of Z_1 and Z_2 must agree in person.

Furthermore, we add

371 Condition INF_2 : T_δ must appear in the **T**-marker if Z_2 is an

$$NP^\frown VP_A^\frown \begin{bmatrix} V_c \\ V_\gamma \end{bmatrix}^\frown \dots,$$

and we see that perhaps "V_c" in the brackets should be replaced by "V_a," depending on a decision as to the grammaticalness of such sentences as **358**. In other cases, T_δ may or may not appear in the **T**-marker.

If the verb of Z_2 in **369** or **370** is a V_b or a V_β, then T_δ is inapplicable by definition even if it appears in the **T**-marker. In this case $\Phi_0{}^P$ (or T_{self}, in **369**) will therefore apply, giving such sentences as "I persuaded myself to try." In this way we derive the sentences **350**.

If the verb of Z_2 is a V_a or a V_α and T_δ does appear in the **T**-marker, then we derive such sentences as "I want to try," "I imagined trying," "I want him to try," etc., and in general, **325**, **328**, **330**, etc.

If the verb of Z_2 is a V_a or a V_α and T_δ does not appear in the **T**-marker, then $\Phi_0{}^P$ (or T_{self}) will apply, giving **357**, **358**, etc.

A sequence of such markers can be used to generate more complex sentences, since transforms can appear in the **P**-basis of a **T**-marker. Since such a sequence can be chosen in any order, we can derive such complex sentences as **336**, **351**, and **354**, and, by continuing the process, even more complex varieties without limit.

With this we can drop statement 10, §72.2, from the kernel grammar, and with it the element VP_B, thus incidentally eliminating a recursive statement. But we have done much more than this. We have described a great number of sentence forms that were not incorporated into the description of phrase structure in §72.2, and which could not have been incorporated without considerable complication and special statements. We have seen that these sentences are all constructible from elementary kernel sentences by a simple set of operations which may be freely applied and reapplied. In addition, we have reduced the sentence form *NP-verb-to-verb phrase* (similarly, *NP-verb-ing-verb phrase*) to a special case of the construction *NP-verb-NP-to-verb phrase* (or *NP-verb-NP-ing-verb phrase*), thus dropping a special restriction on the occurrence of pronouns as objects. We also have the incidental systematic gains noted in §111.3. Finally, as we noted in §111.3, the kernel sentences from which a given complex sentence is derived do give what intuitively is the "content," in some sense, of this complex sentence.

111.7   The investigation of "self" and its distribution will, I think, turn out to be of some importance for the study of transformational structure. The occurrence in a sentence of X-$self$, for some pronoun X, indicates a special relation between this element and some noun or some other pronoun in the sentence. To give a general rule concerning all such cases directly for all sentences may be quite difficult. But we may be able to show that whenever this relation exists between two positions in a complex sentence Z, the elements filling these places have some fixed relation in the kernel structures from which Z is derived (e.g., they may be subject and object). If so, the distribution of $self$ may be stable simply in terms of this kernel sentence relation. The simplification thus introduced can be an important support for transformational analysis, in particular cases. This is just the course we have followed in the preceding discussion.

There are many other instances where this approach can be used to support transformations that we have constructed. There are also cases where problems arise. For instance, the relative order of $\Phi_0{}^P$ and the passive transformation T_p (cf. §99) is unclear. T_p, it will be recalled, preceded all mappings in the formulation we presented above. There is good reason to retain this order even with $\Phi_0{}^P$ added. Thus we cannot have

372   (a)   *himself was seen by John in the mirror*
          (b)   *dinner was eaten by himself*   (from "John ate dinner by
                    himself," by T_p and T_{pd} ; cf. §§99.5, 103.2).

On the other hand, we have seen that $\Phi_0{}^P$ applies in forming the reduced correlate of **T**-markers of the form **369**, and T_p certainly applies to sentences derived from such **T**-markers. If condition 5, §91.5, is dropped, this and several other problems are avoided. On the other hand, we have no good alternative to condition 5. The further investigation of $self$ gives rise to other problems of this nature, and it seems best to put off this study until a specific investigation into the complex of problems surrounding condition 5 is undertaken.

111.8   For similar reasons, we will not present a precise transformational statement of the components $\Phi_i{}^P$ of the mapping Φ^P. There is no particular problem in reformulating the characterization of these components in transformational terms, but, as we have seen, the nature of this formulation depends directly on a decision as to the status of condition 5. In particular, if condition 5 is relaxed sufficiently, it will be possible to avoid the unwelcome necessity of stating the mappings as infinite families of transformations.

Although, for these reasons, we will not undertake to formulate the mappings in an exact way, it is important to recognize that there is no fundamental difficulty in doing so. In Chapter VIII, §72.3, however, there was a fundamental difficulty, since there was no clear sense at that point to the notion of derived constituent structure under mappings, to the process of compounding of elementary components of a mapping, etc. Nor was it clear in what manner and by what precise mechanism a mapping $\Phi_i{}^P$ can refer to the "derivational history" of a sentence. Thus although specific problems remain unresolved, the general problem of giving an effective simple, and systematic analysis of the mapping Φ^P which relates phrase structure and word structure is eliminated by the theory of transformations. In addition, many of the specific difficulties in constructing mappings for English have been eliminated—cf., e.g., §87.5 (iii).

In accordance with the formal condition posed in §110, it is necessary   **112.1**
to eliminate all statements of the tentative kernel grammar of §72.2 that require running through the grammar more than once. Statement 17, the analysis of the adjective phrase AP, still has this property. This statement introduces the possessive noun phrase $NP^\frown S_1$ as one of the forms of AP, but this element leads to a recursion, since one of the forms of NP may be $...NP^\frown S_1....$ In the formulation of statement 17 we discovered independent indications that $NP^\frown S_1$ is a difficult element. In §72.1 we established a simple convention that enabled us to avoid specifying whether or not each substatement of the grammar is obligatory. This convention effects a considerable simplification in a natural manner, but it caused difficulties in statements 16 and 17. Statement 16 has since been dropped, and in statement 17, it is the analysis of the element $NP^\frown S_1$ that is at fault.

$NP^\frown S_1$ has already been eliminated transformationally from the context ——$ing^\frown VP_1$. $NP^\frown S_1{}^\frown ing^\frown VP_1$ has been analyzed above (cf. §99.4) as a transform of $NP^\frown VP_A{}^\frown VP_1$ (e.g., "John's flying" comes from "John flies"). Similarly, we might analyze

373 $NP_1{}^\frown S_1{}^\frown NP_2$ (e.g., "*John's book*")

as a transform of some sentence form

374 $NP_1{}^\frown VP_A{}^\frown V_x{}^\frown NP_2$

The best choice for V_x will have to be made in terms of the selectional relations between NP_1 and NP_2 in 373 and 374. The element which comes closest to giving complete selectional identity is apparently "have." It seems that for a great many noun phrase of the form 373, there is a sentence of the form 374 with $V_x = have$. In fact, certain phrases fail this condition. For example, we have "John's behavior," "John's action," but not "John has behavior," "John has (an) action." But there is another source for phrases 373, where NP_2 is analyzable, in the manner of §107, as verb + nominalizer. In this case, 373 is derived from NP_1-verb. But we do in fact have "John behaves," "John acts," so that this analysis is available in the case of "John's behavior," "John's action." This leads us to the conclusion that such words as "behavior" and "action" are not simple nouns, but are constructed from verbs by a nominalizing morpheme. There is much more to say about this, but it appears to be another instance of an intuitively satisfactory conclusion reached on formal, transformational grounds. It may well be the case that still further sources exist for the construction 373. For instance, NP-is-A may be a further source, accounting for such phrases as "the country's safety," "his sincerity," etc. This matter should be thoroughly investigated, since it may provide a good source for insight into morphology. We will consider here only those instances of 373 for which some sentence of the form 374 with $V_x = have$ provides a transformational origin.

This transformational analysis, aside from eliminating a recursion in the kernel grammar, has several incidental desirable consequences. One artificial feature of the analysis of the construction $NP^\frown S_1$ as an AP was that it was necessary to assume a $\varnothing$ article, so that "$\varnothing$ John's book" was analogous to "a good book." This artificiality is avoided now. A much more significant simplification arising from this transformational analysis would appear had we considered sequence-of-adjective rules in §72.2. $NP^\frown S_1$ must be the first "adjective" in a sequence. Thus we have 375 but not 376:

375   *my old book*

376   *old my book*

This is an automatic consequence of the suggested transformational analysis, but it would have required a special statement in the grammatical statement of §72.2. The essential simplification would appear from the consideration of selectional restrictions, had we gone into sufficient detail in §72.2. Thus we have "John's toothache," "John has a toothache," but not "victory's toothache," "victory has a toothache," etc. Even though the transformational analysis of **373** is necessitated by the nonrecursion requirement of §110, it is interesting and important to note that a careful and detailed argument in terms of simplicity would have led to the same conclusion.

Note that in forming **373** from **374** the article of NP_2 in **374** is dropped.   **112.2**
We thus construct the transformation T_{S_1} such that

377 T_{S_1} is determined by (Q_{S_1}, δ_{S_1}), where

$$Q_{S_1} = \{(NP, VP_A\!\frown\!have, T, X)\} \qquad (X \text{ any string})$$
$$\delta_{S_1} \leftrightarrow (U, S_1, \sigma, U, \sigma, U, U, U)$$

T_{S_1} thus carries $NP\text{-}VP_A\!\frown\!have\text{-}T\text{-}X$ into $NP\!\frown\!S_1\text{-}U\text{-}U\text{-}X = NP\!\frown\!S_1\text{-}X$; e.g., it carries "John has an old car" $(= John\text{–}S\!\frown\!have\text{–}an\text{–}old\!\frown\!car)$ into "John's–old car."

The phrase **373** must now be substituted by a generalized transformation for some segment of a sentence. In general a phrase of the form **373** can appear in a sentence in a given position only if the NP_2 of this phrase can also appear in this position. Hence we have to do here with a family of transformations F_{pos} such that

378 F_{pos} is determined by (C_{pos}, t_{pos}), where $C_{pos}(\alpha_1, \alpha_2, \alpha_3, \alpha_4, \alpha_5)$ if and only if

(i) $\alpha_1 = NP\!\frown\!S_1\!\frown\!X_i$ $(X_i \text{ a string in } \bar{P})$
(ii) $\alpha_2 = \#$
(iii) $\alpha_3 = X_j$
(iv) $\alpha_4 = T\!\frown\!X_i$
(v) $\alpha_5 = X_k$

$t_{pos} \leftrightarrow (\sigma, 0, \sigma, 0, 0, 0, \sigma, 1, 0, 0)$ (i.e., t_{pos} is a *substitution*)

Thus a transformation T_{pos} from the family F_{pos} carries a string of the form **379** into the corresponding string of the form **380**:

379 $NP\!\frown\!S_1\!\frown\!X_i\text{-}\#\text{-}X_j\text{-}T\!\frown\!X_i\text{-}X_k$

380 $U\text{-}U\text{-}X_j\text{-}NP\!\frown\!S_1\!\frown\!X_i\text{-}X_k = X_j\text{-}NP\!\frown\!S_1\!\frown\!X_i\text{-}X_k$

For example, T_{pos} will carry **381** into **382**.

381   *John's old car–#–I saw–the old car–in the lot*

382   *I saw–John's old car–in the lot*

We thus construct **T**-markers of the form

383 $Z_1 \frown K_1 \frown T_{S_1} \text{-} Z_2 \frown K_2 \frown I \text{-} F_{pos} \text{-} \Phi^{\mathbf{P}}$

Where $Z_1 =$ "John has an old car" and $Z_2 =$ "I saw the old car in the lot," the string derived by **383** will be **382**, and "John's old car" will be an *NP* in the transform.

The similarity between **378** and **168** can be exploited in stating them together. Thus, e.g., t_{pos} of **378** is exactly t_A of **168**. Certain conditions will have to be added to **383** to ensure correct and exhaustive generation, and as we noted above, other sources for the $NP \frown S_1 \frown \ldots$ construction must be considered, but we will carry the analysis no further at this point.

112.3   This analysis leaves out one "adjectival" context of $NP \frown S_1$ which was in fact included in the grammatical sketch of §72.2, namely, in such sentences as

384 $NP\text{-}be\text{-}NP \frown S_1$ (e.g., *"it is John's"*)

But further investigation shows that this is an instance of a pattern with a much larger distribution not shared by adjective phrases. Thus we have

385   (a)   *John's is nicer than mine*
         (b)   *I took John's*
         (c)   *I bought it at John's*
             etc.

The only reasonable way to handle such instances as **384** and **385** is by an "elliptical" transformation $T_{S_1 d}$ having much the same relation to T_{S_1} that T_{pd} has to T_p (cf. §§99.5, 103.2).

We define the transformation $T_{S_1 d}$ such that

386 $T_{S_1 d}$ is determined by $(Q_{S_1 d}, \delta_{S_1 d})$, where

$$Q_{S_1 d} = \left\{ \left(X_i \frown NP \frown S_1, N \begin{bmatrix} \emptyset \\ S \end{bmatrix}, X_j \right) \right\}$$

$$\delta_{S_1 d} \leftrightarrow (U, U, \sigma, U, U, U)$$

We can now revise **383**, replacing it by

387   **383** with "$F_{pos} \langle T_{S_1 d} \rangle \Phi^{\mathbf{P}}$" replacing "$F_{pos} \frown \Phi^{\mathbf{P}}$"

If $Z_1 =$ "John has a car" and $Z_2 =$ "I saw the car in the lot," then **387** will yield "I saw John's car in the lot" if $T_{S_1 d}$ does not appear in the **T**-marker, and it will yield "I saw John's in the lot" if $T_{S_1 d}$ does appear in the **T**-marker. $T_{S_1 d}$ deletes the noun that follows the possessive phrase $NP \frown S_1$. Its underlying elementary transformation $\delta_{S_1 d}$ is precisely the underlying transformation δ'_{pd} of **210**, §103.2. We will see below that $T_{S_1 d}$ (and similarly, T_{pd} of §103.2) is just one of a larger class of elliptical transformations based on this elementary transformation.

Actually we should have a family of transformations in place of $T_{S_1 d}$ in **387**, and no doubt certain condition should be placed on these **T**-markers. The sentences **385** are generated in a simple way by this analysis, though they would require a special statement in §72.2. **384** did indeed appear in the grammatical sketch of §72.2 as a form of *NP-be-AP*, but the analysis at which we have arrived here seems intuitively much more adequate. It is intuitively evident that "it is John's" is not a sentence of the same form $it \frown is \frown AP$ as "it is old," but is rather elliptical in the same way as is "I took John's," etc., and this is just the analysis to which we have been led in transformational terms.

The analysis of the adjective phrase provides still another instance of a recursive statement. We did not consider this fact in §72.2, but statement 17 should contain a recursive indication that a sequence of adjectives of any length can precede a noun. This statement must be transformationally eliminated. There are also a variety of selectional restrictions on noun and modifying adjective which we did not consider in the sketch of §72.2. Thus we have **388** but not **389**:

113.1

388 (a) *a talkative man*
     (b) *a flagrant violation*
     (c) *an abundant harvest*

389 (a) $a \begin{Bmatrix} flagrant \\ abundant \end{Bmatrix} man$

     (b) $a \begin{Bmatrix} talkative \\ abundant \end{Bmatrix} violation$

     (c) $a \begin{Bmatrix} talkative \\ flagrant \end{Bmatrix} harvest$

Actually, the distinction between singular and plural is sufficient to establish the fact of selectional relation between noun and modifying adjective, since certain adjectives (e.g., "numerous," "mutually exclusive") occur only with plurals or collectives. Both the fact of selectional relation and the fact that an indefinitely long sequence of adjectives can modify a noun indicate the need for a transformational elimination of the adjective–noun construction.

For any phrase article–adjective–noun $T^\frown A^\frown N$ there is a sentence

390 $T^\frown N\text{-}is\text{-}A$

Thus phrases $T^\frown A^\frown N$ as in **388** can be dropped from the kernel in favor of sentences of the form **390**. Then the selectional relation between noun and modifying adjective need only be stated once, for the construction **390**, and we can drop from the grammar the now-inadmissible recursive statement that allows an indefinitely long sequence of adjectives modifying a noun.

We note at once that this transformational analysis is necessarily unidirectional. That is, we must derive

391 $...T^\frown A^\frown N...$

from **390** as the kernel form, not *vice versa*. If **390** is chosen as the kernel form, then sequences $T^\frown A^\frown A^\frown N$, $T^\frown A^\frown A^\frown A^\frown N$, etc. can be generated by repetition of the transformation that gives **391** from **390**, thus eliminating a recursion in the kernel grammar. But if **390** is derived from kernel sentences of the form **391**, it will be necessary to eliminate this recursion in some other way.[39] Furthermore, the transformational derivation of **391** from **390** follows the familiar pattern of a generalized transformation which substitutes a phrase derived from a sentence for some segment of a second sentence, while the analysis of **390** as a a transform of **391** would require a transformation of a new kind. Similarity of distinct analyses leads to a higher-valued grammar, since since we have defined simplicity in terms of the possibilities of coalescence of distinct statements.

A phrase $T^\frown A^\frown N$ as in **391** is produced by a transformation T_{adj} such that

392 T_{adj} is determined by (Q_{adj}, t_{adj}), where

$$Q_{adj} = \left\{\left(T, N\begin{bmatrix} \emptyset \\ S \end{bmatrix}, VP_A{}^\frown be, AP\right)\right\}$$
$$t_{adj} \leftrightarrow (0, 0, 4, 0, \sigma, 0, \sigma, 0)$$

---

[39] We have sequences $T^\frown A^\frown...^\frown A^\frown and^\frown A^\frown N$ and $T^\frown N^\frown is^\frown A^\frown...^\frown A^\frown and^\frown A$, but these must be considered separately, under the *and*-transformation.

T_{adj} thus carries **393** into **394**:

393 $T\text{-}N\left[\begin{matrix}\emptyset\\S\end{matrix}\right]\text{-}VP_A{}^\frown be\text{-}AP$ (e.g., "*the–boy–is–tall*")

394 $T\text{-}AP^\frown N\left[\begin{matrix}\emptyset\\S\end{matrix}\right]$ (e.g., "*the–tall boy*")

There is one difficulty here. We want the term $AP^\frown N\left[\begin{matrix}\emptyset\\S\end{matrix}\right]$ of the proper analysis of the transform to have the same constituent structure as its root $N\left[\begin{matrix}\emptyset\\S\end{matrix}\right]$, so that it will be possible to reapply the transformation, giving strings of adjectives. This would be an instance like case (iii), §87.5. But as we formulated Definition 30, §87.5, this will be the case only if the root is represented by a prime [cf. (vii), Definition 30, §87.5]. But in the kernel grammar of §72.2 we had no prime representing $N\left[\begin{matrix}\emptyset\\S\end{matrix}\right]$. It is necessary, therefore, either to relax Definition 30 or to introduce into the kernel grammar an intermediate prime representing $N\left[\begin{matrix}\emptyset\\S\end{matrix}\right]$, thus a prime *Noun* representing, e.g., "boy," "boys," or a prime $Noun_s$ representing "boy" and a prime $Noun_p$ representing "boys." For a variety of reasons, the latter alternative seems the best. We thus replace statement 7, §72.2, by

395 $7_1.$ $\left\{\begin{matrix}NP_s\\NP_p\end{matrix}\right\} \rightarrow T\left\{\begin{matrix}Noun_s\\Noun_p\end{matrix}\right\}$[40]

        $7_2.$ $\left\{\begin{matrix}Noun_s\\Noun_p\end{matrix}\right\} \rightarrow N\left\{\begin{matrix}\emptyset\\S\end{matrix}\right\}$

This revision actually permits a slight simplification of **392** and a somewhat more satisfactory statement of several other transformations, but we will not trouble to make the necessary alterations in the transformations discussed previously. In any event, we see that in the transform **394**, $AP^\frown N^\frown\emptyset$ is a $Noun_s$ and $AP^\frown N^\frown S$ is a $Noun_p$. Reformulating Q_{adj} of **392** as

396 $Q_{adj} = \left\{\left(T, \left\{\begin{matrix}Noun_s\\Noun_p\end{matrix}\right\}, VP_A{}^\frown be, AP\right)\right\}$

---

[40] Note that "$\langle PP\rangle$" has already been dropped from statement 7 (cf. §108.3), and "$\langle AP\rangle$" is dropped by the transformational analysis now under discussion.

we see that T_{adj} carries **397** into **398**, since $AP_1{}^\frown N{}^\frown \emptyset$ is a $Noun_s$:

397 $T\text{-}AP_1{}^\frown N{}^\frown \emptyset\text{-}VP_A{}^\frown be\text{-}AP_2$ (*"the–young boy–is–tall"*)

398 $T\text{-}AP_2{}^\frown AP_1{}^\frown N{}^\frown \emptyset$ (*"the–tall young boy"*)

Sequence of adjective restrictions can be given by restricting the order in which such sentences are transformationally derived, i.e., by conditions on **T**-markers in the grammatical statement corresponding to the level **T**.

We must now construct a generalized transformation which will substitute such phrases as **394**, **398** for some segment of a second string, in the familiar manner. The simplest approach seems to be to construct the **T**-markers

399 $Z_1{}^\frown K_1{}^\frown T_{adj}\text{-}Z_2{}^\frown K_2{}^\frown I\text{-}F_{ADJ}\text{-}\Phi^{\mathbf{P}}$

where

400 F_{ADJ} is determined by (C_{ADJ}, t_{ADJ}), where $C_{ADJ}(\alpha_1, \alpha_2, \alpha_3, \alpha_4, \alpha_5)$ if and only if

$\alpha_1 = T{}^\frown AP{}^\frown X_i$ (X_i a string in $\bar{P}$)
$\alpha_2 = \#$
$\alpha_3 = X_j$
$\alpha_4 = T{}^\frown X_i$
$\alpha_5 = X_k$

$t_{ADJ} = t_{pos}$ (of **378**) $= t_A$ (of **168**)

Suppose that we have a **T**-marker of the form **399** with $Z_1 =$ "the boy is tall," $Z_2 =$ "I noticed the boy." Then application of T_{adj} to Z_1 gives "the tall boy," and application of a transformation T_{ADJ} from the family F_{ADJ} to the complex string

401   *the tall boy–#–I noticed–the boy–U*

gives "I noticed the tall boy."

It is necessary to place certain restrictive conditions on **T**-markers of the form **399** as matters now stand. For instance, T_{adj} cannot apply to sentences with pronominal subjects, giving, e.g., "the tall he" from "he is tall." But this is due to a deficiency in our analysis of pronouns. Actually there is good reason to exclude pronouns from the kernel and to introduce them transformationally as substituends for noun phrases.

Thus pronouns, if treated as nouns, not noun phrases, would require special statements to the effect that they occur without article (or with Ø article) and with no modifiers (*AP*'s or *PP*'s).[41] If pronouns are treated transformationally in this way, then no special statement is needed to exclude them from this transformational analysis of adjectives. Transformational introduction of pronouns will also make it possible to simplify certain of the transformational analyses given above. For example, condition K_A of **139**, §99.1 can be dropped if the **T**-marker **137** is reformulated so that the introduction of the pronoun must precede the application of F_A. This is an important subject that should be further investigated.

With this we drop *AP* from the kernel grammar except in the predicate position. This leads to an incidental simplification in the kernel grammar, since in several statements of §72.2 (e.g., statements 9*, 14), it was necessary to refer to *AP* as a part of a restricting context even though this element was not really relevant. The major gains, however, are the elimination of a recursive statement, and avoidance of the necessity of duplicating the statement of selectional relation between noun and modifying adjective, as noted at the outset of this section.

It is important to determine the range of applicability of the transformation T_{adj} that forms *adjective–noun* constructions from sentences of the form *noun–is–adjective*. In statement 17, §67.2, we analyzed the adjective phrase *AP* into six kinds of elements: **113.2**

402
    (a) $NP^\frown S_1$ (*"John's"*)
    (b) $\langle D \rangle\ A$ (*"⟨very⟩ old"*)
    (c) $\langle D \rangle\ ing^\frown V_j$ (*"⟨very⟩ interesting"*)
    (d) $\langle D \rangle\ en^\frown V_k$ (*"⟨very⟩ tired"*)
    (e) $\langle D_2 \rangle\ ing^\frown V_I$ (*"⟨loudly⟩ barking"*)
    (f) $\langle D_2 \rangle\ en^\frown V_T$ (*"⟨completely⟩ forgiven"*)

---

[41] Pronouns are also distinct from other nouns in that they are normally unstressed. The characterization of pronouns in terms of lack of stress suggests interesting possibilities. There are certain nouns that also are normally unstressed in syntactic positions that generally require heavy stress, e.g., "people." Thus we have "hard work matúres people," "adversity stréngthens people," etc., as compared with "hard work matures the mínd," "adversity strengthens the cháracter," etc. If pronouns are transformationally introduced, such words as "people" might well be too. Note that proper nouns share the distributional limitations of pronouns which are under discussion in the text. Proper nouns pose a variety of difficulties on every level which suggest that they may have some special extragrammatical status, but this is a question that we have not investigated.

Form (a) has been dropped from the kernel above in §112, and (f) has been eliminated as a passive in §98. We discussed the derived constituent structure of passives in §87.2, noting in particular that $en^\frown V_T$ is an adjective even if deleted from the kernel, by virtue of its resemblance in form to $en^\frown V_k$, which remains in the kernel as an adjective. Hence T_{adj} as we have defined it will apply to transforms of the form

403 $T\text{-}Noun\text{-}VP_A^\frown be\text{-}en^\frown V_T$ ("*the–man–was–murdered*")

which are derived from kernel sentences by T_p, T_{pd} (cf. §§98.5, 103.2). And in fact we do have such forms as

404   *the murdered man*

We know that this is an instance of **402f**, not **402d** (and hence that it is derived by T_{adj} from **403**, ultimately, from "...murdered the man") since we do not have "the very murdered man" (just as we do not have "the man was very murdered").

The crucial factor in the determination that passives are *AP*'s was the term-by-term resemblance of $en^\frown V_T$ to the kernel adjective $en^\frown V_k$. But this consideration (turning on absolute category comembership) does not hold for such V_T's as "consider a fool," etc. There is no *AP* of the form $en^\frown V^\frown T^\frown Noun$, differing from "considered a fool" (as in "he was considered a fool") word by word in members of the same absolute category and belonging to the kernel. That is, it will not automatically be the case in the kernel grammar that $\rho(AP, en^\frown consider^\frown a^\frown fool)$ as it is automatically the case that $\rho(AP, en^\frown murder)$, as we noted in §87.2. Hence Definition 28, §87.2, will not apply in this case, assigning "considered a fool" to *AP*. Hence T_{adj}, as we have formulated it above, will not apply to such strings as

405 $T\text{-}Noun\text{-}VP_A^\frown be\text{-}en^\frown V_h^\frown NP$ ("*John was considered a fool*")

which, just like **403**, are derived by T_p, T_{pd}. And in fact we do not have such noun phrases as

406   *the considered a fool person*

We note the following difficulty, however. In §87.2 we considered a more general condition, namely, Definition 29, under which constituent structure is assigned. And Definition 29 does in fact apply to "considered a fool," assigning it to *AP*. We conclude, then, that Definition 29 must be weakened in some respect.

The discussion of "consider a fool" can be carried over for all other instances of the constructions *Verb–Complement* that were deleted from the kernel in §109. It will be recalled that the only instances of this construction not deleted from the kernel are those of the form V_{sep}⌒ *Particle* (cf. §100, and the final paragraph of §109). All other cases of *Verb–Complement* fail to qualify as *AP*'s, and thus do not appear as noun modifiers under the transformation T_{adj} .

With respect to the construction V_{sep}⌒*Particle*, however, the situation is less clear. **402d** does appear to have certain instances of this form. If such sentences as

407   *he was very tired out*

are admitted as grammatical, then en⌒V_{sep}⌒*Particle* will be represented in **402d** as en⌒V_k (hence as *AP*), and en⌒V_{sep}⌒*Particle* will qualify as a subconstruction of *AP*, hence subject to T_{adj} if this transformation stands unaltered as in **392, 396**. In this case, noun phrases of the form

408 T-en⌒V_{sep}⌒*Particle-Noun*

will be generated. Certain cases of **408** do seem to occur fairly freely. Thus we have

409   (a)   *a broken down house*
         (b)   *a carefully carried out plan*
                etc.

On the other hand, such phrases as

410   (a)   *the called up people*
         (b)   *a carried out plan*

are hardly acceptable. A much more careful analysis of these phrases appears necessary before we can determine the correct analysis.

Consider now case **402e**. It is necessary to include ⟨D_2⟩ ing⌒V_I as a form of *AP* because of such phrases as "a barking dog," "a sleeping child," etc. Now that cases of T⌒AP⌒*Noun* are derived by T_{adj} from T-*Noun-is-AP*, these phrases will be derived from

411   (a)   *a dog is barking*
         (b)   *a child is sleeping*

But the sentences of the form **411** exist even if case **402e** is not included as a form of AP in the predicate position. **411**a, b are sentences of the form NP-VP_A-V_I, with VP_A taking the form $S^\frown be^\frown ing$. Thus we can drop **402e** from the analysis of AP by revising T_{adj} so that it applies to **411**, thus by replacing **396** by

$$\textbf{412} \quad Q_{adj} = \left\{\left(T, \left\{\begin{matrix} Noun_s \\ Noun_p \end{matrix}\right\}, VP_A^\frown be, \left[_{ing\langle D_2\rangle}^{\quad AP} V_I\right]\right)\right\}$$

But in fact even this elaboration is not necessary if we make an assumption about the absolute analysis (cf. §39 and the analysis of passives in §87.2), which appears to be a reasonable one. Just as we exploited the resemblance between **402f** and **402d** to show that passives $en^\frown V_T$ are AP's, even though deleted from the kernel, we can exploit the resemblance between **402e** and **402c** to show that $ing^\frown V_I$ is an AP, even if not given explicitly in the analysis of AP.

Suppose that we revise the transformational analysis of T-AP-$Noun$ constructions, replacing the **T**-marker schema **399** by

$$\textbf{413} \quad Z_1^\frown K_1^\frown \Phi^{\mathbf{P}}\text{-}T_{adj}\text{-}Z_2^\frown K_2^\frown \Phi^{\mathbf{P}}\text{-}F_{ADJ}$$

The essential change is that both T_{adj} and F_{ADJ} now apply *after*, not before $\Phi^{\mathbf{P}}$, and in particular, after the component $\Phi_5^{\mathbf{P}}$ of $\Phi^{\mathbf{P}}$, which carries $ing^\frown V$ into $V^\frown ing$. Note that **413** is no more complex than **399**, and that the replacement of **399** by **413** leaves our earlier analyses intact. Hence **413** might just as well have been taken in the first place as the **T**-marker schema for this transformational analysis.

In §87.5, (iii), we briefly discussed $\Phi_5^{\mathbf{P}}$, noting that it carries ing-V into U-$V^\frown ing$, with $V^\frown ing$ being a term of the proper analysis of the transform. $\Phi_5^{\mathbf{P}}$ applied to a sentence containing **402c** as predicate gives

$$\textbf{414} \quad NP\text{-}VP_A\text{-}be\text{-}V_j^\frown ing$$

and applied to NP-$S^\frown be^\frown ing$-V_I (e.g., to **411**), it gives

$$\textbf{415} \quad NP\text{-}S^\frown be\text{-}V_I^\frown ing$$

with the proper analysis in each case as given by the dashes. We note that $V_j^\frown ing$ in **414** is an AP, since its root $ing^\frown V_j$ is an AP; hence

$\rho(AP, V_j\frown ing)$.[42] In fact, V_j is a subclass of transitive verbs. If however, it is the case that

416   transitive and intransitive verbs are not distinguished on the absolute level

then Axiom 10, §61 guarantees that $\rho(AP, V_I\frown ing)$ as well. Hence from Definition 28, §87.2, it follows that $V_I\frown ing$ in **415** is an AP.

This argument is perfectly parallel to the argument of §87.2 concerning the adjectival status of the passive. The latter, however, made a much weaker assumption about absolute categories than **416**, since in the case of the passive, it was only necessary to assume that V_k is not distinguished on the absolute level from other transitive verbs. But even the assumption **416** seems to be a reasonable one.

Suppose now that we replace **396** not by **412** but by

417 $Q_{adj} = \left\{ \left(T, \left\{ \begin{array}{c} Noun_s \\ Noun_p \end{array} \right\}, C\frown be, AP \right) \right\}$

where C, it will be recalled, is the element of the auxiliary verb that becomes either the singular or plural element of the verb phrase. **417** differs from **396** in one important respect, namely, in that the status of *be* is ambiguous in **417**—it may be either the main verb or part of the auxiliary. But **417** is no more complex than **396**, and in fact, it could just as well have been given above in place of **396**. But now T_{adj} , with the restricting class **417**, applies to **411** in just the same way as to "the book is interesting."

If we assume **416**, then we replace **396** by **417** and **399** by **413**. Neither of these changes adds to the complexity of the grammar; hence either change can be made independently of this discussion. If we reject **416**, we replace **396** by the somewhat more complex **412**. Either way, then, it is unnecessary to include **402e** as a special form of the adjective phrase.[43] The appearance of $ing\frown V_I$ in the predicate position is guaranteed anyway, because of such forms as **411** (from $NP\text{-}VP_A\text{-}V_I$);

---

[42] Note that we are using here the fact discussed in §87.3 that ρ is recovered in part from ρ^T, which in turn is defined in terms of derived constituent structure. We are also using the fact that the components Φ_i^P of Φ^P are themselves transformations (cf. §88).

[43] Note that we have once more (as in §§94.5, 96.2) made use of the fact that *be* can be either a main verb or part of the auxiliary, as a means of simplifying the statement of transformations.

and one way or another, all occurrences of "barking," "sleeping," etc. are accounted for exactly as in the case of the kernel adjectives "old," "interesting," etc. The fact that only D_2 (i.e., not "very," "rather," etc.) can appear with "barking," "sleeping" (i.e., we do not have "the very sleeping child," though we have "the very interesting book") is accounted for by the fact that these adjectives are derived from the verbal sentences $NP\text{-}VP_A\text{-}V_I$, where (cf. statement 2, §72.2) only D_2 can occur. Thus we do not have "the child–is ing–very sleep" → "the child is very sleeping." We have already seen that the limitation on the occurrence of adverbs in the case of the passives "murdered," "accused," etc. can be explained in exactly the same way.

The fact that adjectives of the form $\langle D_2 \rangle\ ing^\frown V_I$ are dropped from the analysis of the adjective phrase has an important consequence for the intuitive adequacy of the resulting grammar. In §76.2, in reviewing the inadequacies of the grammar which did not go beyond phrase structure, we noted that such sentences as **411** turn out to be cases of constructional homonymity. "The dog is barking" is an instance of the pattern $NP\text{-}VP_A\text{-}V_I$ (like "the dog barks"). But it is also an instance of $NP\text{-}is\text{-}AP$ (like "the dog is mangy"), since $NP\text{-}is\text{-}AP$ is an existing sentence form, and "barking" is in fact an AP because of sentences like "the barking dog . . .," etc. But there is no corresponding structural ambiguity, as there is in other cases of constructional homonymity—the analysis as an instance of $NP\text{-}is\text{-}AP$ has no intuitive support. This intuitive inadequacy suggested some flaw in the conception of linguistic structure that led to the dual analysis. But we see that under transformational analysis, there is no constructional homonymity in these cases. "Barking" is no longer an instance of AP in the kernel. Hence "the dog is barking" has only one analysis—as $NP\text{-}VP_A\text{-}V_I$—and only one **P**-marker. The fact that $\langle D_2 \rangle\ ing^\frown V_I$ occurs as an adjective phrase in other contexts is accounted for by the formal similarity between the occurrence of this phrase as a verb, and the occurrence of adjectives of the form **402c** in the predicate position, T_{adj} applying to both of these cases. With this we see, incidentally, that all of the difficulties noted in §76 have disappeared under transformational analysis.

This leaves only **402b–d** as instances of AP in the grammar of phrase structure for the kernel. This seems to be a satisfactory result. It is clearly the case that intuitively, "the sleeping child" and "the murdered man" have more "verbal force," in some sense, than, respectively, "the interesting book" and "the tired man." There is no explanation for this on lower levels, since these pairs do not differ in any significant way in morphological or constituent structure. But there is a transformational explanation, as we have just seen.

Adjective phrases also occur as predicates of stative verbs such as **113.3** "seem," "become," "act," "look," etc. (cf. Note 24). Thus one of the sentence forms of the kernel will be

418 $NP\text{-}V_{stat}\text{-}AP$

In the kernel, only cases **402**b–d remain as forms of the adjective phrase, and all of these can appear in **418**. Thus we have

419 (a) *he seems old*
    (b) *this seems interesting*
    (c) *he seems tired*

402a, e, f are now introduced transformationally. But the transformational analysis of these adjectival elements as we have developed it in §§112, 113, above, does not provide for the introduction of these elements in the context **418**. This analysis introduces these adjectival elements only as noun modifiers. It is therefore quite interesting to note that these elements **402**a, e, f in fact do *not* occur with stative verbs in the context **418**. We cannot have

420 (a) *it seems John's*
    (b) *it seems barking*
    (c) *he seems forgiven*

On the level of phrase structure, the exclusion of cases **402**a, e, f would have to be given as a special restriction on the selection of AP in **418**, but we see that the correct distributional statement follows automatically from the simplest transformational characterization constructed for the other instances of AP. Again we have an instance where transformational analysis shows an apparently capricious exception to be the result of underlying regularity and structural simplicity.

This discussion does not exhaust the distribution of adjectives. As is the case throughout these applications of transformational analysis, this is only an introductory survey.

Wherever we have a transformation based on a deformation **114.1**

421 $\delta_\epsilon \leftrightarrow (U,\ U,\ \sigma,\ U,\ U,\ U)$

or the like, the result of this transformation will be an "elliptical" sentence. If the restricting class is

422 $Q = (X_1,\ X_2,\ X_3)$

the element X_2 is dropped by the transformation, and a sentence Z of the form $X_1 {}^\frown X_2 {}^\frown X_3$ is carried into the corresponding sentence Z' of the form $X_1 {}^\frown X_3$. In such a case we can expect to find that there is a feeling that X_2 is "understood" in Z'. We have come across two instances of such elliptical transformations. In §98.5 and §103.2 we constructed T_{pd} which carries 423a into 423b:

423 (a) $NP {}^\frown VP_A {}^\frown be {}^\frown en {}^\frown V{-}by {}^\frown NP{-}\langle PP_\alpha \rangle$ ("*the picture was painted–by the artist–⟨by a new technique⟩*")

    (b) $NP {}^\frown VP_A {}^\frown be {}^\frown en {}^\frown V{-}\langle PP_\alpha \rangle$ ("*the picture was painted–⟨by a new technique⟩*")

The second instance is the transformation $T_{S_1 d}$ constructed in §112.3, carrying 424 into 425:

424 $...NP {}^\frown S_1{-}Noun{-}...$ ("*I liked John's–book–better*")

425 $...NP {}^\frown S_1{-}...$ ("*I liked John's–better*")

There are other cases where considerations of simplicity compel us to set up an elliptical transformation. Consider for instance such sentences as

426 (a) *John will*
   (b) *John is*
   (c) *John has*
   (d) *John has been*
   (e) *John does*
     etc.

the answers to "who will go," "who is in the other room," etc.

Intuitively, these appear to be "truncated" sentences, with a verb phrase "understood." But we will see directly that formal analysis leads to the same conclusion, thus providing grounds in formal linguistic structure for this intuition.

Consider the possibility of including 426 in the kernel. We note first that the final elements "will," "be," "have," "do" in 426 cannot be regarded as main verbs which happen to be intransitive. This solution is ruled out by such considerations as the following:

1. If "will" (or any other member of M, e.g., "must," "can") is regarded as a main verb, it is necessary to add a special statement to the effect that auxiliary verbs cannot occur freely with M as they can with all other main verbs. For example, we do not have "John is musting."
2. As main verbs, "be," "have," and "do" can occur with the auxiliary "is⌢ing," as in "John is being nice about it," "John is having breakfast," "John is doing his homework." But we do not have "John is being," "John is having," "John is doing" as forms of **426**. Hence special restrictions must be stated for the "intransitive" use of "be," "have," and "do."
3. As main verbs, "have" and "do" occur with the negative element preceding, as in "he doesn't have a chance," "he doesn't do his work." But in **426** we have only "John hasn't," "John doesn't," as is normal for auxiliaries.
4. "Do" normally takes stress in sentence final position as a main verb (e.g., "what sort of work does John do"). But in **426e** it is unstressed.

Thus if these elements are regarded as main intransitive verbs, rather than as auxiliaries, a variety of special statements will be necessary. In other words, the distributional features of "will," "is," etc., in **426** are precisely those of auxiliaries, and these elements must therefore be regarded as such.

If we recognize that the verbs in **426** are auxiliaries, the only way to retain these sentences in the kernel is to give the analysis of the *Sentence* not as *Sentence* $\rightarrow NP^\frown VP_A^\frown VP_1$ (as in statements 1, 2, §72.2), but as

427   *Sentence* $\rightarrow NP^\frown VP_A \langle VP_1 \rangle$

so that VP_1 may or may not occur, **426** resulting when it does not occur. This would indeed be a possible analysis, and in fact the simplest analysis, were it not for the fact that, as we have seen, the elements *en*, *ing* are best associated with the auxiliary verb, not the main verb. Thus **427** gives not **426**, but

428   (a) *John will*
         (b) *John is ing*
         (c) *John has en*
              etc.

when VP_1 does not occur. This solution is ruled out, then, because the analysis of auxiliary verbs would have to be reformulated with consequent complexities on both the levels **P** and **T**.

It is therefore necessary to delete **426** from the kernel, and provide a transformational analysis with an elliptical transformation. Suppose we set up T_ϵ such that

429 T_ϵ is determined by $(Q_\epsilon, \delta_\epsilon)$, where

$$Q_\epsilon = (NP^\frown VP_A, VP_1)$$
$$\delta_\epsilon \text{ is as in } \mathbf{421}$$

We require that T_ϵ apply after $\Phi_5{}^P$, the mapping that carries $ing^\frown V$ into $V^\frown ing$, etc. We thus construct the **T**-markers

430 $Z^\frown K^\frown \psi_5\text{-}T_\epsilon\text{-}\psi_5'$

ψ_5 carries "John–S will–come" into "John–will–come"; "John–is ing–come" into "John–is–come ing"; "John–has en–come" into "John–has–come en"; etc. [cf. §§72.3, 87.5(iii)], where "will," "is," "has," etc. remain as the VP_A, and "come," "come ing," "come en" (which become "come," "coming," "come," respectively, by the morphological rules $\Phi^{\overline{M}}$) constitute the element VP_1. T_ϵ then carries these strings into **426a–d**.

With **426e**, however, we face a certain problem. ψ_5 carries "John–S come" into "John–come S," and T_ϵ will carry this into "John." Thus T must *precede* the mapping which carries $S^\frown verb$ into $verb^\frown S$, $\emptyset^\frown verb$ into $verb^\frown\emptyset$, and $ed^\frown verb$ into $verb^\frown ed$. But this is again the mapping $\Phi_5{}^P$. The simplest solution is to split $\Phi_5{}^P$ into two mappings $\Phi_5{}^P$ and $\Phi_6{}^P$, where $\Phi_5{}^P$ applies to the affixes en and ing, and $\Phi_6{}^P$ applies in exactly the same way to $\emptyset$, S, ed. (The component of Φ^P which introduces "do" as the bearer of a displaced affix is now renamed "$\Phi_7{}^P$," since it must follow the new $\Phi_6{}^P$). Now, retaining **430**, cases **426a–d** are still handled correctly, but ψ_5 leaves "John S come" unchanged. T_ϵ then carries "John S come" into "John S," and $\Phi_7{}^P$, which introduces "do" as the bearer of a displaced affix, carries "John S" into "John-do S," ultimately, **426e**.

The negatives "John won't," "John isn't," etc. are automatically produced in the correct way with no further changes, since, as we noted in §96.1, if ... is a VP_A, then ...*not*... is a VP_A as well.

We thus have formal grounds for construing the sentences of **426** as elliptical constructions with the verb phrase "understood." Note that it is not always the case when we have sentences $Z = X_1 \frown X_2 \frown X_3$ and $Z' = X_1 \frown X_3$ that Z' is to be derived by an elliptical transformation from Z. For instance, we have seen that $X \frown not \frown Y$ is best derived by a transformation adding *not* to $X \frown Y$, not *vice versa*, and in the case of sentence pairs like "he immediately accepted," "he accepted," the best analysis is evidently to include both in the kernel, giving the analysis of this construction as $NP\langle D\rangle VP$. In these three kinds of instance, then, formal analysis leads to different descriptions. "John will" is derived from "John will Verb Phrase" by an elliptical transformation; "John will not try" is derived from "John will try" by a deformation adding *not*; and "John accepted" and "John immediately accepted" are both kernel sentences. Similarly, "they come" and "they will come" are both kernel sentences. These are the analyses that result from the attempt to construct the simplest possible grammar. But it is quite clear that intuitively, "John will try," "John accepted," "they come," etc. are not derived elliptically from "John will not try," "John immediately accepted," "they will come," respectively, in the same sense in which "John will" is derived from "John–will–Verb Phrase."

The suggested analysis **427** which, if accepted, would have excluded **426** from the class of elliptical constructions, was ruled out because of the fact that the simplest analysis of the auxiliary verb associates *ing, en* with VP_A rather than VP_1. This analysis of VP_A (given originally in §66.2) in itself had little intuitive correspondence to recommend it, though it did enable us to give a very simple description of a fairly complex construction. But we see that this analysis does lead to further analyses that are marked by strong intuitive correspondence. In fact, almost every transformation established hitherto depends to some extent on this analysis of VP_A. It is too much to a expect a point-by-point correspondence between linguistic intuition and the results of applying a given linguistic theory, but just as this theory is supported when in application it leads to intuitively satisfactory analyses, it is also supported when an analysis which itself lacks direct intuitive correspondence serves as the cornerstone for other analyses that do have such correspondence. This is the case with the analysis of VP_A that was systematically motivated by considerations of simplicity.

Imperatives are still another form of elliptical sentences. In imperatives,   **114.2** the noun phrase subject and the auxiliary verb are dropped, leaving only VP_1. Thus we have such imperatives as

431   *give me the record*

But only a restricted set of VP_1's can occur as imperatives. Investigation of the various possibilities serves to determine the restricting class for the transformation T_{imp}. Since we have "give me the record tomorrow" but not "give me the record yesterday," we see that the choice of VP_A in the transformed string is not free. For instance, VP_A can be "will" (since we have "you will give me the record tomorrow" but not "you will give me the record yesterday") but it cannot be "have en" (since we have "you have given me the record yesterday," but not "you have given me the record tomorrow"). It is simplest to restrict VP_A to the element M containing "will," "can," must,"" etc.[44]

Since we have "look at yourself," but not "look at myself," etc., we see that the noun phrase subject of the string which is carried into an imperative must be *you*, and we see that T_{imp} must apply after the mapping Φ_0^P which carries X into X-*self* (where X is a pronoun) in the context X-*verb*—— (cf. §111.5). We might therefore construct the **T**-markers

432 $Z^\frown K^\frown \Phi_0^P - T_{imp} - \psi_0'$

where

433 T_{imp} is determined by (Q_{imp}, δ_{imp}), where

$$Q_{imp} = (you^\frown M, VP_1)$$
$$\delta_{imp} \leftrightarrow (\sigma, U, U, U)$$

T_{imp} thus carries "*you-M-VP_1*" into "*VP_1*"; e.g., it carries "you–will–give me the record tomorrow" into "give me the record tomorrow." It is still necessary to account for such imperatives as

434   (a)   *do come to visit us*
      (b)   *don't come to visit us*

We note that *do* in **434**a always has heavy stress. In §97 we set up an element Ac of the same class as *not* which has the effect of assigning heavy stress to the vowel of the preceding morpheme. **434**a, b could thus be derived from

435   (a)   *do Ac–you–come to visit us*
      (b)   *do n't–you–come to visit us*

---

[44] The auxiliary phrase must contain the element C which carries number, or *ed*, but we will see below that T_{imp} must apply after Φ_2^P which carries $C^\frown M$ into M (cf. §72.3), so that U-$M = M$ is in fact one of the forms of the VP_A at the point where T_{imp} applies.

by deleting *you*. But in §97 we saw that **435**a, b in turn are derived from "you–∅–come to visit us" by application of either the *Ac*-transformation or the *not*-transformation, followed by the question transformation T_q (giving "∅ $\left[\begin{array}{c} Ac \\ not \end{array}\right]$–you–come to visit us"), with the element *do* introduced by $\Phi_7{}^P$ as a bearer of the displaced affix ∅. We can thus reformulate T_{imp} to apply after the question transformation, so that it can apply to **435**. We will see below that this alteration is required for independent reasons. We thus replace **433** by

436 T_{imp} is determined by $(Q'_{imp}, \delta'_{imp})$, where

$$Q'_{imp} = \left\{ \left(\left\{ \begin{array}{c} U, \; \O \; \{Ac\} \\ \{n't\} \\ M, \; U \end{array} \right\}, \, you, \, VP_1 \right) \right\}$$

$$\delta'_{imp} \leftrightarrow (\sigma, \, U, \, U, \, U, \, \sigma, \, U, \, U, \, U)$$

T_{imp} thus carries U-$\O \left[\begin{array}{c} Ac \\ n't \end{array}\right]$-$you$-$VP_1$ into $\O \left[\begin{array}{c} Ac \\ n't \end{array}\right]$-$VP_1$, which upon application of $\Phi_7{}^P$ gives **434**; and it carries M-U-you-VP_1 into VP_1, as before, giving **431**, etc. We must revise the **T**-markers **432** so that T_{imp} follows $\Phi_3{}^P$, since the question transformation must follow $\Phi_3{}^P$, and T_{imp} now applies only to questions. We thus replace **432** by

437 $Z {\frown} K {\frown} \psi_3$-$T_{imp}$-$\psi_3'$

Also to be covered by this analysis are such sentences as

438   (a) *you get it*
         (b) *you be the first volunteer*
         (c) *don't you get it*   (i.e., "*let him get it*")

with heavy stress in all cases on "you." This peculiarity suggests that these sentences be handled uniformly. These sentences are also formed by dropping the auxiliary, and **438**c at least is most simply formed from the question. Hence a uniform treatment is possible only if all are derived from questions. (Note that a further advantage in deriving imperatives from questions is that this treatment excludes them from the context *that*——.) These sentences can be formed by a transformation T_{IMP} such that

439 T_{IMP} is determined by (Q_{IMP}, δ_{IMP}), where

$$Q_{IMP} = \left\{\left(\begin{Bmatrix} U, & \text{Ø}^\frown n't \\ M, & U \end{Bmatrix}, you, VP_1\right)\right\}$$

$$\delta_{IMP} \leftrightarrow (\sigma, U, U, U, U, Ac, U, U)$$

As a **T**-marker schema we have

440 $Z^\frown K^\frown \psi_3 \text{-} T_{IMP} \text{-} \psi_3'$

T_{IMP} carries $\text{Ø}^\frown n't\text{-}you\text{-}VP_1$ (formed by a negative and a question transformation from the kernel sentence $you\text{-}C\text{-}VP_1$) into $\text{Ø}^\frown n't\text{-}you^\frown Ac\text{-}VP_1$, which, by Φ_7^{P} (introducing "do" as a bearer of the displaced Ø) and the morphological analysis of Ac (which adds heavy stress to the preceding morpheme—cf. **96**), becomes **438c**. It also carries $M\text{-}you\text{-}VP_1$ into $you^\frown Ac\text{-}VP_1$, which goes into **438a, b**.

T_{IMP} of **439** is almost identical in its definition with T_{imp} of **436**, and the definitions of these transformations can thus be stated together, The resulting simplification gives a further reason for defining T_{imp} so that it applies after the question transformation. It appears then that imperatives are derived from questions by the elliptical transformation T_{imp} (with an alternative form T_{IMP} differing from T_{imp} in that it adds heavy stress to the subject instead of deleting it). Though this is a fairly simple analysis of this set of sentences, there are enough asymmetries to suggest that there is some better analysis.

115.1   In §74, Chapter VIII, we saw that there was no way to introduce the conjunction rule on the level of phrase structures without excessive complication, or a drastic revision of the form of grammars. Given the nonrecursion requirement of §110, there is of course no hope at all of introducing a rule for conjunction into the kernel grammar. But it is clear from §§90, 91 that this rule can be formulated as a family of generalized transformations.

Fundamentally, the rule for conjunction asserts that any constituent C of a sentence Z can be replaced by $C^\frown and^\frown C'$, where C and C' are both Pr_i's, for some prime Pr_i. But this replacement may be carried out only if C' also appears in the context of C as a Pr_i. In other words, the conjunction rule will effect the transformation

441 $X^\frown C^\frown Y^\frown \#^\frown X^\frown C'^\frown Y \rightarrow X\text{-}C^\frown and^\frown C'\text{-}Y$

where for some Pr_i, C is a Pr_i of $X^\frown C^\frown Y$ and C' is a Pr_i of $X^\frown C'^\frown Y$.

The elementary transformation underlying the family F_{AND} will thus be a generalized transformation that carries $X_1\text{-}X_2\text{-}X_3\text{-}\#\text{-}X_4\text{-}X_5\text{-}X_6$ into $U\text{-}U\text{-}U\text{-}U\text{-}X_4\text{-}X_2{}^\frown and{}^\frown X_5\text{-}X_6$, and F_{AND} will be defined as follows:

442 F_{AND} is determined by (C_{AND}, t_{AND}), where $C_{AND}(\alpha_1, \alpha_2, \alpha_3, \alpha_4, \alpha_5, \alpha_6, \alpha_7)$ if and only if

$$\alpha_1 = \alpha_5$$
$$\alpha_2 = Pr_i = \alpha_6$$
$$\alpha_3 = \alpha_7$$

where Pr_i is a prime

$$t_{AND} = s_{AND}(\delta_{AND})$$

where $\delta_{AND} \leftrightarrow (U, U, U, U, U, U, U, U, U, U, and\ U, U, U)$
$s_{AND} \leftrightarrow (\sigma, 0, \sigma, 0, \sigma, 0, \sigma, 0, 0, 0, 2, 0, 0, 0)$

δ_{AND} is a deformation adding *and*, and s_{AND} is a generalized substitution (cf. Definition 24, §86.4) deleting the first four terms and adjoining the second term to the sixth. It would be possible to extend the definition of substitutions (and to extend Theorem 6, §86.4) so that t_{AND} can be more simply defined as the substitution with the defining sequence

443 $(\sigma, 0, \sigma, 0, \sigma, 0, \sigma, 0, 0, 0, (2, and), 0, 0, 0)$

where this has the obvious meaning.

Since from "John comes" and "John goes" we can form "John comes and goes" by conjunction, if follows that F_{AND} must apply after $\Phi_6{}^P$ (cf. §114.1), which forms $Verb{}^\frown S$ from $S{}^\frown Verb$. We will see below (§115.3) that F_{AND} must precede $\Phi_7{}^P$, the component of Φ^P that introduces "do." We therefore add to the set of **T**-markers all strings

444 $Z_1{}^\frown K_1{}^\frown \psi_6\text{-}Z_2{}^\frown K_2{}^\frown \psi_6\text{-}F_{AND}\text{-}\psi_6'$

Where $\alpha_1 = \alpha_3 = U$ in **442**, a transformation T_{and} of F_{AND} will carry a pair of sentences Z, Z_2 into $Z_1{}^\frown and{}^\frown Z_2$. In other cases, T_{and} will conjoin properly included constituents. There are a good many qualifications and reservations that must be added to **442**, **444**. For one thing, T_{and} cannot apply to certain constituents (e.g., the article τ—we cannot have "the and a boy," etc.). There are many other cases in which the internal analyses of C and C' (i.e., α_2 and α_6 of **442**) are relevant. Thus prepositional phrases cannot be freely conjoined when their initial prepositions are not identical (and if we have a high enough degree of grammaticalness, we will find that there are even certain restrictions when the initial prepositions are identical), and there are restrictions of tense (i.e., of choice of VP_A) when verb phrases are conjoined. Sometimes the transformational history of C and C' must be taken into account. For instance, we noted in §77.1 that sentences of different types cannot be freely conjoined, and now we consider sentences to be of different types when they have distinct transformational histories. Similarly, we note that "recognized," "applauded," "sad," and "tired" are all adjectives, but that only the latter two are still in the kernel. Since we cannot have "very recognized," "very applauded," we know that these adjectives are introduced by the passive transformation in the manner described above. And, although we have **445**, the sentences **446** are not grammatical:

445   (a)   *John was sad and tired*
          (b)   *John was recognized and applauded*

446   (a)   *John was sad and recognized*
          (b)   *John was tired and applauded*
              etc.

It is also interesting to note that though "was applauded" and "was tired" have the same constituent structure, conjunction shows that the passive "was applauded" retains its "verbal force," since it can be conjoined with a verb phrase. Thus we have **447** but not **448**.

447   *the speaker arrived and was applauded*

448   *the speaker arrived and was tired*

The reason for this presumably lies in the verbal origin of "was applauded" under transformation. There are various ways in which this fact, which distinguishes "applauded" from "tired," might be used to simplify the analysis. In general, we see that various conditions must be added to **444** to account for these and other restrictions.

The nature of conjunction is an important matter that deserves a special and detailed investigation. To go into this properly would far exceed the bounds of this study. Though we cannot give the conjunction rule in a precise form at this point, it is important to note that this is in part at least a result not of a theoretical shortcoming, as in Chapter VIII, but simply of lack of data. The specific problems concerning conjunction which were raised in §73 have been overcome, and it appears that the present theoretical framework should be adequate to give a satisfactory account of conjunction, in large measure.

The constructions of this section do not exhaust all cases of conjunction, unless certain subsidiary transformations are given. Thus we have such cases as

449   (a)   *they elected John president and Bill vice-president*
            (b)   *John was elected president, and Bill, vice-president*
            (c)   *he let the dog in and the cat out*
            (d)   *Bill bought candy, and Jim, pretzels*

Cases (b) and (d) suggest a zero pro-verb. (c) and (a) might be handled by transformations that simply rearrange constituent structure (these would be a special class of adjunctions), but it is perhaps more interesting to consider (at least in the case of (a)) the possibility that the original constituent structure of the constituent kernel sentences is somehow taken into account. Further pursuit of this approach, however, leads into areas where our analysis of derived constituent structure appears to be inadequate.

Whether or not all cases of conjunction can with profit be handled by a single family of generalized transformations, only a more detailed study will tell. However this may be, it does not affect the validity of the conjunction criterion for constituent analysis as this has been employed throughout our discussion of English syntax in Chapters VIII and X. It can scarely be doubted that the conjunction rule is tremendously simplified if constituents are chosen in such a way that **442** can be formulated directly in terms of constituents, whether it turns out to be the case that **442, 444** cover all cases of conjunction or only a large majority. And this is the only sense in which conjunction has been used as a criterion for constituent analysis in our study.

We have not yet accounted for the fact that the subject $NP^\frown and^\frown NP$ **115.2** takes a plural verb. Even if F_{AND} is made to precede $\Phi_3{}^P$ (which carries C into $\emptyset$ and S, the number elements of the verb phrase), it is necessary to add a special further transformation to effect this change of the verb from singular to plural, when $NP^\frown and^\frown NP$ is the subject. This can be given either as a component of the mapping Φ^P or as a transformation added to **444** after "F_{AND}."

There are other transformations that can be added to **444** following conjunction. Given "John met Bill" and "John liked Bill," we can form, in the normal way.

450   *John met Bill and liked Bill*

But the more normal form would be

451   *John met Bill and liked him*

In general, it is the case that if conjunction forms a sentence
...$C \frown and \frown C'$..., where C and C' contain the same animate noun in the
same structural position (in some sense to be specified precisely in the
definition of the restricting class of the transformation we are now
considering), then the animate noun in C' is replaced by "he." Once
we have determined the structural requirement, there is no problem in
giving this as an added transformation following "F_{AND}" in **444**, either
obligatory or not, depending on the decision as to the grammaticalness
of **450**. Clearly this phenomenon extends beyond animate nouns. With
inanimate nouns, "it" plays the role of "he" in quite a parallel fashion
(e.g., "I found the book and sent it"). But the element "it" has an even
broader range than this. It can sometimes replace verb phrases (or
perhaps, nominalized verb phrases). Thus in

452   *I visited John and enjoyed it thoroughly*

it is clear intuitively that "it" replaces "visiting John," and it should
be possible to bring transformational analysis to bear on this question.
There are other cases of parallel structures (e.g., "whenever..., then..."),
and investigation of pronoun distribution seems likely to offer a good
deal of insight into the internal structure of the components of such
constructions, in the manner we have just indicated.

115.3   The transformations T_{so} and T_{too} discussed in §94.4 and §96.2 above
are transformations following conjunction and having much the same
status as the pronominal transformation that forms **450**. As we have
seen, "so" is introduced as a pro-element standing for the verb phrase
in such sentences as "John saw him and so did I," "John will be there
and so will I," etc.

T_{so}, incidentally, offers a criterion for determining the analysis
of such elements as "haf to," "ought to," "use to."[45] We might consider
these as some sort of auxiliary verbs, or we might consider them to be
instances of *V-to-V* constructions like "try to," "want to," etc. The
question can be resolved by noting that T_{so} differentiates auxiliaries

[45] As in "I haf to go." This element is distinct from "have to," and an absolute contrast
can be found as "these are the spark plugs we have to (haf to) replace the old ones
(with)." Similarly "use to" is distinct from "used to," as can be seen by substituting
these forms for "have to," "haf to" in the same sentence.

from all main verbs, including those of the *V-to-V* construction (cf. §111 for the final analysis of this construction). Thus we have

453   (a)   *John is coming and so is Bill*
                           (*John–S⌢be⌢ing–come–and–so–S⌢be–Bill*)
          (b)   *John comes and so does Bill*
                           (*John–S–come–and–so–(do)S–Bill*)
          (c)   *John tries to come and so does Bill*
                           (*John–S–try⌢to⌢come–and–so–(do)S–Bill*)
          (d)   *John will come and so will Bill*
             etc.

For "haf to" we have

454   *John has to come and so does Bill*

like **453**c, not **453**d or **453**a. Thus "haf to" is a case of *V-to* like "try to" and not an auxiliary, like "will." Similarly,

455   *John used to come and so did Bill*

shows that "use to" is also such a case. The fact that "does" cannot appear in place of "did" in **455** indicates that "use to" occurs only in the past tense, i.e., that the choice of VP_A with the verb "use" in "use to" is restricted to "ed."

     "Ought to," on the other hand, is an auxiliary verb, not an instance of *V-to* like "try to," since we do not have

456   *John ought to come and so does Bill*

"Ought to" must be in the class *M*, sincewe have "ought to be coming," "ought to have come," etc. But it is limited in distribution. Since we have **457** and not **458**, we might consider it to be a variant of "should":

457   *I ought to come and so should he*

458   *I ought to come and so ought (to) he*

     This classification of these elements coincides with that given by other criteria. Thus we have "I will haf to," but not "I will use to," "I will ought to." However, the restrictions on distribution of these elements require further study.

116   One interesting and highly productive verbal construction that we have not yet considered is the construction *Verb–Preposition* where the preposition is not "separable" as in the cases discussed in §100. As instances of this type we have

459   (a)   *everyone laughed at the clown*
         (b)   *John thought of a good answer*
         (c)   *the staff went over the list*
                etc.[46]

    Investigation of this construction reveals many pecularities and many conflicting criteria by which different and overlapping classifications can be made (e.g., stress on the preposition, occurrence of an adverb or parenthetical expression between verb and preposition, etc.). As only the barest introduction to this complex construction, we can investigate the place of its major constituent break by considering its behavior under certain transformations.

    The conjunction transformation perhaps favors the analysis of **459**a as $NP\text{-}V_I\text{-}PP$, since we have

460   *everyone laughed at the clown and at the elephants*

On the other hand, **461** also appears to be acceptable, at least with certain verbs:

461   *everyone laughed at and mocked the clown*

It is certainly more acceptable than any corresponding form

462   *John worked at and Verb-ed the office*

for the sentence

463   *John worked at the office*

    With other instances of **459** conjunction is indecisive. But the sentences of **459** do not undergo certain transformations characteristic of $NP\text{-}V_I\text{-}PP$ constructions. For example, there is a transformation

---

[46] See Nida, *A Synopsis of English Syntax*, pp. 43, 59 for many examples.

(noted in §103.1) that converts $NP\text{-}V_I\text{-}PP$ into $PP\text{-}NP\text{-}V_I$, converting **463** into

464   *at the office, John worked*

But this transformation does not carry **459**a into

465   *at the clown, everyone laughed*

Furthermore, certain transformations that apply only to $NP\text{-}V_T\text{-}NP$ do apply to **459**. Thus, under the passive transformation, we have

466   (a)   *the clown was laughed at (by everyone)*
         (b)   *an answer was thought of (by John)*
         (c)   *the list was gone over (by the staff)*

but not

467   *the office was worked at (by John), etc.*

This indicates that the sentences of **459** should be analyzed as containing a compound transitive verb $V\text{-}P$. The question transformation also distinguishes **459** from **463** and other instances of $NP\text{-}V_I\text{-}PP$. Thus we have **468** but not **469**:

468   (a)   *whom did everyone laugh at*[47]
         (b)   *what did John think of*
         (c)   *what did the staff go over*

469   *what did John work at*[48]

This is not very convincing evidence, however, since many clear cases of $NP\text{-}V_I\text{-}PP$ are also subject to this transformation. We have "what did John drive away in," from "John drove away in a Cadillac," where "in a Cadillac" must be a PP because of "in a Cadillac, John drove away," "in what did John drive away"; and because of the impossibility of "the Cadillac was driven away in." In fact, it is in general the case that the question transformation applies to the noun in a PP.

---

[47] But also "at whom did everyone laugh," favoring the analysis into $NP\text{-}V_I\text{-}PP$ (cf. §95.3).
[48] But this is a colloquial usage, as the question from "John worked at being a success," etc. But there are clearer cases, e.g., "John left at noon"—"what did John leave at."

These various considerations give some reason to analyze **459** as $NP\text{-}V_T\text{-}NP$, with "laugh at," "think of," "go over," etc., as the transitive verbs. This would seem to match intuition. It will also permit considerable constructional homonymity, since now $NP\text{-}V\text{-}P\text{-}NP$ can be derived from $NP\text{-}V_T\text{-}NP$ (where $V_T \rightarrow V^\frown P$) or from $NP\text{-}V_I\text{-}PP$ (where $PP \rightarrow P^\frown NP$). There is intuitive support for this homonymity in a great many instances. Thus in

470 $NP\text{-}V_T\text{-}NP$ $NP\text{-}V_I\text{-}PP$

they ran after John   *they ran after lunch*
they hoped for peace   *they hoped for three years*
they counted on my support   *they counted on their fingers*

the sentences in the left-hand column have passives, hence are of the form $NP\text{-}V_T\text{-}NP$, while those in the right-hand column, not having passives, are instances of $NP\text{-}V_I\text{-}PP$, and cases where either analysis is possible are easily constructible on these models.[49] The grounds for this intuitively correct analysis are not very firm, as presented above. But it appears that transformational analysis may open up suggestive approaches to the analysis of these forms.

117 The grounds for the validation of any transformational analysis are to be found in considerations of simplicity, given a specification of the form of grammars, and a set of formal requirements that the structure described by the grammar must meet. It is necessary to keep this in mind in considering the relevance to this process of validation of any exceptions to the transformational rules. In one sense, there are no exceptions, since *the* grammar is defined to be the simplest description, meeting fixed formal conditions, for exactly the set of grammatical sentences. If a certain transformational (or other) formulation fails to include certain grammatical sentences, or includes certain ungrammatical ones,

---

[49] This is another instance where extension of the theory to include such phenomena as pitch, stress, and juncture would prove valuable. Though such sentences as "the planes fought over the hills," etc., can be said so as to be ambiguous as to constituent interpretation, they can also be said in an unambiguous manner with intonational features that characterize the left-hand column of **470**, or with features that characterize the right-hand column. These intermittently present intonational features could be transformationally introduced in a more elaborate theory, and the possibilities of one or another intonational transformation could be used as criteria for constituent analysis, in the same way as the segmental transformations we have been discussing. Similarly, the considerations rejected in §65.5 could be reintroduced as criteria of analysis in this way.

then conditions must be added to right the discrepancy.[50] An "exception" to a transformation (i.e., a grammatical form not included, or an included ungrammatical form) will count against the validity of the proposed transformational analysis only if the exception would not have required special statement had the transformational analysis not been adopted. The decision as to whether a sentence belongs to the kernel turns on the relative complexity of the alternative descriptions. If a certain special statement is required under both alternatives, then this statement simply plays no role in the decision between the alternative analyses.

There are many exceptions to the transformations that we have set up. In part, this is due to the insufficiency of our analysis, which makes no attempt to discuss the grammatical structure of English in the required detail. But even in a much more detailed and careful study than this, it will no doubt be the case that if the criteria of grammaticalness are strict enough, there will be many ragged edges in the analysis where special and inelegant formulations will be required. In this discussion of English, these exceptions have not been cited, in part, because of the necessarily sketchy nature of our analysis, and in part because they are irrelevant in the sense of the preceding paragraph. But this is not to say that these exceptions should not be studied. Apparent exceptions may be an important clue, as we have frequently seen above, to deeper underlying regularities.

We might mention several incidental exceptions (whether real or apparent, only future investigation can determine) to the transformations we have constructed. As instances of actives with no corresponding passive we have

471   (a)   *this costs a lot of money*
      (b)   *this weighs three pounds*
      (c)   *John traveled three days*
      (d)   *Mary married John*
      (e)   *misery loves company*
      (f)   *he got his punishment*
      (g)   *he had an accident*
      (h)   *no one foresaw any improvement*
      (i)   *he didn't like either of them*
      (j)   *he only likes certain people*
      (k)   *the artist redecorated it completely*

---

[50] This does not rule out a formulation of linguistic theory in which the simplicity of grammar is a factor in determining the grammatical sentences. But the grammatical sentences must be partially determined by other considerations, if we are to avoid triviality, and the statement in the text holds for the limits of this partially determined set.

From the last four cases it is evident that further analysis of negation and of adverbs is necessary. Suppose that we add a mapping that carries **472** into **473**:

472 $no\frown Noun$ ... $no\frown Noun$

473 $no\frown Noun$ ... $any\frown Noun$

This mapping will account for the fact that case (h) occurs, but not "no one foresees no improvement." And it will also automatically give "no improvement was foreseen by anyone" as the passive of case (h), thus eliminating one discrepancy in what appears to be a simple and intuitively correct manner. Further study is needed of all of the "quantificational" words ("all," "some," "no," "any," etc.).

Case (k) is not handled correctly by our analysis, since its passive should be "it was completely redecorated by the artist." It is thus quite analogous to "John looked it up," which has the passive "it was looked up by John," as we noted in §100. There are also many other indications that certain adverbs can be treated as analogous in their distribution to separable complements.

Consider now cases (a), (b), and (c). We have often noted that the passive transformation offers an effective criterion for the analysis of a sentence as $NP\text{-}V_T\text{-}NP$. When we find a passive that will not be produced unless a certain sentence Z is analyzed as $NP\text{-}V_T\text{-}NP$, we can use this fact to support this analysis of Z. Conversely, when we find a sentence Z which might be analyzed as $NP\text{-}V_T\text{-}NP$, but for which the corresponding passive is not grammatical, we can use this fact as a support for *not* analyzing Z as $NP\text{-}V_T\text{-}NP$. In the cases (h)–(k) there are passives (e.g., "no improvement was foreseen by anyone," "neither of them was liked by him," etc.) which require analysis, and this fact leads us to a further analysis of quantificational words, negatives, and adverbs, as noted. But in cases (a)–(c), there are no passives unaccounted for which could somehow be produced from these sentences, so we may simply refuse to assign the structure $NP\text{-}V_T\text{-}NP$ to these sentences as their constituent analysis. Thus we might analyze these sentences as instances of a construction $NP\text{-}V_I\text{-}Mod$ is a certain type of modifying phrase that occurs after certain intransitive verbs and has a heavily restricted internal structure, with numerals as adjectives, etc. This analysis would make the passive transformation inapplicable in these cases. On lower levels, there is no way to avoid the conclusion that (a)–(c) are cases of transitive verb constructions with objects. But when we employ transformational considerations to determine the simplest analysis of grammatical sentences, we see that this intuitively absurd conclusion is in fact ruled out. This seems to be another case where transformational analysis provides grounds for a strong and unmistakable intuition about linguistic form.

Case (d) is a peculiar instance. Although it has no passive, the sentence "the preacher married John" does.

Case (e) does not really belong here if we can carry through the program suggested in §37. There we suggested grounds for ruling out this sentence as not fully grammatical, and in transformational analysis we are concerned only with fully grammatical sentences. We might take the failure of the passive transformation as a further corroboration for the independently established semigrammaticalness of (e).

Case (f) and (g) have a different sort of interest. It may be significant that the three verbs that are also auxiliaries, i.e., "have," "get," "be,"[51] are impossible or unnatural in the passive, except for certain semicalcified expressions such as "a good time was had by all."

As "passives" with no corresponding active, we find, for example,

474   (a)   *the game was rained out*
          (b)   *John was gone*
          (c)   *John isn't finished yet*
          (d)   *John was really had that time*
                etc.

The first three cases suggest that some fairly productive sentence form has been left out of our analysis.

There are also instances of declaratives with no corresponding questions **475**, and questions with no corresponding declaratives **476**:

475   (a)   *John hardly ever comes*
          (b)   *John almost never comes*
          (c)   *he completely forgot*   (→ *did he forget completely*)

476   (a)   *did your friend leave yet*
          (b)   *did he ever finish*
          (c)   *what did he want to visit them for*
          (d)   *didn't anyone foresee any improvement*
          (e)   *is anyone liked by everybody*

These cases also suggest the need for a more far-reaching analysis of adverbs, negation, and quantificational words. There is no doubt,

---

[51] Though we have in fact seen little reason for calling "be" a verb at all.

on quite independent grounds, that these troublesome words require a great deal more study. Case (d) suggests the need for an extension of the mapping **472–473** discussed above. Case **476c** suggests that "what . . . for" be considered a variant of "why."

These lists can be extended considerably, revealing great gaps in our analysis of English structure. But as far as I have been able to determine, these gaps and exceptions do not negate the major conclusions arrived at in the preceding sections.

118   Sketching briefly the major structural features of English revealed in this analysis, we have a kernel of simple declarative sentences with the two fundamental grammatical relations of subject–predicate and actor–action. The former is subdivided into predicative sentences with *be* (*NP-be-Predicate*) and stative verb constructions with "seem," "act," "become," etc.[52] The actor–action construction is subdivided into transitive constructions (with the grammatical relation transitive verb–object) and intransitive constructions. There is no very good reason to consider *be* to be a verb at all. It shares many of the features of the auxiliary, and we might say that predicate constructions have no main verbs. Transitive verbs are divided into two main structural types, with complement and without complement. The verbs with separable complements are limited to the type "call up," "throw out," etc. The auxiliary verb phrase is retained in full in the kernel. It is probably best to drop adverbs, or at least some classes of adverbs, but this we have barely touched on. "Not" and the related element "*Ac*" are dropped from the kernel, however. Only one type of prepositional phrase remains in the kernel, namely, the "independent" *PP*'s such as "by a new technique," "in the morning," etc., that are added to the verb phrase. Adjectives are limited to the three types A (e.g., "old," "small," etc.), $ing \frown V_j$ (e.g., "surprising"), $en \frown V_k$ (e.g., "tired"), and all can be modified by "very," which remains as a kernel element. Adjectives, however, occur only in the predicate position, never modifying nouns. Noun phrases are all of the type *article–noun*. Pronouns are probably to be dropped from the kernel.

The transformations that produce sentences from simple sentences are the interrogative, elliptical, and passive transformations. A natural classification of simple sentences, based on transformsation, will divide

---

[52] It may be preferable to classify these as instances of the actor–action construction, or as a third independent type. We have touched on these forms too hurriedly for our analysis to have much significance. The terminology "actor–action," borrowed from Bloomfield, *Language*, p. 184*f*, is not to be taken literally as expressing the semantic content of this construction.

them into declaratives and interrogatives. The declaratives include the kernel sentences and the passives, whose derived constituent structure is that of kernel sentences. The basic interrogative sentences are the yes-or-no questions ("did you come," etc.), with inversion. If we apply the *wh*-transformations, with a second inversion, to these questions, we derive a second class of interrogatives, including many types ("who was here," "whom did he see," "what plane did you take," etc.) The *wh*-transformation, applied to declaratives, gives relative clauses. Such sentences as "who saw him," "whom did he see" have the same transformational history, despite the fact that only the second of these contains an inversion. There are several types of elliptical sentences. The verb phrase can be dropped from declaratives, and the final *by*-phrase from passives. The subject *you* can be dropped from yes-or-no questions giving imperatives, by a somewhat more complicated (and more dubious) elliptical transformation.

Other transformations form noun phrases, adjective phrases, and verb phrases. *Ing*-phrases appear as abstract nouns, and the subjects of the sentences from which they are transformationally derived may be retained as possessive "adjectives" (as in the noun phrase "John's refusing to come"). Other transformationally produced noun phrases reproduce the subject–verb relation ("growling of lions," etc.) or the verb–object relation ("reading of good literature," etc.). Similar "nominalizing" transformations give "John's refusal to come," "the sight of men working," etc. *That*-clauses also appear as nouns. We might go on to derive many compound nouns transformationally. Various noun modifiers are introduced, including relative clauses, prepositional phrases, *ing*-phrases, verbal adjectives from the passive ("forgotten," etc.) or from intransitives ("barking," etc.). Adjective phrases appear in noun-modifying position as transforms of *NP-is-AP* sentences.

The most interesting transformational development of the verb phrase is the tremendous extension of the *Verb–Complement* construction, where the complement is separable, and the noun phrase object of the compound verb (e.g., "John" in "I consider John incompetent," where "consider–incompetent" is the compound verb–complement) is the subject of the complement in the underlying simple sentence. This is a highly productive and ramified construction, with many different types of instances. In particular, the *V-to-V* (and *V-ing-V*) constructions, as in "I want to come," "I like reading," etc., are special cases of it, These can be elaborated by simple means into very complex forms (especially, when deletion of pronouns and transformation of *pronoun* to *pronoun-self* is brought into consideration).

Conjunction is the generalized transformation that has by far the broadest scope of all, applying to almost any constituent, and to little else. Further investigation would reveal that parenthetical expressions must also be introduced by transformations. Thus the criteria for constituent analysis stated in §58 reduce to two type, those based on intonational structure (which we have not investigated) and those based on transformational structure. (That these should probably not be sharply distinguished is pointed out in Note 49.) In constructing transformations we discovered many other "criteria" of the transformational type. It appears that the basic reasons for assigning a given constituent structure to a sentence are to be found in the behavior of this sentence under transformation.

This is a crude and incomplete analysis, as a glance at any text in English will quickly show. There are many other phenomena that suggest transformational analysis, and the kernel also requires a considerable amount of further study. But I think that many of the main features of English structure have been touched on in this sketch. In particular, we have seen that all the difficulties and inadequacies sketched in §§76–78 have disappeared with this transformational analysis. We are apparently able to extend the bounds of grammatical description to cover all grammatical sentences without the intolerable complexities and intuitive absurdities that resulted when the devices available on lower levels were extended beyond what in Chapter VIII appeared to be arbitrary and overly narrow limits.

BIBLIOGRAPHY

Bar-Hillel, Yehoshua, "A quasi-arithmetical notation for syntactic description," *Language* **29**, 47–58, 1953.

——, "On recursive definitions in empirical sciences," Proceedings of the Eleventh International Congress of Philosophy, Brussels, 1953, Vol. V, pp. 160–165.

——, "Logical syntax and semantics," *Language* **30**, 230–237, 1954.

Bloch, Bernard, "Phonemic overlapping," *American Speech* **16**, 278–284, 1941.

——, "A set of postulates for phonemic analysis," *Language* **24**, 3–46, 1948.

Bloomfield, Leonard, *Language*, New York, Holt, 1933.

——, "Menomini morphophonemics," *Travaux de cercle linguistique de Prague* **8**, 105–115, 1939.

Chomsky, Noam, *Morphophonemics of Modern Hebrew*, unpublished, 1951; revision of 1951 Master's thesis, University of Pennsylvania.

——, "Systems of syntactic analysis," *Journal of Symbolic Logic* **18**, No. 3, 1953.

——, "Logical syntax and semantics: their linguistic relevance," *Language* **31**, 1955.

——, "Three models for the description of language," *I.R.E. Transactions of Information Theory* **IT-2**, 113–124, 1956.

——, "Review of Hockett, *Manual of Phonology*," *International Journal of American Linguistics* **23**, No. 3, 1957.

——, "Review of Jakobson and Halle, *Fundamentals of Language*," *International Journal of American Linguistics* **23**, No. 3, 1957.

——, *Syntactic Structures*, The Hague, Mouton, 1957.

——, Morris Halle, and Fred Lukoff, "On accent and juncture in English," in M. Halle, H. Lunt, and H. MacLean, eds., *For Roman Jakobson*, The Hague, Mouton, 1956.

Goodman, Nelson, "On the simplicity of ideas," *Journal of Symbolic Logic* **8**, 107–121, 1943.

——, "On likeness of meaning," *Analysis* **10**, No. 1, 1949.

——, *The Structure of Appearance*, Cambridge, Mass., Harvard University Press, 1951.

——, "On some differences about meaning," *Analysis* **13**, No. 4, 1953.

——, *Fact, Fiction and Forecast*, Cambridge, Mass., Harvard University Press, 1955.

——, and W. V. O. Quine, "Steps towards a constructive nominalism," *Journal of Symbolic Logic* **12**, 105–122, 1947.

Halle, Morris, *The Sound Pattern of Russian*, The Hague, Mouton, 1959; revised version of 1955 Harvard University Ph.D. dissertation.

Harris, Zellig, *Methods of Structural Linguistics*, Chicago, University of Chicago Press, 1951.

——, "Discourse analysis," *Language* **28**, 18–23, 1952.

——, "Discourse analysis: a sample text," *Language* **28**, 474–494, 1952.

——, "Distributional structure," *Linguistics Today*, *Word* **10**, 146–162, 1954.

——, "From phoneme to morpheme," *Language* **31**, 190–122, 1955.

——, "Co-occurrence and transformation in linguistic structure," *Language* **33**, 293–340, 1957.

——, and Charles W. Voegelin, "Eliciting," *Southwestern Journal of Anthropology* **9**, 59–75, 1953.

Harwood, F. W., "Axiomatic syntax: the construction and evaluation of a syntactic calculus," *Language* **31**, 409–414, 1955.

Hempel, C. G., "A logical appraisal of operationism," *Scientific Monthly*, October 1954, pp. 215–220.

Hiż, Henry, "Positional algebras and structural linguistics," unpublished.

Hockett, Charles F., "Problems of morphemic analysis," *Language* **23**, 321–343, 1947.

——, "A formal statement of morphemic analysis," *Studies in Linguistics*, **10**, 27–39, 1952.

——, "Two models for grammatical description," *Linguistics Today*, *Word* **10**, 210–234, 1954.

——, *A Manual of Phonology*, Indiana University Publications in Anthropology and Linguistics 11, 1955.

Holt, Anatol W., *Cluster Analysis*, unpublished Master's thesis, Mathematics Department, MIT, 1954.

Householder, Fred, "Review of Harris, *Methods of Structural Linguistics*," *International Journal of American Linguistics* **18**, No. 4, 1952.

Jakobson, Roman, "Russian conjugation," *Word* **4**, 155–167, 1948.

——, Gunnar Fant, and Morris Halle, *Preliminaries to Speech Analysis*, Technical Report No. 13, Acoustics Laboratory, MIT, Cambridge, Mass., January 1952.

——, and Morris Halle, *Fundamentals of Language*, The Hague, Mouton, 1956.

Lounsbury, Floyd G., "Field methods and techniques in linguistics," in A. L. Kroeber, ed., *Anthropology Today*, Chicago, University of Chicago Press, 1953.

Mandelbaum, D. G., ed., *Selected Writings of Edward Sapir*, Berkeley, University of California Press, 1949.

Miller, George A., and J. A. Selfridge, "Verbal context and the recall of meaningful material," *American Journal of Psychology* **63**, 176–185, 1953.

Newman, Stanley S., "On the stress system of English," *Word* **2**, 171–187, 1946.

Nida, Eugene, *Morphology*, University of Michigan Publications in Linguistics 2, 1949.

——, *A Synopsis of English Syntax*, The Hague, Mouton, 1966 (first published: Norman, Oklahoma, Summer Institute of Linguistics, 1960).

Pike, Kenneth L., *The Intonation of American English*, University of Michigan Publications in Linguistics 1, 1945.

Quine, W. V. O., *Mathematical Logic*, Cambridge, Mass., Harvard University Press, revised edition, 1951.

——, "Two dogmas of empiricism," reprinted in *From a Logical Point of View*, Cambridge, Mass., Harvard University Press, 1953.

——, "Meaning in linguistics," in *From a Logical Point of View*.

Rosenbloom, Paul, *The Elements of Mathematical Logic*, New York, Dover, 1950.

Sapir, Edward, "La réalité psychologique des phonèmes," *Journal de Psychologie Normale et Pathologique* **30**, 247–265, 1933; translated in Mandelbaum, ed., *Selected Writings of Edward Sapir*.

Schatz, Carol D., "The role of context in the perception of stops," *Language* **30**, 47–56, 1954.

Trager, George L., and Henry Lee Smith, *An Outline of English Structure*, *Studies in Linguistics*, Occasional Papers 3, 1951.

Wells, Rulon S., "Immediate constitutents," *Language* **23**, 81–117, 1947.

——, "Meaning and use," *Linguistics Today*, *Word* **10**, 235–250, 1954.

Yngve, Victor, "Gap analysis and syntax," *I.R.E. Transactions on Information Theory* **IT-2**, 1956.